T0345326

Sentiment Analysis

Sentiment analysis is the computational study of people's opinions, sentiments, emotions, moods, and attitudes. This fascinating problem offers numerous research challenges, but promises insights useful to anyone interested in opinion analysis and social media analysis. This comprehensive introduction to the topic takes a natural-language-processing point of view to help readers understand the underlying structure of the problem and the language constructs commonly used to express opinions, sentiments, and emotions. The book covers core areas of sentiment analysis as well as related topics such as debate analysis, intention mining, and fake-opinion detection. It will be a valuable resource for researchers and practitioners in natural language processing, computer science, management sciences, and the social sciences.

In addition to traditional computational methods, this second edition includes recent deep learning methods to analyze and summarize sentiments and opinions, and also new material on emotion and mood analysis techniques, emotion-enhanced dialogues, and multimodal emotion analysis.

BING LIU is a distinguished professor of computer science at the University of Illinois at Chicago. His current research interests include sentiment analysis, lifelong machine learning, natural language processing, and data mining. He has published extensively in top conferences and journals, and his research has been cited on the front page of *The New York Times*. Three of his research papers also received Test-of-Time awards. He was the recipient of the ACM SIGKDD Innovation Award in 2018, and he is a Fellow of the ACM, AAAI, and IEEE. He served as the Chair of ACM SIGKDD from 2013 to 2017.

Studies in Natural Language Processing

Sentiment Analysis

Mining Opinions, Sentiments, and Emotions

Second Edition

Bing Liu

University of Illinois at Chicago, and Peking University

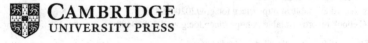

CAMBRIDGE
UNIVERSITY PRESS

Shaftesbury Road, Cambridge CB2 8EA, United Kingdom

One Liberty Plaza, 20th Floor, New York, NY 10006, USA

477 Williamstown Road, Port Melbourne, VIC 3207, Australia

314–321, 3rd Floor, Plot 3, Splendor Forum, Jasola District Centre, New Delhi – 110025, India

103 Penang Road, #05–06/07, Visioncrest Commercial, Singapore 238467

Cambridge University Press is part of Cambridge University Press & Assessment, a department of the University of Cambridge.

We share the University's mission to contribute to society through the pursuit of education, learning and research at the highest international levels of excellence.

www.cambridge.org
Information on this title: www.cambridge.org/9781108486378

DOI: 10.1017/9781108639286

Second edition 2020
First published 2015

A catalogue record for this publication is available from the British Library

Library of Congress Cataloging-in-Publication data
Names: Liu, Bing, 1963– author.
Title: Sentiment analysis : mining opinions, sentiments, and emotions /
    Bing Liu, University of Illinois, Chicago.
Description: Second edition. | Cambridge ; New York : Cambridge University Press,
    2020. | Series: Studies in natural language processing | Includes bibliographical
    references and index.
Identifiers: LCCN 2020009497 (print) | LCCN 2020009498 (ebook) |
    ISBN 9781108486378 (hardback) | ISBN 9781108639286 (epub)
Subjects: LCSH: Natural language processing (Computer science) |
    Computational linguistics. | Public opinion–Data processing. | Data mining. |
    Discourse analysis–Data processing. | Language and emotions.
Classification: LCC QA76.9.N38 L58 2020 (print) | LCC QA76.9.N38 (ebook) |
    DDC 006.3/12–dc23
LC record available at https://lccn.loc.gov/2020009497
LC ebook record available at https://lccn.loc.gov/2020009498

ISBN   978-1-108-48637-8   Hardback

Contents

Preface

Since the first edition of the book was published in 2015, we have witnessed the rapid rise of deep learning, which has resulted in a huge amount of work on using deep learning models to perform sentiment analysis tasks. The goal of this second edition is mainly to update the first edition with the deep learning methods published in the past few years. In addition, many other sections of the book have been updated.

Opinion and sentiment and their related concepts, such as evaluation, appraisal, attitude, affect, emotion, and mood, are about our subjective feelings and beliefs. They are central to human psychology and are key influencers of our behaviors. Our beliefs and perceptions of reality, as well as the choices we make, are to a considerable degree conditioned on how others see and perceive the world. For this reason, our views of the world are very much influenced by others' views. Whenever we need to make a decision, we often seek out others' opinions. This is true not only for individuals but also for organizations. From an application point of view, we naturally want to mine people's opinions and feelings toward any subject matter of interest, which is the task of sentiment analysis. More precisely, sentiment analysis – also called opinion mining – is a field of study that aims to extract opinions and sentiments from natural language text using computational methods.

The inception and rapid growth of sentiment analysis coincide with those of social media on the web, such as reviews, forum discussions, blogs, and microblogs, because for the first time in human history, we have a huge volume of opinionated data recorded in digital forms. These data, also called *user-generated content,* prompted researchers to mine them to discover useful knowledge. This endeavor naturally led to the problem of sentiment analysis or opinion mining because these data are full of opinions. This is not surprising, because the primary reason that people post messages on social media platforms is to express their views and opinions; therefore, sentiment analysis is at the very core of social media analysis. Since the early 2000s, sentiment analysis has grown to be one of the most active research areas in natural language processing. It is also widely studied in the context of data mining, web mining, and information retrieval. In fact, this line of research has expanded from computer science to management science and social science because of its importance to business and society as a whole. Industrial activities surrounding sentiment analysis have also thrived. Numerous start-ups have emerged. Many large corporations – for example, Microsoft, Google, Facebook, Hewlett-Packard, IBM, Adobe, Alibaba, Baidu, and Tencent – have also built their own in-house systems. Sentiment analysis systems have found applications in almost every business, health, government, and social domain.

Although no silver bullet algorithm can solve the sentiment analysis problem, many deployed systems are able to provide useful information to support real-life applications. I believe it is now a good time to document the knowledge that we have obtained through research – and, to some extent, in practice – in a book. Obviously, I don't claim to know everything that is happening in the industry, as businesses do not publish or disclose their algorithms. However, I have built a sentiment analysis system myself in a start-up company and served clients on projects involving social media data sets in a large variety of domains. Over the years, many developers of sentiment analysis systems in the industry have also told me roughly what algorithms they were using. Thus, I have a reasonable knowledge of practical systems and their capabilities and firsthand experience in solving real-life problems. I try to pass along those nonconfidential pieces of information and knowledge in this book.

In writing this book, I aimed to take a balanced approach, analyzing the sentiment analysis problem from a linguistic angle to help readers understand the underlying structure of the problem and the language constructs commonly used to express opinions and sentiments, and presenting computational methods to analyze and summarize opinions. Like many natural language processing tasks, most published computational techniques use machine learning or data mining algorithms with the help of text-specific clues or features. However, if we focus solely on such computational algorithms, we will miss the deep insights of the problem, which in turn will hinder our progress on the computational front. Most existing machine learning algorithms are black boxes; they do not produce human-interpretable models. In turn, when something goes wrong, it is hard to know the cause and how to fix it.

In presenting linguistic constructs and perspectives, I do not follow the linguistic tradition in writing, because the knowledge and the way that the knowledge is presented in the traditional linguistics literature are mainly for people to understand, rather than for computers to operationalize to solve real-life problems. Although the knowledge of human beings and instructions for computers can largely intersect, they also have major differences. As a case in point, when I was working on the problem of mining opinions from conditional sentences, I read several linguistics books about conditionals. To my surprise, I found almost no linguistic knowledge that could be operationalized computationally to help solve the problem. I believe this is partly because the current computation technologies are not mature enough to have the same understanding capability as people and partly because much of the linguistic knowledge was not meant for computers to use.

Another feature of this book is that it is not just about studying the language for human understanding per se, as much of the traditional linguistic literature is; it is also about practical applications of mining sentiment and opinion expressed in natural language, for which we want not only to recognize sentiment or opinion expressions and their polarities (or orientations) but also to extract several other pieces of important information associated with sentiment or opinion. For example, we want to identify the real-world entities or topics that a sentiment or opinion is about. These entities or topics are called *opinion* (or *sentiment*) *targets*. Extracting opinion targets is extremely important in practice. For example, in the sentence "I am disgusted by the tax increase for the poor," if we find only that the sentence expresses a negative sentiment and/or the emotion of *disgust* from the sentence author, it is not that useful in practice. But if we also find that the negative sentiment is toward "tax increase for the poor," which is the target of the negative sentiment or emotion, the information becomes much more valuable. I hope this book can also serve to encourage linguists to develop a comprehensive theory about sentiment, opinion, and emotion, as well as their associated concepts.

I wrote this book as an introductory text for the field of sentiment analysis and as a research survey. In many places, it is one or the other; in other places, it is a mixture of both. The reason for this mixed or somewhat unusual presentational style is that there are few truly mature techniques or algorithms for sentiment analysis, although numerous researchers have attempted to solve each subproblem using many techniques. In many cases, we can see from the accuracy of results of the published papers that they are not yet ready for prime time.

Another reason for the mixed presentational style of this book is that most existing research methods are direct applications of machine learning and data mining algorithms employing text features or the raw text itself. Because many books on machine learning and data mining cover these algorithms extensively, the algorithms are not detailed in this book. This book also does not detail the basics of linguistics or natural language processing, such as part-of-speech tagging, syntactic parsing, shallow parsing, and grammar. Although these topics are very important to sentiment analysis, once again they have been covered in numerous books on natural language processing. This book thus assumes that readers know the basics of machine leaning and natural language processing.

I tried to cover all major developments of the field in this book. It is thus quite comprehensive. Evidence of this is that the book cites more than seven hundred publications from all major conferences and journals. I organized the book as follows.

Chapter 1 introduces the book and gives the motivations for the study of sentiment analysis. We see that sentiment analysis is a fascinating, yet challenging problem with almost unlimited practical applications.

Chapter 2 defines the sentiment analysis problem and discusses many of its related issues. Here we see that although sentiment analysis is a natural language processing problem, it can be defined structurally. Through this definition, we can transform unstructured text to structured data. This facilitates subsequent qualitative and quantitative analyses, which are critical for real-life applications. We also see that sentiment analysis is a multifaceted problem with many challenging and interrelated subproblems.

Chapter 3 studies the popular topic of document-level sentiment classification, which classifies an opinion document (e.g., a product review) as expressing a positive or negative opinion. Chapter 4 studies the same classification problem but focuses on each individual sentence. Related problems of sentiment rating prediction, transfer learning, and multilingual sentiment classification are also discussed in these two chapters.

Chapters 5 and 6 go to a fine-grained level to study the enormously important topic of aspect-based sentiment analysis, which not only classifies sentiment but also identifies the target of sentiment or opinion. Most practical sentiment analysis or opinion mining systems in industry are based on this fine-grained level of analysis. Chapter 5 focuses on aspect sentiment classification, and Chapter 6 addresses aspect or target extraction.

Chapter 7 describes research that compiles sentiment lexicons. A sentiment lexicon is a list of words and phrases (e.g., *good, amazing, bad, horrible*) that people often use to express positive or negative opinions. Chapter 8 studies opinions expressed in comparative sentences. Chapter 9 focuses on opinion summarization and opinion search. Chapter 10 looks into a different type of sentiment (agreement and disagreement) expressed in online debates and discussions, which involve extensive interactive exchanges among participants. Chapter 11 investigates intent mining, which aims to discover intentions expressed in language.

Chapter 12 switches to a very different topic: the detection of fake or deceptive online opinions. Chapter 13 studies the problem of ranking online reviews based on their usefulness so that users can view the most useful reviews first. Chapter 14 concludes the book and discusses some future research.

This book is suitable for students, researchers, and practitioners who are interested in social media analysis and natural language processing in general, and sentiment analysis or opinion mining in particular. It is written not only for the computer science audience, but also for researchers and practitioners in management sciences and social sciences. Consumer sentiments and public opinions are central to many management and social science areas such as marketing, economics, communication, political science, and even history. Lecturers can readily use the book in class for courses on natural language processing, social media analysis, social computing, and text and data mining. Lecture slides are available online.

Acknowledgments

Many researchers assisted me technically while I was writing this book. Without their help, the book might never have become reality. First of all, I would like to thank my former and current students – Zhiyuan Chen, Junsheng Cheng, Xiaowen Ding, Geli Fei, Murthy Ganapathibhotla, Minqing Hu, Wenpeng Hu (Peking University), Nitin Jindal, Zixuan Ke, Gyuhak Kim, Abhinav Kumar, Huayi Li, Guangyi Lv (visiting student from University of Science and Technology China), Nianzu Ma, Sahisnu Mazumder, Arjun Mukherjee, Ramanathan Narayanan (Northwestern University), Qi Qin (Peking University), Guang Qiu (visiting student from Zhejiang University), Sathish Ramadoss, Lei Shu, Jianfeng Si (visiting student from City University of Hong Kong), Vivek Venkataraman, William Underwood, Andrea Vaccari, Hao Wang (visiting student from Southwest Jiaotong University), Shuai Wang, Hu Xu, Zhongwu Zhai (visiting student from Tsinghua University), and Lei Zhang – for contributing numerous research ideas over the years. Discussions with many researchers also helped shape the book: Shuanhu Bai, Jim Blomo, Malu G. Castellanos, Dennis Chong, Umesh Dayal, Eduard Dragut, Boi Faltings, Ronen Feldman, Christiane D. Fellbaum, Zhiqiang Gao, Riddhiman Ghosh, Natalie Glance, Meichun Hsu, Joshua Huang, Minglie Huang, Jing Jiang, Birgit König, Xiao-li Li, Qian Liu, Boia Marina, Sharon Meraz, Tieyun Qian, Jidong Shao, Mehrbod Sharifi, Hao Wang, Jan Wiebe, Qiang Yang, Lixia Yao, Clement Yu, Philip S. Yu, ChengXiang Zhai, Fangwei Zhang, Yuanlin Zhang, Jun Zhao, Xiaoyan Zhu, and Chengqing Zong. Xueying Zhang from Peking University helped greatly tidy up and correct a large number of references. I am also in debt to the two anonymous reviewers; despite their busy schedules, they read the book very carefully and gave me numerous excellent suggestions. I have taken each and every one of those recommendations into consideration while improving this book. Both the web and social media made writing this book so much easier: I have found a great deal of valuable information from them that tremendously helped me in writing the book.

I would also like to express my gratitude to the National Science Foundation, Google, HP Labs, Tencent Holdings, Huawei Technologies, Bosch, and

Microsoft Corporation for their generous support of my research over the years. The Department of Computer Science, University of Illinois at Chicago (UIC), and Wangxuan Institute of Computing Technology, Peking University, provided computing resources and very supportive environments for this project. The new materials of this second edition was mainly written when I was on leave from UIC at Peking University.

On the publication side, it was a pleasure working with the helpful staff of Cambridge University Press. I thank my editors, Lauren Cowles (first edition), Amy He, and Kaitlin Leach (second edition). It has been a wonderful experience working with them. I also thank my copy editor, Holly T. Monteith (first edition) and Jill E. Hobbs (second edition), for helping me improve the presentation and my production editors, Sonika Rai (first edition) and Mathew Rohit (second edition), for guiding me through the final production process.

Finally, I thank my parents, brother, and sister for their constant support and encouragement. My deepest gratitude goes to my own family: Yue, Shelley, and Kate. They have helped me in so many ways. My wife has taken care of almost everything at home and put up with me and the long hours that I have spent on this book. I dedicate this book to them.

1   Introduction

Sentiment analysis, also called opinion mining, is the field of study that analyzes people's opinions, sentiments, appraisals, attitudes, and emotions toward entities and their attributes expressed in written text. The entities can be products, services, organizations, individuals, events, issues, or topics. The field represents a large problem space. Many related names and slightly different tasks – for example, sentiment analysis, opinion mining, opinion analysis, opinion extraction, sentiment mining, subjectivity analysis, affect analysis, emotion analysis, and review mining – are now all under the umbrella of sentiment analysis. The term *sentiment analysis* perhaps first appeared in Nasukawa and Yi (2003), and the term *opinion mining* first appeared in Dave et al. (2003). However, research on sentiment and opinion began earlier (Wiebe, 2000; Das and Chen, 2001; Tong, 2001; Morinaga et al., 2002; Pang et al., 2002; Turney, 2002). Even earlier related work includes interpretation of metaphors; extraction of sentiment adjectives; affective computing; and subjectivity analysis, viewpoints, and affects (Wiebe, 1990, 1994; Hearst, 1992; Hatzivassiloglou and McKeown, 1997; Picard, 1997; Wiebe et al., 1999). An early patent on text classification included sentiment, appropriateness, humor, and many other concepts as possible class labels (Elkan, 2001).

Since existing research and applications of sentiment analysis have focused primarily on written text, it has been an active research field of natural language processing (NLP). However, the topic has also been widely studied in data mining, web mining, and information retrieval because many researchers in these fields deal with text data. In recent years, researchers have studied multimodal sentiment analysis, which uses image/video, text, and audio information to classify people's sentiments and emotions. My own first paper (Hu and Liu, 2004) on the topic was published in the proceedings of the data mining conference KDD (SIGKDD International Conference on Knowledge Discovery and Data Mining) in 2004. This paper defined the problem of aspect-based sentiment analysis and summarization and proposed some basic ideas and algorithms to solve the problem. These are commonly used in academia and industry today.

1

Not surprisingly, there has been some confusion among practitioners and even researchers about the difference between sentiment and opinion and whether the field should be called sentiment analysis or opinion mining. Since the field originated from computer science rather than linguistics, little attention has been given to studying the difference between the two words. In Merriam-Webster's dictionary, *sentiment* is defined as an attitude, thought, or judgment prompted by feeling, whereas *opinion* is defined as a view, judgment, or appraisal formed in the mind about a particular matter. The difference is quite subtle, and each definition contains some elements of the other. The definitions indicate that an opinion is more of a person's concrete view about something, whereas a sentiment is more of a feeling. For example, the sentence "I am concerned about the current state of the economy" expresses a sentiment, whereas the sentence "I think the economy is not doing well" expresses an opinion. In a conversation, if someone says the first sentence, we can respond by saying, "I share your sentiment," but for the second sentence, we would normally say, "I agree/disagree with you." However, the underlying meanings of the two sentences are related because the sentiment depicted in the first sentence is likely to be a feeling caused by the opinion in the second sentence. Conversely, we can also say that the first sentiment sentence implies a negative opinion about the economy, which is what the second sentence is saying. Although in most cases, opinions imply positive or negative sentiments, some opinions do not – for example, "I think he will go to Canada next year."

Regarding the name of the field, *sentiment analysis* is used almost exclusively in industry, whereas both *opinion mining* and *sentiment analysis* are commonly employed in academia. In this book, I use the terms *sentiment analysis* and *opinion mining* interchangeably. Furthermore, I use the term *opinion* to mean the whole concept of sentiment, evaluation, appraisal, or attitude and associated information, such as the opinion target and the person who holds the opinion (see the formal definition in Section 2.1.1), and I use the term *sentiment* to mean the underlying positive or negative feeling implied by an opinion. Sentiment analysis mainly focuses on opinions that express or imply positive or negative sentiments, also called positive or negative opinions in everyday language. This type of opinion is similar to the concept of *attitude* in social psychology. For example, Eagly and Chaiken (1998, p. 1) defined an attitude as "a psychological tendency that is expressed by evaluating a particular entity with some degree of favor or disfavor." In discussing positive and negative sentiments, we must also consider expressions without any implied sentiment, which we call *neutral* expressions. Apart from sentiment and opinion, the concepts of affect, emotion, and mood are also psychological states of mind. We study natural language expressions of such states in detail in Section 2.3.

Sentences expressing opinions or sentiments are usually *subjective* sentences, as opposed to *objective* sentences, which state facts, because opinions and sentiments are inherently subjective. However, objective sentences can imply the positive or negative sentiments of their authors, too, because they may describe desirable or undesirable facts. For example, based on our commonsense knowledge, we know that "I bought the car yesterday and it broke today" and "After sleeping on the mattress for a month, a valley has formed in the middle" describe two undesirable facts, and we can safely infer that the sentence authors feel negatively about the car and the mattress, respectively. Sentiment analysis also studies such objective sentences.

In a nutshell, sentiment analysis or opinion mining aims to identify positive and negative opinions or sentiments expressed in text as well as the targets of these opinions or sentiments (e.g., the car and the mattress in the preceding sentences). A more formal definition is given in Section 2.1.

Although sentiment analysis studies opinion text, there was almost no research into this topic from either the linguistics community or the NLP community before the year 2000, in part because almost no opinionated text was recorded in digital forms before then. Of course, throughout history, spoken or written communications have never had a shortage of opinions. With the explosive growth of the web and social media in the past twenty years, we now have a constant flow of opinionated data recorded in digital forms. Without these data, much of the existing research would not have been possible. It is thus no surprise that the inception and rapid growth of sentiment analysis coincide with the growth of social media on the web.

Over the years, social media systems on the web have provided excellent platforms to facilitate and enable audience participation, engagement, and community, which has resulted in our new participatory culture. From reviews and blogs to YouTube, Facebook, and Twitter, people have embraced these platforms enthusiastically because they enable their users to freely and conveniently voice their opinions and communicate their views on any subject across geographic and spatial boundaries. They also allow people to easily connect with others and to share their information. This participatory web and communications revolution has transformed both our everyday lives and the society as a whole. It has also popularized two major research areas – namely, social network analysis and sentiment analysis. Although social network analysis is not a new research area – it started in the 1940s and 1950s, when management science researchers began to study social actors (people in organizations) and their interactions and relationships – the advent of social media has certainly fueled its explosive growth in the past twenty years. Sentiment analysis, conversely, is a new research area that essentially grew out of social media on the web.

Since the year 2002, research in sentiment analysis has been very active. Apart from the availability of a large amount of opinionated data in social media, opinions and sentiments have a very wide range of applications because opinions are central to almost all human activities. Whenever we need to make a decision, we often seek out others' opinions. This is true not only for individuals but also for organizations. It is thus no surprise that the industry and applications surrounding sentiment analysis have flourished since around 2006. On the one hand, this application need provided a strong motivation for research. On the other hand, sentiment analysis offers numerous challenging and fascinating research problems whose solutions have never before been attempted. In this book, I systematically define and discuss these problems and present the current state-of-the-art techniques for studying them.

Because a key function of social media is for people to express their views and opinions, sentiment analysis is right at the center of research on, and application of, social media. It is now well recognized that, to extract and exploit information in social media, sentiment analysis is a necessary technology. One can even take a sentiment-centric view of social media content analysis because the most important information that one wants to extract from the social media content is what people talk about and what their opinions are. These are exactly the core tasks of sentiment analysis. Furthermore, we can claim that the topics, events, and individuals discussed in social media are unlikely to be important if few people have expressed opinions about them. Human nature being what it is, everything that we consider important arouses our inner feelings or emotions, which are expressed in our opinions and sentiments.

Apart from topics and opinions about topics, social media allows us to study the participants themselves. We can produce a sentiment profile of each social media participant based on his or her topical interests and opinions about these interests expressed in the users' posts because a person's topical interests and opinions reflect the nature and preferences of the person. Such information can be used in many applications – for example, recommending products and services and determining which political candidates for whom a person should vote. Additionally, social media participants can not only post messages but also interact with one another through discussions and debates, which involve sentiments such as *agreement* and *disagreement* (or *contention*). Discovery of such information is of great importance. For example, contentious social and political issues and views of opposing positions can be exploited to frame political issues and to predict election results.

Owing to the importance of opinions in social media, imposters often game the system by posting fake or deceptive opinions to promote some target products, services, and ideological agendas. Detecting such fake or deceptive opinions is an important challenge, which again offers fertile ground for novel research and applications.

Although sentiment analysis originated from computer science, in recent years, it has spread to management sciences and social sciences because of its importance to business and society as a whole. Thus sentiment analysis research not only advances the field of NLP but also advances research in management science, political science, and economics, as these fields are all concerned with consumer and public opinions. It is not hard to imagine that sentiment analysis using social media might profoundly change the direction of research and practice in these fields. This book serves as an up-to-date and introductory text as well as a comprehensive survey of this important and fascinating subject.

1.1   Sentiment Analysis Applications

Opinions are very important to businesses and organizations because they always want to ascertain consumer or public opinions about their products and services. Local and federal governments also want to determine public opinions about their existing or proposed policies. Such opinions will enable relevant government decision makers to respond quickly to fast-changing social, economic, and political climates. In international politics, every government wants to monitor the social media of other countries to find what is happening in these countries and what people's views and sentiments are about current local and international issues and events. Such information is very useful to diplomacy, international relations, and economic decision making. Besides businesses, organizations, and government agencies, individual consumers want to know the opinions of others about products, services, and political candidates before purchasing the products, using the services, and making election decisions.

In the past, when an individual needed opinions, he or she asked friends and family. When an organization or a business needed public or consumer opinions, it conducted surveys, opinion polls, and focus groups. When governments wanted to know what was happening in other countries, they monitored the traditional news media – for example, newspapers, radio, and TV – in these countries, and even sent spies to these countries to collect such information. Acquiring and analyzing public and consumer opinions have long been a huge business for marketing, public relations, and political campaign firms.

Nowadays, individuals, organizations, and government agencies are increasingly using the content in social media for decision making. If an individual wants to buy a consumer product, he or she is no longer limited to asking his or her friends and family for opinions because there are many user reviews and discussions in public forums on the web about the product. For an organization, it may no longer be necessary to conduct surveys, opinion polls, or focus groups to gather public or consumer opinions about the organization's products and services because an abundance of such information is publicly available. Governments can also easily obtain public opinions about their policies and measure the pulses of other nations simply by monitoring their social media.

In recent years, we have witnessed how opinionated posts on social media sites have helped reshape business and sway public sentiment, profoundly impacting our social and political lives. For instance, such posts have mobilized the masses for political change, such as during the Arab Spring in 2011. However, finding and monitoring opinion sites on the web and distilling the information contained in them remains a formidable task because of the diversity of sites. Each site typically contains a huge volume of opinion text that is not always easily deciphered from long blogs and forum posts. The average human reader will have difficulty identifying relevant sites and extracting and summarizing the opinions in them. Automated sentiment analysis systems are thus needed.

Opinionated documents exist not only on the web (often called external data): many organizations have internal data, such as customer feedback collected from e-mails and call centers and results from surveys conducted by the organizations. It is critical to analyze both kinds of data to tease out the key product and service issues and to summarize customer opinions.

In recent years, sentiment analysis applications have spread to almost every possible domain, from consumer products, health care, tourism, hospitality, and financial services to social events and political elections. Hundreds of companies now operate in this space, including both start-up companies and established, large corporations that have built or are in the process of building their own in-house capabilities, such as Google, Microsoft, Hewlett-Packard, Amazon, eBay, SAS, Oracle, Adobe, Bloomberg, Alibaba, Tencent, and SAP. I myself have implemented a sentiment analysis system, called Opinion Parser, in a start-up company and worked on projects for clients in more than forty domains: automobile, mobile phone, earphone, printer, refrigerator, washing machine, stove, Blu-ray, laptop, home theater, television, e-book, Global Positioning System (GPS), liquid-crystal display (LCD) monitor, dieting, hair care product, coffee maker, mattress, paint, cruise, restaurant, hotel, cosmetics, fashion, drug, soft drink, beer and wine, movie, video editing software, financial software, search engine, health insurance, banking, investment, green technology, box-office revenue prediction for new movies, Summer Olympics bidding, gubernatorial election, presidential election, and public mood detection during the 2008–2009 financial crisis.

Applications are also widespread in government agencies. Internally, agencies monitor social media to discover public sentiments and citizen concerns. Such monitoring is especially big in China, where social media have become the most popular channel for the general public to voice their opinions about government policies and to expose corruptions, sex scandals, and other wrong-doings of government officials. It is also the quickest and most popular way to report negative events in everyday lives. Weibo, which literally means "micro-blog" in Chinese and is similar to Twitter, is the most popular platform for such revelations. Several commercial social media monitoring tools are already available. One core technology in these tools is sentiment analysis. Externally, intelligence services discover issues and events being discussed in the social media of other countries and public sentiment about the issues and events by monitoring the main social media sites of these countries.

Besides real-life applications, many application-oriented research papers have been published. For example, several researchers have used sentiment information to predict movie success and box-office revenue. Mishne and Glance (2006) showed that positive sentiment is a better predictor of movie success than simple buzz (keyword) count. Sadikov et al. (2009) made the same prediction using sentiment and other features. Liu et al. (2007) reported a sentiment model for predicting box-office revenue that consists of two steps. The first step builds a topic model based on probabilistic latent semantic analysis (PLSA) (Hofmann, 1999) using only sentiment words in a set of movie reviews. Sentiment words, also called opinion words, are words that indicate desirable or undesirable states. For example, *good*, *great*, and *beautiful* are positive sentiment words, and *bad*, *awful*, and *dreadful* are negative sentiment words. The second step builds an autoregressive model employing both the revenues and sentiment topics in the past few days to predict future revenues. This same revenue prediction problem was also tackled by Asur and Huberman (2010) using both the tweet volume and the tweet sentiment. A linear regression–based approach using movie review text and movie meta-data was reported in Joshi et al. (2010). My own group also used tweet sentiment to predict movie revenues several years ago and found that they could be predicted fairly easily and accurately. We simply applied our Opinion Parser system to identify and combine positive and negative opinions about each movie and user intentions to watch it; no additional model or algorithm was used.

Several researchers have analyzed sentiments of public opinions in the context of electoral politics. For example, O'Connor et al. (2010) computed a sentiment score based simply on counting positive and negative sentiment words; this score was shown to correlate well with presidential approval, political election polls, and consumer confidence surveys. Bermingham and Smeaton (2011) utilized tweet volume and positive and negative tweets as the independent variables and polling results as values for the dependent variable to train a linear regression model to predict election results. Chung and Mustafaraj (2011) and Gayo-Avello et al. (2011) discussed several limitations of current works on using Twitter data to predict political elections, one of them being poor sentiment analysis accuracy. The works in Diakopoulos and Shamma (2010) and Sang and Bos (2012) used manually annotated sentiments of tweets for election prediction. Tumasjan et al. (2010) even showed that simple party mentions on Twitter can be a good predictor of election results. In other related works, Yano and Smith (2010) reported a method for predicting comment volumes of political blogs, Chen et al. (2010) studied political standpoints, and Khoo et al. (2012) analyzed sentiment in political news articles about economic policies and political figures.

Another popular application area is stock market prediction. Das and Chen (2007) identified opinions from message board posts by classifying each post into one of three sentiment classes: bullish (optimistic), bearish (pessimistic), or neutral (neither bullish nor bearish). The resulting sentiments across all stocks were then aggregated and used to predict the Morgan Stanley High-Tech Index. Instead of using bullish and bearish sentiments, Zhang et al. (2010c) identified positive and negative public moods on Twitter and used them to predict the movement of stock market indices such as the Dow Jones Industrial Average (DJIA), S&P 500, and NASDAQ. They showed that when emotions on Twitter fly high – that is, when people express a lot of hope, fear, and worry – the Dow goes down the next day. When people have less hope, fear, and worry, the Dow goes up. Along similar lines, Bollen et al. (2011) used Twitter moods to predict the movement of the DJIA. In particular, the authors analyzed the text content of tweets to generate a six-dimensional daily time series of public mood: calm, alert, sure, vital, kind, and happy. The resulting mood time series were correlated with the DJIA to assess their ability to predict changes in the DJIA over time. Their results indicate that the accuracy of standard stock market prediction models can be significantly improved when certain mood dimensions are included (i.e., calm and happiness), but not others. Instead of treating sentiments from all relevant Twitter authors equally, Bar-Haim et al. (2011) identified expert investors based on their past predictions of bullish and bearish stocks. Such expert investors were then used as one of the features in training stock price movement predictors. Feldman et al. (2011) reported a focused investigation of sentiment analysis of stock-related articles. Zhang and Skiena (2010) used blog and news sentiment to design trading strategies. Si et al. (2013) combined a topic-based sentiment time series and the index time series to predict the S&P 100 index's daily movements using vector autoregression. Their topic-based sentiment analysis system first used a nonparametric topic model to identify daily topics related to stocks and then computed people's sentiments about these topics.

In addition to research in the preceding three popular application areas, numerous papers have been published on using sentiment analysis to facilitate other types of applications. For example, McGlohon et al. (2010) used product reviews to rank products and merchants. Hong and Skiena (2010) studied the relationships between the National Football League betting line and public opinions in blogs and on Twitter. The work of Miller et al. (2011) investigated sentiment flow in social networks. In the study carried out by Mohammad and Yang (2011), sentiments in males were used to find how genders differed on emotional axes. Mohammad's (2011) study tracked emotions in novels and fairy tales. Sakunkoo and Sakunkoo (2009) investigated social influences in online book reviews, and Groh and Hauffa (2011) used sentiment analysis to characterize social relations. A deployed general-purpose sentiment analysis system and some case studies were reported in Castellanos et al. (2011).

1.2 Sentiment Analysis Research

Pervasive real-life applications provide strong motivations for research, but applications alone are not enough to generate strong research interest in academia: researchers also need challenging technical problems. Sentiment analysis has provided plenty of such problems, most of which had not been attempted before, in either the NLP or linguistics communities. The novelty factor coupled with widespread applications and the availability of social media data have attracted numerous researchers to the field. Since the year 2000, the field has grown rapidly to become one of the most active research areas in NLP, data mining, and web mining and is also widely studied in the management sciences (Hu et al., 2006; Archak et al., 2007; Das and Chen, 2007; Dellarocas et al., 2007; Ghose et al., 2007; Park et al., 2007; Chen and Xie, 2008). Although sentiment analysis has been studied in different disciplines, their focuses are not the same. For example, in management sciences, the main focus is the impact of consumer opinions on businesses and ways to exploit such opinions to enhance business practices. In contrast, for NLP and data mining, the objective is to design effective algorithms and models to extract opinions from natural language text and to summarize them suitably.

In terms of natural language understanding, sentiment analysis can be regarded as an important subarea of semantic analysis because its goal is to recognize topics that people talk about and their sentiments toward those topics. In the next few subsections, I briefly describe the key research topics covered in this book and connect sentiment analysis with some general NLP tasks.

1.2.1 Different Levels of Analysis

Sentiment analysis research has been mainly carried out at three levels of granularity: document level, sentence level, and aspect level. We briefly introduce them here.

Document level. The task at the document level is to classify whether a whole opinion document expresses a positive or negative sentiment (Pang et al., 2002; Turney, 2002). It is thus known as *document-level sentiment classification*. For example, given a product review, the system determines whether the review expresses an overall positive or negative opinion about the product. This level of analysis implicitly assumes that each document expresses opinions on a single entity (e.g., a single product or service). Consequently, it is not applicable to documents that evaluate or compare multiple entities, for which more fine-grained analysis is needed. We study document-level sentiment analysis in Chapter 3.

Sentence level. The next level is to determine whether a sentence expresses a positive, negative, or neutral opinion. Note that "neutral opinion" usually means "no opinion." This level of analysis is closely related to subjectivity classification (Wiebe et al., 1999), which distinguishes sentences that express factual information (*objective sentences*) from sentences that express subjective views and opinions (*subjective sentences*). However, subjectivity is not equivalent to sentiment or opinion because, as we discussed earlier, many objective sentences can imply sentiments or opinions – for example, "We bought the car last month and the windshield wiper has fallen off." Conversely, many subjective sentences may not express any opinion or sentiment – for example, "I think he went home after lunch." We study sentence-level sentiment analysis in Chapter 4.

Aspect level. Neither document-level nor sentence-level analyses discover what people like and dislike exactly. In other words, they do not tell what each opinion is about – that is, the target of opinion. For example, if we know only that the sentence "I like the iPhone 5" is positive, it is of limited use unless we know that the positive opinion is about the iPhone 5. One may say that if we can classify a sentence to be positive, everything in the sentence can take the positive opinion. However, that will not work either, because a sentence can have multiple opinions – for example, "Apple is doing very well in this poor economy." It does not make much sense to classify this sentence as positive or negative because it is positive about Apple but negative about the economy. To obtain this level of fine-grained results, we need to go to the aspect level.

This level of analysis was earlier called *feature level,* as in "feature-based opinion mining and summarization" (Hu and Liu, 2004; Liu, 2010), which is now called *aspect-based sentiment analysis*. Instead of looking at language units (documents, paragraphs, sentences, clauses, or phrases), aspect-level analysis directly looks at an opinion and its target (called the *opinion target*). Realizing the importance of the opinion targets enables us to have a much better understanding of the sentiment analysis problem.

Let us see another example sentence: "Although the service is not great, I still love this restaurant." This sentence clearly has a positive tone, but we cannot say that it is entirely positive. We can only say that the sentence is positive about the restaurant (emphasized), but it is still negative about its service (not emphasized). If someone reading the opinion cares a lot about the service, she probably will not go to eat at the restaurant. In applications, opinion targets (e.g., the restaurant and the service in the preceding sentence) are often described by entities (e.g., restaurant) and/or their different aspects (e.g., service of the restaurant). Thus, the goal of this level of analysis is to discover sentiments on entities and/or their aspects. On the basis of this level of analysis, a summary of opinions about entities and their aspects can be produced.

We study aspect-level sentiment analysis in Chapters 5 and 6. Note that in some applications, the user may be interested in only opinions about entities. In that case, the system can just ignore its aspects. Aspect-level analysis is what is needed in applications, and almost all real-life sentiment analysis systems in industry are based on this level of analysis.

Besides different levels of analysis, there are two different types of opinions: regular opinions and comparative opinions (Jindal and Liu, 2006b).

- A *regular opinion* expresses a sentiment about a particular entity or an aspect of the entity. For example, "Coke tastes very good" expresses a positive sentiment or opinion on the aspect taste of Coke. This is the most common type of opinion.
- A *comparative opinion* compares multiple entities based on some of their shared aspects. For example, "Coke tastes better than Pepsi" compares Coke and Pepsi based on their tastes (an aspect) and expresses a preference for Coke (see Chapter 8).

Along with these basic tasks, researchers have studied opinion summarization and opinion search, which we study in Chapter 9.

1.2.2   Sentiment Lexicon and Its Issues

Not surprisingly, the most important indicators of sentiments are sentiment words, also called opinion words. For example, *good, wonderful,* and *amazing* are positive sentiment words, and *bad, poor,* and *terrible* are negative sentiment words. Apart from individual words, phrases and idioms may be indicators of sentiments – for example, *cost an arm and a leg*. Sentiment words and phrases are instrumental to sentiment analysis. A list of such words and phrases is called a *sentiment lexicon* (or *opinion lexicon*). Over the years, researchers have designed numerous algorithms to compile such lexicons. We discuss these algorithms in Chapter 7.

Although sentiment words and phrases are important, they are far from sufficient for accurate sentiment analysis. The problem is much more complex. We highlight several issues in the following:

1. A positive or negative sentiment word may have opposite orientations or polarities in different application domains or sentence contexts. By orientation or polarity, we mean whether a sentiment or opinion is positive, negative, or neutral. For example, *suck* usually indicates negative sentiment (e.g., "This camera sucks"), but can also imply positive sentiment (e.g., "This vacuum cleaner really sucks"). Thus, we say that the orientations of sentiment words can be domain dependent or even sentence context dependent.

2. A sentence containing sentiment words may not express any sentiment. This phenomenon happens in several types of sentences. Question (interrogative) sentences and conditional sentences are two main types – for example, "Can you tell me which Sony camera is good?" and "If I can find a good camera in the shop, I will buy it." Both of these sentences contain the sentiment word *good*, but neither expresses a positive or negative opinion about any specific camera. However, that is not to say that all conditional sentences and interrogative sentences express no opinion or sentiment – for example, "Does anyone know how to repair this terrible printer?" and "If you are looking for a good car, get a Ford Focus." We discuss such sentences further in Chapter 4.

3. Sarcastic sentences with or without sentiment words are hard to deal with – for example, "What a great car! It stopped working in two days." Sarcasm is not so common in consumer reviews about products and services but is common in political discussions, which make political opinions hard to deal with. We discuss such sentences in Chapter 4.

4. Many sentences without sentiment words can imply positive or negative sentiments or opinions of their authors. For example, "This washer uses a lot of water" implies a negative opinion about the washer because it uses a lot of resources (water). Many such sentences are actually objective sentences that express some factual information. For example, "After sleeping on the mattress for two days, a valley has formed in the middle" expresses a negative opinion about the quality of the mattress. This sentence can be regarded as objective because it states a fact, although *valley* is used as a metaphor here. As we can see, these two sentences contain no sentiment words, but both express something undesirable, which indicates negative opinions.

All these issues present major challenges. In fact, these are just some of the difficult problems. More are discussed in Chapter 7.

1.2.3   Analyzing Debates and Comments

There are generally two types of text content in social media: stand-alone posts, such as reviews and blogs, and online dialogues, such as debates and discussions. Online dialogues are conversational and typically involve inter-active exchanges of two or more participants in debates and discussions. In contrast, stand-alone posts are mostly independent of one another. Online dialogues are usually full of opinions. In addition to positive and negative sentiments, they contain *agreements* and *disagreements* (or *contentions*), which are regarded as an interactive form of sentiment or opinion. Further-more, owing to user interactions, additional analyses can be performed. For instance, we can discover the stance of each person in a debate, group people into different ideological camps, mine agreement and disagreement expres-sions, and discover contentious issues and the nature of pairwise user argu-ments (Mukherjee and Liu, 2012b). Because debates or discussions are supposed to be exchanges of arguments and reasoning among participants who are engaged in deliberations to achieve some common goals, we can study whether each participant indeed behaves accordingly – that is, by giving reasoned arguments with justifiable claims or by exhibiting dogmatism and egotistic clashes of ideologies. Such analyses are useful to social scientists, for example, in the fields of political science and communications (Mukherjee et al., 2013).

Comments are posts that comment about a published article (e.g., a news article, a blog post, or a review), a video, a picture, or a piece of music. They often consist of a mixture of stand-alone posts and dialogues. Using comments about an online article, we can observe several types of comment posts – for example, reviews of the article, questions to the author of the article or to other readers, answers to questions, and discussions among readers and between readers and the article author. We study the analysis of debates and comments in Chapter 11.

1.2.4   Mining Intent

Intent is defined as a course of action that a person or a group of persons intends to follow. Mining intents expressed in social media has many applica-tions – for example, making product recommendations and discovering likely voters for a political candidate. Although intent and sentiment are two different concepts, they are related in several ways. First, one may attach some senti-ment or emotion to the involved entity in an intent sentence – for example, "I am dying to see *Life of Pi*." Here the intent of the person has reached the emotional level. Second, when one expresses a desire to get a particular item, one often has a positive opinion about the item. For example, from the statement "I want to buy an iPhone 5," it is probably safe to infer that the person has a good impression about the iPhone 5. These two cases represent a new kind of sentiment, *aspiration*. The two example sentences both expressed positive aspirations. Third, some opinions are expressed as intentions – for example, "I want to throw this camera out of the window" and "I am going to return this camera to the shop." So far, mining of intent has not received much research attention, but I believe it has a great potential for applications. Chapter 12 discusses the problem and presents an intent mining algorithm based on the idea of transfer learning (Chen et al., 2013a).

1.2.5   Opinion Spam Detection and Quality of Reviews

A key feature of social media is that it enables people from anywhere in the world to freely express their views and opinions without disclosing their true identify and without the fear of undesirable consequences. These opinions are thus highly valuable. However, this anonymity comes with a price. It makes it easy for people with hidden agendas or malicious intentions to game the system by posting fake opinions to promote or to discredit some target products, services, organizations, or individuals without disclosing their true intentions, or the person or organization for which they are secretly working. Such individuals are called *opinion spammers,* and their activity is called *opinion spamming* (Jindal and Liu, 2007, 2008).

Opinion spamming has become a major issue in social media. In addition to individuals who give fake opinions in reviews and forum discussions, some commercial companies are in the business of writing fake reviews and bogus blogs for their clients. Several high-profile cases of fake reviews have been reported in the news (Harmon, February 14, 2004; Kost, September 15, 2012; Streitfeld, January 26, 2012; August 25, 2012). It is important to detect such spamming activities to ensure that the opinions on the web are trusted sources of valuable information. Unlike extraction of positive and negative opinions, opinion spam detection is not just a NLP problem but also a data mining problem as it involves analyzing the posting behaviors of reviewers. Besides academic research, some review-hosting companies filter fake reviews on their sites – for example, Yelp.com and Dianping.com. Chapter 13 studies the problem and the current state-of-the-art detection algorithms.

A related research problem is to assess the quality or utility of each online review. The objective here is to identify those reviews that are of high quality and rank them at the top so that the user can read them first to get the maximum information. This topic and its associated algorithms are discussed in Chapter 14.

To end this section, I would like to mention several other books on sentiment analysis or opinion mining: a multiauthor volume *Computing Attitude and Affect in Text: Theory and Applications* (Shanahan et al., 2006), a survey book by Pang and Lee (2008), a newer survey book by Liu (2012), and a monograph by Cambria and Hussain (2012). All four books have excellent content and have helped me in writing this book. However, since the first two books were published, there have been significant advancements. Researchers now have a much better understanding of the whole spectrum of the problem, its structure, and the core issues. Numerous new models and methods have also been proposed. The research in the area has not only deepened but also broadened significantly. Earlier research in the field focused mainly on document- and sentence-level sentiment and subjectivity classification, which is insufficient for real-life applications. Practical applications almost always demand aspect-level analysis. Although the third book, which is also authored by me, is relatively new, it is a research survey. The monograph by Cambria and Hussain (2012) focuses on using commonsense knowledge in opinion mining.

This new book is much more comprehensive. First, it includes details of many important algorithms. By following these algorithms, interested readers can actually implement a practical sentiment analysis system without much difficulty. Second, it goes beyond much of the current analysis on stand-alone (or independent) posts to cover analysis and mining of interactive social media forms (e.g., debates and comments) and intentions. These inclusions significantly broaden the research area and make it more comprehensive.

1.3   Sentiment Analysis As Mini-NLP

Sentiment analysis is commonly seen as a subarea of NLP. Since its inception, sentiment analysis has expanded the NLP research significantly by introducing many challenging research problems that had not been studied before. However, research in the past twenty years seems to indicate that rather than being a subproblem of NLP, sentiment analysis is actually more like a mini-version of the full NLP or a special case of the full NLP. That is, every subproblem of NLP is also a subproblem of sentiment analysis, and vice versa. The reason for this is that sentiment analysis touches every core area of NLP, such as lexical semantics, coreference resolution, word sense disambiguation, discourse analysis, information extraction, and semantic analysis. We discuss some of these general NLP problems in various chapters of this book in the context of sentiment analysis as part of the approaches proposed by researchers to solve the sentiment analysis problem. In this sense, sentiment analysis offers an excellent platform for all NLP researchers to make tangible and focused progress on all fronts of NLP, with the potential of making a huge research and practical impact. Clearly, solving a simpler version of NLP is much more manageable. It is also much easier to achieve major progresses and breakthroughs. A NLP researcher of any area can start to solve a corresponding problem in sentiment analysis without changing her research topic or area. The only thing that she needs to change is the corpus, which should be an opinion corpus.

In general, sentiment analysis is a semantic analysis problem, but it is highly focused and confined because a sentiment analysis system does not need to fully "understand" each sentence or document; it only needs to comprehend some aspects of it – for example, positive and negative opinions and their targets. Owing to some of its special characteristics, sentiment analysis allows much deeper language analyses to be performed to gain better insights into NLP than in the general setting because the complexity of the general setting of NLP is simply overwhelming. Although general natural language understanding is still far from us, with the concerted effort of researchers from different NLP areas, we may be able to solve the sentiment analysis problem, which in turn can give us critical insight into how to deal with the general NLP.

Through this book, I would like to encourage researchers from other areas of NLP to continue working on their favorite NLP problems, but using opinion corpora, which will directly or indirectly help solve the sentiment analysis problem.

1.4   My Approach to Writing This Book

In this book, we explore the fascinating topic of sentiment analysis. Although the book deals with the natural language text, which is called *unstructured data*, I try to take a structured approach to writing this book. The next chapter formally defines the sentiment analysis problem, which allows us to see its structure. From the definition, we will be able to state the key tasks of sentiment analysis. In subsequent chapters, I describe existing techniques for performing the tasks. The book not only discusses key research concepts, but also looks at the technology from an application point of view to help practitioners in the field. This practical guidance is based on my research, consulting, and start-up experiences. When I talk about industrial systems, I will not reveal the names of companies or their systems for confidentiality reasons.

Although I try to cover all major ideas and techniques in this book, fully addressing them has become an impossible task. In the past decade, a huge number of research papers (probably more than two thousand) have been published on the topic. Although most papers appeared at NLP conferences and in NLP journals, many papers have also been published in data mining, web mining, machine learning, information retrieval, e-commerce, management sciences, and many other fields. It is thus almost impossible to write a book that covers the ideas in every published paper. I am sorry if your good ideas or techniques are overlooked in this book.

Finally, background knowledge in the following areas will be helpful in reading this book: NLP (Manning and Schutze, 1999; Indurkhya and Damerau, 2010), machine learning (Mitchell, 1997; Bishop, 2006), data mining (Tan et al., 2005; Liu, 2006, 2011; Han et al., 2011), and information retrieval (Manning et al., 2008). As mentioned earlier, a large number of research papers solve the problem by applying machine learning and data mining algorithms with NLP syntactic and semantic features. For this reason, I do not detail these algorithms in this book.

2   The Problem of Sentiment Analysis

In this chapter, we define an abstraction of the sentiment analysis problem. This abstraction gives us a statement of the problem and enables us to see a rich set of interrelated subproblems. It is often said that if we cannot structure a problem, we probably do not understand the problem. The objective of the definitions is thus to abstract a structure from the complex and intimidating unstructured natural language text. This structure serves as a common framework to unify various existing research directions and enable researchers to design more robust and accurate solution techniques by exploiting the interrelationships of the subproblems. From a practical application point of view, the definitions let practitioners see which subproblems need to be solved in building a sentiment analysis system, how the subproblems are related, and what output should be produced.

Unlike factual information, sentiment and opinion share an important characteristic – namely, they are subjective. This subjectivity comes from many sources. First, different people may have different experiences and thus different opinions. For example, one person may have bought a particular brand of camera and had a very good experience with it. She naturally has a positive opinion or sentiment about the camera. However, another person who bought a camera of the same brand might have had some issues with it because he got unlucky and purchased a defective unit. He thus has a negative opinion. Second, different people may see the same thing in different ways because every issue has at least two sides. For example, when the price of a stock is falling, one person may feel very sad because he bought the stock when the price was high, but another person may be very happy because it is an opportunity to short sell the stock and make a good profit. Furthermore, different people may have different interests or different ideologies.

Owing to such different subjective experiences, views, interests, and ideologies, it is important to examine a collection of opinions from many people rather than only one opinion from a single person, because such an opinion represents only the subjective view of that single person, which is usually not sufficient for action. With a large number of opinions, some form of summary becomes necessary (Hu and Liu, 2004). Thus, the problem definition should state what kind of summary may be desired. Apart from opinion and sentiment, this chapter also discusses the closely related concepts of affect, emotion, and mood.

Throughout this chapter and the whole book, I mainly use product reviews and sentences from such reviews as examples to introduce the key concepts of sentiment analysis, but the ideas and the resulting definitions are general and applicable to all forms of formal and informal opinion text, such as news articles, tweets (Twitter posts), forum discussions, blogs, and Facebook posts, and to all domains, including social and political domains. Because product reviews are highly focused and rich in opinions, they allow us to see different issues more clearly than do other forms of opinion text. Conceptually, there is no fundamental difference between product reviews and other forms of opinion text, except some superficial differences and the degree of difficulty in dealing with them. For example, tweets are short (traditionally limited to 140 characters) and informal: they use many Internet slang terms and emoticons. Owing to the length limit, the authors usually get straight to the point. Thus, it is often easier to achieve better sentiment analysis accuracy for tweets. Reviews are also easier to analyze because they are highly focused with little irrelevant information. Forum discussions are perhaps the hardest to deal with because the users there can discuss anything and often are involved in interactive exchanges with one another.

Different application domains also have different degrees of difficulty. Opinions about products and services are usually the easiest to deal with. By comparison, opinions about social and political issues are much harder to analyze because of their complex topic and sentiment expressions, sarcasm, and use of irony. These often need analysis at the pragmatics level, which is difficult without sufficient background knowledge of the local social and political contexts. These characteristics explain why many commercial systems are able to perform sentiment analysis of opinions about products and services reasonably well but fare poorly on opinionated social and political texts.

2.1   Definition of Opinion

As discussed in Chapter 1, sentiment analysis mainly studies opinions that express or imply positive or negative sentiment. We define the problem in this context. We use the term *opinion* as a broad concept that covers sentiment, evaluation, appraisal, or attitude and associated information such as the opinion target and the person who holds the opinion, and we use the term *sentiment* to mean only the underlying positive or negative feeling implied by opinion. Owing to the need to analyze a large volume of opinions, in defining opinion, we consider two levels of abstraction: *a single opinion* and *a set of opinions*. In this section, we focus on defining a single opinion and describing the tasks involved in extracting an opinion. Section 2.2 focuses on a set of opinions, where we define *opinion summary*.

2.1.1   Opinion Definition

We use the following review (Review A) about a camera to introduce the problem (an ID number is associated with each sentence for easy reference):

> **Review A**: Posted by John Smith
> Date: September 10, 2011
> (1) *I bought a Canon G12 camera six months ago.* (2) *I simply love it.* (3) *The picture quality is amazing.* (4) *The battery life is also long.* (5) *However, my wife thinks it is too heavy for her.*

From this review, we notice the following points.

Opinion, sentiment, and target. Review A has several opinions with positive or negative sentiment about the Canon G12 camera. Sentence 2 expresses a positive sentiment about the Canon camera as a whole. Sentence 3 expresses a positive sentiment about its picture equality. Sentence 4 expresses a positive sentiment about its battery life. Sentence 5 expresses a negative sentiment about the camera's weight.

These opinions enable us to make a crucial observation about sentiment analysis. That is, an opinion has two key components: a target g and a sentiment s on the target – that is, (g, s), where g can be any entity or aspect of the entity about which an opinion has been expressed, and s can be a positive, negative, or neutral sentiment or a numeric rating. "Positive," "negative," and "neutral" are called *sentiment* or *opinion orientations*. For example, the target of the opinion in sentence 2 is the Canon G12 camera, the target of the opinion in sentence 3 is the picture quality of Canon G12, and the target of sentence 5 is the weight of Canon G12 (weight is indicated by "heavy"). The target is also called the *topic* by some researchers.

Opinion holder. Review A contains opinions from two persons, who are called *opinion sources* or *opinion holders* (Kim and Hovy, 2004; Wiebe et al., 2005). The holder of the opinions in sentences 2, 3, and 4 is the author of the review ("John Smith"). For sentence 5, the opinion source is the author's wife.

Time of opinion. The date of the review was September 10, 2011. This date is useful because one often wants to know how opinions change over time or opinion trend.

With this example, we can define the opinion as a quadruple.

Definition 2.1 (Opinion): An *opinion* is a quadruple (g, s, h, t), where g is the sentiment target, s is the sentiment of the opinion about the target g, h is the opinion holder (the person or organization who holds the opinion), and t is the time when the opinion is expressed.

The four components in this quadruple are essential. It is generally problematic if any of them is missing. For example, the time component is often very important in practice because an opinion given two years ago is not the same as an opinion stated today. Not having an opinion holder is also problematic. For example, an opinion from a very important person (VIP) (e.g., the US president) is probably more important than an opinion from the average Joe on the street. An opinion from an organization is typically more important than an opinion from a private individual. For instance, the opinion implied by "Standard & Poor's downgraded the credit rating of Greece" is very important for the international financial market and even for international politics.

One thing that we want to stress about the definition is that *an opinion has a target*. Recognizing this is important for two reasons. First, in a sentence with multiple targets (which are usually expressed as nouns or noun phrases), we need to identify the specific target for each positive or negative sentiment. For example, "Apple is doing very well in this poor economy" contains both a positive sentiment and a negative sentiment. The target for the positive sentiment is Apple, and the target for the negative sentiment is the economy. Second, words or phrases, such as *good, amazing, bad,* and *poor,* that express sentiments (called *sentiment* or *opinion terms or expressions*) and opinion targets often have some specific syntactic relations (Hu and Liu, 2004; Zhuang et al., 2006; Qiu et al., 2011) that allow us to design algorithms to extract both sentiment expressions and opinion targets, which are two core tasks of sentiment analysis (see Section 2.1.6).

The opinion defined here is just one type of opinion, called a *regular opinion* (e.g., "Coke tastes great"). Another type is *comparative opinion* (e.g., "Coke tastes better than Pepsi"), which needs a different definition (Liu, 2006, 2011; Jindal and Liu, 2006b). Section 2.4 further discusses different types of opinions. Chapter 8 defines and analyzes comparative opinions in detail. For the rest of this section, we focus on only regular opinions, which, for simplicity, we just call opinions.

2.1.2   Sentiment Target

Definition 2.2 (Sentiment target): The *sentiment target*, also known as the *opinion target*, of an opinion is the entity or a part or attribute of the entity about which the sentiment has been expressed.

For example, in sentence 3 of Review A, the target is the picture quality of the Canon G12, although the sentence mentioned only the picture quality. The target is not just the picture quality, because without knowing that the picture quality *belongs to the Canon G12 camera*, the opinion in the sentence is of little use.

An entity can be decomposed and represented hierarchically (Liu, 2006, 2011).

Definition 2.3 (Entity): An *entity e* is a product, service, topic, person, organization, issue, or event. It is described with a pair, *e*: (*T*, *W*), where *T* is a hierarchy of parts, subparts, and so on, and *W* is a set of attributes of *e*. Each part or subpart also has its own set of attributes.

For example, a particular camera model is an entity – for example, Canon G12. It has a set of attributes, such as *picture quality*, *size*, and *weight*, and a set of parts, such as *lens*, *viewfinder*, and *battery*. *Battery* also has its own set of attributes – for example, *battery life* and *battery weight*. A topic can be an entity too – for example, *tax increase*, with its subtopics or parts *tax increase for the poor*, *tax increase for the middle class*, and *tax increase for the rich*.

This definition describes an entity hierarchy based on the *part-of* relation. The root node is the name of the entity – for example, Canon G12 in Review A. All the other nodes are parts and subparts. An opinion can be expressed on any node and any attribute of the node. For instance, in Review A, sentence 2 expresses a positive sentiment or opinion about the entity Canon G12 as a whole, and sentence 3 expresses a positive sentiment or opinion about the picture quality attribute of the camera. Clearly, we can also express opinions about any part or component of the camera.

In the research literature, entities are also called *objects*, and attributes are also called *features* (as in product features) (Hu and Liu, 2004; Liu, 2010). We choose not to use the terms *object* and *feature* in this book because "object" can be confused with the term *object* used in grammar, and "feature" can be confused with the term *feature* used in machine learning to mean a data attribute. In recent years, the term *aspect* has become popular and covers both *part* and *attribute* (see Section 2.1.4).

Entities may be called other names in specific application domains. For example, in politics, entities are usually *political candidates*, *issues*, and *events*. There is no term that is perfect for all application domains. The term *entity* is chosen because most current applications of sentiment analysis study opinions about various forms of named entities – for example, products, services, brands, organizations, events, and people.

2.1.3   Sentiment of Opinion

Definition 2.4 (Sentiment): *Sentiment* is the underlying feeling, attitude, evaluation, or emotion associated with an opinion. It is represented as a triple (*y*, *o*, *i*), where *y* is the type of the sentiment, *o* is the orientation of the sentiment, and *i* is the intensity of the sentiment.

Sentiment type. Sentiment can be classified into several types. There are linguistic-based, psychology-based, and consumer research–based classifications. Here I choose to use a consumer research–based classification because I feel it is simple and easy to use in practice. Consumer research classifies sentiment broadly into two categories: rational sentiment and emotional sentiment (Chaudhuri, 2006).

Definition 2.5 (Rational sentiment): *Rational sentiments* stem from rational reasoning, tangible beliefs, and utilitarian attitudes. They express no emotions.

We also call opinions expressing rational sentiment *rational opinions*. The opinions in the following sentences imply rational sentiment: "The voice of this phone is clear" and "This car is worth the price."

Definition 2.6 (Emotional sentiment): *Emotional sentiments* stem from nontangible and emotional responses to entities that go deep into people's psychological states of mind.

We also call opinions expressing emotional sentiment *emotional opinions*. The opinions in the following sentences imply emotional sentiment: "I love the iPhone," "I am so angry with their service people," "This is the best car ever," and "After our team won, I cried."

Emotional sentiment is stronger than rational sentiment and is usually more important in practice. For example, in marketing, to guarantee the success of a new product in the market, positive sentiment from a large population of consumers has to reach the emotional level. Rational positive sentiment may not be sufficient to lead to product success over the long term.

Each of these broad categories can be further divided into smaller categories. There are many types of emotions – for example, anger, joy, fear, and sadness. We will discuss some possible subdivisions of rational sentiment in Section 2.4.2 and different emotions in Section 2.3. In applications, the user is also free to design her own subcategories.

Sentiment orientation. sentiment orientation can be positive, negative, or neutral. "Neutral" usually means the absence of sentiment or no sentiment. Sentiment orientation is also called *polarity*, *semantic orientation*, or *valence* in the research literature.

Sentiment intensity. Sentiment of each type can still have different levels of strength or intensity. People often express intensity of their feelings in text in two different ways. First, they may choose sentiment expressions (words or phrases) with suitable strengths. For example, *good* is weaker than *excellent*, and *dislike* is weaker than *detest*. Recall that sentiment words are words in a language that are often used to express positive or negative sentiments.

For example, *good*, *wonderful*, and *amazing* are positive sentiment words, and *bad*, *poor*, and *terrible* are negative sentiment words. Second, individuals may use *intensifiers* and *diminishers*, which are terms that change the degree of the expressed sentiment. An intensifier increases the intensity of a positive or negative expression, whereas a diminisher decreases the intensity of that expression. Common English intensifiers include *very, so, extremely, dreadfully, really, awfully, terribly*, and so on, and common English diminishers include *slightly, pretty, a little bit, a bit, somewhat, barely*, and so on.

Sentiment rating. In practical applications, we commonly use some sort of discrete rating to express sentiment intensity. For example, five levels (e.g., 1–5 stars) are often employed, which can be interpreted as follows based on the two types of sentiment in Definitions 2.5 and 2.6:

- Emotional positive (+2 or 5 stars)
- Rational positive (+1 or 4 stars)
- Neutral (0 or 3 stars)
- Rational negative (−1 or 2 stars)
- Emotional negative (−2 or 1 star)

Clearly it is possible to have more rating levels based on different intensities in each type of sentiment. However, it then becomes difficult to differentiate the various intensities based on the natural language text alone because of its highly subjective nature, and because people's spoken or written expressions may not fully match their psychological states of mind. For example, the sentence "This is an excellent phone" expresses a stronger rational evaluation of the phone than the sentence "This is a good phone," while "I love this phone" expresses an emotional evaluation about the phone. However, whether "This is an excellent phone" and "I love this phone" represent completely different psychological states of mind of the authors is hard to say. In practice, the five levels are sufficient for most applications. If these five levels are not enough in some applications, I suggest dividing emotional positive sentiment (and, respectively, emotional negative sentiment) into two levels. Such applications are likely to involve sentiment about social or political events or issues on which people can be highly emotional.

2.1.4   Opinion Definition Simplified

Opinion as defined in Definition 2.1, although concise, may not be easy to use in practice, especially in the domain of online reviews of products, services, and brands. Let us first look at the sentiment (or opinion) target. The central concept here is the entity, which is represented as a hierarchy with an arbitrary number of levels. This can be too complex for practical applications because natural language processing (NLP) is a very difficult task. Recognizing parts and attributes of an entity at different levels of detail is extremely hard. Most applications also do not need such a complex analysis. Thus, we simplify the hierarchy to two levels and use the term *aspect* to denote both parts and attributes. In the simplified tree, the root node is still the entity itself, and the second level (also the leaf level) nodes are different aspects of the entity.

The definition of sentiment in Definition 2.4 can be simplified, too. In many applications, positive (denoted by +1), negative (denoted by −1), and neutral (denoted by 0) orientations alone will suffice. In almost all applications, five levels of ratings are sufficient – for example, 1–5 stars. In both cases, sentiment can be represented with a single value. The other two components in the triple can be folded into this value.

This simplified framework is typically used in practical sentiment analysis systems. We now redefine the concept of opinion (Hu and Liu, 2004; Liu, 2010).

Definition 2.7 (Opinion): An *opinion* is a quintuple (*e, a, s, h, t*), where *e* is the target entity, *a* is the target aspect of entity *e* about which the opinion has been given, *s* is the sentiment of the opinion about aspect *a* of entity *e*, *h* is the opinion holder, and *t* is the opinion posting time; here, *s* can be positive, negative, or neutral, or a rating (e.g., 1–5 stars). When an opinion is only about the entity as a whole, the special aspect GENERAL is used to denote it. Here *e* and *a* together represent the opinion target.

Sentiment analysis (or opinion mining) based on this definition is often called *aspect-based sentiment analysis,* or *feature-based sentiment analysis* as it was termed by Hu and Liu (2004) and Liu (2010). We also call this definition the *core definition* of sentiment analysis, as it can be extended for finer-grained analysis to provide opinion reasons and qualifications, which we discuss in the next subsection.

We should note that owing to the simplification, the quintuple representation of opinion may result in information loss. For example, *ink* is a part of *printer*. A printer review might say, "The ink of this printer is expensive." This sentence does not indicate that the printer itself is expensive; instead, *expensive* here indicates the aspect *price*. If one does not care about any attribute of the ink, this sentence just gives a negative opinion about the ink (which is an aspect of the printer entity). This results in information loss. However, if one also wants to study opinions about different aspects of the ink, then the ink needs to be treated as a separate entity. The quintuple representation still applies, but an extra mechanism will be required to record the part-of relationship between the ink and the printer. Of course, conceptually, we can also extend the flat quintuple relation to a *nested relation* to make it more expressive. However, as we explained earlier, an overly complex definition can make the problem extremely difficult to solve in practice. Despite this limitation, Definition 2.7 does cover the essential information of an opinion sufficiently for most applications.

In some applications, it may not be easy to distinguish the entity and an aspect of the entity, or there is no need to distinguish them. Such cases often occur when people discuss political or social issues – for example, "I hate property tax increases." We may deal with them in two ways. First, because we can regard *property tax increase* as a general issue that does not belong to any specific entity, we can treat it as an entity with the aspect GENERAL. Second, we can regard *property tax* as an entity and *property tax increase* as one of its aspects to form a hierarchical relationship. Whether to treat an issue or topic as an aspect or an entity can also depend on the specific context. For example, in commenting about a local government, a person might say, "I hate the proposed property tax increase." Because it is the local government that imposes and levies property taxes, the specific local government may be regarded as the entity and the proposed property tax increase as one of its aspects.

Not all applications need all five components of an opinion. In some applications, the user may not need the aspect information. For example, in brand management, the user typically is interested only in opinions about product brands (entities). This sort of investigation is sometimes called *entity-based sentiment analysis*. In other applications, the user may not need to know the opinion holder or the time of opinion; thus these components can be ignored.

Definition 2.7 provides a framework to transform unstructured text into structured data. The quintuple is basically a database schema, based on which the extracted opinions can be entered into a database table. Then a rich set of qualitative, quantitative, and trend analyses of opinions can be performed using a whole suite of database management systems and online analytical processing (OLAP) tools.

2.1.5   Reason and Qualifier for Opinion

We can in fact perform an even finer-grained analysis of opinions. Let us use the sentence "This car is too small for a tall person" to explain. It expresses a negative sentiment about the *size* aspect of the car. However, only reporting the negative sentiment for size does not tell the whole story because it can mean *too small* or *too big*. In the sentence, we call "too small" the *reason* for the negative sentiment about size. Furthermore, the sentence does not say that the car is too small for everyone but only *for a tall person*. We call "for a tall person" the *qualifier* of the opinion. We now define these concepts.

Definition 2.8 (Reason for opinion): A reason for an opinion is the cause or explanation of the opinion.

In practical applications, discovering the reasons for each positive or negative opinion can be very important because those reasons might enable one to perform actions to remedy the situation. For example, the sentence "I do not like the picture quality of this camera" is not as useful as "I do not like the picture quality of this camera because the pictures are quite dark." The first sentence does not give the reason for the negative sentiment about the picture quality, so it is difficult to know what to do to improve the picture quality. The second sentence is more informative because it gives the reason for the negative sentiment. The camera manufacturer can make use of this piece of information to improve the picture quality of the camera. In most industrial applications, such reasons are called *problems* or *issues*. Knowing the issues allows businesses to find ways to address them. In this regard, Twitter may not be the best source of opinions for businesses because of the length limit of each tweet, which makes it hard for people to express the detailed reasons for their opinions.

In applications, the system should strive to find opinion reasons. In many cases, such reasons are not hard to find. For example, many adjectives and sentiment expressions that modify aspects are the main reasons for the positive or negative opinions – too small (size), blurry picture, low resolution, and so on. To obtain the opinion reasons, one approach is to extract the sentiment expressions and their modified aspects together and report them to the user as follows:

(*sentiment_expression, aspect, sentiment*)

For instance, from the sentence "The resolution is too low," we can extract (low, resolution, negative), or simply (low, resolution). If the output is intended for human users to view rather than for a computer system to analyze, we may omit the sentiment polarity because the reason usually indicates the polarity.

Definition 2.9 (Qualifier of opinion): A qualifier of an opinion limits or modifies the meaning of the opinion.

Knowing the qualifier is also important in practice because it places boundaries on the opinion's utility. For example, "This car is too small for a tall person" does not say that the car is too small for everyone but just for tall people. For a person who is not tall, this opinion does not apply.

However, as we have seen, not every opinion comes with an explicit reason and/or an explicit qualifier. "The picture quality of this camera is not great" does not have a reason or a qualifier. "The picture quality of this camera is not good for night shots" has a qualifier *for night shots*, but does not give a specific reason for the negative sentiment. "The picture quality of this camera is not good for night shots as the pictures are quite dark" has a reason for the negative sentiment (*the pictures are quite dark*) as well as a qualifier (*for night shots*). Sometimes the qualifier and the reason may not appear in the same sentence and/or may be implicit – for example, "The picture quality of this camera is not great. Pictures of night shots are very dark." and "I am six feet five inches tall. This car is too small me." Such reasons and qualifiers are very hard to identify and to extract. An expression can also serve multiple purposes. For example, *too small'* in the preceding sentence simultaneously indicates the *size* aspect of the car, a *negative sentiment* about the size, and the *reason* for the negative sentiment or opinion.

With reason and qualification considered, we can expand the definition of opinion to the following:

$$(e, a, s, r, q, h, t),$$

where *r* represents the reason and *q* represents the qualification.

2.1.6   Objective and Tasks of Sentiment Analysis

With the definitions in Sections 2.1.1–2.1.5, we can now present the core objective and the key tasks of (aspect-based) sentiment analysis.

Objective of sentiment analysis. Given an opinion document *d*, discover all opinion quintuples (*e, a, s, h, t*) in *d*. For more advanced analysis, discover the reason and qualifier for the sentiment in each opinion quintuple.

Key tasks of sentiment analysis. The key tasks of sentiment analysis can be derived from the five components of the quintuple (Definition 2.7). The first component is the entity, and the first task is to extract entities. This task is similar to named entity recognition (NER) in the context of information extraction (Mooney and Bunescu, 2005; Sarawagi, 2008; Hobbs and Riloff, 2010). However, according to Definition 2.3, an entity can also be an event, issue, or topic, which is usually not a named entity. For example, in "I hate the tax increase," the entity is *tax increase*, which is an issue or topic. In such cases, entity extraction is basically the same as aspect extraction, and the difference between the entity and the aspect becomes blurry. In some applications, there may not be a need to distinguish them.

After extraction, we need to categorize the extracted entities, as people often write the same entity in different ways. For example, Motorola may be written as Mot, Moto, and Motorola, but we need to recognize that all refer to the same entity. We detail these in Section 6.7.

Definition 2.10 (Entity category and entity expression): An *entity category* represents a unique entity, whereas an *entity expression* or *mention* is an actual word or phrase that indicates an entity category in the text.

Each entity or entity category should have a unique name in a particular application. The process of grouping or clustering entity expressions into entity categories is called *entity resolution* or *grouping*.

For aspects of entities, the problem is basically the same as for entities. For example, *picture*, *image*, and *photo* refer to the same aspect for cameras. We thus need to extract aspect expressions and resolve them.

Definition 2.11 (Aspect category and aspect expression): An *aspect category* of an entity represents a unique aspect of the entity, whereas an *aspect expression* or *mention* is an actual word or phrase that indicates an aspect category in the text.

Each aspect or aspect category should also have a unique name in a particular application. The process of grouping aspect expressions into aspect categories (aspects) is called *aspect resolution* or *grouping*.

Aspect expressions are usually nouns and noun phrases but can also be verbs, verb phrases, adjectives, adverbs, and other constructions. They can be either explicit or implicit (Hu and Liu, 2004).

Definition 2.12 (Explicit aspect expression): Aspect expressions that appear in an opinion text as nouns and noun phrases are called *explicit aspect expressions*.

For example, *picture quality* in "The picture quality of this camera is great" is an explicit aspect expression.

Definition 2.13 (Implicit aspect expression): Aspect expressions that are not nouns or noun phrases but indicate some aspects are called *implicit aspect expressions*.

For example, *expensive* is an implicit aspect expression in "This camera is expensive." It implies the aspect *price*. Many implicit aspect expressions are adjectives and adverbs used to describe or qualify some specific aspects – for example, *expensive* (price), and *reliably* (reliability). They can also be verb and verb phrases – for example, "I can install the software easily" and "This machine can play DVDs, which is its best feature." *Install* indicates the aspect of *installation*, and *can play DVDs* indicates the function aspect of *playing DVDs*. Implicit aspect expressions are not just adjectives, adverbs, verbs, and verb phrases; they can be arbitrarily complex. For example, in "This camera will not easily fit in my pocket," *fit in my pocket* indicates the aspect *size* (and/ or *shape*). In the sentence "This restaurant closes too early," *closes too early* indicates the aspect of *closing time* of the restaurant. In both cases, some commonsense knowledge may be needed to recognize them.

Aspect extraction is a very challenging problem, especially when it involves verbs and verb phrases. In some cases, even human beings find it very hard to recognize and annotate aspects. For example, in a vacuum cleaner review, an individual wrote, "The vacuum cleaner does not get the crumbs out of thick carpet," which seems to describe only one very specific aspect, *get the crumbs out of thick carpet*. However, in practice, it may be more useful to decompose this function into two different aspects indicated by (1) *get the crumbs* and (2) *thick carpet*. Aspect 1 represents *the suction power* of the vacuum cleaner about *crumbs*, and aspect 2 represents *suction* related to *thick carpet*. Both aspects are important and useful because the user may be interested in knowing whether the vacuum can suck crumbs and whether it works well with thick carpets.

The third component of the opinion definition is the sentiment. To obtain this information, we need to perform sentiment classification or regression to determine the sentiment orientation or score on the involved aspect and/or entity. The fourth and fifth components are the opinion holder and the opinion posting time, respectively. Both of these components also have expressions and categories as entities and aspects. (I will not repeat their definitions here.) Note that the opinion holder (Bethard et al., 2004; Kim and Hovy, 2004; Choi et al., 2005) is also called the *opinion source* (Wiebe et al., 2005). For product reviews and blogs, opinion holders are usually the authors of the posts and are easy to extract. By comparison, opinion holders are more difficult to extract from news articles, which often explicitly state the person or organization that holds an opinion.

On the basis of the preceding discussion, we can now define a model of entity and a model of opinion document (Liu, 2006, 2011) and summarize the main sentiment analysis tasks.

Model of entity. An entity e is represented by itself as a whole and a finite set of its aspects $A = \{a_1, a_2, \ldots, a_n\}$; e can be expressed in text with any one of a finite set of its entity expressions $\{ee_1, ee_2, \ldots, ee_s\}$. Each aspect $a \in A$ of entity e can be expressed with any one of its finite set of aspect expressions $\{ae_1, ae_2, \ldots, ae_m\}$.

Model of opinion document. An opinion document d contains opinions about a set of entities $\{e_1, e_2, \ldots, e_r\}$ and a subset of aspects of each entity. The opinions are from a set of opinion holders $\{h_1, h_2, \ldots, h_p\}$ and are given at a particular time point t.

Given a set of opinion documents D, sentiment analysis performs the following tasks:

Task 1: entity extraction and resolution. Extract all entity expressions in D, and group synonymous entity expressions into entity clusters (or categories). Each entity expression cluster refers to a unique entity e.

Task 2: aspect extraction and resolution. Extract all aspect expressions of the entities, and group these aspect expressions into clusters. Each aspect expression cluster of entity e represents a unique aspect a.

Task 3: opinion holder extraction and resolution. Extract the holder expressing each opinion from the text or structured data, and group these opinion holders into clusters. This task is analogous to tasks 1 and 2.

Task 4: time extraction and standardization. Extract the posting time for each opinion and standardize different time formats.

Task 5: aspect sentiment classification or regression. Determine whether an opinion about an aspect *a* (or entity *e*) is positive, negative, or neutral (classification), or assign a numeric sentiment rating score to the aspect (or entity) (regression).

Task 6: opinion quintuple generation. Produce all opinion quintuples (*e*, *a*, *s*, *h*, *t*) expressed in *D* based on the results from tasks 1–5. This task might seem simple but it is actually quite difficult in many cases, as Review B (following) shows.

For more advanced analysis, we can also perform the following two tasks, which are analogous to task 2:

Task 7: opinion reason extraction and resolution. Extract reason expressions for each opinion, and group all reason expressions into clusters. Each cluster represents a unique reason for the opinion.

Task 8: opinion qualifier extraction and resolution. Extract qualifier expressions for each opinion, and group all qualifier expressions into clusters. Each cluster represents a unique qualifier for the opinion.

Although reasons for and qualifiers of opinions are useful, their extraction and grouping are very challenging. Little research has been done about them so far.

We use an example review to illustrate the tasks (a sentence number is again associated with each sentence) and the analysis results.

> **Review B:** Posted by bigJohn
> Date: September 15, 2011
> (1) I bought a Samsung camera and my friend brought a Canon camera yesterday. (2) In the past week, we both used the cameras a lot. (3) The photos from my Samy are not clear for night shots, and the battery life is short too. (4) My friend was very happy with his camera and loves its picture quality. (5) I want a camera that can take good photos. (6) I am going to return it tomorrow.

Task 1 should extract the entity expressions *Samsung*, *Samy*, and *Canon* and group *Samsung* and *Samy* together because they represent the same entity. Task 2 should extract the aspect expressions *picture*, *photo*, and *battery life* and group *picture* and *photo* together, as both are synonyms for cameras. Task 3 should find that the holder of the opinions in sentence 3 is bigJohn (the blog author) and that the holder of the opinions in sentence 4 is bigJohn's friend.

Task 4 should find that the time when the blog was posted is September 15, 2011. Task 5 should find that sentence 3 gives a negative opinion of the *picture quality* of the Samsung camera as well as a negative opinion of its *battery life*. Sentence 4 gives a positive opinion of the *Canon camera* as a whole and also of its *picture quality*. Sentence 5 seemingly expresses a positive opinion, but actually does not.

To generate opinion quintuples for sentence 4, we need to know what *his camera* and *its* refer to. Task 6 should finally generate the following opinion quintuples:

1. (Samsung, picture_quality, negative, bigJohn, Sept-15-2011)
2. (Samsung, battery_life, negative, bigJohn, Sept-15-2011)
3. (Canon, GENERAL, positive, bigJohn's_friend, Sept-15-2011)
4. (Canon, picture_quality, positive, bigJohn's_friend, Sept-15-2011)

With more advanced mining and analysis, we can also find the reasons and qualifiers of opinions. *None* means unspecified.

1. (Samsung, picture_quality, negative, bigJohn, Sept-15-2011)
   Reason for opinion: picture not clear
   Qualifier of opinion: night shots
2. (Samsung, battery_life, negative, bigJohn, Sept-15-2011)
   Reason for opinion: short battery life
   Qualifier of opinion: none
3. (Canon, GENERAL, positive, bigJohn's_friend, Sept-15-2011)
   Reason for opinion: none
   Qualifier of opinion: none
4. (Canon, picture_quality, positive, bigJohn's_friend, Sept-15-2011)
   Reason for opinion: none
   Qualifier of opinion: none

2.2   Definition of Opinion Summary

Unlike facts, opinions are subjective (although they may not be all expressed in subjective sentences). An opinion from a single opinion holder is usually not sufficient for action. In almost all applications, the user needs to analyze opinions from a large number of opinion holders. This tells us that some form of summary of opinions is necessary – but what form that opinion summary should take remains a question. On the surface, an opinion summary is just like a multidocument summary because we need to summarize multiple opinion documents (e.g., reviews). Yet it is also very different from a traditional multidocument summary. Although informal descriptions may be developed for a traditional multidocument summary, it is never formally defined. Instead, a traditional multidocument summary is often just "defined" operationally based on each specific algorithm that produces the summary. Thus different algorithms produce different kinds of summaries. The resulting summaries are also hard to evaluate.

Conversely, an opinion summary in its core form can be defined precisely based on the quintuple definition of the opinion, and can be easily evaluated. That is, all opinion summarization algorithms should aim to produce the same summary. Differences in their final summaries will be due to their different accuracies. This core form of opinion summary is called the *aspect-based opinion summary* (or *feature-based opinion summary*) (Hu and Liu, 2004; Liu et al., 2005).

Definition 2.11 (Aspect-based opinion summary): The *aspect-based opinion summary* about an entity *e* is of the following form:

GENERAL: number of opinion holders who are positive about entity *e*

number of opinion holders who are negative about entity *e*

Aspect 1: number of opinion holders who are positive about aspect 1 of entity *e*

number of opinion holders who are negative about aspect 1 of entity *e*

. . .

Aspect *n*: number of opinion holders who are positive about aspect *n* of entity *e*

number of opinion holders who are negative about aspect *n* of entity *e*

where GENERAL represents the entity *e* itself and *n* is the total number of aspects of *e*.

The key features of this opinion summary definition are that it is based on positive and negative opinions about each entity and its aspects and that it is quantitative. The quantitative perspective is reflected by the numbers of positive or negative opinions. In an application, these number counts can be replaced by percentages, if desired. The quantitative perspective is especially important in practice. For example, 20 percent of people positive about a product is very different from 80 percent of people positive about the product.

To illustrate this form of summary, we summarize a set of reviews of a digital camera, called digital camera 1, in Figure 2.1. This figure depicts a *structured summary,* in contrast to a traditional text summary of a short document generated from one or multiple long documents. In the figure, 105 reviews expressed positive opinions about the camera itself, denoted by GENERAL, and twelve reviews expressed negative opinions. *Picture quality*

Digital Camera 1:

Aspect: **GENERAL**
Positive: 105   \<Individual review sentences\>
Negative: 12   \<Individual review sentences\>

Aspect: **Picture quality**
Positive: 75   \<Individual review sentences\>
Negative: 42   \<Individual review sentences\>

Aspect: **Battery life**
Positive: 50   \<Individual review sentences\>
Negative: 9   \<Individual review sentences\>
...

Figure 2.1 An aspect-based opinion summary.

and *battery life* are two camera aspects. Seventy-five reviews expressed positive opinions about the picture quality, and forty-two reviews expressed negative opinions. We also added \<Individual review sentences\>, which can be a link pointing to the sentences and/or the whole reviews that contain the opinions (Hu and Liu, 2004; Liu et al., 2005). With this summary, we can easily see how existing customers feel about the camera. To obtain information on a particular aspect and additional details, we can drill down by following the \<Individual review sentences\> link to see the actual opinion sentences or reviews.

In a more advanced analysis, we can also summarize opinion reasons and qualifiers in a similar way. On the basis of my experience, qualifiers for opinion statements are rare, but reasons for opinions are quite common. To perform this task, we need another level of summary. For example, in Figure 2.1, we may want to summarize the reasons for the poor picture quality based on the sentences in \<Individual review sentences\>. We might find that thirty-five people say the pictures are not bright enough and seven people say the pictures are blurry. This kind of summary is particularly useful in practice because both businesses and individual consumers want to know the main issues with a product. However, this level of detail is more difficult to extract because a reason may take the form of a phrase, a clause, or even a sentence.

Based on the idea of aspect-based summary, researchers have proposed many opinion summarization algorithms. They have also extended this form of summary to some other, more specialized forms. We study them in Chapter 9.

2.3   Affect, Emotion, and Mood

We now discuss emotional sentiment, which includes affect, emotion, and mood. These concepts have been studied extensively in several fields, including psychology, philosophy, and sociology. However, investigations in these fields are seldom concerned with the language used to express such feelings. Instead, their main concerns are people's psychological states of mind; theorizing what affect, emotion, and mood are; what constitutes basic emotions; the physiological reactions that occur (e.g., heart rate change, blood pressure, sweating); the facial expressions, gestures, and postures used; and the impact of such mental states. These mental states have also been exploited extensively in application areas such as marketing, economics, and education.

However, despite the extensive research in this area, these concepts remain slippery and confusing because different theorists may have somewhat different definitions for them and may not even agree about what emotion, mood, and affect are. For example, diverse theorists have proposed that there are from two to twenty basic human emotions, and some do not believe there is such a thing as basic emotions at all (Ortony and Turner, 1990). In most cases, emotion and affect are regarded as synonymous, but all three terms are sometimes used interchangeably. Affect is also used as an all-encompassing term for topics related to emotion, feeling, and mood. To make matters worse, in applications, researchers and practitioners use these concepts loosely in whatever way they feel like without following any established definitions. Thus one is often left puzzled by just what an author means when the word *emotion*, *mood*, or *affect* is used. In most cases, the definition of each term also incorporates one or more of the other terms, resulting in circular definitions, which cause further confusion. The good news for NLP researchers and practitioners is that in practical applications of sentiment analysis, we needn't be too concerned with such an unsettled state of affairs; instead, we can pick and use whatever emotion or mood states that are suitable for the application at hand.

This section first clarifies these concepts and their relationships for our NLP tasks in general and sentiment analysis in particular. It then situates these concepts within the context of sentiment analysis and discusses how they can be handled in sentiment analysis. In addition, we present some other human feelings that are not commonly studied in sentiment analysis.

2.3.1 Affect, Emotion, and Mood in Psychology

We start the discussion with the dictionary definitions of *affect*, *emotion*, and *mood*.[1] The concept of *feeling* is also included, as all three concepts deal with human feelings. From the definitions, we can see how difficult it is to explain or articulate these concepts:

---

[1] www.thefreedictionary.com/subjective

- *Affect:* Feeling or emotion, especially as manifested by facial expression or body language.
- *Emotion:* A mental state that arises spontaneously rather than through conscious effort and is often accompanied by physiological changes.
- *Mood:* A state of mind or emotion.
- *Feeling:* An affective state of consciousness, such as that resulting from emotions, sentiments, or desires.

These definitions are confusing from a scientific point of view because we do not see a clear demarcation for each concept. Thus we turn to the field of psychology to look for better definitions of these terms. The convergence of views and ideas among theorists in the past twenty years gives us a workable classification scheme.

Affect is commonly defined as a neurophysiological state consciously accessible as the simplest raw (nonreflective) feeling evident in moods and emotions (Russell, 2003). The key point here is that such a feeling is primitive and not directed at an object. For example, suppose you are watching a scary movie. If you are affected, it moves you and you experience a feeling of being scared. Your mind further processes this feeling and expresses it to yourself and the world around you. The feeling is then displayed as an *emotion*, such as crying, shock, and screaming.

Emotion is thus the indicator of affect. Owing to cognitive processing, emotion is a compound (rather than primitive) feeling concerned with a specific object, such as a person, an event, a thing, or a topic. It tends to be intense and focused and lasts a short period of time.

Mood, like emotion, is a feeling or affective state, but it typically lasts longer than emotion and tends to be more unfocused and diffused. Mood is also less intense than emotion. For example, you may wake up feeling happy and stay that way for most of the day.

In short, emotions are quick and tense, whereas moods are more diffused and prolonged feelings. For example, we can get very angry very quickly, but it is difficult to stay very angry for a long time. The anger emotion, however, may subside into an irritable mood that can last for quite a long time. An emotion is usually very specific, triggered by noticeable events, which means that an emotion has a specific target. In this sense, emotion is like a rational opinion. Conversely, a mood can be caused by multiple events, and sometimes it may not have any specific targets or causes. Mood typically also has a dimension of future expectation. It can involve a structured set of beliefs about general expectations of a future experience of pleasure or pain, or of positive or negative affect in the future (Batson et al., 1992).

Sentiment analysis is not overly concerned with affect as defined here. Thus, in the following discussion, we focus only on emotion and mood in the psychological context. Let us start with emotion.

Table 2.1 *Basic Emotions Identified by Different Theorists*

Source	Basic Emotions
Arnold (1960)	Anger, aversion, courage, dejection, desire, despair, fear, hate, hope, love, sadness
Ekman et al. (1982)	Anger, disgust, fear, joy, sadness, surprise
Gray (1982)	Anxiety, joy, rage, terror
Izard (1971)	Anger, contempt, disgust, distress, fear, guilt, interest, joy, shame, surprise
James (1884)	Fear, grief, love, rage
McDougall (1926)	Anger, disgust, elation, fear, subjection, tender emotion, wonder
Mowrer (1960)	Pain, pleasure
Oatley and Johnson-Laird (1987)	Anger, disgust, anxiety, happiness, sadness
Panksepp (1982)	Expectancy, fear, rage, panic
Parrott (2001)	Anger, fear, joy, love, sadness, surprise
Plutchik (1980)	Acceptance, anger, anticipation, disgust, joy, fear, sadness, surprise
Tomkins (1984)	Anger, interest, contempt, disgust, distress, fear, joy, shame, surprise
Watson (1930)	Fear, love, rage
Weiner and Graham (1984)	Happiness, sadness

2.3.2 Emotion

Emotion has been studied extensively in sentiment analysis. Because it has a target or an involved entity (or object), it fits the sentiment analysis context naturally. Almost all applications are interested in opinions and emotions associated with some target entities or objects.

Theorists in psychology have grouped emotions into various categories. However, as mentioned earlier, no consensus among theorists has been reached about the set of basic (or primary) emotions. Ortony and Turner (1990) compiled the basic emotions proposed by several theorists in an effort to show their disagreement. We reproduce this summary in Table 2.1.

In addition to the basic emotions, Parrott (2001) proposed the existence of secondary and tertiary emotions (Table 2.2). These secondary and tertiary emotions are useful in some sentiment analysis applications because the set of basic emotions may not be fine-grained enough. For example, in one of the applications that I worked on, the client was interested in detecting *optimism* in the financial market. Optimism is not a basic emotion found in the list of any theorist, but it is a secondary emotion for *joy*, as noted in Table 2.2. Note that although the words in Table 2.2 describe different emotions or states of mind, they can also be used as part of an emotion lexicon in sentiment analysis to

Table 2.2 *Primary, Secondary, and Tertiary Emotions Identified by Parrott (2001)*

Primary Emotion	Secondary Emotion	Tertiary Emotion
Anger	Disgust	Contempt, loathing, revulsion
	Envy	Jealousy
	Exasperation	Frustration
	Irritability	Aggravation, agitation, annoyance, crosspatch, grouchy, grumpy
	Rage	Anger, bitter, dislike, ferocity, fury, hatred, hostility, outrage, resentment, scorn, spite, vengefulness, wrath
	Torment	Torment
Fear	Horror	Alarm, fear, fright, horror, hysteria, mortification, panic, shock, terror
	Nervousness	Anxiety, apprehension (fear), distress, dread, suspense, uneasiness, worry
Joy	Cheerfulness	Amusement, bliss, gaiety, glee, jolliness, joviality, joy, delight, enjoyment, gladness, happiness, jubilation, elation, satisfaction, ecstasy, euphoria
	Contentment	Pleasure
	Enthrallment	Enthrallment, rapture
	Optimism	Eagerness, hope
	Pride	Triumph
	Relief	Relief
	Zest	Enthusiasm, excitement, exhilaration, thrill, zeal
Love	Affection	Adoration, attractiveness, caring, compassion, fondness, liking, sentimentality, tenderness
	Longing	Longing
	Lust/sexual desire	Desire, infatuation, passion
Sadness	Disappointment	Dismay, displeasure
	Neglect	Alienation, defeatism, dejection, embarrassment, homesickness, humiliation, insecurity, insult, isolation, loneliness, rejection
	Sadness	Depression, despair, gloom, glumness, grief, melancholy, misery, sorrow, unhappy, woe
	Shame	Guilt, regret, remorse
	Suffering	Agony, anguish, hurt
	Sympathy	Pity, sympathy
Surprise	Surprise	Amazement, astonishment

Table 2.3 *HUMAINE Polarity Annotations of Emotions*

Negative and Forceful	Negative and Passive	Quiet and Positive
Anger	Boredom	Calm
Annoyance	Despair	Content
Contempt	Disappointment	Relaxed
Disgust	Hurt	Relieved
Irritation	Sadness	Serene
Negative and Not in Control	**Positive and Lively**	**Caring**
Anxiety	Amusement	Affection
Embarrassment	Delight	Empathy
Fear	Elation	Friendliness
Helplessness	Excitement	Love
Powerlessness	Happiness	
Worry	Joy	
	Pleasure	
Negative Thoughts	**Positive Thoughts**	**Reactive**
Doubt	Courage	Interest
Envy	Hope	Politeness
Frustration	Pride	Surprised
Guilt	Satisfaction	
Shame	Trust	
Agitation		
Stress		
Shock		
Tension		

spot different kinds of emotions. Clearly, they need to be significantly expanded to include a sufficient set of synonymous words and phrases to form a reasonably complete emotion lexicon. In fact, researchers have already compiled some emotion lexicons, which we discuss in Section 4.8.

For the purposes of sentiment analysis, we do not need to be concerned with the disagreement of theorists regarding the basic emotions. That is, for a particular application, we can choose the types of emotions that are useful to our specific application. We also do not need to worry about whether those emotions are primary, second, or tertiary.

The *emotion annotation and representation language* (EARL) proposed by the Human–Machine Interaction Network on Emotion (HUMAINE) (HUMAINE, 2006) has classified forty-eight emotions into different kinds of positive and negative orientations or valences (Table 2.3). This is useful to us because sentiment analysis is mainly interested in expressions with positive or negative orientations or polarities (also called *valences*). However, we should take note that some emotions do not have either positive or negative orientations – for example, *surprise* and *interest*. Some psychologists suggest that these should not be regarded as emotions (Ortony and Turner, 1990) simply because they do not have positive or negative orientations or valences. For the same reason, they are not commonly used in sentiment analysis.

2.3.3　Mood

We now turn to mood. The types of moods are similar to the types of emotions, but emotions that last only momentarily will not usually be moods – for example, surprise and shock. Thus, the words or phrases used to express moods are similar to those used for emotions. However, because mood is a feeling that lasts a relatively long time, is diffused, and may not have a clear cause or target object, it is hard to recognize unless a person explicitly declares it – for example, "I feel sad today." We can also monitor someone's writings over a period of time to assess his or her prevailing mood during the period, which can help discover people with prolonged mental or other medical conditions (e.g., chronic depression) and even the tendency to commit suicides or crimes.

It is also interesting to discover the mood of the general population – for example, public mood – and the general atmosphere between organizations or countries – for example, the mood of US and Russian relations – by monitoring the traditional news media and/or social media over a period of time.

Desmet et al. (2012) gave a detailed discussion of mood based on the work of Watson and Tellegen (1985), who proposed the use of two factors to describe and explain mood. These two factors, which were identified from numerous studies, have been used extensively in research that relies on self-reported mood (Watson, Clark, and Tellegen, 1988). These two factors, valence (pleasure–displeasure) and arousal (high energy–low energy), generate four basic mood categories (Figure 2.2).

The energized-pleasant mood represents a state in which a person feels enthusiastic, active, and alert. This is a state of excitement and pleasure, whereas the opposite mood, calm-unpleasant, is a state of sadness and lethargy. The energized-unpleasant mood represents a state in which a person feels tense, nervous, and upset. It is a distress or unpleasant state, whereas the opposite mood, calm-pleasant, is a state of serenity and peacefulness. Together, the four mood states account for roughly one-half to three-quarters of the common variance in mood terms (Watson and Tellegen, 1985; Watson, 1988).

Desmet et al. (2012) simplified the categories and assembled a set of eight basic mood types, two for each category (Table 2.4). This set balances fine-grained distinctions between different moods, yet is also concise and adds nuance to the four basic categories. This set of mood states represents the general variety of human moods, although it is not complete and does not capture every nuance.

Table 2.4 *Eight Mood Types in Four Mood Categories (Desmet et al., 2012)*

	Pleasant	Unpleasant
Energized	(1) Excited – lively	(3) Tense – nervous
	(2) Cheerful – happy	(4) Irritated – annoyed
Calm	(7) Calm – serene	(5) Sad – gloomy
	(8) Relaxed – carefree	(6) Bored – weary

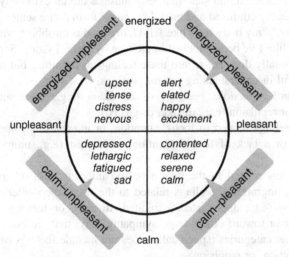

Figure 2.2 Four basic mood categories proposed by Watson and Tellegen (1985), with examples of moods (in the circle) from Russell (1980) and Barrett and Russell (1999).

2.3.4 Feeling

Although sentiment analysis is mainly concerned with feelings of affect, emotion, and mood, other human feelings may be useful in some applications. Feeling is a perception or mental representation of physiological or bodily states (LeDoux, 2012; Damasio and Carvalho, 2013; Nummenmaa et al., 2014), processes inside (e.g., psychological processes) and outside the central nervous system, and/or environmental circumstances. Thus, in addition to the concepts of affect, emotion, and mood, feeling includes many other mental or bodily states. Siddharthan et al. (2019) gave the following list of feeling categories: physiological/bodily states, actions, anticipatory, arousal, social, hedonics (pleasure), hedonics (pain), motivation (approach), motivation (neutral), motivation (avoidance), general well-being (positive), general well-being (negative), self, other. Siddharthan et al. (2019) further described some of the categories in detail, as summarized here.

Physiological or bodily states: Feelings related to specific physiological/ bodily states (e.g., hungry, warm, nauseous) include feelings related to the current status of mental function (e.g., dizzy, forgetful) and feelings related to energy levels (e.g., vital, tired). However, this category does not include levels of arousal (e.g., excited, relaxed). Feelings of such physiological states are particularly common in medical domains. For example, patients might state that "My muscles are all extremely sore," "I'm extremely confused and tired," "I cannot form entire sentences that make sense," "my body feels like Jell-O, my head is throbbing with pain, and I feel like I've been punched in the face by Mike Tyson." Sentiment analysis usually does not regard these feelings as opinions, but they are quite useful in understanding patient postings.

Attraction and repulsion: Feelings of attraction (e.g., love, attracted, hooked) or repulsion (e.g., dislike, disgusted).

Attention: Feelings related to focus, attention, or interest (e.g., interested, curious), or a lack of focus, attention, or interest (e.g., uninterested, apathetic).

Social: Feelings related to the way a person interacts with others (e.g., accepting, ungrateful), feelings related to the way others interact with that person (e.g., appreciated, exploited, trusted), or feelings of one person for or toward others (e.g., sympathy, pity) that are not covered by the other categories (specifically, does not include feelings of anger, fear, attraction, or repulsion).

Actions and prospects: Feelings related to goals, tasks, and actions (e.g., purpose, inspired), including feelings related to planning of actions or goals (e.g., ambitious); feelings related to readiness and capacity for planned actions (e.g., ready, daunted); feelings related to levels of arousal, typically involving changes in heart rate, blood pressure, or alertness; physical and mental states of calmness and excitement (e.g., relaxed, peaceful, excited); feelings related to a person's approach, progress, or unfolding circumstances as related to tasks/goals within the context of the surrounding environment (e.g., organized, over- whelmed, surprised, cautious); and feelings related to prospects (e.g., afraid, anxious, pessimistic, optimistic, hopeful, tense).

Hedonics: Feelings that relate to pleasurable and painful sensations and states of mind, where "pleasurable" includes milder feelings related to comfort and pleasure (e.g., comfortable, soothed) and "painful" includes feelings related to discomfort and suffering (e.g., suffering, uncomfort- able) in addition to pain.

Most of these feelings have already been touched upon by sentiment analysis for specific applications. Perhaps the main exceptions are the physiological or bodily states, which can be analyzed or extracted similarly and may be useful in health or medical applications.

We should also note that the preceding categories are by no means exhaustive. Moreover, feelings can be categorized in other ways. For example, we can use the feelings wheel developed by Willcox (1982). This wheel consists of a core, a secondary ring, and an outer ring. The core has six basic feelings: *mad*, *scared*, *joyful*, *powerful*, *peaceful*, and *sad*. The secondary ring of words helps narrow those core feelings down. The third, outer ring gets even more specific. In all, this tool includes seventy-two adjectives linked to feelings. However, these feelings do not include the physiological or bodily states described earlier.

2.3.5 Affect, Emotion, and Mood in Sentiment Analysis

The preceding discussions are only about people's states of mind, which are the subjects of study of psychologists. However, for sentiment analysis, we need to know how such feelings are expressed in natural language and how they can be recognized. This leads us to the linguistics of affect, emotion, and mood. Affect as defined by psychologists – that is, as a primitive response or feeling with no target – is not much of interest to us: almost everything written in text or displayed in the form of facial expressions and other visible signs has already gone through some cognitive processing to become an emotion or mood. However, we note that the term *affect* is still commonly used in linguistics and many other fields to mean emotion and mood.

Wikipedia has a good page describing the linguistic aspect of emotion and mood. Humans express themselves in two major ways: speech and writing. In addition to making choices about grammatical and lexical expressions, which are common to both speech and writing (discussed later), speaker emotion can be conveyed through paralinguistic mechanisms such as intonations, facial expressions, body movements, biophysical signals, or changes, gestures, and posture. In writing, special punctuation (e.g., repeated exclamation marks, !!!!), capitalization of all letters of a word, emoticons, lengthening of words (e.g., *sloooooow*), and so on, are frequently used to convey emotion, especially in social media.

Regarding choices of grammatical and lexical expressions, there are several common ways in which people express emotions or moods:

1. Use emotion or mood words or phrases such as *love*, *disgust*, *angry*, and *upset*.
2. Describe emotion-related behaviors – for example, "He cried after he saw his mother" and "After he received the news, he jumped up and down for a few minutes like a small boy."

3. Use intensifiers. As discussed in Section 2.1.3, common English intensifiers include *very, so, extremely, dreadfully, really, awfully* (e.g., *awfully bad*), *terribly* (e.g., *terribly good*), *never* (e.g., "I will never buy any product from them again"), *the sheer number of, on earth* (e.g., "What on earth do you think you are doing?"), *the hell* (e.g., "What the hell are you doing?"), *a hell of a,* and so on. To emphasize emotions even further, intensifiers may be repeated – for example, "This car is very very good."

4. Use superlatives. Arguably, many superlative expressions also express emotions – for example, "This car is simply the best."

5. Use pejorative (e.g., "He is a fascist"), laudatory (e.g., "He is a saint"), and sarcastic expressions (e.g., "What a great car; it broke the second day").

6. Use swearing, cursing, insulting, blaming, accusing, and threatening expressions.

My experience is that using these clues is sufficient for recognizing emotion and mood in text. In linguistics, adversative forms, honorific and deferential language, interrogatives, tag questions, and the like may also be employed to express emotional feelings, but their uses are rare and difficult to recognize computationally.

In Sections 3.6 and 4.8, we study existing methods for recognizing or classifying emotions in text. To design new emotion-detection algorithms, in addition to considering the preceding clues, we should be aware of the cognitive gap between people's true psychological states of mind and the language they use to express such states. They may not fully match for many reasons (e.g., being polite and not wanting people to know one's true feelings). Thus, language does not always represent psychological reality. For example, when someone says, "I am happy with this car," that person may not have any emotional reaction toward the car, although the emotion word *happy* is used. Furthermore, emotion and mood are difficult to distinguish in written text (Alm, 2008). We normally do not distinguish between them; that is, when we say "emotion," we mean *emotion or mood*.

Because emotions have targets, and because most of them also imply positive or negative sentiment, they can be represented and handled in very much the same way as rational opinions. Although a rational opinion emphasizes a person's evaluation of an entity and an emotion emphasizes a person's feeling caused by an entity, emotion can essentially be regarded as sentiment with a stronger intensity (see Section 2.1.3). It is often the case that when the sentiment of a person becomes strong, she becomes emotional. For example, "The hotel manager is not professional" expresses a rational opinion, whereas "I almost cried when the hotel manager talked to me in a hostile manner" indicates that the author's sentiment reached the emotional level of *sadness* and/or *anger*. The sentiment orientation of an emotion naturally inherits the polarity of the emotion; for example, *sad, anger, disgust,* and *fear* are negative, whereas *love* and *joy* are positive. Clearly, at the emotional level, sentiment becomes more fine-grained. Additional mechanisms are needed to recognize different types of emotions in writing, as we discussed earlier.

Owing to the similarity of emotion and rational opinion in essence, we can still use the quadruple or quintuple representation of opinion (Definitions 2.1 and 2.7) to represent emotion. However, if we want to be more precise, we can give it a separate definition based on the quadruple (Definition 2.1) or quintuple (Definition 2.7) definitions, as the meanings of some components in the tuple differ somewhat from their counterparts' meanings in the opinion definition: the reason is that emotions focus on personal feelings, whereas rational opinions focus on evaluations of external entities.

Definition 2.14 (Emotion): An *emotion* is a quintuple (e, a, m, f, t), where e is the target entity, a is the target aspect of e that is responsible for the emotion, m is the emotion type or a pair representing an emotion type and an intensity level, f is the feeler of the emotion, and t is the time when the emotion is expressed.

For example, for the emotion expressed in the sentence "I am so upset with the manager of the hotel," the entity is *the hotel,* the aspect is *the manager* of the hotel, the emotion type is *anger,* and the emotion feeler is *I* (the sentence author). If we know the time when the emotion was expressed, we can add it to the quintuple representation. As another example, in "After hearing his brother's death, he burst into tears," the target entity is *his brother's death,* which is an event, and there is no aspect. The emotion type is *sadness* and the emotion feeler is *he.*

In practical applications, we should integrate the analysis of rational opinions and emotions. We should also include the sentiment orientation or polarity of each emotion – that is, whether it is positive (desirable) or negative (undesirable) for the feeler. If that is required, a sentiment component can be included in Definition 2.14 to make it a sextuple.

Cause of emotion. In Section 2.1.5, we discussed reasons for opinions. In a similar way, emotions have causes: they are usually caused by some internal or external event. Here we use the word *cause* instead of *reason* because an emotion is an effect produced by a cause (usually an event) rather than a justification or explanation in support of an opinion. In "After hearing his brother's death, he burst into tears," *his brother's death* is the cause for his sadness emotion. Actually, *his brother's death* is both the target entity and the cause. In many other cases, the target and the cause of an emotion are different. For example, in "I am so mad with the hotel manager because he refused to refund my booking fee," the target entity is *the hotel,* the target aspect is *the manager* of the hotel, and the cause of the *anger* emotion is *he refused to refund my booking fee.*

There is a subtle difference between *his brother's death* and *he refused to refund my booking fee*. The latter states an action performed by *he* (the *hotel manager*) that causes the *sadness* emotion. He is the agent of the undesirable action. The sentiment for the hotel manager is negative. The sentence also explicitly states the anger is directed toward the hotel manager. In the case of *his brother's death*, *his brother* or *death* alone is not the target of the emotion. Instead, the whole event is the target and the cause of the sadness emotion.

Unlike in rational opinions, the authors of many emotion and mood sentences may not explicitly state the entities (e.g., named entities, topics, issues, actions, and events) that are responsible for the emotions or moods – for example, "I felt a bit sad this morning" and "There is sadness in her eyes." Since a rational opinion sentence focuses on both the opinion target and the sentiment for the target, the opinion holder is often omitted (e.g., "The pictures from this camera are great"). In contrast, an emotion sentence focuses on the feeling of the feeler (e.g., "There is sadness in her eyes"). This means that a rational opinion sentence contains both sentiments and their targets explicitly, but may or may not give the opinion holder. An emotion sentence always has feelers and emotion expressions, but may or may not state the emotion target or the cause (e.g., "I love this car" and "I felt sad this morning"). This does not mean that some emotions do not have targets and/or causes. They do, but the targets and/or causes may be expressed in previous sentences or implied by the context, which makes extracting targets and/or causes difficult. In the case of mood, the causes may be implicit or even unknown and, therefore, are not stated in the text.

2.4   Different Types of Opinions

Opinions can actually be classified along many dimensions. We discuss some main classifications in this section.

2.4.1   Regular and Comparative Opinions

The type of opinion that we have defined is called the *regular opinion* (Liu, 2006, 2011). Another type is *comparative opinion* (Jindal and Liu, 2006b).

Regular opinion. A *regular opinion* is often referred to simply as an *opinion* in the literature. It has two main subtypes (Liu, 2006, 2011), as follows.

> *Direct opinion.* A direct opinion is expressed directly on an entity or an entity aspect – for example, "The picture quality is great."
> *Indirect opinion.* An indirect opinion is expressed indirectly on an entity or an aspect of an entity based on some positive or negative effects on some

other entities. This subtype often occurs in the medical domain. For example, the sentence "After injection of the drug, my joints felt worse" describes an undesirable effect of the drug on *my joints*, which indirectly gives a negative opinion or sentiment for the drug. In this case, the entity is *the drug* and the aspect is *effect on joints*. Indirect opinions also occur in other domains, although less frequently. In these cases, they are typically expressed as benefits (positive) or issues (negative) of entities – for example, "With this machine, I can finish my work in one hour, which used to take me five hours" and "After switching to this laptop, my eyes felt much better." In marketing, benefits of a product or service are regarded as major selling points of the product or service. Thus, extracting such benefits is of practical interest.

Current research mainly focuses on direct opinions, which are easier to deal with. Indirect opinions are often harder to handle. For instance, in the drug domain, the system needs to know whether a desirable or undesirable state occurs before or after using a drug. The sentence "Since my joints were painful, my doctor put me on this drug" does not express any opinion about the drug because *painful joints* happened before using *this drug*.

Comparative opinion. A *comparative opinion* expresses a relation of similarities or differences between two or more entities and/or a preference of the opinion holder based on some shared aspects of the entities (Jindal and Liu, 2006a, 2006b). For example, the sentences "Coke tastes better than Pepsi" and "Coke tastes the best" express two comparative opinions. A comparative opinion is usually expressed using the *comparative* or *superlative* form of an adjective or adverb, although not always (e.g., *prefer*). The definitions in Sections 2.1 and 2.2 do not cover comparative opinions. Comparative opinions have many types; we define and discuss them in Chapter 8.

2.4.2   Subjective and Fact-Implied Opinions

Opinions and sentiments are, by nature, subjective because they are about people's subjective views, appraisals, evaluations, and feelings. But when they are expressed in actual text, they do not have to appear as subjective sentences. People can use objective or factual sentences to express their happiness and displeasure because facts can be desirable or undesirable. Conversely, not all subjective sentences express positive or negative sentiments. For example, "I think he went home" states a belief and has no orientation. On the basis of subjectivity, we can classify opinions into two types, subjective and fact-implied.

Subjective opinion. A *subjective opinion* is a regular or comparative opinion given in a subjective statement – for example,

> "Coke tastes great."
> "I think Google's profit will go up next month."
> "This camera is a masterpiece."
> "We are seriously concerned about this new policy."
> "Coke tastes better than Pepsi."

We broadly classified subjective opinions into two categories: rational opinions and emotional opinions (Section 2.1.3). Section 2.3 describes the different emotions, but rational opinions can also be categorized. Here we discuss one classification scheme based on the appraisal system of Martin and White (2005), who categorized opinions (which they called *attitudes*) into three types: affect, judgment, and appreciation. *Affect* concerns emotions; *judgment* concerns opinions about intelligent entities, such as people in the social and ethical domains; and *appreciation* concerns opinions about nonintelligent entities in the aesthetic domain. Here, we discuss only judgment and appreciation.

Judgment can be further divided into normality, capacity, tenacity, veracity, and propriety:

- *Normality* is about how *special* one is. It covers positive opinions related to concepts such as *lucky, fortunate, cool, predictable, fashionable,* and *celebrated,* and negative opinions related to concepts such as *unlucky, odd, eccentric, unpredictable,* and *obscure.*
- *Capacity* is about how *capable* one is. It covers positive opinions related to concepts such as *powerful, vigorous, insightful, clever,* and *accomplished,* and negative opinions related to concepts such as *weak, unsound, crippled, silly, foolish,* and *ignorant.*
- *Tenacity* is about how *dependable* one is. It covers positive opinions related to concepts such as *brave, cautious, dependable,* and *adaptable,* and negative opinions related to concepts such as *cowardly, rash, impatient, undependable,* and *stubborn.*
- *Veracity* is about how *honest* one is. It covers positive opinions related to concepts such as *truthful, honest, credible, frank,* and *candid,* and negative opinions related to concepts such as *dishonest, deceitful, lying, deceptive,* and *manipulative.*
- *Propriety* is about how *ethical* one is. It covers positive opinions related to concepts such as *moral, ethical, law abiding, fair, modest,* and *polite,* and negative opinions related to concepts such as *immoral, evil, corrupt, unfair, arrogant,* and *rude.*

Appreciation can be divided into reaction, composition, and valuation. Reaction and composition also have two subtypes each.

- *Reaction (impact)* focuses on the question "Did it attract me?" It covers positive opinions related to concepts such as *arresting, engaging, fascinating, exciting,* and *lively,* and negative opinions related to concepts such as *dull, boring, tedious, uninviting,* and *unremarkable.*

- *Reaction (quality)* deals with the question "Did I like it?" It covers positive opinions related to concepts such as *fine, good, lovely, beautiful,* and *welcome,* and negative opinions related to concepts such as *bad, yuk, plain, ugly,* and *repulsive.*
- *Composition (balance)* addresses the question "Did it hang together?" It covers positive opinions related to concepts such as *balanced, harmonious, consistent, logical,* and *curvaceous,* and negative opinions related to concepts such as *unbalanced, discordant, uneven, contradictory,* and *distorted.*
- *Composition (complexity)* answers the question "Was it hard to follow?" It covers positive opinions related to concepts such as *simple, pure, elegant, intricate, precise,* and *detailed,* and negative opinions related to concepts such as *ornate, extravagant, byzantine, plain, monolithic,* and *simplistic.*
- *Valuation* relates to the question "Was it worthwhile?" It covers positive opinions related to concepts such as *deep, profound, innovative, valuable, priceless, worthwhile, timely,* and *helpful,* and negative opinions related to concepts such as *shallow, fake, conventional, pricey, worthless, shoddy, dated,* and *useless.*

In applications, we can choose some of these categories based on our application needs. We are also free to design our own scheme, as there is no universally accepted classification. Another linguistic-based classification scheme is described in Asher et al. (2009). However, such generic classifications are often too coarse for real applications, so we should use them with care. For example, based on the definition of valuation, the opinions expressed in the following four sentences all belong to the category of *valuation*:

> "This camera is pricey."
> "The cost of this camera is very high."
> "This camera is old-fashioned."
> "The camera case is useless."

However, these examples talk about very different things with different sentiment targets. In normal applications, they should not be grouped together because they have very different target aspects. Only sentences 1 and 2 have the same target aspect of *price* (or *cost*). The aspects in sentences 1 and 3 are actually implicit – *price* and *design*, respectively.

Fact-implied opinion. A *fact-implied opinion* is a regular or comparative opinion implied in an objective or factual statement. Such an objective statement expresses a desirable or undesirable fact or action. This type of opinion can be further divided into two subtypes:

1. *Personal fact-implied opinion.* Such an opinion is implied by a factual statement about someone's personal experience – for example,

> "I bought the mattress a week ago, and a valley has formed in the middle."
> "I bought the toy yesterday and I have already thrown it into the trash can."
> "My dad bought the car yesterday and it broke today."
> "The battery life of this phone is longer than my previous Samsung phone."

Although factual, these sentences tell us whether the opinion holder is positive or negative about the product or his or her preference among different products. Thus, the opinions implied by these factual sentences are no different from subjective opinions.

2. *Nonpersonal fact-implied opinion.* This type is entirely different, as it does not imply any personal opinion. It often comes from fact reporting, and the reported fact does not give any opinion from anyone – for example,

> "Google's revenue went up by 30 percent."
> "The unemployment rate came down last week."
> "Google made more money than Yahoo! last month."

Unlike personal facts, these sentences do not express any experience or evaluation from any person. For instance, the first sentence does not have the same meaning as a sentiment from a person who has used a Google product and expresses a desirable or undesirable fact about the Google product. Because these sentences do not give any personal opinion, they do not have opinion holders, although they do have sources of information. For example, the source of the information in the first sentence is likely to be Google itself, but it is a fact, not Google's subjective opinion.

We can still treat them as a type of opinion sentence for the following two reasons:

- Each of the sentences indicates a desirable and/or undesirable state for the involved entities or topics (i.e., *Google, Yahoo!,* and *unemployment rate*) based on commonsense knowledge.
- The persons who post the sentences might be expressing positive or negative opinions implicitly about the involved entities. For example, the person who posted the first sentence on Twitter is likely to have a positive sentiment about Google; otherwise, the person would probably not post the fact. This kind of post occurs very frequently on Twitter, where Twitter users pick up some news headlines from the traditional media and post them on Twitter. Many people may also retweet them.

As we can see, it is important to distinguish personal facts and nonpersonal facts, as opinions induced from nonpersonal facts represent a very different type of opinion and need special treatment. The best way to deal with such facts depends on the specific application. My recommendation is to assign a positive or negative orientation based on our commonsense knowledge of whether a sentence is about a fact desirable or undesirable to the involved entity – for example, Google. Users of the sentiment analysis system should be made aware of the convention so that they can make use the opinion appropriately based on their applications.

Sometimes the author who posts such a fact may also give an explicit opinion – for example,

"I am so upset that Google's share price went up today."

The clause *Google's share price went up today* gives a nonpersonal fact-implied positive opinion about Google, but the author is negative about it. This is called a *meta-opinion*, an opinion about an opinion. We discuss ways to deal with meta-opinions in Section 2.4.4.

If we turn the preceding facts into subjective sentences, the meanings become very different:

"I think that Google's revenue will go up by at least 30 percent in the next quarter."
"The unemployment rate will come down soon."
"I think Google will make more money than Yahoo!"

These sentences express only personal opinions.

Subjective opinions are usually easier to deal with because the number of words and phrases that can be used to explicitly express subjective feelings is limited, but this is not the case for fact-implied opinions. There seem to be an infinite number of desirable and undesirable facts, and every domain is different. However, some patterns can still be exploited to infer opinions, as we discuss in Chapter 5. That being said, much of the existing research has focused only on subjective opinions, and only limited work has been done on fact-implied opinions (Zhang and Liu, 2011b).

2.4.3   First-Person and Non-First-Person Opinions

In some applications, it is important to distinguish those statements expressing one's own opinions from those statements expressing beliefs about someone else's opinions. For example, in a political election, a voter makes ballot choices based on his or her belief of each candidate's stances on issues rather than based on the true stances of the candidate, which may or may not be the same.

1. *First-person opinion.* Such an opinion states one's own attitude toward an entity. It can be from a person, a representative of a group, or an organization. Here are some example sentences expressing first-person opinions:

"The tax increase is bad for the economy."
"I think Google's profit will go up next month."
"We are seriously concerned about this new policy."
"Coke tastes better than Pepsi."

Notice that not every sentence needs to explicitly use the first-person pronoun *I* or *we* or to mention an organization name.

2. *Non-first-person opinion.* Such an opinion is expressed by a person stating someone else's opinion. That is, it is a belief of someone else's opinion about some entities or topics – for example,

"I think John likes Lenovo PCs."
"Jim loves his iPhone."
"President Obama supports tax increase."
"I believe Obama does not like wars."

2.4.4   Meta-Opinions

Meta-opinions are opinions about opinions. That is, a meta-opinion's target is also an opinion, which is usually contained in a subordinate clause. The opinion in the subordinate clause can express either a fact with an implied opinion or a subjective opinion. Let us see some examples:

"I am so upset that Google's profit went up."
"I am very happy that my daughter loves her new Ford car."
"I am so sad that Germany lost the game."

These sentences look quite different from the opinion sentences presented earlier, yet they still adhere to the same definition of opinion provided in Definition 2.7. It is just that the target of the meta-opinion in the main clause is now an opinion itself in the subordinate clause. For example, in the first sentence, the author is negative about *Google's profit went up*, which is the target of the meta-opinion in the main clause. Thus the meta-opinion is negative. However, its target is a regular fact-implied positive opinion about *Google's profit*. In practice, these two types of opinions should be treated differently. Because meta-opinions are rare, little research or practical work has been done on them.

2.5   Author and Reader Standpoint

We can look at an opinion from two perspectives: that of the author (opinion holder) who posted the opinion and that of the reader who reads the opinion. Because opinions are subjective, naturally the author and the reader may not see the same thing in the same way. Let us use the following two example sentences to illustrate the point:

"This car is too small for me."
"Google's profits went up by 30 percent."

Because the author (opinion holder) of the first sentence felt the car was too small, a sentiment analysis system should output a negative opinion about the size of the car. However, this does not mean that the car is too small for everyone. A reader may actually like the small size and feel positive about it. This causes a problem because if the system outputs only a negative opinion about size, the reader will not know whether the car was too small or too large, and then she would not see this positive aspect for her. Fortunately, this problem can be remedied by mining and summarizing opinion reasons (see Section 2.1.5). Here *too small* not only indicates a negative opinion about the size but also the reason for the negative opinion. With the reason in hand, the reader can see a more complete picture of the opinion, which will help her make a better decision. In a slightly related work, Greene and Resnik (2009) studied the influence of syntactic choices on perceptions of implicit sentiments. For example, for the same story, different headlines can imply different sentiments.

The second sentence represents a nonpersonal fact-implied opinion. As discussed in Section 2.4.1, the person who posts this fact is likely to be positive about Google. However, the readers may have different feelings. Those who have a financial interest in Google should feel happy, but Google's competitors will not be thrilled. In Section 2.4.2, we choose to assign positive sentiment to the opinion because our commonsense knowledge says that the fact is desirable for Google. Users can decide how to use the opinion based on their application needs.

2.6   Summary

This chapter mainly defined the concepts of opinion and sentiment, the main tasks of sentiment analysis, and the framework of opinion summarization. The definitions abstracted a structure from the complex unstructured natural language text that forms the foundation of the field and serves as a common framework to unify various research directions.

Sentiment analysis is multifaceted problem with many interrelated subproblems, rather than just a single problem. Researchers can exploit the relationships to design more robust and accurate solution techniques for sentiment analysis, and practitioners can see what is needed in building a sentiment analysis system. This chapter also classified and discussed different types of opinions, which may require different solution techniques to analyze them.

Along with these definitions and discussions, the important concepts of affect, emotion, and mood were introduced and defined. They are closely related to, yet also different from, conventional rational opinions. Opinions emphasize evaluation or appraisal of some target objects, events, or topics (collectively called "entities" in this chapter), whereas emotions emphasize people's feelings caused by such entities. In almost all cases, emotions can be regarded as sentiments with strong intensities that have aroused people's inner or basic feelings. Emotions are also more fine-grained than positive or negative opinions, as many types of emotions exist. However, some emotions do not have a positive or negative orientation or polarity – for example, *surprise*. Although one can be positively or negatively surprised, it is also possible that one is just surprised without a positive or negative polarity of feeling. As we mentioned in Section 2.3, there is no single set of basic emotions on which all researchers agree, but this conceptual confusion among psychologists does not concern us too much: we can pick and choose emotion or mood types useful to our particular application and deal with them just as we would any other opinion.

After reading this chapter, you would likely agree with me that on the one hand, sentiment analysis is a highly challenging area of research involving many different tasks and perspectives, and on the other hand, it is highly subjective in nature. But I do not expect that you would completely agree with me on everything in the chapter. I also do not claim that this chapter has covered all the important aspects of sentiment and opinion. My goal is to present a reasonably precise definition of sentiment analysis (or opinion mining) and its related concepts, issues, and tasks. I hope I have succeeded.

3   Document Sentiment Classification

Starting from this chapter, we discuss the main research topics of sentiment analysis and their state-of-the-art algorithms. *Document sentiment classification* (or *document-level sentiment analysis*) is perhaps the most extensively studied topic in the field of sentiment analysis so far, especially in its early days (see the surveys by Pang and Lee, 2008a; Liu, 2012). It aims to classify an opinion document (e.g., a product review) as expressing a positive or a negative opinion (or sentiment), which are called *sentiment orientations* or *polarities*. This task is referred to as document-level analysis because it considers each document as a whole and does not study entities or aspects inside the document or determine sentiments expressed about them. Arguably, this task is the one that popularized sentiment analysis research. Its limitations also motivated the fine-grained task of aspect-based sentiment analysis (Hu and Liu, 2004) (Chapters 5 and 6), which is widely used in practice today.

Document sentiment classification is considered the simplest sentiment analysis task because it treats sentiment classification as a traditional text classification problem with sentiment orientations or polarities as the classes. Thus, any supervised learning algorithms can be applied directly to solve the problem. In most cases, the features used in classification are the same as those used in traditional text classification. Owing to its simple problem definition and equivalence to text classification, document sentiment classification has served as the base task for several other research directions adapted from the general text classification – for example, cross-lingual and cross-domain sentiment classification.

To ensure that the task is meaningful in practice, existing literature on document sentiment classification makes the following implicit assumption (Liu, 2010).

Assumption 3.1: Document sentiment classification assumes that the opinion document d (e.g., a product review) expresses opinions on a single entity e and contains opinions from a single opinion holder h.

Thus, strictly speaking, document sentiment classification can be applied only to a special type of opinion documents. We make this assumption explicit in the task definition.

Definition 3.1 (Document sentiment classification): Given an opinion
document d evaluating an entity, determine the overall sentiment s of
the opinion holder about the entity. In other words, we determine
sentiment s expressed on aspect GENERAL in the quintuple opinion
definition from Section 2.1.1: (_, *GENERAL*, s, _, _), where the entity,
opinion holder, and time of opinion are assumed to be either known or
irrelevant.

There are actually two popular formulations of document-level sentiment analysis based on the type of values that s takes. If s takes categorical values (e.g., positive and negative), it is a classification problem. If s takes numeric values or ordinal scores within a given range (e.g., one to five stars), the problem becomes a regression.

On the basis of the preceding discussions, we can see that this task is somewhat restrictive because, in general, an opinion document can evaluate more than one entity and the sentiment orientations on different entities can be different. The opinion holder may be positive about some entities and negative about others. In such a case, the task of document sentiment classification becomes less meaningful because it is not so useful to assign one sentiment to the entire document. Likewise, the task is not so meaningful if multiple opinion holders express opinions in a single document because their opinions can be different, too – for example, "Jane has used this camera for a few months. She said that she loved it. However, my experience has not been great with the camera. The pictures are all quite dark."

Assumption 3.1 holds well for online reviews of products and services because each review usually focuses on evaluating a single product or service and is written by a single reviewer. However, this assumption may not hold for a forum discussion or blog post because in such a post, the author may express opinions on multiple entities and compare them. That explains why most researchers have used online reviews to perform the task of classification or regression.

In Sections 3.1 and 3.2, we discuss the classification problem of predicting categorical class labels. In Section 3.3, we discuss the regression problem of predicting sentiment rating scores. Most existing techniques for document-level classification use supervised learning, although some unsupervised methods also exist. Sentiment regression has been done mainly using supervised learning. Several extensions to this research have also been attempted, most notably *cross-domain sentiment classification* (or *domain adaptation*) and *cross-language sentiment classification*, which we discuss in Sections 3.4 and 3.5, respectively.

Although this chapter describes several basic techniques in detail, it is mainly written in a survey style because there are a very large number of published papers, and most existing techniques are direct applications of machine learning algorithms with feature engineering. No comprehensive evaluation has been conducted to assess the effectiveness or accuracy of these large numbers of proposed techniques.

3.1   Supervised Sentiment Classification

Sentiment classification is usually formulated as a two-class classification problem: positive or negative. The training and testing data used are normally product reviews. Because every online review has a rating score assigned by its reviewer (e.g., one to five stars), positive and negative classes can be determined easily using the ratings. A review with four or five stars is considered a positive review, and a review with one to two stars is considered a negative review. Most research papers do not use the neutral class (three-star ratings) so as to make the classification problem easier.

Sentiment classification is basically a text classification problem. However, traditional text classification mainly classifies documents on different topics – for example, politics, sciences, and sports. In such classifications, topic-related words are the key features. In contrast, in sentiment classification, sentiment or opinion words that indicate positive or negative opinions are more important – for example, *great*, *excellent*, *amazing*, *horrible*, *bad*, and *worst*. In this section, we present two approaches: (1) applying a standard supervised machine learning algorithm and (2) using a classification method designed specifically for sentiment classification.

3.1.1   Classification Using Traditional Machine Learning Algorithms

Because sentiment classification is a text classification problem, any existing supervised learning method can be directly applied, such as naïve Bayes (NB) classification or support vector machines (SVM) (Joachims, 1999; Shawe-Taylor and Cristianini, 2000). In this subsection, we focus on methods that use traditional supervised learning or classification methods. In Section 3.1.3, we cover deep learning methods.

Pang et al. (2002) took the supervised learning approach in classifying movie reviews into positive and negative classes, showing that using unigrams (a bag of words) as features in classification performed quite well with either NB or SVM, although the authors also tried a number of other feature options. In subsequent research, a large number of researchers have sought to apply many more features and learning algorithms. Like most supervised learning

Table 3.1 *Penn Treebank Part-of-Speech (POS) Tags*

Tag	Description	Tag	Description
CC	Coordinating conjunction	PRP$	Possessive pronoun
CD	Cardinal number	RB	Adverb
DT	Determiner	RBR	Adverb, comparative
EX	Existential *there*	RBS	Adverb, superlative
FW	Foreign word	RP	Particle
IN	Preposition or subordinating conjunction	SYM	Symbol
JJ	Adjective	TO	*to*
JJR	Adjective, comparative	UH	Interjection
JJS	Adjective, superlative	VB	Verb, base form
LS	List item marker	VBD	Verb, past tense
MD	Modal	VBG	Verb, gerund or present participle
NN	Noun, singular or mass	VBN	Verb, past participle
NNP	Proper noun, singular	VBP	Verb, non–third person singular present
NNPS	Proper noun, plural	VBZ	Verb, third person singular present
NNS	Noun, plural	WDT	Wh-determiner
PDT	Predeterminer	WP	Wh-pronoun
POS	Possessive ending	WP$	Possessive wh-pronoun
PRP	Personal pronoun	WRB	Wh-adverb

applications, the key for sentiment classification is the engineering of effective features. Some of the example features are as follows:

Terms and their frequency. These features consist of individual words (unigram) and their *n*-grams with associated frequency counts. They are also the most common features used in traditional, topic-based text classification. In some cases, word positions may also be considered. The TFIDF weighting scheme from information retrieval may be applied as well. As in traditional text classification, these features have been shown to be highly effective for sentiment classification.

Part of speech. The part of speech (POS) of each word is another class of features. Adjectives are important indicators of opinion and sentiment, so some researchers have treated adjectives as special features. However, one can also use all POS tags and their *n*-grams as features. In this book, we use the standard Penn Treebank POS tags, as shown in Table 3.1 (Santorini, 1990), to denote different parts of speech. The Penn Treebank site is www.cis.upenn.edu/~treebank/home.html.

Sentiment words and phrases. Sentiment words are natural features, as they are words in a language for expressing positive or negative sentiments.

For example, *good*, *wonderful*, and *amazing* are positive sentiment words, and *bad*, *poor*, and *terrible* are negative sentiment words. Most sentiment words are adjectives and adverbs, but nouns (e.g., *rubbish*, *junk*, and *crap*) and verbs (e.g., *hate* and *love*) can also be used to express sentiments. Besides individual words, sentiment phrases and idioms are possible – for example, *cost someone an arm and a leg*.

Rules of opinion. In addition to sentiment words and phrases, many other constructs or language compositions can be used to express or imply sentiment and opinion. We list and discuss some of these expressions in Section 5.2.

Sentiment shifters. These expressions are used to change sentiment orientations from positive to negative, or vice versa. Negation words are the most important class of sentiment shifters. For example, the sentence "I don't like this camera" is negative, although the word *like* is positive. Several other types of sentiment shifters also exist, as discussed in Sections 5.2, 5.3, and 5.4. Sentiment shifters also need to be handled with care because not all occurrences of such words mean sentiment changes. For example, *not* in "not only … but also" does not change sentiment orientation.

Syntactic dependency. Researchers have also investigated words' dependency-based features generated from parsing or dependency trees.

A large number of papers have been published on the topic using machine learning algorithms. Here we can only briefly introduce some of them.

Gamon (2004b) performed classification of customer feedback data, which are usually short and noisy compared to reviews, and showed that deep linguistic features are beneficial to classification in addition to the surface features of word *n*-grams. Feature selection is useful as well. The deep linguistic features were extracted from the phrase structure tree produced by NLPWin, a natural language processing (NLP) system from Microsoft Research. The features included POS trigrams, constituent specific length measures (length of sentence, clause, adverbial/adjectival phrase, and noun phrase), constituent structure in the form of context-free phrase structure patterns for each constituent in a parse tree (e.g., DECL::NP VERB NP, a declarative sentence consisting of a noun phrase, a verbal head, and a second noun phrase), POS information coupled with semantic relations (e.g., "verb–subject–noun" indicating a nominal subject to a verbal predicate), and logical form features provided by NLPWin, such as transitivity of a predicate and tense information.

Mullen and Collier (2004) introduced a set of sophisticated features to combine with *n*-grams. These new features are categorized into three main classes: (1) features related to sentiment values of words or phrases computed using pointwise mutual information (PMI) (Turney, 2002), (2) values of adjectives for the three factors introduced by Osgood et al. (1957), and (3) sentiment values of words or phrases in 1 and 2 that are near or in the sentence that mentions the entities being reviewed. The three Osgood factors are *potency* (strong or weak), *activity* (active or passive), and *evaluative* (good or bad), with values derived using WordNet relationships (Kamps et al., 2002). These additional features show some – but not a great deal of – improvements over lemmatized unigrams. We discuss PMI in Section 3.2.1.

In the research conducted by Joshi and Penstein-Rosé (2009), *dependency relations* and their generalizations were used as features in addition to word unigrams. The dependency parse for a given sentence is essentially a set of triples, each of which comprises a grammatical relation and a pair of words from the sentence between which the grammatical relation holds: $\{rel_i, w_j, w_k\}$, where rel_i is a dependency relation between words w_j and w_k. Word w_j is usually referred to as the *head word,* and w_k is usually referred to as the *modifier word.* A feature generated from such a dependency relation is of the fôrm RELATION_HEAD_MODIFIER, which is then used as a standard bag-of-words (BoW) type of binary or frequency-based feature. For example, "This is a great car" has an adjectival modifier (amod) relation between *great* and *car*, which generates the feature amod_car_great. However, this feature is too specific and can be used only for *car*. We can back off or generalize the head word with its POS tag, amod_NN_great, which is a more general feature and can be applied to any noun.

In the work by Xia and Zong (2010), this was generalized further by using N to represent NN, NNS, NNP, NNPS, or PRP; J to represent JJ, JJS, or JJR; R to represent RB, RBS, or RBR; V to represent VB, VBZ, VBD, VBN, VBG, or VBP; and O to represent all other POS tags. The rel_i was also discarded so that, for example, amod_car_great was turned into two features, N_great and car_J. The same generalization strategy was also applied to traditional word bigrams. For classification, an ensemble model was proposed, which improved classification.

An earlier work in Ng et al. (2006) also used dependency relations (adjective–noun, subject–verb, and verb–object), but did not apply back-off generalization. These authors' features also included unigrams, bigrams, trigrams, sentiment words, and objective terms. Feature selection based on weighted log-likelihood ratio was performed as well.

Mejova and Srinivasan (2011) compared various feature definitions and selection strategies. They first tested stemming, term frequency versus binary weighting, negation-enriched features, and *n*-grams or phrases. They then moved to feature selection using frequency-based vocabulary trimming, POS, and lexicon selection. Experiments based on three product and movie review data sets of various sizes showed that some techniques were more beneficial for larger data sets than for smaller ones. For large data sets, a classifier trained only on a small number of features that were ranked high by mutual information (MI) outperformed the classifier trained on all features. However, for small data sets, this did not prove to be true.

Earlier work by Cui et al. (2006) described an evaluation using several classification algorithms and high-order n-grams, up to 6-grams. It applied a chi-square-based feature selection algorithm and showed that high-order n-grams help achieve better classification accuracy. High-order n-grams were also utilized successfully by Bespalov et al. (2011), who applied a deep neutral network approach to build a unified discriminative framework for classification. In the study by Abbasi et al. (2008), a genetic-algorithm–based feature selection algorithm was proposed for sentiment classification in different languages. In addition to the usual n-gram features, these authors used stylistic features such as vocabulary richness and function words.

In the context of microblog sentiment classification, Kouloumpis et al. (2011) used four types of features: (1) n-grams; (2) a Multi-Perspective Question Answering (MPQA) subjectivity lexicon (Wilson et al., 2009); (3) counts of the number of verbs, adverbs, adjectives, nouns, and any other parts of speech; and (4) binary features that capture the presence of positive, negative, and neutral emoticons, abbreviations, and intensifiers (e.g., all caps and character repetitions).

Instead of using the full review for classification, Pang and Lee (2004) proposed application of a machine learning method only to the subjective portions of each review. Such portions are more likely to contain opinions or sentiments. To identify the subjective portions in a review, a simple approach is to use a standard classification algorithm to classify each individual sentence in the review as subjective or objective, treating individual sentences independently. However, neighboring sentences do have some relationships in a document. Considering proximity relations between sentences enables the algorithm to leverage *coherence*: text spans occurring near each other may share the same subjectivity status (subjective or objective), other things being equal.

To consider the proximity relation, the authors represented sentences with a graph. Let the sequence of sentences in a review be $x_1, \ldots, x_n$. Each sentence belongs to one of the two classes C_1 (subjective) or C_2 (objective). The algorithm also has access to two types of information:

- *Individual score $ind_j(x_i)$*: a non-negative estimate of each x_i's preference for being in C_j based on just the features of x_i alone
- *Association score $assoc(x_i, x_k)$*: a non-negative estimate of how important it is that x_i and x_k are in the same class

Using these pieces of information, an undirected flow graph G is constructed with vertices $\{v_1, \ldots, v_n, s, t\}$, where $v_1, \ldots, v_n$ denote the sentences and s and t denote the *source* and the *sink*, respectively. The algorithm then adds n edges (s, v_i) to the graph, each with weight $ind_1(x_i)$, and n edges (v_i, t), each with weight $ind_2(x_i)$. Finally, it adds $\binom{n}{2}$ edges (v_i, v_k), each with weight $assoc(x_i, x_k)$.

The optimization problem for the final classification was set up in such a way that the classification result is the outcome of a *minimum cut* of the graph. The individual score $ind_j(x_i)$ is produced based on a sentence-level subjectivity classifier – for example, NB – that will give the probabilities for being in each class, and the probabilities are $ind_1(x_i)$ and $ind_2(x_i) (= 1 - ind_1(x_i))$. The association score $assoc(x_i, x_k)$ is computed based on the distance between the two sentences. The final review sentiment classification uses only the subjective sentences produced by the minimum cut algorithm. The classification produced this way was shown to be more accurate than that produced by using the whole review.

Related work along the same lines has used annotator rationales to help classification. A rationale is defined as a text span in a document highlighted by human annotators or by an automated system, then used as support or evidence for the document's positive or negative sentiment, which is similar to the subjective portion. In Zaidan et al.'s (2007) research, human annotators were used to label the rationales, whereas Yessenalina et al. (2010a) employed an automated method based on a sentiment lexicon to label rationales. The technique used by Yessenalina et al. (2010b) also tried to identify opinionated or subjective sentences for document sentiment classification. It used a two-level joint model (sentence level and document level) based on structural SVMs (Yu and Joachims, 2009) and directly optimized the document-level classification. The sentence-level sentiment was treated as latent, so no annotations at the sentence level were needed. The work by McDonald et al. (2007) was similar, but it required sentence-level annotations.

In the study by Liu et al. (2010), different linguistic features were compared for blog and review sentiment classification. These researchers found that results on blogs were much worse than on reviews because a review usually focuses on evaluating a single entity, whereas a blog can evaluate multiple entities. Opinions can be positive on some entities, but negative on some others. The authors then studied two methods to improve the classification accuracy for blogs. The first approach involved an information retrieval method that finds relevant sentences to a given topic in each blog and discards the irrelevant sentences before classification. The second method was a simple domain adaption technique that first trains several classifiers from some review domains and then incorporates the hypotheses of the classifiers on the blog data as additional features for training on the blog data. These argumentations resulted in higher classification accuracy for the blog data.

Becker and Aharonson (2010) showed that sentiment classification should focus on the final portion of the text (e.g., the last sentence in a review) based on psycholinguistic and psychophysical experiments using human subjects. However, no computational studies were carried out to verify the claim.

All existing methods use n-gram (usually unigram) features and assign values to features using various term-weighting schemes in information retrieval. Kim et al. (2009) tested various combinations of these schemes: PRESENCE (binary indicator for presence), TF (term frequency), VS.TF [normalized TF as in vector space model (VS)], BM25.TF (normalized TF as in BM25; Robertson and Zaragoza, 2009), IDF (inverse document frequency), VS.IDF (normalized IDF as in VS), and BM25.IDF (normalized IDF as in BM25). The results showed that PRESENCE did very well. The best combination was BM25.TF·VS.IDF, which needs quite a bit of parameter tuning, and offers a minor improvement over PRESENCE (about 1.5 percent).

Martineau and Finin (2009) proposed a new term-weighting scheme called Delta TFIDF, which produced quite good results. In this scheme, the feature value ($V_{t,d}$) for a term/word t in a document d is the difference of that term's TFIDF scores in the positive and negative training corpora:

$$V_{t,d} = tf_{t,d} \times \log_2 \frac{N^+}{df_{t,+}} - tf_{t,d} \times \log_2 \frac{N^-}{df_{t,-}} = tf_{t,d} \times \log_2 \frac{N^+}{df_{t,+}} \frac{df_{t,-}}{N^-} \quad (3.1)$$

where $tf_{t,d}$ is the number of times term t occurs in document d (term frequency), $df_{t,+}$ is the number of positive documents in the training set containing term t, N^+ is the total number positive documents in the training set, $df_{t,-}$ is the number of negative documents in the training set containing term t, and N^- is the total number of negative documents. This term frequency transformation boosts the importance of words that are unevenly distributed between the positive and negative classes and discounts evenly distributed words. This better represents their true importance within the document for sentiment classification.

A comprehensive set of experiments was carried out by Paltoglou and Thelwall (2010) to evaluate the effectiveness of a large number of term-weighting schemes. These included the TF and IDF variants in the SMART system (Salton, 1971) and the variants in BM25 (Robertson and Zaragoza, 2009), their SMART Delta TFIDF versions, and their BM25 Delta TFIDF variants. Smoothing was also applied. The results showed that the Delta versions with smoothing performed significantly better than other variants.

In Li et al.'s (2010f) research, personal (*I, we*) and impersonal (*it, this product*) sentences were exploited to help classification. Specifically, the authors defined a sentence as personal if the subject of the sentence is (or represents) a person and as impersonal if the subject of the sentence is not (or does not represent) a person. Three classifiers – f_1, f_2, and f_3 – were constructed by using only the personal sentences, only the impersonal sentences, and all sentences in each review, respectively. The three base classifiers were then combined by multiplying their posterior possibilities, and the multiplied probability was finally used for classification.

Li et al. (2010d) explored negations and some other sentiment shifters to help improve document-level sentiment classification. Unlike the lexicon-based approach used by Kennedy and Inkpen (2006), which we discuss in Section 3.2.2, these authors took a supervised learning approach, which does not explicitly identify individual words or phrases that are sentiment shifters. Instead, it separates sentences in a document into sentiment-shifted sentences and sentiment-unshifted sentences using classification. This classification required no manually labeled data, but rather simply exploited the original document-level sentiment labels and a feature selection method. The two types of sentences were then used to build two independent sentiment classifiers, which were finally combined to produce the final results. Xia et al. (2013) also proposed a method to make good use of negation words in classification.

Qiu et al. (2009b) proposed an integrated approach of lexicon-based and self-learning methods (the lexicon-based approach is discussed in Section 3.2.2). Briefly, a lexicon-based method uses sentiment words and phrases to determine the sentiment of a document or sentence. The algorithm developed by Qiu et al. (2009b) consists of two phases. The first phase uses a lexicon-based iterative method, in which some reviews are initially classified based on a sentiment lexicon, and then more reviews are classified through an iterative process with a negative/positive ratio control. In the second phase, a supervised classifier is learned by utilizing some reviews classified in the first phase as training data. The learned classifier is then applied to other reviews to revise the classifications produced in the first phase. The advantage of this approach is that it needs no manually labeled data, so it is essentially an unsupervised method using a supervised technique and can be applied to any domain. By contrast, the corpus-based classification methods need manually labeled positive and negative reviews from every domain to which the algorithm is applied.

Li and Zong (2008) showed how to perform sentiment classification by exploiting training data from multiple domains. They proposed two approaches. The first approach combines features from multiple training domains, whereas the second approach combines classifiers built from individual domains. Their results showed that the classifier-level combination performed better than single-domain classification (using the training data from only its own domain).

Li et al. (2009) proposed a non-negative matrix trifactorization model for sentiment classification. In this model, an $m \times n$ term document matrix X is approximated by three factors that specify soft membership of terms and documents in one of k classes; that is, $X \approx FSG^T$. F is an $m \times k$ non-negative matrix representing knowledge in the word space; that is, the ith row of F represents the posterior probabilities of word i belonging to the k classes. G is an $n \times k$ non-negative matrix representing knowledge in the document space; that is, the ith row of G represents the posterior probabilities of document i belonging to the k classes, and S is a $k \times k$ non-negative matrix providing a condensed view of X. In the case of two-class classification, $k = 2$. We can obtain G and F matrices through factorization. G provides the sentiment classification of each document, and F provides the sentiment association of each term (or word). Without any initial knowledge, this is an unsupervised model. Li et al. (2009) also experimented with some supervision – for example, using a small set of sentiment words and a small set of document labels – to constrain the factorization model. If word i is a positive word, the model sets $(F_0)_{i1} = 1$; if it is negative, the model sets $(F_0)_{i2} = 1$. Here F_0 is the initial F matrix. The factorization process is iterative, based on three updating rules. Some known document labels can also be used in the same way. That is, $(G_0)_{i1} = 1$ if the ith document expresses a positive sentiment, and $(G_0)_{i2} = -1$ if the ith document expresses a negative sentiment. These semi-supervised options perform classification quite well.

Bickerstaffe and Zukerman (2010) considered the more general problem of multiway sentiment classification for discrete, ordinal rating scales, focusing on the document level – that is, the problem of predicting the "star" rating associated with each review. Because the classes are ordinal, the algorithm considered interclass similarity in its classification.

Other work on document-level sentiment classification has sought to use semi-supervised learning and/or active learning (Dasgupta and Ng, 2009; Zhou et al., 2010; Li et al., 2011b), labeling features rather than documents (He, 2010), using word vectors to capture latent aspects of words to help classification (Maas et al., 2011), classifying tonality of news article statements (Scholz and Conrad, 2013), and performing word clustering first to reduce feature sparsity and then building models and classifying using the word clusters as features (Popat et al., 2013). In the work described by Li et al. (2012b), active learning was applied for imbalanced sentiment classification. In the study by Tokuhisa et al. (2008), emotion classification of dialogue utterances was also investigated. It first performed sentiment classification of three classes (positive, negative, and neutral) and then classified positive and negative utterances into ten emotion categories. Aly and Atiya (2013) crawled and prepared a large set of Arabic book reviews (63,257); they then performed some initial experiments of sentiment classification and rating prediction on their data set.

3.1.2 Classification Using a Custom Score Function

As an alternative to using a standard machine learning method, researchers have proposed customized techniques specifically for sentiment classification of reviews. The score function described by Dave et al. (2003) is one such technique. It is based on words in positive and negative reviews. The algorithm consists of two steps:

Step 1. Score each term (unigram or n-gram) in the training set using the following equation:

$$\text{score}(t_i) = \frac{\Pr(t_i|C) - \Pr(t_i|C')}{\Pr(t_i|C) + \Pr(t_i|C')} \tag{3.2}$$

where t_i is a term; C is a class; C' is its complement – that is, not C; and $\Pr(t_i|C)$ is the conditional probability of term t_i in class C, which is computed by taking the number of times that a term t_i occurs in class C reviews and dividing it by the total number of terms in the reviews of class C. A term score is thus a measure of the term's bias toward either class ranging from -1 to 1.

Step 2. Classify a new document $d_i = t_1 \ldots t_n$ by summing up the scores of all terms and using the sign of the total to determine the class:

$$\text{class}(d_i) = \begin{cases} C & \text{eval}(d_i) > 0 \\ C' & \text{otherwise} \end{cases} \tag{3.3}$$

where

$$\text{eval}(d_i) = \sum_j \text{score}(t_j) \tag{3.4}$$

Experiments were conducted based on more than 13,000 reviews of seven types of products. The results showed that bigrams (two consecutive words) and trigrams (three consecutive words) as terms gave (similar) best accuracies (84.6–88.3 percent) on two different review data sets. No stemming or stopword removal was applied.

The authors also experimented with many alternative classification techniques – for example, NB, SVM, and several variant score functions. In addition, they tried some word substitution strategies to improve generalization:

- Replace product names with a token ("_productname")
- Replace rare words with a token ("_unique")
- Replace category-specific words with a token ("_producttypeword")
- Replace numeric tokens with NUMBER

Some linguistic modifications using WordNet, stemming, negation, and collocation were tested as well. However, these were not helpful and actually degraded the classification accuracy.

3.1.3 Classification Using Deep Learning

In recent years, due to the popularity of deep learning, many deep learning or neural network methods have been proposed for sentiment classification. This subsection summarizes this body of work. The writing here is based on our survey of deep learning for sentiment analysis (Zhang, Wang, and Liu, 2018).

One of the key contributions of deep learning to sentiment classification or any other learning task is the representation learning. Traditionally, the BoW (bag of words) and TF-IDF scheme was used to generate text representations in NLP and text mining. Early neural networks also adopted this document representation scheme.

However, BoW has several disadvantages. First, it ignores the word order, which means that two documents can have exactly the same representation if they share the same words. Bag-of-n-grams, an extension of BoW, can consider the word order in a short context (n-gram), but suffers from data sparsity and high dimensionality. Second, BoW can barely encode the semantics of words. For example, the words "smart", "clever," and "book" have equal distance between them in BoW, but "smart" should be closer to "clever" than to "book" semantically.

To tackle the shortcomings of BoW, word embedding techniques based on neural networks (Mikolov et al., 2013b) were proposed to generate dense vectors (or low-dimensional vectors) for word representation, which are able to encode some semantic and syntactic properties of words. With word embeddings as input of words, document representation as a dense vector (also called a dense document vector) can be derived using neural networks.

Notice that in addition to applying the two approaches just described (i.e., using BoW and learning dense vectors for documents through word embeddings), one can learn a dense document vector directly from BoW. We distinguish different approaches used in related studies in Table 3.2.

When documents are properly represented, sentiment classification can be conducted by using a variety of neural network models within the traditional supervised learning setting. In some cases, neural networks may be used only to extract text features/text representations, and these features are fed into a non-neural classifier (e.g., SVM) to obtain a final globally optimal classifier. The properties of neural networks and SVM complement each other in such a way that their advantages are combined.

Table 3.2 *Example Deep Learning Methods for Document-Level Sentiment Classification*

Research Work	Document/Text Representation	Neural Network Model	Use Attention Mechanism	Joint Modelling with Sentiment
Moraes et al. (2013)	BoW	ANN (artificial neural network)	No	–
Le and Mikolov (2014)	Dense vector at sentence, paragraph, document level	Paragraph vector	No	–
Glorot et al. (2011)	BoW to dense document vector	SDA (stacked denoising autoencoder)	No	Unsupervised data representation from target domains (in the transfer learning setting)
Zhai and Zhang (2016)	BoW to dense document vector	DAE (denoising autoencoder)	No	–
Johnson and Zhang (2015)	BoW to dense document vector	BoW-CNN and Seq-CNN	No	–
Tang et al. (2015a)	Word embeddings to dense document vector	CNN/LSTM (to learn sentence representation) + GRU (to learn document representation)	No	–
Tang et al. (2015b)	Word embeddings to dense document vector	UPNN (user product neutral network) based on CNN	No	User information and product information
Chen et al. (2016a)	Word embeddings to dense document vector	UPA (user product attention) based on LSTM	Yes	User information and product Information
Dou (2017)	Word embeddings to dense document vector	Memory network	Yes	User information and product Information
Xu et al. (2016)	Word embeddings to dense document vector	LSTM	No	–
Yang et al. (2016)	Word embeddings to dense document vector	GRU-based sequence encoder	Hierarchical attention	–
Yin et al. (2017)	Word embeddings to dense document vector	Input encoder and LSTM	Hierarchical attention	Aspect/target information
Zhou et al. (2016)	Word embeddings to dense document vector	LSTM	Hierarchical attention	Cross-lingual information
Li et al. (2017)	Word embeddings to dense document vectors	Memory network	Yes	Cross-domain information

Besides sophisticated document/text representations, researchers have also leveraged characteristics of the data for the purposes of sentiment classification. For product reviews, several researchers found it beneficial to jointly model sentiment and some other information (e.g., user information and product information) for classification. Additionally, since a document often contains long dependency relations, the attention mechanism is also frequently employed. Table 3.2 summarizes some existing techniques. Next, we give a brief description of some representative works.

Moraes et al. (2013) made an empirical comparison between SVM and artificial neural networks (ANN) for document-level sentiment classification, which demonstrated that ANN produced competitive results to SVM in most cases.

To overcome the weaknesses of BoW, Le and Mikolov (2014) proposed paragraph vector, an unsupervised learning algorithm that learns vector representations for variable-length texts such as sentences, paragraphs, and documents. The vector representations are learned by predicting the surrounding words in contexts sampled from the paragraph. The vector representations of documents are then used in classification.

Zhai and Zhang (2016) introduced a semi-supervised autoencoder, which further considers the sentiment information in its learning stage to obtain better document vectors. These vectors are then used in sentiment classification. More specifically, the model learns a task-specific representation of the textual data by relaxing the loss function in the autoencoder to the Bregman divergence and also deriving a discriminative loss function from the label information.

Johnson and Zhang (2015) proposed a CNN variant named BoW-CNN that employs BoW conversion in the convolution layer. They also designed a new model, called Seq-CNN, to maintain the sequential information of words by concatenating the vector of multiple words.

Tang et al. (2015a) proposed a neural network to learn document representation, which provides for consideration of sentence relationships. This model first learns the sentence representation with CNN or LSTM from word embeddings. Then a GRU is utilized to adaptively encode semantics of sentences and their inherent relations in document representations for sentiment classification.

Tang et al. (2015b) applied user representations and product representations in review classification. The idea is that those representations can capture important global clues such as individual preferences of users and overall qualities of products, which can provide better text representations.

Chen et al. (2016a) also incorporated user information and product information for classification but via word- and sentence-level attentions, which can take into account the global user preference and product characteristics at both the word level and the semantic level. Likewise, Dou (2017) used a deep memory network to capture the user and product information. The proposed model can be divided into two separate parts. In the first part, LSTM is applied to learn a document representation. In the second part, a deep memory network consisting of multiple computational layers (hops) is used to predict the review rating for each document.

Xu et al. (2016) proposed a cached LSTM model to capture the overall semantic information in a long text. The memory in this model is divided into several groups with different forgetting rates. The intuition is to enable the memory groups with low forgetting rates to capture global semantic features and those with high forgetting rates to learn local semantic features.

3.1.4   Classification Based on Lifelong Learning

Lifelong learning is an emerging machine learning paradigm that learns a sequence of tasks, with the knowledge learned from previous tasks being retained and used in learning the new task. It contrasts with the traditional machine learning paradigm, which builds a model based on only a single data set with no knowledge retention or use of prior knowledge – an approach called *isolated single task learning*. Lifelong learning tries to imitate human learning: humans always continue to learn and accumulate knowledge, and they use their knowledge to help subsequent learning and problem solving. We never learn in isolation or from scratch. Details about lifelong learning can be found in the first and second editions of Chen and Liu's (2016, 2018) book.

In the context of sentiment classification, each task is the classification of reviews of a particular type of products. The goal of lifelong learning for sentiment classification is to learn from each task, to retain or accumulate the learned sentiment knowledge, and to use the shared knowledge to improve the learning of the new task.

Definition (Lifelong learning): Lifelong learning (LL) is a continuous learning process. At any time point, the learner has learned a sequence of N tasks, $T_1, T_2, \ldots, T_N$. These tasks, which are also called the previous tasks, have their corresponding data sets $D_1, D_2, \ldots, D_N$. When faced with the $(N+1)$th task T_{N+1} (called the new or current task) with its data D_{N+1}, the learner can leverage the past knowledge in the knowledge base (KB) to help learn T_{N+1}. KB maintains the knowledge learned and accumulated from learning the previous tasks. After learning T_{N+1}, KB is updated with the knowledge gained from learning T_{N+1}.

In the work (Chen, Ma, and Liu, 2015), a lifelong learning method, called lifelong sentiment classification (LSC), was proposed for document-level sentiment classification. Assume that we have already performed supervised learning in many past domains (each type of products is regarded as a domain).

(We use the terms *domain* and *task* interchangeably in this setting.) The knowledge learned in these past domains is retained in a knowledge base *KB*. *KB* is then used to improve sentiment classification in the new or target domain D^t, which also has its labeled training data. After learning D^t, its knowledge is also incorporated into the *KB*.

The method proposed by Chen, Ma, and Liu (2015) is based on NB classification. NB is a natural fit for LL because past knowledge can serve as priors for the probabilities of the new task, which is the underlying idea of LSC.

Let us answer two specific questions in the context of sentiment classification. The first question is why the past learning can contribute to the new/current task classification given that the current task already has labeled training data. The answer is that the training data may not be fully representative of the test data due to *sample selection bias* [Heckman, 1979; Shimodaira, 2000; Zadrozny, 2004] and/or small training data set size, which is the case in Chen, Ma, and Liu's (2015) work. For example, in a sentiment classification application, the test data may contain some sentiment words that are not present in the training data, but these sentiment words have appeared in the review data in some previous tasks. So the past knowledge can provide the prior sentiment polarity information for the new task.

The second question is why the past knowledge can help even if the past domains are very diverse and not very similar to the current domain. The main reason is that in sentiment classification, sentiment words and expressions are largely domain independent. That is, their polarities (positive or negative) are often shared across domains. Hence, having worked on a large number of previous/past domains, the system has learned a lot of positive and negative sentiment words. Note that knowledge from only one or two past domains may not be sufficient because of the low coverage of sentiment words in the limited domains.

The paper by Chen, Ma, and Liu (2015) proposed a method that uses two forms of knowledge – document-level knowledge and domain-level knowledge – gained from the previous tasks to help learn the new task. One important technique is to find the previous knowledge that is applicable to the new task. If the knowledge is not applicable, it can harm the learning of the new task. Chen, Ma, and Liu (2015) proposed a frequency-based method to deal with this problem. Their experimental results, using reviews of twenty domains (or tasks), show that this method does, indeed, facilitate future learning.

Wang et al. (2019b) improved this approach further. Their proposed algorithm can improve not only the learning of the new task, but also the performance of any previous task without retraining using the data of that previous task. That is, the algorithm can improve learning forward and backward. The training data for a task does not need to be saved once it is used in learning.

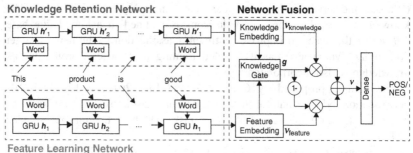

Figure 3.1 SRK architecture.

The main idea is that since NB is a generative model, which is governed by a set of parameters, it should be possible to mine applicable and useful knowledge from the generative model parameters of previous and subsequent tasks (not the original data) and then use it to adjust the parameters of the model for the target task to improve its performance. The target task can be a new task or a previous task. Notably, the generative model for each task is independent of other tasks and the model parameters for each task are saved. Thus no retraining is required when going back to improve the model of any past task.

Lv et al. (2019) proposed a lifelong learning method based on deep learning, called SRK (**S**entiment classification by leveraging the **R**etained **K**nowledge). This method also deals with catastrophic forgetting (CF) in an effort to improve the classification performance. CF is a major problem for neural networks when learning a sequence of tasks. The issue is that the learning of each new task will likely overwrite the weights learned for previous tasks, which degrades the model accuracy for previous tasks. Without solving the CF problem, it is hard to use neural networks for lifelong learning.

The architecture of SRK is given in Figure 3.1. SRK consists of two main networks – a feature learning network and a knowledge retention network – plus a network fusion component.

Feature Learning Network (FLN). FLN is used to learn document representations to perform classification. As shown in Figure 3.1, this network is structured as a conventional gated recurrent units (GRU) cell (Cho et al., 2014).

Knowledge Retention Network (KRN). KRN is used to learn and to retain domain-specific knowledge from previous tasks. Similar to FLN, the structure of this network is a GRU cell that has the same input x and gives out states $\{h'_1, h'_2, \ldots, h'_l\}$. The final state h'_l is used as the knowledge embedding $v_{knowledge} = h'_l$. To retain knowledge, a different learning method, called *partial update*, is proposed; it is described below.

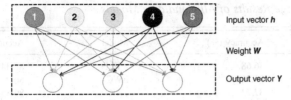

Figure 3.2 An example of a dense layer from a network. The darkness level of the input neuron indicates the activation value. Darker color means a higher activation value.

Network Fusion Component (NFC). NFC is a knowledge gate that integrates the two kinds of representations from FLN and KRN to produce the final result. More specifically, by using the knowledge gate, the relevant information for the current task from both two networks will be selectively combined to make the final decision.

The core of SRK is the KRN. To perform sentiment classification tasks sequentially, the KRN learns and retains domain-specific knowledge from each task. However, conventional neural networks have poor performance because they often suffer from catastrophic forgetting. In a pilot study, it was found that even though neural network–based models have the ability to learn knowledge from tasks, they have a tendency to remember only knowledge that is common across all tasks rather than important specific features in specific tasks. They also tend to remember more of the last task learned due to catastrophic forgetting. Thus, a partial update mechanism is proposed to solve the problem. This idea is inspired by the observation of activation sparsity in neural networks. That is, only a small number of hidden nodes have very high degrees of activation. Most hidden nodes have relatively tiny activation values. This phenomenon becomes more obvious as the number of model parameters grows.

This observation indicates that it is possible to exploit the property of activation sparsity for knowledge learning and sharing among tasks. Specifically, for any network converged on task (D_i, T_i), we compute some statistical information for every layer. As shown in Figure 3.2, the output weights corresponding to those less activated neurons (neurons 2 and 3) can be regarded as less important to task (D_i, T_i). At the same time, those weights corresponding to those frequently activated neurons (neurons 1, 4, and 5) store much of the important knowledge of the task. It is easy to understand that in a matrix multiplication form $y = Wh$, when h_2 and h_3 have tiny values, any modification for columns 2 and 3 in matrix W will have relatively little impact on the output y. Thus, when we train matrix multiplication–based networks like RNNs, we can keep some columns in the weight matrix unchanged, and update only those less important ones.

Table 3.3 *Average Results of All Candidate Models*

Model	Accuracy (%)	Model	Accuracy (%)
LSC	86.68	2-FLN	88.44
I-RNN	83.86	EWC	86.29
FLN	87.73	SRK	89.85

The partial update mechanism consists of two steps: free neuron detection and gradient mask. Free neuron detection basically finds those neurons that are not important for previous tasks. Gradient mask then tries to avoid changing the weights for those nonfree neurons in training to learn the new task. The details of this mechanism are quite involved, but interested readers may refer to Lv et al. (2019).

When experiments were conducted using reviews from twenty domains (or categories of products), they yielded the results summarized in Table 3.3. In the table, LSC is the lifelong learning method in (Chen et al., 2015). Isolated RNN (I-RNN) is the classic RNN model performing each task individually in isolation. It does not use knowledge sharing between multiple tasks, and each task is viewed as an isolated one. The FLN model uses only the FLN of the proposed SRK. 2-FLN uses two identical feature learning networks (i.e., replacing the knowledge retention network with another FLN). EWC is a well-known lifelong learning algorithm that deals with catastrophic forgetting (Kirkpatrick et al., 2017). From the results in Table 3.3, we can see that SRK significantly outperforms other models, which shows that lifelong learning is effective for sentiment classification.

3.2   Unsupervised Sentiment Classification

Because sentiment words and phrases are often the dominating factor for sentiment classification, it is not hard to imagine using them for sentiment classification in an unsupervised manner. We discuss two methods here. The first, based on the method described by Turney (2002), performs classification using some fixed syntactic patterns that are likely to express opinions. The second is based on a sentiment lexicon, which is a list of positive and negative sentiment words and phrases.

3.2.1   *Classification Using Syntactic Patterns and Web Search*

As described by Turney (2002), each syntactic pattern is a sequence of POS tags with some constraints (Table 3.4). The algorithm consists of three steps:

Table 3.4 *Patterns of POS Tags for Extracting Two-Word Phrases*

	First Word	Second Word	Third Word (Not Extracted)
1	JJ	NN or NNS	Anything
2	RB, RBR, or RBS	JJ	Not NN nor NNS
3	JJ	JJ	Not NN nor NNS
4	NN or NNS	JJ	Not NN nor NNS
5	RB, RBR, or RBS	VB, VBD, VBN, or VBG	Anything

Step 1. Two consecutive words are extracted if their POS tags conform to any of the patterns in Table 3.4. For example, pattern 2 means that two consecutive words are extracted if the first word is an adverb, the second word is an adjective, and the third word (not extracted) is not a noun. For example, in the sentence "This piano produces beautiful sounds," *beautiful sounds* will be extracted because it satisfies the first pattern. These patterns are used because JJ, RB, RBR, and RBS words often express opinions or sentiments. The nouns or verbs act as the contexts because in different contexts, a JJ, RB, RBR, and RBS word may express different sentiments. For example, the adjective (JJ) *unpredictable* may have a negative sentiment in a car review (e.g., "unpredictable steering"), but a positive sentiment in a movie review (e.g., "unpredictable plot").

Step 2. The sentiment orientation (SO) of the extracted phrases is estimated using the PMI measure:

$$\text{PMI}(\text{term}_1, \text{term}_2) = \log_2 \left(\frac{\Pr(\text{term}_1 \wedge \text{term}_2)}{\Pr(\text{term}_1)\Pr(\text{term}_2)} \right) \tag{3.5}$$

PMI measures the degree of statistical dependence between two terms. Here $\Pr(\text{term}_1 \wedge \text{term}_2)$ is the actual co-occurrence probability of term_1 and term_2, and $\Pr(\text{term}_1)\Pr(\text{term}_2)$ is the co-occurrence probability of the two terms if they are statistically independent. The SO of a phrase is computed based on its association with the positive reference word *excellent* and the negative reference word *poor*:

$$\text{SO(phrase)} = \text{PMI(phrase, "excellent")} - \text{PMI(phrase, "poor")} \tag{3.6}$$

The probabilities are calculated by issuing queries to a search engine and collecting the number of *hits*. For each search query, a search engine usually gives the number of relevant documents to the query, called hits.

Thus, by searching for the two terms both together and separately, the probabilities in Equation (3.5) can be estimated. In Turney's (2002) study, the author used the AltaVista search engine because it had a NEAR operator to constrain the search to return documents that contain the words within ten words of one another in either order. Let *hits*(*query*) be the number of hits returned. Equation (3.6) can be rewritten as

$$SO(\text{phrase}) = \log_2 \left(\frac{\text{hits}(\text{phrase } NEAR \text{ "excellent"})\text{hits}(\text{"poor"})}{\text{hits}(\text{phrase } NEAR \text{ "poor"})\text{hits}(\text{"excellent"})} \right)$$

(3.7)

Step 3. Given a review, the average SO score of all phrases in the review is computed, and the review is classified as positive if the average SO value is positive and negative otherwise.

Final classification accuracies on reviews from various domains range from 84 percent for automobile reviews to 66 percent for movie reviews.

Feng et al. (2013a) compared PMI with three other association measures using different corpora – namely, Jaccard, Dice, and normalized Google distance. The corpora were Google indexed pages, Google Web IT 5-grams, Wikipedia, and Twitter. The authors' experimental results show that PMI with the Twitter corpus produces the best results.

3.2.2   *Classification Using Sentiment Lexicons*

Another unsupervised approach is based on sentiment lexicons and is called the *lexicon-based approach*. This approach performs classification based on a dictionary of sentiment words and phrases, called a *sentiment lexicon* or *opinion lexicon*, with their associated sentiment orientations and strengths. It may also incorporate intensification and negation to compute a sentiment score for each document (Kennedy and Inkpen, 2006; Taboada et al., 2006, 2011). This approach was used earlier for aspect-level sentiment classification (Hu and Liu, 2004) and for sentence-level sentiment classification (Kim and Hovy, 2004). A sentiment word can be an adjective, noun, verb, or adverb. Each positive expression (a word or phrase) is assigned a positive SO value, and each negative expression is assigned a negative SO value.

In its base form, to classify a document, the SO values of all sentiment expressions in the document are summed. The SO of the document is then classified positive if the sum is positive, negative if the sum is negative, and neutral if the final sum is 0. Many variations of this approach are possible, which mainly differ in what value is assigned to each sentiment expression, how negations are handled, and whether additional information is considered. In the work by Hu and Liu (2004) and Kim and Hovy (2004), each positive sentiment expression is given the SO value of +1, and each negative sentiment expression is given the SO value of −1. Negation words (also called *negators*), such as *not* and *never*, reverse the SO value. For example, *good* is +1 and *not good* is −1. Polanyi and Zaenen (2004) showed that other factors in addition to negation words can also affect whether a particular expression is positive or negative. *Sentiment shifters* (called *valence shifters* by Polanyi and Zaenen, 2004) are expressions that can change the SO value of another expression. There are, in fact, many more sentiment shifters than those identified by Polanyi and Zaenen (2004). We describe them and additional ways that sentiments may be expressed or implied beyond just sentiment expressions in Sections 5.2, 5.3, and 5.4.

The work by Kennedy and Inkpen (2006) implemented some of the ideas from Polanyi and Zaenen's (2004) research. In addition to negations, which switch or reverse the sentiment of positive or negative expressions, they considered intensifiers and diminishers, which can alter the SO values of sentiment expressions. Intensifiers and diminishers are expressions that change the degree of the expressed sentiment. An intensifier increases the intensity of a positive or negative expression, whereas a diminisher decreases the intensity of that expression. For example, in the sentence "This movie is very good," the phrase *very good* is more positive than just *good*, whereas in the sentence "This movie is barely any good," the word *barely* is a diminisher that makes this statement less positive. To allow for intensifiers and diminishers, Kennedy and Inkpen's (2006) paper gives all positive sentiment expressions the value of 2. If they are preceded by an intensifier in the same clause, then they are given the value of 3. If the expressions are preceded by a diminisher in the same clause, then they are given the value of 1. Negative sentiment expressions are given the value of −2 by default and a value of −1 or −3 if preceded by a diminisher or an intensifier, respectively.

Taboada et al. (2011) extended this method further by considering finer cases. The SO value for each sentiment expression is assigned a value in the range of −5 (extremely negative) to +5 (extremely positive). The value of 0 is not used. Each intensifier or diminisher is associated with a positive or negative percentage weight, respectively. For example, *slightly* is −50, *somewhat* is −30, *pretty* is −10, *really* is +15, *very* is +25, *extraordinarily* is +50, and *(the) most* is +100. If *excellent* has an SO value of 5, *most excellent* would have an SO value of $5 \times (100\% + 100\%) = 10$. Intensifiers and diminishers are applied recursively, starting from the one placed closest to the SO-valued expression: if *good* has an SO value of 3, then *really very good* has a SO value of $(3 \times [100\% + 25\%]) \times (100\% + 15\%) = 4.3$. There are two main types of intensifying and diminishing cases: an SO-valued adjective with an adverbial modifier (e.g., *very good*) and an SO-valued noun with an adjectival modifier (e.g., *total failure*). In addition to adverbs and adjectives, other intensifiers and diminishers used in Taboada et al. (2011) are quantifiers (*a great deal of*), all capital letters, exclamation marks, and discourse-connective *but* (to indicate more salient information).

Simply reversing the SO value to handle negation can be problematic in some cases. Consider *excellent*, a +5 adjective: if we negate it, we get *not excellent*, which is a far cry from *atrocious*, a −5 adjective. In fact, *not excellent* seems more positive than *not good*, which would negate to a −3. To capture these pragmatic intuitions, instead of changing the sign, the SO value is shifted toward the opposite polarity by a fixed amount (e.g., 4). Thus a +2 adjective is negated to a −2, but the negation of a −3 adjective (e.g., *sleazy*) is only slightly positive (i.e., +1). Following are a few examples:

It's not terrific (5 − 4 = 1) but not terrible (−5 + 4 = −1) either.
I have to admit it's not bad (−3 + 4 = 1).
This CD is not horrid (−5 + 4 = −1).

The idea is that it is difficult to negate a strongly positive word without implying that a less positive one is to some extent true. Thus the negator becomes a diminisher.

As noted by Kennedy and Inkpen (2006), lexicon-based sentiment classifiers generally show a positive bias. To compensate for this bias, negative expressions, being relatively rare, are given more weight in Taboada et al.'s (2011) study by increasing the final SO value of any negative expression (after other modifiers have applied) by 50 percent.

A number of markers may also indicate that the words appearing in a sentence are not reliable for the purposes of sentiment analysis. Usually included to indicate nonfactual contexts, they are referred to as *irrealis* markers. The list of irrealis markers includes modals, conditional markers (*if*), negative polarity items like *any* and *anything*, certain (mostly intensional) verbs (*expect*, *doubt*), questions, and words enclosed in quotation marks (which may not be factual but not necessarily reflective of the author's opinion). The SO value of any word in the scope of an irrealis marker (i.e., within the same clause) is ignored, a strategy called *irrealis blocking*. This does not mean that such sentences or clauses express no sentiment. In fact, many such sentences do bear sentiments – for example, "Anyone know how to repair this lousy car?" However, it is hard to reliably determine when such sentences express sentiment and when they do not. Consequently, they are ignored. We discuss these issues further when we deal with sentence-level and aspect-level sentiment classification.

In addition to the preceding methods, manual approaches may be employed for specific applications. For example, Tong (2001) reported a system that generates sentiment timelines. The system tracked online discussions about movies and displayed a plot of the number of positive and negative messages (*Y*-axis) over time (*X*-axis). Messages were classified by matching specific phrases that indicate the sentiment of the author toward a movie – for example, *great acting*, *wonderful visuals*, *uneven editing*, and *highly recommend it*. The phrases were manually compiled as indicating positive or negative sentiments in the application. The resulting lexicon is thus specific to the domain and needs to be compiled anew for each new domain.

If labeled training data for a particular domain are available, supervised learning usually provides superior classification accuracy because it can consider domain-dependent sentiment expressions automatically. Lexicon-based methods cannot easily consider domain-dependent sentiment expressions unless an algorithm is available that can discover such expressions and determine their orientations automatically. Some work has been done on this issue (Zhang and Liu, 2011a, 2011b), but it remains quite immature. Supervised learning also has its weaknesses. In particular, the classifier trained from one domain usually does not work in another domain (see Section 3.4). Thus, for effective classification, training data are required for each application domain. Because lexicon-based methods do not need training data, they have an edge when no training data are available.

3.3 Sentiment Rating Prediction

Classifying opinion documents only as positive or negative may not be sufficient in some applications, where the user may need the degree of positivity or negativity. For this purpose, researchers have studied the problem of predicting rating scores (e.g., one to five stars) of reviews (Pang and Lee, 2005). In this case, the problem is typically formulated as a regression problem because the rating scores are ordinal, although not all researchers solve the problem using regression techniques. Pang and Lee (2005) experimented with SVM regression, SVM multiclass classification using the one-versus-all (OVA) strategy, and a meta-learning method called metric labeling; their results showed that OVA-based classification is significantly poorer than the other two approaches. This outcome is understandable, as numerical ratings are not categorical values.

Goldberg and Zhu (2006) improved on this approach by modeling rating prediction as a graph-based semi-supervised learning problem with both labeled (with ratings) and unlabeled (without ratings) reviews. The unlabeled reviews were the test reviews whose ratings needed to be predicted. In the graph, each node is a document (review), and the link between two nodes is the similarity value between the two documents. A large similarity weight implies that two documents tend to have the same sentiment rating. The authors experimented with several different similarity schemes. They also assumed that, initially, a separate learner had already predicted the numerical ratings of the unlabeled documents. Their graph-based method simply improves the initial predictions by revising the ratings through solving an optimization problem to force ratings to be smooth throughout the graph with regard to both the ratings and the link weights.

Qu et al. (2010) modified the traditional BoW representation to introduce a bag-of-opinions representation of documents to capture the strength of n-grams with opinions. Each of the opinions is a triple, consisting of a sentiment word, a modifier, and a negator. For example, in "not very good," *good* is the sentiment word, *very* is the modifier, and *not* is the negator. For sentiment classification of two classes (positive and negative), opinion modifiers are not crucial. By comparison, for rating prediction, they are very important, as is the impact of negation words. A constrained ridge regression method was developed to learn the sentiment score or strength of each opinion from domain-independent corpora (of multiple domains) of rated reviews. The key idea was to exploit an available opinion lexicon and the review ratings. To transfer the regression model to a newly given domain-dependent application, the algorithm derives a set of statistics over the opinion scores and then uses them as additional features together with the standard unigrams for rating prediction.

Prior to this work, Liu and Seneff (2009) proposed an approach to extracting adverb–adjective–noun phrases (e.g., "very nice car") based on the clause structure obtained by parsing sentences into a hierarchical representation. Rather than using learning, they assigned sentiment scores based on a heuristic method that computes the contributions of adjectives, adverbials, and negations to the sentiment degree based on the ratings of reviews where these words occurred.

Snyder and Barzilay (2007) studied the problem of predicting the rating for each aspect instead of predicting the rating of each review. A simple approach to this task would be to use a standard regression or classification technique. However, this approach does not exploit the dependencies between users' judgments across different aspects, which are useful for accurate prediction. Thus this article proposed two models: an aspect model (which works on individual aspects) and an agreement model (which models the rating agreement among aspects). Both models were combined in learning. The features used for training were lexical features such as unigram and bigrams from each review.

Long et al. (2010) used a similar approach to that applied by Pang and Lee (2005) but employed a Bayesian network classifier for rating prediction of each aspect in a review. To ensure good accuracy, instead of predicting ratings for every review, they focused on predicting only aspect ratings for a selected subset of reviews that comprehensively evaluated the aspects because the other reviews did not have sufficient information. The review selection method used an information measure based on Kolmogorov complexity. The aspect rating prediction for the selected reviews used machine learning. The features for training were only from those aspect-related sentences. The aspect extraction was done using a similar method to that described by Hu and Liu (2004).

In the past few years, several deep learning–based methods have also been introduced. For example, Yang et al. (2016) proposed a hierarchical attention network for document-level sentiment rating prediction of reviews. Their model includes two levels of attention mechanisms: one at the word level and the other at the sentence level. These mechanisms allow the model to pay more or less attention to individual words or sentences in constructing the representation of a document. Yin et al. (2017) formulated the document-level aspect-sentiment rating prediction task as a machine comprehension problem and proposed a hierarchical interactive attention-based model. Specifically, documents and pseudo aspect-questions are interleaved to learn aspect-aware document representation for aspect rating prediction.

3.4 Cross-Domain Sentiment Classification

Sentiment classification is highly sensitive to the domain from which the training data are extracted. Indeed, a classifier trained using opinion documents from one domain often performs poorly on test data from another domain because words and even language constructs used for expressing opinions in different domains can be quite different. To make matters worse, the same word may be positive in one domain but negative in another. Thus domain adaptation or transfer learning is needed.

Existing research on this problem is mainly based on two settings. The first setting needs a small amount of labeled training data for the new domain (Aue and Gamon, 2005). The second needs no labeled data for the new domain (Blitzer et al., 2007; Tan et al., 2007). The original domain with labelled training data is often called the *source domain*, and the new domain used for testing is called the *target domain*.

Aue and Gamon (2005) proposed the transfer of sentiment classifiers to new domains in the absence of large amounts of labeled data in these domains. They experimented with four strategies: (1) training on a mixture of labeled reviews from other domains where such data are available and testing on the target domain; (2) training a classifier as in strategy 1, but limiting the set of features to only those observed in the target domain; (3) using ensembles of classifiers from domains with available labeled data and testing on the target domain; and (4) combining small amounts of labeled data with large amounts of unlabeled data in the target domain (i.e., the traditional semi-supervised learning setting). SVM was used for the first three strategies, and expectation maximization (EM) for semi-supervised learning (Nigam et al., 2000) was used for the fourth strategy. Aue and Gamon's (2005) experiments showed that strategy 4 provided the best performance, because it was able to make use of both the labeled and unlabeled data in the target domain.

In Yang et al.'s (2006) research, a simple strategy based on feature selection was proposed for transfer learning for sentence-level classification. Their method first used two fully labeled training sets from two domains to select features that were highly ranked in both domains. These selected features were considered to be domain-independent features. A classifier built using these features was then applied to any target or test domains. Another simple strategy was proposed by Tan et al. (2007), which first trains a base classifier using the labeled data from the source domain and then uses the classifier to label some informative examples in the target domain. On the basis of the selected examples in the target domain, a new classifier is learned, which is finally applied to classify the test cases in the target domain.

Blitzer et al. (2007) used a method called structural correspondence learning (SCL) for domain adaptation, which had been proposed earlier (Blitzer et al., 2006). Given labeled reviews from a source domain and unlabeled reviews from both the source and target domains, SCL first chooses a set of m features that occur frequently in both domains and are also good predictors of the source labels; in the article, these were the features with the highest mutual information (MI) values with the source labels. These *pivot features* represent the shared feature space of the two domains. SCL then computes the correlations of each pivot feature with other nonpivot features in both domains. This produces a correlation matrix $\mathbf{W}$, where row i is a vector of correlation values of nonpivot features with the ith pivot feature. Intuitively, positive values indicate that those nonpivot features are positively correlated with the ith pivot feature in the source domain or in the new domain. This establishes a feature correspondence between the two domains. After that, singular value decomposition (SVD) is employed to compute a low-dimensional linear approximation θ (the top k left singular vectors, transposed) of $\mathbf{W}$. The final set of features for training and for testing is the original set of features $\mathbf{x}$ combined with $\theta \mathbf{x}$, which produces k real-valued features. The classifier built using the combined features and labeled data in the source domain should work in both the source and target domains.

Pan et al. (2010) proposed a method similar to SCL at the high level. Their algorithm works in the setting where there are only labeled examples in the source domain and unlabeled examples in the target domain. It bridges the gap between the domains by using a spectral feature alignment (SFA) algorithm to *align* domain-specific words from different domains into unified clusters, with domain-independent words acting as the bridge. Domain-independent words are akin to the pivot words utilized by Blitzer et al. (2007) and can be selected similarly. SFA works by first constructing a bipartite graph with the domain-independent words as one set of nodes and the domain-specific words as the other set of nodes. A domain-specific word is linked to a domain-independent word if the words co-occur either in the same document or within the same window. The link weight is the frequency of their co-occurrence. A spectral clustering algorithm is then applied on the bipartite graph to co-align domain-specific and domain-independent words into a set of feature clusters. The idea is that if two domain-specific words have connections to more common domain-independent words in the graph, they tend to be aligned or clustered together with a higher probability. Similarly, if two domain-independent words have connections to more common domain-specific words in the graph, they have a higher probability of alignment. For the final cross-domain training and testing, all data examples are represented with the combination of these clusters and the original set of features.

Along the same lines, He et al. (2011) used joint topic modeling to identify opinion topics (which are similar to the clusters described earlier) from both domains to bridge them. The resulting topics, which cover both domains, are used as additional features to augment the original set of features for classification. Gao and Li (2011) likewise used topic modeling to find a common semantic space based on domain term correspondences and term co-occurrences in the two domains. This common semantic space was then used to learn a classifier, which was applied to the target domain.

Bollegala et al. (2011) reported a method to automatically create a sentiment-sensitive thesaurus using both labeled and unlabeled data from multiple source domains to find the association between words that express similar sentiments in different domains. This thesaurus is then used to expand the original feature vectors to train a binary sentiment classifier.

Yoshida et al. (2011) devised a method to transfer from multiple source domains to multiple target domains by identifying domain-dependent and domain-independent word sentiments. Andreevskaia and Bergler (2008) used an ensemble of two classifiers: the first classifier was built using a dictionary, and the second was built using a small amount of in-domain training data.

Wu et al. (2009a) described a graph-based method that uses the idea of label propagation on a similarity graph (Zhu and Ghahramani, 2002) to perform the transfer. In the graph, each document is a node, and each link between two nodes is a weight computed using the cosine similarity of the two documents. Initially, every document in the old domain has a label score of +1 (positive) or −1 (negative); each document in the new domain is assigned a label score based a normal sentiment classifier, which can be learned from the old domain. The algorithm then iteratively updates the label score of each new domain document i by finding k nearest neighbors in the old domain and k nearest neighbors in the new domain. A linear combination of the neighbor label scores and link weights is used to assign a new score to node i. The iterative process stops when the label scores converge. The sentiment orientations of the new domain documents are determined by their label scores. Ponomareva and Thelwall (2012) compared graph-based methods with several other state-of-the-art methods and concluded that graph-based representations offer a competitive solution to the domain adaptation problem.

Xia and Zong (2011) found that across different domains, features of some types of POS tags are usually domain dependent, whereas others are not tied to a particular domain. Based on this observation, they presented a POS-based ensemble model to integrate features with different types of POS tags to improve the classification performance.

Glorot et al. (2011) proposed a deep learning system based on a stacked denoising autoencoder with sparse rectifier units to perform an unsupervised text feature or representation extraction using both labeled and unlabeled data. The features are highly beneficial for domain adaption of sentiment classifiers.

Li et al. (2017) proposed an adversarial memory network for cross-domain sentiment classification, where the data from the source and the target domains are modeled together. This network jointly trains two networks for sentiment classification and domain classification (i.e., whether a document is from the source or target domain).

3.5   Cross-Language Sentiment Classification

Cross-language sentiment classification is sentiment classification of opinion documents in multiple languages. Two main motivations for cross-language classification exist. First, researchers from different countries want to build sentiment analysis systems in their own languages, but much of the research has been done in English. Few resources or tools in other languages are available that can be used to build good sentiment classifiers quickly in these languages. The natural question is whether it is possible to leverage the automated machine translation capability and existing sentiment analysis resources and tools available in English to help build sentiment analysis systems in other languages. Second, in many applications, companies want to determine and compare consumer opinions about their products and services in different countries. If they already have a sentiment analysis system in English, they want to quickly build sentiment analysis systems in other languages through translation.

Several researchers have studied this problem. Much of the current work focuses on sentiment classification at the document level and on subjectivity and sentiment classification at the sentence level. Limited work has been done at the aspect level, except that by Guo et al. (2010). In this section, we focus on cross-language document-level sentiment classification. Section 4.6 addresses the sentence level.

In Wan's (2008) study, sentiment resources in English were exploited to perform classification of Chinese reviews. The first step of the algorithm translates each Chinese review into English using multiple translators, which produce different English versions. It then uses a lexicon-based approach to classify each translated English version. The lexicon consists of a set of positive expressions, a set of negative expressions, a set of negation expressions, and a set of intensifiers. The algorithm then sums up the sentiment scores of the expressions in the review considering negations and intensifiers. If the final score is less than 0, the review is negative; otherwise, it is positive. For the final classification of each review, the algorithm combines the scores of different translated versions using various ensemble methods (e.g., average, max, weighted average, voting). If a Chinese lexicon is also available, the same technique can be applied to the Chinese version. Its result may then be combined with the results of those English translations. The results show that the ensemble technique is effective. Brooke et al. (2009) also experimented with translation (using only one translator) from the source language (English) to the target language (Spanish) and then used a lexicon-based approach or machine learning for target language document sentiment classification.

Wan (2009) reported on a co-training method that uses an annotated English corpus for classification of Chinese reviews in a supervised manner. No Chinese resources were used in this study. In training, the input consisted of a set of labeled English reviews and a set of unlabeled Chinese reviews. The labeled English reviews were translated into labeled Chinese reviews, and the unlabeled Chinese reviews were translated into unlabeled English reviews. Each review was thus associated with an English version and a Chinese version. English features and Chinese features for each review were considered as two independent and redundant views of the review. A co-training algorithm using SVM was then applied to learn two classifiers, which were subsequently combined into a single classifier. In the classification phase, each unlabeled Chinese review for testing was first translated into an English review, and then the learned classifier was applied to classify the review as either positive or negative. In Wan's 2013 study, a co-regression method was presented for cross-language review rating prediction. The method was again based on the co-training idea.

Wei and Pal (2010) used a transfer learning method for cross-language sentiment classification. Because machine translation is still far from perfect, to minimize the noise introduced during translation, they proposed using the SCL method (Blitzer et al., 2007) to find a small set of core features shared by both languages (English and Chinese). To alleviate the problem of data and feature sparseness, they issued queries to a search engine to find other features highly correlated to those in the core feature set, and then used the newly discovered features to create extra pseudo-examples for training.

Boyd-Graber and Resnik (2010) extended the topic modeling method known as supervised latent Dirichlet allocation (SLDA) (Blei and McAuliffe, 2007) to work on reviews from multiple languages for review rating prediction. SLDA is able to consider the user rating of each review in topic modeling. An extended model, known as MLSLDA, creates topics using documents from multiple languages at the same time. The resulting multilanguage topics are globally consistent across languages. To bridge topic terms in different languages in topic modeling, the model uses the aligned WordNets of different languages or dictionaries.

In the work by Guo et al. (2010), a topic model–based method was employed to group a set of given aspect expressions in different languages into aspect clusters (categories) for aspect-based sentiment comparison of opinions from different countries.

In the paper by Duh et al. (2011), the authors presented their opinions on the research into cross-language sentiment classification. On the basis of their analysis, they claimed that domain mismatch was not caused by machine translation (MT) errors, and accuracy degradation would occur even with perfect MT. They also argued that the cross-language adaptation problem was qualitatively different from other (monolingual) adaptation problems in NLP; thus new adaptation algorithms should be considered.

Zhou et al. (2016) designed an attention-based LSTM network for cross-lingual sentiment classification at the document level. The model consists of two attention-based LSTMs for bilingual representation, and each LSTM is also hierarchically structured. In this setting, the network effectively adapts the sentiment information from a resource-rich language (English) to a resource-poor language (Chinese) and helps improve the sentiment classification performance.

3.6   Emotion Classification of Documents

Let us now turn to classification of emotion and mood, which is a considerably harder task because (1) there are many more classes – that is, types of emotions and moods and (2) different types of emotions or moods have many similarities, which makes it difficult to separate them. In writing, it is not easy to distinguish emotion and mood (Alm, 2008); thus we will not distinguish between them in this section.

Existing approaches to emotion or mood classification at the document level are mainly based on supervised learning. For example, Mishne and de Rijke

(2006) performed mood classification on a collection of blog posts from LiveJournal.com. On LiveJournal.com, authors can tag each of their posts with a mood type. Thus the blog posts can be naturally used for supervised classification. The main features used in learning are a set of discriminative terms (words or n-grams) for each mood. These terms are computed as follows: for each mood m, two probability distributions, θ_m and $\theta_{\neg m}$, are produced; θ_m is the distribution of all words in the blog posts tagged with mood m, and $\theta_{\neg m}$ is the distribution of all words in the rest of the blog posts. All words in θ_m are ranked according to their log-likelihood measure, as compared with $\theta_{\neg m}$: this produces a ranked list of "characteristic terms" for mood m. Once this process has been carried out for all moods, a single feature set of "discriminating terms" is created by selecting the terms that appear in the top-N position of the separate rank lists for individual moods. Several other features are also used – for example, the hour of the day when the blog was posted and whether the posting date was a weekend. For model building, pace regression (Wang and Witten, 1999) was applied.

Lin et al. (2007) classified news articles provided by Yahoo! Chinese news. Readers had voted on the articles based on the readers' perceived emotions. The algorithm used supervised learning with SVM and employed four feature sets. The first set consisted of all Chinese character bigrams. The second set contained all words produced by a Chinese word segmentation tool. The third set comprised the meta-data of the articles – for example, news reporter, news category, location of the news event, publication time, and name of the news agency. The fourth set was the emotion categories of words, which were obtained from an emotion lexicon that has been previously constructed by the authors (Yang et al., 2007).

Supervised learning was also employed by Strapparava and Mihalcea (2008), who used NB classification. Likewise, Kim et al. (2013) developed a supervised method based on manifold. These authors' learning algorithm is different from those used in the previously mentioned articles, in that those methods treated mood prediction as a multiclass classification problem with discrete labels. Kim et al.'s (2013) article assumes a continuous mood manifold and, therefore, involves an inherently different learning paradigm.

Several other studies have focused on emotions, including, for example, emotion lexicon construction; WordNet-Affect (Strapparava and Valitutti, 2004), which was constructed in the context of WordNet; and the lexicon constructed using crowdsourcing (Mohammad and Turney, 2010). Researchers also studied issues in emotion corpus annotation. Some emotion analysis work (no classification) using different kinds of online texts was also performed in Mihalcea and Liu (2006) and Mohammad (2011).

3.7   Summary

Sentiment classification at the document level detects the overall opinion or sentiment expressed in a document. This problem has been studied extensively by a large number of researchers. However, this level of classification has two main shortcomings.

First, it is not concerned with sentiment or opinion targets. Although it is generally applicable to reviews, because each review usually evaluates a single entity, it is not easily applicable to nonreviews, such as forum discussions, blogs, and news articles, because many such posts evaluate multiple entities and compare the entities using comparative sentences. In many cases, it is hard to determine whether a post actually evaluates the entity in which the user is interested and whether the post expresses any opinion at all: unlike reviews, a forum post may only give some product description, making it difficult to determine the sentiment about the entity. Document-level sentiment classification does not perform such fine-grained tasks, which require in-depth NLP rather than just text classification. In fact, online reviews do not need sentiment classification because almost every review on the web has a user-assigned star rating. In practice, it is the forum discussions and blogs that really need sentiment classification to determine people's opinions.

Second, even if it is known that a document evaluates a single entity, in most applications the user wants to know additional details – for example, what aspects of the entity are liked and disliked by consumers. In a typical opinion document, such details are provided, but document-level sentiment classification does not extract them for the user. These details can be very important for decision making. For example, a particular camera might get all positive reviews (four or five stars), but some reviewers mention the short battery life in their reviews. If a potential buyer wants long battery life, he probably will not buy the camera, even though every review of the camera is positive.

4   Sentence Subjectivity and Sentiment Classification

As discussed in Chapter 3, document-level sentiment classification is too coarse for practical applications. We now move to the sentence level and look at methods that classify sentiment expressed in each sentence. The goal is to classify each sentence in an opinion document (e.g., a product review) as expressing a positive, negative, or neutral opinion. This gets us closer to real-life sentiment analysis applications, which require opinions about sentiment targets. Sentence-level classification is about the same as document-level classification because sentences can be regarded as short documents. Sentence-level classification, however, is often harder because the information contained in a typical sentence is much less than that contained in a typical document owing to their length difference. Most document-level sentiment classification research papers ignore the neutral class mainly because it is more difficult to perform three-class classification (positive, neutral, and negative) accurately. However, for sentence-level classification, the neutral class cannot be ignored because an opinion document can contain many sentences that express no opinion or sentiment. Note that neutral opinion often means no opinion or sentiment expressed.

One implicit assumption that researchers make about sentence-level classification is that a sentence expresses a single sentiment. Let us start our discussion with an example review:

> I bought a Lenovo Ultrabook T431s two weeks ago. It is really light, quiet, and cool. The new touchpad is great, too. It is the best laptop that I have ever had, although it is a bit expensive.

The first sentence expresses no sentiment or opinion, as it simply states a fact. It is thus neutral. All other sentences express some sentiment. Sentence-level sentiment classification is defined as follows:

Definition 4.1 (Sentence sentiment classification): Given a sentence x, determine whether x expresses a positive, negative, or neutral (or no) opinion.

As we can see, like document-level sentiment classification, sentence-level sentiment classification does not consider opinion or sentiment targets.

However, in most cases, if the system is given a set of entities and their aspects, the sentiment about them in a sentence can just take the sentiment of the sentence. Of course, this is not always the case. For example, there is no opinion on Chrome in the sentence "Trying out Chrome because Firefox keeps crashing." This definition also cannot handle sentences with opposite opinions – for example, "Apple is doing well in this bad economy." This sentence is often regarded as containing a mixed opinion. Thus, like document sentiment classification, the problem of sentence sentiment classification is somewhat restrictive because it is not applicable to many types of sentences owing to its ignorance of sentiment (or opinion) targets. It can still be useful, however, because most sentences in practice express a single opinion or sentiment.

Definition 4.1 does not use the quintuple (e, a, s, h, t) notation because sentence-level classification is an intermediate step in the overall sentiment analysis task. Specifically, it is not concerned with the opinion target (entity or aspect), the opinion holder, or the time when the opinion is posted.

Sentence sentiment classification can be solved either as a three-class classification problem or as two separate two-class classification problems. In the latter case, the first problem (also called the first step) is to classify whether a sentence expresses an opinion. The second problem (also called the second step) classifies those opinion sentences into positive and negative classes. The first problem is often called *subjectivity classification* in the research literature; such classification determines whether a sentence expresses a piece of subjective information or objective (or factual) information (Hatzivassiloglou and Wiebe, 2000; Riloff and Wiebe, 2003; Yu and Hatzivassiloglou, 2003; Wiebe et al., 2004; Wilson et al., 2004; Riloff et al., 2006; Wilson et al., 2006). Many researchers regard subjectivity and sentiment as the same concept. This is problematic, as we discussed in Section 2.4.2, because many objective sentences can imply opinions, and many subjective sentences contain no positive or negative opinions. Thus, it is perhaps more appropriate for the first step to classify each sentence as *opinionated* or *not-opinionated* (Liu, 2010), regardless of whether it is a subjective or an objective sentence.

Definition 4.2 (Opinionated): A sentence is opinionated if it expresses or implies a positive or negative sentiment.

Definition 4.3 (Not-opinionated): A sentence is not-opinionated if it expresses or implies no positive or negative sentiment.

However, the common practice is still to use the term *subjectivity classification*. In the following, we first discuss the concept of subjectivity (Section 4.1) and then the existing work on sentence-level subjectivity classification (Section 4.2) and sentiment classification (Section 4.3).

Like Chapter 3, this chapter is written in a survey style owing to the large number of published papers, most of which use supervised machine learning and thus focus on feature engineering. There is still no independent and comprehensive experimental evaluation of the existing techniques and feature sets to assess their effectiveness.

4.1   Subjectivity

Subjectivity is a concept that has been widely used in sentiment analysis. It has also caused some confusion among researchers. In many papers, being subjective and being sentiment bearing are regarded as equivalent, but they are not the same. Let us define sentence subjectivity here. Because this concept depends on the definitions of both subjective and objective, we give the dictionary definitions of these two terms first:[1]

Definition 4.4 (Subjective): Proceeding from or taking place in a person's mind rather than the external world.
Definition 4.5 (Objective): Having actual existence or reality.

On the basis of these definitions, we can define sentence subjectivity as follows:

Definition 4.6 (Sentence subjectivity): An *objective sentence* states some factual information, whereas a *subjective sentence* expresses some personal feelings, views, judgments, or beliefs.

An example of an objective sentence is "The iPhone is an Apple product." An example subjective sentence is "I like the iPhone." Subjectivity classification is the task of determining whether a sentence is subjective or objective (Wiebe and Riloff, 2005). However, we should note the following:

- A subjective sentence may not express any positive or negative sentiment. Subjective expressions can express opinions, appraisals, evaluations, allegations, desires, beliefs, suspicions, speculations, and stances (Wiebe, 2000; Riloff et al., 2006). Some of these concepts indicate positive or negative sentiments, and some of them do not. For example, "I think he went home" is a subjective sentence: it expresses a belief but does not express or imply any positive or negative sentiment. The sentence "I want to buy a camera that can take good photos" is also subjective and even contains a sentiment word *good*, but again it does not give a positive or negative sentiment about anything. It actually expresses a desire or intent (we discuss intent mining in Chapter 11).
- Objective sentences can imply opinions or sentiments due to desirable and undesirable facts (Zhang and Liu, 2011b). For example, the following two

---

[1] www.thefreedictionary.com/

sentences, which state some facts, clearly imply negative sentiments about the respective products because the facts are undesirable:

> "The earphone broke in two days."
> "I bought the mattress a week ago and a valley has formed in the middle."

Apart from positive and negative sentiment, many other types of subjectivity have been studied in various communities, although not as extensively as sentiment – for example, affect, emotion, mood, judgment, appreciation, speculation, hedge, perspective, arguing, agreement and disagreement, and political stances (Lin et al., 2006; Medlock and Briscoe, 2007; Alm, 2008; Ganter and Strube, 2009; Greene and Resnik, 2009; Somasundaran and Wiebe, 2009; Hardisty et al., 2010; Murakami and Raymond, 2010; Neviarouskaya et al., 2010; Mukherjee and Liu, 2012b). Many of them may also imply opinions or sentiments. We discussed affect, emotion, and mood in Section 2.3. We discuss arguing, agreement, disagreement, and stance in Chapter 10.

In summary, the concepts of subjectivity and sentiment are not equivalent, although they have a large intersection. Most people would agree that, from a psychological perspective, sentiment is a kind of subjective feeling; in addition, subjectivity is a superconcept of sentiment and sentiment is a subconcept of subjectivity. However, one does not always need to use subjective sentences to express sentiment because our commonsense knowledge and pragmatics in communication can tell us what facts are desirable and what facts are undesirable in a particular context.

4.2   Sentence Subjectivity Classification

Subjectivity classification classifies sentences into two classes: subjective and objective (Wiebe et al., 1999). Early research solved subjectivity classification as a stand-alone problem, rather than for the purpose of sentiment classification. More recently, researchers and practitioners have treated it as the first step of sentence-level sentiment classification by using it to remove objective sentences that are assumed to express or imply no opinion. In this case, as we discussed earlier, *subjective* and *objective* should really mean *opinionated* and *not-opinionated,* respectively.

Most existing approaches to subjectivity classification are based on supervised learning. For example, the early work reported by Wiebe et al. (1999) performed subjectivity classification using the naïve Bayes classifier with a set of binary features – for example, the presence in the sentence of a pronoun, an adjective, a cardinal number, a modal other than *will,* and an adverb other than *not.* Subsequent research used other learning algorithms and more sophisticated features.

Wiebe (2000) proposed an unsupervised method for subjectivity classification that simply used the presence of subjective expressions in a sentence to determine the subjectivity of a sentence. Because there was not a complete set of such expressions, it provided some seeds and then used distributional similarity (Lin, 1998) to find similar words, which were also likely to be subjectivity indicators. However, words found this way had low precision and high recall. Then, the method of Hatzivassiloglou and McKeown (1997) and the gradeability of Hatzivassiloglou and Wiebe (2000) were applied to filter the wrong subjective expressions. We discuss the method developed by Hatzivassiloglou and McKeown (1997) in Section 6.2.

Gradability is a semantic property that enables a word to appear in a comparative construct and to accept modifying expressions that act as intensifiers or diminishers. Gradable adjectives express properties in varying degrees of strength, relative to a norm either explicitly mentioned or implicitly supplied by the modified noun (for example, a *small planet* is usually much larger than a *large house*). Gradable adjectives can be found using a seed list of manually compiled adverbs and noun phrases (such as *a little, exceedingly, somewhat,* and *very*) that are frequently used as grading modifiers. Such gradable adjectives are good indicators of subjectivity.

Yu and Hatzivassiloglou (2003) performed subjectivity classifications using sentence similarity and a naïve Bayes classifier. The sentence similarity method was based on the assumption that subjective or opinion sentences are more similar to other opinion sentences than to factual sentences. They used the SIMFINDER system described by Hatzivassiloglou et al. (2001) to measure sentence similarity based on shared words, phrases, and WordNet synsets. For naïve Bayes classification, they used features such as words (unigram), bigrams, trigrams, parts of speech (POS), the presence of sentiment words, the counts of the polarities (or orientations) of sequences of sentiment words (e.g., "++" for two consecutive positively oriented words), and the counts of POS combined with sentiment information (e.g., "JJ+" for positive adjective), as well as features encoding the sentiment (if any) of the head verb, the main subject, and their immediate modifiers. They also performed sentiment classification to determine whether a subjective sentence is positive or negative, as we discuss in the next section.

One of the bottlenecks in applying supervised learning is the manual effort involved in annotating a large number of training examples. To save the manual labeling effort, a bootstrapping approach to label training data automatically was proposed by Riloff and Wiebe (2003). This algorithm works by first using two high-precision classifiers (HP-Subj and HP-Obj) to automatically identify some subjective and objective sentences. The high-precision classifiers use lists of lexical items (single words or *n*-grams) that are good subjectivity clues. HP-Subj classifies a sentence as subjective if it contains two or more strong subjective clues. HP-Obj classifies a sentence as objective if there are no strong subjective clues. These classifiers provide for very high precision but low recall. The extracted sentences are then added to the training data to learn patterns. These patterns (which form the subjectivity classifiers in the next iteration) are used to automatically identify more subjective and objective sentences, which are then added to the training set, and the next iteration of the algorithm begins.

For pattern learning, a set of syntactic templates is used to restrict the kinds of patterns to be learned. Some example syntactic templates and example patterns are as follows:

Syntactic Template	Example Pattern
<subj> passive-verb	<subj> was satisfied
<subj> active-verb	<subj> complained
active-verb <dobj>	endorsed <dobj>
noun aux <dobj>	fact is <dobj>
passive-verb prep <np>	was worried about <np>

Wiebe and Riloff (2005) used the discovered patterns to generate a rule-based method that produces training data for subjectivity classification. The rule-based subjective classifier classifies a sentence as subjective if it contains two or more strong subjective clues; otherwise, it does not label the sentence. In contrast, the rule-based objective classifier looks for the absence of clues: it classifies a sentence as objective if there are no strong subjective clues in the sentence and it meets several other conditions. The system also learns new patterns about objective sentences using the information extraction system AutoSlog-TS (Riloff, 1996), which finds patterns based on some fixed syntactic templates. The data produced by the rule-based classifiers were used to train a naïve Bayes classifier. A related study was also reported by Wiebe et al. (2004), who used a more comprehensive set of features or subjectivity clues for subjectivity classification.

Riloff et al. (2006) studied relationships among different features. They defined subsumption relationships among unigrams, n-grams, and lexico-syntactic patterns. If one feature is subsumed by another, the subsumed feature is not needed. This can remove many redundant features.

Pang and Lee (2004) proposed a mincut-based algorithm to classify each sentence as being subjective or objective. This algorithm works on a sentence graph of an opinion document – for example, a review. The graph is first built based on local labeling consistencies (which produces an association score of two sentences) and an individual sentence subjectivity score computed based on the probability produced by a traditional classification method (which yields a score for each sentence). Local labeling consistency means that sentences close to each other are more likely to have the same class label (subjective or objective). The mincut approach is able to improve individual sentence-based subjectivity classification because of the local labeling consistencies. The purpose of this work was to remove objective sentences from reviews to improve document-level sentiment classification.

A study by Scheible and Schütze (2013) employed a similar approach. However, it did not classify sentences based on *subjective* and *objective* classes, but rather as *opinionated* and *not-opinionated*, which the authors called *sentiment relevance* and *sentiment irrelevance,* respectively. The set of features used was also different.

Barbosa and Feng (2010) classified the subjectivity of tweets (posts on Twitter) based on traditional features with the inclusion of some Twitter-specific clues such as retweets, hashtags, links, uppercase words, emoticons, and exclamation and question marks. For sentiment classification of subjective tweets, the same set of features was used.

Interestingly, in the study by Raaijmakers and Kraaij (2008), the authors found that character *n*-grams of subwords, rather than word *n*-grams, can be used to perform sentiment and subjectivity classification well. For example, for the sentence "This car rocks," subword character bigrams are th, hi, is, ca, ar, ro, oc, ck, ks. In the work by Raaijmakers et al. (2008) and Wilson and Raaijmakers (2008), word *n*-grams, character *n*-grams, and phoneme *n*-grams were all compared for subjectivity classification. BoosTexter (Schapire and Singer, 2000) was used as the learning algorithm. Surprisingly, these studies showed that character *n*-grams performed the best and that phoneme *n*-grams performed similarly to word *n*-grams.

Wilson et al. (2004) pointed out that a single sentence may contain both subjective and objective clauses. It is useful to pinpoint such clauses as well as to identify the strength of subjectivity. Wilson et al.'s study of automatic subjectivity classification sought to classify clauses of a sentence into four levels of strength of subjectivity expressed in individual clauses (*neutral, low, medium,* and *high*). Strength classification thus subsumes the task of classifying a sentence as subjective or objective. For classification, the authors used supervised learning. Their features included subjectivity indicating words and phrases and syntactic clues generated from the dependency parse tree.

Benamara et al. (2011) performed subjectivity classification with four classes, *S, OO, O,* and *SN,* where *S* means subjective and evaluative (the sentiment can be positive or negative), *OO* means positive or negative opinion implied in an objective sentence or sentence segment, *O* means objective with no opinion, and *SN* means subjective but not evaluative (no positive or negative sentiment). This classification conforms to our discussion in Sections 4.1 and 2.4, which showed that a subjective sentence may not necessarily be evaluative (with positive or negative sentiment) and that an objective sentence can imply sentiment as well.

Additional work on subjectivity classification of sentences has been done in Arabic (Abdul-Mageed et al., 2011) and Urdu languages (Mukund and Srihari, 2010) based on different machine learning algorithms using general and language-specific features.

4.3   Sentence Sentiment Classification

We now turn to sentence sentiment classification. That is, if a sentence is classified as subjective (or, alternatively, opinionated), we determine whether it expresses a positive or negative opinion. Supervised learning again can be applied to solve the problem similarly to document-level sentiment classification, as can lexicon-based methods. If an application needs opinions about some desired target entities or entity aspects, the system can simply assign the overall sentiment of each sentence to the target entities and aspects in the sentences. This assignment can be problematic, however, as we discuss in Section 4.3.1.

4.3.1   Assumption of Sentence Sentiment Classification

As discussed at the beginning of the chapter, sentence-level sentiment classification makes the following important assumption, which is often not explicitly stated in research papers:

Assumption 4.7: A sentence expresses a single opinion or sentiment.

As is the case with document-level analysis, sentence-level analysis does not consider the opinion (or sentiment) target. This assumption imposes several other restrictions, which makes it difficult for sentence-level sentiment classification to be applied to several types of complex sentences:

1. The assumption is only appropriate for simple sentences (subject–verb–object) with one sentiment – for example, "The picture quality of this camera is amazing." It is not appropriate for simple sentences with more than one sentiment – for example, "Lenovo is doing quite well in this poor PC market." It is often not applicable to compound or complex sentences because they often express more than one sentiment in a sentence. For example, the sentence "The picture quality of this camera is amazing and so is the battery life, but the viewfinder is a little small for such a great camera" expresses both positive and negative sentiments. For *picture quality* and *battery life*, the sentence is positive, but for *viewfinder*, it is negative. It is also positive about the *camera* as a whole (the GENERAL aspect described in Section 2.1). Because of this multiple-sentiment problem, some researchers regard such sentences as having a mixed sentiment and use a separate

class called MIXED to represent or label this type of sentence. However, mixed-class sentences are not easy to use in practice.

2. Sentence-level analysis may detect an overall positive or negative tone from a sentence but ignore the details, which causes problems in applications. For example, many researchers regard the following sentence as positive and expect a sentiment classifier to classify it as such (Neviarouskaya et al., 2010; Zhou et al., 2011): "Despite the high unemployment rate, the economy is doing well." It is true that the overall tone of this sentence is positive, as the author emphasizes her positive sentiment on *the economy*, but it does not mean that the sentence is positive about everything mentioned in the sentence. It is actually negative about the *unemployment rate*, which we must not ignore because practical applications often need opinions and their targets. In the context of an application, simply assigning *unemployment rate* the same positive sentiment as the whole sentence is clearly wrong. However, if we go to the aspect-level sentiment analysis and consider the opinion target explicitly for each opinion, the problem is solved (see Chapter 5).

3. Sentence-level sentiment classification can be applied only to sentences expressing regular opinions; it cannot be applied to sentences expressing comparative opinions – for example, "Coke tastes better than Pepsi." This example sentence clearly expresses an opinion, but we cannot simply classify the sentence as being positive, negative, or neutral. We need different methods to extract and analyze comparative opinions as they have different semantic meanings (see Chapter 8).

4.3.2   Traditional Classification Methods

For sentiment classification of subjective sentences, Yu and Hatzivassiloglou (2003) used a method similar to that employed by Turney (2002), which we discussed in Section 3.2. However, instead of using one seed word for positive and one for negative, as Turney (2002) did, this work used a large set of seed adjectives. Furthermore, instead of using pointwise mutual information (PMI), this work used a modified log-likelihood ratio to determine the positive or negative orientation for each adjective, adverb, noun, or verb. To assign an orientation to each sentence, it used the average log-likelihood scores of its words. Two thresholds were chosen using the training data and applied to determine whether the sentence has a positive, negative, or neutral orientation. The same problem was also studied by Hatzivassiloglou and Wiebe (2000), who considered gradable adjectives.

Hu and Liu (2004) proposed a lexicon-based algorithm for aspect-level sentiment classification, but their method was also able to determine the sentiment orientation of a sentence. It was based on a sentiment lexicon generated using a bootstrapping strategy with some given positive and negative sentiment word seeds and the synonyms and antonyms relations in WordNet. We discuss various methods for generating sentiment lexicons in Chapter 6. The sentiment orientation of a sentence was determined by summing up the orientation scores of all sentiment words in the sentence. A positive word was given a sentiment score of +1 and a negative word was given a sentiment score of −1. Negation words and contrary words (e.g., *but* and *however*) were also considered.

Kim and Hovy (2004) used a similar approach, including a similar method for compiling a sentiment lexicon. However, they determined the sentiment orientation of a sentence by multiplying the scores of the sentiment words in the sentence. These authors also experimented with two other methods of aggregating sentiment scores, but found that they were inferior.

In the studies conducted by Kim and Hovy (2004, 2007) and Kim et al. (2006), supervised learning was used to identify several specific types of opinions. In Nigam and Hurst's (2004) research, the authors applied a domain-specific lexicon and a shallow natural language processing approach to assess the sentence sentiment orientation.

Gamon et al. (2005) used a semi-supervised learning algorithm to learn from a small set of labeled sentences and a large set of unlabeled sentences. The learning algorithm was based on EM using the naïve Bayes classifier as the base classifier (Nigam et al., 2000). This work utilized three classes: positive, negative, and "other" (no opinion or mixed opinion).

McDonald et al. (2007) proposed a hierarchical sequence learning model similar to conditional random fields (CRF) (Lafferty et al., 2001) to jointly learn and infer sentiment at both the sentence level and the document level. In the training data, each sentence was labeled with a sentiment, and each whole review was also labeled with a sentiment. The authors showed that learning both levels jointly improved accuracy for both levels of classification. Täckström and McDonald (2011b) further reported a method that learns only from the document-level labeling but performs both sentence-level and document-level sentiment classifications. In the research by Täckström and McDonald (2011a), the authors integrated a fully supervised model and a partially supervised model to perform multilevel sentiment classification.

Hassan et al. (2010) proposed an algorithm to identify attitudes about participants in online discussions. Because the authors were interested in the discussion recipient, the algorithm used only sentence segments with second person pronouns. Its first step finds sentences with attitudes using supervised learning. The features were generated using Markov models. Its second step determines the orientation (positive or negative) of the attitudes. For this purpose, the study used a lexicon-based method similar to that described by Ding et al. (2008), except that the shortest path in the dependence tree was utilized to determine the orientation when the sentence contained conflicting sentiment words, whereas Ding et al. (2008) used word distance (see Section 5.1).

Finally, many researchers have studied Twitter post (or tweet) sentiment classification, as each tweet is quite short and can be regarded as a sentence. For example, Davidov et al. (2010) performed sentiment classification of tweets using the traditional *n*-gram features as well as hashtags, smileys, punctuation, and their frequent patterns. These additional features were shown to be quite effective. Volkova et al. (2013a) investigated gender differences in the use of subjective or opinionated languages, emoticons, and hashtags for male and female users. Their experiments showed that gender-aware or gender-dependent classification gives better results than gender-independent classification. Hu et al. (2013) presented a supervised approach to sentiment classification of microblogs by taking advantage of social relations, which are mainly used to tackle the high level of noise in microblogs.

Other interesting work includes the study of character–character sentiments toward each other in Shakespeare's plays using a sentiment lexicon (Nalisnick and Baird, 2013) and multimodal sentiment classification of utterances extracted from video reviews of products (Perez-Rosas et al., 2013). Features used in classification include transcribed text of utterances, acoustic signals, and facial expressions.

4.3.3   Deep Learning–Based Methods

Just as in document-level sentiment classification, sentence representation produced by neural networks is important for sentence-level sentiment classification. Additionally, since a sentence is usually short compared to a document, some syntactic and semantic information (e.g., parse trees, opinion lexicons, and POS tags) may be used in classification. Additional information such as review ratings, social relationships, and cross-domain information may be used as well. For example, social relationships have been exploited in discovering sentiments in tweets.

In the early research, parse trees (which provide some semantic and syntactic information) were used together with the original words as the input to neural models, so that the sentiment composition can be better inferred. More recently, CNN and RNN become more popular: they do not need parse trees to extract features from sentences. CNN and RNN use word embeddings as input, which already encode some semantic and syntactic information. Moreover, the model architecture of CNN and RNN can help learn intrinsic relationships between words in a sentence. Some representative works are introduced in detail in this subsection.

Socher et al. (2011a) first proposed a semi-supervised recursive autoencoders network (RAE) for sentence-level sentiment classification, which obtains a reduced dimensional vector representation for a sentence. Later, Socher et al. (2012) proposed a matrix-vector recursive neural network (MV-RNN), where each word is additionally associated with a matrix representation (besides a vector representation) in a tree structure. The tree structure is obtained from an external parser. Socher et al. (2013) then introduced the recursive neural tensor network (RNTN), where tensor-based compositional functions are used to better capture the interactions between elements. Qian et al. (2015) proposed two more advanced models: the tag-guided recursive neural network (TG-RNN), which chooses a composition function according to the POS tags of a phrase, and the tag-embedded recursive neural network / recursive neural tenser network (TE-RNN/RNTN), which learns tag embeddings and then combines the tag and word embeddings.

Kalchbrenner et al. (2014) proposed a dynamic CNN (DCNN) for semantic modelling of sentences. DCNN uses the dynamic K-Max pooling operator as a nonlinear subsampling function. The feature graph induced by the network is able to capture word relations. Kim (2014) proposed to use CNN for sentence-level sentiment classification and experimented with several variants: CNN-rand (where word embeddings are randomly initialized), CNN-static (where word embeddings are pretrained and fixed), CNN-non-static (where word embeddings are pretrained and fine-tuned), and CNN-multichannel (where multiple sets of word embeddings are used). Wang et al. (2016c) described a joint CNN and RNN architecture for sentiment classification of short texts, which takes advantage of the coarse-grained local features generated by CNN and long-distance dependencies learned via RNN. Huang et al. (2017) proposed to encode the syntactic knowledge (e.g., POS tags) in a tree-structured LSTM to enhance phrase and sentence representation. Dahou et al. (2016) used word embeddings and a CNN-based model for Arabic sentiment classification at the sentence level.

Santos and Gatti (2014) proposed a character to sentence CNN (CharSCNN) model. CharSCNN uses two convolutional layers to extract relevant features from words and sentences of any size to perform sentiment analysis of short texts. Wang et al. (2015) utilized LSTM for Twitter sentiment classification by simulating the interactions of words during the compositional process. Multiplicative operations between word embeddings through gate structures are used to provide more flexibility and to produce better compositional results compared to the additive ones in simple RNN. Similar to bidirectional RNN, the unidirectional LSTM can be extended to a bidirectional LSTM (Graves and Jurgen, 2005) by allowing bidirectional connections in the hidden layer.

Guan et al. (2016) employed a weakly supervised CNN for sentence-level (and also aspect-level) sentiment classification. It involves a two-step learning process: it first learns a sentence representation weakly supervised by overall review ratings, and then uses the sentence-level (and aspect-level) labels for fine-tuning and classification. Wu et al., (2017) and Angelidis and Lapata (2018) proposed two more weakly supervised methods that exploit document-level review ratings to perform sentence sentiment classification. Wang et al. (2019a) introduced a method to remove noise in the training data to improve sentence sentiment classification accuracy.

Teng et al. (2016) proposed a context-sensitive lexicon-based method for sentiment classification based on a simple weighted-sum model, using bidirectional LSTM to learn the sentiment strength, intensification, and negation of lexicon sentiments in composing the sentiment value of a sentence. Qian et al. (2017) presented a linguistically regularized LSTM to handle this task. Their model incorporates linguistic resources such as sentiment lexicon, negation words, and intensity words into the LSTM so as to capture the sentiment effect in sentences more accurately.

Zhao et al. (2017) introduced a recurrent random walk network learning approach for sentiment classification of opinionated tweets that exploits the deep semantic representation of both user-posted tweets and their social relationships. Mishra et al. (2017) utilized CNN to automatically extract cognitive features from the eye-movement (or gaze) data of human readers reading the text and used them as enriched features along with textual features for sentiment classification.

Additionally, Yu and Jiang (2016) studied the problem of learning generalized sentence embeddings for cross-domain sentence sentiment classification. They designed a neural network model containing two separated CNNs that jointly learn two hidden feature representations from both the labeled and unlabeled data. Guggilla et al. (2016) presented a LSTM- and CNN-based deep neural network model, which utilizes word2vec and linguistic embeddings for claim classification (classifying sentences to be factual or feeling). Wang et al. (2016a) proposed a regional CNN-LSTM model, which consists of two parts: regional CNN and LSTM, to predict the valence arousal ratings of text. Akhtar et al. (2017) proposed several multilayer perceptron-based ensemble models for fine-gained sentiment classification of financial microblogs and news.

Deep learning models have also been used in sentiment classification for resource-poor languages (compared to English) and have achieved significant progress. For example, Akhtar et al. (2016) reported a CNN-based hybrid architecture for sentence- and aspect-level sentiment classification in a resource-poor language, Hindi.

However, Wang et al (2018b) found an important problem with the current MNs (memory networks) in performing the ASC (aspect sentiment classification) task – and simply improving the attention mechanism will not solve it. This problem is referred to as target-sensitive sentiment, which means that the sentiment polarity of the (detected) context is dependent on the given target and cannot be inferred from the context alone. To tackle this problem, Wang et al. (2018b) proposed the use of target-sensitive memory networks (TMNs). Several alternative techniques were designed for the implementation of TMNs.

4.4   Dealing with Conditional Sentences

Much of the existing research on sentence-level subjectivity classification or sentiment classification focuses on solving the general problem without considering that different types of sentences may need different treatments. Narayanan et al. (2009) argued that a one-technique-fits-all solution is unlikely to be practical, because different types of sentences express sentiments in very different ways. A divide-and-conquer approach may be needed – that is, focused studies on different types of sentences. Narayanan et al.'s (2009) paper focused on conditional sentences, which have some unique characteristics that make it hard for a system to determine sentiment orientations.

Conditional sentences describe implications or hypothetical situations and their consequences. Such a sentence typically contains two clauses that are dependent on each other: the condition clause and the consequent clause. Their relationship has significant impact on whether the sentence expresses a positive or negative sentiment. A simple observation is that sentiment words (e.g., *great, beautiful, bad*) alone cannot distinguish an opinion sentence from a non-opinion one. As examples, consider the sentences "If someone makes a reliable car, I will buy it" and "If your Nokia phone is not good, buy this Samsung phone." The first sentence expresses no sentiment toward any particular car, although *reliable* is a positive sentiment word. The second sentence is positive about the Samsung phone, but does not express an opinion about the Nokia phone (although the owner of the Nokia phone may be negative about it). Hence, a method for determining sentiments in nonconditional sentences will not work for conditional sentences. Narayanan et al. (2009) proposed a supervised learning approach to deal with this problem using a set of linguistic features – for example, sentiment words or phrases and their locations, POS tags of sentiment words, tense patterns, and conditional connectives.

Here we list a set of interesting patterns in conditional sentences that often indicate sentiment. This set of patterns is particularly useful for reviews, online discussions, and blogs about products. They are not frequently used in other types of domains. Each of these patterns must appear in the consequent clause. The conditional clause often expresses a conditional intent to buy a particular type of product – for example, "If you are looking for a great car," "If you are in the market for a good car," and "If you like fast cars." The patterns are as follows:

POSITIVE	:: =	ENTITY is for you
		ENTITY is it
		ENTITY is the one
		ENTITY is your baby
		go (with | for) ENTITY
		ENTITY is the way to go
		this is it
		(search | look) no more
		CHOOSE ENTITY
		check ENTITY out
NEGATIVE	:: =	forget (this | it | ENTITY)
		keep looking
		look elsewhere
		CHOOSE (another one | something else)
CHOOSE	:: =	select | grab | choose | get | buy | purchase | pick | check | check out
ENTITY	: =	this | this ENTITY_TYPE | ENTITY_NAME

POSITIVE and NEGATIVE are the sentiments. ENTITY_TYPE is a product type, such as car or phone. ENTITY_NAME is a named entity, such as iPhone or Motorola. Here negation is not included; it should be handled in standard ways, as discussed in Section 5.3. In most cases, the entity names are not mentioned in such sentences; that is, either they are mentioned in earlier sentences or they are actually the product being reviewed. However, the target aspects of opinions are frequently mentioned in the conditional clause. For example, the sentence "If you want a beautiful and reliable car, look no further" gives positive opinions of both the *appearance* and the *reliability* aspects of the car.

Although these patterns are quite useful for recognizing sentiments in conditional sentences, they can be unsafe for nonconditional sentences. Thus they should not be used for nonconditional sentences. Clearly, some other types of conditional sentences can also express opinions or sentiments – for example, "If you do not mind the price, this is a great car." This sentence expresses two opinions: one negative for the *price* and one positive for the *car*. However, most conditional sentences containing sentiment words express no opinions. To recognize them is still very challenging. Incidentally, sentences expressing uncertainty using *if* and *whether* usually express no positive or negative sentiment either – for example, "I wonder if the new phone from Motorola is good." Here, *wonder* can be replaced by many other words or phrases, such as *am not sure, am unsure, am not certain, am uncertain, am not clear,* and *am unclear*.

Another type of difficult sentence is the interrogative sentence, or question. For example, "Can anyone tell me where I can find a good Nokia phone?"

clearly offers no opinion about any particular phone. However, "Can anyone tell me how to fix this lousy Nokia phone?" presents a negative opinion about the Nokia phone. Many rhetorical questions are also opinionated, such as "Aren't HP Minis pretty?" and "Who on earth wants to live in this building?" To my knowledge, little work has been done in this area.

To summarize, I believe that for more accurate sentiment analysis, we need to handle different types of sentences differently. Much further research is needed in this direction.

4.5   Dealing with Sarcastic Sentences

Sarcasm is a sophisticated form of speech act in which the speakers or the writers say or write the opposite of what they mean. Sarcasm has been studied in linguistics, psychology, and cognitive science (Gibbs, 1986; Kreuz and Glucksberg, 1989; Utsumi, 2000; Gibbs and Colston, 2007; Kreuz and Caucci, 2007). In the context of sentiment analysis, sarcasm means that when one says something positive, one actually means something negative, and vice versa. Sarcastic sentences are very difficult to deal with in sentiment analysis because commonsense knowledge and discourse analysis are often required to recognize them. Some initial attempts have been made to handle sarcasm in recent years (Tsur et al., 2010; González-Ibáñez et al., 2011), but our knowledge about this sort of analysis is still very limited. On the basis of my own experiences, sarcastic sentences are not common in reviews of products and services, but they can be found quite frequently in online discussions and commentaries about politics.

Tsur et al. (2010) proposed a semi-supervised learning approach to identify sarcasms. Their paper also gives a number of nice examples of sarcastic titles of reviews:

1. "[I] Love the Cover" (book)
2. "Where am I?" (GPS device)
3. "Be sure to save your purchase receipt" (smartphone)
4. "Are these iPods designed to die after two years?" (music player)
5. "Great for insomniacs" (book)
6. "All the features you want. Too bad they don't work!" (smartphone)
7. "Great idea, now try again with a real product development team" (e-reader)

Example 1 is sarcastic because of the expression "don't judge a book by its cover." Choosing a variant of this idiom as the title of the review reveals that the author is negative about the book. Example 2 requires knowledge of the context (review of a GPS device). Example 3 might seem borderline between suggesting a good practice and a sarcastic utterance; however, as in example 1, placing it as the title of the review leaves no doubt about its sarcastic meaning. It implies poor quality of the phone and that the purchaser needs to be prepared to return it. In example 4, the sarcasm emerges from the naïve-like question that assumes the general expectation that goods should last. In example 5, the sarcasm requires commonsense knowledge (insomnia $\rightarrow$ boredom). In examples 6 and 7, the sarcasm is conveyed by the explicit contradiction. Note that example 7 contains an explicit positive sentiment (*great idea*), whereas the positive sentiment in example 6 is not explicit. From these sentences, we can clearly see the difficulty of dealing with sarcasm.

The sarcasm detection algorithm proposed by Tsur et al. (2010) uses a small set of labeled sentences (seeds) but does not use unlabeled examples. Instead, it expands the seed set automatically through web search. The authors posited that sarcastic sentences frequently co-occur in texts with other sarcastic sentences. An automated web search using each sentence in the seed training set as a query was performed. The system then collected up to fifty search engine snippets for each seed example and added the collected sentences to the training set. This enriched training set was then used for learning and classification. For learning, it relied on two types of features: pattern-based features and punctuation-based features. A pattern is an ordered sequence of high-frequency words similar to sequential patterns in data mining (Liu, 2006, 2011). Two criteria were also designed to remove too-general and too-specific patterns. Punctuation-based features included the number of "!," "?," and quotation marks and the number of capitalized or all-capital words in the sentence. For classification, a kNN-based method was employed. This work, however, did not perform sentiment classification, but only separated sarcastic and nonsarcastic sentences.

González-Ibáñez et al. (2011) studied the Twitter data to distinguish sarcastic tweets and nonsarcastic tweets that directly convey positive or negative opinions (neutral utterances were not considered). Again, a supervised learning approach was taken using SVM and logistic regression. As features, these authors used unigrams and some dictionary-based information. The dictionary-based features included word categories (Pennebaker et al., 2007), WordNet-affect (WNA) (Strapparava and Valitutti, 2004), and a list of interjections (e.g., *ah, oh, yeah*) and punctuation (e.g., !, ?). Features like emoticons and *ToUser* (which marks if a tweet is a reply to another tweet, signaled by $<$@user$>$) were also used. Experimental results for three-way classification (sarcastic, positive, and negative) showed that the problem is very challenging. The best accuracy was only 57 percent. Again, this work did not classify sarcastic sentences into positive and negative classes.

Riloff et al. (2013) proposed a bootstrapping method to identify a specific type of sarcastic tweets characterized by positive sentiment followed by a negative situation. For example, in "I love waiting forever for a doctor," *love* indicates a positive sentiment and *waiting forever* indicates a negative situation. It was found that this type of sarcastic tweet is very common on Twitter. The authors further limited their study to positive sentiments that are expressed as verb phrases or as predicative expressions (predicate adjective or predicate nominal) and negative situation phrases that are complements to verb phrases. The bootstrapping learning process relies on the assumption that a positive sentiment phrase usually appears to the left of a negative situation phrase and in close proximity (usually, but not always, adjacent) to it:

[+ VERB PHRASE] [− SITUATION PHRASE]

The proposed bootstrapping algorithm starts with a single seed – a positive sentiment verb, *love*. Using a manually labeled sarcastic and nonsarcastic tweets corpus, it first finds a set of candidate negative situation phrases that are *n*-grams following *love* (on the right-hand side) and are verb complement phrases of certain forms, which are defined as some bigram POS patterns. It then scores each candidate phrase based on the manually labeled tweets. Those that pass the score threshold are added to the set of negative situation phrases. This set of negative situation phrases is then used to find the two types of positive sentiment phrases in a similar way. The bootstrapping process alternately learns positive sentiments and negative situations until no more phrases can be found. The resulting sets of positive sentiment phrases and negative situation phrases are then used to identify sarcastic tweets.

In recent years, sarcasm detection has been attempted using deep learning techniques. Zhang et al. (2016a) constructed a deep neural network model for tweet sarcasm detection. Their network first uses a bidirectional GRU model to capture the syntactic and semantic information over tweets locally, and then employs a pooling neural network to extract contextual features automatically from history tweets for detecting sarcastic tweets. Joshi et al. (2016b) investigated word embeddings–based features for sarcasm detection. They experimented with four past algorithms for sarcasm detection plus augmented word embeddings features, an approach that showed promising results. Poria et al. (2016b) developed a CNN-based model for sarcasm detection (sarcastic or nonsarcastic tweets classification) by jointly modeling pretrained emotion, sentiment, and personality features, along with the textual information in a tweet. Peled and Reichart (2017) proposed to interpret sarcasm tweets based on a RNN neural machine translation model. Ghosh and Veale (2017) presented a CNN and bidirectional LSTM hybrid for sarcasm detection in tweets, which models both linguistic and psychological contexts. Mishra et al. (2017) utilized CNN to automatically extract cognitive features from the eye-movement (or gaze) data to enrich information for sarcasm detection. Word embeddings have also been used for irony recognition in English tweets (Van Hee et al., 2016) and for controversial words identification in debates (Chen et al., 2016b).

4.6   Cross-Language Subjectivity and Sentiment Classification

Researchers have also studied cross-language subjectivity classification and sentiment classification at the sentence level as well as at the document level. Once again, this area of research focuses on using the extensive resources and tools available in English and automated translations to help build sentiment analysis systems in other languages that have few resources or tools. Current research has proposed three main strategies:

1. Translate test sentences in the target language into the source language, and then classify them using a source language classifier.
2. Translate a source language training corpus into the target language, and then build a corpus-based classifier in the target language.
3. Translate a sentiment or subjectivity lexicon in the source language into the target language, and then build a lexicon-based classifier in the target language.

Kim and Hovy (2006a) experimented with strategy 1, translating German e-mails into English and then applying English sentiment words to determine sentiment orientation, and with strategy 2, translating English sentiment words into German sentiment words and then analyzing German e-mails using German sentiment words.

Mihalcea et al. (2007) also experimented with translating English subjectivity words and phrases into the target language. They actually tried two translation strategies for cross-language subjectivity classification. First, they derived a subjectivity lexicon for the target language (in their case, Romanian) using an English subjectivity lexicon through translation. A rule-based subjectivity classifier similar to that developed by Riloff and Wiebe (2003) was then applied to classify Romanian sentences into subjective and objective classes. The precision was not bad, but the recall was poor. Second, they derived a subjectivity-annotated corpus in the target language using a manually translated parallel corpus. They first automatically classified English sentences in the corpus into subjective and objective classes using some existing tools, and then projected the subjectivity class labels onto the Romanian sentences in the parallel corpus using the available sentence-level alignment in the parallel corpus. A subjectivity classifier based on supervised learning was then built in Romanian to classify Romanian sentences. In this case, the result was better than the first approach.

The research by Banea et al. (2008) reported three sets of experiments. First, a labeled corpus in the source language (English) was automatically translated into the target language (Romanian). The subjectivity labels in the source language were then mapped to the translated version in the target language. Second, the source language text was automatically labeled for subjectivity and then translated into the target language. In both cases, the translated version with subjectivity labels in the target language was used to train a subjectivity classifier in the target language. Third, the target language was translated into the source language, and then a subjectivity classification tool was used to classify the automatically translated source language text. After classification, the labels were mapped back to the target language. The resulting labeled corpus was subsequently used to train a subjectivity classifier in the target language. The final classification results were quite similar for the three strategies.

Banea et al. (2010) conducted extensive experiments in cross-language sentence-level subjectivity classification by translating from a labeled English corpus to five other languages. First, they showed that using the translated corpus for training worked reasonably well and consistently for all five languages. Combining the translated versions in different languages with the original English version to form a single training corpus was also seen to improve the original English subjectivity classification itself. Second, these authors demonstrated that by combining the predictions made by monolingual classifiers using a majority vote, it is possible to generate a high-precision sentence-level subjectivity classifier.

The technique used in the study by Bautin et al. (2008) was also to translate documents in the target language into English and use an English lexicon-based method to determine the sentiment orientation for each sentence containing an entity. This technique actually worked at the aspect level. The sentiment classification method was similar to that employed by Hu and Liu (2004).

Kim et al. (2010) introduced multilingual comparability as a means to evaluate multilingual subjectivity analysis systems. This concept was defined as the level of agreement in the classification results of a pair of multilingual texts with an identical subjective meaning. Using a parallel corpus, the authors studied the agreement among the classification results of the source language and the target language using Cohen's kappa. For the target language classification, they tried several existing translation-based cross-language subjectivity classification methods. The results showed that classifiers trained on corpora translated from English to the target languages performed well for both subjectivity classification and multilingual comparability.

Lu et al. (2011) attempted to solve a slightly different problem. Their paper assumes that a certain amount of sentiment-labeled data is available for both the source and target languages, along with an unlabeled parallel corpus. The authors used a maximum entropy-based EM algorithm that jointly learns two monolingual sentiment classifiers: it treats the sentiment labels in the unlabeled parallel text as unobserved latent variables and maximizes the regularized joint likelihood of the language-specific labeled data together with the inferred sentiment labels of the parallel text. In learning, it exploits the intuition that two sentences or documents that are parallel (i.e., translations of each other) should exhibit the same sentiment. This method can simultaneously improve sentiment classification for both languages.

Deep learning models have also been used in cross-lingual setting. For example, Singhal and Bhattacharyya (2016) designed a solution for multilingual sentiment classification at the sentence level and experimented with multiple languages, including Hindi, Marathi, Russian, Dutch, French, Spanish, Italian, German, and Portuguese. The authors applied machine translation tools to translate these languages into English and then used English word embeddings, polarities from a sentiment lexicon, and a CNN model for classification. Joshi et al. (2016a) introduced a sub-word-level representation in an LSTM architecture for sentiment classification of Hindi–English code-mixed sentences.

4.7   Using Discourse Information for Sentiment Classification

Most existing works on both document-level and sentence-level sentiment classification do not use the discourse information either among sentences or among clauses in the same sentence. However, in many cases, such analysis is necessary. For example, in the segment

> "I'm not tryna be funny, but I'm scared for this country. Romney is winning."

if there is no intersentential discourse analysis, we will not be able to find out that the author is negative about *Romney*. Current research on discourse analysis remains at a primitive stage and cannot handle this kind of case.

Sentiment annotation at the discourse level was studied by Asher et al. (2008) and Somasundaran et al. (2008). Asher et al. (2008) used five types of rhetorical relations – *contrast, correction, support, result,* and *continuation* – with attached sentiment information for annotation. Somasundaran et al. (2008) proposed a concept called *opinion frames*; the components of opinion frames are opinions and the relationships with their targets.

Somasundaran et al. (2009) performed sentiment classification based on the opinion frame annotation using the *collective classification* algorithm developed by Bilgic et al. (2007), which is described in detail in Section 6.2.2. Collective classification performs classification on a graph, in which the nodes are sentences (or other expressions) that need to be classified and the links are relations. In the discourse context, they are sentiment-related discourse relations. These relations can be used to generate a set of relational features for learning. Each node itself also generates a set of local features. The relational features allow the classification of one node to affect the classification of other nodes in the collective classification scheme.

In the study by Zhou et al. (2011), the discourse information within a single compound sentence was used to perform sentiment classification of the sentence. For example, the sentence "Although Fujimori was criticized by the international community, he was loved by the domestic population because people hated the corrupted ruling class" is a positive sentence, even though it contains more negative opinion words (see also Section 4.7). This paper used pattern mining to find discourse patterns for classification.

Zirn et al. (2011) proposed a method to classify discourse segments. Each segment expresses a single (positive or negative) opinion. Markov logic networks were used for classification, as they can utilize not only a sentiment lexicon but also the local/neighboring discourse context.

4.8   Emotion Classification of Sentences

Like emotion classification at the document level, sentence-level emotion classification is considerably more challenging than sentence-level sentiment classification. The classification accuracy of most published works is less than 50 percent due to many more classes and similarity or relatedness of different emotion types. Emotions are also highly subjective, which makes it difficult even to manually label them in sentences. Like sentence-level sentiment classification, both supervised learning and lexicon-based approaches have been applied to emotion classification. We discuss some existing works using supervised learning first.

Alm et al. (2005) classified the emotional affinity of sentences in the narrative domain of children's fairy tales using supervised learning. Their classification method involved a variation of the Winnow algorithm. The features were not the traditional word n-grams, but rather fourteen groups of Boolean features about each sentence and its context in the document. Only two classes were used in this study: neutral and emotional.

Additional work was reported by Alm (2008), who used individual types of emotion as class labels. Aman and Szpakowicz (2007) also performed classification at the sentence level using only two classes. Their research experimented with sentiment words, emotional words, and all words as features. The researchers found that using all words as features gave the best results with SVM.

In the study by Mohammad (2012), a Twitter data set was annotated with emotion types based on emotion word hashtags in Twitter posts; classification was performed using SVM with binary features that capture the presence or absence of unigrams and bigrams. Chaffar and Inkpen (2011) compared the effectiveness of a few classification methods (i.e., decision trees, naïve Bayes, and SVM) on several document-level and sentence-level classification data sets. In their study, SVM performed consistently better.

Using a lexicon-based approach, Yang et al. (2007) first constructed an emotion lexicon and then performed emotion classification at the sentence level using the lexicon. For constructing the emotion lexicon, the proposed algorithm relies on only sentences with a single user-provided emoticon. For a word, it computes a collocation (or association) strength of the word with each emoticon using a measure similar to PMI. The top-scored words are very likely to indicate different types of emotion. For emotion classification of sentences, Yang et al. (2007) experimented with two approaches. The first approach was similar to the lexicon-based approach to sentiment classification. For each sentence, the algorithm uses the emoticon collocation strength scores of the words in the sentence and several voting strategies to decide the emotion type of the sentence. The second approach used supervised learning with SVM; the features were only the top *k* emotion words. The results showed that SVM performed better.

A related method was reported by Liu et al. (2003), who proposed a more sophisticated lexicon-based approach. This algorithm first uses a small lexicon of emotion words for six emotion types (i.e., *happy, sad, anger, fear, disgust,* and *surprise*; from Ekman, 1993) to extract sentences from a commonsense knowledge base called open mind common sense (OMCS) (Singh, 2002). The lexicon words and their emotion values in the sentences are then propagated to other related words in the sentences based on some commonsense relation rules. Finally, the expanded lexicon and the emotion values of its emotion words are used with a set of rules (called models in the paper) to classify emotions.

Earlier work by Zhe and Boucouvalas (2002) used a lexicon-based method as well, with a set of accompanying rules for special handling of different types of language constructs and different types of sentences. A similar approach was taken by Neviarouskaya et al. (2009), who used a set of more fine-grained rules to handle constructs at various grammatical levels. Specifically, their approach followed the compositionality principle and developed a rule-based algorithm for emotion classification. At the individual word level, this algorithm uses an emotion lexicon and a list of emotion-indicating items such as emoticons, abbreviations, acronyms, interjections, question and exclamation marks, repeated punctuation, and capital letters. At the phrase level, rules are designed to deal with emotions expressed in adjective phrases, noun phrases, and verb plus adverbial phrases, verb plus noun phrases, and verb plus adjective phrases. At the sentence level, rules are designed to deal with sentence clues indicating no emotions, such as those involving *think, believe, may,* and conditional statements. To classify a sentence into an emotion type, another set of rules is applied to aggregate the emotion scores from the components of the sentence following certain precedence. This technique showed very good accuracy in classification of emotions expressed in sentences extracted from blog posts.

Many deep learning methods have also been designed for emotion classification and emotion cause discovery. Wang et al. (2016f) built a bilingual attention network model for code-switched emotion prediction. These authors first used an LSTM model to construct a document-level representation of each post, and then applied the attention mechanism to capture the informative words from both the monolingual and bilingual contexts. Abdul-Mageed and Ungar (2017) first built a large data set for emotion detection automatically by using distant supervision and then used a GRU network for fine-grained emotion detection. Felbo et al. (2017) used millions of emoji occurrences in social media to pretrain neural models to learn better representations of emotional contexts.

A question–answer approach has also been proposed using a deep memory network for emotion cause extraction. This task aims to identify the reasons behind a certain emotion expressed in text. Xia and Ding (2019) further proposed a deep learning model for joint extraction of emotion and emotion cause.

Zhou et al. (2018) proposed a major application of emotion classification in dialogue systems. It is well known that human dialogues are full of emotions. To build a dialogue system for human–machine conversation, it is highly desirable to generate emotional responses that exhibit empathy. The method developed by Zhou et al. (2018) performs exactly this task. It first carries out emotion classification on the utterance from the human user and then generates an empathetic response. I am aware that some practical dialogue systems have already been built and deployed with this capability in some companies for their customer support operations, although they may not use deep learning for dialogue generation.

4.9 Multimodal Sentiment and Emotion Classification

Multimodal data, which may carry textual, visual, and acoustic information, have been used to facilitate sentiment analysis in recent years, as such data provide sentiment or emotion signals that complement the traditional text features. Since deep learning models are very effective at mapping inputs to some latent space for feature representation, it is fairly easy to project the multimodal inputs simultaneously to fuss them – for example, by using feature concatenation, joint latent space, or other more sophisticated fusion techniques. There is now a growing trend of using multimodal data with deep learning techniques.

Yang et al. (2017a) developed two algorithms based on a conditional probability neural network to analyze visual sentiment in images. Zhu et al. (2017) proposed a unified CNN-RNN model for visual emotion recognition. The architecture leverages CNN with multiple layers to extract different levels of features (e.g., color, texture, object) within a multitask learning framework. A bidirectional RNN was proposed to then integrate the learned features from different layers in the CNN model. You et al. (2017) adopted the attention mechanism for visual sentiment analysis, which can jointly discover relevant local image regions and build a sentiment classifier on top of these local regions. Bertero et al. (2016) described another CNN model for emotion and sentiment recognition in acoustic data from interactive dialogue systems.

Poria et al. (2015) proposed a way of extracting features from short texts based on the activation values of an inner layer of CNN. The main idea was to first use a deep CNN to extract features from the text and then use multiple kernel learning (MKL) to classify heterogeneous multimodal fused feature vectors. Poria et al. (2017) further proposed a deep learning model for video sentiment analysis based on utterance sequence and context in the video. Fung et al. (2016) demonstrated a virtual interaction dialogue system that incorporates sentiment, emotion, and personality recognition capabilities trained by deep learning models.

Wang et al. (2016b) reported a CNN structured deep network, called a deep coupled adjective and noun (DCAN) neural network, for visual sentiment classification based on images. The key idea underlying the use of DCAN is to harness the adjective and noun text descriptions, treating them as two (weak) supervision signals to learn two intermediate sentiment representations. These learned representations are then concatenated and used together with the images for sentiment classification.

Tripathi et al. (2017) used deep CNN-based models for emotion classification on a multimodal data set DEAP, which contains electroencephalogram and peripheral physiological and video signals. Zadeh et al. (2017) formulated the problem of multimodal sentiment analysis as modeling intramodality and intermodality dynamics and introduced a new neural model, called the tensor fusion network, to tackle it. Long et al. (2017) proposed an attention neural model trained with cognition-grounded eye-tracking data for sentence-level sentiment classification. A cognition-based attention (CBA) layer was built for neural sentiment analysis.

Wang et al. (2017a) proposed a select-additive learning (SAL) approach to tackle the confounding factor problem in multimodal sentiment analysis. This method removes the individual specific latent representations learned by neural networks (e.g., CNN). To achieve this goal, two learning phases are involved: a selection phase to identify confounding factors and a removal phase to eliminate those factors.

4.10 Summary

Sentence-level subjectivity classification, sentiment classification, and emotion classification go further than document-level classification, as they move closer to opinion targets and sentiments about the targets. However, because they are still not concerned with opinion targets, they have several shortcomings in real-life applications:

- In most applications, the user needs to know what the opinions are about – that is, what entities or aspects of entities are liked and disliked. As at the document level, the sentence-level analysis does not identify entities, their aspects, and opinions about them, which are key to applications.
- Ideally, if we knew the opinion targets (e.g., entities and aspects, or topics), we could simply assign the sentiment orientation of the sentence to the targets in the sentence. However, this is problematic, as discussed in Section 4.3.1. Sentence-level classification is suitable only for simple sentences with a single opinion in each sentence. It is not applicable to compound and complex sentences such as "Trying out Chrome because Firefox keeps crashing" and "Apple is doing very well in this poor economy": in these sentences, the opinions are different for different targets. Even for sentences with a single overall tone, different parts of the sentence can still express different opinions. For example, the sentence "Despite the high unemployment rate, the economy is doing well" has an overall positive tone, but it does not have a positive opinion about the *unemployment rate*.
- Sentence-level classification cannot deal with opinions or sentiment in comparative sentences, such as "Coke tastes better than Pepsi." Although this sentence clearly expresses an opinion, we cannot simply classify the sentence as being positive, negative, or neutral. We need different methods to deal with such cases, as they have quite different semantic meanings from regular opinions.

To solve all these problems, we need aspect-level analysis; that is, we need to perform sentiment analysis following the full definition given in Section 2.1. We discuss aspect-level sentiment analysis in the next two chapters and the analysis of comparative opinions in Chapter 8.

5   Aspect Sentiment Classification

Following the natural progression of chapters, this chapter should focus on expression-level (word or phrase) sentiment classification, as the last two chapters were about document-level and sentence-level classifications. However, we leave that topic to Chapter 7. In this and the next chapter, we focus on *aspect-based sentiment analysis* (or opinion mining) to deal with the full sentiment analysis problem as defined in Section 2.1 – that is, classifying sentiments and extracting sentiment or opinion targets (entities and aspects).

As we discussed in Chapters 3 and 4, classifying opinion text at the document level or at the sentence level as positive or negative is insufficient for most applications because these classifications do not identify sentiment or opinion targets or assign sentiments to the targets. Even if we know that each document evaluates a single entity, a positive opinion document about an entity does not mean that the author is positive about every aspect of the entity. Likewise, a negative opinion document does not mean that the author is negative about everything. For more complete analysis, we need to discover aspects and determine whether the sentiment is positive, negative, or neutral about each aspect. To obtain such details, we need aspect-based sentiment analysis, which is the full model defined in Section 2.1. Aspect-based sentiment analysis was earlier called *feature-based opinion mining* by Hu and Liu (2004).

In the most general case (Definition 2.1 in Section 2.1.1), an opinion is defined as a quadruple (g, s, h, t), where g is the opinion target, s is the sentiment about the target, h is the opinion holder, and t is the time when the opinion is given. However, in many cases, it is useful to decompose an opinion target to an entity and one of its aspects. This gives the quintuple definition of (e, a, s, h, t), where e is an entity and a is one of its aspects (Definition 2.7 in Section 2.1.4). When the opinion is only about the entity e and not any of its aspects, we assign the GENERAL to the aspect component in the quintuple to indicate the fact. For example, for the opinion in the sentence "I love the iPhone," the entity is *iPhone* and the aspect is GENERAL because the opinion is about *iPhone* in general or as a whole. However, for the sentence "The iPhone's voice quality is great," the entity is still *iPhone* but the aspect is *voice quality,* because in this case, the opinion is not about the *iPhone* as a whole but about its voice quality.

In different application domains, aspect-based sentiment analysis may be called different names because no single term sounds natural in every application domain. For example, in some applications, the term *topic-based sentiment analysis* is used, where a topic means an aspect. In some other applications, because the users are interested only in sentiment about entities, they may use the term *entity-based sentiment analysis*, which is actually covered by aspect-based sentiment analysis because the quintuple definition includes both entities and aspects. Some researchers even use the term *target-based sentiment analysis*. In this book, we use the descriptor *aspect-based sentiment analysis* throughout.

To achieve the goal of aspect-based sentiment analysis, we need to perform six basic tasks (Section 2.1.6), which are all highly challenging and require deep NLP capabilities. Among them, two tasks have received the most research attention: aspect extraction and aspect sentiment classification:

- *Aspect extraction.* This task is to extract aspects and entities that have been evaluated. For example, in the sentence "The voice quality of this phone is amazing," we should extract *voice quality* as an aspect of the entity represented by *this phone*. For simplicity of presentation, we often omit entities in our discussions and focus only on aspects. But bear in mind that whenever we talk about an aspect, we must know the entity to which it belongs; otherwise, the aspect is not meaningful. Hence aspect extraction covers entity extraction. Note that *this phone* here does not indicate the aspect GENERAL because the evaluation is not about the phone as a whole but about its voice quality. The sentence "I love this phone" evaluates the whole phone – that is, the GENERAL aspect of the entity indicated by *this phone*.
- *Aspect sentiment classification.* This task determines whether the opinions about different aspects are positive, negative, or neutral. In the first example sentence, the opinion about the *voice quality* aspect is positive. In the second (i.e., "I love this phone"), the opinion about the aspect GENERAL (the entire entity) is also positive.

This chapter focuses on the second task. Chapter 6 discusses aspect extraction, where we will also cover existing research on the other extraction tasks identified in Section 2.1.6.

5.1   Aspect Sentiment Classification

As with sentiment classification at the sentence and document levels, aspect-level sentiment classification involves two main approaches: the supervised learning approach and the unsupervised lexicon-based approach. However, these approaches are not the same as their counterparts at the sentence level or the document level, because we now need to consider opinion targets in the classification. In the next three subsections, we first describe the two approaches and then their advantages and disadvantages.

5.1.1 Supervised Learning

Although we still use the same machine learning algorithms, such as SVM and naïve Bayes classification, the kinds of features used for sentence-level and clause-level sentiment classification are no longer sufficient or appropriate. The key reason is that those features do not consider (or are independent of) the opinion target (entity and/or aspect) and are thus unable to determine to which target an opinion refers. To remedy this problem, we need to add the ability to consider opinion target in learning, which is quite challenging. Two approaches may be employed. The first approach is to generate a set of features that are dependent on the target entity or aspect in a sentence. Clearly, these features cannot used in sentence- or document-level classifications because their features are *target independent*. The second approach is to determine the application scope of each sentiment expression to determine whether it covers the target entity or aspect in the sentence. For example, in the sentence "Apple is doing very well in this bad economy," the sentiment word *bad*'s application scope covers *economy* but not *Apple* (i.e., *bad* does not modify *Apple*). This approach assumes that the system knows each sentiment expression.

The currently used supervised learning methods mainly rely on the first approach but also have a flavor of the second approach. For example, Jiang et al. (2011) used a syntactic parse tree to generate a set of target-dependent features that represent some syntactic relationships of the target entity or aspect words and other words. This parse tree assumes that the target entity or aspect is already given or has been discovered beforehand. Let w_i be a word and T be the target entity or aspect. Some example target-dependent features cited by Jiang et al. (2011) are as follows: if w_i is a transitive verb and T is its object, the feature w_i_arg2 is generated, where arg means argument. For example, if *iPhone* is the target entity, for the sentence "I love the iPhone," the feature $love\_arg2$ is generated. If w_i is a transitive verb and T is its subject, the feature w_i_arg1 is generated. If w_i is an intransitive verb and T is its subject, the feature $w_i\_it\_arg1$ is generated. If w_i is an adjective or noun and T is its head, the feature w_i_arg1 is generated. Apart from these and other target-dependent features, the technique described by Jiang et al. (2011) also employs conventional target-independent features used in sentence-level or document-level classifications.

A related approach introduced by Boiy and Moens (2009) computed the feature weight (value) for each word feature based on the distance between the word feature and the target entity or aspect. Three alternative weights were defined based on the following characteristics:

1. *Depth difference*. The feature weight is inversely proportional to the difference in depth between the word feature and the entity of interest in the parse tree.
2. *Path distance*. If the parse tree is seen as a graph, the weight of a word feature is inversely proportional to the length of the path between the feature and the entity of interest using a breadth-first search.
3. *Simple distance*. The weight of a word feature is inversely proportional to its distance to the entity of interest in the sentence. In this case, no parse tree is used.

In recent years, many deep learning models have been proposed to handle this task. The key is to deal with the challenge of modeling the semantic relatedness of a target aspect with its surrounding context words. Different context words have different influences on the sentiment polarity of a sentence toward the target aspect. Therefore, it is necessary to capture semantic connections between the aspect words and the context words when building learning models using neural networks.

There are three important tasks in aspect-level sentiment classification using neural networks. The first task is to represent the context of a target, where the context means the contextual words in a sentence or document. This issue can be similarly addressed using the text representation approaches discussed for document- and sentence-level sentiment classification. The second task is to generate a target representation, which can properly interact with its context. A general solution is to learn target embedding, which is similar to word embedding. The third task is to identify the important sentiment context (words) for a specified target. For example, in the sentence "The screen of the iPhone is clear but the battery life is short", *clear* is the important context word for *screen* and *short* is the important context word for *battery life*. This task is usually addressed using the attention mechanism. Although many deep learning techniques have been proposed to deal with aspect-level sentiment classification, no techniques appear to dominate in the literature. Representative works and their main focuses are introduced here.

Dong et al. (2014) proposed an adaptive recursive neural network (AdaRNN) for target-dependent Twitter sentiment classification, which learns to propagate the sentiments of words toward the target depending on the context and the syntactic structure. It uses the representation of the root node as the features, and feeds them into the softmax classifier to predict the distribution over classes.

Vo and Zhang (2015) studied aspect-based Twitter sentiment classification by making use of rich automatic features, which are additional features obtained using unsupervised learning methods. Their paper showed that multiple embeddings, multiple pooling functions, and sentiment lexicons can offer rich sources of feature information and help achieve performance gains.

Since LSTM can capture semantic relations between the target and its context words in a more flexible way, Tang et al. (2016b) proposed target-dependent LSTM (TD-LSTM) and target-connection LSTM (TC-LSTM) to extend LSTM by taking the target into consideration. They regarded the given target as a feature and concatenated it with the context features for aspect sentiment classification.

Ruder et al. (2016) proposed to use a hierarchical and bidirectional LSTM model, which is able to leverage both intra- and inter-sentence relations. The sole dependence on sentences and their structures within a review renders the proposed model language-independent. Word embeddings are fed into a sentence-level bidirectional LSTM. Final states of a forward and backward LSTM are concatenated together with the target embedding and fed into a bidirectional review-level LSTM. Specifically, at every time step, the outputs of the forward and backward LSTMs are concatenated and fed into the final layer, which outputs a probability distribution over the sentiment classes.

Considering the limitations of work done by Dong et al. (2014) and Vo and Zhang (2015), Zhang et al. (2016b) proposed a sentence-level neural model to address the weakness of pooling functions, which do not explicitly model tweet-level semantics. To achieve that goal, the model includes two gated neural networks. First, a bidirectional gated neural network is used to connect the words in a tweet so that pooling functions can be applied over the hidden layer instead of words for better representation of the target and its context. Second, a three-way gated neural network is used to model the interaction between the target mention and its surrounding context, addressing the limitations by using gated neural network structures to model the syntax and semantics of the enclosing tweet, and the interaction between the surrounding contexts and the target, respectively. Gated neural networks have been shown to reduce the bias of standard recurrent neural networks toward the end of a sequence through better propagation of gradients.

Wang et al. (2016e) proposed an attention-based LSTM method with target embedding, which proved to be an effective way to enforce the neural model to attend to the related part of the sentence. The attention mechanism prompts the model to attend to the important part of the sentence, in response to a specific aspect. Likewise, Yang et al. (2017b) proposed two attention-based bidirectional LSTMs to improve the classification performance. Liu and Zhang (2017) extended the attention modeling by differentiating the attention obtained from the left context and from the right context of a given target aspect. They further controlled their attention contribution by adding multiple gates.

Tang et al. (2016a) introduced an end-to-end memory network for aspect-level sentiment classification, which employs an attention mechanism with external memory to capture the importance of each context word with respect to the given target aspect. This approach explicitly identifies the importance of each context word when inferring the sentiment polarity of the aspect. The importance degree and text representation are calculated with multiple computational layers, each of which consists of a neural attention model over an external memory.

Lei et al. (2016) proposed a neural network approach to extract pieces of input text as rationales (reasons) for review ratings. Their model consists of a generator and a decoder. The generator specifies a distribution over possible rationales (extracted text), while the encoder maps any such text to a task-specific target vector. For multi-aspect sentiment analysis, each coordinate of the target vector represents the response or rating pertaining to the associated aspect.

Li et al. (2017) integrated the target identification task into the sentiment classification task to better model aspect–sentiment interaction. They showed that sentiment identification can be solved with an end-to-end model, in which the two subtasks are interleaved by a deep memory network. In this way, signals produced in target detection provide clues for polarity classification; conversely, the predicted polarity provides feedback to the identification of targets.

Ma et al. (2017) proposed an interactive attention network (IAN) that considers attentions to both target and context. That is, it uses two attention networks to interactively detect the important words of the target expression/description and the important words of its full context.

Chen et al. (2017) proposed use of a recurrent attention network to better capture the sentiment of complicated contexts. To achieve that goal, their proposed model uses a recurrent/dynamic attention structure and learns the nonlinear combination of the attention in GRUs.

Tay et al. (2017) designed a dyadic memory network (DyMemNN) to model dyadic interactions between aspect and context. This network uses either neural tensor compositions or holographic compositions for memory selection operations.

Tang, Qin, and Liu (2016) proposed an aspect sentiment classification model based on memory networks and attention mechanism. It is capable of explicitly capturing the importance of context words for a given target aspect and using that information to build up features for the sentence for the sentiment classification. Chen and Qian (2019) proposed a capsule-based method.

As we see, most existing work on using deep learning models for aspect sentiment classification has relied on an attention mechanism. Wang et al.

(2018b) showed that simply improving this attention mechanism is not enough due to the problem of target-sensitive sentiment – that is, the sentiment polarity of the (detected) context depends on the given target aspect and it cannot be inferred from the context alone. To tackle this problem, these authors proposed use of target-sensitive memory networks (TMNs). Several alternative techniques have been designed to implement TMNs.

The target and sentiment expression dependency was also noted by Wang et al. (2016e), who designed an aspect-to-sentence attention mechanism that can concentrate on the key part of a sentence given the target aspect. This method is not as direct or specific as that described by Wang et al. (2018b) in dealing with the dependency problem.

Wang et al. (2018a) proposed a lifelong learning method that can exploit a large unlabeled data set. The key idea is to make a memory network learn knowledge from the unlabeled data from multiple domains (regarded as past tasks in lifelong learning) and to then use the learned knowledge to better guide future task learning. Two types of knowledge are involved: aspect–sentiment attention and context–sentiment effect.

5.1.2 Lexicon-Based Approach

Although we still use the terminology of the lexicon-based approach, the approach described in this subsection is not the same as that of document-level or sentence-level sentiment classification. Again, the key difference is that we now need to explicitly consider the opinion target, which is absent at the document level or sentence level. To consider the opinion target, both approaches mentioned previously can be used. That is, we can compute the sentiment orientation on a target in a sentence by using a sentiment aggregation function that can account for the distances of the sentiment expressions (words or phrases) and the target entity or aspect in the sentence. We can also find the application scope of each sentiment expression to determine whether it covers the target entity or aspect in the sentence. This is typically done by exploiting the syntactic relationships of sentiment expressions and opinion targets. Moreover, we can also combine the two approaches.

The lexicon-based approach to aspect sentiment classification can be stated as follows: it uses (1) a lexicon of sentiment expressions including sentiment words, phases, idioms, and composition rules (Section 5.2); (2) a set of rules for handling different language constructs (e.g., *sentiment shifters* and *but-clauses*) and types of sentences; and (3) a sentiment aggregation function or a set of sentiment and target relationships derived from the parse tree to determine the sentiment orientation on each aspect in a sentence (Ding et al., 2008; Liu, 2010). Extension and adaptation of the approach to analyzing comparative sentences are provided in Section 8.2.

Here we introduce a simple lexicon-based method (Ding et al., 2008) – which improves upon the method given by Hu and Liu, 2004 – to give a flavor of this approach. We assume that the target entities and aspects are known, being either given or extracted beforehand. Aspect extraction is discussed in Chapter 6. The method consists of four steps:

1. *Mark sentiment expressions (words and phrases).* All sentiment expressions are marked in each sentence that contains one or more aspects (including entities). Each positive expression is assigned a sentiment score of +1 and each negative expression is assigned a sentiment score of −1. For example, after this step, the sentence "The voice quality of this phone is not good, but the battery life is long" becomes "The *voice quality* of this phone is not **good** [+1], but the *battery life* is long" because *good* is a positive sentiment word (the aspects in the sentence are italicized). Note that *long* here is not a sentiment word, but we can infer its sentiment in this context shortly. In fact, we can regard *long* as a context-dependent sentiment word, which we discuss in Chapter 7.

2. *Apply sentiment shifters.* Sentiment shifters [also called *valence shifters* by Polanyi and Zaenen (2004)] are words and phrases that can change sentiment orientations. Several types of such shifters exist. Negation words like *not, never, none, nobody, nowhere, neither,* and *cannot* are the most common type. This step turns our sentence into "The *voice quality* of this phone is **not good** [−1], but the *battery life* is long" owing to the negation word *not.* We discuss several other types of sentiment shifters in Section 5.3. Note that not every appearance of a sentiment shifter changes the sentiment orientation – for example, "not only ... but also." Such phrases need to be identified beforehand based on a precompiled lexicon and skipped in sentiment classification.

3. *Handle but-clauses.* Words or phrases that indicate *contrary* need special handling because they often change sentiment orientations. The most commonly used contrary word in English is *but.* A sentence containing a contrary word or phrase is handled by applying the following rule: the sentiment orientations before the contrary word (e.g., *but*) and after the contrary word are opposite to each other if the opinion on one side cannot be determined. The if-condition in the rule is used because contrary words and phrases do not always indicate an opinion change – for example, "Car-x is great, but Car-y is better." After this step, our sentence is turned into "The *voice quality* of this phone is **not good** [−1], **but** the *battery life* is *long* [+1]," where [+1] is added at the end of the but-clause. Here we can infer that *long* is positive for *battery life.* In addition to *but,* words and phrases such as *however, with the exception of, except that,* and *except for* also have the meaning of contrary and are handled in the same way. As in the case of

negation, not every *but* means contrary – for example, "not only ... but also." Such non-but phrases containing *but* also need to be identified beforehand based on a precompiled lexicon and should be skipped.

4. *Aggregate sentiment scores.* In this last step, a sentiment or opinion aggregation function is applied to the resulting sentiment scores to determine the final orientation of the sentiment on each aspect in the sentence. Given a sentence s containing a set of aspects $\{a_1, \ldots, a_m\}$ and a set of sentiment expressions $\{se_1, \ldots, se_n\}$ with their sentiment scores obtained from steps 1–3, the sentiment orientation for each aspect a_i in sentence s is determined by the following aggregation function:

$$\text{score}(a_i, s) = \sum_{ow_j \in s} \frac{se_j.ss}{\text{dist}(se_j, a_i)} \tag{5.1}$$

where se_j is a sentiment expression in sentence s, dist(se_j, a_i) is the word distance between aspect a_i and sentiment expression se_j in s, and $se_j.ss$ is the sentiment score of se_j. The multiplicative inverse is used to give lower weights to sentiment expressions that are far away from aspect a_i. If the final score is positive, then the opinion for aspect a_i in s is positive. If the final score is negative, then the sentiment for the aspect is negative. It is neutral otherwise.

This simple algorithm performs quite well in practice. It can handle the sentence "Apple is doing very well in this bad economy" without any problem. There are also other aggregation functions. For example, Hu and Liu (2004) simply summed up the sentiment scores of all sentiment expressions in a sentence or sentence segment. Kim and Hovy (2004) used a method involving the multiplication of sentiment scores of words. Similar methods were employed later by Wan (2008) and Zhu et al. (2009). However, Equation (5.1) seems to work better in general.

To make this method more effective, we can determine the scope of each individual sentiment expression instead of simply using word distance to ensure that sentiments and their targets are matched more accurately. One obvious method is to exploit the relationships between sentiment expressions and their targets. Many such relationships are possible, which can be grouped into three categories.

1. *Syntactic dependencies.* This type mainly involves adjective–noun dependency relations and verb–adverb dependency relations. For example, for the sentence "This camera takes great pictures," we can use the dependency relation of adjective *great* and noun *picture* to identify the target (*picture*) of the opinion or sentiment indicated by *great*. Another example of an adjective–noun relation is "The picture quality is great." Here *picture quality* is the aspect expression or the target of the opinion indicated by *great*. An example of verb–adverb relations is "I can install this software

easily." Again, the dependency relation of the adverb *easily* and the verb *install* can be utilized to identify the target of the opinion (the *installation* aspect of the software). The aspect is indicated by the verb *install*. We discuss these relations in Section 6.2 when we study how to use them to extract aspects.

2. *Sentiment word itself as target aspect.* In many cases, a sentiment word serves two roles: as a sentiment word and as an aspect indicator. Many adjective sentiment words are such words. Apart from some general adjective sentiment words such as *great, good, amazing*, and *bad*, which can modify anything, most adjectives describe some specific attributes or properties of entities – for example, *expensive* describes *price*, and *beautiful* describes *appearance*. *Price* and *appearance* are called the *attribute nouns* of the adjectives *expensive* and *beautiful*, respectively. For example, in the sentence "A BMW is expensive," the sentiment is indicated by *expensive*, which also implies the aspect *price*, the target aspect of the sentiment or opinion. *BMW* is the target entity, which has a syntactic dependency with *expensive*, as discussed earlier (see also Section 6.2). Adjectives and their attribute nouns are discussed further in Section 6.4.

3. *Semantic relations.* This category of relations is hard to recognize in general, except for a small subset, because they are based on the meaning and/or usage patterns of individual words or phrases. For example, in "John admires Jean," the positive opinion indicated by *admires* has the target of *Jean*. There is no sentiment about *John,* who is actually the opinion holder. However, if we change the word *admires* to *murdered*, the opinion target becomes *John*. Notice that this is a fact-implied opinion. Most sentiment composition rules discussed in Section 5.2 fall into this semantic relation category. In general, semantic relations indicating opinions and targets can be arbitrarily complex.

To make use of these relations (except the second category), a syntactic parse tree is typically needed to first identify them. Of course, in a practical implementation, one can also employ a shallow parser to help identify the relations approximately. Apart from parsing-based methods, Liu et al. (2012) proposed a word alignment method to align or to pair sentiment expressions and sentiment targets (see Section 6.2.1). Later, Yang and Cardie (2013) proposed a supervised learning method to link sentiment and target.

Another way to improve the preceding lexicon-based sentiment classification method is to automatically discover the sentiment orientation of context-dependent (sentiment) words such as *long*. The algorithm introduced by Ding et al. (2008) offers a technique to handle this task. More details about this topic are given in Chapter 7.

Other related work includes that of Blair-Goldensohn et al. (2008), who integrated the lexicon-based method with supervised learning. Kessler and Nicolov (2009) experimented with four different strategies for determining the sentiment for each aspect and target. Using a large set of manually annotated data, they also produced several interesting statistics that show why it is so hard to link sentiment words to their targets. Although the preceding methods were not developed for comparative sentences, it is not difficult to adapt them for comparative sentences. In fact, Ganapathibhotla and Liu (2008) as well as Ding et al. (2009) performed this adaption, as discussed in Chapter 8.

Along with aspect-level sentiment classification, researchers have studied aspect sentiment rating prediction. However, this thread of work has mainly been pursued in conjunction with aspect extraction in the context of topic modeling, which we cover in Chapter 6.

5.1.3 Pros and Cons of the Two Approaches

We now shed some light on the advantages and disadvantages of the supervised learning approach and the lexicon-based approach. The key advantage of the learning-based approach is that a learning algorithm can automatically learn from all kinds of features for classification through optimization. A lexicon-based method finds it difficult to use most such features, because people do not know how to apply them without an algorithm to figure it out. Supervised learning is, however, dependent on the training data, which need to be manually labeled for each domain. As discussed in Section 3.4, a sentiment classifier trained from the labeled data in one domain often does not work in another domain. Although researchers have studied domain adaptation (or transfer learning) and lifelong learning, the existing techniques are still too immature for practical use. The current domain adaptation and lifelong learning methods are also mainly appropriate for document-level sentiment classification, as documents are long and contain more features for classification than do individual sentences or clauses. Supervised learning is thus difficult to scale up to a large number of application domains. Another shortcoming is that it is hard to learn things that do not occur frequently.

The lexicon-based approach is able to avoid some of these issues to some extent, and has been shown to perform well in a large number of applications. Most industrial systems are based on this approach. The key advantage of the lexicon-based approach is its domain independence, which enables it to be applied to any domain. It does not need the user to manually label a large number of sentences for each application domain, as is required in the supervised learning approach. The lexicon-based method is also flexible in the sense that the system can be easily extended and improved. If an error occurs, the user can simply correct some existing rules and/or add new rules to the system's rule base. By comparison, supervised learning is more challenging to extend or improve because the problem sentences have to appear frequently for a learning algorithm to pick up the right patterns.

However, the lexicon-based approach also has its disadvantages. A heavy investment of time and effort is required to build the initial knowledge base of lexicon, patterns, and rules. The next few sections present some of these underpinnings, which I have accumulated over the years, and should help a programmer build an initial sentiment analysis system fairly easily. Furthermore, although the lexicon-based approach claims to be domain-independent, some additional work is still needed to take care of the idiosyncrasies of each domain. However, after one has worked on a large number of domains, increasingly less additional work is required for each new domain. The main idiosyncrasy that poses an ongoing challenge is domain- or context-dependent sentiment words and phrases. For example, the word *suck* usually indicates a negative opinion, but in the domain of vacuum cleaner reviews, it might express a positive opinion about the suction power. Although some data mining techniques have been proposed to discover such words and their orientations, the currently available methods have poor accuracy. Nevertheless, this presents a very promising research direction. If one can make good progress in attacking this problem, sentiment classification accuracy can be improved dramatically.

Machine learning has a greater potential for the future, although a great deal of research is still needed. By "machine learning," I do not mean just the existing supervised classification or unsupervised clustering approaches. In fact, the current approaches are not likely to suffice for making major progress in this field. With a huge number of data sets available, more sophisticated or even new kinds of machine learning algorithms should be designed to make major breakthroughs in learning domain–independent and domain-specific knowledge needed for sentiment analysis. In this sense, lifelong learning may be a promising direction to improve sentiment classification.

5.2   Rules of Sentiment Composition

As indicated earlier, in addition to sentiment words and phrases, many other types of language constructs can convey or imply sentiments. Most of them are also harder to deal with. This section discusses some of them, which were called *rules of opinion* in Liu (2010). In this book, we call them *sentiment composition rules* to stress the complexity and compositionality of sentiment expressions. We also add a large number of new rules to the list in Liu (2010). For completeness, individual sentiment words and phrases are covered as well.

These rules can be utilized by both the lexicon-based approach and the supervised learning-based approach:

- These composition rules together with a sentiment lexicon form the core of the lexicon-based approach for aspect-based sentiment classification. As mentioned earlier, this approach is widely used in commercial sentiment analysis systems (although their levels of sophistication and algorithmic details may vary) because of its flexibility and domain-independent nature.
- They can serve as effective features for supervised learning. Some commercial systems also use supervised learning with manually labeled data for training.

In a nutshell, a sentiment composition rule represents a scenario that implies a positive or negative sentiment. It can be as simple as a sentiment word with a given orientation or as complex as a composite expression that may need domain knowledge to determine its sentiment orientation. From these rules, we can see why sentiment analysis is a difficult problem and why simply using a sentiment lexicon for analysis is far from sufficient.

This section presents the rules at the conceptual level, meaning that the rules are meant to be language-independent. However, because this book is written in English, I also list English constructs that are often used to express the concepts; they not only help reader understanding but also can be employed directly in building an actual sentiment analysis system in English. For other languages, these rules can be adapted and instantiated with words and phrases in those languages. For example, I have tried to map each of these rules to Chinese with no difficulty. However, the actual expressions used in different languages are obviously very different.

One way to represent these rules is to use the idea of compositional semantics (Montague, 1974; Dowty et al., 1981), which states that the meaning of a compound expression is a function of the meaning of its constituents and of the syntactic rules by which they are combined. Several researchers have also studied compositionality in the context sentiment analysis. However, the representation schemes used in existing research (see Section 5.2.6) are far from sufficient for handling the sophistication required to represent most, if not all, sentiment composition rules listed in this section. I still do not have a good way to represent them formally in a grammar framework because of their diversity and complexity. In what follows, I first describe the rules conceptually without considering how they may be represented in an actual system. After discussing the impact of negation, modality, and the coordination conjunction *but* on sentiment, Section 5.7 offers a representation scheme to code these rules at the expression level so that they can be used in an actual sentiment analysis system.

Besides introducing sentiment, many of these rules give good indications where the opinion targets (entities and aspects) are. This information is extremely valuable for two reasons. First, it allows us to perform opinion target (entity and aspect) extraction based on sentiment rules, which we discuss in Chapter 6. Second, it enables the system to find the right targets for opinions. For example, in the sentence "This doctor forced me to take the medicine," the negative opinion is not about *the medicine* but about *this doctor*. We discuss target specification in Section 5.7 when we describe rule representation at the expression level, which can be directly used in a sentiment analysis system.

5.2.1   Sentiment Composition Rules

We present the rules using a specification language similar to the Backus–Naur form (BNF). This pseudo-BNF is used mainly for convenience, as it is easy to represent alternative concepts. It allows us to get the gist of the ideas and avoid details, which we discuss in Section 5.7. Because there are a large number of rules, we discuss only a subset of them here to facilitate reading; the rest are given in the Appendix. To aid in understanding, we also group the rules into categories. To save space, we generally list only lexemes in the rules. *Lexemes* are words that can act as dictionary entries. Words that perform particular grammatical roles (e.g., past tense) are called *inflectional forms*. For example, for the lexeme *solve*, its inflectional forms include *solve, solves, solving*, and *solved*. However, these rules almost always apply to inflectional forms as well as the lexemes.

1. *General sentiment rules*. These top-level or most general rules decide the final assignment of positive (POSITIVE) or negative (NEGATIVE) sentiment to each expression. They are expanded by subsequent rules and discussed in more detail in the next few sections. Some of the rules are highly involved, and their applications can be context dependent.

POSITIVE	:: =	PO
	|	NEGATION NE
	|	MODAL NE
	|	# BUT NE
	|	NE BUT #
NEGATIVE	:: =	NE
	|	NEGATION PO
	|	MODAL PO
	|	# BUT NE
	|	NE BUT #
NE	:: =	N
PO	:: =	P

POSITIVE and NEGATIVE. These are the final sentiments used to determine the sentiment orientations on the targets or aspects in a sentence.

P and PO. These nonterminals represent two types of *positive sentiment expressions*. P represents an atomic positive sentiment expression, which can be a sentiment word, phrase, or idiom in a sentiment lexicon. PO can be P or a compound positive sentiment expression to be defined in subsequent rules. The positive sentiment lexicon is defined as

> P :: = amazing | beautiful | excellent | expensive feel | expressive look | good | make someone special | stand above the rest | stand out | . . .

N and NE. These nonterminals are analogous to P and PO, respectively, but represent two types of *negative sentiment expressions*. Additional expressions for NE are defined in the following. The negative sentiment lexicon is defined as

> N :: = bad | cheap feel | cheap look | cost an arm and a leg | pain | painful | poor | smell a rat | take a beating | terrible | ugly | . . .

NEGATION NE (or PO). This pattern represents the negation of a negative (or positive) sentiment expression. Negation is an involved topic. We dedicate Section 5.3 to it.

MODAL NE (or PO). This pattern represents the composition of a modal auxiliary verb and a negative (or positive) expression – for example, "This car should have a better engine." Modality and sentiment also form a complex topic, which is explored in Section 5.4.

 # BUT NE (or PO). This pattern is about sentiment related to the coordinating conjunction *but*, which is also called a *contrary word*. The # symbol represents the sentence segment before *but*. That is, the POSITIVE sentiment of the rule POSITIVE ::= # BUT NE is only applicable to the sentence segment before *but*. However, the interaction between *but* and sentiment is more complicated than this, and we detail it in Section 5.5.

NE (or PO) BUT #. This pattern is similar to the preceding one, but here the implied sentiment is applicable only to the sentence segment after *but*.

The rest of the rules in this subsection, including those in the Appendix, define PO and NE. Note that we use words of all uppercase letters to denote nonterminals and words of all lowercase letters to denote terminals.

2. *Decreasing or increasing the quantity of a sentiment item (PO or NE).* This set of rules says that decreasing or increasing the quantity of a sentiment item (often expressed as nouns and noun phrases) can change the sentiment orientation. For example, in the sentence "This drug reduced my pain significantly," *pain* is a negative sentiment word and the *reduction* of *pain* indicates a desirable or positive effect of the drug.

PO   :: =   DECREASE NE | INCREASE PO
NE   :: =   DECREASE PO | INCREASE NE

The actual words or phrases representing the concepts of DECREASE and INCREASE are highly diverse and numerous. We discuss them in Section 5.2.2.

Note that INCREASE PO and INCREASE NE do not change sentiment orientations, but can increase the sentiment intensity. Also, expressions with the decreasing or increasing meaning in a sentence may appear before or after PO/NE. For example:

> "My pain has subsided after taking the drug."
> "This drug has reduced my pain."
> "This earphone can isolate noise."

Sentences of this type usually use verbs to express the meaning of decreasing or increasing, but they can use other parts of speech, too. The concept of *decreasing* also extends to verbs such as *disappeared* and *removed*. For example:

> "My pain disappeared after taking the drug."
> "My pain has gone after taking the drug."
> "After taking the drug, I am now pain free."
> "After taking the drug, I am now free of/from pain completely."

In these example sentences, we can see where the opinion targets or aspects are – that is, those nouns and noun phrases in the NE and PO expressions. These sentences all represent indirect opinions and the aspect in each sentence is indicated by *pain*.

3. *Decreasing or increasing the quantity of a positive potential item (PPI) or a negative potential item (NPI).* For some items, increasing (or decreasing) their quantities is positive (or negative). For example,

> "Lenovo has cut its revenue forecast."
> "Lenovo has increased the battery life of its laptops."
> "This song has climbed the chart by several places."

Here *revenue, battery life,* and *chart places* are called a PPI because increasing them is desirable. However, for some other items, increasing (or decreasing) their values/quantities is negative (or positive). For example:

> "Sony has increased the price of the camera."

Here *price* is called an NPI because a large value for it is not desirable (to consumers). These example sentences are factual statements and have fact-implied opinions (see Section 2.4.2).

The following rules represent these concepts:

PO	:: =	DECREASE NPI I INCREASE PPI
NE	:: =	DECREASE PPI I INCREASE NPI
PPI	:: =	access I answer I budget I benefit I choice I class I color I connection I credit I diversity I developed I dividend I durability I economy I efficiency I feature I functionality I GDP I growth I help I insurance I opportunity I option I profit I quality I revenue I yield I reliability I security I selection I solution I spirit I strength I usefulness I standard I ...
NPI	:: =	charge I cost I duplicate I effort I expense I fee I hesitation I jobless I maintenance I price I repair I spender I the need I tax I unemployment I ...

Again, the concept of decreasing extends to disappearing and removing. For example:

> "My hope has gone."
> "The fee has been waived."
> "After the action, all duplicates disappeared."

The difference between PO/NE and PPI/NPI is that PPI and NPI items do not possess sentiment themselves, whereas PO and NE items do. The example PPI and NPI expressions were extracted from many different domains. In a specific application, they need to be discovered from the domain corpus. For example, in the economy domain, *growth* and *budget* are PPIs; in the mortgage domain, *interest rate* and *down payment* are NPIs for borrowers.

PPIs and NPIs can be discovered automatically or semi-automatically, or compiled manually. Wen and Wu (2011) published a bootstrapping cum classification algorithm for this purpose using Chinese text with some success.

4. *Less or more quantity of a sentiment item (PO or NE).* Similar to rules 2 and 3, less quantity of a positive (or negative) item is negative (or positive) and more quantity of a positive (or negative) item is positive (or negative). Some example sentences follow:

> "This production line produces fewer defects."
> "This drug has reduced more pain than my previous drug."

We have the following composition rules:

PO :: = LESS NE I MORE PO
NE :: = LESS PO I MORE NE

Note that MORE PO and MORE NE do not change sentiment orientations. We include them for completeness. We also want to highlight two other issues. First, for these rules, the sentiment words are usually nouns or noun phrases. Second, an additional level of composition may be present in an actual sentence. For example, the second example sentence involves another level of composition – that is, *more pain* is negative, but reducing the negative becomes positive. Note that the aspect or the opinion target in this case is *pain* (not *more pain*).

Many expressions can describe the general concepts of LESS and MORE, and we study them in detail in Section 5.2.3. This set of rules is closely related to comparative opinions, which we study in Chapter 8.

5. *Small or less and large or more quantity of a PPI (or NPI).* This is similar to rule 4, as shown in the following example sentences:

> "The battery life is short."
> "This phone gives me more battery life."
> "The price of the car is high."
> "I won't buy this phone due to the high cost."

Battery life is a PPI, and *price* and *cost* are an NPI.

> PO :: = SMALL_OR_LESS NPI | LARGE_OR_MORE PPI
> NE :: = SMALL_OR_LESS PPI | LARGE_OR_MORE NPI

Many expressions can express the concepts of SMALL_OR_LESS and LARGE_OR_MORE, and we study these expressions in Section 5.2.3. This set of rules is also related to comparative opinions, discussed in Chapter 8.

6. *Producing and consuming resource and waste.* If an entity produces a large quantity of resources, it is desirable or positive. If it consumes a large quantity of resources, it is undesirable or negative. For example, *electricity* is a resource, and the sentence "This computer uses a lot of electricity" gives a negative opinion about the power consumption of the computer. Likewise, if an entity produces a large quantity of waste, it is negative. If it consumes a large quantity of wastes, it is positive.

PO	:: =	PRODUCE LARGE_MORE RESOURCE
	|	PRODUCE SMALL_LESS WASTE
	|	CONSUME LARGE_MORE WASTE
	|	CONSUME SMALL_LESS RESOURCE
NE	:: =	PRODUCE SMALL_LESS RESOURCE
	|	PRODUCE LARGE_MORE WASTE
	|	CONSUME SMALL_LESS WASTE
	|	CONSUME LARGE_MORE RESOURCE
PRODUCE	:: =	generate | produce | . . .
CONSUME	:: =	consume | need | require | spend | use | take | . . .
RESOURCE	:: =	attention | effort | energy | gas | oil | money | power | resource | room | space | electricity | service | water | opportunity | . . .
WASTE	:: =	waste | dust | rubbish | . . .

Resources are also a kind of PPI and waste is a kind of NPI (rule 3). They thus can be governed by other rules concerning PPI and NPI – for example, "This device reduces the gas consumption by 20 percent."

Any particular domain may contain other resources and wastes that need to be discovered. For example, in the washer domain, detergent is a resource; in the printer domain, ink is a resource. We discuss resource term discovery in Section 6.2.1.

7. *Desirable or undesirable fact.* As mentioned earlier, many objective or factual expressions can imply positive or negative sentiment because they describe desirable and undesirable facts. Such sentences use no sentiment words – for example, "After sleeping on the mattress for two weeks, I saw a valley in the middle" and "After taking the drug, my blood pressure went up to 410." The first sentence implies a negative opinion about the mattress, even though it does not include a sentiment word, because a *valley in the middle* is not desirable. The second sentence is also negative because of the very high blood pressure. Thus we have the following composition rules:

> PO :: = DESIRABLE_FACT
> NE :: = UNDESIRABLE_FACT

Desirable and undesirable facts are very hard to deal with because they are different in different domains. For example, in the mattress domain, the following words often indicate undesirable facts: *mountain, hill, valley, hole*, and *body impression*. For an application, such words have to be either discovered automatically or compiled manually. Zhang and Liu (2011b) proposed an initial automated method to discover aspect nouns that also indicate sentiment.

8. *Performing desirable or undesirable action.* Similar to desirable and undesirable facts, if an entity performs a desirable action or function, it is positive; if it performs an undesirable action, it is negative. Then we have

> PO :: = DESIRABLE_ACTION
> NE :: = UNDESIRABLE_ACTION

Desirable and undesirable actions are also hard to deal with, as they, too, are domain-dependent. In a domain, some verbs and verb phrases usually indicate desirable or undesirable actions. For example, the first of the following sentences is positive due to *hiring*, and the rest are negative due to *laying off, buy my votes*, and *skips frames*, respectively:

> "HP is hiring."
> "Motorola is planning to lay off more people."
> "She wants to buy my vote."
> "This player skips frames."

9. *Meeting expectations.* In many cases, people have expectations about an entity. If the entity meets or exceeds their expectations, it is positive; otherwise, it is negative.

PO	:: =	MEET EXPECTATION
MEET	:: =	above I beyond I exceed I live up to I meet I satisfy I surpass I . . .
EXPECTATION	:: =	expectation I my need I my requirement I . . .

The following are some example sentences:

"It meets my need/requirement."
"It lives up to my expectations."
"The performance of this product is above/beyond my expectation."
"I find them to work as advertised/expected."
"It works exactly the way that I wanted."
"It provides everything you need."
"It gives what you look for."
"Everything is going as planned."

10. *Part and overall sentiment.* Sentences that satisfy this set of rules are usually compound sentences with different sentiments in different parts of the sentence. The second part often serves to summarize the overall sentiment on an entity, but we should not ignore the sentiment in the first part. For example:

"Despite the high price, I still like this phone very much."
"Although there are some minuses with the seats, this is still my car of choice."
"The price of this phone is high, but overall it is a great phone."
"Although the car has great engine, I do not like it because it has so many other issues."

We single out this type of sentence and treat it as special because it often gives an overall sentiment about the entity being evaluated. This is useful because in some applications, the user is interested only in the entity-level analysis (e.g., in brand management) and not in sentiment about entity aspects:

NE	: =	PO* BUT_OVERALL_IS NE
PO	: =	NE* BUT_OVERALL_IS PO

"BUT_OVERALL_IS NE (PO)" means it is overall negative (NE) or positive (PO). To recognize "BUT_OVERALL_IS NE (PO)," the system needs to detect some special kinds of sentences, such as the preceding examples. One strong clue is that the dominant clause usually mentions the entity type (e.g., *car*) or even the entity name. We should also note two important considerations. First, although each such sentence focuses on the dominant sentiment, it does not mean that the sentiment expressed in the secondary clause should be ignored. We use * to indicate that. Second, it is not always true that the second part of the sentence signifies the dominant sentiment. In fact, the reverse order also occurs – for example, "This is my car of choice despite some minuses with the seats."

Additional rules are given in the Appendix. These additional rules are not less important; in fact, all of the rules are highly important in building a sentiment analysis system. Such conceptual rules can appear in many forms and be expressed using different words and phrases. Moreover, they may manifest differently in different domains. Most of them are hard to recognize and hence not easy to apply. Furthermore, we make no claim that this set of rules is the complete set that governs opinion or sentiment. In fact, there are many others, and with further research, even more rules will be discovered.

Like individual sentiment words, an occurrence of an opinion rule in a sentence does not always indicate opinion or sentiment. For example, the sentence "I want a car with high reliability" does not express a positive or negative opinion about any specific car, but rather a desire of the author, although *high reliability* is positive and covered by our rules. Another class of sentences that contains sentiment expressions but expresses no evaluation or sentiment is the class that describes purposes. For example:

> "We used the system to solve the formatting problem."
> "This drug is for treating stomach pain."
> "This drug is for the treatment of stomach pain."

Yet another class comprises the how-to sentences. For example:

> "How to solve this problem is a difficult question."
> "How to win a game is hard to know."

The Opinion Parser system has mechanisms to detect such cases using rules specified in the specification language described in Section 5.7.

5.2.2   DECREASE and INCREASE Expressions

As we discussed in the context of rules 2 and 3, decreasing (DECREASE) and increasing (INCREASE) expressions (words and phrases) are crucial for sentiment analysis. This subsection explores these expressions, listing some of the commonly used such English words and phrases. We study DECREASE expressions first, and then INCREASE expressions. The following is a list of commonly used DECREASE expressions that act as verbs:

> alleviate, attenuate, block, cancel, cease, combat, come down, crackdown, crack down, cut, cut back, cut down, cut off, cut out, decrease, deduct, die off, die out, diminish, disappear, discontinue, discount, downgrade, drop, dwindle, eliminate, fade, fall, filter, get around, get off, get over, go away, go down, halt, have gone, improve, isolate, lack, lessen, limit, lock, lose, minimize, miss, mitigate, omit, pass off, pay off, plunge, prevent, quit, reduce, relieve, remove, resolve, shrink, shut out, slide, slip, smooth, soothe, stop, subside, suppress, take away, take off, to be down, undo, vanish, weed out, waive, wipe out, wither

These words can appear either before or after a PO/NE/PPI/NPI expression. They can be further grouped based on their usage characteristics.

DECREASE expressions that mainly decrease NPI and NE items (DECREASE-N). These DECREASE expressions are used almost exclusively with negative sentiment items. Commonly used DECREASE-N expressions include *alleviate, avoid, handle, lessen, mitigate, relieve, resolve, soothe, subside, waive,* and so on. The following are some example sentences:

> "The noise level has subsided."
> "The school waived my tuition fees."
> "This device can mitigate the impact of the crash."
> "This drug relieved my shoulder pain."

DECREASE expressions that mainly decrease PPI and PO items (DECREASE-P). These DECREASE expressions are used almost only with positive sentiment items. DECREASE-P expressions (or words) include *lack, lose, omit, miss,* and so on. The following are some example sentences:

> "This phone lacks magic."
> "The company has missed a great opportunity."
> "This phone omitted one important detail."
> "I really miss the smoothing capability of the old version."
> "He lost our trust."
> "The company loses a good customer."

DECREASE expressions that mainly appear after PO/NE/PPI/NPI items (DECREASE-after). These DECREASE expressions are mainly used in active sentences with PO/NE/PPI/NPI items appearing before such expressions. Examples of DECREASE-after expressions include *die off, die out, disappear, dwindle, fade, fall, go away, pass off, slide, slip, to be down, vanish, wither,* and so on. Some example sentences follow:

> "The unemployment rate has fallen."
> "My neck pain has disappeared."

"The noise problem went away."
"All their profits have vanished."
"The economy is down."

When these verbs and verb phrases are used in the gerund form to form a phrase, the PO/NE/PPI/NPI expression can occur after the DECREASE expressions. For example:

"The company is experiencing a period of dwindling profits."

DECREASE expressions that mainly appear before PO/NE/PPI/NPI items (DECREASE-before). These DECREASE expressions are mainly used in active sentences with PO/NE/PPI/NPI items appearing after such expressions. Examples of after-DECREASE expressions include *quit* and *stop*:

"This machine quit working on the second day."

Most DECREASE expressions can act on PO/PPI and NE/NPI and can also appear before or after PO/NE/PPI/NPI items, which is mostly determined by active or passive voices of sentences.

Active and passive voice. If a sentence is in active voice, then the DECREASE verb normally occurs before the PO/NE/PPI/NPI expressions. For example:

"The earphone can block surrounding noise."

If a sentence is in passive voice, the situation is the opposite. For example:

"The surrounding noise is blocked by the earphone effectively."

Thus knowing whether a sentence is active or passive is important because the system will know where to look for PO/NE/PPI/NPI expressions, which usually are also the opinion targets. For example:

"Standard and Poor's downgraded Greece's credit rating."

Because this is an active voice sentence, we know that the opinion target appears after *downgrade*. The sentence does not express any opinion about *Standard and Poor's*, but only a negative opinion about *Greece's credit rating*. *Standard and Poor's* is actually the opinion holder.

Detecting active and passive voice requires accurate parsing. This can be challenging because of the poor grammar of social media posts, inaccuracy of parsers, and the fact that most verbs in English have the same past simple and past participle forms.

Noun DECREASE expressions. The DECREASE expressions discussed so far are verbs and phrases acting as verbs, but DECREASE expressions can be nouns, too – usually noun forms of verbs, such as *remove* (verb) and *removal* (noun), and *reduce* (verb) and *reduction* (noun). Here are two example sentences using noun DECREASE expressions:

> "This drug resulted in a decrease in my stomach pain."
> "This promotion offers a big price reduction."

In the first sentence, the NE word *pain* appears after the DECREASE expression *decrease*. In the second sentence, the NPI word *price* appears before the DECREASE word *reduction*.

We now turn to INCREASE verbs. INCREASE verbs behave similarly to DECREASE verbs. Commonly used verbs or verb phrases in the category include the following:

> build up, burst, climb, come back, elevate, enlarge, escalate, expand, extend, go up, grow, increase, intensify, mark up, pile up, progress, raise, return, rise, soar, surge, to be up

Some example sentences are as follows:

> "The pain comes back."
> "My pain has returned within two days."
> "The profits of the company surged last month."
> "The price of this car has been marked up by two thousand dollars."
> "Google's stock price soared yesterday."

The types of INCREASE expressions are similar to the types of DECREASE expressions. Like DECREASE expressions, INCREASE expressions can be nouns (e.g., *increase* and *upsurge*). However, there are fewer INCREASE expressions.

5.2.3   *SMALL_OR_LESS and LARGE_OR_MORE Expressions*

Adjectival expressions (words and phrases) about quantity, size, length, weight, and speed are important for determining or implying sentiment when they are combined with PO/NE/PPI/NPI items, resources, and wastes. They form the LESS, MORE, SMALL_OR_LESS, and LARGE_OR_MORE expressions used in rules 4 and 5 in Section 5.2.1. In this subsection, we list some of the commonly used such expressions.

Adjectival expressions of quantity. Also called quantifiers, these expressions consist of *small* quantity quantifiers (denoted by SMALL-Qs), *neutral* quantifiers (denoted by NEUTRAL-Qs), and *large* quantity quantifiers (denoted by LARGE-Qs). We extend the meaning by also including expressions like *no, free of,* and *free from,* as they function similarly.

SMALL-Qs. These words and phrases include few, only a few, little, only a little, a/one little bit, a small number of, a fraction of, free, free of, free from, no, nonexistent, nonexistent, not many, not much, rare, a small amount of, a small quantity of, a tiny amount of, and tight. Note that small quantities include a zero quantity. The following are some example sentences that use such expressions and express or imply positive or negative sentiment:

> "This bank is very tight on credit."
> "This vacuum cleaner uses no bag."
> "After taking the drug, I am now pain free."
> "This washer uses a tiny amount of water."

In some cases, fractions are also employed to express small quantities. For example:

> "The price is only one third of what it was two years ago."
> "The price is only 40 percent of what it was two years ago."
> "The price is only a small fraction of what it was two years ago."

Such sentences can be recognized by some fixed patterns used to express fractions.

NEUTRAL-Qs. These words and phrases of quantity include expressions like *some, any, several, a fair amount of, a number of,* and *enough.* They are not commonly used to compose sentiment expressions, except for the word *enough.* For example:

> "They provide enough space for kids to play around."

Here *space* is a resource and also a PPI.

LARGE-Qs. These expressions include *an awful lot of, a bundle of, a great/good deal of, a great/good many of, a huge amount of, a large amount of, a large quantity of, a load of, loads of, a lot of, lots of, many, much, a plenty of, a ton of,* and *tons of.* Some example sentences with explicit or implicit/implied sentiment follow:

> "This machine uses a lot of electricity."
> "This program needs a huge amount of disk space."

In some cases, multiples are employed to express a large quantity. For example:

> "The price now is three times that of two years ago."

In comparative sentences, comparative quantifiers, denoted by MORE-Qs and LESS-Qs, are used in a similar way.

MORE-Qs. These words and phrases include *more, most, a larger number of, a lot more, plenty more, a larger amount of, a larger quantity of,* and so on.

LESS-Qs. These words and phrases include *fewer, least, fewest, less, a smaller number of, a smaller amount of, a smaller quantity of,* and so on.

Adjectival expressions of size. We use two concepts to represent size, LARGE and SMALL, which can be expressed with many words and phrases:

LARGE: *big, enormous, hefty, huge, large, massive,* and so on
SMALL: *meager, minimum, small, tiny,* and so on

For their comparative forms, LARGER and SMALLER, we have

LARGER: *bigger, greater, larger,* and so on
SMALLER: *smaller, lesser, tinier,* and so on

Adjectival expressions of weight.

HEAVY: *heavy, weighted, weighty,* and so on
LIGHT: *light, featherweight, lightweight, weightless,* and so on

For their comparative forms, HEAVIER and LIGHTER, we have

HEAVIER: *heavier*
LIGHTER: *lighter*

Adjectival expressions of length.

LONG: *long*
SHORT: *short*

For their comparative forms, LONGER and SHORTER, we have

LONGER: *longer*
SHORTER: *shorter*

Adjectival expressions of height.

HIGH: *high*
LOW: *low*

For the comparative forms, HIGHER and LOWER, we have

HIGHER: *higher*
LOWER: *lower*

Adjectival expressions of speed.

FAST: *fast, immediate, quick, swift,* and *rapid*
SLOW: *crawling, like a snail, like a tortoise, lagging, slow, slow-moving, snaillike, tortoise-like,* and so on

For their comparative forms, FASTER and SLOWER, we have

FASTER: *faster*
SLOWER: *slower*

Finally, the concepts of LESS, MORE, SMALL_OR_LESS, and LARGE_OR_MORE are defined as follows:

SMALL_OR_LESS	:: =	SMALL_SPEC | LESS
LARGE_OR_MORE	:: =	LARGE_SPEC | MORE
SMALL_SPEC	:: =	SMALL-Q | SMALL | LOW | LONG | LIGHT | SLOW
LARGE_SPEC	:: =	LARGE-Q | LARGE | LONG | HIGH | HEAVY | FAST
LESS	:: =	LESS-Q | SMALLER | LOWER | LONGER |
LIGHTER | SLOWER		
MORE	:: =	LARGER-Q | LARGER | LONGER | HIGHER |
		HEAVIER | FASTER

So far, we have only discussed words and phrases that function as adjectives modifying nouns. Their corresponding adverbials can be used as well, to modify verbs. In this case, verbs are PO/NE items or PPI/NPI items. The following examples illustrate their use:

> "This phone is highly priced."
> "This phone costs a lot."
> "This printer prints very fast."

We will not discuss them further because the ideas are similar.

5.2.4 Emotion and Sentiment Intensity

As discussed in Section 2.3, there are many basic human emotions. Analyzing these emotions is an important part of sentiment analysis. On the basis of my experience, emotions can be handled in the same way as normal sentiments, except that an additional lexicon is required for each emotion, and the analysis also needs to account for the sentiment intensity.

For example, for the emotions *anger, joy,* and *sad,* we have the following indicating words:

Anger: *absurd, awful, crap, crappy, disgraceful, disgusted, disgusting, furious, garbage, gruesome, hate, horrible, horrid, horrify, horrific,* and so on

Joy: *adorable, amazed, attractive, awesome, beautiful, beautifully, breathtaking, brilliance, brilliant, charm, delight, elegant, elegance, excited, exciting,* and so on

Sad: *bitter, despair, despondent, disconsolate, dismal, distress, doleful, downcast, dreary, gloomy, sad, unhappy,* and so on

Given these lexicons (there are also many phrases), any lexicon-based sentiment analysis system can mine emotions.

If we want to reflect different levels of intensities of emotions and rational sentiments or opinions using multiple ratings, intensifiers and diminishers should be considered. The ideas in Sections 2.1.3, 2.3.5, and 3.2.2 are applicable. For example, the sentence "This product is very bad" is more negative than the sentence "This product is bad," and the emotion in the sentence "I am somewhat unhappy with their service" is weaker than that in the sentence "I am unhappy about their service," where *very* is an intensifier and *somewhat* is a diminisher. Because this topic has been covered in Sections 2.1.3, 2.3.5, and 3.2.2, we will not discuss it further here, except to stress that when a rational sentiment expression is modified by an intensifier, the rational sentiment can be turned into an emotional sentiment (see Section 2.3.5).

Distinguishing rational and emotional sentiments, however, is subjective. There is still no standard methodology for their separation. In a practical system, the system designer is free to design his or her own scheme. In Opinion Parser, I used sentiment and emotion words and phrases to identify five rating scales for sentiment classification – that is, emotional positive, rational positive, neutral, rational negative, and emotional negative. My experience is that the five ratings are sufficient for most practical applications. Of course, one can design finer-grained ratings.

5.2.5   Senses of Sentiment Words

Sentiment words and phrases are instrumental for sentiment analysis. However, few such sentiment words, if any, actually express sentiment in all possible contexts. A word can have multiple meanings or senses, including some in which it may not have any sentiment. For example, *great* is a positive sentiment word, but *great* as in *great-grandfather* does not express any sentiment. Because word sense disambiguation remains a very difficult problem in NLP, we cannot depend on it to solve our problem. In fact, we may have to ignore word sense disambiguation entirely and use some other clues to determine whether a sentiment word actually expresses a sentiment in a particular context. Although the POS of a word can indicate whether a sentiment word expresses sentiment in some cases, in other cases the same POS may imply sentiment in some senses and not in others. In the rest of this section, we use some common sentiment words to further illustrate the point and describe how they may be suitably used in a sentiment analysis system. In the next section, we discuss how to represent sentiment words and other opinion rules.

Pretty and terribly. When *pretty* is used as an adjective, verb, or noun, it has a positive orientation, except when it appears in some special phrases or idioms – for example, *cost a pretty penny*, which means something costs a lot of money (i.e., it has the same meaning as *cost an arm and a leg* and *cost the earth*). However, when this word is used as an adverb modifying an adjective, it

does not indicate a positive or negative sentiment but only qualifies the sentiment of the adjective – for example, *pretty good, pretty bad*, and *pretty sure*. In
this case, it has the meaning of *to a fairly or moderately high degree*. Specifically, when *pretty* is followed by an adjective or adverb, its own default sentiment
should be ignored. However, owing to POS tag errors, we cannot completely
depend on POS tags produced by a tagger. The system may need to see the POS
tag of the word after it and whether the word after it expresses sentiment.

The adverb *terribly* functions in a similar way, although it is not as frequently used as *pretty*. In *terribly bad* and *terribly good*, it has the sense or
meaning of *very* or *extremely*. However, when it is not modifying an adjective,
it is a strong negative sentiment word with the meaning of *very badly* – for
example, "This car is terribly built."

Easily, clearly, and well. These three words usually have a positive orientation, but in some senses they may not indicate sentiment. However, it is
difficult to determine in which sense each of the words is being used in an
actual sentence. We often have to use some other clues to make this decision.

Easily and *clearly* are often positive when they are used with verbs having
no sentiment. However, when they are used with sentiment verbs, they no
longer exhibit sentiment themselves but instead intensify the context sentiment. Furthermore, when they modify a *be* verb in an active voice, they also do
not exhibit sentiment. The following sentences give some examples:

> "This software can be installed easily."
> "This machine gets damaged easily."
> "He explains everything clearly."
> "This is clearly a bad phone."

Many other words in English have similar usage – for example, *fast* and
quickly. Sometimes the positions where such words appear in a sentence can
give a good indication whether they express sentiment. For example, when
clearly appears as the first word in a sentence, it just means *obviously,* and the
sentiment of the sentence should usually be determined from the rest of the
sentence. The word *well* as an adverb functions similarly:

> "Clearly, this is a problem for the car."
> "Clearly, this is not my car."
> "Well, I do not think this is a good car."

Incredible. *Incredible* is a hard case. It is mostly positive in informal text,
meaning *astonishing* and *amazing*. In a negative context, however, it means
unbelievable and can even be negative. For example:

> "This car is incredible."
> "It is incredible that this guy murdered so many people."
> "It is incredible that Apple sold so many iPhones."

Incredible in the first sentence expresses a positive opinion by default, but in the second and the third sentences, it means *beyond belief*. The second sentence is negative and the third sentence is positive.

Thus, *incredible* can be handled in a sentiment analysis system as follows: when the sentence has other sentiment-bearing words or phrases, *incredible* only reinforces the sentiment, and its default positive sentiment should be ignored. However, in some cases, it can be hard to detect the meaning of *incredible* because its context may appear in a previous sentence. For example:

> "He murdered ten people. This is an incredible case."

Smell. *Smell* can be either a verb or a noun. It is an interesting word in English as far as sentiment is concerned:

> "This car smells."
> "This perfume smells good."
> "This room smells bad."
> "This room has a smell."
> "This room has a foul smell."
> "This room has a nice smell."

When there is no associated positive or negative sentiment word, *smell* is often negative regardless of whether it acts as a verb or a noun. But when such an associated word is present, *smell* does not have a sentiment. That is, the sentiment of the sentence or clause depends on the sentiment of the adjective before or after *smell*. There is also an idiom involving *smell* – *smell a rat* – which should override the sentiment of *smell*.

5.2.6   Survey of Other Approaches

Early work on sentiment or opinion rules mainly dealt with sentiment word and negation word combinations (Hu and Liu, 2004; Kim and Hovy, 2004), which led to the general concept of *sentiment reversal* resulting from the compositions of sentiment shifters and positive or negative sentiment words – for example, "*not*" & POS("*good*") => NEG("*not good*") and "*fail to*" & POS ("*impress*") => NEG("*fail to impress*"). An extension to sentiment reversal is similar to rule category 3 in Section 5.2.1 – for example, "*reduced*" & NEG ("*pain*") = > POS("*reduced pain*").

Moilanen and Pulman (2007) introduced the notion of *sentiment conflict*, which is used when multiple-sentiment words occur together – for example, *terribly good*. Conflict resolution is achieved by ranking the constituents on the basis of relative weights assigned to them dictating which constituent is more important with respect to sentiment.

Neviarouskaya et al. (2010) introduced six types of composition rules: sentiment reversal, aggregation, propagation, domination, neutralization, and intensification. *Aggregation* is similar to sentiment conflict but is defined differently. If the sentiments of words in adjective–noun, noun–noun, adverb–adjective, or adverb–verb phrases have opposite orientations or polarities, then mixed polarity with the dominant polarity of the pre-modifier is assigned to the phrase – for example, POS("*beautiful*") & NEG("*fight*") = > POSneg("*beautiful fight*").

The rule of *propagation* is applied when a verb of propagation or transfer type is used in a phrase/clause and the sentiment of an argument that has prior neutral polarity needs to be determined – for example, PROP-POS("*to admire*") & "*his behavior*" = > POS("*his behavior*"); "*Mr. X*" & TRANS ("*supports*") & NEG("*crime business*") = > NEG("*Mr. X*"). We can see this covers the opinion target.

The rules of *domination* are as follows: (1) if polarities of a verb and an object in a clause have opposite directions, the polarity of verb prevails [e.g., NEG("*to deceive*") & POS("*hopes*") = > NEG("*to deceive hopes*")]; (2) if a compound sentence joins clauses using the coordinate connector *but*, the attitude features of the clause following the connector are dominant [e.g., 'NEG("*It was hard to climb a mountain all night long*"), but POS("*a magnificent view rewarded the traveler in the morning*").' = > POS(whole sentence)].

The rule of *neutralization* is applied when a preposition-modifier or condition operator relates to a sentiment statement – for example, "*despite*" & NEG('*worries*') = > NEUT("*despite worries*"). The rule of *intensification* strengthens or weakens a sentiment score (intensity) – for example, Positive_score("*happy*") < Positive_score("*extremely happy*").

Additional related works can be found in the literature (Nasukawa and Yi, 2003; Polanyi and Zaenen, 2004; Choi and Cardie, 2008; Ganapathibhotla and Liu, 2008; Neviarouskaya et al., 2009; Nakagawa et al., 2010; Min and Park, 2011; Socher et al., 2011a; Yessenalina and Cardie, 2011).

As we can see, many of the sentiment composition rules discussed in Section 5.2.1 and the Appendix have not been expressed with compositions in the literature – for example, those about resource usage and about desirable and undesirable facts. Existing rules are also too restrictive for practical use because we need to deal with the potential problem of other words intervening between the component words in a rule. For example, in "The drug reduced a lot of my shoulder pain," the words *reduced* and *pain* in the rule, "*reduced*" & NEG("*pain*") = > POS("*reduced pain*"), do not appear next to each other in the sentence. Thus, the rule is hard to apply. We need to know what expression is allowed in between and whether the application scope of *reduced* actually covers *pain*. In fact, we need a more sophisticated, yet flexible representation language to code the rules, which we discuss in Section 5.7. By "flexible,"

I mean that the representation language should not depend too much on correct grammar or correct parse trees because much of the opinion text from social media is informal, containing numerous grammatical and other types of errors.

5.3   Negation and Sentiment

Sentiment shifters [or valence shifters, as they are called by Polanyi and Zaenen (2004)] often change sentiments to their opposite directions. Negation words like *no, not, never, none, nobody, nowhere, neither-nor, nothing*, and *cannot* are the most common type of sentiment shifters. However, as we saw in Section 5.2, sentiment change can be achieved in many ways. In Section 5.4, we will see that modality can have a major impact on sentiment, too.

In this section, we will not use rules as in Section 5.2.1 to represent the applications of negations, as they can be largely described using the dependency grammar. The dependency parse tree of a sentence can also help us determine the application scope of each negation word or phrase in the sentence, which we discuss in Section 5.3.5. However, knowing the application scope of each negation word or phrase does not mean that we can easily determine whether the negated expression implies a positive or negative sentiment. This is beyond the traditional study of negation or modality in the literature – a point that we will see shortly.

5.3.1   Negation Words

A negation word can affect the sentiment expressed in a sentence in many ways. The following three ways are very common:

1. A negation word directly negates a positive or negative sentiment expression. For example:

> "This car is not good."
> "This Sony camera is not as bad as people think it is."
> "Nobody likes this car."
> "No race could John win."
> "John cannot win any race."
> "Nothing works on this computer."
> "The fridge is small enough not to take up a lot of space."

In these sentences, the negation words simply reverse the sentiments indicated by the sentiment words or phrases in the sentences. Note that "take up a lot of space" is a negative sentiment expression by the resource usage rule 6 in Section 5.2.

However, this sentiment reversal should not be treated as a general rule. In many cases, simply reversing the sentiment orientation is problematic.

For example, "I am not angry" does not mean "I am happy," and "This is not the best car" does not mean "This is a bad car." We discussed this issue in Section 3.2.2, where one method was described to deal with the problem. However, there is still no standard way to solve the problem.

2. A negation word indicates that some expected or desirable functions or actions cannot be performed. Such sentences often do not use any sentiment words.

> "When I click the start button, the program does not launch."
> "My car does not start in a few occasions."
> "The fridge door cannot be opened."
> "Nowhere can I find out how to use the display function."
> "You can do nothing on an iPad."

The sentiments in these sentences can be quite hard to recognize because it is often very difficult to know what the expected or desirable functions or actions are for a particular entity or aspect in a domain. The negation words here do not function as sentiment shifters, as they do in case 1, because there is no sentiment from a sentiment word to shift in any of the preceding sentences.

Hard to, difficult to, and *have difficulty in* function similarly to negation words in this context, but have a weaker strength or intensity.

3. A negation word negates a desirable or undesirable state expressed without using a sentiment word:

> "The water that comes out of the refrigerator is not cold."
> "No bag is used on this vacuum cleaner anymore."

The sentiments in such sentences are also hard to determine because it is difficult to decide what the desirable or undesirable state is or what is expected in a particular domain without an explicit sentiment word or phrase being present in the sentence. For example, in the second sentence, without the knowledge that older vacuum cleaners hold dust in bags, one needs to change them frequently, and changing the bags is very troublesome, it is hard to know whether the sentence is positive or negative.

In what follows, we discuss a few other issues about negation expressions.

Negation in comparative sentences. Negating a comparative or superlative opinion word can be tricky in some cases. For example:

> "This car is not better than my previous car."
> "This car is not the best car in the market."

The first sentence may not have a negative opinion about *this car* because the two cars could be equally good. The situation in the second sentence is similar.

However, on the basis of my experience, treating both of them as negative for *this car* is acceptable in practice, although in some cases their meanings can be affected by the context. For example:

> "This car is not the best car in the market, but it is quite good."

When an equative comparison is negated, the orientation usually reverses – for example, "This car is not as good as my previous car." For definitions of different types of comparisons, refer to Chapter 8.

In some cases, negating a comparative does not change sentiment orientation. For example:

> "It does not get better/worse than this."
> "Nothing I have seen could rival the pyramids."
> "Nothing is better than an iPhone."

These sentences are usually easy to deal with because *than* (or *rival*, which signifies a comparison here) splits a sentence into two segments, with one side being positive and the other negative. Note that the first sentence does not mention the target entity, which should have been mentioned in a previous sentence.

Double negation. Sentences involving double negation are often difficult to deal with. For example:

> "This is not the reason for not providing a good service."
> "It is not that I do not like it."
> "There is nothing that it cannot do."

Not followed by a noun phrase. In this case, *not* usually does not change or introduce sentiment about the entity or aspect represented by the noun phrase unless the noun phrase is a sentiment word or phrase. For example:

> "I hate Audi, not Mini."
> "It is not a Sony, but a Samsung."
> "Evo runs Android, not the Windows mobile software."
> "She is not a beauty."
> "She is not a nice person."

Not in the first three sentence does not change or introduce any sentiment, as there is no sentiment to be changed in the application scope of *not*. *Not* in the last two sentences does change their sentiment orientations because the noun phrases express desirable states.

There are also some rather complex cases. For example:

> "Evo runs Android and not the creaky Windows mobile software."
> "Well, Touchpad is not an iPad."

For the first sentence, it is easy to know that the opinion (or sentiment) target of *creaky* is the *Windows mobile software*. But the hard part is to realize that *not* does not change the orientation of *creaky*, which is a negative sentiment word. The second sentence is even harder to deal with because it depends on people's general impression of *iPad*. In this case, the opinion about *Touchpad* is negative because the impression among consumers is that *iPad* is a very good product.

Negation words in imperative sentences. Because imperative sentences give commands or make requests, they usually do not express sentiment. Thus, negation words in them also do not change sentiment:

> "No bigotry please."
> "Do not bring a calculator."

But such sentences can express sentiment in some cases. For example:

> "Do not waste time on this movie."

The author of this sentence is negative about the movie.

Negation words in idioms or phrases. Negation words in idioms and phrases should be treated as integral parts of the idioms or phrases rather than independent negation words. Here is a list of some commonly used idioms and phrases containing negation words:

> believe it or not, by no means, can stand no more, cannot wait to, do not apply, do not get me started, do not get me wrong, do not mind, do not push too hard, for no reason, have nothing to do with, if not better, if not impossible, if not the best/worst, last but not (the) least, look no further, never-ending story, no avail, no bearing, no big deal, no brainer, no change, no comparison, no difference, no doubt, no end, no exception, no exaggeration, no fun, no idea, no issue, no matter, no question, no question asked, no stranger, no time, no way, no soul, no luck, not looking back, no problem, no rush, no stake, no substitute, no such thing as, no use, no wonder, not alone, not a big deal, not a deal breaker, not a fan of, not huge on something, not just, not least of, not only, not possible without, not the least, not the only, not to mention, not until, nothing to do, second to none, why not

As we can see, sentences involving negation words may or may not express any explicit or implied sentiment. But it should be safe to say that if a sentence does not use a sentiment word or an expression of a desirable or undesirable state or action, it usually does not have a clear sentiment. The problem is that it is often hard to identify whether there is an expression stating a desirable or undesirable state or action and what is expected in a domain.

5.3.2   *Never*

The negation word *never* is special. Although it is mainly used as a negation word to express a strong positive or negative opinion, it can also function in other ways. The following examples show its base use as a strong negation word:

> "This vacuum never loses suction."
> "I will never buy another product from eBay."
> "This printer never worked properly."
> "I never liked any Apple products."
> "I have never heard a good thing about this car."

However, *never* can function in diverse ways, many of which do not change sentiment orientations at all. It thus needs special treatment. In the following, we study several cases.

1. Express a positive opinion about a single entity by dismissing all others.

> "I will never buy anything else."
> "I will never buy any other brand of vacuum."
> "I will never switch back to another brand."

The target of the opinion is not given in any of these sentences, but it usually can be inferred easily from the previous sentences. Of course, one may explicitly mention the opinion target sometimes using *except, besides*, and *but*. For example:

> "I have never liked any other smartphone except iPhone."
> "Once you buy this phone, you will never want another phone."

Expressions like *anything else, any other*, and *another* are the key here, as they do not include the entity in question itself. Any change to them could result in a completely different meaning. For example:

> "I would never spend such an exorbitant amount of money on any phone."

2. Express an opinion that something has never been *so good/bad* (or *this/that good* or *bad*) or *better/worse* (using comparatives). In such a sentence, the use of a sentiment word or some desirable or desirable state expression is important. For example:

> "My carpets were never this clean."
> "I have never had such a clean house."
> "I have never owned a car that is so fun to drive."
> "I never knew how bad this phone was until I bought a Nokia phone."
> "This car has never been better."

The first two sentences are from reviews of a vacuum cleaner. They actually express indirect opinions or benefits because the opinion targets in the sentences are the vacuum cleaner, which is not even mentioned. Thus, discourse-level analysis is needed. The words *so, this*, and *such* are crucial in the first three sentences, which express some surprising or unexpected results. Without them, the meaning and the sentiment orientation of these sentences can be completely different, or at least ambiguous. The fourth sentence expresses a contrast (see also Section 5.5). The sentiment about *this phone* is negative, but that about the *Nokia phone* is positive. The last sentence uses a comparative (*better*) to express the current superior state of the car.

3. Express something desirable or undesirable that has never been experienced before.

> "I never had a vacuum blowing out a clean smell before."

Again, in such a sentence, the use of a sentiment word or some expression of a desirable or desirable state is important.

To deal with these special uses of *never*, the first step is to recognize them in the sentences. These cases should not be difficult to recognize using patterns. Once they are recognized, we can just ignore the negation sense of *never*.

5.3.3 Some Other Common Sentiment Shifters

Hardly, barely, rarely, seldom. These are *presuppositional* words. They can also change a sentiment orientation. We can compare "It works" with "It hardly works." *Works* indicates a positive sentiment, but *hardly works* does not: it presupposes that better was expected.

Little, few, rare. These words change the sentiment orientation in a similar way:

> "The Fed has little room left to revive growth."
> "Few people like this product."
> "The problem is rare."

We first encountered these words in Section 5.2.3; we discuss them again here for completeness in the context of negation. Note that *a little* and *a few* do not have this meaning, and when *little* or *few* is used with other senses/meanings, they may not express sentiment. For example:

> "This little machine is great."
> "I went to Chicago in the past few days."
> "We had that little house in the South."

Fail to, refuse to, omit, neglect. These words and phrases often change sentiment orientations. They function similarly to presuppositional words:

> "This camera fails to impress me."
> "The fridge door refuses to open."
> "This camera never failed to impress me."

The last sentence can be regarded as a double negation case.

Far from, nowhere (even) near/close. These phrases function just like negation words and indicate sentiment change. For example:

> "This car is nowhere near perfect."
> "This car is far from perfect."

5.3.4   Shifted or Transferred Negations

In English, when expressing negation with verbs like *think, believe*, and so on, it is preferable to negate the first verb instead of the second. That is, we shift or transfer the negation from the second verb to the first. Take, for example, the following sentences:

> "I do not think this is a good car."
> "I do not believe that this car is worth the price."

Interestingly, when modality is used, the opinion may not be reversed in some cases. For example:

> "I did not believe that this car could work so well."

In fact, modal auxiliary verbs such as *would, should, could, might, need, must*, and *ought to* are another type of sentiment shifter. We study them in Section 5.4.

Sarcasm often changes sentiment orientations, too – for example, "What a great car, it failed to start the first day." Although it may not be hard to recognize such shifters manually, spotting them in actual sentences and handling them correctly automatically is very challenging (see Section 4.5).

5.3.5   Scope of Negations

We have discussed many cases where, when a negation word and a sentiment word or phrase are present in a sentence, the sentiment should not be reversed. Besides these cases, there is yet another reason to avoid sentiment reversal: the sentiment word may not be in the application scope of the negation word. For example, in the following sentence, the negation word *not* does not change the orientation of the sentiment word *horrible* because *horrible* is beyond the scope of *not*:

> "I did not drive my car on that horrible road."

In the following sentence, *not* applies to *like* but not to *ugly*:

> "I do not like this car because it is ugly."

In most cases, simple syntactic rules can determine the application scope of a negation word quite well. For example, Jia et al. (2009) proposed several rules based on using a dependency parse tree. It defines the scope to be the word span between the negation expression (word or phrase) and another word or punctuation after it. The key is to determine the end of the span. The main rule basically says that the ending should not cross the independent clause where the negation expression resides or its next subordinate clause. This rule is further refined with four additional rules to restrict the scope or to reduce the span further.

Sentiment verb rule. Whenever a negation expression in a sentence negates a sentiment verb, the word immediately after the verb is the end of the scope.

Sentiment adjective rule. Whenever a sentiment adjective forms a "cop" or "xcomp" typed dependency with the closest preceding copula or verb, which is negated by a negation expression, the expression immediately after this adjective is the end of the scope. Here "cop" means copula and "xcomp" means open clausal complement (de Marneffe and Manning, 2008).

Sentiment noun rule. Whenever a sentiment noun acts as the object of a verb negated by a negation expression, the expression immediately after this noun is the end of the scope.

Double object rule. Whenever a negation expression negates a verb taking double objects, only the direct object should be in the scope, and the indirect object should be excluded.

Jia et al. (2009) also describe several exceptions, which are cases where negative words should not be treated as such – for example, *not only* and *not just*. We discussed these in the preceding subsections. Note that here the scope does not include shifted negations, which should be handled separately, as discussed previously. In the work by Ikeda et al. (2008) and Li et al. (2010g), supervised classification was used to determine whether a negation expression should change the sentiment in a sentence. The scope of negation has also been studied in the general NLP context by researchers. For example, in the research of Rosenberg and Bergler (2012) and Rosenberg et al. (2012), some heuristic rules were proposed based on syntactic dependency trees.

Although many cases of negation have been covered here, many more certainly exist. Even the cases discussed in this section are not easy to deal with: a large number of sentences are objective sentences, which require some understanding of the application domain to analyze them correctly. In that sense, I have actually presented many problems but provide few solutions. Much further research is needed.

5.4 Modality and Sentiment

Modal verbs or expressions in sentences can have a significant impact on the sentiment expressed in those sentences. This is quite natural because modality expresses notions such as possibility, probability, necessity and obligation, permission, ability, and intent – all of which are subjective in nature and closely related to sentiment and feeling. There are three types of modality in English: deontic, epidemic, and dynamic (Aarts, 2011).

Deontic modality. Deontic modality is concerned with getting people to do things or (not) allowing them to do things – that is, with such notations as *obligation* and *permission*. For example:

> "Sony must improve the reliability of its laptops."
> "This company should reduce the price of its products."
> "You may return the phone to us."

Epidemic modality. Epidemic modality expresses some kind of inferencing or judgment about the truth of a proposition. For example:

> "Sony may produce good cameras."
> "Sony might have solved its picture quality problem."

Dynamic modality. This type of modality is often concerned with *ability* and *volition*. For example:

> "The camera can take great pictures."
> "I cannot tell whether this is a good car."

In English, there are nine core modal verbs:

> can, could, may, might, will, would, shall, should, must

Can, may, will, shall, and *must* are in present tense, and *could, might, would*, and *should* are the past tense forms of *can, may, will*, and *shall*, respectively. However, *could, might, would*, and *should* also have specialized meanings in which they do not function as the past tense forms of *can, may, will*, and *shall*. All of them can be combined with negation to form interesting combinations, which have important impact on sentiment analysis. There are also some *marginal modal verbs*,

> dare, need, ought (to)

and modal idioms,

> have (got) to, had better/best, would rather, and so on

So far, little research has been done about how modals influence sentiment. An exception is the work by Liu et al. (2013), which proposes a supervised learning method to perform sentiment classification of sentences with modals. However, owing to the use of supervised learning, it does not help us understand modality's impact on sentiment. Although extensive studies of modality have been performed in linguistics, they were not conducted for sentiment analysis purposes. Here our focus is only on the use of modals in sentiment or opinion sentences and how they affect sentiment orientations.

On the basis of these definitions, we can see that sentences of epidemic modality using *may* or *might* usually do not express clear sentiment because of the uncertainty involved in such sentences. Deontic modality and dynamic modality are closely related to sentiment. Before we go into details, we make three observations:

- Most modal sentences expressing negative opinions do not use negation words.
- Most modal sentences expressing positive opinions use negation words.
- As a result, in sentences with negative sentiment, modal verbs typically serve as sentiment shifters, and such sentences often involve comparatives (e.g., *-er* words) or words and phrases with comparative meanings.

Can and could. In many cases, the ability to do something – that is, dynamic modality – is positive:

> "I can count on Apple."
> "This device can deal with the connection problem."
> "This phone can do speed dialing but my previous phone cannot."

Could and *can* often combine with a comparative (JJR or RBR) to express negative sentiment, but such sentences are not comparative sentences:

> "The touchscreen could be better."
> "I can find a better GPS for this amount of money."
> "The voice quality could be improved."

Although *improved* is not a comparative word, it does express a more desirable state. When a negation word is combined with a comparative, the sentence can be either positive or negative, depending on the comparative in the sentence:

> "I cannot be happier with this product."
> "It cannot be worse than this."
> "I cannot praise this product more highly."

There are also many other common ways that *cannot* and *could not* are used to express sentiment. In many cases, *cannot* may be replaced with *could not*:

> "Their service agent cannot be bothered to serve me."
> "I cannot wait to see this movie."
> "This phone cannot compare with my old phone."
> "I cannot live without this phone."
> "This is a deal that I cannot resist/refuse."
> "You cannot beat the price."
> "I cannot stand this movie."

> "I can stand no more."
> "You cannot find anything else for this price/money."
> "I cannot find anything in X to compare with Y."

Clearly, *cannot* and *could not* can also be treated simply as normal negations, as in "This car cannot do fast reverse." However, in some cases, the negation may not affect sentiment. That is the case in the sentence "I cannot say whether this camera is good or not," because the scope of *cannot* does not go beyond *say* in this sentence.

Will and would. *Will* does not seem to have clear patterns that indicate sentiment. However, like *could, would* can be used together with positive sentiment words to imply negative sentiment. It can also be combined with a comparative (JJR or RBR) to express a negative sentiment:

> "I would have loved this product."
> "It would have been a good car."
> "I would like something better than this."
> "I would like something prettier."

The following examples show some other special uses of *would* to indicate sentiment:

> "I would not buy any other car than this."
> "I would not buy this car."
> "I would not like anything else."
> "Without Google, I would be failing every exam."
> "I did not believe that this phone would work so/this well."

The last sentence, which gives a positive opinion about *this phone*, also shows that the verb tense of the sentence can have a big impact on sentiment. If the sentence is changed to "I do not believe that the phone will work well," it becomes negative.

Shall and should. Like *will/would, shall* does not seem to have clear patterns that indicate sentiment, whereas *should* functions similarly to *could*. *Should* often combines with a comparative (JJR or RBR) to express a negative sentiment. Such sentences are not comparative sentences:

> "This car should be less expensive."
> "Apple should know better."
> "Apple should have done better."
> "iPhone should have a bigger screen."
> "Sony should improve its products."
> "Sony should reduce the price of its products."

Unlike with *could*, when negation is used with *should*, it often still expresses negative sentiment:

> "They should not make the screen so big."
> "They should not have done this terrible thing."
> "Nobody should buy this product."

The modal *ought to* functions similarly to *should*.

Need and must. The use of *need* for sentiment is similar to *should* when no negation word is involved. In some cases, *must* can be used in place of *need* with the addition of a verb. For simplicity, we do not distinguish *need*'s use as a modal from its other uses here:

> "This phone needs a good/better screen."
> "This phone needs work or improvement."
> "Sony needs to improve its products."
> "This car needs more gas."
> "Sony must have a better screen to compete in this market."
> "Sony must improve its products."
> "What they need is a big screen."

When negation or a similar word is used, *need* often expresses positive sentiment:

> "Sony needn't further improve its TV."
> "iPhone allows you to make a call without the need of using your figures."
> "Touchscreens eliminate the need of a mouse."

Have to, had better, and better. These modal idioms can express or change opinions just as *must* does. For example:

> "Sony had better improve its products."
> "Sony has to reduce the price of its TV to sell it."
> "All you have to do is to press the button and everything will be done."

Interestingly, their negations are often used to express positive opinion. For example:

> "With this feature, you no longer have to use your fingers."
> "You do not have to use many programs to perform this task anymore."

Sometimes such a modal may not indicate any opinion itself, although the other part of the sentence may express opinions. For example:

> "I have to admit/say/confess/agree that this is a great car."

Have to can also combine with other modal verbs to express opinions. For example:

> "It is a faulty phone and I should not have to pay to send it back to the dealer."

Want, wish, hope, and like. These English verbs can express modality but are not modal verbs because they are not auxiliaries. For example, the following sentences all express negative opinions about the screen. They involve some words of comparison:

> "I wish the iPhone had a bigger screen."
> "I hope they can improve their screen."
> "I want a bigger screen from the iPhone."

5.5   Coordinating Conjunction *But*

Conjunctions are words that are used to link other words or larger expressions. Two types of conjunctions are distinguished: *coordinating conjunctions* and *subordinating conjunctions*. Coordinating conjunctions are *and, or, but,* and related words. Subordinating conjunctions are *after, because, when, where, that, which,* and so on; they are used to introduce subordinate clauses in sentences. Coordinating conjunction *but* is of particular interest to sentiment analysis because its use is very frequent in opinion documents and it usually connects contrasting constituents with opposite opinions. Thus the ability to effectively deal with complex sentences involving *but* can make a major difference in the sentiment analysis accuracy.

In general, *but* has two distinct senses.

But as preposition. In this sense, *but* is used as an alternative to *except* (*for*), *apart from,* and *bar* to introduce the only thing or person that the main part of the sentence does not include:

> "I like all Honda models but the CRV."
> "I would not want anything but the iPhone."

This use of *but* often follows words such as *everyone, nobody, anything, anywhere, all, no, none, any,* and *every.* It raises the question of how we should deal with words that represent a set of hidden entities. For example, in the first sentence, the author is positive about every car model of *Honda* except the *CRV* (negative). If the system knows all of the *Honda* car models, each of them can be given a positive opinion. However, in most applications, the system does not know the complete set of entities. Hence, to simplify the analysis, only the explicit entity and opinion are used – that is, negative about the *CRV* and positive about the *iPhone*.

But as conjunction. This is the most common use of *but*. It links two contrastive clauses:

> "The picture quality of this camera is great, but the battery life is short."
> "The voice quality of the iPhone is not great, but it sure looks pretty."

We can see from these examples that the opinions before and after *but* are opposite to each other. This characteristic can be exploited for several purposes. First, if we can determine the sentiment orientation of one side, we can infer the orientation on the other side. For example, in the first sentence, it is easy to discover that the clause before *but* is positive because of the sentiment word *great*. Then, we can imply a negative sentiment for the clause after *but*. Second, we can use this characteristic to help determine the sentiment orientation of some context-dependent opinion word. For example, from the positive sentiment before *but*, we can infer that *short* is negative for *battery life*.

But here also has the sense of negation. It collates frequently with negative expressions. In such sentences, the contrastive meanings before and after *but* are often quite obvious:

> "The seat is slightly uncomfortable but not too bad."
> "Fuel economy is very good but not what is stated."
> "They are not cheap but definitely worth it."
> "I hate Audi but not Honda."
> "I'm not a HP fan but that new HP Envy is no joke – a full music laptop."

From these sentences, we can see something quite tricky. For example, the clause after *but* in the first sentence only weakens the negative sentiment about the seat but does not really change it. The second sentence is similar. To get this level of fine detail is challenging. One simple and reasonable strategy is to still give opposite opinions before and after *but* for the same aspect.

Some other more complex cases make the rule of thumb (opinions on both sides of *but* are opposite to each other) difficult to apply in practice because contrast does not always mean opposite. Here are some example sentences, which highlight the issue:

> "The phone worked well at first, but after a short while the sound deteriorated quickly."
> "He promised us work but gave us none."
> "The phone functions well so far, but we will have to wait and see if it will last."
> "The engine is very powerful but it is still quiet."
> "I knew this phone's battery life is not long but not this bad."
> "This is a great phone, but the iPhone is better."
> "I thought I needed an SUV, but the Prius has been great."

The first three sentences involve a sequence of events. To identify the sentiment expressed in them, it is important to know the expressions of time (i.e., *at first* and *so far*), which indicate the sequence of sentiments. The first two sentences are negative, but in the third sentence, the clause after *but* expresses no opinion. The fourth sentence has two positive opinions: one before *but* and one after *but*. The fifth sentence is similar but with negative opinion on both sides of *but*. The sixth sentence is also similar but expresses a comparative opinion. The last sentence expresses no opinion in the first part.

But can also be used as an adverb, but this is quite rare. The expression *but for* may be used as a preposition and has the meaning of a negated if-clause – for example, "But for their help, I would not have a phone to use." *But* is also becoming more commonly used to link two contrastive sentences. In this case, *but* is normally the first word of the second sentence with a similar meaning to *however*: in terms of sentiment analysis, the sentiment orientations in the two sentences are typically different.

Finally, many other words and phrases can have similar meaning or sense as *but* – for example, *although, aside from, despite, except, except for, except that, however, instead of, oddly, on the other hand, other than, otherwise, rather than, until, whereas,* and *with exception of.* We must also be aware that *but* in many idioms and phrases may or may not indicate explicit contrast – for example, *no (other) choice but, no other way but, not only . . . but also, cannot help but, last but not least,* and *nothing but.* In such cases, one can just ignore *but.*

5.6   Sentiment Words in Non-Opinion Contexts

In this section, we highlight several situations where sentiment words indicate no sentiment.

Entity names containing sentiment words. Many businesses choose their names to project a positive image. This causes a problem for sentiment analysis, especially in informal text such as social media, where people often do not use capitalization to indicate entity names. For example, an insurance company is called *Progressive*, an electronic store is called *Best Buy*, a Hollywood movie is called *Pretty Woman*, and a salon is called *Elegant Beauty Salon & Spa*. The name of a particular type of business may also contain sentiment words. For example, *beauty salon, beauty parlor*, and *beauty shop* are names of a kind of business. The word *beauty* can cause problems for sentiment classification because it is usually regarded as a positive sentiment word, as in "This car is a beauty."

Function names containing sentiment words. One should also be mindful of the names of some functions. For example, video players include a button called *fast forward* or *fast rewind*. If *fast*'s default sentiment polarity is positive, a sentence containing *fast forward* may result in a sentiment classification error. Another example is *beauty treatment*, which is the name of a class of procedures that enhance someone's personal beauty. If *beauty* is used as a positive sentiment word by default, it can cause errors. Some functions of software may also include sentiment words – for example, "I am feeling lucky" in Google search.

A preprocessing step should be applied to identify such entity and function names. Entity names are slightly easier to identify, but function names are difficult to recognize because people never use capitalization to indicate them. Grammar-based methods need to be applied. For example, if a sentiment noun like *beauty* is followed by another noun, it usually does not express any sentiment. However, there are exceptions. For example, the sentence "She is a beauty queen" would lead one to automatically have a positive opinion about her appearance.

Greetings and good wishes. Every language includes numerous expressions for greetings and good wishes. Such expressions almost always contain sentiment words. For example, English has *good morning, good day, happy birthday, happy anniversary, warm regards, best regards, best wishes, good luck, have a great weekend, hope you get well soon,* and so on.

These expressions do not express any positive or negative opinion and should thus be ignored in sentiment analysis. One can compile a good set of such expressions fairly easily and mask them in the preprocessing stage. To automatically discover them is also an option, because many of them appear at the end of a message.

Authors' self-description. In many cases, authors describe themselves, and these descriptions can contain sentiment words. In these sentences, it is natural to mention some entity names and/or their aspects. However, the opinions in the sentences are not about the entities or their aspects, but rather about the authors themselves. Such sentences are hard to recognize. Compare the following two sentences:

> "I know Lenovo laptops very well."
> "Lenovo knows the needs of its customers very well."

In the first sentence, the sentiment word *well* describes the author himself. Thus it has nothing to do with Lenovo laptops. However, in the second sentence, the opinion is positive about Lenovo. In product reviews, sentences describing the authors themselves and also using sentiment words in the sentences are rare. In contrast, in forum discussions, such sentences are common because authors in forums could be experts or experienced users of the discussed products or services and they come to answer questions and provide advice. These sentences are not easy to deal with because when first-person pronouns (*I* and *we*) are used, the sentences often express personal experiences and opinions about the entities involved and not about the authors themselves.

> "I have used several Lenovo laptops and am very happy about their reliability."

To deal with these sentences, parsing can help identify opinion targets. We discuss the topic in Section 6.2.

In addition, there are a large number of other contexts in which sentiment expressions express no opinion. The following are some examples.

- Uncertainty: "I am not sure whether iPhone is the best phone for me or not."
- Action intent: "I am looking for a good iPhone case."
- General fact: "No insurance means that you have to pay high cost."
- Commercial advertisement: "Buy this great camera and win a trip to Hawaii."
- Past impression: "I thought this car was not good, but after driving it for a few weeks, I simply love it."
- Author's own mistakes: "I made some stupid mistakes in using this camera."

Because little study has been done about these types of sentences or expressions, it is hard to know the percentage of such expressions or sentences that express no sentiment. Furthermore, although conceptually we humans can understand these cases fairly easily, spotting them automatically by an algorithm is challenging.

5.7   Rule Representation

We are now ready to discuss how to represent complex sentiment-bearing expressions and rules in a sentiment analysis system. The representation should ideally cover all intrinsic details needed for effective recognition of such expressions and rules and for applying them to arrive at the right sentiment for the right target aspects and/or entities.

Although some research has been done on rule representation, as described in Section 5.2.6, current proposals from the research community are too simplistic for practical use. Systems in industry use much more sophisticated representations. For example, the rule representation or specification language in my Opinion Parser system, which uses a lexicon-based approach, employs regular expressions to represent rules. Each symbol in regular expressions is also attached to a set of constraints and actions.

The rule specification language discussed in this section is based on the language used in Opinion Parser. This language follows a *default-and-exception* scheme. Such a scheme is employed because, as discussed in Section 5.2.5, almost no sentiment word has a fixed sentiment orientation in all senses and/or contexts. Each word's sentiment orientation is thus represented with a default orientation (the most frequently used orientation or polarity) and a set of exceptions. That is, the default sentiment orientation can be overwritten by exceptions with different orientations or no sentiment at all. The exception rules basically represent different special contexts and their corresponding sentiment orientations. This default-and-exception scheme also applies to sentiment composition rules.

We do not discuss regular expressions further, as they are standard. Instead, we discuss only how each symbol is represented. A symbol, denoted by SYMBOL, can be either a word, denoted by WORD_spec, or a gap in between two important words, denoted by GAP_spec. A gap cannot be the first or the last symbol of a rule in the regular expression. The grammar for SYMBOL is as follows:

SYMBOL	:: =	WORD_spec | GAP_spec
WORD_spec	:: =	"(" word WORD POS VOICE LOC_range TARGET_loc ACTION ")"
WORD	:: =	WORD_set | ("(" not WORD_set ")") | + | − | ASPECT | ENTITY | nil
POS	:: =	POS_set | ("(" not POS_set ")") | nil
VOICE	:: =	active | passive | nil
LOC_range	:: =	"(" (start | end) START END ")" | nil
TARGET_loc	:: =	self | left | right | nil
ACTION	:: =	+ | − | nil
GAP_spec	:: =	"(" gap RANGE POS ")"
RANGE	:: =	("(" MIN MAX ")") | CHUNK | nil
CHUNK	:: =	np | vp | pp | clause | nil

WORD_SPEC: the specification of a word, which has seven components.
word: indicator of a word specification.
WORD: a set of possible or alterative words (WORD_list), or not any word of the set indicated by (not WORD_set).
+ and −: positive and negative sentiment, respectively.
ASPECT or ENTITY: the word being an aspect or an entity.
nil: nothing to specify.
POS: a set of alternative POS tags (POS_list) for the word, or not any POS tag of the set indicated by (not POS_set).
VOICE: either active or passive voice.
LOC_range: location of the word in the sentence, which should be in the range between the number START and the number END, counting from the first word (indicated by *start*) or the last word (indicated by *end*) of the sentence.
TARGET_loc: indicating where the opinion target should be. *self* means this word, *left* means to the *left* of this word, and *right* means to the *right* of this word.
ACTION: sentiment to be attached to this word; +, −, and *nil* are negative, positive, and neutral (or no) sentiment, respectively.
GAP_spec: represents a gap specification. It consists of three components.
gap: a fixed word indicating a gap specification.
RANGE: the range of the gap. MIN means the minimum gap size (e.g., 0, no gap) and MAX means the maximum gap size (e.g., 5, five words gap).

CHUNK: a noun phrase (np), a verb phrase (vb), a prepositional phrase (pp), or a clause (clause).

For example, suppose we want to express the rule that *throwing something away* is negative. We can use the following regular expression rule to represent it:

```
(  (word ("throw") nil active nil right −)
   (gap np nil)
   (word ("away") nil nil nil left nil) )
```

The sentence "I want to throw the iPhone away" matches this rule. After it is matched, the negative sentiment sign − is attached to *throw* as the rule's action. The opinion target is between *throw* and *away*. The gap should be a noun phrase; that is, there should be a noun phrase between *throw* and *away*.

Although the language is fairly expressive, some complex sentiment compositions or contexts cannot be specified by using it. For example, it does not allow intersentence discourse-level specifications as required by this segment of two sentences: "I'm not tryna be funny, but I'm scared for this country. Romney is winning." Furthermore, because Opinion Parser uses only shallow parsing, it does not allow specification of rules based on parse trees. The reason is that the current syntactic parsers are too slow for practical use unless one has a large number of machines. Additionally, many social media posts, such as tweets and discussions, are full of grammatical errors and other language irregularities, which make parsing highly error-prone. We also note that this specification language does not cover the specification for emotions, but that can be easily added. Sentiment and emotion intensities can be incorporated, too.

5.8   Word Sense Disambiguation and Coreference Resolution

So far, we have not studied any core NLP problems and their effects on aspect sentiment classification. Because sentiment analysis works with the natural language text, it inevitably encounters all issues and difficulties of NLP. This section highlights the NLP issues in the sentiment analysis context using two popular NLP tasks, *word sense disambiguation* and *coreference resolution*, and presents some existing work on them.

As discussed earlier, whether a word indicates sentiment and what orientation it expresses in a particular sentence context are, to a great extent, determined by the sense of the word in that context. Also, in determining opinion targets, coreference resolution plays a major role because, in many cases, the opinion targets are mentioned not in the sentences where sentiments are expressed, but rather in the previous sentences. These targets thus need to be discovered through coreference resolution. Unfortunately, neither of the two tasks has received much research attention in the sentiment analysis community.

Akkaya et al. (2009) first studied *subjectivity word sense disambiguation* (SWSD). Their task was to automatically determine which word instances in a corpus are being used with subjective senses and which are being used with objective senses. Currently, most subjectivity or sentiment lexicons are compiled as lists of words without their specific senses (meanings). However, many words have both subjective and objective senses. False hits – subjectivity clues used with objective senses – are a significant source of error in subjectivity and sentiment analysis. Akkaya et al. (2009) built a supervised SWSD model to disambiguate members of a subjectivity lexicon as having a subjective sense or an objective sense in a corpus context. Their algorithm relies on common machine learning features for word sense disambiguation (WSD). However, the performance was substantially better than the performance of full WSD on the same data, suggesting that the SWSD task is feasible and that subjectivity provides a natural coarse-grained grouping of senses. These authors also showed that SWSD can subsequently facilitate subjectivity and sentiment analysis.

Coreference resolution has been studied extensively in the NLP community in general. It refers to the problem of determining multiple expressions in a sentence or document referring to the same thing – that is, they have the same "referent." For example, in "I bought an iPhone two days ago. It looks very nice. I made many calls in the past two days. They were great," *it* in the second sentence refers to *iPhone*, which is an entity, and *they* in the fourth sentence refers to *calls*, which is an aspect. Recognizing these coreference relationships is clearly very important for aspect-based sentiment analysis. If we do not resolve them, but only consider the opinion in each sentence in isolation, we lose in recall. Although we know that the second and fourth sentences in this piece of text express opinions, we do not know about what and we thus get no useful opinion; in fact, the text expresses a positive opinion about the iPhone itself as well as a positive opinion about its call quality.

Ding and Liu (2010) proposed a supervised learning approach to the problem of *entity and aspect coreference resolution* – that is, the quest to determine which mentions of entities and/or aspects the pronouns refer to. The most interesting point of their work was the design and testing of two opinion-related features that used sentiment analysis for the purpose of coreference resolution. The two features are semantic features that current general coreference resolution methods do not consider, and they can help improve the coreference resolution accuracy.

The first feature is based on sentiment analysis of regular sentences and comparative sentences and the idea of *sentiment consistency*. Consider these sentences: "The Nokia phone is better than this Motorola phone. It is cheap, too." Our common sense tells us that *it* means *Nokia phone* because, in the first sentence, the sentiment about *Nokia phone* is positive (comparative positive), but the sentiment is negative (comparative negative) for *Motorola phone*, and the second sentence is positive. Thus we conclude that *it* refers to *Nokia phone* because people usually express sentiments in a consistent way. It is unlikely that *it* refers to *Motorola phone*. However, if we change "It is cheap, too" to "It is also expensive," then *it* probably now refers to *Motorola phone*. To obtain this feature, the system needs to have the ability to determine positive and negative opinions expressed in both regular and comparative sentences.

The second feature considers which entities and aspects are modified by which opinion words. Consider these sentences: "I bought a Nokia phone yesterday. The sound quality is good. It is cheap, too." The question is whether *it* refers to *sound quality* or the *Nokia phone*. We know that *it* refers to *Nokia phone* because *sound quality* cannot be cheap. To obtain this feature, the system needs to identify which sentiment words are usually associated with which entities or aspects. Such relationships have to be mined from the corpus.

Stoyanov and Cardie (2006) proposed the problem of *source coreference resolution,* which is the task of determining which mentions of opinion holders (sources) refer to the same entity. These authors used existing coreference resolution features described by Ng and Cardie (2002). However, instead of simply employing supervised learning, they used partially supervised clustering.

5.9   Summary

Aspect-level sentiment analysis provides the level of detail required by most practical applications. Although a great deal of work has been done in the research community and many systems have been built in industry, the problem is still far from solved. Every subproblem remains highly challenging. As one CEO put it, "Our sentiment analysis system is as bad as everyone else's" – a nice portrayal of the current situation and the difficulty of the problem.

Two key problems are aspect extraction and aspect sentiment classification. This chapter focused on aspect sentiment classification. In particular, we presented a large number of linguistic patterns that imply opinion and sentiment, which we call rules of sentiment composition or rules of opinions. They can be used in both the supervised learning approach and the lexicon-based approach to aspect sentiment classification. In addition, we studied negation handling and the influence of modality on sentiment. Unfortunately, the classification accuracy of most existing systems is still not high enough for many application domains: existing algorithms cannot deal with complex sentences that require more than sentiment words and simple parsing, or handle factual sentences that imply opinions.

Although this chapter presented a large number of rules, they are still insufficient for practical applications. First, many rules are hard to recognize in an actual sentence and thus are not easy to apply. Second, many other rules are not easily described. Third, identifying targets of opinions remains challenging, which results in opinions being given to wrong entities and/or aspects.

On the whole, we seem to have witnessed a long-tail situation. While sentiment words can handle about 60 percent of the cases (more in some domains and less in others), the remaining cases are highly diverse, numerous, and infrequent, which makes it hard for statistical machine learning algorithms to learn patterns because there are simply not enough training data. People seem to use an unlimited number of ways to express positive and negative opinions. Every domain appears to have something special. To address this dilemma, Wu et al. (2011) proposed a more complex graph-based representation of opinions, which requires even more sophisticated solution methods.

So far, the research community has mainly focused on opinions about electronic products, hotels, and restaurants. These domains are easier (although not easy) to analyze, and reasonable accuracy can be achieved if one can focus on each domain and take care of its special cases. When one moves to other domains – for example, mattresses or paint – the situations get considerably harder, because in these domains, many factual statements imply opinions. One may need to compile a different lexicon for each domain. Political and social domains are another can of worms. Political sentiments are particularly difficult to determine because of the complex mixture of factual reporting and subjective opinions, sarcasm, and the need for background knowledge.

In terms of the type of social media, researchers working on aspect-based sentiment analysis have focused mainly on reviews and tweets from Twitter. These forms of data are also easier (again, not easy) to handle because reviews are opinion rich and contain little irrelevant information, whereas tweets are very short and often straight to the point. Other forms of opinion text, such as forum discussions and commentaries, are much more problematic because sentiments are mixed with all kinds of non-opinion content, and texts often deal with multiple entities and even involve user interactions.

This leads us to another major issue that we have not discussed so far, as limited research has tackled it: the data noise. Almost all forms of social media are very noisy (except reviews) and full of all kinds of spelling, grammatical, and punctuation errors. Most NLP tools, such as POS taggers and parsers, need clean data to perform accurately. Thus a significant amount of preprocessing is needed before any analysis is carried out. Dey and Haque (2008) have identified some preprocessing tasks and methods.

To make significant progress, we still need novel ideas to study opinion text in a wide range of domains. Successful algorithms are likely to require a good integration of machine learning and domain linguistic knowledge.

6   Aspect and Entity Extraction

This is the second chapter about aspect-based sentiment analysis. In Section 2.1.1, we defined each opinion as a quintuple (*e, a, s, h, t*), where *e* is an entity and *a* is one of its aspects, *s* is the sentiment about the aspect *a, h* is the opinion holder, and *t* is the time when the opinion is expressed. Chapter 5 focused on aspect-based sentiment classification, which determines *s*. This chapter addresses extraction of entities and aspects about which sentiments or opinions have been expressed.

Entity and aspect extractions are often regarded as two separate tasks because the methods and features used for their recognition are usually different owing to their individual specific characteristics. Entities commonly refer to names of products, services, individuals, events, and organizations, whereas aspects commonly refer to the attributes and components of entities. The two tasks are also collectively called *opinion target extraction* in sentiment analysis because they together form the targets of opinions. After their extraction, a resolution step is performed to group synonymous entities and aspects together to facilitate opinion summarization. Let us use two example sentences to ground the tasks:

"I brought a Motorola X phone yesterday, and its voice quality is great."
"The sound from this Moto X phone is great."

The entities in these two sentences are *Motorola X* and *Moto X*, and the aspects are *voice quality* and *sound*. The entity and aspect extraction tasks aim to find these entities and aspects. The resolution step should group *Motorola X* and *Moto X* together because they refer to the same entity, and *voice quality* and *sound* together because they refer to the same aspect. This chapter will not discuss how to determine sentiments about entities or aspects, as this topic was covered in Chapter 5.

In general, both aspect extraction and entity extraction are information extraction tasks. However, in the context of sentiment analysis, some specific characteristics of the problem can facilitate their extractions. A key characteristic is that an opinion always has a target. This target is an aspect or an entity. We can exploit some syntactic structures often used to depict opinion and

168

target relationships to help extraction. In this chapter, we first focus on extracting explicit aspects, which are nouns or noun phrases (see Section 2.1.2); we then discuss implicit aspects in Section 6.4.

There are four main approaches to extracting explicit aspects:

1. Extraction by finding frequent nouns and noun phrases.
2. Extraction by exploiting syntactic relations. There are two main types of relations:
   i. Syntactic dependencies depicting opinion and target relations.
   ii. Lexico-syntactic patterns encoding entity and part/attribute relations.
3. Extraction using supervised learning.
4. Extraction using topic models.

The chapter is divided into two main parts, dealing with aspect extraction and entity extraction, respectively. Although the preceding approaches can be used for both tasks, focused work on entity extraction in the context of sentiment analysis is limited because it has been researched extensively in other communities. In the second part of the chapter, we review those existing work from other communities about entity extraction. Along with these two main tasks, this chapter discusses existing research into opinion holder and time extraction.

Throughout the chapter, I use product reviews to develop the ideas and to illustrate the concepts because entities and aspects are clearly identifiable, and entities and aspects are often easily separable. In some other domains, the boundary between entities and aspects is fuzzy. For example, in the political domain, individual candidates are clearly entities. Thus, we can mine public opinions about them and their aspects such as their experiences, personal attributes, and families. For political issues, however, it is often hard to distinguish entities and aspects unless there is a clear hierarchical relationship between issues. For example, we may regard *tax increase* as an entity, and *tax increase for the rich* and *tax increase for the poor* as two aspects of the entity. When such hierarchical relationships are not clear or it is unnecessary to distinguish between entities and aspects, we can simply treat all issues as entities or aspects.

6.1 Frequency-Based Aspect Extraction

Frequency-based aspect extraction finds *explicit aspect expressions* that are nouns and noun phrases from a large number of reviews in a given domain. This approach first identifies nouns and noun phrases using a POS tagger, and then counts their occurrence frequencies using a data mining algorithm, keeping only the frequent nouns and noun phrases using an experimentally determined frequency threshold. Hu and Liu (2004) used association rule mining for this purpose. Such an approach works because aspects are usually expressed as nouns and noun phrases. Moreover, when people comment on different aspects of an entity, the vocabulary that they use typically converges. Thus, frequently occurring nouns and noun phrases are usually genuine and important aspects. Irrelevant contents in reviews tend to be quite different in different reviews. Hence, those infrequently occurring nouns are likely to be nonaspects or less important aspects. This approach is also applicable to entity extraction because in English, an entity name is often written with the first letter of each word in uppercase. Such phrases are usually important named entities in the domain.

The assumptions made by this approach are that the corpus has a reasonable number of reviews and that the reviews are about the same product or at least about the same type of products – for example, phones. This method will not work if the corpus includes a mixture of very different products and/or if each product has only one or two reviews: in those cases, few noun phrases will be repeatedly encountered.

Although this method is very simple, it is quite effective. Some commercial companies are already using this method with some enhancements, such as combining it with the method described in Section 6.2, which was also used by Hu and Liu (2004). Those candidate aspects with the highest frequency counts are almost always the most important aspects of the product.

The precision of this algorithm can be improved by removing noun phrases that may not be aspects of entities. Popescu and Etzioni (2005) evaluated each discovered noun phrase by computing a PMI score between the phrase and some *meronymy discriminators* associated with the entity class. For example, the meronymy discriminators for the camera class are "of camera," "camera has," "camera comes with," and so on; these discriminators can be used to find camera components in a web search. The idea is that those discovered phrases (candidate aspects) that often co-occur with these *part-of* relation indicators are likely to be correct aspects. The PMI measure is a simplified version of Equation (3.5) in Section 3.2:

$$PMI(a, d) = \frac{hits(a \wedge d)}{hits(a)hits(d)} \tag{6.1}$$

where a is a candidate aspect identified using the frequency approach and d is a discriminator. Web searches can be used to find the number of hits for individual expressions as well as their co-occurrences. If the PMI value of a candidate aspect is too low, it may not be a component of the product because a and d do not co-occur frequently. The algorithm also distinguishes components/parts from attributes using WordNet's *is-a* hierarchy (which enumerates different kinds of properties) and morphological cues (e.g., *-iness* and *-ity* suffixes).

A refinement of the frequent noun and noun phrase approach is to consider mainly those noun phrases that appear in sentiment-bearing sentences or occur in some syntactic patterns that indicate sentiments (Blair-Goldensohn et al., 2008). In their work, Blair-Goldensohn et al. (2008) also applied several filters to remove unlikely aspects – for example, dropping aspects that do not have sufficient mentions alongside known sentiment words. They also collapsed aspects at the word stem level and ranked the discovered aspects by a manually tuned weighted sum of their frequency in sentiment-bearing sentences and the type of sentiment phrases/patterns, with appearances in phrases carrying a greater weight. Using sentiment sentences is related to the approach explored in Section 6.2.

Other frequency-based approaches include that introduced by Ku et al. (2006), who made use of a TFIDF scheme and considered expressions at both the document level and the paragraph level. Moghaddam and Ester (2010) augmented the frequency-based approach with an additional pattern-based filter to remove some nonaspect expressions; they also predicted aspect ratings. Scaffidi et al. (2007) proposed a method that compares the frequency of the extracted frequent nouns and noun phrases in a review corpus with their occurrence rates in a generic English corpus to identify true aspects.

Zhu et al. (2009) proposed a method based on the Cvalue measure from Frantzi et al. (2000) for extracting multiword aspects. The Cvalue method is also based on frequency, but considers the frequency of multiword expression t, the length of t, and other expressions that contain t. After Cvalue finds a set of candidates, the set is refined using a bootstrapping technique with a set of given seed aspects. The idea of refinement is based on each candidate's co-occurrence with the seeds.

Long et al. (2010) extracted aspects (nouns) based on frequency and information distance. Their method first finds the core aspect words using the frequency-based method. It then uses the information distance introduced by Cilibrasi and Vitanyi (2007) to find other related words to an aspect. For example, for aspect *price*, it may find "$" and "*dollars.*"

6.2   Exploiting Syntactic Relations

Because opinions have targets, it is no surprise that there are many syntactic relations between sentiment expressions and their sentiment or opinion targets, which can be identified by a syntactic parser. For example, in the sentence "This camera takes great photos," the opinion or sentiment expression is *great*, and the opinion target is *photos*. Here the targets can be either entities or aspects of entities. Such relationships can be exploited to extract aspects and entities because sentiment words and phrases are often known and most of them are domain independent. In fact, if some sentiment words are unknown, these relations can be used to extract sentiment expressions, too (see Section 7.2). In addition to these relations, the general conjunctions can be exploited. The most useful one is *and* because the conjoined expressions are usually of the same type. For example, in the sentence "Picture quality and battery life are great," if we know that *battery life* (or *picture quality*) is an aspect, we can infer that *picture quality* (or *battery life*) is an aspect as well.

There is yet another type of relation that we can exploit. Because aspects are components and attributes of entities, and because linguistic constructions are commonly used to express such semantic relationships, we can use these linguistic constructions for aspect and entity extraction. For example, in the sentence "The voice quality of the iPhone is not as good as I expected," if we know that *voice quality* is an aspect, we can extract *iPhone* as an entity; likewise, if we know that *iPhone* is an entity, we can extract *voice quality* as an aspect. In English, a common way to express such relationships is through the use of genitives. Apart from genitives, some other patterns also exist.

This section explores some of these relations and the existing extraction techniques that exploit them. In Section 6.2.1, we examine some techniques that make use of the opinion and target relations and conjunctions for aspect extraction. In Section 6.2.2, we study part-of and attribute-of relations and their application to aspect extraction.

6.2.1   Using Opinion and Target Relations

The frequency-based aspect extraction method described in Section 6.1 (Hu and Liu, 2004) also has a technique to extract infrequent aspects based on opinion and target relations. This technique is based on the idea that sentiment words often describe or modify aspects in a sentence. If a sentence does not have a frequent aspect but does have some sentiment words, the nearest noun or noun phrase to a sentiment word is extracted as an aspect. Because no parser was used in the work by Hu and Liu (2004), the "nearest" function approximates the dependency relation between the sentiment word and the noun or noun phrase that the sentiment word modifies, which usually works well. For example, in the sentence "The software is amazing," if we know that *amazing* is a sentiment word, then *software* is extracted as an aspect. This idea turns out to be very useful in practice even when it is applied alone. The sentiment pattern method developed by Blair-Goldensohn et al. (2008) uses a similar idea.

To make this method more principled, a dependency parser can be used to identify the dependency relations of sentiment (or opinion) words and opinion targets to extract *aspect–sentiment* pairs (Zhuang et al., 2006). After being parsed by a dependency parser (e.g., using MINIPAR; Lin, 2007), words in a sentence are linked by dependency relations. Figure 6.1 shows the

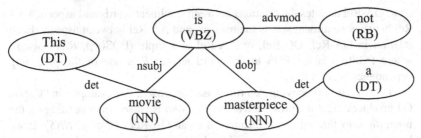

Figure 6.1 An example of a dependency graph.

dependency graph of the sentence "This movie is not a masterpiece." If *movie* and *masterpiece* are labeled as aspect and sentiment words, respectively, a dependency relation can be found as the sequence "NN–nsubj–VB–dobj–NN," where NN and VB are POS tags, and *nsubj* and *dobj* are dependency relation tags. The algorithm first identifies reliable dependency relation templates from the training data and then uses them to identify valid aspect–sentiment pairs in the test data. Somasundaran and Wiebe (2009) and Kobayashi et al. (2006) employed a similar approach. The dependency idea was further generalized into the double propagation (DP) method for simultaneous extraction of both sentiment words and opinion targets (including both entities and aspects) in Qiu et al. (2009a, 2011). We discuss the DP method next.

Double propagation (DP). DP is a bootstrapping method for extracting both sentiment words and aspects at the same time by exploiting certain dependency relations between sentiments and targets (Qiu et al. (2009a, 2011). It needs only a small set of seed sentiment words (which are adjectives) as input; no seed aspects are required.

Dependency relations between sentiments/opinions and their targets (or aspects) allow sentiment words to be recognized by identified aspects, and aspects to be identified by known sentiment words. The extracted sentiment words and aspects are used to identify new sentiment words and new aspects, which are used again to extract more sentiment words and aspects. This propagation process ends when no more sentiment words or aspects can be found. As the process involves propagation through both sentiment words and aspects, the method is thus called *DP*. Extraction rules are based on some special dependency relations.

The method also imposes some constraints on the rules. Sentiment words are assumed to be adjectives and aspects are assumed to be nouns or noun phrases. The dependency relations between sentiment words and aspects include *mod, pnmod, subj, s, obj, obj2*, and *desc*, whereas the relations for sentiment words and aspects themselves include only the conjunction relation *conj.* OA-Rel denotes the relations between sentiment words and aspects, OO-Rel between sentiment words themselves, and AA-Rel between aspects. Each relation in OA-Rel, OO-Rel, or AA-Rel is a triple $\langle POS(w_i), R, POS(w_j)\rangle$, where $POS(w_i)$ is the POS tag of word w_i and R is one of the preceding dependency relations.

The extraction process uses a rule-based approach. For example, in "Canon G3 produces great pictures," the adjective *great* is parsed as depending on the noun *pictures* through *mod*, formulated as an OA-Rel $\langle JJ, mod, NNS\rangle$. If we know that *great* is a sentiment word, and if we are given the rule that a noun on which a sentiment word directly depends through *mod* is taken as an aspect, we can extract *pictures* as an aspect. Similarly, if we know that *picture* is an aspect, we can extract *great* as an opinion word using a similar rule. The propagation performs four subtasks:

1. Extract aspects using sentiment words
2. Extract aspects using extracted aspects
3. Extract sentiment words using extracted aspects
4. Extract sentiment words using both given and extracted opinion words

OA-Rels are used for tasks 1 and 3, AA-Rels for task 2, and OO-Rels for task 4. Four types of rules are defined for these four subtasks (shown in Table 6.1). In the table, *o* (or *a*) stands for the output (or extracted) sentiment word (or aspect). $\{O\}$ (or $\{A\}$) is the set of known sentiment words (or aspects) either given or extracted. *H* means any word. $POS(O(\text{or } A))$ and $O(\text{or } A)\text{-}Dep$ stand for the POS tag and the dependency relation of the word O (or A), respectively. $\{JJ\}$ and $\{NN\}$ are sets of POS tags of potential sentiment words and aspects, respectively. $\{JJ\}$ contains *JJ*, *JJR*, and *JJS*; $\{NN\}$ contains *NN* and *NNS*. $\{MR\}$ consists of dependency relations, which is the set $\{mod, pnmod, subj, s, obj, obj2, desc\}$. $\{CONJ\}$ contains only *conj*. The arrows indicate a dependency. For example, $O \rightarrow O\text{-}Dep \rightarrow A$ means O depends on A through the relation $O\text{-}Dep$. Specifically, $R1_i$ is employed to extract aspects (a) using sentiment words (O), $R2_i$ to extract opinion words (o) using aspects (A), $R3_i$ to extract aspects (a) using extracted aspects (A_i), and $R4_i$ to extract sentiment words (o) using known sentiment words (O_i).

This DP method was originally designed for English, but it has also been applied successfully to Chinese online discussions (Zhai et al., 2011c). In addition, this method can be reduced for finding aspects only using a large sentiment lexicon (without any propagation).

Wang and Wang (2008) proposed a similar method to perform the task. Given a list of seed sentiment words, they used a bootstrapping algorithm to identify both product aspects and sentiment words in an alternating fashion. In their method, MI is employed to measure the association between potential aspects and sentiment words, and vice versa. Additionally, linguistic rules are

Table 6.1 *Rules for Aspect and Opinion Word Extraction*

Rule ID	Observed Relation (Line 1) and Constraints (Lines 2–4)	Output	Examples
$R1_1$ (OA-Rel)	$O \rightarrow O\text{-}Dep \rightarrow A$ s.t. $O \in \{O\}$, $O\text{-}Dep \in \{MR\}$, $POS(A) \in \{NN\}$	$a = A$	The phone has a good "screen." *good→mod→screen*
$R1_2$ (OA-Rel)	$O \rightarrow O\text{-}Dep \rightarrow H \leftarrow A\text{-}Dep \leftarrow A$ s.t. $O \in \{O\}$, $O/A\text{-}Dep \in \{MR\}$, $POS(A) \in \{NN\}$	$a = A$	"iPod" is the best MP3 player. *best→mod→player←subj←iPod*
$R2_1$ (OA-Rel)	$O \rightarrow O\text{-}Dep \rightarrow A$ s.t. $A \in \{A\}$, $O\text{-}Dep \in \{MR\}$, $POS(O) \in \{JJ\}$	$o = O$	Same as $R1_1$ with *screen* as the known word and *good* as the extracted word
$R2_2$ (OA-Rel)	$O \rightarrow O\text{-}Dep \rightarrow H \leftarrow A\text{-}Dep \leftarrow A$ s.t. $A \in \{A\}$, $O/A\text{-}Dep \in \{MR\}$, $POS(O) \in \{JJ\}$	$o = O$	Same as $R1_2$ with *iPod* as the known word and *best* as the extract word
$R3_1$ (AA-Rel)	$A_{i(j)} \rightarrow A_{i(j)}\text{-}Dep \rightarrow A_{j(i)}$ s.t. $A_{j(i)} \in \{A\}$, $A_{i(j)}\text{-}Dep \in \{CONJ\}$, $POS(A_{i(j)}) \in \{NN\}$	$a = A_{i(j)}$	Does the player play DVDs with audio and "video"? *video→conj→audio*
$R3_2$ (AA-Rel)	$A_i \rightarrow A_i\text{-}Dep \rightarrow H \leftarrow A_j\text{-}Dep \leftarrow A_j$ s.t. $A_i \in \{A\}$, $A_i\text{-}Dep = A_j\text{-}Dep$ OR ($A_i\text{-}Dep = subj$ AND $A_j\text{-}Dep = obj$), $POS(A_j) \in \{NN\}$	$a = A_j$	Canon "G3" has a great lens. *len→obj→has←subj←G3*
$R4_1$ (OO-Rel)	$O_{i(j)} \rightarrow O_{i(j)}\text{-}Dep \rightarrow O_{j(i)}$ s.t. $O_{j(i)} \in \{O\}$, $O_{i(j)}\text{-}Dep \in \{CONJ\}$, $POS(O_{i(j)}) \in \{JJ\}$	$o = O_{i(j)}$	The camera is amazing and "easy" to use. *easy→conj→amazing*
$R4_2$ (OO-Rel)	$O_i \rightarrow O_i\text{-}Dep \rightarrow H \leftarrow O_j\text{-}Dep \leftarrow O_j$ s.t. $O_i \in \{O\}$, $O_i\text{-}Dep = O_j\text{-}Dep$ OR ($O_i /O_j\text{-}Dep \in \{pnmod, mod\}$), $POS(O_j) \in \{JJ\}$	$o = O_j$	If you want to buy a sexy, "cool," accessory-available MP3 player, you can choose iPod. *sexy→mod→player←mod←cool*

Note. Column 1 is the rule ID, column 2 is the observed relation (line 1) and the constraints that it must satisfy (lines 2–4), column 3 is the output, and column 4 is an example. In each example, the underlined word is the known word and the word in double quotation marks is the extracted word. The corresponding instantiated relation is given immediately below the example.

extracted to identify infrequent aspects and sentiment words. A similar idea was employed by Hai et al. (2012). However, instead of relying on a set of sentiment words as seeds, their method starts with a small set of aspects as seeds, on which the algorithm iteratively enlarges by mining aspect–opinion, aspect–aspect, and opinion–opinion dependency relations. Two association models – namely, likelihood ratio tests and latent semantic analysis – were used to compute pairwise associations between expressions (aspects or opinions). The whole algorithm bootstraps the initial seeds to find more aspects.

Xu et al. (2013) proposed a sophisticated algorithm to improve the DP method in three ways: (1) detecting general and frequent opinion targets that are incorrect – for example, *thing* and *people*; (2) discovering more long-tail or infrequent targets; and (3) detecting discovered adjectives that are not sentiment words – for example, *every* and *many*. The algorithm involves two steps. Step 1 first utilizes the opinion and target relations similar to those in the DP method to extract opinion words and targets from the corpus. The extraction results are then used to build a sentiment graph. A graph propagation method based on reinforcement relationships among the items is executed on the graph to rank the candidate opinion targets and opinion words. Those items ranked higher are more likely to be correct. In step 2, the algorithm builds a self-learning classifier to refine the candidate opinion targets discovered in the first step. The refined results for opinion targets are subsequently exploited to refine the discovered candidate opinion words.

Li et al. (2012a) extended the DP method to perform cross-domain extraction of opinion words and opinion targets. They proposed a new bootstrapping method for the task. In each iteration, the algorithm uses a cross-domain classifier and opinion and target syntactic patterns to identify opinion words and opinion targets for which the confidence is highest. The cross-domain classifier is trained on the source domain lexicons and the extracted lexicons in the new domain to predict the labels of the unlabeled data in the new domain.

Wu et al. (2009b) employed a phrase dependency parser rather than a normal dependency parser to extract noun phrases and verb phrases, which form candidate aspects. The system then uses a language model to filter out those unlikely aspects. Note that a normal dependency parser identifies only the dependency of individual words, whereas a phrase dependency parser identifies the dependency of phrases, which can be more suitable for aspect extraction. The idea of using dependency relations has been explored by many researchers for many different purposes (Kessler and Nicolov, 2009).

For practical use, the set of relations in Table 6.1 can be significantly expanded by the following:

1. *Adding verb- and noun-based relations.* The DP method uses only adjectives as sentiment words, though verb and noun sentiment words may be used as well. For example, using the sentiment verb *hate*, we can extract the entity *iPhone* from the sentence "I hate the iPhone" because *iPhone* is the object of *hate* and the target of the opinion expressed by *hate*. Using the sentiment noun *masterpiece*, we can also extract *iPhone 5* as the opinion target from the sentence "The iPhone 5 is a masterpiece." However, we must note that allowing verb and noun as sentiment words to participate in

propagation can be quite dangerous, as a large number of wrong aspects may be extracted.

2. *Adding comparative- and superlative-based relations.* So far, we have only used relations in regular opinion sentences. For comparative sentences, some dependency relations used in regular opinion sentences are still applicable. For example, $R1_1$ in Table 6.1 can be used to extract aspect *voice quality* from the sentence "The iPhone 5 has better voice quality than Moto X." For a regular opinion sentence, if opinion targets are entities, then there is usually only one opinion target unless the sentence includes conjunctions connecting multiple entities. However, for comparative sentences, there are usually two entities, both of which are opinion targets – for example, "The iPhone 5 is better than Moto X." We can design comparative dependency relations to extract both *iPhone 5* and *Moto X* as entities because they are both opinion targets.

3. *Adding the composition rules in Section 5.2.1.* For most of those opinion rules, it is fairly easy to identify the dependency relations among their constituents and the locations of opinion targets. These relations can then be applied for aspect extraction and even entity extraction. For example, in the sentence "Enbrel has reduced my joint pain," it is easy to extract both the entity *Enbrel* and the aspect *joint pain* based on the composition rule: decreasing (reduced) negative (joint pain) is positive. As another example, from the sentence "This car consumes a lot of gas," we can extract *gas* as a (resource) aspect because it satisfies the composition rule of consuming a large quantity of resource. However, blindly applying such rules can result in many errors. Zhang and Liu (2011a) proposed a more sophisticated method for more accurate extraction of resource usage aspects.

Identify resource usage aspects. In many applications, resource usage is an important aspect – for example, "This washer uses a lot of water." Here *water usage* is an aspect of the *washer*, and this sentence indicates a negative opinion about water usage because consuming too much resource is undesirable. The sentence does not contain any opinion word, however.

Discovering resource words or phrases, called *resource expressions*, is an important problem for sentiment analysis. In Section 5.2.1, we presented some opinion rules involving resources. We reproduce two of them here:

> PO :: = CONSUME SMALL_LESS RESOURCE
> NE :: = CONSUME LARGE_MORE RESOURCE

In our example, *water* should be extracted as a resource expression.

Zhang and Liu (2011a) formulated the resource expression extraction problem based on a bipartite graph and proposed an iterative algorithm to solve it based on the following observation:

Observation: The sentiment or opinion expressed in a sentence about resource usage is determined by the triple (*usage_verb, quantifier, resource_noun*), where *resource_noun* is a noun or noun phrase, which is often the resource name.

For example, in "This washer uses a lot of water," *uses* is the main verb, *a lot of* is a quantifier phrase, and *water* is the noun representing a resource. However, simply applying this rule or pattern can often lead to error – for example, in the case of "This filter will cause a lot of trouble for you," where *trouble* is not a resource.

The method used by Zhang and Liu (2011a) performs the extraction by exploiting a special reinforcement relationship between *resource usage verbs* (e.g., *consume*) and *resource expressions* (e.g., *water*) based on the bipartite graph. The quantifiers are not used in the computation but are employed to identify candidate verbs and candidate resource expressions. The algorithm assumes that a list of quantifiers was given (see Section 5.2.3). The problem was solved using an iterative algorithm similar to the HITS algorithm given by Kleinberg (1999). To start the iterative computation, some global *seed resource expressions* are employed to find and score some strong resource usage verbs. These scores are then applied as the initialization for the iterative computation for any application domain. When the algorithm converges, a ranked list of candidate resource expressions is identified.

Note that to identify grammar relations for extraction, a full parsing is needed. However, parsing is a very expensive operation in NLP. If one wants to fully parse a large number of opinion documents, doing so is impractical without a large number of machines because a parser can parse only a small number of sentences (typically fewer than twenty) per second. However, in practice, it is possible to do without full parsing. Shallow parsing or even just POS tagging may be sufficient in such a case. Because the dependency relations can be approximated by linear patterns of words and POS tags, a good pattern matching algorithm can do the extraction job.

For informal texts found in social media, parsing errors can be serious and thereby harm the extraction. Liu et al. (2012) proposed a method based on word alignment in machine translation (MT) to discover opinion targets. Word alignment is a common MT method that tries to align words in sentences of different languages (parallel corpora). In this work, only monolingual alignment is applied; that is, a sentence is aligned with itself. However, the alignment is constrained in such a way that adjectives in one sentence are aligned with nouns in the other sentence (both are the same sentence). Like the method described by Qiu et al. (2009a, 2011), Liu et al.'s (2012) method assumes that sentiment words are adjectives and opinion targets are nouns and noun phrases. Because the alignment is based on statistical information of the corpus, it does not require parsing and thus will not be affected by parsing errors.

Instead of using a purely unsupervised alignment model, Liu et al. (2013), integrated the opinion and target relationship patterns described by Qiu et al. (2009a, 2011) with the alignment model. The idea was to use some high-precision patterns to identify an initial set of seed alignments (which are incomplete) and use them as constraints to construct the full alignments using the EM algorithm. When the EM algorithm converges, we have the complete alignments, which are a set of opinion expression–opinion target pairs. This method also includes a second step that computes the confidence of each opinion target based on the bipartite graph constructed with the discovered candidate opinion expression–opinion target pairs and a random walk algorithm.

Greetings. It is important to discard relations that represent greetings or good wishes, such as *good morning, good afternoon, good night, happy birthday, happy anniversary, happy holidays, good luck, best of luck, warm regards*, and so on. Clearly *morning, afternoon, night, luck,* and so on. These greetings and good wishes contexts are not aspects in any application domain. Every language has a large number of such greetings, which can be either manually compiled or discovered through data mining.

6.2.2   Using Part-of and Attribute-of Relations

In any language, there are probably some lexico-syntactic patterns that are frequently used to express part-of and attribute-of relations – for example, "the battery of the iPhone" (part-of) and "the voice quality of the iPhone" (attribute-of). Expressions that depict such relations can clearly be exploited for aspect extraction because aspects are often parts or attributes of entities. Zhang et al. (2010a) proposed several such lexico-syntactic patterns in addition to the opinion and target relations described in Section 6.2.2 for aspect extraction to improve the recall of the DP algorithm. Using lexico-syntactic patterns to recognize part-of relations (Moldovan and Badulescu, 2005; Girju et al., 2006) and attribute-of relations has actually been investigated in several different contexts (Almuhareb, 2006; Hartung and Frank, 2010).

It turns out that the patterns used for recognizing part-of and attribute-of relations are quite similar. The most frequently used patterns are related to genitives. In English, there are two kinds of genitives: *s-genitives* and *of-genitives*. For s-genitives, the modifier is morphologically linked to the possessive clitic and precedes the head noun (i.e., NP_{modif}'s NP_{head}), whereas for of-genitive, the modifier is syntactically marked by the preposition *of* and follows the head noun (i.e., NP_{head} of NP_{modif}) (Moldovan and Badulescu, 2005). However, the semantic meanings of these genitive constructions and the other patterns (as discussed later) can be quite diverse. Although researchers have studied the genitive constructions for a long time, the specific meaning of a genitive in a particular context remains hard to pin down. For example, genitive constructions can encode relations such as *part-of* (iPhone's battery), *possession* (John's iPhone), *attribute-of* (iPhone's price), *kinship* (John's brother), *source-from* (John's birth city), or *make-produce* (Apple's phone) (Girju et al., 2006). In applications, it is very difficult to determine the correct semantic relation in each context, as the system needs to analyze the two noun constituents and use some commonsense knowledge. There is some slightly good news for sentiment analysis: for aspect extraction, we do not need to recognize whether a relation is part-of, attribute-of, or even make-produce.

For our purposes, we want to restrict NP_{modif} to be a *named entity* or a *class concept phrase* (CP). By class CP, we mean the name of an entity type. For example, if we are analyzing car reviews, the CP is *car* or synonyms of *car* – for example, *vehicle* or *automobile*. It can also be general terms such as *product* or *unit* – for example, "the price of this unit" and "the price of this product." For simplicity of presentation, we use CP to represent both the class concept and the named entity (e.g., iPhone). The following lexico-syntactic patterns were proposed by Zhang et al. (2010a), and cover of-genitives but not s-genitives. In all of them, the NP is the aspect (part or attribute).

NP Prep CP. NP and CP are connected by a preposition word (Prep). For example, "battery of the camera" is an instance of this pattern where *battery* (NP) is the part and *camera* (CP) is the class concept noun. Notice that we ignore determiners here. In Zhang et al. (2010a), only three prepositions – *of, on*, and *in* – were used; for example, "I did not see the price of the car," "There is a valley on the mattress," and "I found a hole in my mattress."

CP with NP. For example, in the phrase "mattress with a cover," *cover* is an aspect for *mattress*.

CP NP. For example, in "car seat," *seat* is an aspect of *car*, which is a CP. CP can be a named entity as well – for example, "iPhone battery."

CP Verb NP. The verbs (Verb) include *has, have, include, contain, consist*, and *comprise*. These verbs usually indicate a *part-of* relation. For example, in a sentence "The phone has a big screen," we can infer that *screen* is an aspect for *phone*, which is a class concept.

To use these patterns, the class CP for a domain corpus needs to be identified. This is a fairly easy task because the noun phrase with the highest frequency in the corpus is almost always the most used class CP. In an application, the user can provide it without any problem. It is also useful to know the entity names in the corpus. Extraction of named entities is discussed in detail in Section 6.7.

Because these patterns may not always extract the correct aspects, the resulting aspects extracted using these patterns are just candidates. The algorithm developed by Zhang et al. (2010a), which uses the DP method for extraction, ranks aspect candidates by aspect importance. That is, if an aspect candidate is genuine and important, it should be ranked high. In contrast, an unimportant aspect or noise should be ranked low.

Two major factors were used to determine aspect importance: aspect relevance and aspect frequency. *Aspect relevance* describes how likely an aspect candidate is a genuine aspect, as indicated by three clues. First, if an aspect is modified by multiple sentiment words, it is more likely to be relevant. For example, in the mattress reviews domain, *delivery* is modified by *quick, cumbersome,* and *timely*. This shows that reviewers put emphasis on the word *delivery*. Thus, *delivery* is likely to be a genuine aspect. Second, if an aspect was extracted by multiple lexico-syntactic patterns, it is more likely to be relevant. For example, in the car reviews domain, if we have the sentences "The engine of the car is large" and "The car has a big engine," we can infer that *engine* is very likely to be an aspect of the car because both sentences contain part-of relations indicating that *engine* is a part of the car. Third, if an aspect is extracted by both a sentiment word modification relation and a lexico-syntactic pattern in the same sentence, then it is more likely to be correct. For example, the sentence "There is a bad hole in the mattress" strongly indicates that *hole* is an aspect for the mattress because it is modified by the sentiment word *bad* and also satisfies the "NP Prep CP" pattern.

Zhang et al. (2010a) also showed that there are mutual enforcement relations between opinion words, lexico-syntactic patterns, and aspects. That is, an adjective is more likely to be a sentiment word if it modifies many genuine aspects. Likewise, if an aspect candidate can be extracted by many sentiment words and lexico-syntactic patterns, it is more likely to be a genuine aspect. Thus, the HITS algorithm (Kleinberg, 1999) can be used to measure aspect relevance.

Aspect frequency is another important factor affecting aspect ranking. It is desirable to rank those frequent aspects more highly than infrequent aspects. The final ranking score for a candidate aspect a ($S(a)$) is the score of aspect relevancy ($r(a)$) multiplied by the log of aspect frequency ($f(a)$):

$$S(a) = r(a) \log (f(a)) \tag{6.2}$$

The idea is to push the frequent candidate aspects up by multiplying the log of frequency. The log is taken to reduce the effect of large frequency count numbers.

Many applications share certain aspects. For example, all products have a *price*, and most electronics products have *batteries*. Thus aspects are accumulative, and can be organized as an ontology for different products or product categories either semi-automatically or manually. However, automated discovery is still necessary because products and services and their aspects change constantly due to changes or improvements to the products. An old or fixed ontology will not be up-to-date. Furthermore, fixed ontologies may not be able to cover some specific usage experiences of users.

Lifelong learning (Chen and Liu, 2018) precisely exploits the sharing of aspects across different product categories for improved extraction. Liu et al. (2016) proposed an unsupervised lifelong learning method for this purpose. The main idea is to first use the (unsupervised) DP method (Qiu et al. 2011) to extract a set of aspects with high precision (but low recall) as well as a set of aspects with high recall (but low precision) from the given data. The method then exploits the aspects extracted from many previous domains to improve the recall of the high precision set. This is done using two strategies, semantic similarity and aspect association.

6.3   Using Supervised Learning

Aspect extraction is a special information extraction problem. Many algorithms based on supervised learning for information extraction (Mooney and Bunescu, 2005; Sarawagi, 2008; Hobbs and Riloff, 2010) are clearly applicable to aspect extraction. The most dominant methods are those based on *sequential learning* (or *sequential labeling*). Like all supervised techniques, they need manually labeled data for training – that is, manually annotated aspects and non-aspects in each sentence of a training corpus. The current state-of-the-art sequential learning methods include *hidden Markov models* (HMM) (Rabiner, 1989) and *conditional random fields* (CRF) (Lafferty et al., 2001); they are explored in this section.

6.3.1   Hidden Markov Model

The HMM is a directed sequence model for a wide range of state series data. It has been successfully applied to many sequence labeling problems such as NER and POS tagging in NLP. A generic HMM model is illustrated in Figure 6.2, where

$\mathbf{y} = <y_0, y_1, \ldots y_t>$: hidden state sequence
$\mathbf{x} = <x_0, x_1, \ldots x_t>$: observation sequence

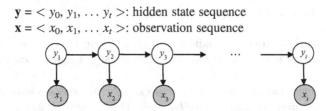

Figure 6.2 Hidden Markov model.

A HMM of a sequence of observations **x** assumes the existence of a *hidden* sequence of states **y**. Observations are dependent on the hidden states. Each state has a probability distribution over the possible observations. Two independence assumptions are made to model the joint distribution $p(\mathbf{y},\mathbf{x})$. First, state y_i only depends on its immediate predecessor state y_{i-1}; y_i is independent of all its ancestor $y_1, y_2, y_3, \ldots, y_{i-2}$. This is called the *Markov* property. Second, the observation x_i only depends on the current state y_i. With these assumptions, we can specify the HMM using three probability distributions: $p(y_0)$ over the initial state, a state transition distribution $p(y_i|y_{i-1})$, and an observation distribution $p(x_i|y_i)$. The joint probability of a state sequence **y** and an observation sequence **x** factorizes as follows:

$$p(\mathbf{y},\mathbf{x}) = \prod_{i=1}^{t} p(y_i|y_{i-1})p(x_i|y_i) \tag{6.3}$$

where we write the initial state distribution $p(y_1)$ as $p(y_1|y_0)$ (Sutton and McCallum, 2011).

Given some observation sequences, we can learn the model parameter of the HMM that maximizes the observation probability. That is, the learning can be done by building a model to best fit the training data. With the learned model, we can find an optimal state sequence for a new observation sequence.

In aspect extraction, we can regard the words or phrases in a review as observations and the aspect or opinion expression as underlying states. Jin and Ho (2009) utilized a lexicalized HMM to extract product aspects and opinion expressions from reviews; their model integrates linguistic features such as POS and lexical patterns. For example, an observable state for the lexicalized HMM is represented by a pair [$word_i$, POS($word_i$)], where POS($word_i$) represents the part of speech of $word_i$.

6.3.2 Conditional Random Fields

One limitation of the HMM is that its assumptions may not be adequate for real-life problems, which leads to reduced accuracy. To address this limitation, linear-chain CRF (Lafferty et al., 2001) was proposed as an undirected sequence model; it models a conditional probability $p(\mathbf{y}|\mathbf{x})$ over hidden sequence **y** given observation sequence **x** (Sutton and McCallum, 2011). That is, the conditional model is trained to label an unknown observation sequence **x** by selecting the hidden sequence **y** that maximizes $p(\mathbf{y}|\mathbf{x})$. The model thereby allows relaxation of the HMM's strong assumptions of independence. The linear-chain CRF model is illustrated in Figure 6.3, where

$\mathbf{y} = \; < y_0, y_1, \ldots y_t >$: hidden state sequence
$\mathbf{x} = \; < x_0, x_1, \ldots x_t >$: observation sequence

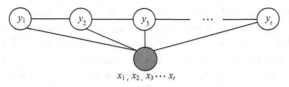

Figure 6.3 Linear-chain conditional random fields.

The conditional distribution $p(\mathbf{y}|\mathbf{x})$ takes the form

$$p(\mathbf{y}|\mathbf{x}) = \frac{1}{Z(\mathbf{x})} \prod_{i=1}^{t} \exp\left\{ \sum_{k=1}^{K} \lambda_k f_k(y_i, y_{i-1}, \mathbf{x}_i) \right\} \qquad (6.4)$$

where $Z(\mathbf{x})$ is a normalization function

$$Z(\mathbf{x}) = \sum_{\mathbf{y}} \prod_{i=1}^{t} \exp\left\{ \sum_{k=1}^{k} \lambda_k f_k(y_i, y_{i-1}, \mathbf{x}_i) \right\} \qquad (6.5)$$

CRF introduces the concept of *feature functions*. Each feature function has the form $f_k(y_i, y_{i-1}, \mathbf{x}_i)$ and λ_k is its corresponding weight. Figure 6.3 indicates that CRF makes independence assumption among $\mathbf{y}$, but not among $\mathbf{x}$. One argument for the feature function f_k is the vector $\mathbf{x}_i$, which means that each feature function can depend on observation $\mathbf{x}$ from any step. That is, all the components of the global observations $\mathbf{x}$ are needed in computing feature function f_k at step i. Thus, CRF can introduce more features than the HMM can at each step.

Jakob and Gurevych (2010) utilized CRF to extract opinion targets (or aspects) from sentences that contain an opinion expression. They employed the following features as input for their CRF-based approach:

Token. The string of the current token.
Part of speech. The POS tag of the current token.
Short dependency path. Because sentiment expressions and their targets are often related syntactically, this feature captures several direct dependencies that link tokens with each sentiment expression in a sentence.
Word distance. Because noun phrases are good candidates for opinion targets in product reviews, this feature captures the closest tokens to each sentiment expression in a sentence.

The possible class labels are represented following the inside–outside–begin (IOB) labeling scheme: *B-Target*, identifying the beginning of an opinion target; *I-Target*, identifying the continuation of a target; and *O* for other (nontarget) tokens.

Similar work has also been done by Li et al. (2010b). To model the long-distance dependency with conjunctions (e.g., *and, or, but*) at the sentence level and the deep syntactic dependencies for aspects, positive opinions, and negative opinions, they integrated two CRF variations, skip-chain CRF and tree-CRF, to extract both aspects and opinions. Unlike the original CRF, which can use only word sequences in learning, skip-chain CRF and tree-CRF enable CRF to exploit structure features. CRF was also used in the research by Choi and Cardie (2010) and Qiu et al. (2009a, 2011).

Yang and Cardie (2013) proposed a method to jointly extract opinion targets, opinion (or sentiment) expressions, and opinion holders, and also to identify the associated opinion linking relations, IS-ABOUT and IS-FROM. The IS-ABOUT relation is the opinion and target relation, whereas the IS-FROM relation is the opinion and its holder relation. The extraction of opinion targets, opinion expressions, and opinion holders uses CRF. In contrast, the identification of relations relies on supervised learning. Each relation is basically represented as a pair. An opinion expression and its target form an IS-ABOUT relation, and an opinion expression and its opinion holder form an IS-FROM relation. The classification identifies the appropriate pairs. Because all these tasks are related to each other, a joint optimization framework was proposed to perform all the tasks together, rather than in a pipelined or sequential manner in which the interaction between different extraction tasks cannot be exploited and error propagation cannot be controlled.

Besides HMM and CRF, researchers have used several other supervised learning methods. Liu et al. (2005) and Jindal and Liu (2006b) used sequential rules, which are based on supervised sequential pattern mining with class labels. Kobayashi et al. (2007) used a tree-structured classification method. Their method first finds candidate aspect–opinion word pairs using a dependency parse tree; it then employs the tree-structured classification method to learn and to classify the candidate pairs as being an aspect and evaluation relation (or not). Aspects are extracted from the highest scored pairs. The features used in learning include contextual clues and statistical co-occurrence clues, among others. Yu et al. (2011a) used a partially supervised learning method, called one-class SVM (Manevitz and Yousef, 2002), to extract aspects from "pros and cons" of reviews. Ghani et al. (2006) used both traditional supervised learning and semi-supervised learning for aspect extraction. Kovelamudi et al. (2011) employed a supervised learning method but also exploited some relevant information from Wikipedia. Klinger and Cimiano (2013) applied factor graphs to extract both target entities and opinion expressions. Similar work was done by Mitchell et al. (2013) based on CRF. Zhou et al. (2013) proposed an unsupervised label propagation method to extract opinion targets from Chinese microblogs. This method differs from the commonly used label propagation method described by Zhu and Ghahramani (2002), which is a semi-supervised algorithm that spreads label distributions throughout the graph from a small set of nodes seeded with some initial label information.

Shu et al. (2017) also proposed a lifelong learning method based on CRF for aspect extraction. Shu et al. (2016) further proposed a lifelong learning method to classify or to separate entities and aspects.

6.3.3   Deep Learning–Based Methods

This subsection discusses some existing work on aspect extraction (or aspect term extraction) using deep learning models. One of the main reasons why deep learning is helpful for this task is its superb feature or representation learning capability. When an aspect is properly characterized in some feature space – for example, in one or more hidden layers of a deep learning model – the semantics or correlation between an aspect and its context can be well captured by the interplay between their corresponding feature representations. In other words, deep learning provides a superior approach to automated feature engineering without human involvement.

One simple way to apply deep learning is to use it to perform feature learning only. The resulting features are fed into a CRF model to build a CRF extraction model. This method works remarkably well – indeed, significantly better than CRF using traditional features. Several existing deep learning–based methods use CRF. For example, Zhang et al. (2015) extended CRF using a neural network to jointly extract aspects and corresponding sentiments. The proposed CRF variant replaces the original discrete features in CRF with continuous word embeddings, and adds a neural layer between the input and output nodes. Yin et al. (2016) proposed a method that first learns word embeddings by considering the dependency path connecting words. They then employed embedding features considering the linear context and the dependency context to build a CRF-based aspect extraction model. Wang et al. (2016c) developed a different joint model that integrates recursive neural networks and CRF for explicit aspect and opinion terms co-extraction. Wang et al. (2016f) proposed yet another joint model integrating RNN and CRF to co-extract aspects and opinion terms (or expressions).

Since aspect and opinion terms are often related within a sentence, it is natural to jointly extract both. Many algorithms have used this approach. For example, Katiyar and Cardie (2016) investigated the use of deep bidirectional LSTMs for joint extraction of opinion entities and relationships that connect the entities. Their proposed model learns high-level discriminative features and double-propagates information between aspect and opinion terms simultaneously for their extraction. Wang et al. (2017b) proposed a coupled multi-layer attention model (CMLA) that can also co-extract aspect and opinion terms. This model consists of an aspect attention and an opinion attention using GRU units. An improved LSTM-based approach was reported by Li and Lam (2017), specifically for aspect term extraction. It consists of three LSTMs, of which two LSTMs capture aspect and sentiment interactions. The third LSTM uses the sentiment polarity information as an additional guidance to extract aspects. Wang et al. (2017c) described an end-to-end neural network solution that does not require any parsers or other linguistic resources for preprocessing. Their model is a multilayer attention network, where each layer consists of a couple of attentions with tensor operators. One attention seeks to extract aspect terms, while the other focuses on extracting opinion terms. A joint model for extracting both aspect and opinion terms was also presented in the work by Luo et al. (2019).

Many other papers have addressed either aspect extraction alone or additional tasks. Poria et al. (2016a) proposed to use CNN for aspect extraction. They developed a seven-layer-deep convolutional neural network to tag each word in opinionated sentences as either an aspect or non-aspect word. Some linguistic patterns are also integrated into this model for its further improvement. Ding et al. (2017) proposed two RNN-based models for cross-domain aspect extraction. They first used a rule-based method to generate an auxiliary label sequence for each sentence. They then trained the models using both the true labels and auxiliary labels – an approach that produced promising results. Li et al. (2018) proposed a novel method that exploits two pieces of information: opinion summary and aspect detection history. Opinion summary is distilled from the whole input sentence, conditioned on each current token for aspect prediction. This summary can help aspect prediction for this token. Aspect detection history is distilled from the previous aspect predictions so as to leverage the coordinate structure and tagging schema constraints to upgrade the aspect prediction.

Xu et al. (2018) proposed a simple CNN model employing two types of pretrained embeddings for aspect extraction: general-purpose embeddings and domain-specific embeddings. Without using any additional supervision or sophisticated models, this method achieves surprisingly good results, outperforming the existing sophisticated, state-of-the-art methods. Xu et al. (2019) proposed a post-training method for the popular language model BERT that enhances the performance by fine-tuning of BERT. Although this paper and the technique were primarily directed toward review reading comprehension, the proposed post-training is general and also works well on aspect extraction and aspect sentiment classification, producing state-of-the-art results.

For extraction and grouping of aspect terms, Zhou et al. (2015) proposed a semi-supervised word embedding learning method to obtain continuous word representations on a large set of reviews with noisy labels. Once the word vectors are learned, deeper and hybrid features are then learned by stacking on the word vectors through a neural network. Finally, a logistic regression classifier trained with the hybrid features is used to predict aspect categories.

Xiong et al. (2016) proposed an attention-based deep-distance metric learning model to group aspect terms. Their attention-based model seeks to learn feature representation in contexts. Both aspect term embedding and context embedding are used to learn a deep feature subspace metric for K-means clustering.

Apart from these supervised methods, unsupervised methods have been introduced. For example, He et al. (2017) proposed an unsupervised method to extract aspects. At a high level, the idea is similar to topic modeling, but uses a neural network. The algorithm starts with neural word embeddings that map words co-occurring within the same context to nearby points in the embedding space. It then filters the word embeddings within a sentence using an attention mechanism and uses the filtered words to construct aspect embeddings, while using an autoencoder for aspect identification and grouping.

6.4   Mapping Implicit Aspects

In Section 2.1, we called aspect expressions that are expressed as nouns and noun phrases the *explicit aspects* – for example, *picture quality* in "The picture quality of this camera is great." All other expressions that indicate aspects are called *implicit aspects* (not including pronouns that need coreference resolution). Many types of implicit aspect expressions exist. Adjectives and adverbs are perhaps the most common types because most adjectives describe some specific attributes or properties of entities; for example, *expensive* describes *price*, and *beautiful* describes *appearance*. *Price* and *appearance* are called *attribute nouns* of *expensive* and *beautiful*, respectively. Implicit aspects can be verbs, too. In general, implicit aspect expressions can be arbitrarily complex; for example, in "This camera will not easily fit in a pocket," *fit in a pocket* indicates the aspect *size*.

Researchers have worked on mapping adjectives to noun aspects, but have done little to map verbs or discover verb or verb phrase indicated aspects – for example, "The machine can play DVDs, which is its best feature." I am also not aware of any research that investigates more complex implicit aspect expressions such as "fit in a pocket." In what follows, we discuss some existing approaches to mapping adjectives to noun aspects.

6.4.1   Corpus-Based Approach

Su et al. (2008) proposed a clustering method to map implicit aspect expressions, assumed to be sentiment adjectives, to their corresponding explicit aspects. This method exploits the mutual reinforcement relationship between an explicit aspect and a sentiment word forming a co-occurring pair in a sentence. Such a pair may indicate that the sentiment word describes the aspect, or that the aspect is associated with the sentiment word. The algorithm finds the mapping by iteratively clustering the set of explicit aspects and the set of sentiment words separately. In each iteration, before clustering one set, the clustering results for the other set are used to update the pairwise similarity of the set. The pairwise similarity in a set is determined by a linear combination of intra-set similarity and inter-set similarity. The intra-set similarity of two items is the traditional similarity. The inter-set similarity of two items is computed based on the degree of association between aspects and sentiment words. The association (or mutual reinforcement relationship) is modeled using a bipartite graph. An aspect and an opinion word are linked if they have co-occurred in a sentence. In addition, the links are weighted based on the co-occurrence frequency. After the iterative clustering, the strongest n links between aspects and sentiment word groups form the mapping.

Hai et al. (2011) proposed a two-phase co-occurrence association rule mining approach to match implicit aspects (assumed to be sentiment words) with explicit aspects. In the first phase, this approach generates association rules involving each sentiment (adjective) word as the condition and an explicit aspect as the consequence; this sentiment word and aspect co-occur frequently in the sentences of a corpus. In the second phase, these authors' method clusters the rule consequents (explicit aspects) to generate more robust rules for each sentiment word. For application or testing, given a sentiment word with no explicit aspect, it finds the best rule cluster and then assigns the representative word of the cluster as the final identified aspect.

Use of these corpus-based approaches by themselves has some weaknesses (Fei et al., 2012):

- It is difficult to discover attributes that do not co-occur with their adjectives due to linguistic conventions. For example, in English, people do not say, "The price of the iPhone is expensive." Instead, they say, "The iPhone is expensive" or "The price of the iPhone is high." It is thus hard for a corpus-based approach to find *price* as an attribute of *expensive*. Instead, it may wrongly find *price* as an attribute of *high*.
- Even if an adjective and one of its attribute nouns do appear in a corpus, if the corpus is limited in size (e.g., the number of reviews for a product can be very small), they may not co-occur in many sentences and thus may not be associated reliably.

6.4.2   Dictionary-Based Approach

Fei et al. (2012) proposed a dictionary-based approach to complement the corpus-based approach and address the preceding problems. Dictionaries typically define adjectives using their attributes – which resolves the first problem. For example, *expensive* is defined as "Marked by high prices" in thefreedictionary.com. In addition, dictionaries are not restricted by any specific corpus (which has limited coverage) – which handles the second problem. Each adjective in the dictionary can be studied individually.

Although not all attribute nouns of an adjective may appear in a single dictionary, multiple dictionaries can be employed to improve the coverage. In

Fei et al.'s (2012) experiments, the investigators used five online dictionaries. The goal was to find all attribute nouns for an adjective. This approach did not identify the specific mapping of an adjective with one or more suitable attribute nouns in a specific sentence due to different senses. However, it did provide a more complete set of attributes of an adjective amenable to analysis with an existing corpus-based approach, such as that described by Hartung and Frank (2010, 2011).

Instead of using the traditional supervised learning classification, Fei et al. (2012) employed a relational learning method called *collective classification* (Sen et al., 2008), which can take advantage of the rich lexical relationships between words in dictionaries for classification. In traditional supervised learning, each instance is drawn independently of others (Mitchell, 1997). However, in real-life data, instances are often not independent of each other. Such data are often represented as a graph, where the nodes consist of instances and the links are their relations. In this type of graph, the classification of one node can influence the classification of its neighboring nodes. Collective classification performs classification based on the graph in an iterative fashion. Each iteration uses the classification results of the previous iteration as additional or enhanced features to improve the accuracy.

In the context of our task, we have synonym, antonym, hyponym, and hypernym relations among words, which naturally form a graph. Each instance denotes a pair consisting of an adjective A_i and one of its candidate attribute nouns c_{ij} – that is, (A_i, c_{ij}). The candidate attribute nouns of each adjective are nouns found in the dictionary definitions of the adjective. Owing to the relational features (which will be detailed later), Fei et al. (2012) used a graph representation of instances with a set of nodes (pairs), $V = \{(A_i, c_{ij}) \mid c_{ij} \in C_i, A_i \in A\}$, and a neighborhood function N where $N_{ij} \subseteq V - \{(A_i, c_{ij})\}$. Each node [a pair (A_i, c_{ij})] in V is represented with a vector $\mathbf{x}_{ij}$ of features, $f_1, f_2, \ldots, f_n$, and an associated class label y_{ij} in the domain of $\{+1, -1\}$. The $+1$ class means *attribute noun*, and the -1 class means *not attribute noun*. V is further divided into two sets of nodes: L, labeled nodes, and U, unlabeled nodes. The task is to predict the label for each node $u_{ij} \in U$.

A collective classification algorithm called the *iterative classification algorithm* (ICA; Figure 6.4) (Sen et al. 2008) was employed to solve this problem. Its training process (not shown in Figure 6.4) trains a classifier h just like traditional supervised learning, using the labeled set L with all features. The classification or testing step constitutes the core of the algorithm.

In testing, the learned classifier h assigns a class label to each node $u_{ij} \in U$ in the test data (lines 1–4). Line 2 computes the feature vector $\mathbf{x}_{ij}$ for u_{ij}. This (and also line 8) is an important step of this algorithm, and one that distinguishes it from the conventional supervised learning. It computes all the relational features for u_{ij} using the neighbors of u_{ij}. Note that relational features are not

Algorithm 6.1 ICA - Iterative classification
1. for each node $u_{ij} \in U$ // each node is a pair
2.   compute $\mathbf{x}_{ij}$ using only $L \cap N_{ij}$
3. $y_{ij} \leftarrow h(\mathbf{x}_{ij})$
4. endfor
5. repeat // iterative classification
6.   generate an ordering O over pairs in U
7.   for each node $o_{ij} \in O$ do
8.   compute $\mathbf{x}_{ij}$ using current assignments to N_{ij}
9. $y_{ij} \leftarrow h(\mathbf{x}_{ij})$
10.   endfor
11. until all class labels do not change

Figure 6.4 Iterative classification algorithm (ICA).

detailed here, as they are quite involved. Interested readers can refer to the original paper for details. Line 2 is slightly different from line 8: in line 2, not all nodes have been assigned class labels, so we compute $\mathbf{x}_{ij}$ based on the intersection of the labeled nodes (L) and u_{ij}'s neighbors. Line 3 uses h to assign a class (y_{ij}) to node u_{ij}. Lines 1–4 are considered to be the initialization step.

After initialization, the classifier is run iteratively (lines 5–11) until the class labels of all nodes no longer change. The iterations are needed because some relational features of a node depend on the class labels of the node's neighbors. Such labels are assigned in each iteration and may change from one iteration to the next. In each iteration (lines 6–10), the algorithm first generates an ordering of nodes to be classified. We order them randomly to reduce bias, as random ordering makes the process stochastic. Line 8 does the same job as line 2; line 9 does the same job as line 3. Classifier h does not change in the iterations.

Figure 6.5 shows a simple example of a graph based on some relationships of words. It can be considered a snapshot of an iteration of ICA. Each oval node denotes an instance (an adjective and attribute pair). Each dash-lined box encloses all pairs that belong to the same adjective. A link between two oval nodes denotes a relationship between two (candidate) attribute nouns, and a link between two dash-lined boxes denotes a relationship between two adjectives. Thin lines connect synonyms and thick lines connect antonyms. The dark shaded nodes denote those labeled pairs, the lightly shaded nodes denote those candidate attribute nouns whose labels have been predicted (unlabeled at the beginning), and the unshaded oval nodes denote those candidate attribute nouns whose labels have not yet been predicted in the iteration. In the figure, adjectives A_k and A_j are synonyms, attribute noun c_{k2} (labeled) and candidate attribute noun c_{j1} are synonyms, and candidate attribute nouns c_{j1} and c_{j2} are antonyms. In the previous iteration, ICA predicted/labeled c_{j2} as an attribute noun of A_j. Because c_{j2}, c_{j1}, and c_{k2} are related, the label of c_{j1} will be affected by the labels of c_{j2} and c_{k2} in this iteration.

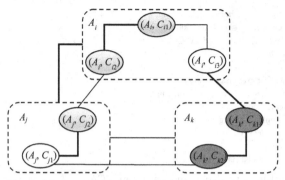

Figure 6.5 An example of a graph of word relations and an ICA iteration.

6.5   Grouping Aspects into Categories

Clearly, people use different words or phrases to describe the same aspect (or aspect category). For example, *sound quality* and *voice quality* refer to the same aspect of phones. We call *sound quality* and *voice quality* aspect expressions (see Section 2.1.6). After aspect expressions have been extracted, they need to be grouped or clustered into synonymous aspect categories. Each category represents a unique aspect (see Section 2.1.6). Grouping aspect expressions is critical for opinion analysis and summary.

The most obvious approach to solve this problem is to use WordNet or another thesaurus dictionary to find synonymous expressions. However, this approach is far from sufficient for the following reasons:

- Many synonyms are domain dependent (Liu et al., 2005). For example, *movie* and *picture* are synonyms in movie reviews, but they are not synonyms in camera reviews. In the latter case, *picture* is more likely to be synonymous with *photo,* and *movie* synonymous with *video.*
- Many aspect expressions are multiword phrases, which cannot be easily handled with dictionaries.
- Many aspect expressions describing the same aspect are not general or domain-specific synonyms. For example, *expensive* and *cheap* can both indicate the aspect *price* but they are antonyms, not synonyms of each other or of *price* (see Section 6.4).
- In most practical applications, the task of aspect grouping cannot be solved completely in an unsupervised manner because it is often a subjective task. That is, different applications or even different users may have different categories in mind depending on the application needs. In some cases, this is due to different levels of granularity in analysis. For example, in a real-life application of car reviews, one user might group aspect expressions related

to *exterior design* or *interior design* into one category and call it *design*, but another user might keep them separate, because the two users are in charge of different tasks. If two categories are used, when one says "The design of the car is great," we have to assign it to both the interior and exterior design categories. In some other cases, it is not easy to decide which category an aspect expression belongs to. Consider whether these four sentences are describing the same aspect or different aspects: "This car works very well," "This car is reliable," "The quality of this car is great," and "The car broke down the next day." Different people may have different answers to this question.

Carenini et al. (2005) proposed a method to solve this problem. Their method was based on several similarity metrics defined using string similarity, synonyms, and lexical distances measured using WordNet. It requires a given taxonomy of aspects (more specifically, aspect categories) for a particular domain. Its objective is to merge each discovered aspect expression with an aspect node in the taxonomy based on the similarities. Experiments based on digital camera and DVD reviews showed promising results. In the study by Yu et al. (2011b), a more sophisticated method used publicly available aspect hierarchies/taxonomies of products and the actual product reviews to produce the final aspect hierarchies. A set of distance measures was also combined using an optimization strategy.

Zhai et al. (2010) proposed a semi-supervised learning method to group aspect expressions into some user-specified aspect categories. To reflect the user needs, they first manually labeled a small number of seed aspect expressions for each category. The system then assigned the rest of the aspect expressions to suitable categories using a semi-supervised learning method working with labeled and unlabeled examples. The method uses the Expectation Maximization (EM) algorithm developed by Nigam et al. (2000). It also employed two pieces of prior knowledge to provide a better initialization for EM: (1) aspect expressions sharing some common words, which are likely to belong to the same group – for example, *battery life* and *battery power*, and (2) aspect expressions that are synonyms in a dictionary, which are likely to belong to the same group – for example, *movie* and *picture*. These two pieces of knowledge help EM produce better classification results.

In the study by Zhai et al. (2011b), soft constraints were used to help label some initial examples. The constraints were generated based on sharing of words and lexical similarity (Jiang and Conrath, 1997). The learning method also used EM, but it eliminated the need to task the user to provide seeds.

Guo et al. (2009) presented a method called multilevel latent semantic association. At the first level, all the words in aspect expressions are grouped into a set of concepts/topics using the topic model known as Latent Dirichlet

Allocation (LDA) (Blei et al., 2003). We will provide more details on LDA in Section 6.6. Basically, LDA groups words in documents into clusters, where each cluster represents a topic. The results from the first level are used to build latent topic structures for aspect expressions. For example, suppose we have four aspect expressions: *day photos, day photo, daytime photos,* and *daytime photo*. If LDA groups the individual words *day* and *daytime* into topic10, and *photo* and *photos* into topic12, the system will group all four aspect expressions into a single group, topic10-topic12, which is a latent topic structure. At the second level, aspect expressions are grouped by LDA again but according to their latent topic structures produced at level 1 and their context snippets in reviews. In the preceding example, *day photos, day photo, daytime photos,* and *daytime photo* in topic10-topic12 combined with their surrounding words form a document. LDA then analyzes such documents to produce the final result. In the research described by Guo et al. (2010), a similar idea was used to group aspect expressions from different languages into aspect categories, which can be used to compare opinions along different aspects from different languages (or countries).

In the study by Zhai et al. (2011a), a topic model called Constrained-LDA was proposed for grouping or clustering aspect expressions. This algorithm assumes that the aspect expressions have already been discovered by another system. Constrained-LDA basically incorporates two forms of constraints into LDA: *must-links* and *cannot-links*. A must-link constraint means that two aspect expressions should be in the same cluster. A cannot-link constraint means that two aspect expressions should be in different clusters. The constraints are extracted automatically. This method can handle a large number of must-link and cannot-link constraints. The constraints can also be relaxed; that is, they may be treated as soft (rather than hard) constraints and may not be satisfied. For aspect categorization, constrained-LDA uses the following constraints: (1) if two aspect expressions share one or more words, they are assumed to form a must-link – that is, they should be in the same topic, such as "battery power" and "battery life"; and (2) if two aspect expressions occur in the same sentence and are not connected by *and*, they form a cannot-link. The second constraint is appropriate because people normally do not repeat the same aspect in the same sentence. We will describe the Constrained-LDA model in detail in Section 6.6.5 for a different but similar purpose.

6.6   Exploiting Topic Models

As discussed in the preceding sections and in Section 2.1.6, aspect extraction has two tasks: aspect expression extraction and grouping. In terms of aspect expression extraction, we need to extract both explicit and implicit expressions. The two tasks are usually performed in two separate steps. However, statistical topic modeling performs both tasks simultaneously in a single step and also handles explicit as well as implicit aspects to some extent – a highly desirable characteristic. In this section, we explore topic models for aspect extraction and aspect-based sentiment analysis.

Topic modeling is a principled approach for discovering topics from a large corpus of text documents. The most common outputs of a topic model are a set of word clusters and a topic distribution for each document. Each word cluster is called a *topic* and is a probability distribution over words (also called *topical terms*) in the corpus. The topic distribution of a document gives the proportion of each topic in the document. There are two basic topic models, *probabilistic latent semantic analysis* (pLSA) (Hofmann, 1999) and *Latent Dirichlet Allocation* (LDA) (Blei et al., 2003), both of which are unsupervised methods. Although they are primarily used to model and extract topics from text documents, they can be extended to model many other types of information. For readers who are not familiar with topic models, graphical models, and Bayesian networks, besides the various papers in the topic modeling literature, the book *Pattern Recognition and Machine Learning* by Christopher M. Bishop (2006) is an excellent source of background knowledge.

In the sentiment analysis context, topics are basically aspects (or, more precisely, aspect categories). Each topical term or word in a topic is an aspect word (or expression). In most current topic models, a topical term is an individual word or unigram. We discuss topical terms that can be phrases in Section 6.6.5. Theoretically speaking, the key advantage of topic modeling for aspect extraction is that it can perform both explicit and implicit aspect expression extraction and, at the same time, group them. For example, it may extract and group *price, cost, expensive,* and *cheap* together under one aspect or topic. These capabilities are very useful for sentiment analysis. In addition to models for aspect extraction, researchers have proposed many joint models that model both aspects and sentiments based on the idea that sentiments or opinions have targets.

This section first introduces the LDA model because most existing topic models for aspect extraction and sentiment analysis are based on this approach. Section 6.6.2 then gives an overview of the current models. In Section 6.6.3, we describe some weaknesses of unsupervised models and present several *knowledge-based topic models*, also called *semi-supervised topic models*, to overcome these weaknesses. These models have been proposed to exploit prior domain knowledge from the user to guide model inference so as to produce better results. In Section 6.6.4, we take a major step forward to mine prior domain knowledge from big data, which makes the knowledge-based topic modeling approach fully automatic. This also introduces the important new concept of *lifelong topic modeling* to machine learning. Finally, we discuss two models that can consider aspect expressions that are multiword phrases. Multiword phrases are important in practice because many aspects cannot be expressed with single words. For example, if *battery life* is split into two separate words *battery* and *life*, the meaning of *battery life* is lost.

6.6.1   Latent Dirichlet Allocation

LDA is an unsupervised learning model that assumes each document consists of a mixture of topics and each topic is a probability distribution over words. It is a document-generative model that specifies a probabilistic procedure by which documents are generated. Like most other topic models, LDA can be depicted graphically and is based on Bayesian networks.

The input to LDA is a corpus consisting of a set of documents D. The outputs from LDA are a distribution over topics for each document, called *document-topic* distribution θ, and a distribution over words for each topic, called *topic-word* distribution ϕ. Both θ and ϕ are assumed to follow multinomial distributions. To smooth the distributions, it is also assumed that they have Dirichlet priors with hyperparameters α and β, respectively. Because Dirichlet distribution is the conjugate prior of multinomial distribution, using Dirichlet priors simplifies the problem of statistical inference. Note that Dirichlet distribution has, in fact, a vector of parameters, and that each parameter can have a different value. In LDA, however, most researchers have used the same value for all parameters. Such a Dirichlet distribution is commonly called a symmetric Dirichlet distribution.

Let the number of topics be T (usually specified by the user). The topics are indexed by $\{1, \ldots, T\}$, and the entries in the vocabulary of the corpus are indexed by $\{1, \ldots, V\}$, where V is the number of unique words in the entire document corpus. The corpus has D documents. Each document d is a sequence of N_d words. w is the bag of all observed words with cardinality, $|w| = \sum_d N_d$. z denotes the topic assignments of all words in all documents, and z_i denotes the topic assignment of ith word w_i in document d. For simplicity of notations, we omit the subscript of document d for w_i and z_i.

As a generative model, LDA's procedure for generating documents is as follows:

> **for** each topic $t \in \{1, \ldots, T\}$ **do**
>   draw a word distribution for topic t, $\phi_t \sim Dirichlet(\beta)$
> **for** each document $d \in \{1, \ldots, D\}$ **do**
>   draw a topic distribution for document d, $\theta_d \sim Dirichlet(\alpha)$
>   **for** each term w_i, $i \in \{1, \ldots, N_d\}$ **do**
>   draw a topic for the word, $z_i \sim Multinomial(\theta_d)$
>   draw a word, $w_i \sim Multinomial(\phi_{zi})$

The graphical or plate notation of LDA is given in Figure 6.6, where θ, ϕ, and z are latent variables, and word w is observed. Dirichlet hyperparameters α and β are regarded as constants and, therefore, are also observed. All the observed value nodes are shaded, and all latent variable nodes are not shaded.

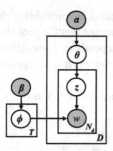

Figure 6.6 Graphical representation of LDA in plate notation.

To obtain the distributions θ and ϕ, two main algorithms were proposed: variational inference (Blei et al., 2003) and Gibbs sampling (Griffiths and Steyvers, 2004). These methods do not directly estimate distributions θ and ϕ. Instead, they estimate the posterior distribution over z (the assignment of topics to words), given the observed words w, while marginalizing out θ and ϕ. Each z_i gives an integer value $\{1 \ldots T\}$ for the topic to which each word w_i in a document d is assigned. From the topic assignments z, we can compute distributions θ and ϕ. Because Gibbs sampling – a Markov Chain Monte Carlo (MCMC) algorithm – is more commonly used, we briefly describe it here.

For Gibbs sampling–based LDA, the most important process is the updating of topic for each word w_i in each document d according to the probabilities calculated as follows:

$$P\left(z_i = t | z^{-i}, w\right) \propto \frac{\left(n_{t,d}^{-i} + \alpha\right)}{\sum_{t'=1}^{T}\left(n_{t',d}^{-i} + \alpha\right)} \frac{n_{w_i,t}^{-i} + \beta}{\sum_{v'=1}^{V}\left(n_{v',t}^{-i} + \beta\right)} \qquad (6.6)$$

where $z_i = t$ represents the assignment of topic t to the ith word (w_i) in document d (i.e., z_i indicates the topic assignment for word w_i), and z^{-i} represents the topic assignments for all words in the corpus except the ith word w_i in d. $n_{t,d}^{-i}$ is the number of times that topic t has been assigned to words in document d, excluding the ith word w_i. $n_{w_i,t}^{-i}$ is the number of times that word $v = w_i$ has been assigned to topic t, excluding the current instance w_i. In other words, it is the number of times that topic t has been assigned to the vocabulary word $v = w_i$, excluding the current instance w_i of v. Here v is the corresponding vocabulary word for w_i.

Deriving the preceding sampling equation is quite involved (see the Wikipedia entry for LDA; see also Griffiths and Steyvers, 2004; Steyvers and Griffiths, 2007; Carpenter, 2010). But the final equation is quite intuitive. It basically consists of two parts. The left part is the probability that topic t is assigned to the words in document d. The right part is the probability that word w_i is assigned to topic t. From the equation, we can see that the probability of a word in a document being assigned to a topic depends on how dominant the topic is in the document, as well as how likely the word is to appear for the topic in the corpus.

In fact, Equation (6.6) can be further simplified to Equation (6.7) because $\sum_{t'=1}^{T}\left(n_{t',d}^{-i}+\alpha\right)$ is a constant for all topics:

$$P\left(z_i = t|z^{-i},w\right) \propto \left(n_{t,d}^{-i}+\alpha\right)\frac{n_{w_i,t}^{-i}+\beta}{\sum_{v'=1}^{V}\left(n_{v',t}^{-i}+\beta\right)} \tag{6.7}$$

To compute the final probability for each topic, we need to perform normalization.

$$P\left(z_i = t|z^{-i},w\right) = \frac{\left(n_{t,d}^{-i}+\alpha\right)\dfrac{n_{w_i,t}^{-i}+\beta}{\sum_{v'=1}^{V}\left(n_{v',t}^{-i}+\beta\right)}}{\sum_{t'}^{T}\left(n_{t',d}^{-i}+\alpha\right)\dfrac{n_{w_i,t'}^{-i}+\beta}{\sum_{v'=1}^{V}\left(n_{v',t'}^{-i}+\beta\right)}} \tag{6.8}$$

The algorithm for Gibbs sampling is given in Figure 6.7, which represents one sweep of the documents in the corpus. Note that the superscript $-i$ is not used for counts because the related counts have been decremented in lines 3 and 4.

After a large number of iterations of Gibbs sampling for words in all documents, we obtain the estimated topic distribution for each document, called the *document-topic* distribution $\hat{\theta}$, and the word distribution in

1. **for** each document $d \in D$ **do**
2.   **for** each word w_i in document d **do**
3. $n_{z_i,d} \leftarrow n_{z_i,d} - 1$
4. $n_{w_i,z_i} \leftarrow n_{w_i,z_i} - 1$
5.   sample z_i from $P\left(z_i = t \mid z^{-i},w\right) \propto \left(n_{t,d}+\alpha\right)\dfrac{n_{w_i,t}+\beta}{\sum_{v'=1}^{V}(n_{v',t}+\beta)}$, for $t \in \{1, ... T\}$
6. $n_{z_i,d} \leftarrow n_{z_i,d} + 1$
7. $n_{w_i,z_i} \leftarrow n_{w_i,z_i} + 1$
8.   **endfor**
9. **endfor**

Figure 6.7 One sweep of Gibbs sampling in LDA.

each topic, called the *topic-word* distribution $\hat{\phi}$, using Equations (6.9) and (6.10):

$$\hat{\theta}_{t,d} = \frac{(n_{t,d} + \alpha)}{\sum_{t'=1}^{T} \left(n_{t',d}^{-i} + \alpha \right)} \tag{6.9}$$

$$\hat{\phi}_{v,t} = \frac{n_{v,t} + \beta}{\sum_{v'=1}^{V} \left(n_{v',t} + \beta \right)} \tag{6.10}$$

Here, $\hat{\theta}_{t,d}$ represents the predictive probability or distribution of sampling topic t in document d, and $\hat{\phi}_{v,t}$ represents the predictive probability or distribution of sampling a new instance of vocabulary word v from topic t.

In most applications, the user is interested in $\hat{\phi}_{v,t}$, which gives a list of words (the vocabulary) under each topic t ranked according to their probability values in $\hat{\phi}_{v,t}$. The top-ranked words often provide a good indication of the topic label. For example, in a set of reviews, suppose LDA finds the following top-ranked words for a topic: *price, money, expensive, cost, cheap, purchase, deal*. We can see that the topic is about product *price*, and then we can label the topic with *price*.

6.6.2 Using Unsupervised Topic Models

Various topic models, which are mostly extensions of LDA, have been proposed for aspect extraction, joint modeling of both aspect and sentiment words, and joint modeling of aspects and sentiment ratings of those aspects. We discuss each of them in turn.

Titov and McDonald (2008a) first applied LDA and pLSA directly to review corpora for aspect extraction. They showed that global topic models such as LDA are not suitable for detecting aspects because they depend on topic distribution differences and word co-occurrences among documents to identify topics and word probability distribution in each topic. However, opinion documents such as reviews of a particular type of product are quite homogenous, meaning that every document or review basically talks about the same set of aspects for the product. This makes global topic models ineffective for discovering aspects but more effective for discovering entities (e.g., different brands or product names). Thus, treating each review as a document for topic modeling is ineffective.

As an alternative, Titov and McDonald (2008a) proposed a multigrained topic model. With this approach, the global model discovers entities while the local model discovers aspects by treating a few sentences (or a sliding text window) as a document. Each discovered aspect is a topic (also called a unigram language model, a multinomial distribution over words). Different words expressing the same or related facets are automatically grouped together under the same aspect. This technique does not separate aspects and sentiment words.

Branavan et al. (2008) reported a method that makes use of the aspect descriptions in keyphrases in "pros and cons" sections of reviews to help find aspects in the detailed review text. Their model consists of two parts. The first part clusters the keyphrases in pros and cons into aspect categories based on distributional similarity. The second part builds a topic model that encompasses the topics or aspects in the review text. Their final topic model integrates these two parts based on the idea that the model biases or constrains the assignment of hidden topics in the review text to be similar to the topics represented by the keyphrases in the review's pros and cons, yet also permits some words in the document to be drawn from other topics not represented by the keyphrases. This flexibility in the coupling allows the model to learn effectively in the presence of incomplete keyphrases, while still encouraging the keyphrase clustering to cohere with the topics supported by the review text. Clearly, this approach also does not separate aspects and sentiments. Likewise, several other papers on aspect extraction do not distinguish aspect and sentiment words (Chen et al., 2013b, 2013c). This approach is reasonable because most adjective sentiment words actually describe or modify some aspects of entities (see Section 6.4.2). For example, when we say "This car is expensive," we refer to the *price* aspect of the car; when we say "This car is beautiful," we refer to the *appearance* aspect.

Most existing topic models for sentiment analysis are actually joint models that model both aspects and sentiments, although they may not separate the two types of words. Mei et al. (2007) built the first aspect–sentiment mixture model based on an aspect model, a positive sentiment model, and a negative sentiment model learned with the help of some external training data. Their model was based on pLSA.

Here we describe two representative joint models in some detail to give a flavor of them. The first model is the aspect and sentiment unification model (ASUM) (Jo and Oh, 2011), and the second model is the MaxEnt-LDA model developed by Zhao et al. (2010). Both models are extensions of LDA. The main difference between them is that ASUM does not separate aspect words and sentiment words, whereas MaxEnt-LDA does.

The ASUM model produces a set of sentiment–aspect topics. Each topic consists of a mixture of sentiment words of a particular polarity or orientation (positive or negative) and aspect words associated with a particular aspect for the sentiment polarity. In other words, a topic is a multinomial distribution over both aspect and sentiment words. ASUM achieves this outcome by constraining the words in a sentence to come from one topic. Aspect words and sentiment words are not explicitly separated under each topic. We will see this in the graphical model and the generative process of ASUM.

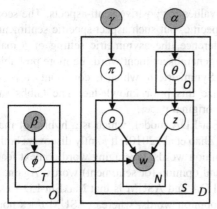

Figure 6.8 Plate notation of ASUM.

Let the number of aspects be T. The aspects or topics are indexed by $\{1, \ldots, T\}$. Let the number of documents in the corpus be D. Each document d consists of S sentences. Each sentence s in d consists of N words. Let the number of sentiment or opinion orientations be O (positive and negative). The model has five latent variables: θ, ϕ, π, z, and o. (Their meanings will be explained in the generative process.) There are also the usual hyperparameters: α, β, and γ. The graphical representation of ASUM in plate notation is given in Figure 6.8.

The generative process of ASUM is as follows:

> **for** every pair of sentiment $o \in \{1, \ldots, O\}$ and aspect $z \in \{1, \ldots, T\}$ **do**
> > Draw a word distribution $\phi_{o,z} \sim Dirichlet(\beta_o)$
>
> **for** each document $d \in \{1, \ldots, D\}$ **do**
> > Draw the document d's sentiment distribution $\pi_d \sim Dirichlet(\gamma)$
> > **for** each sentiment o **do**
> > > Draw an aspect distribution $\theta_{d,o} \sim Dirichlet(\alpha)$
> >
> > **for** each sentence $s \in \{1, \ldots, S\}$ **do**
> > > Choose a sentiment $j \sim Multinomial(\pi_d)$
> > > Given sentiment j, choose an aspect $t \sim Multinomial(\theta_{d,j})$
> > > **for** each w_i, $i \in \{1, \ldots, N\}$ **do**
> > > > Generate word $w_i \sim Multinomial(\phi_{j,t})$

To separate positive and negative sentiment polarities, ASUM exploits some prior sentiment words and uses an asymmetric β. For example, we expect that the words *good* and *great* likely will not appear in negative expressions; similarly, the words *bad* and *annoying* are not likely to be found in positive expressions. A set of given general seed postive and negative words is used to set β. Specifically, the seed words are encoded into β for each sentiment such that the elements of β corresponding to the general positive sentiment words have small values for negative senti-aspects, and the general negative sentiment words have small values for positive senti-aspects. The seed senti-ment words are not aspect specific, but such aspect-specific sentiment words should be discovered. In inference, the asymmetric setting of β makes the words that co-occur with the general sentiment words be more probable in the corresponding senti-aspects. Symmetric β, which is commonly used in most other models, does not utilize this prior knowledge. The Gibbs sampling equation can be found in the original paper.

We now turn to the MaxEnt-LDA model, which is a hybrid of maximum entropy (MaxEnt) and LDA (Zhao et al., 2010). It jointly discovers both aspect words and aspect-specific opinion words, leveraging word context features to help separate aspect words and opinion (or sentiment) words. Again, the key difference between MaxEnt-LDA and ASUM is that MaxEnt-LDA explicitly separates aspect words and opinion words, whereas ASUM does not. How-ever, MaxEnt-LDA does not separate positive and negative sentiment orienta-tions or polarities, whereas ASUM does. Aspect and opinion word separation in MaxEnt-LDA is achieved through an *indicator variable* (also called a *switch variable*) drawn from a multinomial distribution governed by a set of param-eters. This indicator variable determines whether a word in a sentence is an aspect word, an opinion word, or a background word. It uses MaxEnt on some labeled training data to learn the parameters of the distribution from which the indicator variable's value is drawn. A second indicator variable is used to determine general and specific types of aspect or opinion. Thus MaxEnt-LDA represents a rather fine-grained model.

For example, in a restaurant review, each word in a sentence s of the review can be one of a few types. The word may be a specific aspect word (e.g., *waiter* for the *staff* aspect), a general aspect word (e.g., *restaurant*), an opinion word specific to the aspect (e.g., *friendly*), a generic opinion word (e.g., *great*), or a commonly used background word (e.g., *know*).

A graphical representation of MaxEnt-LDA in plate notation is given in Figure 6.9. Subscripts and superscripts are used in the plates to explicitly indicate the nested structure and different kinds of distributions. The genera-tive process of MaxEnt-LDA is as follows:

Draw a background word distribution $\phi^B \sim Dirichlet(\beta)$
Draw a general aspect word distribution $\phi^{A,g} \sim Dirichlet(\beta)$
Draw a general opinion word distribution $\phi^{O,g} \sim Dirichlet(\beta)$
Draw a specific (0) and generic (1) type distribution $p \sim Beta(\gamma)$
for each aspect $t \in \{1, \ldots, T\}$ **do**
    Draw an aspect word distribution for aspect t, $\phi^{A,t} \sim Dirichlet(\beta)$
    Draw an aspect-specific opinion word distribution for aspect t, $\phi^{O,t} \sim Dirichlet(\beta)$
for each document $d \in \{1, \ldots, D\}$ **do**

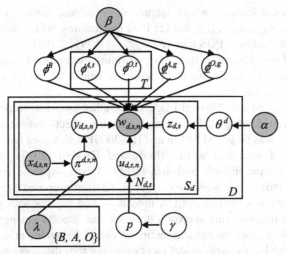

Figure 6.9 Plate notation of MaxEnt-LDA.

Draw an aspect distribution for document d, $\theta^d \sim Dirichlet(\alpha)$
for each sentence $s \in \{1, \ldots, S_d\}$ **do**
    Draw an aspect assignment $z_{d,s} \sim Multinomial(\theta^d)$
    for each word $w_{d,s,n}$ in sentence s, $n \in \{1, \ldots, N_{d,s}\}$ **do**
        Set background (0), aspect (1) and opinion (2) type distribution

$$\pi_{d,s,n} \leftarrow \text{MaxEnt}(xd,s,n,\ \lambda)$$

        Draw an assignment for indicator $y_{d,s,n} \sim Multinomial(\pi_{d,s,n})$
        Draw an assignment for indicator $u_{d,s,n} \sim Bernoulli(p)$

$$\text{Draw } w_{d,s,n} \sim \begin{cases} Multinomial(\phi^B) & if y_{d,s,n} = 0 \\ Multinomial(\phi^{A,z_{d,s}}) & if y_{d,s,n} = 1, u_{d,s,n} = 0 \\ Multinomial(\phi^{A,g}) & if y_{d,s,n} = 1, u_{d,s,n} = 1 \\ Multinomial(\phi^{O,z_{d,s}}) & if y_{d,s,n} = 2, u_{d,s,n} = 0 \\ Multinomial(\phi^{O,g}) & if y_{d,s,n} = 2, u_{d,s,n} = 1 \end{cases}$$

The distribution $\pi_{d,s,n}$ needs additional explanation. It is produced by a MaxEnt classifier. The training data consist of a set of sentences with labeled background words, opinion words, and aspect words in the sentences. The classifier is built based on the observation that aspect words and opinion words usually play different syntactic roles in a sentence. Aspect words tend to be nouns, whereas opinion words tend to be adjectives – although words of other parts of speech can serve as sentiment words as well, such as *hate* and *dislike*. The feature vector, represented by $x_{d,s,n}$, can be any arbitrary clues extracted from the sentence contexts of these words. Zhao et al. (2010) used two types of features: (1) lexical features, which include the previous, current, and next words $\{w_{d,s,n-1}, w_{d,s,n}, w_{d,s,n+1}\}$; and (2) POS tag features, which include the previous, current, and next POS tags $\{POS_{d,s,n-1}, POS_{d,s,n}, POS_{d,s,n+1}\}$. Here, λ_l are the model weights for $l = 0, 1, 2$, representing, background, aspect, and sentiment classes. The detailed Gibbs sampling equations for inference can be found in Zhao et al. (2010).

Apart from ASUM and MaxEnt-LDA, many other aspect–sentiment joint models have been developed. For example, a joint aspect–sentiment model similar to ASUM was proposed by Lin and He (2009); it also does not separate aspect words and sentiment words. Brody and Elhadad (2010) identified aspects by using topic models, and then identified aspect-specific sentiment words by considering only adjectives. Li et al. (2010c) proposed Sentiment-LDA and Dependency-Sentiment-LDA models to find aspects with positive and negative sentiments. This approach does not find aspects independently, nor does it separate aspect words and sentiment words. Lazaridou et al. (2013) improved Lin and He's (2009) model by considering four discourse relations, which enables the model to handle sentiment or aspect changes in the same sentence due to the contrast indicated by *but*. Sauper et al. (2011) worked on short snippets extracted from reviews – for example, "battery life is the best I've found." Their method combines topic modeling with a HMM, where the HMM models the sequence of words with types (aspect word, sentiment word, or background word). This model is related to the HMM-LDA proposed by Griffiths et al. (2005), which models the word sequence as well. Variations of the joint topic modeling approach were also described by Liu et al. (2007) and Lu and Zhai (2008).

Another line of research that uses topic modeling for sentiment analysis aims to associate aspects with opinion/sentiment ratings – that is, to predict aspect ratings based on joint modeling of aspects and ratings. Titov and McDonald (2008b) proposed a model that both discovers aspects from reviews and extracts textual evidence supporting each aspect rating. Lu et al. (2009) defined the problem of rated aspect summarization of short comments from eBay.com. Their aspect extraction is based on a topic model called structured pLSA, which can model the dependency structure of phrases in short comments. To predict the rating for each aspect in a comment, it combines the overall rating of the comment and the classification result of a learned classifier for the aspect based on all the comments.

Wang et al. (2010) reported a probabilistic rating regression model that assigns ratings to aspects. Their method first uses some given seed aspects to find more aspect words through a heuristic bootstrapping technique. It then predicts aspect ratings using the proposed probabilistic rating regression model, which is also a graphical model. The model makes use of review ratings and assumes that the overall rating of a review is a linear combination of its aspect ratings. The model parameters are estimated using the maximum likelihood estimator and an EM-style algorithm.

A series of joint models were also proposed by Lakkaraju et al. (2011) based on the composite topic model of HMM-LDA developed by Griffiths et al. (2005), which considers both word sequence and word-bag. The models thus can capture syntactic structures as well as semantic dependencies, much like the model proposed by Sauper et al. (2011). They are able to discover latent aspects and their corresponding sentiment ratings. Moghaddam and Ester (2011) reported a joint topic model for finding and grouping aspects, as well as deriving their ratings.

6.6.3   Using Prior Domain Knowledge in Modeling

Although topic modeling is a principled approach based on probabilistic inferencing and can be extended to model many types of information using joint models, it does have some weaknesses that limit its practical use in sentiment analysis applications. One major issue is that it needs a large volume of data and a significant amount of tuning to achieve reasonable results. Owing to this large data requirement, one often has to collect opinion documents for many entities of the same category. For example, suppose we are interested in opinions about a particular hotel, but that hotel does not have available the thousands of reviews needed for effective topic modeling. We have to supplement the existing reviews with reviews from a large number of other hotels. With such a large data set, it is not hard for topic modeling to find very general and frequent topics or aspects. However, it becomes very difficult to find locally frequent but globally infrequent aspects – such as those specific aspects of the hotel that the user is really interested in – because every hotel is different. Such locally frequent aspects are often most useful because they tell the user about specific pros and cons of the particular hotel. General and frequent aspects can also be easily found by using the non-topic modeling–based methods discussed in earlier sections; in addition, those methods may find less frequent aspects without the need for a large data set.

In short, the results from current topic models are usually not granular or specific enough for most practical sentiment analysis applications. However, they do allow users to get some high-level ideas about what a document collection is about.

That being said, topic modeling remains a powerful and flexible tool with a great potential if it is improved. Continued research will undoubtedly make it more useful in practice. One promising research direction is *knowledge-based topic modeling* (*KBTM*), also known as *semi-supervised topic modeling*. KBTM can incorporate existing natural language and prior domain knowledge in modeling to guide the model inference, thereby generating better topics without a need for large volumes of data. Some initial work has been done in this area (Andrzejewski and Zhu, 2009; Andrzejewski et al., 2009; Zhai et al., 2011a; Mukherjee and Liu, 2012a; Chen et al., 2013b, 2013c). DF-LDA (Andrzejewski et al., 2009), which is not specific to aspect extraction, is perhaps the first model that can incorporate prior domain knowledge in modeling. The knowledge is in the form of *must-links* (state that two words should belong to the same topic) and *cannot-links* (indicate that two words should not be in the same topic). In the study by Andrzejewski et al. (2011), more general knowledge in the form of first-order logic was used. Seeded models were proposed by Lu et al. (2011), Burns et al. (2012), Jagarlamudi et al. (2012), and Mukherjee and Liu (2012a), which allow the user to specify some prior seed terms for some topics. Petterson et al. (2010) also used word similarity as priors. However, these knowledge-based models have three major shortcomings.

Inability to handle multiple senses. A word typically has multiple meanings or senses. For example, *light* can mean "of little weight" or "something that makes things visible." DF-LDA (Andrzejewski et al., 2009) cannot handle multiple senses because its definition of a must-link is transitive. That is, if A and B form a must-link, and B and C form a must-link, that implies a must-link between A and C, indicating A, B, and C should be in the same topic. For example, the word *light* can have two must-links indicating two distinct senses: {light, heavy} and {light, bright}. Transitivity will force the words *heavy* and *bright* to belong to the same topic, which is wrong. This case also applies to the models developed by Petterson et al. (2010), Andrzejewski et al. (2011), and Mukherjee and Liu (2012a). Although Jagarlamudi et al.'s (2012) model allows multiple senses, it requires that each topic has at most one seed set, which is restrictive because the amount of knowledge should not be limited.

Sensitivity to the adverse effect of knowledge. When using must-links or seed sets, existing models basically try to ensure that the words in a must-link or a seed set have similar probabilities under a topic. This causes a serious problem. If a must-link consists of a frequent word and an infrequent word, the probability of the frequent word under a topic will decrease, while the probability of the infrequent word will increase due to the redistribution of the probability mass. This harms the final topics/aspects because the attenuation of the frequent (often domain-important) words may result in some irrelevant words being ranked higher (with higher probabilities) (Chen et al., 2013d).

Inability to create additional topics when needed. This issue is caused by cannot-links. Two types of cannot-links are possible: consistent or inconsistent with the corpus domain. For example, in the reviews of domain "Computer," a topic model may generate two topics, *Battery* and *Screen*, that represent two different aspects. A cannot-link {battery, screen} is thus consistent with the corpus. However, the words *Amazon* and *Price* may appear in the same topic due to their high co-occurrences in the review corpus. To separate them, a cannot-link {amazon, price} can be added, though it is inconsistent with the corpus. In this case, the number of topics needs to be *increased* by one because the mixed topic needs to be separated into two individual topics *Amazon* and *Price*. In almost all existing KBTM models, the number of topics is specified by the user and cannot be changed in the modeling process.

To address these shortcomings, Chen et al. (2013c) first defined *m-set* (*must-set*) as a set of words that should belong to the same topic, and *c-set* (*cannot-set*) as a set of words that should not be in the same topic. They are similar to must-link and cannot-link, respectively, but m-sets do not enforce transitivity (which causes the first shortcoming). M-sets and c-sets are also more expressive in providing knowledge in the context of a set rather than just a link pair. The same authors then proposed the topic model *MC-LDA* (LDA with m-set and c-set). MC-LDA adds a new latent variable s in LDA to distinguish multiple senses.

Next, deviating from the standard topic modeling approaches (which are based on a simple Pólya urn sampling scheme), Chen et al. (2013c) utilized the *generalized Pólya urn* (GPU) model (Mahmoud, 2008) was used to address the second shortcoming of adverse effect of knowledge. However, these extensions are unable to deal with c-sets, for which an *extended GPU* (E-GPU) model was proposed. E-GPU extends the GPU model to enable multi-urn interactions, which is necessary for handling c-sets and for adjusting the number of topics.

Requiring prior domain knowledge from the user can be quite demanding because the user must know the domain very well. Even if she knows the domain well, she may not be able to provide knowledge suitable for topic models. Chen et al. (2013b) thus proposed to exploit domain-independent general knowledge from dictionaries. Specifically, they used one form of general knowledge – the lexical semantic relations of words such as synonym, antonym, and adjective–attribute relations – to help produce more coherent topics. Using such general knowledge, however, causes a major difficulty for topic models. That is, a word can have multiple meanings/senses, each with a different set of synonyms and antonyms. However, not every meaning or sense is suitable or correct for a particular domain. Wrong knowledge can result in poor-quality topics. To deal with this problem, a new model, called GK-LDA, was proposed in an effort to identify wrong knowledge during modeling (Chen et al., 2013b).

6.6.4 Lifelong Topic Models: Learn As Humans Do

Although KBTM can achieve better results, acquiring user knowledge is not always easy because the user may not know the domain well or may be unwilling to provide any knowledge because he wants the system to discover knowledge for him. General knowledge such as lexical semantic relations in dictionaries can help to some extent, but it often contains too many errors owing to multiple word senses and lack of specificity for the application.

Lifelong topic modeling, proposed by Chen and Liu (2014a), aims to mine prior knowledge automatically from the results of past modeling without the need for the user to input any prior domain knowledge. This approach works like human learning. Here we use the term *learning* because topic modeling is an unsupervised learning method. We humans always retain the results learned in the past and use them to help future learning. In machine learning, this paradigm is called *lifelong learning*. In our case, we expand the name to *lifelong topic modeling* because we use topic models. This approach represents an important step forward because it closes the modeling loop, in the sense that the whole KBTM process is made fully automatic.

Lifelong learning for topic modeling assumes that the system performs topic modeling continuously in different task domains. After each modeling task is completed, it stores all the resulting topics in a *topic base*. In performing the next or new modeling task in a particular domain, the system finds some prior knowledge from the topic base to help the new modeling. We can find useful prior knowledge from the topic base because, although every task domain may be different, there is a decent amount of concept or aspect overlapping across domains (Chen et al., 2014). For example, every product review domain has the aspect or topic *price*, reviews of most electronic products also share the aspect of *battery*, and reviews of some products share the aspect of *screen*. Aspects produced from a single domain can be erroneous (i.e., an aspect or topic may contain some irrelevant words in its top-ranked positions), but if we can find a set of shared words among some aspects or topics generated from multiple domains, these shared words are more likely to be correct or coherent for a particular aspect or topic. They can serve as a piece of prior knowledge for improving topic modeling in the new domain, also called the *target domain*.

As an example, suppose we have product reviews from three domains. We run LDA to generate a set of topics from each domain. Every domain has a topic about *price*, which is listed as follows with its top four words (words are ranked based on their probabilities under each topic):

Domain 1: price, color, cost, life
Domain 2: cost, picture, price, expensive
Domain 3: price, money, customer, expensive

These topics are clearly not perfect due to the incoherent words *color, life, picture,* and *customer*. However, if we want those topical words that appear together at least in two topics from two different domains, we can find the following two sets:

{*price, cost*} and {*price, expensive*}.

The words in each set are likely to belong to the same topic. Then, {*price, cost*} and {*price, expensive*} can serve as prior knowledge or must-links for a knowledge-based topic model to help improve the output topics for each of the three domains or a new domain.

For example, after running a knowledge-based model on the reviews of Domain 1, we may find a new topic, {*price, cost, expensive, color*}, which has three coherent words in the top four positions rather than only two words as in the original topic. This represents a good topic improvement (although the topic still includes the incoherent word *color*, that word may be pushed down if more prior knowledge is discovered). Note that here Domain 1 also serves as the target domain, but the target domain can be a completely new domain in other cases.

The preceding discussion indicates that lifelong topic modeling needs document collections from a large number of domains to mine topics from each of them and put them into a *topic base*. We then use the topics in the topic base to discover reliable must-links and cannot-links that can help improve topic modeling in the current new or test domain. The resulting topics are added to the topic base for future use. Chen and Liu's (2014a, 2014b) lifelong topic modeling methods took a two-phase approach:

Phase 1 (*initialization*). Given n prior document collections $D = \{D_1, \ldots, D_n\}$, we first run a topic model (e.g., LDA) on each collection $D_i \in D$ to produce a set of topics S_i. Let $S = \bigcup S_i$, which we call the *topic base* with all *prior topics* (or *p-topics* for short). This phase is needed only for initialization. In subsequent modeling, it will not be used.

Phase 2 (*lifelong topic modeling*). Given in a new document collection D^t, we first mine some prior knowledge K from all p-topics in topic base S. We then run a KBTM guided by the prior knowledge K to generate a set of topics A^t for the new collection D^t. To enable lifelong modeling or learning, the resulting topics A^t are incorporated or added into S. Thus, in a long run, S becomes bigger and bigger.

Phase 1 is very simple, as it just runs a topic model on each domain corpus $D_i \in D$. We will not discuss it further. Here we elaborate on the two substeps of phrase 2.

Step 1: Mining quality knowledge from all p-topics S. Without quality knowledge to guide the modeling process, we will not obtain quality aspects. As stated earlier, knowledge from only a single domain can be erroneous. However, if the knowledge is shared by multiple domains, it is more likely to be of high quality. Chen et al. (2014) proposed to first use a clustering method to group p-topics (topics in the topic base), and then use the topics in each cluster to find sets of shared topical words. Each set of words, which is a must-set, serves as a piece of prior knowledge that can guide the modeling to extract aspects in the target domain. In their experiments, these authors used reviews from thirty-six types of products or domains and showed promising results. Chen and Liu (2014a) proposed an even more effective method, which embeds Step 1 in Step 2 to mine more targeted knowledge. We discuss this method in Step 2. In this case, the authors used reviews from fifty domains in their experiments and showed that the new method produced superior results.

Step 2: Modeling guided by mined knowledge. For reliable aspect extraction or modeling using the mined prior knowledge, we need to deal with possible errors in the knowledge base. In particular, a piece of automatically mined knowledge may be wrong or domain specific (i.e., the words in a piece of knowledge – for example, a must-link – may be semantically coherent in some domains but not in others). In leveraging such knowledge in a new aspect extraction process, the system must detect those inappropriate pieces of knowledge; otherwise, the discovered aspects will be incoherent. Chen et al. (2014) proposed a new topic model, called automated knowledge LDA (AKL), which can exploit the automatically learned prior knowledge and also deal with the issue of incorrect knowledge to produce superior topics/aspects.

Chen and Liu (2014a) introduced a more effective model called lifelong topic modeling (LTM) that can omit the clustering in Step 1 – setting the right number of clusters is very difficult. As mentioned earlier, LTM embeds Step 1 inside Step 2 to find more targeted knowledge. Specifically, the algorithm first runs a KBTM on the test document collection D^t without any knowledge (which is equivalent to LDA) until its topics (A^t) stabilize. To distinguish these topics from p-topics (topics in the topic base), they are called the *current topics* (or *c-topics* for short). For each c-topic $a_j \in A^t$, the algorithm finds a set of matching or similar p-topics M_j^t of a_j in S (the topic base – the set of all p-topics). It then mines M_j^t to generate a set of prior knowledge sets K_j^t or must-links, for c-topic a_j specifically. Next, it continues the execution of the KBTM on D^t, which is now guided by the must-links in K^t (which is the union of all K_j^t), to generate better c-topics (Chen and Liu, 2014a). The intuition of this method is as follows: After running a model on D^t with no knowledge, we obtain its initial topics A^t. To improve each topic $a_j \in A^t$, we find only those p-topics M_j^t in all p-topics S that are similar to a_j. We then mine must-links from M_j^t for topic a_j. These must-links are thus targeted and should be of high quality for topic a_j.

Chen and Liu (2014b) proposed another technique to mine cannot-links, which enable a KBTM to produce even better results, especially when the test document collection is small. These two techniques are quite involved. Interested readers should refer to the original papers, which include mechanisms for handling wrong knowledge and multiple senses of words.

Lifelong learning or modeling is quite suitable for aspect extraction because a great deal of aspect sharing occurs among different entities, and such sharing can be exploited to produce better aspects from a review corpus. To end this subsection, I would like to make a few remarks about lifelong learning.

First, the key to lifelong modeling is to find quality knowledge from past modeling results and to recognize possible wrong knowledge. Without these capabilities, a lifelong topic model will not produce good results.

Second, although related, the lifelong learning described here differs from traditional transfer learning or domain adaptation in a key sense: in transfer learning, knowledge from a single source domain is used to help learning in a target domain. This has at least two shortcomings. First, it is very hard to obtain high-quality knowledge from only a single source domain, as we have seen from our example topics. Second, a single source domain may not have many shared concepts or topics with the target domain. In most cases, the user has to find a very similar source domain for the target domain to enable effective transfer learning. These weaknesses make transfer learning hard to apply to real-life situations. In contrast, the lifelong learning approaches explored by Chen and Liu (2014a, 2014b) exploit a large number of source domains to deal with the two problems. They can find high-quality prior knowledge from any source domain that is relevant or useful to the target/new domain.

Third, in general, NLP tasks seem to be ideal for lifelong learning or modeling because a word appearing in different domains or contexts often has the same meaning and represents the same concept. Without such shared concepts, lifelong learning or modeling will not be possible. Lifelong topic modeling techniques basically transfer concepts across domains. Although a word can have multiple senses, such senses can be recognized (Chen and Liu, 2014a, 2014b).

6.6.5   Using Phrases As Topical Terms

Most current topic models are based on individual words, but many aspect expressions in real-life applications are multiword phrases – for example, *hotel staff*. If *hotel* and *staff* are treated as two separate words, *staff* is still fine, but *hotel* and *hotel staff'* have very different meanings and should belong to different aspects. If *hotel* and *staff* are put in the same topic, that decision is not appropriate. But putting *hotel* and *staff* in two separate topics also creates a problem: when the system sees *hotel staff*, it may treat them as two separate aspects.

One way to consider phrases in topic models is to use *n*-grams. However, using *n*-grams makes the space highly sparse, which can result in poor clustering or topic formation. By "sparse," we mean two things. First, because a phrase can consist of any number of words, we may need 1- to 4-grams, inclusive, which gives a huge number of terms. Second, each 2-, 3-, or 4-gram is much less frequent than each individual word, which makes it difficult to connect terms and find their semantic relations in topic modeling. In other words, due to the sparsity, the higher-level co-occurrences – which serve as the basis for the topic models (Heinrich, 2009) – are adversely affected, which in turn can produce poor topics. Higher-order co-occurrences of terms refers to how often they co-occur in different contexts. For example, w_1 co-occurring with w_2, which in turn co-occurs with w_3, denotes a second-order co-occurrence between w_1 and w_3. Although some topic models do model bigram orders (Wallach, 2006), they are hard to scale to arbitrary *n*-grams because all possible ordering sequences of *n*-grams need to be sampled in inferencing. Other approaches use statistical correlation of unigram topics to form multiword phrases (Blei and Lafferty, 2009; Andrzejewski and Buttler, 2011; Zhao et al., 2011). Statistical correlation, however, does not necessarily guarantee to generate semantically coherent phrases.

Here we describe two approaches that find phrases first and then run two special topic models, respectively. The first model is the constrained-LDA model described by Zhai et al. (2011a), and the second model is the LDA (p_GPU) model based on the *generalized Pólya urn (GPU)* model (Fei et al., 2014). To find phrases in the first step, we can use a chunking or shallow parsing tool, or we can even use an existing aspect extraction method, such as CRF (Jakob and Gurevych, 2010), which is a supervised method, or DP (Qiu et al., 2011), which is an unsupervised method. These methods can find phrases as aspect expressions, but they do not perform aspect grouping or clustering. However, the resulting phrases are usually too sparse for effective modeling.

To deal with the sparsity problem, Constrained-LDA introduces a bias to guide the inference process (e.g., using an approximate Gibbs distribution) so that a term's topic assignment focuses on topics with similar terms to this term. Here, *term* means a word or phrase. The intuition is that similar terms should be assigned to similar topics. The sparsity problem is solved with similarity because similarity in effect increases the co-occurrence space or frequency of similar terms.

Many similarity functions can be used in this context. For example, one function is the sharing of words. In particular, two expressions are considered to be similar if they share some words – for example, *picture* and *picture quality*. More generally, if two terms have synonymous words, they are more likely to be similar – for example, *picture* and *photo quality*. In the topic updating process of the Gibbs sampling, we can consider similarity relationships and assign similar terms to similar topics based on their similarity value. There are multiple ways to do this. One strategy is to intervene in the Gibbs sampler so that when it updates the topic assignment for each term in a document, the system alters the conditional probability so that it focuses the term on some specific or similar topics. The original Gibbs sampler for LDA is

$$P(z_i = t | z^{-i}, w) \propto (n_{t,d}^{-i} + \alpha) \frac{n_{w_i,t}^{-i} + \beta}{\sum_{v'=1}^{V} \left(n_{v',t}^{-i} + \beta \right)} \tag{6.11}$$

where $z_i = t$ represents the assignment of topic $t \in \{1, \ldots, T\}$ to the ith word (w_i) in document d (i.e., z_i indicates the topic assignment for word w_i), and z^{-i} represents topic assignments for all words in the corpus except the ith word w_i in d. w is the bag of all observed words in the corpus; $n_{t,d}^{-i}$ is the number of times that topic t has been assigned to words in document d, excluding the ith word w_i; and $n_{w_i,t}^{-i}$ is the number of times that vocabulary word $v = w_i$ has been assigned to topic t, excluding the current instance w_i of v. Here v is the corresponding vocabulary word for w_i. T is the number of topics (which is an input parameter specified by the user), and V is the vocabulary size of the corpus. Variables α and β are the hyperparameters for the document-topic and topic-word Dirichlet distributions, respectively.

To guide topic assignment in LDA by allowing similarity functions to be encoded, we augment Equation (6.11) with a bias function. That is, if a term w_i is assigned to particular topic t, then another term that is similar to w_i should be given a high probability of belonging to topic t. To achieve this goal in topic updating, a bias function $f(z_i = t)$ is multiplied by the probability calculated by the original Gibbs sampler [Equation (6.11)] to produce the final probability for topic updating. This gives Equation (6.12):

$$P(z_i = t | z^{-i}, w) \propto f(z_i = t)(n_{t,d}^{-i} + \alpha) \frac{n_{w_i,t}^{-i} + \beta}{\sum_{v'=1}^{V} \left(n_{v',t}^{-i} + \beta \right)} \tag{6.12}$$

In this equation, $f(z_i = t)$ can be seen as encoding some preexisting knowledge or constraints into the model. The computation of this bias function depends on the types of similarities.

This augmented topic model, called constrained-*LDA* (Zhai et al., 2011a), models similarity with must-links and cannot-links. Recall that a must-link constraint means that two terms should belong to the same topic, while a cannot-link constraint means that two terms cannot belong to the same topic.

$f(z_i = t)$ is computed as follows: For a term w_i, if w_i is not constrained by any must-links or cannot-links, $f(z_i = t) = 1$; otherwise, $f(z_i = t)$ is calculated in four steps:

Step 1. Computing must-topics' and cannot-topics' weights for w_i. Here must-topics mean the topics to which the term w_i should be assigned, while cannot-topics mean the topics to which the term w_i should not be assigned. For a given term w_i, its *must-linked terms* and *cannot-linked terms* are first found by querying must-links and cannot-links stores, which are the sets of other terms in the must-links and cannot-links that contain w_i, respectively. Next, the topics of these terms are obtained from the current topic models. Then, w_i's must-topics and cannot-topics weights are calculated.

For example, w_i's must-linked (and, respectively, cannot-linked) *terms* that the sampler has assigned to topic t thus far are M_1 and M_2 (and C_1, C_2, and C_3). So, for topic t, w_i's must-topics' and cannot-topics' weights are $m\_weight_k(w_i) = |\{M_1,M_2\}| = 2$ and $c\_weight_k(w_i) = |\{C_1, C_2, C_3\}| = 3$, respectively. Here, $m\_weight_k(w_i)$ and $c\_weight_k(w_i)$ are interpreted as the weights that w_i should or should not be assigned to topic t, respectively.

Step 2. Adjust the relative influences between the must-link category and the cannot-link category. In extracting the two types of constraints (discussed later), the qualities of must-links and cannot-links may be different from each other. A damping factor λ is used to adjust the relative influences based on the constraint qualities. Specifically, all the must-topics' weights are multiplied by λ, while the cannot-topics' weights are multiplied by $(1 - \lambda)$. Following the example in step 1, $c\_weight_k(w_i)$ is adjusted to 2λ, while $m\_weight_k(w_i)$ is adjusted to $3(1 - \lambda)$. In the work by Zhai et al. (2011a), the default value for λ was empirically set to 0.3.

On the basis of the results of these two steps, Steps 3 and 4 convert the *weights* of must-topics and cannot-topics to biases $f(z_i = t)$, $t = 1, \ldots, T$.

Step 3. Aggregate the weights for each candidate topic. For the given term w_i, its candidate topics can be one of three types: must-topics, unconstrained topics, or cannot-topics. Must-topics are the topics that w_i should be assigned to, whereas cannot-topics are the topics that w_i should not be assigned to. Thus, if t is a must-topic, we add $m\_weight_k(w_i)$ to $f(z_i = k)$ to increase the probability that w_i is assigned to topic t. If t is a cannot-topic, we subtract $c\_weight_k(w_i)$ from $f(z_i = t)$ to decrease the probability that w_i will be assigned to topic t. In the preceding example, for the candidate topic k, the value for $f(z_i = t)$ is calculated as follows: $0 + c\_weight(w_i) - m\_weight(w_i) = 2\lambda - 3(1 - \lambda) = 5\lambda - 3$.

Step 4. Normalize and relax the weight of each candidate topic. Because the constraints are not guaranteed to be correct, especially when the constraints are extracted automatically (discussed later), a parameter should adjust the constraint's strength according to the quality of the constraints. If the constraints are completely correct, the model should treat these constraints as hard-constraints. If the constraints are all wrong, the model should discard them. To achieve this aim, $\{f(z_i = t) \mid t = 1, \ldots, T\}$ are adjusted by the relaxation factor η using the following procedure: First, before being relaxed, $\{f(z_i = t) \mid t = 1, \ldots, T\}$ are normalized to [0, 1] using Equation (6.13). In this equation, max and min represent the maximum and minimum values of $\{f(z_i = t) \mid t = 1, \ldots, T\}$, respectively:

$$f(z_i = t) = \frac{f(z_i = t) - \min}{\max - \min} \tag{6.13}$$

Then, $\{f(z_i = t) \mid t = 1, \ldots, T\}$ are relaxed by the relaxation factor η based on Equation (6.14). The default value of η is set to 0.9 in the model developed by Zhai et al. (2011a):

$$f(z_i = t) = f(z_i = t) \times \eta + (1 - \eta) \tag{6.14}$$

Extracting constraints. In Zhai et al.'s (2011a) model, must-link and cannot-link constraints are automatically extracted based on two observations.

Observation 1: Two noun phrases (or terms) w_i and w_j that share one or more words are likely to belong to the same topic – for example, *battery life* and *battery power*. That is, w_i and w_j form a must-link constraint. It is possible to extend this observation of word sharing to synonyms, but doing so could result in more errors because many dictionary synonyms are not synonyms in a particular domain.

Observation 2: A sentence may comment on several product aspects – for example, "I like the picture quality, the battery life, and the zoom of this camera" and "The picture quality is great, the battery life is also long, but the zoom is not good." From either of the sentences, we can infer that *picture quality, battery life*, and *zoom* are unlikely to be synonyms or to belong to the same topic simply because people normally will not repeat the same aspect in the same sentence. This observation allows us to form many cannot-link constraints automatically. Specifically, if two terms w_i and w_j occur in the same sentence, the two terms form a cannot-link; that is, they should be in different topics.

Clearly, the must-links and cannot-links generated from the two observations are not perfect, so Constrained-LDA allows constraints to be relaxed. Incidentally, *adjectives* and their *attribute nouns* can also form must-set constraints. As we discussed in Section 6.4.2, most adjectives describe some specific attributes of objects. For example, *expensive* and *cheap* usually describe the *price* attribute of an object, and *beautiful* describes the *appearance* or *look* of an object, which allow us to generate two must-link constraints, {*expensive, cheap, price*} and {*beautiful, appearance, look*}.

Fei et al. (2014) proposed another modeling approach. Its model inference is based on the GPU model (Mahmoud, 2008). The algorithm treats phrases as individual terms and allows their component words to have some connections or co-occurrences with them. The intuition is that when the algorithm sees a phrase, it assumes it also sees a small fraction of its component words; and when it sees each individual word, it assumes it also sees a small fraction of its related phrases. Furthermore, not all words in a phrase are equally important. For example, in the phrase *hotel staff"*, *staff* is more important because it is the head noun, which represents the semantic category of the phrase. The GPU model can realize this idea easily in the topic model context.

To conclude this section, we note that besides the methods discussed in this section and those in Sections 6.1, 6.2, and 6.3, there are still other works on aspect extraction. For example, Yi et al. (2003) used a mixture-language model and likelihood ratio to extract product aspects. Fang and Huang (2012) performed aspect-based analysis using latent structural models. Ma and Wan (2010) used centering theory and supervised learning. Meng and Wang (2009) extracted aspects from product specifications, which are structured data. Kim and Hovy (2006b) used semantic role labeling. Stoyanov and Cardie (2008) exploited coreference resolution. Toprak et al. (2010) designed a comprehensive annotation scheme for aspect-based opinion annotation. Earlier annotations were partial and mainly for the special needs of individual papers. Carvalho et al. (2011) annotated a collection of political debates with aspects and other information.

6.7   Entity Extraction and Resolution

Entity extraction in the sentiment analysis context is similar to the classic problem of *named entity recognition* (NER). In fact, the opinion target extraction methods are also able to extract many entities, as entities may be opinion targets in some cases. For example, in the sentence "The iPhone 5 is great," *iPhone* is the target of the sentiment word *great*. In this section, we focus solely on entity extraction.

NER has been studied extensively in several fields, including information retrieval, text mining, data mining, machine learning, and NLP, under the name of information extraction (Mooney and Bunescu, 2005; Sarawagi, 2008; Hobbs and Riloff, 2010). There are two main approaches to information extraction: rule-based and statistical. Early extraction systems were mainly based on rules (e.g., Riloff, 1993). More recent approaches primarily use statistical machine learning. The most popular learning models used in these approaches are hidden Markov models (HMMs; Rabiner, 1989) and conditional random fields (CRFs; Lafferty et al., 2001). Both HMM and CRF are supervised sequence learning methods, which we briefly introduced in Section 6.3. A comprehensive survey of the general information extraction tasks and algorithms can be found in Sarawagi (2008). Owing to the prior work on the topic, specific work in the context of sentiment analysis is not extensive. This section examines the problems in the context of sentiment analysis and surveys the general approaches from other research areas.

6.7.1 The Problem of Entity Extraction and Resolution

The most general entity extraction problem in sentiment analysis can be stated as follows:

Problem statement 6.1: Given a corpus C, we want to solve the following two subproblems:

1. Identify all entity expressions or mentions M in corpus C.
2. Cluster all entity expressions in M into synonymous groups. Each group represents a unique real-world object or entity.

The first subproblem is the traditional NER problem, while the second subproblem is the traditional *entity resolution* (ER) problem.

In truth, few real-life sentiment analysis applications need to solve this general problem. Instead, in a typical application, the user wants to find opinions about a set of entities of interest – for example, products or services. For example, a smartphone producer may want to find consumer opinions about a set of smartphones, which may be a subset of its own phones, a subset of its competitors' phones, or a combination of both. A political candidate may want to find public sentiments about herself and her political rivals. Thus, most sentiment analysis applications need to solve the following problem:

Problem statement 6.2: Given a corpus C and a set of desired entities $E = \{e_1, e_2, \ldots, e_n\}$, identify all manifestations or mentions, denoted by M_i, of each entity e_i in E from C.

Each mention m_{ij} ($\in (M_i)$ is a unique entity expression that refers to entity e_i. For example, the brand *Motorola* is an entity, which is the official name of the Motorola brand, but it may be written as Motorola, Moto, or Mot in different social media posts and/or even different sentences.

This problem is similar to, but also different from, traditional NER and ER problems. In traditional NER, the objective is to recognize or extract all named entities of certain types in a corpus, such as names of people or names of organizations. However, in our case, we are interested in only the manifestations or mentions of the set of desired entity E, which is a subset of all entities that exist in corpus C. For example, the user may be interested in only some particular car brands rather than all cars in the market. The problem thus requires *entity linking*, a special case of ER. The problem (Problem 6.2) is solved in two steps:

1. *Entity extraction.* Identify all entities – more specifically, entity mentions M – in C. This is a full NER step.
2. *Entity linking.* For each *entity mention* (also called *entity expression*) m ($\in M$) with its associated context document where the entity expression occurs and a set of desired entities E, the system identifies the entry in E to which m belongs, or *nil* if there is no corresponding entry in E. This task is the same as traditional entity linking (also known as *entity disambiguation*) (McNamee and Dang, 2009).

For example, suppose we have the following review:

> I brought a Moto phone two months ago. I had been very satisfied with the phone until today. It stopped working in the morning. I called the Mot service center. The service rep said I can get a replacement right away if I post the phone to the Motorola collection center in Illinois. My old Nokia phone never had any problem.

Step 1 should find *Moto, Mot, Motorola*, and *Nokia* as entity mentions. If the desired set of entities E is only {Motorola}, step 2 should link *Moto, Mot*, and *Motorola* with *Motorola* in E. For *Nokia*, the algorithm should return nil because it does not refer to any entity in E.

Because the entity extraction task is fairly clear, in what follows, we provide some additional discussion of the entity linking task. Entity linking basically resolves two name ambiguity problems (Dredze et al., 2010; Gottipati and Jiang, 2011):

1. *Polysemy.* This refers to the case where more than one entity shares the same name. For example, *Apple* may refer to *Apple Inc.* (the maker of the iPhone and iPad), *Apple Daily* (a Hong Kong newspaper), or anything else that uses *Apple* in its name.
2. *Synonymy.* This refers to the case where there are multiple name variations (or orthographically different mentions) for an entity, as in the Motorola example. These include abbreviations (Chicago Symphony Orchestra vs. CSO), shortened forms (Volkswagen vs. Vwagen), aliases or alternative names (New York vs. the Big Apple) and alternative spellings (Osama vs. Ussamah vs. Oussama).

When the task is performed with a set of entity mentions without the set E of desired entities, it is called entity resolution. ER clusters entity mentions, where each cluster corresponds to a single real-world entity. In the next two subsections, we describe some existing research in solving these two problems.

Before proceeding, it is useful to understand the types and the nature of the data or corpora that are often used in sentiment analysis, which has an impact on whether we need to perform both the entity extraction and entity linking tasks. There are three main types of corpora:

1. *Entity-focused corpora.* These corpora include online reviews of products and services. Because reviews are usually listed under their respective products or services in web pages, we can use the meta-data scraped from the review page to determine which entity that a set of reviews evaluates. In this case, entity extraction may not be needed because we know the entity that each review evaluates. Some other entities may be mentioned in the review text, but they are rare. Of course, if we want more accurate analysis, entity extraction and entity linking should be carried out for each review to identify mentions of other entities (often used for comparison purposes) and even mentions of the reviewed entity because it can have name variations.
2. *Domain-focused corpora.* Such a corpus mainly includes forum discussions. A forum site normally focuses on discussions of a particular type of product or topic. For example, HowardForums.com hosts discussions about mobile phones. Entity extraction is needed in this case because, unlike for reviews, there are no meta-data to show the entities discussed in each post except for the text content. Clearly, entity linking is needed as well.
3. *Open domain corpora.* In this case, the corpus can contain documents of any entity or topic. Twitter is such a corpus. People can post tweets about anything they want. Again there are few meta-data to identify what each post talks about, except for the hashtags that may be used in a small number of tweets to indicate topics. In this case, both entity extraction and entity linking are required.

For different types of corpora, entity extraction and linking may be performed differently. The size of the corpus also plays an important role. For reviews, entity extraction may not be necessary (although we can still do both extraction and linking for improved sentiment analysis accuracy). For domain-focused corpora, we will need both extraction and linking. However, for a huge corpus, we may not be able to perform extraction or linking from the whole corpus due to computational and other difficulties. In such cases, a *keyword search* is often undertaken as the first step, where the keywords (often compiled manually) are usually name variations of the desired entities in E. The entity keywords are used to search the corpus to retrieve relevant posts. As it is often the case that different entities usually have different names in the same domain (i.e., entity names are unambiguous), entity linking may not be necessary because the entity names are manually compiled.

For open domain corpora, the situation is similar to that for domain-focused corpora. In this case, the corpus is often very large, which renders it almost impossible to perform entity extraction on the whole corpus. Twitter and Weibo, for example, have hundreds of millions of posts per day. Even if you have the computational power needed to perform NER, the data owner (e.g., twitter.com or weibo.com) may not give you the whole corpus unless you pay it an exorbitant amount of money. However, they do allow you to search their data using keywords either for free or for a small fee. Because it is hard to perform NER on the whole corpus, a comprehensive list of name variations for each desired entity is needed as keywords to perform searches on the corpus and extract relevant posts.

In this case, the keywords representing entities of interest are likely to be ambiguous due to the diverse topics covered within the corpus. Consequently, a classification step is needed to identify those posts containing the desired entities. For example, searching for all posts related to Google using the keyword "google" is probably unambiguous, as there is no other entity called Google apart from the Google search engine. In contrast, searching for Apple Inc. (the consumer electronics company) using "apple" as the keyword may retrieve many irrelevant posts. Classification can be used to separate those relevant and irrelevant posts. Entity linking may also be used to solve this problem, as we discuss later.

For the last two types of corpora, it is still advisable to perform an entity extraction in the reduced corpus because the posts in the corpus may also contain unrelated entities. Some opinions in a post may be directed at them rather than the desired entities, even though the desired entities are mentioned in the post. Recognizing such undesired entities helps identify the target of each opinion. Furthermore, as discussed earlier, many entity names contain sentiment words – for example, *Best Buy* (the name of a store in the United States) and *Pretty Woman* (a movie title) – because many companies and organizations use auspicious names to project a positive image for their brands, products, or services. Such sentiment words (e.g., *best* and *pretty* in the preceding examples) in entity names can cause real problems for sentiment classification if they are not identified.

6.7.2   Entity Extraction

Although the most effective approaches for entity extraction are HMM (Rabiner, 1989) and CRF (Lafferty et al., 2001), these supervised methods require labeling of training data to learn a model to perform the extraction task on the test data, which is not always possible. Here we focus on two semi-supervised approaches that have been applied to extract entities from opinion documents; they are based on the machine learning models known as *learning from positive and unlabeled examples* (also called *PU learning*) and *Bayesian Sets.*

For both these models, the user does not have to label any training data. Instead, the user needs only to provide some unambiguous seed entity names, meaning that the appearances of these names in the given corpus represent the same entity of interest. The objective of these models is to identify all named entities of the same type as the seeds from a given corpus.

PU learning is a two-class classification model. It is stated as follows Liu et al. (2002): given a set P of positive examples of a particular class and a set U of unlabeled examples (containing hidden positive and negative cases), build a classifier using P and U for classifying the data in U or future test cases. The results can be either binary decisions (whether each test case belongs to the positive class or not) or a ranking (based on how likely it is that each test case belongs to the positive class represented by P).

The entities in E or an extended E can serve as the seeds. In most applications, the entities in E are of the same type such as phones or cars. Li et al. (2010h) used this approach. Their algorithm first identifies candidate entities D from the corpus, which are single words or phrases with the following POS tags: NNP (proper noun), NNPS (plural proper noun), and CD (cardinal number). A phrase with a sequence of NNP, NNPS, and CD tags is regarded as one candidate entity (CD cannot be the first word unless it starts with a letter). For example, "Windows/NNP 7/CD" and "Nokia/NNP N97/CD" are regarded as two candidates: "Windows 7" and "Nokia N97."

For each seed $e_i \in E$, every mention or occurrence of e_i in the corpus forms a vector representing a positive example in P. The vector is made from the surrounding words context of the seed mention. Similarly, for each candidate entity $d \in D$, every occurrence also forms a vector as an unlabeled example in U. Thus, each unique seed or candidate entity may produce multiple feature vectors, depending on the number of times that it appears in the corpus. The components in the feature vectors are term frequencies.

Using the P and U sets, the PU learning algorithm S-EM given by Liu et al. (2002) was applied to learn a model to label the unlabeled examples in U. Those positively labeled examples in U are entities of interest. The algorithm can also rank the discovered entities based on how likely they are to belong to the seed set S using the classification results. Note that S-EM is based on the EM algorithm with naïve Bayes classification as its base classifier. Clearly, many other PU learning algorithms can be used as well (Liu, 2006, 2011).

In the study by Zhang and Liu (2011c), Bayesian sets (Ghahramani and Heller, 2005) were employed. However, two heuristic changes were made to the original Bayesian Sets algorithm by identifying high-quality features and by raising weights of some features. The algorithm produced a final ranking of candidate entities.

The classic method of distributional similarity (Lee, 1999; Pantel et al., 2009) from NLP can also be adapted to solve the problem by first comparing the similarity of the surrounding words of each candidate entity with those of the seed entities, and then ranking the candidate entities based on the similarity values. Li et al. (2010h) and Zhang and Liu (2011c) showed that PU learning and Bayesian sets markedly outperform distributional similarity.

In summary, the main advantage of using semi-supervised learning is that the user does not need to label any training data – a labor-intensive, time-consuming process that has to be done for each application domain. To provide a set of seed entities is fairly easy if the user knows the domain to some extent.

6.7.3   Entity Linking

Once entity mentions are found, entity linking is performed. Owing to polysemy, even in cases where the entity names are manually compiled for keyword search, entity linking may still be needed on the returned posts to ensure that each keyword in the context of the post actually refers to a desired entity.

There is a fairly long history of study of entity linking in the NLP community. Most investigations of entity linking in recent years have stemmed from the evaluation task of the Text Analysis Conference (TAC). The entity linking task of TAC is defined as follows (Ji et al., 2010):

> Given a query Q that consists of a name string N_q (which we call an entity expression), a background document B_q in which the name appears, and a knowledge base KB of known entities, the system is required to identify the KB entry to which the query name string N_q refers; or nil if there is no corresponding KB entry. Each entry of the knowledge base KB consists of a name string N_e (which may be regarded as the official name of an entity e), an entry type T_e [which can be PER (person), ORG (organization), GRE (geopolitical entity), or UKN (unknown)], and some disambiguating text D_e (e.g., text from the Wikipedia page of the entity).

This is the same as the entity linking problem in which we are interested. However, depending on the application, the user's desired entities for sentiment analysis may or may not be names of persons, organizations, or geopolitical entities, but may instead be products, services, or brands. In our case, if we attach each desired entity with a disambiguating text and type, our desired entity becomes an entry in the KB.

Many approaches have been proposed in recent years to solve the entity linking problem. For example, a "learning to rank" approach has been proposed by Dredze et al. (2010) and Zheng et al. (2010). Both of their algorithms consist of three main steps: candidate generation, candidate ranking, and determining NIL. The candidate generation step selects a set of likely KB entries for each query based on a set of heuristic rules. Candidate ranking uses the supervised learning-to-rank approach. This step treats each pair of the query and a candidate entity (a KB entry) for the query as an example and represents the pair as a feature vector. Each feature is a relationship between the two – for example, similarity of context texts, similarity of entity name strings, or whether they have the same entity type. The learned ranker is applied to rank the test set, which are also pairs for each query. In the research of Zheng et al. (2010), the top-ranked candidate entity is the predicted KB entry for the query. To deal with a return value of nil (when there is no KB entry for a query), a separate binary classifier is learned to determine whether the top-ranked candidate entity is the corresponding entity for the query. Dredze et al. (2010) took a different approach to handling nil by actually including nil as a KB entry for ranking. An additional set of features indicating nil is included.

Instead of treating entity linking as a ranking problem, Zhang et al. (2010b) treated it as a classification problem. They also used the pair (query, entity) as an example, just like the preceding approaches. For the class label, if the entity is the corresponding KB entry for the query, it is positive; otherwise, it is negative. Next, a two-class classifier is trained to directly predict the KB entry entity for a query. If no pair for a query is predicted to be positive, then the query has no corresponding entry in KB; that is, it is nil. A similar approach was also described by Milne and Witten (2008).

To use supervised learning, one needs to carefully engineer a large number of features and to label many training examples. Gottipati and Jiang (2011) proposed an unsupervised approach based on statistical language model-based information retrieval – specifically, a KL-divergence based retrieval model. The same approach also performs query expansion. The top-ranked KB entry with the same entity type as the query and with a score value greater than a threshold is assigned to the query as its corresponding entity in the KB. If no such KB entry is found, a value of nil is returned to indicate that there is no corresponding entity in the KB for the query. More recent research has also used graph propagation (Hoffart et al., 2011; Liu et al., 2012) and topic modeling to solve this problem (Han and Sun, 2012; Yogatama et al., 2012).

In sentiment analysis applications involving consumer products, there is usually another level of complexity because products typically have brands and models, which form a hierarchical relationship. For example, if a user wants to find consumer opinions about Apple Inc., opinions about its iPad and iPhone products may also be relevant. Then we may need to identify the brands and the product models under each brand. However, separating brands and models and discovering what models are under what brands are usually not difficult. Some heuristic rules should be able to do the job.

6.7.4   Entity Search and Linking

As discussed earlier, if the corpus is very large and contains a large and diverse set of entities or topics, we need to use keyword search to find relevant posts for sentiment analysis. In such cases, we only need to deal with the polysemy problem; that is, we do not need to deal with the synonym problem because the set of alternative names for an entity has been compiled as keywords and used in search. Then the entity linking problem becomes the following Davis et al. (2012):

> Given a large corpus C, and a set of alternative names $n_1, n_2, \ldots, n_m$ of an desired entity e. These names (treated as keywords) are used to search in C. Each returned document containing n_i needs to be classified as relevant or not relevant to e. In other words, we need to determine whether the mention of n_i in the returned document actually refers to e or not.

This problem clearly can be solved using the standard supervised classification approach. That is, after searching C using $n_1, n_2, \ldots, n_m$, some returned documents can be manually labeled. Documents referring to the desired entity e are labeled positive and others are labeled negative. A supervised learning algorithm such as SVM can be applied to the training data to build a classifier that is used to classify each future or test document containing n_i.

In the study by Davis et al. (2012), the problem is instead formulated as a PU learning problem. These authors argued that supervised learning needs a large number of manually labeled posts or tweets, but manual labeling is both time consuming and labor intensive. However, in many cases, acquiring some positive examples is relatively easy or inexpensive. For instance, if the corpus C is a stream of Twitter posts (tweets), it is possible to use hashtags of the entity to search for relevant tweets. Using this set of possibly noisy positive examples and other retrieved tweets as the set of unlabeled examples, PU learning can be performed to identify additional positive examples in the unlabeled set. In their paper, the authors use the EM algorithm with an association rule-based classifier (Velosoa et al., 2006), which consists of a set of class association rules (Liu et al., 1998).

6.8   Opinion Holder and Time Extraction

Like entity extraction, opinion holder and time extraction is a classic NER task, because both person names and times are named entities. These can be dealt with using current named extraction techniques. However, in most applications that use social media, we do not need to extract opinion holders and posting times from the text content, as opinion holders are usually the authors of the reviews, blogs, or discussion posts and their login ids are known.

The date and time when a post is submitted are also known; indeed, they are often displayed on the web page where the post appears. They can be scraped fairly easily from the page using structured data extraction techniques (Liu, 2006, 2011). It is only when opinion holders and times appear in the actual text – for example, in news articles – that they need to be extracted using NER techniques. We give a survey of existing work on news article corpora here.

Kim and Hovy (2004) considered person and organization as the only possible opinion holders and used a named entity recognizer to identify them. Choi et al. (2006) used CRF for their extraction. To train CRF, they used features such as surrounding words, POS of surrounding words, grammatical roles, and sentiment words.

Kim and Hovy (2006b) proposed a method that first generates all possible holder candidates in a sentence – that is, all noun phrases, including common noun phrases, named entities, and pronouns – and then parses the sentence and extracts a set of features from the parse tree. Next, a learned maximum entropy (ME) model scores all holder candidates using their features. On the basis of the ME scores, all holder candidates are ranked. The one with the highest score is selected as the holder of the opinion in the sentence.

Several other related works also exist. For example, Johansson and Moschitti (2010) dealt with the problem using SVM, Wiegand and Klakow (2010) applied convolution kernels, and Lu (2010) employed a dependency parser. Ruppenhofer et al. (2008) discussed the issue of using automatic semantic role labeling (ASRL) for identifying opinion holders. They argued that ASRL is insufficient and that other linguistic phenomena, such as discourse structures, may need to be considered. Kim and Hovy (2006b) actually used semantic role labeling for this purpose. Yang and Cardie (2013) proposed a method to jointly extract opinion holders, opinion expressions, and opinion targets, and their associated linking relations using CRF and an optimization framework (see Section 6.3.2).

6.9   Summary

Aspect and entity extraction and their resolution are important sentiment analysis tasks, as they represent opinion targets or what people talk about in opinion documents. Without their discovery, positive or negative opinions are of limited use. Although these tasks can be regarded as general information extraction problems, most existing methods exploit specific characteristics of the opinion domain (e.g., opinions having targets) for extraction and resolution.

Despite substantial research, resolving these problems remains a highly challenging endeavor. In many domains, the accuracy of existing algorithms is still low. Additionally, the current approaches mainly focus on extracting aspects that are nouns and noun phrases. In domains where many aspects are verb expressions or their aspects cannot be stated with simple nouns or noun phrases, such as political and social domains, these extraction algorithms are not very effective.

In the past few years, many unsupervised and semi-supervised topic models have been devised and applied to aspect extraction and joint modeling of sentiments and aspects. However, the current models are still not accurate enough for practical use. Most of these models are based on unigrams, but a large number of aspects in real-life data are multiword phrases. Despite the current shortcomings, future research into these learning models (not necessarily topic models) will likely be able to exploit a large number of data sets to make major breakthroughs. That is, in the big data age, we can exploit large volumes of data to discover commonsense and domain-specific knowledge, which are crucial for aspect and entity extraction and for their resolution.

Along with aspect and entity extraction, this chapter reviewed opinion holder and time extraction research. Although a large body of literature addresses these extraction tasks, some closely related tasks have received little research attention. For example, limited work has been done on discovering reasons or qualifications for opinions, with some notable exceptions. Zhang et al. (2013) made an attempt to discover opinion reasons using Markov logic networks. Clearly, much more research is needed to explore these important areas.

7   Sentiment Lexicon Generation

By now, it should be quite clear that words and phrases that convey positive or negative sentiment are instrumental for sentiment analysis. This chapter discusses how to compile such word lists. In the research literature, *sentiment words* are also called *opinion words, polar words*, or *opinion-bearing words*. Positive sentiment words such as *beautiful, wonderful*, and *amazing* are used to express some desired states or qualities, while negative sentiment words such as *bad, awful*, and *poor* are used to express some undesired states or qualities. In addition to individual words, there are sentiment phrases and idioms – for example, *cost an arm and a leg*. Collectively, they are called the *sentiment lexicon* (or *opinion lexicon*). From now on, when we say sentiment words, we mean both individual words and phrases.

Sentiment words can be divided into two types: *base type* and *comparative type*. All of the preceding example words are of the base type. Sentiment words of the comparative type (which include the superlative type) are used to express comparative and superlative opinions. Examples of such words include *better, worse, best*, and *worst*, which are comparative and superlative forms of the base adjectives or adverbs such as *good* and *bad*. We discuss comparative and superlative sentiment words further in Chapter 8. This chapter focuses on sentiment words of the base type.

There are three main approaches to compiling sentiment words: the *manual approach*, the *dictionary-based approach* (discussed in Section 7.1), and the *corpus-based approach* (discussed in Section 7.2). The manual approach is both labor intensive and time consuming, so it is typically used as a check on automated approaches – because automated approaches make mistakes. In Section 7.4, we will also discuss the issue of factual statements implying opinions, which has largely been overlooked by the research community.

This chapter is written in a survey style because past research has constructed numerous sentiment lexicons in many languages. Most of them are publicly available (see Section 7.5 for a list of them in English). Even if a particular language does not have a lexicon, compiling one is not hard. The real problems for sentiment analysis with regard to sentiment words are twofold: (1) how to identify and deal with words and phrases that have domain- or context-dependent sentiment orientations, and (2) how to spot factual words and phrases that imply sentiment in a domain context. For the first problem, there are almost always some sentiment words or phrases in a domain that express different orientations in some contexts than their default orientations in a general-purpose lexicon. If these words and their contexts are not identified and dealt with in an application, they can cause major drops in sentiment analysis accuracy. The second problem is even harder to solve because there are too many possibilities, and because it often needs analysis at the pragmatics level and prior domain knowledge to comprehend (see Section 7.4). These two problems represent key obstacles to accurate and domain-independent sentiment analysis. Unfortunately, not much research has been done to solve them.

7.1   Dictionary-Based Approach

Using a dictionary to compile sentiment words is an obvious approach because most dictionaries (e.g., WordNet; Miller et al., 1990) list synonyms and antonyms for each word. Thus, a simple technique is to use a few seed sentiment words to bootstrap based on the synonym and antonym structure of a dictionary. Specifically, this method works as follows: A small set of sentiment words (seeds) with known positive or negative orientations (or polarities) is first collected manually, which is very easy. The algorithm then grows this set by searching in WordNet or another online dictionary for their synonyms and antonyms. The newly found words are added to the seed list, and the next iteration begins. The iterative process ends when no more new words can be found (Hu and Liu, 2004; Valitutti et al., 2004). After the process is complete, a manual inspection step is performed to clean up the list (remove errors). The list can also be cleaned up by assigning a sentiment strength to each word using a probabilistic method (Kim and Hovy, 2004). Mohammad et al. (2009) additionally exploited many antonym-generating affix patterns like X and dis$X$ (e.g., honest–dishonest) to increase the coverage.

Kamps et al. (2004) proposed a more sophisticated approach that uses a WordNet distance-based method to determine the sentiment orientation of a given adjective. The distance $d(t_1, t_2)$ between words t_1 and t_2 is the length of the shortest path that connects t_1 and t_2 in WordNet. The orientation of an adjective word t is determined by its relative distance from two reference (or seed) words *good* and *bad* – that is, $SO(t) = [d(t, \text{bad}) - d(t, \text{good})]/d(\text{good}, \text{bad})$. t is positive iff $SO(t) > 0$, and is negative otherwise. The absolute value of $SO(t)$ gives the strength of the sentiment. Along similar lines, Williams and Anand (2009) studied the problem of assigning sentiment strength to each word.

Blair-Goldensohn et al. (2008) presented a different bootstrapping method that uses a positive seed set, a negative seed set, and a neutral seed set. This approach is based on a directed, weighted semantic graph where neighboring nodes are synonyms or antonyms of words in WordNet and are not part of the neutral seed set. The neutral set is used to stop the propagation of sentiment through neutral words. The edge weights are preassigned based on a scaling parameter for different types of edges – that is, synonym or antonym edges. Each word is then scored (given a sentiment value) using a modified version of the label propagation algorithm described by Zhu and Ghahramani (2002). At the beginning, each positive seed word is given a score of +1, each negative seed is given a score of −1, and all other words are given a score of 0. The scores are then revised during the propagation process. When the propagation stops after a number of iterations, the final scores after logarithmic scaling are assigned to words as their degrees of being positive or negative.

In the study by Rao and Ravichandran (2009), three graph-based semi-supervised learning methods were employed to separate positive and negative words given a positive seed set, a negative seed set, and a synonym graph extracted from WordNet. The three algorithms were mincut (Blum and Chawla, 2001), randomized mincut (Blum et al., 2004), and label propagation (Zhu and Ghahramani, 2002). It was shown that mincut and randomized mincut produced better F scores, but label propagation gave significantly higher precision with low recall.

Hassan and Radev (2010) presented a Markov random walk model over a word-relatedness graph to produce a sentiment estimate for a given word. It first uses WordNet synonyms and hypernyms to build a word-relatedness graph. It then defines a measure, called the *mean hitting time* $h(i|S)$, and uses the measure to gauge the distance from a node i to a set of nodes (words) S, which is the average number of steps that a random walker, starting in state $i \notin S$, will take to enter a state $k \in S$ for the first time. Given a set of positive seed words S^+ and a set of negative seed words S^-, to estimate the sentiment orientation of a given word w, it computes the hitting times $h(w|S^+)$ and $h(w|S^-)$. If $h(w|S^+)$ is greater than $h(w|S^-)$, the word is classified as negative. All other outcomes are classified as positive. Hassan et al. (2011) applied the same method to find the sentiment orientations of foreign words. For this purpose, a multilingual word graph was created with both English words and foreign words. Words in different languages are connected based on their meanings in dictionaries. Other methods based on graphs include those described by Takamura et al. (2005, 2006, 2007).

In the work by Turney and Littman (2003), the same PMI-based method employed by Turney (2002) was used to compute the sentiment orientation of a given word. Specifically, this method computes the orientation of the word from the strength of its association with a set of positive words (*good, nice, excellent, positive, fortunate, correct*, and *superior*), minus the strength of its association with a set of negative words (*bad, nasty, poor, negative, unfortunate, wrong*, and *inferior*). The association strength is measured using PMI.

Esuli and Sebastiani (2005) used supervised learning to classify words into positive and negative classes. Given a set P of positive seed words and a set N of negative seed words, the two seed sets are first expanded using synonym and antonym relations in an online dictionary (e.g., WordNet) to generate the expanded sets P' and N', which form the training set. The algorithm then uses all the glosses in the dictionary for each word in $P' \cup N'$ to generate a feature vector. A binary classifier is built using different learning algorithms. This process can also be run iteratively. That is, after the newly identified positive and negative words and their synonyms and antonyms are added to the training set, an updated classifier can be constructed and so on.

In the study by Esuli and Sebastiani (2006a), the authors also included the category *objective* (no sentiment). To expand the objective seed set, hyponyms were used in addition to synonyms and antonyms. They then tried different strategies to do the three-class classification. In the study by Esuli and Sebastiani (2006b), a committee of classifiers based on the preceding method was utilized to build SentiWordNet, a lexical resource in which each synset of WordNet is associated with three numerical scores Obj(s), Pos(s) and Neg(s), describing the degrees to which each word contained in the synset are Objective, Positive, and Negative, respectively.

Kim and Hovy's (2004, 2006c) method likewise starts with three seed sets of positive, negative, and neutral words, which are then used to find synonyms in WordNet. The expanded sets, however, have many errors. This method then uses a Bayesian formula to compute the closeness of each word to each category (positive, negative, and neutral) to determine the most probable class for the word.

Guerini et al. (2013) proposed a classification method that assigns a sentiment orientation to each word based on the positive and negative scores of each sense of the word in SentiWordNet and various aggregations of the scores as features. Gatti and Guerini (2012) went even further, predicting the sentiment strength of each word.

Andreevskaia and Bergler (2006) proposed a more sophisticated bootstrapping method with several techniques to expand the initial positive and negative seed sets and to clean up the expanded sets (removing nonadjectives and words in both positive and negative sets). In addition, their algorithm performs multiple runs of the bootstrapping process using some nonoverlapping seed subsets. Each run typically finds a slightly different set of sentiment words. A net overlapping score for each word is then computed based on how many times the word is discovered in the runs as a positive word and as a negative word. The score is then normalized to [0, 1] based on fuzzy set theory.

In the research conducted by Kaji and Kitsuregawa (2006, 2007), many heuristics were used to build a sentiment lexicon from HTML documents based on web page layout structures. For example, a table in a web page may have a column clearly indicating the positive or negative orientations (e.g., pros and cons) of the surrounding text. These clues can be exploited to extract a large number of candidate positive and negative opinion sentences from a large set of web pages. Adjective phrases can then be extracted from these sentences and assigned sentiment orientations based on different statistics of their occurrences in the positive and negative sentence sets, respectively.

Velikovich et al. (2010) also proposed a method to construct a sentiment lexicon using web pages. It was based on a graph propagation algorithm over a phrase similarity graph. It again assumed as input a set of positive seed phrases and a set of negative seed phrases. The nodes in the phrase graph were the candidate phrases selected from all n-grams up to length ten extracted from four billion web pages. Only twenty million candidate phrases were selected using several heuristics – for example, frequency and mutual information of word boundaries. A context vector for each candidate phrase was then constructed based on a word window of size six aggregated over all mentions of the phrase in the four billion documents. The edge set was constructed through cosine similarity computation of the context vectors of the candidate phrases. All edges (v_i, v_j) were discarded if they were not one of the twenty-five highest-weighted edges adjacent to either node v_i or v_j. The edge weight was set to the corresponding cosine similarity value. A graph propagation method was used to calculate the sentiment of each phrase as the aggregate of all the best paths to the seed words.

Dragut et al. (2010) proposed yet another, albeit very different, bootstrapping method using WordNet. Given a set of seed words, instead of simply following the dictionary, the authors proposed a set of sophisticated inference rules to determine other words' sentiment orientations through a deductive process. That is, the algorithm takes words with known sentiment orientations (the seeds) as input and produces synsets (sets of synonyms) with orientations. The synsets with the deduced orientations can then be used to further deduce the polarities of other words.

Peng and Park (2011) presented a sentiment lexicon generation method using constrained symmetric non-negative matrix factorization (CSNMF). Their method first applies bootstrapping to find a set of candidate sentiment words in a dictionary; it then uses a large corpus to assign polarity scores to each word. This method thus uses both dictionary and corpus. Xu et al. (2010) presented several integrated methods also using dictionaries and corpora to find emotion words. Their method is based on label propagation in a similarity graph (Zhu and Ghahramani, 2002).

Although many dictionary-based approaches to sentiment lexicon generation have been proposed, I am not aware of any existing study that evaluated these methods independently. Thus, it is hard to tell which one is the best. In general, we note that the advantage of using a dictionary-based approach is that one can easily and quickly find a large number of sentiment words along with their orientations. Although the resulting list may have many errors, manual checking can be performed to clean it up. The manual cleanup is a time-consuming, but one-time-only effort that requires just a few days for a native speaker.

The main disadvantage of the dictionary-based approach is that the sentiment orientations of words collected this way are general or domain and context independent. Many sentiment words actually have context-dependent orientations. For example, if a speaker phone is quiet, it usually indicates a negative sentiment. However, if a car is quiet, it is positive. Thus, the sentiment orientation of *quiet* is domain or context dependent. The corpus-based approach can help deal with this problem.

7.2   Corpus-Based Approach

The corpus-based approach has been applied to two main scenarios: (1) given a seed list of known (often general-purpose) sentiment words, discover other sentiment words and their orientations from a domain corpus, and (2) adapt a general-purpose sentiment lexicon to a new one using a domain corpus for sentiment analysis applications in the domain. In practice, the issue can be more complicated than just building a domain-specific sentiment lexicon because in the same domain the same word can be positive in one context but negative in another.

In this section, we discuss some of the existing work that deals with these problems. Although the corpus-based approach may also be used to build a general-purpose sentiment lexicon, if a very large and very diverse corpus is available, the dictionary-based approach is usually more effective because a dictionary contains all words.

7.2.1   Identifying Sentiment Words from a Corpus

Two major ideas have been applied to identify sentiment words in a given corpus. The first idea is to exploit some linguistic rules or conventions on connectives to simultaneously identify sentiment words and determine their orientations from a given corpus. The second idea is to use syntactic relations of opinions and targets to extract sentiment words.

The first idea was proposed by Hatzivassiloglou and McKeown (1997). It relies on a set of seed adjectives with known orientations and a corpus to find additional sentiment adjectives in the corpus. One of the rules focuses on the conjunction AND, stating that conjoined adjectives usually have the same orientation. For example, in the sentence, "This car is beautiful and spacious," if *beautiful* is known to be positive, it can be inferred that *spacious* is also positive. This is so because people usually express the same sentiment on both sides of a conjunction. The following sentence, however, is not very likely: "This car is beautiful and difficult to drive." It is more acceptable if it is changed to "This car is beautiful but difficult to drive." Hatzivassiloglou and McKeown also designed rules for other connectives – that is, OR, BUT, EITHER–OR, and NEITHER–NOR.

The underling idea is called *sentiment consistency*, though in practice it is not always consistent. To overcome this difficulty, Hatzivassiloglou and McKeown (1997) applied a machine learning step to determine if two conjoined adjectives have the same or different orientations. First, a graph was formed with same- and different-orientation links between adjectives. Clustering was then performed on the graph to produce two sets of words: positive and negative.

Kanayama and Nasukawa (2006) extended this approach by introducing the concepts of intrasentential (within a sentence) and intersentential (between neighboring sentences) sentiment consistency, which they collectively call *coherency*. The intrasentential consistency is similar to the idea described in the previous graph, while intersentential consistency applies this idea to neighboring sentences. That is, the same sentiment orientation is usually expressed in consecutive sentences. Sentiment changes are indicated by adversative expressions such as *but* and *however*. Some criteria were also proposed to determine whether to add a word to the positive or negative lexicon. This study was based on Japanese text and was used to find domain-dependent sentiment words and their orientations. Other related work includes that by Kaji and Kitsuregawa (2006, 2007).

The second idea – that is, using syntactic relations of opinions and targets for extraction – was originally proposed for extracting aspects or opinion targets (Hu and Liu, 2004; Zhuang et al., 2006). It was later adapted to extract both sentiment words and their opinion targets (aspects) by Wang and Wang (2008) and Qiu et al. (2009a, 2011). In fact, both ideas were employed by Qiu et al. (2009a, 2011). Because we described this approach in detail in Section 6.2.1, we will not discuss it further here.

Volkova et al. (2013b) proposed another corpus-based bootstrapping method to generate sentiment lexicon from tweets. Their algorithm employs a set of polarity-labeled tweets, so it is a semi-supervised method. However, this method does not use opinion and target relations. Other related work includes that by Hamilton et al. (2016) and by Wang et al. (2017c).

7.2.2 Dealing with Context-Dependent Sentiment Words

Although finding domain-specific sentiment words and their orientations is useful, it is insufficient in practice. Ding et al. (2008) showed that many words in the same domain can have different orientations in different contexts. In fact, this phenomenon was captured by the basic rules of opinions in Section 5.2. For example, in the camera domain, the word "long" clearly expresses opposite opinions in the following two sentences:

"The battery life is long." (positive)
"It takes a long time to focus." (negative)

Such situations often occur with quantity adjectives – for example, *long, short, large, small*, and so on – and sometimes with other adjectives, too. For example, in a car review, the sentence "This car is very quiet" is positive, whereas the sentence "The audio system in the car is very quiet" is negative. Thus, finding domain-dependent sentiment words and their orientations is insufficient. The example sentences tell us that both the aspect and the sentiment expressing words or phrases are important. Ding et al. (2008) proposed to use the pair

(*context_sentiment_word, aspect*)

as the *opinion context* – for example, (*long, battery life*). Their method determines sentiment words and their orientations together with the aspects that they modify. In determining whether a pair is positive or negative, the preceding intrasentential and intersentential sentiment consistency rules about connectives are still applied.

The work of Ganapathibhotla and Liu (2008) adopted the same context definition but used it for analyzing comparative sentences. Lu et al. (2011) also used the same context definition and performed the task using a review corpus. Like Ding et al. (2008), they assumed that the set of aspects was given. They formulated the problem of assigning each pair a positive or negative sentiment as an optimization problem with a number of constraints. The objective function and constraints were designed based on clues such as a general-purpose sentiment lexicon, the overall sentiment rating of each review, synonyms and antonyms, and conjunction "and" rules, "but" rules, and "negation" rules.

Wu and Wen (2010) dealt with a similar problem in Chinese. They focused on pairs in which adjectives are quantifiers such as *big, small, low,* and *high*. Their method is based on syntactic patterns, as in the study by Turney (2002) (see Section 3.2.1), and also uses web search hit counts to solve the problem.

Zhao et al. (2012) used web searches for this task as well. However, they performed query expansion to include more relevant queries. For example, for the context pair (*long, battery life*), they searched using four queries: "long battery life," "battery life is long," "the battery life is very long," and "the battery life is not long." Instead of using the Google general search capabilities, they employed Google's advanced search features to focus on forum sites that discuss some specific products. They then collected the top one hundred snippets and performed sentiment analysis on them using the lexicon-based method described by Hu and Liu (2004). If there are more snippets that are positive, the pair [e.g., (*long, battery life*)] is assigned a positive sentiment; otherwise, it is assigned a negative sentiment.

The methods utilized by Turney (2002) and Takamura et al. (2007) can be considered methods for finding context-specific opinions, too, but they do not explicitly use the sentiment consistency idea. Instead, they use web searches to find sentiment orientations (see Section 3.2.1). We should note that all these context definitions are still not sufficient for all cases, as the basic rules of opinions discussed in Section 5.2 show. Many contexts can be more complex – for example, consuming a small or large quantity of resources (Zhang and Liu, 2011a) owing to the use of a triple as the opinion context:

$$(usage\_verb, quantifier, resource\_noun),$$

where *resource_noun* is a noun or a noun phrase representing a resource, and *usage_verb* is a verb expressing the concept of consumption. This context indicates a sentiment and an aspect. For example, in the sentence "This washer uses a lot of water," *uses* is the *usage_verb, a lot of* is a quantifier phrase, and *water* is the resource. This context represents a negative sentiment and a *water resource usage* aspect. Another example is "This car eats a lot of gas." Unfortunately, no systematic study has been conducted to identify all such sentiment contexts.

A similar problem is to identify contextual subjectivities and sentiments at the phrase or expression level. Contextual sentiment means that although a word or phrase in a lexicon is marked as positive or negative, in the context of the sentence expression it may have no sentiment or have the opposite sentiment. Wilson et al. (2005) studied this problem. Their algorithm first labeled the subjective expressions in the corpus that contain subjective words or phrases in a given subjectivity lexicon. A subjectivity lexicon is slightly different from a sentiment lexicon because it may contain words that indicate only subjectivity but no sentiment – for example, *feel* and *think*. These authors' paper took a supervised learning approach comprising two steps. The first step determines whether the expression is subjective or objective. The second step determines whether the subjective expression is positive, negative, both, or neutral. *Both* means the expression has both positive and negative sentiments. *Neutral* is still included as an option because the first step can make mistakes and leave some neutral expressions unidentified. For subjectivity classification, a large and rich set of features was used, including *word features, modification features* (dependency features), *structure features* (dependency tree–based patterns), *sentence features*, and *document features*. For the second step of sentiment classification, the study used features such as *word tokens, word prior sentiments, negations, modified by polarity, conj polarity*, and so on. In both steps, the machine learning algorithm BoosTexter AdaBoost.HM (Schapire and Singer, 2000) was employed to build classifiers.

A related problem is expression-level sentiment classification, which determines the sentiment orientation of expressions. Choi and Cardie (2008) classified the expressions annotated in the MPQA corpus (Wiebe et al., 2005). Both lexicon-based classification and supervised learning were used in this experiment.

Along similar lines, Kessler and Schütze (2012) used supervised classification to determine sentiment words that have different orientations in specific sentence contexts. Breck et al. (2007) studied the problem of extracting sentiment expressions with any number of words using CRF (Lafferty et al., 2001). Yang and Cardie's (2012) study used semi-Markov conditional random fields (semi-CRF; Sarawagi and Cohen, 2004) to extract opinion expressions. Semi-CRF is more powerful than CRF for the extraction task because semi-CRF allows one to construct features to capture characteristics of the subsequences of a sentence.

7.2.3   Lexicon Adaptation

Several researchers have studied how to adapt a general sentiment lexicon to a particular domain. Choi and Cardie (2009) investigated the adaptation of a general lexicon to a new one for domain-specific expression-level sentiment classification. Their technique adapts the word-level polarities of a general-purpose sentiment lexicon for a particular domain by utilizing the expression-level polarities in the domain. In return, the adapted word-level polarities are used to improve the expression-level polarities. The word-level and the expression-level polarity relationships are modeled as a set of constraints, with the problem then being solved using integer linear programming. This work assumes that there is a given general-purpose polarity lexicon L, and a polarity classification algorithm $f(e_l, L)$ that can determine the polarity of the opinion expression e_l based on the words in e_l and L. Jijkoun et al. (2010) proposed a related method to adapt a general sentiment lexicon to a topic-specific one.

Du et al. (2010) studied the problem of adapting the sentiment lexicon from one domain (not a general-purpose lexicon) to another domain. As input, the algorithm assumes the availability of a set of in-domain sentiment-labeled documents, a set of sentiment words from these in-domain documents, and a set of out-of-domain documents. The task is to adapt the in-domain sentiment lexicon for the out-of-domain documents. Two ideas are used. First, a document should be positive (or negative) if it contains many positive (or negative) words, and a word should be positive (or negative) if it appears in many positive (or negative) documents. These are mutually reinforcing relationships. Second, even though the two domains may be under different distributions, it is possible to identify a common part between them (e.g., the same word has the same orientation). The sentiment lexicon adaption was solved using the information bottleneck framework. The same problem was also dealt with in the work by Du and Tan (2009).

7.2.4   Some Other Related Work

Word sense and subjectivity. Wiebe and Mihalcea (2006) investigated the possibility of assigning subjectivity labels to word senses based on a corpus. They first investigated the agreement between annotators who manually assigned the labels *subjective, objective,* or *both* to WordNet senses. They then evaluated a method based on distributional similarity (Lin, 1998) to automatically assign subjectivity labels/scores to word senses. Their work showed that subjectivity is a property that can be associated with word senses, and word sense disambiguation (WSD) can directly benefit from subjectivity annotations. Subsequent work was reported in the paper by Akkaya et al. (2009). Su and Markert (2008) also studied the problem and performed a case study for subjectivity recognition. Su and Markert (2010) further investigated this problem and applied it in a cross-lingual environment.

Connotation lexicon. Feng et al. (2011) studied the problem of producing a connotation lexicon, consisting of words with positive or negative connotations. A connotation lexicon differs from a sentiment lexicon in that the latter concerns words that express sentiment either explicitly or implicitly, while the former concerns words that are often associated with a specific polarity of sentiment. For example, *award* and *promotion* have positive connotations, whereas *cancer* and *war* have negative connotations. Many are even objective words such as *intelligence, human,* and *cheesecake*. The authors proposed a graph-based method exploiting mutual reinforcement to solve the problem.

Feng et al. (2013b) improved upon this approach by using linear programming and integer linear programming encoding a diverse set of linguistic insights (semantic prosody, distributional similarity, and semantic parallelism of coordination) and prior knowledge drawn from lexical resources as constraints, to construct a broad-coverage connotation lexicon. They also experimented with and compared these algorithms with themselves and with some popular graph-based methods such as HITS, PageRankk and label propagation. The results showed that linear programming gave the best results.

Brody and Diakopoulos (2011) studied the lengthening of words (e.g., slooooow) in microblogs. They showed that lengthening is strongly associated with subjectivity and sentiment, and presented an automatic way to leverage this association to detect domain sentiment and emotion words. Mohtarami et al. (2013) proposed a method to infer sentiment similarity between a pair of words – that is, whether they have the same orientation and intensity. Meng et al. (2012) and Lai et al. (2012) studied how to translate sentiment words from one language to another.

7.3   Sentiment Word Embedding

It is well known that word embeddings play an important role in deep learning–based text classification. That is also the case for sentiment classification. Interestingly, it has been shown that even without using deep learning models for the final classification, word embeddings can be employed as features for non-neural learning models for various tasks to obtain improved results. This section highlights the word embedding research specific to sentiment analysis.

For sentiment analysis, directly applying regular word embedding methods such as CBOW and Skip-gram (Mikolov et al., 2013a) to learn word embeddings from the context can encounter problems, because words with similar contexts but opposite sentiment polarities (e.g., *good* or *bad*) may be mapped to nearby vectors in the embedding space. Therefore, sentiment-encoded word embedding methods have been proposed. Mass el al. (2011) introduced word embeddings that can capture both semantic and sentiment information. Bespalov et al. (2011) showed that an *n*-gram model combined with latent representation would produce a more suitable embedding for sentiment classification. Labutov and Lipson (2013) re-embedded existing word embeddings with logistic regression by regarding sentiment supervision of sentences as a regularization term.

Le and Mikolov (2014) proposed the concept of paragraph vectors to first learn the fixed-length representation for variable-length pieces of texts, including sentences, paragraphs, and documents. They experimented with both sentence- and document-level sentiment classification tasks and achieved performance gains, which demonstrates the merit of paragraph vectors in capturing more semantic information to help sentiment classification.

Tang et al. (2014) and Tang et al. (2016c) presented models to learn sentiment-specific word embeddings (SSWE), in which both the semantic and sentiment information is embedded in the learned word vectors. Wang and Xia (2017b) developed a neural architecture to train a sentiment-bearing word embedding by integrating the sentiment supervision at both the document and word levels. Yu et al. (2017) adopted a refinement strategy to obtain joint semantic/sentiment-bearing word vectors.

Feature enrichment and multisense word embeddings have also been investigated as means to improve sentiment analysis. Vo and Zhang (2015) studied aspect-based Twitter sentiment classification by making use of rich automatic features, which are additional features obtained using unsupervised learning techniques. Li and Jurafsky (2015) experimented with the utilization of multisense word embeddings on various NLP tasks. Experimental results show that while such embeddings do improve the performance of some tasks, they offer little benefit for sentiment classification tasks. Ren et al. (2016) proposed methods to learn topic-enriched multiple-prototype word embeddings for Twitter sentiment classification.

Multilinguistic word embeddings have also been applied to sentiment analysis. Zhou et al. (2015) reported a bilingual sentiment word embedding (BSWE) model for cross-language sentiment classification. It incorporates the sentiment information into English–Chinese bilingual embeddings by employing labeled corpora and their translation, instead of large-scale parallel corpora. Barnes et al. (2016) compared several types of bilingual word embeddings and neural machine translation techniques for cross-lingual aspect-based sentiment classification.

Zhang et al. (2016c) integrated word embeddings with matrix factorization for personalized review-based rating prediction. Specifically, these authors refined existing semantics-oriented word vectors [e.g., word2vec (Mikolov et al., 2013b) and GloVe (Pennington et al. 2014)] using sentiment lexicons. Sharma et al. (2017) proposed a semi-supervised technique to use sentiment-bearing word embeddings for ranking the sentiment intensity of adjectives. Additional work on using word embedding techniques to improve various sentiment analysis related tasks can be found in the reports by Wang et al. (2015); Teng et al. (2016); Zhou et al. (2016); Xiong et al. (2016); and Liu et al. (2015).

7.4   Desirable and Undesirable Facts

The sentiment words and expressions that we have discussed so far are mainly subjective words and expressions that indicate positive or negative sentiment. However, many objective words and expressions can imply sentiment as well, because they can represent desirable or undesirable facts in some specific domains or contexts. To understand whether a fact is desirable or not desirable, we often need prior domain knowledge – which means we need pragmatics analysis. Because pragmatics analysis is extremely difficult due to the need for commonsense knowledge, we must resort to other signs or clues to achieve our objective.

Zhang and Liu (2011b) proposed a technique to identify nouns and noun phrases that indicate aspects and also imply positive or negative sentiment in a particular domain context. These noun phrases (including individual nouns) exhibit no sentiment when they stand alone, but in the domain context they may represent desirable or undesirable facts. For example, the words *valley* and *mountain* themselves do not have any sentiment connotation in general; that is, they are objective. However, in the domain of mattress reviews, they often imply negative sentiment as in "Within a month, a valley formed in the middle of the mattress." Here, *valley*, used as a *metaphor*, implies a negative sentiment about the mattress quality. Identifying sentiment orientations of such noun phrases is very challenging but critical for effective sentiment analysis in many domains.

The algorithm introduced by Zhang and Liu (2011b) is based on the following idea: although many sentences involving such noun phrases read like objective sentences with no explicit sentiment, in some cases the authors may also express explicit sentiment – for example, "Within a month, a valley formed in the middle of the mattress, which is terrible." The context of this sentence indicates that *valley* may not be desirable. These sentiment contexts can be exploited to determine what sentiment a noun phrase may imply. However, the problem with this approach is that noun phrases with no implied sentiment appear frequently in positive or negative sentiment contexts – for example, *voice quality* in "The voice quality is poor." To distinguish these two cases, the following observation was used:

> **Observation.** For normal noun phrases that imply no positive or negative sentiment, people can express both positive and negative opinions about them. For example, for the noun phrase "voice quality," some people may say "good voice quality" and some may say "bad voice quality." However, a noun phrase representing a desirable or undesirable fact is often associated with only a single sentiment orientation, either positive or negative, but not both. For example, it is unlikely that both of the following sentences would appear in the same domain: "A bad valley has formed" and "A good valley has formed."

With this observation in mind, Zhang and Liu's (2011b) approach proceeds in two steps:

1. *Candidate identification.* The algorithm first identifies all noun phrases in the corpus and determines the surrounding sentiment context for each of the noun phrases. If a noun phrase occurs in negative (respectively positive) sentiment contexts significantly more frequently than in positive (or negative) sentiment contexts in a large domain corpus, this finding infers that the noun phrase's sentiment polarity or orientation is likely to be negative (or positive). The significance is assessed using a statistical test. This step produces a list of candidate noun phrases with positive sentiment and a list of candidate noun phrases with negative sentiment.
2. *Pruning.* The algorithm then prunes the two lists based on the preceding observation. If a noun phrase has been directly modified by both positive and negative sentiment words in the corpus, it is unlikely to imply any sentiment and should be pruned. Two types of dependency relations are used to detect such direct modifications.

Type 1: O → O-Dep → N

means that O depends on N through relation O-Dep – for example, "This TV has *good* picture quality."

Type 2: O → O-Dep → H ← N-Dep ← N

means that both O and N depend on H through relations O-Dep and N-Dep, respectively – for example, "The springs of the mattress are *bad*." O is a sentiment or opinion word, O-Dep and N-Dep are dependency relations, N is a noun phrase, and H means any word.

For the first example sentence, given the noun phrase *picture quality*, we can identify its modification sentiment word *good*. For the second example, given the noun *springs*, we can obtain its modification sentiment word *bad*.

This work was just the first attempt to tackle the problem, and its accuracy is not high. Much further research is needed.

7.5   Summary

Owing to the contributions of many researchers, several general-purpose subjectivity, sentiment, and emotion lexicons have been constructed. Some of them are also publicly available.

- General Inquirer lexicon (Stone, 1968): www.wjh.harvard.edu/~inquirer/ spreadsheet_guide.htm
- Sentiment lexicon (Hu and Liu, 2004): www.cs.uic.edu/~liub/FBS/senti ment-analysis.html
- MPQA subjectivity lexicon (Wilson et al., 2005): www.cs.pitt.edu/mpqa/ subj_lexicon.html
- SentiWordNet (Esuli and Sebastiani, 2006b): http://sentiwordnet.isti.cnr.it/
- Emotion lexicon (Mohammad and Turney, 2010): www.purl.org/net/ emolex

With many lexicons, inconsistency and errors are inevitable. Dragut et al. (2012) studied the problem of polarity or orientation consistency checking in sentiment lexicons or dictionaries and found considerable inconsistencies in the lexicons that they have studied. They then proposed a fast SAT solver-based method to detect such inconsistencies.

Despite a significant amount of research, challenging problems related to sentiment lexicon generation remain. First, there is still not an effective method for discovering and determining domain- and context-dependent sentiments. For example, *suck* is in general negative, but for vacuum cleaners, it is often positive. Furthermore, in different sentence contexts, the same word may exhibit different sentiments, as we discussed earlier. Besides the techniques discussed in Section 7.2, recent works have tried to use word vectors and matrix to capture the contextual information of sentiment words (Maas et al., 2011; Yessenalina and Cardie, 2011). However, the existing techniques are still not accurate enough for practical use.

Second, in almost every domain, there are some objective words or phrases that describe some desirable and undesirable states or qualities and thus imply positive or negative sentiment, respectively (see Section 7.4). We still do not have a good method to identify such objective words and phrases.

Third, having a sentiment lexicon (even with domain-specific orientations) does not mean that every word in the lexicon always expresses an opinion/ sentiment in a sentence. For example, in "I am looking for a good car to buy," *good* does not express either a positive or negative sentiment about any particular car because the sentence actually expresses a desire or intent.

8   Analysis of Comparative Opinions

Apart from directly expressing positive or negative opinions about an entity and/or its aspects, one can also express opinions by comparing similar entities. Such opinions are called *comparative opinions* (Jindal and Liu, 2006a, 2006b). Comparative opinions have different semantic meanings from regular opinions as well as different syntactic forms. For example, a typical regular opinion sentence is "The voice quality of this phone is amazing," and a typical comparative opinion sentence is "The voice quality of Moto X is better than that of iPhone 5." This comparative sentence does not say that any phone's voice quality is good or bad, but simply states a relative ordering in terms of voice quality of the two smartphones. Like regular sentences, comparative sentences can be opinionated or not-opinionated. The preceding comparative sentence is clearly opinionated because it explicitly expresses a comparative sentiment, while the sentence "Samsung Galaxy 4 is larger than iPhone 5" expresses no sentiment, at least not explicitly.

In this chapter, we first define the problem of comparative opinion mining and then present some existing methods for solving the problem. We will study *superlative opinions* as well because their semantic meanings and handling methods are similar.

8.1   Problem Definition

A comparative sentence usually expresses a relation based on the similarities or differences for more than one entity. Linguists have studied comparatives in the English language for a long time. Lerner and Pinkal (1992) defined comparatives as universal quantifiers over degrees. For example, in the sentence "John is taller than he was," the degree d is John's height and John is tall to degree d. In other words, comparatives are used to express explicit orderings between objects with respect to the degree or amount to which they possess some gradable property (Kennedy, 2005). The two broad types of comparatives are as follows:[1]

---

[1] www.cis.upenn.edu/~xtag/release-8.31.98-html/node189.html

1. *Metalinguistic comparatives.* Compare the extent to which an entity has one property to a greater or lesser extent than another property. Example: "Ronaldo is angrier than upset."
2. *Propositional comparatives.* Make a comparison between two propositions. This category has three subcategories:
   a. *Nominal comparatives.* Compare the cardinality of two sets of objects denoted by nominal phrases. Example: "Paul ate more grapes than bananas."
   b. *Adjectival comparatives.* Usually use words that end with *-er, more, less*, and so on (occurring with the conjugate *than*) and equative *as* (e.g., *as good as*). Example: "Ford is cheaper than Volvo."
   c. *Adverbial comparatives.* Similar to nominal and adjectival ones except that they generally occur after a verb phrase. Example: "Tom ate more quickly than Jane."

Then there are superlatives, which are a form of adjective or adverb that expresses the highest or a very high degree of quality of what is being described. They have two categories:

1. *Adjectival superlatives.* Express that an entity has the most of a particular quality within a group or of its kind. Example: "John is the tallest person."
2. *Adverbial superlatives.* Express that an entity does something to the greatest degree within a group or of its kind. Example: "Jill did her homework most frequently."

We can also look at comparisons from the gradability point of view, from which we can group comparisons into two categories: *gradable comparison* and *nongradable comparison* (Kennedy, 2005; Jindal and Liu, 2006a).

Gradable comparison. Expresses an ordering relationship of entities being compared. It has three subtypes:

1. *Nonequal gradable comparison.* Expresses a relation of the type *greater* or *less than*, which ranks a set of entities over another set of entities based on some of their shared aspects – for example, "Coke tastes better than Pepsi." This type also includes preference – for example, "I prefer Coke to Pepsi."
2. *Equative comparison.* Expresses a relation of the type *equal to*, which states that two or more entities are equal based on some of their shared aspects. Example: "Coke and Pepsi taste the same."
3. *Superlative comparison.* Expresses a relation of the type greater or less than all others, which ranks one entity over all others. Example: "Coke tastes the best among all soft drinks."

Nongradable comparison. Expresses a relation of two or more entities but does not grade them. There are three main subtypes:

1. Entity *A* is similar to or different from entity *B* based on some of their shared aspects. Example: "Coke tastes differently from Pepsi."
2. Entity *A* has aspect a_1, and entity *B* has aspect a_2 (a_1 and a_2 are usually substitutable). Example: "Desktop PCs use external speakers but laptops use internal speakers."
3. Entity *A* has aspect *a*, but entity *B* does not have. Example: "Nokia phones come with earpieces, but iPhones do not."

This chapter focuses on gradable comparisons. Nongradable comparisons may also express opinions but they are often more subtle and difficult to determine.

In English, comparisons are typically expressed using *comparative words* (also called *comparatives*) and *superlative words* (also called *superlatives*). Comparatives are formed by adding the suffix *-er* and superlatives are formed by adding the suffix *-est* to their *base adjectives* and *base adverbs*. For example, in "The battery life of Huawei phones is longer than that of Samsung phones," *longer* is the comparative form of the adjective *long*. *Longer* (with *than*) here also indicates that this is a comparative sentence. In "The battery life of Nokia phones is the longest," *longest* is the superlative form of the adjective *long*, and it indicates that this is a superlative sentence. We call these types of comparatives and superlatives *Type 1 comparatives* and *Type 1 superlatives,* respectively. For simplicity, we often use *comparative* to mean both *comparative* and *superlative* if superlative is not explicitly stated.

Adjectives and adverbs that have two syllables or more and do not end in *y* do not form comparatives or superlatives by adding *-er* or *-est*. Instead, the qualifiers *more*, *most*, *less*, and *least* are used before such words – for example, *more beautiful*. We call these types of comparatives and superlatives *Type 2 comparatives* and *Type 2 superlatives,* respectively. Both Type 1 and Type 2 are called *regular comparatives* and *superlatives*.

English also has *irregular comparatives* and *superlatives* – that is, *more, most, less, least, better, best, worse, worst, further/farther,* and *furthest/farthest*, which do not follow the preceding rules. However, they behave similarly to Type 1 comparatives and, therefore, are grouped under Type 1.

These standard comparatives and superlatives are only some of the words that indicate comparison. In fact, many other words and phrases can be used to express comparisons – for example, *prefer* and *superior*. For example, the sentence "The iPhone's voice quality is superior to that of BlackBerry" says that the iPhone has a better voice quality and is preferred. Jindal and Liu (2006a) compiled a list of such words and phrases (still incomplete). Because these words and phrases usually behave similarly to Type 1 comparatives, they are also grouped under Type 1. All these words and phrases plus the preceding standard comparatives (*-er* words) and superlatives (*-est* words) are collectively called *comparative keywords*.

Comparative keywords used in nonequal gradable comparisons can be further divided into two groups. This grouping is very useful in sentiment analysis.

- *Increasing comparative.* Expresses an increased quantity of some property – for example, *more* and *longer.*
- *Decreasing comparative.* Expresses a decreased quantity – for example, *less* and *fewer.*

Objective of mining comparative opinions (Jindal and Liu, 2006b; Liu, 2010). Given an opinion document d, discover in d all comparative opinion sextuples of the form

$$(E_1, E_2, A, PE, h, t),$$

where E_1 and E_2 are the entity sets being compared based on their shared aspects A (entities in E_1 appear before entities in E_2 in the sentence), PE ($\in \{E_1, E_2\}$) is the preferred entity set of the opinion holder h, and t is the time when the comparative opinion is expressed. In other words, the representation says that the aspects A of entity sets E_1 and E_2 are compared, and the opinion holder h's opinion at time t is that entity set PE's ($PE \in \{E_1, E_2\}$) aspects A are superior. For a superlative comparison, we can use a special universal set U to denote an implicit entity set that is not given in the text. For an equative comparison, we can use the special symbol EQUAL as the value for PE.

As an example, consider the comparative sentence "Canon's picture quality is better than those of LG and Sony," written by Jim on 9-25-2011. The extracted comparative opinion is

({Canon}, {LG, Sony}, {picture_quality}, {Canon}, Jim, 9-25-2011)

The preceding representation may not be easily put into a database due to the use of sets, but it can be easily converted to multiple tuples with no sets. The sets based sextuples can be expanded into two tuples:

(Canon, LG, picture_quality, Canon, Jim, 9-25-2011)
(Canon, Sony, picture_quality, Canon, Jim, 9-25–2011)

As when mining regular opinions, to mine comparative opinions we need to extract entities, aspects, opinion holders, and times. The techniques used are similar, too. In fact, these tasks are often easier for comparative sentences because entities usually appear on the two sides of the comparative keyword, and aspects are also nearby. However, for sentiment analysis to identify the preferred entity set, we need a different method, which we will discuss in Section 8.3. We also need to identify comparative sentences themselves because not all sentences containing comparative keywords express comparisons and many comparative keywords and phrases are hard to identify

(Jindal and Liu, 2006b). In what follows, we focus on studying two comparative opinion–specific problems: identifying comparative sentences and determining the preferred entity set.

8.2   Identifying Comparative Sentences

Although most comparative sentences contain comparative and superlative keywords, such as *better*, *superior*, and *best*, many sentences that contain such words are not comparative sentences – for example, "I cannot agree with you more." Jindal and Liu (2006a) showed that almost every comparative sentence has a keyword (a word or phrase) indicating comparison. Using a set of keywords, they were able to identify 98 percent of comparative sentences (recall = 98 percent) with a precision of 32 percent based on their data set. The keywords were as follows:

1. Comparative adjectives (JJR) and comparative adverbs (RBR), such as *more*, *less*, *better*, and words ending with *-er*. These are counted as only two keywords.
2. Superlative adjectives (JJS) and superlative adverbs (RBS), such as *most*, *least*, *best*, and words ending with *-est*. These are also counted as only two keywords.
3. Other nonstandard indicative words and phrases such as *favor*, *beat*, *win*, *exceed*, *outperform*, *prefer*, *ahead*, *than*, *superior*, *inferior*, *number one*, *up against*, and so on. These are counted individually in the number of keywords.

Because keywords alone are able to achieve a high recall, they can be used to filter out those sentences that are unlikely to be comparative sentences. We just need to improve the precision for the remaining sentences.

Jindal and Liu (2006a) observed that comparative sentences have strong patterns involving comparative keywords, which is not surprising. These patterns can be used as features in learning. To discover these patterns, class sequential rule (CSR) mining was employed in the study by Jindal and Liu (2006a). CSR mining is a special kind of sequential pattern mining (Liu, 2006, 2011). Each training example is a pair (s_i, y_i), where s_i is a sequence and y_i is a class label – that is, $y_i \in$ {comparison, noncomparison}. The sequence is generated from a sentence. Using the training data, CSRs can be generated. For classification model building, the left-hand side sequence patterns of the CSRs with high conditional probabilities were used as features by Jindal and Liu (2006a). Naïve Bayes was employed for model building. Yang and Ko (2011) studied the same problem but in the context of the Korean language; they used a transformation-based learning algorithm, which also produces rules.

Classifying comparative sentences into four types. After comparative sentences are identified, the algorithm classifies them into four types: *nonequal gradable*, *equative*, *superlative*, and *nongradable*. For this task, Jindal and Liu (2006a) showed that keywords and keyphrases as features were sufficient. SVM gave the best results.

Over the years, several other researchers have studied this and related classification problems. For example, Li et al. (2010e) examined the problem of identifying comparative questions and the entities (which they called comparators) that are compared, but did not decide the types of comparison. For comparative sentences identification, they also used sequential patterns/ rules. However, their patterns were different: they decided whether a question is a comparative question and found the entities being compared at the same time. For example, the question "Which city is better, New York or Chicago?" satisfies the sequential pattern <which NN is better, \$C or \$C ?>, where \$C is an entity. These authors used the weakly supervised learning method introduced by Ravichandran and Hovy (2002) to learn such patterns. This algorithm is based on bootstrapping, which starts with a user-given pattern. From this pattern, it extracts a set of initial seed entity (comparators) pairs. For each entity pair, all questions containing the pair are retrieved from the question collection and regarded as comparative questions. From the comparative questions and entity pairs, all possible sequential patterns are learned and evaluated. The learning process is the traditional generalization and specialization process. Any words or phrases that match \$C in a sentence are extracted as entities. Both Jindal and Liu (2006b) and Yang and Ko (2011) also extracted compared entities, which we discuss in Section 8.5.

8.3   Identifying the Preferred Entity Set

Unlike with regular opinions, it does not make much sense to perform sentiment classification on a comparative opinion sentence as a whole, because such a sentence does not express a direct positive or negative opinion. Instead, it compares some shared aspects of multiple entities by ranking them to give a *comparative opinion*. In other words, it expresses a preference order of the entities based on their aspect comparison. Because most comparative sentences compare two sets of entities, the analysis of an opinionated comparative sentence seeks to identify the preferred entity set. For application purposes, one may assign positive opinions to the aspects of the entities in the preferred set, and negative opinions to the aspects of the entities in the not-preferred set. In what follows, we describe a method for identifying the preferred entity set based on the methods proposed by Ding et al. (2009) and Ganapathibhotla and Liu (2008).

These authors' methods extend the lexicon-based approach to aspect-based sentiment classification of regular opinions to classification of comparative opinions. In turn, they need a sentiment lexicon for comparative opinions. Just as with opinion (or sentiment) words of the base type, we can divide comparative opinion words into two categories:

1. *General-purpose comparative sentiment words.* For Type 1 comparatives, this category includes words like *better, worse,* and so on, which often have domain-independent positive or negative sentiments. In sentences involving such words, it is often easy to determine which entity set is preferred. In the case of Type 2 comparatives (formed by adding *more, less, most,* or *least* before adjectives/adverbs), the preferred entity sets are determined by both words. The following rules apply:

> Comparative Negative :: = Increasing_Comparative NE
> | Decreasing_Comparative PO
> Comparative Positive :: = Increasing_Comparative PO
> | Decreasing_Comparative NE

Here, PO (or NE) denotes a positive (negative) sentiment word or phrase of the base type. The first rule says that the combination of an increasing comparative (e.g., *more*) and a negative sentiment word (e.g., *awful*) implies a *comparative negative opinion* (on the left), so the entities on the left of the comparative keyword are not preferred. The other rules have similar meanings. Note that the preceding rules were discussed as composition rules for opinions in Section 5.2, where we used MORE for Increasing_Comparative, and LESS for Decreasing_Comparative.

2. *Context-dependent comparative sentiment words.* In the case of Type 1 comparatives, such words include *higher, lower,* and so on. For example, "Nokia phones have a longer battery life than Motorola phones" carries a comparative positive sentiment about *Nokia phones* and a comparative negative sentiment about *Motorola phones*; that is, *Nokia phones* are preferred with respect to the *battery life* aspect. However, without domain knowledge it is hard to know whether *longer* is positive or negative for *battery life.* This issue also arises with regular opinions, and this case was included in the composition rules for opinions in Section 5.2. Here, *battery life* is considered as a *PPI.*

   In the case of Type 2 comparatives, the situation is similar. However, in this case the comparative word (*more, most, less,* or *least*), the adjective/adverb, and the aspect are all important in determining the preference. If we know whether the comparative word is an increasing or decreasing comparative (which is easy to determine because there are only four of them), then the opinion can be determined by applying the four rules in point 1.

To deal with *context-dependent comparative sentiment words*, we refer to Section 6.2, where we used the pair (*aspect, context_sentiment_word*) as an opinion context. To determine whether a pair is positive or negative, Ganapathibhotla and Liu's (2008) algorithm uses a large external corpus of pros and cons from product reviews to determine whether the *aspect* and the *context_sentiment_word* are more associated with each other in pros or in cons. If they are more associated in pros, *context_sentiment_word* is most likely to be positive; otherwise, it is likely to be negative. However, because pros and cons seldom use comparative opinions, we must convert context-dependent comparative sentiment words in a comparative sentence to their base forms (e.g., from *longer* to *long*) before analyzing them using the pros and cons corpus. This conversion can be done using WordNet with the help of English comparative formation rules. This conversion is meaningful because of the following observation.

> **Observation.** If a base adjective or adverb is positive (or negative), its comparative or superlative form is also positive (or negative) – for example, *good, better*, and *best*.

After the comparative sentiment words and their orientations are identified, determining which entity set in a sentence is preferred is a fairly simple task. Without negation, if the comparative is positive (or negative), then the entities before (or after) *than* are preferred. Otherwise, the entities after (or before) *than* are preferred. For superlative sentences, the situation is similar except that the second entity set E_2 may not be explicitly given in the sentence – for example, "Dell laptops are the worst." In that case, we use the universal set U to indicate that.

8.4   Special Types of Comparisons

In dealing with comparative opinions, one of the biggest problems is how to identify whether a sentence expresses a comparative opinion and where the separation of the two sides of the comparison occurs. In this section, we focus on gradable comparisons, as they are most useful in practice. For those sentences using standard comparative (*-er*) and superlative (*-est*) adjectives and adverbs, it is relatively easy to determine whether a sentence expresses a comparison; likewise, it is relatively easy to identify the separation point, which is usually the *than* word. However, some special comparisons require special handling.

8.4.1   Nonstandard Comparisons

Although most comparative sentences in English use *-er* and *-est* words (plus *more, most, less*, and *least*), there are still a large number of comparisons that

do not rely on such words. These comparisons typically express user preferences, superiorities, winning or losing in contests, and so on. They may also
look syntactically different from standard comparisons, although they have the
same or similar meanings. Many such sentences actually give objective (rather
than subjective) information that expresses some desirable or undesirable state
for the entities involved. Thus, they represent fact-implied positive or negative
comparative opinions (see Section 2.4.2).

In what follows, we first list some phrases and then individual words that are
often used to express explicit or implicit comparisons. For each phrase, we
provide an example sentence to show its usage context.

ahead of
"In terms of processor speed, Intel is way ahead of AMD."
blow away
"AMD blows Intel away."
blow out of the water
"Intel blows AMD out of the water."
(buy | choose | grab | pick | purchase | select | stick to) over
"I would select Intel over AMD."
"I would stick to Intel over AMD."
X can do something positive Y cannot
"This earphone can filter high-frequency noise that Sony earphones
cannot."
cannot race against
"TouchPad cannot race against iPad."
cannot compete with
"Motorola cannot compete with Nokia."
(drop | dump) something for
"I dumped my TouchPad for a Coolpad."
(edge | lead | take) past
"AMD edged past Intel."
edge out
"Apple edged out BlackBerry."
get rid of something for
"I got rid of my BlackBerry for an iPhone."
gain from
"BlackBerry gained some market shares from iPhone."
(inferior | superior) to
"In terms of quality, BlackBerry is superior to iPhone."
"In terms of quality, BlackBerry is inferior to iPhone."
lag behind
"iPhones lag behind Samsung phones."
lead against
"Team A leads 3–2 against Team B."
lead by
"Team A leads Team B by 3–2."
lose to | against

"Team A lost the race to Team B."
on [a] par with
"TouchPad is on par with iPad."
(not | nothing) like
"My iPhone is not like my ugly old Droid phone."
"My iPhone is nothing like my ugly old Droid phone."
prefer to | over
"I prefer the BlackBerry to the iPhone."
subpar with
"iPhone is subpar with BlackBerry."
suck against
"iPhone sucks against BlackBerry."
take over
"iPhone takes over BlackBerry."
vulnerable to
"BlackBerry is vulnerable to iPhone's attack."
win against
"Apple wins the game against Samsung."

Apart from these phrases, many individual words can be used to express similar meanings. We list some of the words here: *beat, defeat, destroy, kill, lead, rival, trump, outclass, outdo, outperform, outplay, overtake, top, smack, subdue, surpass, win,* and so on.

"Honda beats Volkswagen in quality."
"BMW is killing Nissan."
"BlackBerry cannot rival iPhone."

Sentences containing such words must be analyzed with care because many of them do not express comparisons in some contexts due to different senses, idioms, and some specific usages. For example, the word *beat* used in the context of comparison has the sense of *defeat, subdue, superior to,* or *better than,* but *beat* can also mean music beat. The word appears in several idioms as well – for example, "beat me," "beat a dead horse," and "beat around/about the bush."

Determining whether a sentence using such a word expresses a comparison can be a challenge. One of the strong clues is whether more than one entity set is mentioned in the sentence. If no entity appears on each side of the word, the sentence is not likely to be a comparative sentence. This check is itself not simple because it requires the system to have entity recognition capability, and in many cases coreference resolution capability as well because an entity might have appeared in a previous sentence.

Other nonstandard comparisons remain hard to recognize. For example, the sentence "With the iPhone, I no longer need my iPad" is a kind of comparison, but it does not seem to include any strong clue that can be used to recognize this comparison in practice, except for the presence of two entities in the sentence.

8.4.2 Cross-Type Comparison

Comparative, equative, or superlative words and phrases are typically used to express their corresponding comparisons of comparative, equative, or superlative meanings. However, that is not always the case. One type of comparisons may be expressed using another type of comparative constructs.

Superlatives expressed using comparatives. Use comparative words to express superlative meanings in two main ways:

1. By explicitly or implicitly comparing with every other entity. For example:

   "This phone is *better than* every other phone."

   This sentence actually says "This phone is the best." In analyzing such sentences, the system should realize that the second entity set in the comparison is the universal set U, as *every other phone* appeared after the comparative word *better*.
2. By combining negation and comparison involving a phrase expressing the meaning of "everything else." For example:

   "You *cannot* find anything *better than* iPhone."
   "It does *not* get any *better than* iPhone."
   "*No* phone works *better than* iPhone."

   As in point 1, these sentences express superlative meanings. However, in this case, the first entity set is the universal set U. Such sentences often use *find* and *get* as their main verbs, although not always (e.g., the third sentence). The preferred entity sets often appear after the comparative words – for example, *better*.

Comparatives expressed with negated equatives. Combine a negation word and an equative expression to express a nonequal gradable comparison. For example:

   "The iPhone is not as good as this phone."

Regular opinions expressed with negated superlatives. When a negation word negates a superlative word in an opinion sentence, the sentence usually expresses a regular opinion rather than a comparative or superlative opinion. For example:

   "Moto X is not the best phone in the world."

Without any context, this sentence can be treated as negative about *Moto X*. But such sentences are really ambiguous. In some cases, the author may add a clause or even a separate sentence to clarify his real sentiment. For example:

   "Moto X is not the best phone in the world, but it is quite good."

In sentiment analysis, we can ignore the sentiment expressed in the first part of the sentence.

8.4.3   Single-Entity Comparison

In Section 8.1, we defined comparisons based on two entity sets and some of their shared aspects. However, some types of comparisons involve only one entity set. In dealing with such comparisons, if they express opinions, we can treat them as regular opinions rather than comparative opinions. It is not known how many types of such comparisons exist, but we list a few of them here. Our classification is not based on semantic meanings for human under-standing, but rather on how they can be recognized syntactically and dealt with in a sentiment analysis system – for example, based on POS tags and some specific words.

1. More or less than normal, usual, sufficient, enough, and so on.

> "This camera's build-in memory is *more than sufficient*."
> "iPhone provides *more than the usual* amount of memory."
> "After taking the drug, my blood pressure went much *higher than normal*."

2. More or less than a particular quality grade.

> "This car is *more than* just *beautiful*."
> "Lenovo's service agents are *more than happy* to help."

3. More or less than a particular quantity.

> "I have used this machine for *more than five* years."
> "This car cost *more than $150,000.*"

4. Comparing with some expectations or anticipations.

> "This car is more *beautiful than I expected*."

5. Comparing with the same entity or aspect in the past.

> "This phone works *better than in the past*."

6. Comparing with the feeling in the past.

> "I love this car *more than before* (or *ever*)."

7. Comparing different aspects.

> "This car is *more beautiful than lasting*."

This type of comparison needs special handling because it does not compare different entities, but rather two or more aspects of the same entity. For example, the author of the preceding example sentence is more positive about the appearance (or beauty) of the car than about its durability. This case is not covered by our definition in Section 8.1. Of course, it is possible to propose a new definition to cover this case, but it may not be necessary given that comparisons do not appear frequently. In practice, we can simply treat this as two regular opinions: positive about *appearance* and negative about *durability*.

8. Comparative or superlative words in idioms.

> "It is easier said than done."

In addition, many phrases and idioms contain *than*, but do not indicate any gradable comparison – for example, "other than," "rather than," "different than," and "look no further than."

8.4.4   *Sentences Involving* Compare *or* Comparison

It is no surprise that words *compare* and *comparison* are commonly used to express comparisons. However, sentences that use these words have very different syntactic forms than standard comparisons. They may or may not use any comparative or superlative words. I single out this type of sentence because of this reason, and also because they need a different method to analyze them. In fact, they are harder to deal with than the cases in which other comparison-type words are used.

In what follows, we list four kinds of phrases involving *compare* or *comparison*, classified mainly based on their syntactic differences. These differences help researchers to recognize them and deal with them individually. Their semantic meanings are similar except the last one.

(Compared | comparing) (with | to | and): used as participle phrases; that is, *compared* or *comparing* is not used as the main verb of the sentence.

> "Comparing the Camry with the Audi, the Audi is more fun to drive."
> "Compared to everything else in its class, BMW sets the standard."
> "Compared to the Camry the BMW is wonderful."
> "After comparing the Camry with the Prius we settled on the Prius."

Only the first sentence uses a comparative word (i.e., *more*); the other sentences do not use any comparative or superlative word. The first two sentences are easier to handle but the third and fourth sentences are difficult to deal with because no comma separates the two clauses in each sentence. Without the comma, the parser often makes mistakes, which causes errors in determining which entity set is preferred.

In these sentences, past participle (in the first three sentences) and present participle phrases (in the fourth sentence) appear before the main clauses of the sentences, but they can also appear after the main clauses.

"Hondas feel like tin cans compared to Volkswagens."
"The exterior of the Camry gives it a sleek look compared to the Accord."
"BMW is outstanding compared to Audi and Lexus."

In comparison (of | with): functions similarly to the preceding phrases.

"Mini is good in comparison with Smart."
"In comparison with BMW, Lexus is a better choice."
"In a comparison of the iPhone and (or to) the Lumia, Lumia has a good voice quality."

Compare (with | to | and | over): *compare* is used either as the main verb of the sentence or in the infinitive form. Such sentences are often hard to deal with because the clauses expressing the comparison may not indicate any sentiment or opinion. For instance, in the first example shown here, the opinion is expressed in the second sentence. This causes difficulty because the compared entities do not appear in the same sentence. To deal with such sentences, we need discourse-level analysis. In the second example, the sentiment is expressed in the second clause after *and*; in the third example, the opinion is only implied in the before clause. The fourth example uses an infinitive phrase of *compare* and it does not express any opinion.

"I drove and compared the BMW and the Lexus. I found the BMW is more fun to drive."
"I compared the BMW and the Lexus and found that the Lexus offers far more features."
"I compared the BMW and the Lexus before buying the BMW."
"I prepared a spreadsheet to compare the fuel and cost savings between the BMW and the Lexus."

No comparison | cannot compare: usually express opinions and are relatively easy to deal with.

"There is no comparison with the BMW when it comes to the interior space."
"The BMW cannot compare with the Audi."

However, in some cases they express no sentiment and can be hard to spot. For example:

"You cannot compare BMW and Lexus as they are for different purposes."
"I have no comparison results for these two cars."

8.5   Entity and Aspect Extraction

As mentioned at the beginning of Chapter 6, there are four main approaches to aspect and entity extraction, which is also called *opinion target extraction*. We reproduce them here:

1. Extraction based on frequent nouns and noun phrases.
2. Extraction by exploiting grammatical relations. There are two main types of relations: (a) syntactic dependencies depicting opinion and target relations, and (b) lexico-syntactic patterns encoding entity and part/attribute relations.
3. Extraction using supervised learning.
4. Extraction using topic models.

For target extraction from comparative sentences, these approaches still apply. In fact, the detailed methods discussed in Chapter 6 (for regular opinion sentences) for the first and fourth approaches can be directly used here with no modifications. The third approach is applicable as well, except that the features used for the two types of sentences may be different. The second approach is likewise applicable, except that the relations used for the two types of sentences have differences, but there is also a large intersection between them (see Section 6.2.1). Here we highlight three main differences.

1. The opinion and target relations used in Section 6.2.1 need to be extended because a comparative sentence compares two sets of entities. Thus, there is usually more than one opinion target. For example, in "Coke is better than Pepsi," the targets of the comparative opinion (represented by *better*) are *Coke* and *Pepsi*. Clearly, this special relation can be exploited for aspect and entity extraction.
2. A comparative sentence contains at least one entity, and usually two or more, except some special types of comparisons. A regular opinion sentence, however, may not mention any entity or even a pronoun refer-ring to it. For example, in "I brought a Lenovo laptop yesterday. The screen is really cool," the opinion target of the second sentence is *screen* but the sentence does not mention the entity to which it belongs; that entity appears in the first sentence. However, it is unlikely that a compara-tive sentence will not mention any entity. For example, in "I brought a Lenovo laptop yesterday. The screen is better than that of a Dell," if the second sentence does not mention a *Dell*, it will not be a comparative sentence.
3. Special characteristics of different types of comparisons can be exploited in extraction because they usually have different syntactic forms and thus

different dependencies between opinion (or sentiment) expressions and their targets. That is, targets and opinions are connected with their specific relations. For example, as we can see from Section 8.4.4, different ways of using *compare* or *comparison* require different relations for extraction.

To consider these observations in entity and aspect extraction using opinion and target relations, we simply need to design some additional dependency relations. That is fairly easy to do, and we will not discuss these relations further here. Obviously, such relations can be used as features for supervised learning as well.

8.6   Summary

Although some work has been done in this area, comparative opinions have not been studied as extensively as many other topics in sentiment analysis. Apart from identifying comparative sentences and their types, as we discussed earlier, several researchers have investigated the extraction of compared entities, compared aspects, and comparative words. Jindal and Liu (2006b) used label sequential rule mining, which is a supervised learning method based on sequential patterns. Yang and Ko (2011) applied the ME and SVM learning algorithms. Fiszman et al. (2007) attempted to identify entities with more of certain aspects in comparative sentences found in biomedical texts, but they did not analyze opinions in comparisons.

In general, standard comparisons involving *-er* and *-est* words and other words functioning similarly to them (e.g., *prefer* and *superior*) are relatively easy to analyze. Two problems are, however, especially challenging. The first problem involves comparative sentences using the word *compare* or *comparison*. Because their use can be very flexible, identifying aspects and/or entities that have been compared and the preferred entity set is not easy. The second problem is that many nonstandard comparison words have multiple senses. In some senses, they express comparison; in other senses, they do not. It is not easy to perform accurate word sense disambiguation. Using simple patterns to perform the task is usually not sufficient. Further research in this area is needed.

9   Opinion Summarization and Search

As discussed in Chapter 2, in most sentiment analysis applications, one needs to study opinions from many people; due to the subjective nature of opinions, looking at only the opinion from a single person is usually not sufficient. To understand a large number of opinions, some form of summary is necessary. Definition 2.10 in Chapter 2 defined a structured opinion summary called *aspect-based summary*, also known as *feature-based summary* in the reports by Hu and Liu (2004) and Liu et al. (2005). Much of the opinion summarization research is based on this definition. This form of summary is also widely used in industry. For example, both Microsoft Bing and Google Product Search use aspect-based summary in their opinion analysis systems.

In general, opinion summarization can be seen as a kind of *multidocument text summarization*. Traditional text summarization has been studied extensively in NLP (Das, 2007). However, an opinion summary is quite different from a conventional single document or multidocument summary (of factual information). Notably, an opinion summary should be (1) centered on entities and aspects and sentiments about them and (2) be quantitative. Traditional single-document summarization produces a short document from a long document by extracting some "important" sentences, while traditional multidocument summarization finds differences among documents and discards repeated information. Neither of them *explicitly* captures different topics/entities and their aspects discussed in the documents, nor do they have a quantitative perspective. The "importance" of a sentence in traditional text summarization is typically defined operationally, based on the summarization algorithms and measures used in each system. Opinion summary, in contrast, can be defined formally in a structured form and represented as structured objects (see Definition 2.10). Even output opinion summaries that consist of short text documents should still contain explicit structures.

After discussing summarization, we address the topic of opinion search or retrieval in this chapter. As the general web search has proven to be an extremely valuable service on the web, it is not hard to imagine that the opinion search will be of great use as well. However, an opinion search is very different from a general web search, and is considerably harder to

259

perform. Ideally, the opinion search should return summarized opinions for the user's search query. Sections 9.6 and 9.7 examines the current algorithms for opinion search, many of which originated from the TREC Blog Track evaluations.

9.1   Aspect-Based Opinion Summarization

Aspect-based opinion summarization has two main characteristics (Hu and Liu, 2004). First, it captures the essence of opinions: opinion targets (entities and their aspects) and sentiments about them. Second, it is quantitative, giving the number or percentage of people who hold positive or negative opinions about the entities and aspects. The quantitative side is crucial because of the subjective nature of opinions. The resulting opinion summary is a form of structured summary produced from the opinion quintuple introduced in Section 2.1. Figure 9.1 reproduces the opinion summary example in Section 2.2 about a digital camera. The aspect GENERAL represents opinions about the camera entity as a whole. For each aspect (e.g., picture quality), it shows the number of people who hold positive and negative opinions. <Individual review sentences> links to the actual sentences or full reviews or blogs. Because it is a structured form of summary, it can be easily visualized (Liu et al., 2005).

Figure 9.2a uses a bar chart to visualize the summary in Figure 9.1. In this figure, each bar above the X-axis shows the number of positive opinions about the aspect given at the top. The corresponding bar below the X-axis shows the number of negative opinions on the same aspect. Clicking on each bar, we can see the individual sentences and full reviews. Obviously, other forms of visualizations are also possible, such as pie charts.

Digital Camera 1:

    Aspect: **GENERAL**

Positive:	105	<individual review sentences>
Negative:	12	<individual review sentences>

    Aspect: **Picture quality**

Positive:	95	<individual review sentences>
Negative:	10	<individual review sentences>

    Aspect: **Battery life**

Positive:	50	<individual review sentences>
Negative:	9	<individual review sentences>

    ...

Figure 9.1 An aspect-based opinion summary.

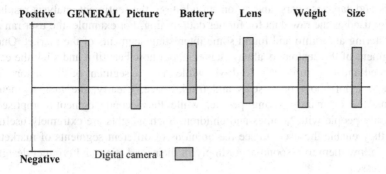

(a) Visualization of aspect-based summary of opinions about a digital camera

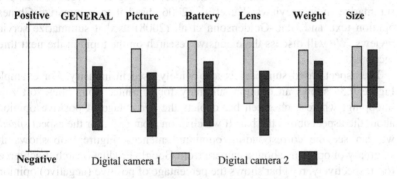

(b) Visual opinion comparison of two digital cameras

Figure 9.2 Visualization of aspect-based summaries of opinions.

Comparing opinion summaries for a few entities is even more interesting (Liu et al., 2005). Figure 9.2b shows the visual opinion comparison of two digital cameras. We can see how consumers felt about each of them along different aspect dimensions including the entities (the digital cameras) themselves.

Opinion quintuples actually allow one to provide many more forms of structured summaries. For example, by extracting time, one can show the trend of opinions on different aspects. Even without using sentiments, one can see the buzz (frequency) of each aspect mention, which gives the user an idea of which aspects people are most concerned about. In fact, a full range of database and OLAP tools can be applied to slice and dice the data for all kinds of qualitative and quantitative analyses.

For example, in one practical sentiment analysis application in the automobile domain, opinion quintuples of individual cars were mined first. The user then compared sentiments about small cars and medium-sized cars, German cars and Japanese cars, and so on. In addition, the sentiment analysis results were used as the raw data for further data mining. For example, the user ran a clustering algorithm and found some interesting segments of the market. One segment of the customers always talked about how beautiful and slick the car looked and how fun it was to drive, while another segment of the customers talked a lot about back seats and trunk space. Clearly, the first segment consisted of mainly young people, while the second segment comprised mainly people with families and children. Such insights are extremely useful as they enable the users to see the opinions of different segments of markets and allow them to respond accordingly in their marketing and product design processes.

Aspect-based summary has been the main summarization framework used in sentiment analysis research, for example, Zhuang et al. (2006) used it to summarize movie reviews, Ku et al. (2006) used it to summarize Chinese opinion text, and Blair-Goldensohn et al. (2008) used it summarize service reviews. We will discuss the extensive research on the topic in the next three sections.

The aspect-based summary is also widely used in industry. For example, Figure 9.3a shows an opinion summary for a printer from Microsoft Bing Shopping, where each green bar depicts the percentage of positive opinions about the aspect above the bar. If we click on a bar (e.g., for the aspect *speed*), we can see the corresponding opinion sentences. Figure 9.3b shows the summary of opinions about a camera from Google Product Search. Each green (or, respectively, red) bar shows the percentage of positive (negative) opinions about the aspect on the left. Clicking on an aspect or a bar causes the system to display its corresponding opinion sentences. Unfortunately, neither system can visualize comparisons of opinions on multiple products like that in Figure 9.2b, which I believe is a major weakness. Without a side-by-side comparison, it is hard for a user to know which product is better.

9.2   Enhancements to Aspect-Based Summaries

Over the years, researchers have suggested several improvements and refinements to the basic aspect-based summary. Carenini et al. (2006) proposed to integrate aspect-based summarization with two traditional text summarization approaches for factual documents – namely, sentence selection (or extraction) and sentence generation. We discuss the integration with the sentence selection approach first.

Carenini et al.'s (2006) system first identifies aspect expressions from reviews of a particular entity (e.g., a product) using the method described by Hu and Liu (2004). It then maps the aspect expressions to some given aspect categories organized as an ontology tree for the entity. These aspects in the tree

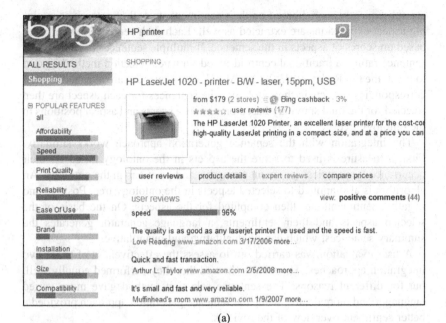

(a)

(b)

Figure 9.3 Opinion summaries of (a) Bing Shopping and (b) Google Product Search.

are subsequently scored based on their sentiment strength. Sentences containing aspect expressions are extracted as well. Each such sentence is then rated based on scores of aspects in the sentence. If multiple sentences have the same sentence rating, a traditional centroid-based sentence selection method is used to break the tie (Radev et al., 2003). All relevant sentences are attached to their corresponding aspects in the ontology. The sentences for each aspect are then selected for the final summary based on sentence scores and aspect positions in the ontology tree.

The integration with the sentence generation approach works similarly. First, a measure is used to score the aspects in the ontology based on their occurrence frequencies, sentiment strengths, and positions in the ontology. An algorithm is also applied to selected aspects in the ontology tree. Positive and negative sentiments are then computed for the aspects. On the basis of the selected aspects and their sentiments, a language generator generates the summary sentences, which can be qualitative and quantitative.

A user evaluation was carried out to assess the effectiveness of these two integration approaches. The results showed that they performed equally well, but for different reasons. The sentence selection method gave more varied languages and more details, while the sentence generation approach provided a better sentiment overview of the reviews.

In the study carried out by Tata and Di Eugenio (2010), the authors produced an opinion summary of song reviews similar to that in Hu and Liu (2004), but for each aspect and each sentiment (positive or negative) they first selected a representative sentence for the group. This sentence was expected to mention the fewest aspects, so that the representative sentence was tightly focused. The researchers then ordered the sentences using a given domain ontology by mapping sentences to the ontology nodes. Note that the ontology basically encodes the key domain concepts and their relations. The sentences were ordered and organized into paragraphs following the tree such that they appear in a conceptually coherent fashion.

Lu et al. (2010a) also used an online ontology of entities and aspects to organize and summarize opinions. Their method was related to the preceding two approach, yet also different. Their system first selected aspects that capture major opinions. The selection was done using frequency, opinion coverage (no redundancy), or conditional entropy. The system then ordered aspects and their corresponding sentences based on a coherence measure, which tried to optimize the ordering to best follow the sequences of aspect appearances in their original posts.

Ku et al. (2006) performed blog opinion summarization, and produced two types of summaries – brief and detailed – based on extracted topics (aspects) and sentiments on the topics. For the brief summary, their method picked up the document/article with the largest number of positive or negative sentences and used its headline to represent the overall summary of positive-topical or negative-topical sentences. For the detailed summary, it listed positive-topical and negative-topical sentences with high sentiment degrees.

Lerman et al. (2009) defined opinion summarization in a slightly different way. Given a set of documents D (e.g., reviews) that contains opinions about some entity of interest, the goal of an opinion summarization system is to generate a summary S of that entity that is representative of the average opinion and speaks to its important aspects. This paper proposed three different models, all of which choose some set of sentences from a review, to perform summarization of reviews of a product. The first model, called *sentiment match* (SM), extracts sentences so that the average sentiment of the summary is as close as possible to the average sentiment rating of the reviews of the entity. The second model, called *sentiment match + aspect coverage* (SMAC), builds a summary that trades off between maximally covering important aspects and matching the overall sentiment of the entity. The third model, called *sentiment-aspect match* (SAM), attempts not only to cover important aspects, but to cover them with appropriate sentiment. A comprehensive evaluation using human users was conducted to compare the three types of summaries. The investigators found that although the SAM model was the best, it was not significantly better than the others.

Nishikawa et al. (2010b) presented a more sophisticated summarization technique that generates a traditional text summary by selecting and ordering sentences taken from multiple reviews, considering both the informativeness and the readability of the final summary. Informativeness was defined as the sum of frequency of each aspect–sentiment pair. Readability was defined as the natural sequence of sentences, which was measured as the sum of the connectivity of all adjacent sentences in the sequence. The problem was then solved through optimization. The authors further studied this problem using an integer linear programming formulation (Nishikawa et al., 2010a).

Ganesan et al. (2010) proposed a graphical model–based method to generate an abstractive summary of opinions. Yatani et al. (2011) extracted adjective–noun pairs as the summary.

For more advanced analysis, the summarization should include the reasons and qualifications for opinions. However, little work has been done on extracting and summarizing opinions at this level. One simple way to include these two types of information in the overall opinion summary is to first discover and cluster reasons and qualifications; the system should then present the main reasons (which represent problems or issues with the product being reviewed) and the main qualifications for the opinions. Opinion reasons are fairly frequent, but qualifications are rare and also harder to identify.

To visualize this type of summary, we can use Figure 9.2. When the user clicks the positive or negative bar, the system could show the clusters of reasons and qualifications ranked according to the sizes of the clusters.

9.3   Contrastive View Summarization

Several researchers have studied the problem of summarizing opinions by finding contrastive viewpoints. For example, a reviewer might give a positive opinion about the voice quality of an iPhone by saying, "The voice quality of the iPhone is really good"; another reviewer might say the opposite, "The voice quality of my iPhone is very bad." Such pairs can give the reader a direct comparative view of different opinions.

This problem was proposed by Kim and Zhai (2009). Given a positive sentence set and a negative sentence set, they performed contrastive opinion summarization by extracting a set of k contrastive sentence pairs from the sets. A pair of opinionated sentences (x, y) is called a *contrastive sentence pair* if sentence x and sentence y are about the same aspect, but have opposite sentiment orientations. The k chosen sentence pairs must represent both the positive and negative sentence sets well. Kim and Zhai formulated the summarization as an optimization problem and solved it based on several similarity functions.

Paul et al. (2010) explored this problem further. Their algorithm generates a macro multiview summary and a micro multiview summary. A macro multiview summary contains multiple sets of sentences, each representing a different opinion. A micro multiview summary contains a set of pairs of contrastive sentences, where each pair consists of two sentences representing two different opinions. The algorithm works in two steps. In the first step, it uses a topic modeling approach to extract both topics (aspects) and sentiments. In the second step, a random walk formulation (similar to PageRank; Page et al., 1999) is employed to score sentences and pairs of sentences from opposite viewpoints based on both their representativeness and their contrastiveness with each other. Along similar lines, Park et al. (2011) reported another method for generating contrastive summaries of opposing views in news articles.

In the study by Lerman and McDonald (2009), a different contrastive summarization problem was formulated. These authors wanted to produce contrastive summaries of opinions about two different products to highlight the differences of opinions about them. Their approach jointly models the two summarization tasks with the objective to explicitly optimize the summaries so that they maximally contract each other.

9.4   Traditional Summarization

Several researchers have studied opinion summarization in the traditional fashion – for example, producing a short text summary with limited or no explicit consideration of aspects (or topics) and sentiments about those aspects.

Beineke et al. (2003) proposed a supervised learning method to select import-ant sentences in reviews. Seki et al. (2006) proposed a paragraph-clustering algorithm for the same task.

Wang and Liu (2011) studied extractive summarization (selecting important sentences) of opinions in conversations. They experimented with both the traditional sentence ranking and graph-based approaches, but also considered features such as topic relevance, sentiments, and dialogue structure.

A weakness of such traditional summaries is that they give only limited or no consideration to target entities and aspects, and sentiments about them. Thus, they may select sentences that are not related to sentiments or aspects. Another issue is that such a summary is not quantitative. As we discussed earlier, the quantitative perspective is important in practice because one out of ten people hating something is very different from eight out of ten people hating something.

9.5   Summarization of Comparative Opinions

According to the definition of comparative opinions given in Section 8.1, comparisons are essentially preference orders. Thus, a graph-based summary is more appropriate to visualize them. In the graph, each node is an entity (e.g., a product or a business), and each direct edge between two nodes represents the mined pairwise preference order between the two nodes. Two pieces of information can be attached to the edge: (1) the specific aspect that has been compared about the two entities and (2) the ratio of the comparative positive opinion count and the total number of comparisons that have been made about this aspect. Because multiple aspects may be compared, multiple links may occur between two nodes, and their link directions may be different as well. The reasons for the comparative opinions and opinion qualifications can also be attached to each link.

So far, little work has been done on summarization of comparative opinions. Li et al. (2011c) made an attempt to study the problem using a similar but simpler approach. Future research or practice should give us a better idea about what might be a good way to summarize and present comparisons.

9.6   Opinion Search

We now turn to the problem of opinion search or retrieval. As with the general web search, it is easy to imagine that an opinion search will be of great use. Wouldn't it be nice if whenever you wanted to find opinions about an entity or topic, you could just submit a query to an opinion search engine with the name of the entity or topic, and the search engine would return the summarized opinions with attached reasons? Unfortunately, this ideal scenario is still far from reality because of the many challenges discussed in the preceding chapters.

In general, at least two types of opinion searches are of interest in practice:

1. Find public opinions about a particular entity or an aspect of the entity – for example, a particular digital camera or the picture quality of the digital camera, or a political candidate or issue.
2. Find opinions of a particular person or organization (i.e., opinion holder) about a specific entity or an aspect of the entity (or topic) – for example, Barack Obama's opinion about abortion. This type of search is particularly relevant to news articles, where individuals or organizations that have expressed opinions are explicitly stated.

For the first type of search, the user simply gives the name of the entity or the name of the aspect together with the name of the entity as the search query. For the second type of search, the user needs to additionally give the name of the opinion holder as the search query.

Similar to a general web search, an opinion search needs to perform two main tasks: (1) retrieve documents/sentences relevant to the user query and (2) rank the retrieved documents or sentences. However, there are also major differences. On retrieval, opinion search needs to perform two subtasks:

1. Find documents or sentences that are relevant to the query. This is the only task performed in the traditional search.
2. Determine whether the documents or sentences express opinions on the query topic (entity and/or aspect) and whether those opinions are positive or negative. This is the task of sentiment analysis. Traditional search does not perform this subtask.

Traditional web search engines rank web pages based on authority and relevance scores (Liu, 2006, 2011). The basic premise is that the top-ranked pages (ideally the first page) contain sufficient information to satisfy the user's information need. This paradigm is adequate for factual information searches because *one fact equals any number of the same fact*. That is, if the first page contains the required information, there is no need to see the rest of the relevant pages. For opinion searches, this paradigm suffices only for the second type of queries because an opinion holder usually has only one opinion about a particular entity or topic, and that opinion is contained in a single document or page. However, for the first type of opinion queries, this paradigm needs to be modified because ranking in opinion searches has two objectives. First, it needs to rank those opinionated documents or sentences with high utility or information content at the top (see Chapter 13). Second, it needs to reflect the natural distribution of positive and negative opinions. This second objective is important because in most applications the actual proportions of positive and negative opinions are critical pieces of information. Only reading the top-ranked result as in the traditional search is problematic, because the top result represents the opinion of just a single opinion holder. Thus, ranking in opinion searches needs to capture the natural distribution of positive and negative sentiments of the whole population in a summarized form. One simple solution to this problem is to produce two rankings, one for positive opinions and one for negative opinions, and to also display the numbers of positive and negative opinions.

Providing an aspect-based summary for each opinion search would be even better. However, this is an extremely challenging problem. As we have seen, generating an aspect-based opinion summary is already very difficult even with given entities and relevant corpora. It becomes ever more complex when we must account for arbitrary query entities or topics from the user and a general corpus containing opinions about all kinds of entities and topics.

9.7 Existing Opinion Retrieval Techniques

Current research related to opinion retrieval typically treats the task as a two-stage process. In the first stage, documents are ranked by topical relevance only, which is what a traditional information retrieval or search system does. In the second stage, candidate relevant documents are ranked again by their opinion scores. These scores can be acquired by using either a machine learning–based sentiment classifier, such as SVM, or a lexicon-based sentiment classifier using a sentiment lexicon and a score aggregation function that combines sentiment word scores and query term–sentiment word proximity scores. More advanced research models topic relevance and opinion simultaneously, and produces rankings based on their integrated scores.

To give a flavor of opinion search, we present an example system (Zhang and Yu, 2007), which was the winner of the blog track in the 2007 TREC evaluation (http://trec.nist.gov/). The task addressed was precisely opinion search (or retrieval). This system has two components: one for retrieving relevant documents for each query, and the second for classifying the retrieved documents as being opinionated or not-opinionated. The opinionated documents are further classified as positive, negative, or mixed (containing both positive and negative opinions).

Retrieval component. This component performs the traditional information retrieval (IR) task. It uses both keywords and concepts. Concepts are named entities (e.g., names of people or organizations) or various types of phrases from dictionaries and other sources (e.g., Wikipedia entries). The strategy for processing a user query is as follows (Zhang and Yu, 2007; Zhang et al., 2008). First, the algorithm recognizes and disambiguates the concepts within the user query before broadening the search query with its synonyms. Then, it recognizes concepts in the retrieved documents and performs pseudo-feedback so that relevant words are automatically extracted from the top-ranked documents to expand the query. Finally, it computes a similarity (or relevance) score for each document. with the expanded query using both concepts and keywords.

Opinion classification component. This component performs two tasks: (1) classifying each document into one of the two categories, opinionated or not-opinionated, and (2) classifying each opinionated document as expressing a positive, negative, or mixed opinion. For both tasks, the system uses supervised learning. For the first task, it obtains a large amount of opinionated (subjective) training data from review sites such as rateitall.com and epinions.com. Data are also collected from different domains involving consumer goods and services as well as government policies and political viewpoints. The not-opinionated training data are obtained from sites that give objective information, such as Wikipedia. From these training data, a SVM classifier is constructed.

This classifier is then applied to each retrieved document as follows. The document is first partitioned into sentences. The SVM classifier then classifies each sentence as opinionated or not-opinionated. If a sentence is classified as opinionated, its strength, as determined by SVM, is noted. A document is regarded as opinionated if it contains at least one sentence that is classified as opinionated. To ensure that the opinion of the sentence is directed at the query topic, the system requires enough query concepts/words to be found in its vicinity. The totality of the opinionated sentences and their strengths in a document, together with the document's similarity as assessed by the query, are used to rank the document.

To determine whether an opinionated document expresses a positive, negative or mixed opinion, a second classifier is constructed using reviews from review sites containing review ratings (e.g., rateitall.com) as the training data. A low rating indicates a negative opinion, while a high rating indicates a positive opinion. Using positive and negative reviews as training data, a sentiment classifier is built to classify each document as expressing a positive, negative, or mixed opinion.

Other approaches to opinion retrieval have also been explored in TREC evaluations. Readers are encouraged to read the papers at the TREC website (http://trec.nist.gov/). For a summary of TREC evaluations, refer to the overview papers from the 2006 TREC blog track (Ounis et al., 2006), the 2007 TREC blog track (Macdonald et al., 2007), and the 2008 TREC blog track (Ounis et al., 2008). In what follows, we discuss research published in some other forums.

Eguchi and Lavrenko (2006) proposed a sentiment retrieval technique based on generative language modeling. In their approach, the user first provides a set of query terms representing a particular topic of interest, along with the sentiment polarity (orientation) of interest represented either as a set of seed sentiment words or a particular sentiment orientation (positive or negative). Instead of treating topic relevance and sentiment classification as two separate problems, these authors' language modeling approach combines sentiment relevance models and topic relevance models with model parameters estimated from the training data, considering the topic dependence of the sentiment. Their experiments showed that explicitly modeling the dependency between topic (or aspect) and sentiment produced better retrieval results than treating them independently. A similar approach was proposed by Huang and Croft (2009), which scores the relevance of a document using a topic relevance model and an opinion relevance model. Both these works employed a linear combination of topic relevance and sentiment relevance for the final ranking.

Zhang and Ye (2008) used the product of the two relevance scores. The relevance formulation is also based on language modeling.

Na et al. (2009) used a lexicon-based approach for opinion retrieval. They also attempted to deal with the domain-dependent lexicon construction issue. A relevant feedback–style learning for generating a query-specific sentiment lexicon was proposed, which made use of a set of top-ranked documents in response to a query.

Liu et al. (2009) explored various lexical and sentiment features and different learning algorithms to identify opinionated blogs. They also presented results for a strategy combining both the opinion analysis and the retrieval components for retrieving relevant and opinionated blogs.

Li et al. (2010a) took a different approach. Their algorithm first finds topic and sentiment word pairs from each sentence of a document, then builds a bipartite graph to link such pairs with the documents that contain the pairs. The graph-based ranking algorithm HITS (Kleinberg, 1999) was applied to rank the documents, with documents being considered as authorities and pairs being considered as hubs. Each link connecting a pair and a document was weighted based on the contribution of the pair to the document.

In the study by Pang and Lee (2008b), a simple method was proposed for review search, which reranks only the top k topic-based search results by using an *idiosyncrasy* measure, defined based on the rarity of terms appeared in the initial search results. The rationale for this measure was explained in the paper. The assumption is that the search engine has already found good results and only reranking is needed to put reviews at the top. The proposed method is unsupervised and does not use any preexisting lexicon.

9.8 Summary

Unlike traditional text summarization, which produces short abstracts from long documents, opinion summarization needs to identify aspects and sentiments and to be quantitative (proportions of positive and negative opinions). So far, a great deal of research has sought to produce structured summaries based on aspect-based summarization framework.

In some applications, human users also like to have readable summaries. Structured summaries are clearly not suitable for human reading. Although several researchers have attempted to address the readability issue, the existing work is still not mature. One possible option is to generate natural language sentences based on the structured summary described in Section 9.1 using some language templates. For instance, the first bar in Figure 9.2b can be written as "70 percent of the people are positive about digital camera 1 as a whole." This, however, may not be the best sentence for people's reading pleasure. We expect future research to produce more human-readable opinion summaries that also provide quantitative data about aspects and sentiments. However, we should note that opinion summarization research cannot progress alone. It critically depends on results and techniques from other areas of the research on sentiment analysis – for example, aspect and entity extraction and aspect-based sentiment classification. Work in all these directions must go hand-in-hand.

In terms of opinion search, it would be very useful if a web search engine such as Google or Microsoft Bing could provide a general opinion search service. Both Google and Microsoft Bing already produce opinion summaries for reviews of some products, but their coverage remains limited. For entities and topics not covered at present, it is not easy to find opinions about them, because such opinions are scattered all over the Internet. Finding and extracting such opinions are formidable tasks because of the proliferation of diverse sites and the difficulty of identifying opinions that are relevant to searched entities or topics. Much further research is needed in this area.

10   Analysis of Debates and Comments

Opinion documents come in many different forms. So far, we have implicitly assumed that individual documents are independent of each other or have no relationships. In this chapter, we move on to two forms of social media contexts that involve extensive interactions of their participants and are also full of expressions of sentiments and opinions: debates/discussions and comments. However, the key characteristic of the documents in such media forms is that they are not independent of each other, in contrast to stand-alone documents such as reviews and blog posts. The interactive exchanges and discussions among participants make these media forms much richer targets for analysis. Such interactions can be seen as relationships or links both among participants and among posts. Thus, we can not only perform sentiment analysis, as discussed in previous chapters, but also carry out other types of analyses that are characteristic of interactions – for example, grouping people into camps, discovering contentious issues of debates, mining agreement and disagreement expressions, discovering pairwise arguing nature, and so on. Because debates are exchanges of arguments and reasoning among participants who may be engaged in some kind of deliberation to achieve a common goal, it is interesting to study whether each participant in online debate forums gives reasoned arguments with justifiable claims via constructive debates, or whether a participant just exhibits dogmatism and egotistical clashes of ideologies. These tasks are important for many fields of social science, such as political science and communications. Central to these tasks are the sentiments of agreement and disagreement, which are instrumental to these analyses. These additional types of analyses are the focus of this chapter.

Comments are posts that address online articles (e.g., news articles, blog posts, and reviews), videos, images, and so on. We use comments about online articles in our study in this chapter. Comments typically contain many types of information, such as views and opinions from the readers of the article about the article and/or its subject matter, questions to the author of the article or to other readers, and discussions among readers and between readers and the author of the article. Hence, comments comprise a mixture of reviews (of the article), debates/discussions, and questions and answers. In other words, they contain more types of dialogue acts than do debates/discussions. Although in general the topic of the article can be anything, articles on controversial topics often generate a large number of comments.

This chapter studies the existing mining and analysis research about debates and comments. It covers both the traditional supervised classification approach to solving some specific problems in this context and probabilistic modeling approaches that aim to capture both the rich content and complex user interactions.

10.1   Recognizing Stances in Debates

One of the interesting issues in debate analysis is to identify the stances of the participants. Researchers have attempted to address two main variations of the problem. Given a debate/discussion topic, such as "Do you support a tax increase?", and a set of debate posts from a set of participants:

1. Classify the participants into some predefined groups – for example, those who take a for-increase stance and those who take an against-increase stance.
2. Classify the posts into some predefined groups – for example, those that are for-increase and those that are against-increase.

Most techniques have exploited the interactions among participants to model the problem as a graph and used graph theoretical algorithms to perform the classification task. For example, Agrawal et al. (2003) proposed a graph theoretical algorithm to categorize newsgroup discussion participants for a topic into two classes: those who are "for" the topic and those who are "against" the topic. Thus, this approach solves the first problem. An interesting feature of this work is that it completely ignores the text content of the discussions. The authors observed that quoting and replying activities usually show disagreement with previous authors, which are used as clues for grouping. The graph is constructed as follows. Each participant forms a node, and each edge (i, j) between node i and node j represents that participant i has responded to a post by participant j. The algorithm then bipartitions the graph into two subsets F (for) and A (against) of participants. Specifically, the two sets are associated with a cut function $f(F, A)$, which is the number of edges crossing from F to A. It was shown that the optimal choice of F and A maximizes $f(F, A)$, which is the classic *maxcut* problem. However, to solve the problem more efficiently, Agrawal et al. (2003) used a spectral partitioning algorithm to partition the graph into two groups (or camps).

A solution of the second problem was attempted in the work by Thomas et al. (2006). Their technique aimed to determine from the transcripts of U.S. Congressional floor debates whether each speech represents support for or opposition to a proposed piece of legislation. This work integrated two factors in the classification: (1) each individual speech segment (analogous to a debate post in social media) classification based on traditional n-gram features and (2) the relationship among labels of speech segments that are characteristic of conversations. The whole classification problem was modeled as a graph, where each node represents a speech segment and each link represents a relationship constraint with a weight.

The algorithm developed by Thomas et al. (2006) comprises three steps. The first step trains a SVM classifier in which unigrams are used to classify each speech segment. The second step adds links to the graph by setting some constraints between nodes. Two types of constraints are used (1) speech segments from the same speaker should be labeled the same and (2) different-speaker agreement. In a debate, a speaker may refer to another speaker and express agreement or disagreement with him or her. Thus the system needs to classify agreement and disagreement, which is done with another SVM classifier based on the surrounding text where the referenced speaker was mentioned. The class labels (agree and disagree) are determined based on whether the two persons voted the same way. The SVM classification scores are used to add more links to the graph. The third step of the algorithm solves an optimization problem by finding graph minimum cuts.

Murakami and Raymond (2010) proposed another graph-based method that exploits the reply relationship and some local information to build the graph. The local information between two participants includes the number of agree, disagree, and neutral pairs in their exchanges. The three numbers are combined linearly to produce the link weight between two participants. The graph is then partitioned using a maxcut algorithm to separate supporting and opposing participants. This work thus solves the first problem.

Earlier work by Galley et al. (2004) classified posts into agreement, disagreement, backchannel, and other classes. It also exploited the relationships (called dependencies in the paper) among posts, along with many other traditional features in a Bayesian network–based classification method. Bayesian networks facilitate the encoding of dependencies. An example relationship is that if speaker B disagrees with speaker A, B is likely to disagree with A in his or her next speech addressing A.

These methods basically used the relational information between posts and between participants in addition to traditional features to solve the problems. They can all be seen as instances of *collective classification* (Sen et al., 2008), a relational learning framework for modeling and solving such problems. Several existing learning algorithms exist for collective classification, which work on a graph $G = (V, E)$, where $V = \{V_1, \ldots, V_n\}$ is a set of nodes and each node V_i is a random variable with a value domain, which is the set of class labels $C = \{C_1, .., C_k\}$. Each node typically is also associated with a set of features $F = \{F_1, .., F_m\}$. E is a set of edges, where each edge (V_i, V_j) represents a relationship. V is further divided into two subsets of nodes: L, labeled nodes, and U, unlabeled nodes. The task is to predict the label of each unlabeled node in $U(\subseteq V)$.

One of the simplest machine learning algorithms for solving this problem is the iterative classification algorithm (ICA). Unlike traditional instance-based classification, which has only features about each instance or example, the feature set for a node in ICA includes a set of relational features that are computed based on the neighbors of the node and its relationships with the neighbors. The algorithm runs iteratively because the labels of the nodes and the relational features can change in the classification process. We described the ICA method in Section 6.4.

Markov random fields (Kindermann and Snell, 1980) using the inference method of *loopy belief propagation* and the *mean-field* method can also be applied to the problem. Burfoot et al. (2011) performed a comparative study to compare Markov random fields and the mincut method used by Thomas et al. (2006) to analyze the congressional voting data. The results showed that Markov random fields and the mean-field method gave better results.

Somasundaran and Wiebe (2010) adopted the traditional supervised learning approach to solve the first problem of classifying stances of participants, but used sentiment lexicon and arguing expression features as the basis for the classification. Arguing expression features had not been used prior to this paper. The following types of features were used in the paper:

- *Arguing-lexicon features.* To produce these features, an arguing subjectivity-annotated corpus (Wilson and Wiebe, 2005) is first used to construct an arguing lexicon. Then, for each sentence of a post, the algorithm finds all positive and negative arguing expressions and determines the primary polarity or orientation. Finally, it attaches a label to each content word (noun, verb, adjective, or adverb): *ap* (for positive polarity) or *an* (for negative polarity).
- *Modal verb features for arguing.* Modal verbs such as *must, should,* and *ought* are usually good indicators of arguing. For every modal in a sentence, three features are created by combining the modal word with its subject and object.
- *Sentiment-based features.* This approach uses the subjectivity lexicon developed by Wilson et al. (2005), which contains not only positive and negative sentiment words, but also many neutral subjective words such as *absolutely, amplify, believe,* and *think.*

Unsupervised learning approaches can be used to solve the problem of determining stances in debates, too. Such an approach was proposed by Somasundaran and Wiebe (2009), who primarily used sentiment analysis to identify user stances in discussions about products, which are different from ideological discussions. For each side, it first mines the web to discover opinion target pairs that are associated with a preference for that side. This information and some discourse information are then combined in an integer linear programming framework to arrive at stance classifications.

Abu-Jbara et al. (2012) attempted a related but slightly different problem. They grouped the discussion participants into subgroups. Their unsupervised technique, also based on sentiment analysis, attempted to find opinion (or attitude) and target pairs. The target of an opinion can be an entity or another participant (or discussant). Two methods were used to find targets. The first method found frequent noun phrases in a manner similar to one of the methods introduced by Hu and Liu (2004). The second method used a named entity recognition system to identify named entities. The opinion target pair was produced based on dependency relations similar to those employed in the studies by Zhuang et al. (2006) and Qiu et al. (2011). Each participant was then represented with an attitude profile, a feature vector consisting of counts of positive/negative attitudes expressed by the discussant toward each of the targets. Using the vectors, clustering was applied to find groups. Further work reported by Abu-Jbara et al. (2013) performed the task of identifying how the participants in a discussion split into subgroups with contrasting opinions.

Other related work studying dialogue and discourse in discussions has focused on authority recognition (Mayfield and Rose, 2011), participant characteristics classification based on their posting contributions (Lui and Baldwin, 2010), dialogue acts segmentation and classification (Boyer et al., 2011; Morbini and Sagae, 2011), dialogue acts classification (Kim et al., 2010), and thread discourse structure (including interpost links and dialogue acts) prediction (Wang et al., 2011). These tasks, however, are not related to sentiment. In the next section, we will see that dialogue acts and topics can be modeled in a single framework, which can also identify language expressions that are indicative of these dialogue acts.

10.2   Modeling Debates/Discussions

Online debate/discussion forums allow people with common interests to freely ask and answer questions, to express their views and opinions on any subject matter, and to discuss issues of common interest. A large part of such discussions focuses on social, political, and religious issues. Such issues often inspire heated discussions/debates, in which people vigorously agree or disagree and argue with one another. These types of online ideological discussions on a myriad of social and political issues have practical implications in the fields of communication and political science, as they give social scientists an opportunity to study real-life discussions/debates on almost any issue and to analyze the behaviors of participants in a large scale. In this section, we discuss modeling of this form of interactive social media (Mukherjee and Liu, 2012c; Mukherjee et al., 2013c). Given a set of discussion/debate posts, we aim to perform the following tasks:

1. Discover expressions that people often use to express *agreement* (e.g., "I agree" and "you're right") and *disagreement* (e.g., "I disagree" and "you speak nonsense"). This will help produce a lexicon of agreement and disagreement (or contention) expressions, which is useful for many tasks of debate/discussion analysis.
2. Discover contentious topics or issues, which have the most disagreements among participants. This is important because a large part of social media is devoted to discussions/debates of contentious issues. Discovery of contentious issues has abundant applications. For example, in a political election, such issues can separate voters into different camps and be used to determine voters' political leanings or orientations. It is thus important for political candidates to obtain data on such issues.
3. Discover the nature of interactions between each pair of participants who have engaged in discussions or debates on certain issues. By *nature of interaction*, we mean whether the two participants mostly agree or disagree with each other in their exchanges.
4. Identify tolerant and intolerant participants in debates/discussions. Tolerance is a psycholinguistic phenomenon of discussions, and an important concept in the field of communications. This subfacet of deliberation refers to critical thinking and the exchange of rational arguments on an issue among participants who seek to achieve a consensus/solution (Habermas, 1984).

Although agreement and disagreement expressions are distinct from traditional sentiment expressions (words and phrases) such as *good, excellent, bad,* and *horrible,* they clearly express a kind of sentiment. These expressions are usually emitted during an interactive exchange of arguments. We then introduce the concept of *agreement–disagreement sentiment* (*AD-sentiment*) and explore analysis of debates as an extension to the traditional sentiment analysis. Agreement expressions are defined as having *positive* polarity, whereas disagreement expressions are defined as having *negative* polarity. Agreement and disagreement expressions are known as *AD-sentiment expressions* (*AD-expressions*). AD-expressions are instrumental for the analysis of debates.

Mukherjee and Liu (2012b) and Mukherjee et al. (2013c) proposed three statistical or graphical models to perform the aforementioned tasks. The first model, called the joint topic–expression (JTE) model, jointly models both discussion topics and AD-expressions. It thus provides a general framework for discovering discussion topics and AD-expressions simultaneously. Its generative process separates topics and AD-expressions by using maximum entropy priors to guide the separation. However, this model does not consider a key characteristic of discussions/debates – namely, authors quoting or mentioning the claims/views of other authors and expressing contention with or agreement on those claims/views. That is, interactions among authors and topics occur through the reply-to relation. To consider the reply-to relation, JTE was extended to the JTE-R model. Furthermore, the JTE-P model was proposed to consider author-pair structures.

10.2.1 JTE Model

The JTE model jointly model topics and AD-expressions. It belongs to the family of generative models for text where words and phrases (n-grams) are viewed as random variables. Each document is viewed as a bag of n-grams, and each n-gram (word/phrase) takes one value from a predefined vocabulary. Up to 4-grams (i.e., $n = 1, 2, 3, 4$) have been used in JTE. Note that topics in most topic models like LDA are usually unigram distributions over words, and they assume words to be exchangeable at the word level. Arguably, this offers a great computational advantage over more complex models taking word order into account for discovering significant n-grams (Wallach, 2006). The JTE model enhances the expressiveness by considering n-grams and preserving the advantages of exchangeable modeling (rather than modeling n-gram word order). Thus, both words and n-gram phrases are considered in the vocabulary.

For notational convenience, from now on we use *terms* to denote both *words* (unigrams) and *phrases* (n-grams). We denote the entries in the vocabulary by $v_{1...V}$, where V is the number of unique terms in the vocabulary. The corpus (document collection) of study is composed of $d_{1...D}$ documents. A document (e.g., debate/discussion post) d is represented as a vector of terms w_d with N_d entries. W is the bag of all observed terms in the corpus, with cardinality $|W| = \sum_d N_d$. Z denotes the topic assignments of all terms in all documents. Note that here we use different notations than those in Section 6.6 just to conform to the notations used in the original papers (Mukherjee and Liu, 2012b; Mukherjee et al., 2013c). For example, W and Z are w and z, respectively, in Section 6.6.1.

The JTE model is motivated by the joint occurrence of AD-expression types (i.e., *agreement* and *disagreement*) and topics in debate posts. A typical debate post mentions a few topics (using semantically related topical terms) and expresses some viewpoints with one or more AD-expression types (using semantically related agreement and/or disagreement expressions). This observation motivates the generative process of the model, in which documents are represented as random mixtures of latent topics and AD-expression types. Each topic or AD-expression type is characterized by a distribution over terms.

Assume we have $t = 1, \ldots, T$ topics and $e = 1, \ldots, E$ expression types in the corpus. In the case of discussion/debate forums, based on reading of posts, Mukherjee and Liu (2012b) hypothesized that $E = 2$. In such forums, one mostly finds two expression types: agreement and disagreement. However, the JTE and other models are general and can be used with any number of expression types.

Let $\psi_{d,j}$ denote the probability of $w_{d,j}$ being a topical term, with $r_{d,j} \in \{\hat{t}, \hat{e}\}$ denoting the binary indicator variable (topic or AD-expression) for the jth term of d, $w_{d,j}$. $z_{d,j}$ denotes the appropriate topic or AD-expression type index to which $w_{d,j}$ belongs. JTE parameterizes multinomials over topics using a matrix $\Theta^T_{D \times T}$, whose elements $\theta^T_{d,t}$ signify the probability of document d exhibiting topic t. For simplicity of notation, we will drop the latter subscript (t in this case) when convenient and use θ^T_d to stand for the dth row of Θ^T. Similarly, we define multinomials over AD-expression types using a matrix $\Theta^E_{D \times E}$. The multinomials over terms associated with each topic are parameterized by a matrix $\Phi^T_{T \times V}$, whose elements $\varphi^T_{t,v}$ denote the probability of generating v from topic t. Likewise, multinomials over terms associated with each AD-expression type are parameterized by a matrix $\Phi^E_{E \times V}$.

We now define the generative process of JTE (see Figure 10.1 for plate notation of JTE).

1. For each AD-expression type e, draw $\varphi^E_e \sim \text{Dir}(\beta_E)$
2. For each topic t, draw $\varphi^T_t \sim \text{Dir}(\beta_T)$
3. For each forum discussion post $d \in \{1 \ldots D\}$:
      i. Draw $\theta^E_d \sim \text{Dir}(\alpha_E)$
      ii. Draw $\theta^T_d \sim \text{Dir}(\alpha_T)$

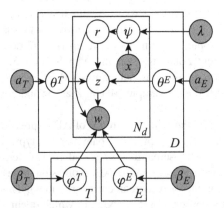

Figure 10.1 The JTE model in the plate notation. Shaded and unshaded nodes indicate observed and latent variables, respectively.

iii. For each term $w_{d,j}, j \in \{1 \ldots N_d\}$:

    a. Set $\psi_{d,j} \leftarrow MaxEnt(x_{d,j}; \lambda)$

    b. Draw $r_{d,j} \sim Bernoulli(\psi_{d,j})$

    c. If ($r_{d,j} = \hat{e}$)   // $w_{d,j}$ is an AD-expression term

        Draw $z_{d,j} \sim \text{Mult}\left(\theta_d^E\right)$

      else // $r_{d,j} = \hat{t}$, $w_{d,j}$ is a topical term

        Draw $z_{d,j} \sim \text{Mult}\left(\theta_d^T\right)$

    d. Emit $w_{d,j} \sim \text{Mult}\left(\varphi_{z_{d,j}}^{r_{d,j}}\right)$

The maximum entropy (Max-Ent) model was used to set $\psi_{d,j}$. The Max-Ent parameters can be learned from a small number of labeled topical and AD-expression terms that serve as good priors. The idea is motivated by the following observation: topical and AD-expression terms usually play different syntactic roles in a sentence. Topical terms (e.g., *U.S. Senate, sea level, marriage, income tax*) tend to be noun and noun phrases, whereas AD-expression terms (e.g., *I refute, how can you say, probably agree*) usually contain pronouns, verbs, wh-determiners, and modals. To utilize POS tag information, we place $\psi_{d,j}$ (the prior over the indicator variable $r_{d,j}$) in the word plate (see Figure 10.1) and draw it from a Max-Ent model conditioned on the observed context $x_{d,j}$ associated with $w_{d,j}$ and the learned Max-Ent parameters λ based on a set of feature functions defined on $x_{d,j}$. $x_{d,j}$ can encode arbitrary contextual information that may be discriminative. In the work by Mukherjee and Liu (2012b), the authors used the previous, current, and next POS tags and lexemes of the term $w_{d,j}$; that is, $x_{d,j} = [POS_{w_{d,j-1}}, POS_{w_{d,j}}, POS_{w_{d,j+1}}, w_{d,j-1}, w_{d,j}, w_{d,j+1}]$. For phrasal terms (*n*-grams), all POS tags and lexemes of $w_{d,j}$ are included. To learn the JTE model from data, exact inference is not possible. Instead, approximate inference using collapsed Gibbs sampling (Griffiths and Steyvers, 2004) has been employed. In what follows, we first give the joint distribution and then the Gibbs sampler.

To derive the joint distribution, we factor the joint according to the conditional distributions (causalities) governed by the Bayesian network of the proposed generative model [R denotes the topical ($\hat{t}$) or AD-expression ($\hat{e}$) assignments of all terms in the corpus].

$$P(W, Z, R) = P(W \mid Z, R) \times P(Z \mid R) \times P(R) \tag{10.1}$$

As a collapsed Gibbs sampler is used, θ and φ are integrated out to give the joint as follows.

$$P(W,Z,R) = \left[\prod_{t=1}^{T}\frac{B(n_t^{TV}+\beta_T)}{B(\beta_T)} \times \prod_{e=1}^{E}\frac{B(n_e^{EV}+\beta_E)}{B(\beta_E)}\right] \times \qquad (10.2)$$

$$\left[\prod_{d=1}^{D}\left(\frac{B(n_d^{DT}+\alpha_T)}{B(\alpha_T)} \times \frac{B(n_d^{DE}+\alpha_E)}{B(\alpha_E)}\right)\right] \times \left[\prod_{d=1}^{D}\prod_{j=1}^{N_d}p(r_{d,j}|\psi_{d,j})\right] \quad (10.2)$$

where $p(r_{d,j}|\psi_{d,j}) = (\psi_{d,j,\hat{\imath}})^u(\psi_{d,j,\hat{e}})^{1-u}$; $u = \begin{cases} 1, r_{d,j}=\hat{\imath} \\ 0, r_{d,j}=\hat{e} \end{cases}$ and the outcome probabilities of the Max-Ent model are given by (y is the prediction/class variable):

$$\psi_{d,j,\hat{\imath}} = p(y=\hat{\imath}\,|x_{d,j})$$

$$\psi_{d,j,\hat{e}} = p(y=\hat{e}\,|x_{d,j})$$

$$p(y|x_{d,j}) = \frac{\exp\left(\sum_{i=1}^{n}\lambda_i f_i(x_{d,j},y)\right)}{\sum_{y\in\{\hat{\imath},\hat{e}\}}\exp\left(\sum_{i=1}^{n}\lambda_i f_i(x_{d,j},y)\right)}$$

Here, $\lambda_{1...n}$ are the parameters of the learned Max-Ent model corresponding to the n binary feature functions $f_{1...n}$ from Max-Ent. $n_{t,v}^{TV}$ and $n_{e,v}^{EV}$ denote the number of times term v was assigned to topic t and expression type e, respectively. $B(\cdot)$ is the multinomial Beta function $B(\vec{x}) = \frac{\prod_{i=1}^{\dim(\vec{x})}\Gamma(x_i)}{\Gamma\left(\sum_{i=1}^{\dim(\vec{x})}x_i\right)}$.

$n_{d,t}^{DT}$ and $n_{d,e}^{DE}$ denote the number of terms in document d that were assigned to topic t and AD-expression type e, respectively. n_t^{TV}, n_e^{EV}, n_d^{DT}, and n_d^{DE} denote the corresponding row vectors.

Posterior inference is done using Gibbs sampling, a form of the Markov Chain Monte Carlo (MCMC) method in which a Markov chain is constructed to have a particular stationary distribution. In our case, we want to construct a Markov chain that converges to the posterior distribution over R and Z conditioned on the observed data. We only need to sample z and r, as we use collapsed Gibbs sampling and the dependencies of θ and φ have already been integrated out analytically in the joint. Denoting the random variables $\{w,z,r\}$ by singular subscripts $\{w_k, z_k, r_k\}$, $k_{1...K}$, $K = \sum_d N_d$, a single iteration consists of performing the following sampling:

$$p(z_k = t, r_k = \hat{t}|Z_{\neg k}, W_{\neg k}, R_{\neg k}, w_k = v) \propto$$

$$\frac{n_{d,t\neg k}^{DT} + \alpha_T}{n_{d,(\cdot)\neg k}^{DT} + T\alpha_T} \times \frac{n_{t,v\neg k}^{TV} + \beta_T}{n_{t,(\cdot)\neg k}^{TV} + V\beta_T} \times \frac{\exp\left(\sum_{i=1}^n \lambda_i f_i(x_{d,j}, \hat{t})\right)}{\sum_{y \in \{\hat{t},\hat{e}\}} \exp\left(\sum_{i=1}^n \lambda_i f_i(x_{d,j}, y)\right)} \quad (10.3)$$

$$p(z_k = e, r_k = \hat{e}|Z_{\neg k}, W_{\neg k}, R_{\neg k}, w_k = v) \propto$$

$$\frac{n_{d,e\neg k}^{DE} + \alpha_E}{n_{d,(\cdot)\neg k}^{DE} + E\alpha_E} \times \frac{n_{e,v\neg k}^{EV} + \beta_E}{n_{e,(\cdot)\neg k}^{EV} + V\beta_E} \times \frac{\exp\left(\sum_{i=1}^n \lambda_i f_i(x_{d,j}, \hat{e})\right)}{\sum_{y \in \{\hat{t},\hat{e}\}} \exp\left(\sum_{i=1}^n \lambda_i f_i(x_{d,j}, y)\right)} \quad (10.4)$$

where $k = (d, j)$ denotes the jth term of document d, and the subscript $\neg k$ denotes assignments excluding the term at k. Omission of the latter index denoted by $(\cdot)$ represents the marginalized sum over the latter index. The conditional probabilities in Equation (10.3) and Equation (10.4) were derived by applying the chain rule on the joint distribution. A blocked sampler was employed in which r and z were sampled jointly, as this improves convergence and reduces autocorrelation of the Gibbs sampler (Rosen-Zvi et al., 2004).

Here we give a list of disagreement or AD-expressions and a list of agreement expressions discovered by JTE from a debate data set.

Contention expressions, $\Phi_{Contention}^E$: disagree, I don't, oppose, I disagree, reject, I reject, I refute, I refuse, doubt, nonsense, I contest, dispute, completely disagree, don't accept, don't agree, your claim isn't, incorrect, hogwash, ridiculous, I would disagree, false, I don't buy your, I really doubt, your nonsense, can you prove, argument fails, you fail to, your assertions, bullshit, sheer nonsense, doesn't make sense, why do you, you have no clue, how can you say, do you even, absolute nonsense, contradict yourself, absolutely not, you don't understand

Agreement expressions, $\Phi_{Agreement}^E$: agree, correct, yes, true, accept, I agree, right, indeed correct, I accept, are right, valid, I concede, is valid, you are right, would agree, agree completely, yes indeed, you're correct, valid point, proves, do accept, support, agree with you, I do support, rightly said, absolutely, completely agree, well put, very true, well said, personally agree, exactly, very well put, absolutely correct, kudos, acknowledge, point taken, partially agree, agree entirely, and so on.

10.2.2   JTE-R Model: Encoding Reply Relations

The JTE model does not consider interactions among participants, which contain rich information that can be exploited in modeling. We now improve upon JTE by encoding the reply-to relations. Authors usually reply to each other's viewpoints by explicitly mentioning the user name using @name and/or by quoting others' posts. For easy presentation, we refer both cases as *quoting* from now on. Considering reply-to relations, the new model is called JTE-R (Figure 10.2). This model is based on the following observation:

> **Observation.** Whenever a post d replies to the viewpoints in some other posts by quoting them, d and the posts quoted by d should have similar topic distributions.

This observation indicates that the JTE-R model needs to depart from typical topic models where there is no topical interaction among documents; that is, documents are treated as being independent of one another. Let q_d be the set of posts quoted by post d. Clearly, q_d is observed. When encoding this reply-to relation into JTE-R, the key challenge is to somehow constrain the topic distribution of d, θ_d^T to be similar to the topic distributions of posts in q_d. Specifically, we must constrain θ_d^T to be similar to $\theta_{d'}^T$, where $d' \in q_d$ (i.e., constraining topic assignments to documents) during inference while the topic distributions of both θ_d^T and $\theta_{d'}^T$, $d' \in q_d$ are latent and unknown a priori. To solve our problem, Mukherjee and Liu (2012b) exploited the following salient features of the Dirichlet distribution:

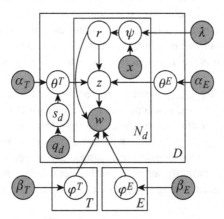

Figure 10.2 The JTE-R model.

1. Because $\theta_d^T \sim Dir(\alpha_T)$, we have $\sum_t \theta_{d,t}^T = 1$. Thus, it suffices that θ_d^T can act as a base measure for Dirichlet distributions of the same order.
2. The expected probability mass associated with each dimension of the Dirichlet distribution is proportional to the corresponding component of its base measure. That is, taking moments on $(X_1 \ldots X_n) \sim Dir(\alpha_1 \ldots \alpha_n)$, we get $E[X_i] = \frac{\alpha_i}{\sum \alpha_i}$. Thus, $E[X_i] \propto \alpha_i$.

Thus, to constrain a post d's topic distribution to be similar to the posts that it replies/quotes (i.e., posts in q_d), we need functional base measures, which govern the expected mass associated with each topical dimension in θ_d^T. One way to employ functional base measures is to draw $\theta_d^T \sim Dir(\alpha_T s_d)$, where $s_d = \sum_{d \in q_d} \theta_d^T / |q_d|$ (the expected topical distribution of posts in q_d). For posts that do not quote any other post, we simply draw $\theta_d^T \sim Dir(\alpha_T)$.

For a topic model with functional Dirichlet base measures, the sampling distribution is more complicated due to the topic interaction of the current post and quoted posts. Specifically, the document-topic distribution θ_d^T is no longer a simple predictive distribution; that is, when sampling z_n^d, the implication of each quoted document related to d by reply-to relations and their topic assignments must be considered because the sampling distribution for z_n^d in document d must consider its effect on the joint probability of the entire model. Unfortunately, this, too, can be computationally expensive for large corpora.

To circumvent this issue, it is possible to hierarchically sample documents based on the reply-to relation network using a sequential Monte Carlo method (Canini et al., 2009), or to approximate the true Gibbs sampling distribution by updating the original smoothing parameter (α_T) to reflect the expected topic distributions of quoted documents (s_d, α_T), where $s_{d,t}$ is the tth component of the base measure s_d, which is computed at runtime during sampling. The latter approach is taken in the study by Mukherjee and Liu (2012b) [see Equation (10.5)]. Experiments show that this approximation performs well empirically. The approximate Gibbs distribution for JTE-R while sampling $z_k^d = t$ is given by

$$p(z_k = t, r_k = \hat{\imath} | Z_{\neg k}, W_{\neg k}, R_{\neg k}, w_k = v) \propto$$

$$\frac{n_{d,t\,\neg k}^{DT} + s_{d,t}\alpha_T}{\sum_{t=1}^T \left(n_{d,t\,\neg k}^{DT} + s_{d,t}\alpha_T \right)} \times \frac{n_{t,v\,\neg k}^{TV} + \beta_T}{n_{t,(\cdot)\neg k}^{TV} + V\beta_T} \times \frac{\exp\left(\sum_{i=1}^n \lambda_i f_i(x_{d,j}, \hat{\imath}) \right)}{\sum_{y \in \{\hat{\imath}, \hat{e}\}} \exp\left(\sum_{i=1}^n \lambda_i f_i(x_{d,j}, y) \right)}$$

$$(10.5)$$

Discovering points of contention. On the basis of the model results, we can identify points of contention – topical terms on which contentions or disagreements have been expressed. The JTE and JTE-R models can be employed in the following manner with the estimated θ_d^T.

Given a contentious post d, the algorithm first selects the top m topics that are mentioned in d according to its topic distribution, θ_d^T. Let T_d denote the set of these top k topics in d. Then, for each disagreement expression $e \in d \cap \varphi_{Disagreemnt}^E$, we emit the topical terms of topics in T_d appearing within a word window of v from e in d. More precisely, we emit the set $H = \{w | w \in d \cap \varphi_t^T, t \in T_d, |posi(w) - posi(e)| \le v\}$, where $posi(\cdot)$ returns the position index of the word/phrase in document d. To compute the intersection $d \cap \varphi_t^T$ (and also $d \cap \varphi_{Disagreemnt}^E$), we need a threshold. This is necessary because the Dirichlet distribution has a smoothing effect that assigns some nonzero probability mass to every term in the vocabulary for each topic t. So for computing the intersection, we considered only terms in φ_t^T that have $p(v|t) = \varphi_{t,v}^T > 0.001$, as probability masses lower than 0.001 are due more to the smoothing effect of the Dirichlet distribution than to a true correlation. In an actual application, the values for m and v can be set according to the user's need. In the experiment, $m = 3$ and $v = 5$ were used, which are reasonable because a post normally does not discuss many topics (k), and the contention points (topical terms) should appear quite close to the contentious expressions. The JTE-R model was shown to produce better results (points of contention) than the JTE model.

10.2.3   JTE-P Model: Encoding Pair Structures

JTE-R builds upon the JTE model by encoding reply-to relations to constrain a post to have similar topic distributions to the posts it quotes. An alternative strategy is to make θ^T and θ^E author-pair specific, so as to estimate the nature of the pairwise interaction. The idea is motivated by the following observation.

> **Observation.** When authors reply to others' viewpoints (by @name or by quoting other authors' posts), they typically direct their own topical viewpoints with contentious (or disagreeing) or agreeing expressions to those authors. Such exchanges can go back and forth between pairs of authors. The discussion topics and AD-expressions emitted are thus caused by the author-pairs' topical interests and their nature of interactions.

Let a_d be the author of a post d, and $b_d = [b_{1...n}]$ be the list of *target authors* (we will call them *targets* for short) to whom a_d replies to or quotes in d. The pairs of the form $p = (a_d, c), c \in b_d$ essentially shape both the topics and AD-expressions emitted in d, as contention with or agreement on topical viewpoints is almost always directed toward certain target authors. For example, if c claims something, a_d quotes the claim in his post d and disagrees/agrees by emitting AD-expressions like "you have no clue," "yes, I agree," and "I don't think." Clearly, this pair structure is an important feature of discussion/debate forums. Each pair has its unique and shared topical interests and interaction nature (by which we mean contention/disagreement or agreement). Thus, it is appropriate to condition θ^T and θ^E over author-pairs. Standard topic models do not consider this piece of information.

The JTE model was extended to incorporate the pair structure. The new JTE-P model conditions the multinomial distributions over topics and AD-expression types (θ^T, θ^E) on authors and targets as pairs rather than on documents, as in the JTE and JTE-R models. In its generative process, for each post, the author a_d and the set of targets b_d are observed. To generate each term $w_{d,j}$, a target $c \sim Uni(b_d)$ is chosen at uniform from b_d, forming a pair $p = (a_d, c)$. Then, depending on the switch variable $r_{d,j}$, a topic or an expression type index z is chosen from a multinomial over topic distribution θ_p^T or AD-expression type distribution θ_p^E, where the subscript p denotes the fact that the distributions are specific to the author-target pair p who shape topics and AD-expressions. Finally, the term is emitted by sampling from topic or AD-expression specific multinomial distribution $\varphi_{z_{d,j}}^{r_{d,j}}$.

Figure 10.3 depicts the graphical model in plate notation corresponding to the preceding process.

Clearly, in JTE-P, the discovery of topics and AD-expressions is guided by the pair structure of the reply-to relations from which the collection of posts was generated. For posterior inference, we again use Gibbs sampling. Note that as a_d is observed, sampling c is equivalent to sampling the pair $p = (a_d, c)$. Its Gibbs sampler is given by

$$p(z_k = t, p_k = p, r_k = \hat{t} | Z_{\neg k}, W_{\neg k}, P_{\neg k}, R_{\neg k}, w_k = v) \propto$$

$$\frac{1}{|b_d|} \times \frac{n_{p,t \neg k}^{PT} + \alpha_T}{n_{p,(\cdot) \neg k}^{PT} + T\alpha_T} \times \frac{n_{t,v \neg k}^{TV} + \beta_T}{n_{t,(\cdot) \neg k}^{TV} + V\beta_T} \times \frac{\exp\left(\sum_{i=1}^n \lambda_i f_i(x_{d,j}, \hat{t})\right)}{\sum_{y \in \{\hat{t}, \hat{e}\}} \exp\left(\sum_{i=1}^n \lambda_i f_i(x_{d,j}, y)\right)}$$

(10.6)

$$p(z_k = e, p_k = p, r_k = \hat{e} | Z_{\neg k}, W_{\neg k}, P_{\neg k}, R_{\neg k}, w_k = v) \propto$$

$$\frac{1}{|b_d|} \times \frac{n_{p,e \neg k}^{PE} + \alpha_E}{n_{p,(\cdot) \neg k}^{PE} + E\alpha_E} \times \frac{n_{e,v \neg k}^{EV} + \beta_E}{n_{e,(\cdot) \neg k}^{EV} + V\beta_E} \times \frac{\exp\left(\sum_{i=1}^n \lambda_i f_i(x_{d,j}, \hat{e})\right)}{\sum_{y \in \{\hat{t}, \hat{e}\}} \exp\left(\sum_{i=1}^n \lambda_i f_i(x_{d,j}, y)\right)}$$

(10.7)

where $n_{p,t}^{PT}$ and $n_{p,e}^{PE}$ denote the number of times the pair p was assigned to topic t and expression type e, respectively. As JTE-P assumes that each pair has a specific topic and expression distribution, we see that Equations (10.6) and (10.7) share topics and expression types across pairs. Note also, that given A authors, there are $\binom{A}{2}$ possible pairs. However, the actual number of pairs

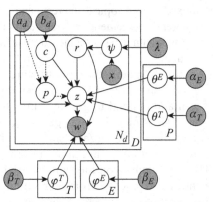

Figure 10.3 The JTE-P model. Note that the pair variable p is introduced for derivational convenience' thus its causalities are shown by dotted arrows.

(i.e., where the authors have communicated at least once) is much less than $\binom{A}{2}$. The experimental data used in Mukherjee and Liu (2012b) consist of 1,824 authors and 7,684 actual pairs.

Classify pair interaction nature. The model posterior on θ_p^E for JTE-P actually gives an estimate of the overall interaction nature of a pair – that is, the probability masses assigned to expression types $e = Ag$ (Agreement) and $e = DisAg$ (Disagreement). As $\theta_p^E \sim \text{Dir}(\alpha_E)$, we have $\theta_{p,e=Ag}^E + \theta_{p,e=DisAg}^E = 1$. Hence, if the probability mass assigned to any one of the expression types (agreement, disagreement) > 0.5, then according to the model posterior, that expression type is dominant; in other words, if $\theta_{p,Ag}^E > 0.5$, the pair is agreeing or else disagreeing. However, this approach is not the best possible strategy.

Mukherjee and Liu (2013) adopted a supervised learning approach, which gave better results. These authors randomly sampled 500 pairs from their data for labeling. The manual labeling resulted in 320 disagreeing and 152 agreeing pairs. The rest of the pairs were hard to classify by human labelers and were not used in the evaluation. The features were the top 2,000 AD-expressions from φ^E. Fove-fold cross-validation using SVM achieved an F-score of 0.78 for agreement and an F-score of 0.89 for disagreement.

10.2.4   Analysis of Tolerance in Online Discussions

We now discuss a different and important concept of debate: the psycholinguistic phenomenon of *tolerance*. Tolerance is a subfacet of *deliberation*, which refers to critical thinking and exchange of rational arguments on an issue among participants who seek to achieve a consensus/solution (Habermas, 1984).

Perhaps the most widely accepted definition of tolerance was developed Gastil (2005, 2007), who defined tolerance as a means to engage (in written or spoken communication) in critical thinking, judicious argument, sound reasoning, and justifiable claims through constructive discussion as opposed to mere coercion/egotistic clashes of ideologies. Mukherjee et al. (2013) adopted this definition, and also employed the following characteristics of tolerance (known as a "code of conduct") (Gutmann and Thompson, 1996; Crocker, 2005) in judging whether a debate participant is tolerant.

- *Reciprocity*. Each member (or participant) offers proposals and justifications in terms that others can understand and accept.
- *Publicity*. Each member engages in a process that is transparent to all, and each member knows with whom he is agreeing or disagreeing.
- *Accountability*. Each member gives acceptable and sound reasons to others on the various claims or proposals suggested by the member.
- *Mutual respect and civic integrity*. Each member's speech should be morally acceptable – that is, use proper language irrespective of agreement or disagreement of views.

Although the issue of tolerance has been actively researched in the field of communications for the past two decades, and has been investigated in multiple dimensions, existing studies are typically qualitative and focus on theorizing the socio-linguistic aspects of tolerance (Mukherjee et al., 2013c).

With the rapid growth of social media, the large volumes of online discussions/debates offer a golden opportunity to investigate people's implicit psyche in discussions quantitatively based on real-life data. That is, such data enable researchers to investigate their tolerance levels and their arguing nature, which are of fundamental interest to fields such as communications, marketing, politics, and sociology (Moxey and Sanford, 2000; Dahlgren, 2005; Gastil, 2005). Communication and political scholars are hopeful that technologies capable of identifying people's tolerance levels on social issues (often discussed in online forums) can provide statistics vital to predicting outcomes in political elections and in tailoring voting campaigns and agendas to maximize winning chances (Dahlgren, 2002).

Mukherjee et al. (2013c) studied the problem of classifying tolerant and intolerant participants in discussions. For their classification experiments, these authors manually labeled 436 participants from a political domain and 501 participants from a religion domain as tolerant or intolerant based on their posts in the debate forum volconvo.com. The guidelines for labeling were the "code of conduct" described earlier. Owing to the complex and interactive nature of debates/discussions, the traditional n-gram features were not sufficient for accurate classification.

As an alternative, Mukherjee et al. (2013c) proposed a generative model called the debate topic model (DTM) to discover some key pieces of information; DTM is a variation of the JTE model. The information revealed by the model was used to generate a set of novel features from the estimated latent variables of DTM that are capable of capturing authors' tolerance or intolerance psyche during discussions. These features include word and POS n-grams, factor expressions that are indicative of tolerance and intolerance, AD-expressions, overall arguing nature of the participant, behavioral response, equality of speech, and topic shift. The features were used in learning to identify tolerant and intolerant authors. They were quite involved, as surface features could not be directly extracted from the text or the posting behavior. Instead, most of them needed various posteriors of the DMT model to define them. Interested readers are encouraged to refer to the original paper for detailed explanations of the features and their formulas.

The final classification was done using SVM. Mukherjee et al. (2013c) found that the set of features was highly effective and outperformed several baseline feature sets.

10.3   Modeling Comments

We now turn to modeling of comments. This section is based on the work by Mukherjee and Liu (2012b), which models comments of online reviews. Online reviews enable consumers to evaluate the products and services that they have used. These reviews are also used by other consumers and businesses as a valuable source of opinions. However, such posts give only the evaluations and experiences of the specific reviewers. This is problematic because a reviewer may not be an expert of the product and may misuse the product or make other mistakes. Reviews may also omit opinions on certain aspects of the product that are interesting to readers. Some reviewers may even write fake reviews to promote or demote some products, a practice called *opinion spamming* (Jindal and Liu, 2008).

To improve their online review systems and user experiences, many review hosting sites allow readers to write comments about reviews. However, many reviews receive a large number of comments. It is difficult for a reader to read all of them and get their gist, so an automated comment analysis would be very helpful.

Review comments mainly contain the following information:

- *Thumbs-up or thumbs-down.* Some readers may comment on whether they find the review useful in helping them make purchase decisions.

- *Agreement or disagreement.* Some readers who comment on a review for a product may be users of the product themselves. They can state whether they agree or disagree with the review. Such comments are valuable as they provide a second opinion, which may even help identify fake reviews because a genuine user often can easily spot reviewers who have never used the product.
- *Question and answer.* A commenter may ask for clarification or about some aspects of the product that are not covered in the review.

Similar to debate modeling, here we want to model comment topics and different types of expressions, which indicate different types of comment posts:

1. Thumbs-up (e.g., "review helped me").
2. Thumbs-down (e.g., "poor review").
3. *Question* (e.g., "how to").
4. *Answer acknowledgment* (e.g., "thank you for clarifying"). Note that the lack of an expression for the answer: there are usually no specific phrases indicating that a post answers a question, except possibly starting with the name of the person who asked the question. However, typical phrases for acknowledging answers do exist, so there are *answer acknowledgment* expressions.
5. Disagreement (contention) (e.g., "I disagree").
6. *Agreement* (e.g., "I agree").

These expressions are called *comment expressions* (or *C-expressions*). The JTE model can be used for comment modeling as well, but with one caveat: C-expressions have six types ($E = 6$), whereas debate expressions have only two types ($E = 2$). Thus, JTE provides a model for extracting both these six pieces of information and debate topics. Its generative process separates topics and the six C-expression types by using a switch variable, and treats posts as random mixtures over latent topics and C-expression types. Maximum entropy priors are used to guide topic/C-expression switching. The topics in the comment context are usually product aspects.

The extracted C-expressions and topics from review comments are very useful in practice. First, C-expressions enable accurate comment classification. The thumbs-up, thumbs-down, and disagreeing posts can give us a good evaluation of the review quality and credibility. For example, a review with many *disagreeing* and *thumbs-down* comments is dubious. Second, the extracted C-expressions and topics help identify the key product aspects that trouble people in disagreements and in questions. With these pieces of information, comments for a review can be summarized. The summary may include, but is not limited to, the following:

1. Percentage of people who give the review a thumbs-up or thumbs-down
2. Percentage of people who agree or disagree (or contend) with the reviewer
3. Contentious (disagreed) aspects (or topics)
4. Aspects of the product about which people often have questions

These summaries are related to, but also different from, comment summarization works that summarize comments based on topics and clustering in relation to their associated articles (Hu et al., 2008; Khabiri et al., 2011; Ma et al., 2012).

10.4   Summary

In this chapter, we explored some current techniques for mining and analyzing debates/discussions and comments, which are important social media forms. Existing research is still in an early stage, and has mainly been done in computer science. For this area of research to truly flourish, we will need the participation of social scientists: they are the ones who truly understand the problems and their implications, and can set meaningful research agendas. I have been fortunate to have the opportunity to collaborate with some social science researchers. Through these collaborations, I realized that much remains to be done. In what follows, I use politics as an example to describe some research issues that are of interest to political scientists. Their current analytical methods are still primitive and mainly based on keyword search and manual coding and analysis, which cannot keep up with the rapid growth of online political discussions and participations.

Political scientists are interested in knowing the dynamics of how online conversation elevates issues, perspectives, and participants. They are also interested in understanding how the changing scope and means of participation influence the political agenda, public attitudes and preferences, and the resolution of conflict. More specific to this chapter, they want to analyze many features of debates and discussions, such as positions taken, contentious issues, frames/interpretations used to describe issues, beliefs about the implications of policies, and so on, and to examine the dynamics of interaction and the nature of exchange among participants. The Internet seems to hold the potential to invigorate public discussions of controversial issues, but it is important to study whether web publics engage in the hallmark features of deliberation. Specifically, does conversation move toward consensus on particular understandings or interpretations of issues? Do participants of opposing positions exhibit tolerance toward diverse perspectives? In other words, to what extent do partisan publics seem willing to bridge political groups and engage in healthy intergroup political discussion?

Political scientists are also seeking insight into why certain ideas gain popularity and why some individuals attain greater celebrity online. Moreover, the analysis of large-scale data sets about debates, discussions, and comments can help them understand the nature of the competition among arguments and claims in politics, in particular the extent to which popularity and durability are related to the source of ideas, their content and framing, and the context in which they are expressed. The knowledge gained from such analyses can help politicians, political organizations, think tanks, and the government better understand the dynamics of online preferences formation, enabling more informed policy decisions through speedy data processing of public opinions toward social, political, and economic issues.

Several existing works in computer science have ventured into some of these areas. I have discussed them in this chapter, but they are still quite preliminary and much more research remains to be done. Clearly, there is a tremendous scope for collaboration with social scientists to conduct funda-mental and impactful research. Although political science was used as an example here, I have no doubt that related studies will be of great utility to many other social sciences fields.

11 Mining Intent

Before performing an action, we almost always have the intent to perform the action first. In many cases, we also talk about or write about our intents. Although the concept of intent has been investigated in philosophy and psychology, researchers in these fields are usually not concerned with the language used to state intent or how to infer intent from written language computationally, which is our objective in this chapter. Studying intent computationally is just beginning, and our understanding of the problem remains limited.

Although intent and sentiment are generally regarded as different concepts, they are closely related, as we discuss in Section 11.1. Mining intent also has many practical applications. For example, if we find that a large number of Twitter posts say something like "I am dying to see *Life of Pi*," we can predict that the movie will do well at the box office. If someone writes, "I am looking for a car to replace my old Ford Focus, any suggestions?", that person clearly wants to buy a car and a car dealer can quickly recommend some new car models. If the dealer also has reviews of these cars, these reviews can be shown to this perspective buyer to act as persuasion at the same time. Mining intent information is also useful to social media hosting sites, which often use their user-generated content (posts) for advertising. If user intent can be recognized automatically, advertising can be based on intent and, therefore, should be much more targeted and effective.

This chapter is organized as follows. Section 11.1 defines the intent mining problem. Section 11.2 studies an existing method for identifying intent posts in social media based on transfer learning. Section 11.3 suggests a simple method to mine fine-grained intents of any kind in a massive scale from any social media site.

11.1 The Problem of Intent Mining

This section defines the concept of *intent*. Two definitions are presented: (1) a dictionary definition for human understanding and (2) a structured definition to help a computer identify the core components of an intent to operationalize the task of intent mining.

Definition 11.1 (Intent): *Intent* has two main meanings or senses:[1]

1. A course of action that a person or a group of persons intends to follow.
2. The goal or purpose behind a specific action or set of actions.

The intents expressed in the following sentences have the first meaning:

> "I really want to buy an iPhone 5."
> "I am in the market for a new car."

The following sentences have the second meaning:

> "He bought this car just to please his girlfriend."
> "This policy is to help the smart kids."

For this second type, some intents may be hidden, especially unethical intents. For example:

> "I love this car and it is definitely the best car ever."

The author of this sentence may have either one of the two intents: (1) to provide an honest opinion about the car or (2) to promote the car by writing a fake review.

In this chapter, we focus on the first sense of intent, partly because there are more commercial interests in the first sense, and partly because the intent in the second sense may be hidden and its analysis is highly subjective. In Chapter 12, we will deal with hidden intents of reviews by exploring ways to detect fake or deceptive reviews. From now on, when we use the word *intent*, we refer to its first sense/meaning.

Although intent and sentiment are different concepts, they are related in several ways. First, a person often has some positive or negative sentiment toward the involved entities before deciding the intended course of action about the entities. For example:

> "I am dying to see *Life of Pi*."
> "I am going to join the PROTEST in the city square tomorrow!!!!!!"

The intent in the first sentence is emotional, and the author also is likely to have a positive sentiment about the movie *Life of Pi*. The second sentence is emotional as well, because the author capitalized every letter of *protest* and used multiple exclamation marks. We call them *emotional intents*.

---

[1] www.thefreedictionary.com/

Second, even if someone is not emotional about a particular item, when that person expresses a desire to get a specific item, he or she should have a positive impression about the item. For example:

"I want to buy an iPhone 5."

Although this sentence shows no sign of sentiment or emotion explicitly, it should be safe to infer from this sentence that the person has a positive impression about *iPhone 5* because she has the desire to purchase it.

In fact, these examples represent the *sentiment of desire*, which differs from the traditional evaluation or appraisal type of sentiment in that the sentence authors have not had first-hand experience with the entities. Such sentiment of desire is important for many applications. For example, it can be used to assess how successful a marketing campaign is in arousing people's buying interests or how many people may be enthusiastic voters for a political candidate.

One interesting thing to note in the preceding example sentence is that the author wants to buy a specific product, *iPhone 5*, which we call the intent target. It is also possible that the intent target is not specific:

"I need to get a new camera."
"I am in the market for a new car."

In these cases, it is not clear whether the authors have any sentiment attached. We call the intents implied in the preceding three examples the *rational intents*, which may or may not imply any sentiment.

Third, some evaluative opinions are expressed as intents. For example:

"I want to throw this camera out of the window."
"I am going to return this camera to the shop."

The author of the first sentence does not literally mean to throw the camera out of the window, but rather is using a figure of speech to express a strong negative sentiment about the camera. This kind of "pseudo" intent is quite common in opinion documents.

We are now ready to provide a structured definition of intent, which will help operationalize the task of intent mining from text.

Definition 11.2 (Intent): An intent is a quintuple (*intended-action, intent-target, intent-intensity, holder, time*), where *intended-action* is the action that is intended, *intent-target* is the object of the intent, *intent-intensity* is the intensity of the intent (e.g., rational intent or emotional intent), *holder* is the person or the group of persons who has the intent, and *time* is the time when the intent is posted.

For example, in "*I plan to buy a camera*," the holder is *I*, the intended-action is *to buy*, the intent-target is *a camera*, and the intent-intensity is *rational*.

Following are some remarks about this definition:

- All five components are useful, although the first and the second are probably more important in practice, and form the core of an intent. Intended action is crucial because different actions mean very different things. For example, *to buy* and *to fix* a computer have completely different implications. Similarly, the target of intent is important. For example, *to buy* a *computer* is very different from *to buy* a *camera* for applications. The holder is also useful because the author's own intent is more meaningful to an application than someone else's intent described by the author. For example, "I plan to buy a new car" and "My friend plans to buy a new car" mean quite different things for advertisers because the author may or may not have any influence on her friend. Thus, showing an advertisement to the author may have little effect.
- Intent target can be specific (e.g., *iPhone 5*) or nonspecific (e.g., *a smart-phone*), which also has implications for applications. For example, in advertising, the two types of targets need different advertising actions. Thus discovering such information is useful.
- The scales of intent intensity can be designed according to the application need. In the preceding example, we used two scales, *rational intent* and *emotional intent*, which are analogous to the rational and emotion evaluations in Section 2.1.3.

The following definition distinguishes explicit and implicit intents.

Definition 11.3 (Explicit intent and implicit intent): An *explicit intent* is an intent explicitly stated in the text. An *implicit intent* is an intent that may be implied or inferred from the text. An implicit intent is uncertain.

For example, the sentence "I want to buy a new phone" explicitly expresses a buying intent. The sentence "How long is the battery life of an iPhone?" may or may not suggest an implicit intent of buying an iPhone. This sentence clearly has the explicit intent of finding out the battery life of an iPhone.

Most interrogative sentences actually have two possible intents: (1) an *explicit intent* of getting an answer to the question and (2) an *implicit intent* of doing something based on the answer. Of course, both intents of a question sentence can be explicit– for example, "Anyone know where I can buy an iPhone?" The sentence author wants to find a store and also wants to buy an iPhone. Because an explicit intent does not mean absolute certainty, there is no clear demarcation line between explicit and implicit intents. Their judgment is based on commonsense and pragmatics.

Intent mining can be seen as an instance of the information extraction problem (Sarawagi, 2008; Hobbs and Riloff, 2010). Traditional supervised sequence learning methods such as conditional random fields (CRFs) (Lafferty et al., 2001) and hidden Markov models (HMMs) (Rabiner, 1989) can be applied. Likewise, pattern-based methods are applicable because most intent sentences are indicated by some linguistic patterns as we can see from the preceding example sentences. A preliminary study by my group showed that by using a set of manually compiled linguistic patterns on a forum discussion data set, we could find buying intents with a recall of 95 percent and a precision of about 30 percent.

Section 11.2 discusses an intent mining study based on machine learning, which aimed to identify social media posts expressing some intents of interest (Chen et al., 2013a). This task, called *intent classification*, can be considered one step toward solving the intent mining problem because extracting individual components of intents should be done only in the intent posts. A start-up company called Aiaioo Labs already uses intent analysis for business applications. It presented a demonstration at the Coling-2012 conference (Carlos and Yalamanchi, 2012). However, neither of these systems extracts the intent components in the quintuple definition.

11.2   Intent Classification

In Chen et al. (2013a), intent classification is formulated as a two-class classification problem because an application may be interested in only a particular intent. *Intent posts* (positive class) are defined as posts that explicitly express a particular intent of interest. The other posts are treated as *nonintent posts* (negative class), although some of these posts may express some other kinds of intents. In Chen et al.'s experiments, the positive class was the intent *to buy*.

An important characteristic about this problem makes it amenable to transfer learning. For a particular kind of intent such as buying intent, very similar ways are used to express the intent in different application domains. This idea can be exploited to build a classifier based on labeled data in other domains and apply it to any new/target domain without labeling training data in the new/target domain. This problem, however, has two difficulties that make it hard for existing general transfer learning methods:

- In an intent post, the intent is typically expressed in only one or two sentences; that is, most sentences do not express intent. Additionally, words/phrases that indicate intents are limited compared to other types of expressions. In consequence, the set of shared features in different domains is small. Because most transfer learning methods try to extract and exploit these shared features, having just a small number of such features can make it hard for the methods to find them accurately, which in turn can result in weak classifiers.

- As mentioned earlier, in different domains, the means used to express the same intent are often similar. However, only the positive (or intent) features may be shared among different domains, while features indicating the negative (nonintent) class in different domains can be quite diverse. This gives a feature imbalance problem: the shared features mostly indicate the positive class, which also makes it difficult for a general transfer learning method to work accurately.

Chen et al. (2013a) proposed a specific transfer learning (or domain adaptation) method for intent classification, called Co-Class, to deal with these difficulties. This algorithm works by using labeled data from one or more domains, called *source domains* or *source data*, to help classify the *target domain* data, which have no labels.

Co-Class avoids the first problem by using a naïve Bayes–based EM-like (Nigam et al., 2000) algorithm to iteratively transfer learning from the source domains to the target domain, while exploiting feature selection in the target domain to focus on the important features in the target domain. Co-Class is also inspired by Co-Training (Blum et al., 2004), as it builds two classifiers and makes them work together on the target data. The algorithm starts by first building a classifier h using the labeled data combined from all source domains, and then applying the classifier to classify the unlabeled target (domain) data. On the basis of the target data labeled or classified by h, it performs a feature selection on the target data. The selected set of features is used to build two classifiers: h_S, from the labeled source data, and h_T, from the target data that have been labeled by h. The two classifiers h_S and h_T then work together to perform classification on the target data. The process runs iteratively until the labels assigned to the target data stabilize. In each iteration, both classifiers are built using the same set of features selected from the target domain; thus, the process is forced to focus on the target domain, and the knowledge in the source domains transfers gradually/iteratively to the target domain.

The detailed Co-Class algorithm is given in Figure 11.1. First, it selects a feature set Δ from the labeled source data D_L to build an initial naïve Bayes classifier h (lines 1 and 2). The feature selection is based on information gain (IG) (Yang and Pedersen, 1997). Next, h classifies each document in the target data D_U to obtain its predicted class (lines 3–5). A new target data set D_P is produced in line 6, which is D_U with added class labels (predicted in line 5). Line 8 selects a set of new features Δ from D_P. Two naïve Bayes classifiers, h_L and h_P, are then built using the source data D_L and predicted target data D_P, respectively, with the same set of features Δ (lines 9–10). Lines 11–13 classify each target domain document d_i again using the two classifiers.

Algorithm Co-class
Input: Labeled data D_L and unlabeled data D_U
1   Select a feature set Δ based on IG from D_L;
2   Learn an initial naïve Bayes classifier h from D_L based on Δ;
3   **for** each document d_i in D_U **do**
4         $c_i = h(d_i)$; // predict the class of d_i using h
5   **end**
6   Produce data D_P based on the predicted classed of D_U;
7   **repeat**
8   Select a new feature set Δ from D_P;
9   Build a naïve Bayes classifier h_L using Δ and D_L;
10   Build a naïve Bayes classifier h_P using Δ and D_P;
11   **for** each document d_i in D_U **do**
12            $c_i = \Phi(h_L(d_i), h_P(d_i))$; // Aggregate function
13   **end**
14   Produce data D_P based on the predicted class of D_U;
15   **until** the predicted classes of D_U stabilize

Figure 11.1 The Co-Class algorithm.

$\Phi(h_L(d_i), h_P(d_i))$ is the aggregation function to combine the results of two classifiers. It is defined as

$$\Phi\left(h_L(d_i), h_P(d_i)\right) = \begin{cases} + & h_L(d_i) = h_P(d_i) = + \\ - & Otherwise \end{cases}$$

The function Φ assigns the positive class to the document d_i if both classifiers classify it as being positive. Otherwise, it is classified as being negative. This is a crucial step for dealing with the second problem of feature imbalance – that is, strong positive features and weak negative features. This function restricts the positive class to require both classifiers to give positive predictions. After the algorithm converges, the classification results of the target domain data are the class labels produced in the last iteration.

Although the study of intent mining in full-text documents remains in its infancy, many researchers have studied the problem of *user* (or *query*) *intent classification* in web searches. The task in this case is to classify each query submitted to a search engine to determine what the user is searching for and/or whether she has a commercial intent such as to buy and to sell. Such intents are typically highly implicit, because people usually do not issue a search query like "I want to buy a digital camera." Instead, they just type the keywords *digital camera*. Current classification methods use user keyword queries, click-through data, and external data sources such as Wikipedia to build machine learning models for classification (Chen et al., 2002; Dai et al., 2006; Shen et al., 2006; Li et al., 2008; Arguello et al., 2009; Hu et al.,

2009). The intents discussed in this chapter are different, as they are explicitly stated in full-text documents.

11.3 Fine-Grained Mining of Intent

As mentioned earlier, little research has been done on fine-grained mining of intent components as defined in Section 11.1. In this section, we suggest a simple approach to performing this detailed level of mining on a social media platform, which usually includes a massive amount of data or user posts.

On a typical social media platform such as Twitter or Facebook, people consciously or unconsciously express their intents all the time. If you issue the search query "I want to buy" to the Twitter search engine, you will find a large number of Twitter posts (tweets) that express the desire or intent to buy all kinds of products. If you issue the query "I want to watch," you will find a large number of people who want to watch all kinds of movies and TV shows. If you issue some variations of these queries, you will get even more of such intent posts.

Knowing user intent can help merchants and advertisers promote their products and services online more accurately. It can also save time and effort for the users or post authors, because they do not have to find the needed information, products, or services by using a general search engine such as Google and browsing a large number of returned pages in the conventional manner. Instead, merchants or advertisers can directly respond to users' intents by showing them their relevant products and services.

The preceding search queries suggest a simple pattern matching–based method to mine fine-grained intent. This approach is reasonable because our earlier study showed that using manually crafted patterns can yield a very high recall of 95 percent in identifying intent sentences. Owing to the huge number of posts at any social media site, search is perhaps the most efficient method to get relevant information. However, because search has a low precision – only about 30 percent – we need more than just search. Search also cannot extract intent targets and other needed information.

As an alternative, we suggest the following simple approach:

1. Use a set of manually crafted patterns to extract candidate intent sentences. As the types of intents can be very broad (e.g., intents to buy, to watch, to go, to eat, and to stay), the patterns should reflect the desired intents of the application user.
2. Manually label some training intent and nonintent sentences from the search result to build a classifier. The classifier will classify the future candidate intent sentences to find those true intent sentences.
3. Extract intent targets from intent sentences using a supervised sequence learning method such as CRF. We do not need to extract intent type

because the patterns already include the information about the intent type. For example, if we use the pattern "I want to buy" or its variations such as "I plan to purchase" and "I intend to buy" to find buying intent posts, we already know the intent type – that is, *to buy*. Thus, we only need to extract intent targets in this step.

If an application also needs intent holders and times when intents are expressed, those data can be extracted as well. They are usually the authors of the posts and the times when the posts are made, which are simple to extract from posting pages of any social media site.

This approach has not been tested or validated using real-life experiments. Ideally, someone will build a system based on the approach in the near future. Researchers could also couple this system with an application. For example, once fine-grained intents are extracted, the site advertisers can provide the intent holders (or the authors) with information on their needed products or services right after they have posted their messages. For example, if I want to eat French food, I can post "I want to eat French food this evening" on Twitter. Twitter immediately recognizes my intent and gives me the information about local French restaurants and the customer reviews of the restaurants. Technically, it is already possible to build such a system.

This simple approach can be employed to do large-scale or massive intent mining on one or multiple social media sites because both the search (pattern matching) and the classification can be done very efficiently. With a wide range of applications, this may represent a good business opportunity for social media sites and their advertisers.

11.4   Summary

Intent has a tremendous potential for commercial applications. Advertising and recommendations are perhaps the two most direct applications. On social media platforms such as Twitter, Facebook, and discussion forums, people express their intents constantly. However, the research on intent mining is just starting.

This chapter discussed a machine learning approach for discovering intent posts. We are still unable to do fine-grained mining of intent components as defined Definition 11.2 in Section 11.1. A simple pattern-based approach has been suggested to mine intent at the fine-grained level. Such mining can be carried out at a massive scale because it is easy to design patterns for all possible domains.

Finally, we note that this chapter studied only explicit intents. The topic of recognizing implicit intents presents a much greater challenge due to the highly subjective nature and the difficulty of evaluation. The recent popularity of dialogue systems and chatbots makes intent mining even more important, however: to answer user questions or simply to chat with the user, the system must understand the intent of the user based on his or her utterance. Most task-oriented dialogue systems deal with this problem by using deep learning models. In addition, some stand-alone systems classify intents.

12   Detecting Fake or Deceptive Opinions

Opinions from social media are increasingly used by individuals and organizations for making purchase decisions and making choices at elections and for marketing and product design. Positive opinions often mean profits and fames for businesses and individuals. Unfortunately, that gives imposters a strong incentive to game the system by posting *fake reviews* or *opinions* to promote or to discredit some target products, services, organizations, individuals, and even ideas without disclosing their true intentions, or the person or organization for which they are secretly working. Such individuals are called *opinion spammers* and their activities are called *opinion spamming* (Jindal and Liu, 2007, 2008). An opinion spammer is also called a *shill*, a *plant*, or a *stooge* in the social media environment, and opinion spamming is also called *shilling* or *astroturfing*. Opinion spamming can not only hurt consumers and damage businesses, but also warp opinions and mobilize masses into positions counter to legal or ethical mores. This can be frightening, especially when spamming is about opinions on social and political issues. It is safe to say that as opinions in social media are increasingly used in practice, opinion spamming is becoming more and more sophisticated, which presents a major challenge for its detection. However, such offenses must be detected to ensure that social media continue to be a trusted source of public opinions, rather than being full of fakes, lies, and deceptions.

The good news is that both the industry and the research community have made a tremendous progress in combating opinion spamming. Several major review hosting sites are now able to detect a good proportion of fake reviews and fake reviewers. These efforts have already acted as a deterrent to opinion spamming and made it difficult for inexperienced spammers to succeed. However, the problem is still huge and a great deal of research is needed.

Spam detection in general has been studied in many fields. Web spam and e-mail spam are perhaps the two most widely studied types of spam. Opinion spam, however, is very different. There are two main types of web spam: *link spam* and *content spam* (Liu, 2006, 2011; Castillo and Davison, 2010). Link spam is spam on hyperlinks, which hardly exist in online reviews. Although advertising links are common in Twitter and forum discussions, they are relatively easy to detect, and are not considered to be opinion spam. Content spam adds popular (but irrelevant) words in target web pages to fool search engines into making them relevant to many search queries, but this hardly occurs in opinion posts – opinion posts are intended for human beings to read rather than for machines to consume. It thus does not make sense to add irrelevant words.

E-mail spam refers to unsolicited explicit advertisements. Opinion spam, especially posts aimed at promoting some target products and services, can be thought of as a form of advertisement. However, they are highly implicit and pretend to be honest opinions from real users or customers. This leads us to the major challenge of opinion spam detection:

> *Challenge of opinion spam detection.* Unlike other forms of spam, it is very hard – if not impossible – to recognize fake opinions by manually reading them. This makes it difficult to find gold-standard data to help design and evaluate detection algorithms. For other forms of spam, one can recognize them fairly easily.

In the extreme case, it is logically impossible to recognize spam by simply reading it. For example, one can write a truthful review for a good restaurant and post it as a fake review for a bad restaurant to promote it. There is no way to detect this fake review without considering information beyond the review text itself, simply because the same review cannot be both truthful and fake at the same time. Following are three example reviews. Can you, as a reader, figure out which reviews are fake? The answer is at the end of the chapter.

> *Review 1.* I want to make this review to comment on the excellent service that my mother and I received on the Serenade of the Seas, a cruise line for Royal Caribbean. There was a lot of things to do in the morning and afternoon portion for the 7 days that we were on the ship. We went to 6 different islands and saw some amazing sites! It was definitely worth the effort of planning beforehand. The dinner service was 5 star for sure. One of our main waiters, Muhammad was one of the nicest people I have ever met. However, I am not one for clubbing, drinking, or gambling, so the nights were pretty slow for me because there was not much else to do. Either than that, I recommend the Serenade to anyone who is looking for excellent service, excellent food, and a week full of amazing day-activities!

> *Review 2.* This movie starring big names – Tom Hanks, Sandra Bullock, Viola Davis, and John Goodman – is one of the most emotionally endearing films of 2012. While some might argue that this film was "too Hollywood" and others might see the film solely because of the cast, it is Thomas Horn's performance as young Oskar that is deserving

of awards. The story is about a 9-year-old boy on a journey to make sense of his father's tragic death in the 9/11 attacks on the World Trade Center. Oskar is a bright and nervous adventurer calmed only by the rattle of a tambourine in his ear. "I got tested once to see if I had Asperger's disease," the boy offers in explanation of his odd behavior. "The tests weren't definitive." One year after the tragedy, Oskar finds a key in his father's closet and thus begins a quest to find the missing lock. Oskar's battle to control his emotional anxiety and form and mend relationships proves difficult, even with his mother. "If the sun were to explode, you wouldn't even know about it for eight minutes," Oskar narrates. "For eight minutes, the world would still be bright and it would still feel warm." Those fleeting eight minutes Oskar has left of his father make for two hours and nine minutes of Extremely Emotional and Incredibly Inspiring film. Leaving the theater, emotionally drained, it is a wonder where a movie like this has been. We saw *Fahrenheit 9/11* and *United 93*, but finally here is the story of a New York family's struggle to understand why on "the worst day" innocent people would die. I highly recommend this movie as a must see.

Review 3. High Points: Guacamole burger was quite tall; clam chowder was tasty. The decor was pretty good, but not worth the downsides. Low Points: Noisy, noisy, noisy. The appetizers weren't very good at all. And the service kind of lagged. A cross between Las Vegas and Disney world, but on the cheesy side. This Cafe is a place where you eat inside a plastic rain forest. The walls are lined with fake trees, plants, and wildlife, including animatronic animals. A flowing waterfall makes sure that you won't hear the conversations of your neighbors without yelling. I could see it being fun for a child's birthday party (there were several that occurred during our meal), but not a place to go if you're looking for a good meal.

I am sure that you would agree with me that it is really hard to decide. This chapter uses the context of online reviews to study the opinion spam detection problem. Although not much research has been done in the contexts of other forms of social media, the ideas described in the chapter are applicable to other forms of social media such as forum discussions, blogs, and microblogs. Of course, each of these forms also has its special characteristics or features that can be exploited in the detection process. For example, for microblogs, social network structures are quite useful for detection. Likewise, each of them also has specific challenges that do not exist in reviews. Review ratings, for instance, are quite helpful in detecting fake reviews, but such ratings are not available in other social media forms. If sentiment ratings are needed in a detection algorithm, then an accurate sentiment analysis system is required.

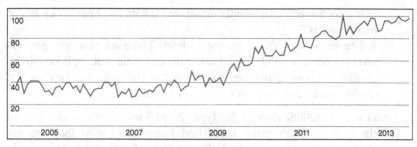

Figure 12.1 Google Trend result for the search query "fake review."

In recent years, numerous high-profile fake review cases have been reported in the news media. In some cases, fake reviewers even bluntly admitted that they wrote a large number of fake reviews. Most cases involve businesses (even highly reputable ones) that pay people to write fake reviews for them to promote their products/services and/or to discredit their competitors. Fake reviews are thus harmful not only to consumers, but also to businesses. I personally know of some fake negative reviews that caused real grief to businesses. Such reviews are especially damaging for small businesses, as they usually have only a few reviews available. Even one nasty fake review can potentially destroy a small business.

Increasingly, consumers are also becoming wary of fake reviews. The Google Trend chart for the query "fake review" (Figure 12.1) clearly shows a growing concern about fake reviews from the general public. This chapter examines this problem and presents current state-of-the-art detection algorithms.

12.1 Different Types of Spam

According to Jindal and Liu (2008), there are three main types of spam reviews:

Type 1 (fake reviews). These untruthful reviews are written not based on the reviewers' genuine experiences of using the products or services, but rather with hidden motives. They often contain undeserving positive opinions about some target entities (products or services) to promote the entities and/or unjust or false negative opinions about some other entities to damage their reputations.

Type 2 (reviews about brands only). These reviews do not comment on the specific products or services that they are supposed to review, but only comment on the brands or the manufacturers of the products. Although they may be genuine, they are considered as spam because they are not targeted at the specific products and are often biased. For example, a review for a specific HP printer might say, "I hate HP. I never buy any of their products."

Type 3 (nonreviews). These are not reviews. There are two subtypes: (1) advertisements and (2) irrelevant texts containing no opinions (e.g., questions, answers, and random texts). Strictly speaking, they are not opinion spam, as they do not give user opinions.

Jindal and Liu (2008) showed that types 2 and 3 spam reviews are rare and relatively easy to detect using supervised learning. Even if they are not detected, they do not pose a major problem because human readers can easily spot them during reading. This chapter thus focuses on type 1 spam, fake reviews.

12.1.1 Harmful Fake Reviews

Not all fake reviews are equally harmful. Table 12.1 gives a conceptual view of different kinds of fake reviews. Here we assume we know the true quality of the product. The objective of fake reviews in regions 1, 3, and 5 is to promote the product. Although opinions expressed in region 1 may be true, the reviewers do not disclose their conflicts of interest or hidden motives. The goal of fake reviews in regions 2, 4, and 6 is to damage the reputation of the product. Although opinions in region 6 may be true, the reviewers have malicious intentions. Fake reviews in regions 1 and 6 are not damaging, but fake reviews in regions 2, 3, 4, and 5 are very harmful. Thus, fake review detection algorithms should focus on identifying reviews in these regions. Some existing detection algorithms have already used this idea by employing some rating deviation features. Note that a fake neutral reviews category is not included in Table 12.1 because such fake reviews hardly serve the purpose of spamming and therefore seldom occur.

By separating regions 1 and 6 from regions 2, 3, 4, and 5, we also want to stress that those damaging fake reviews are only a subset of all fake reviews. Fake reviews in regions 2, 3, 4, and 5 are all harmful to consumers, but only those reviews in regions 2 and 4 are damaging to businesses. Because no one knows the percentage of harmful fake reviews and no one can tell which

Table 12.1 *Fake Review versus Product Quality*

	Fake Positive Review	Fake Negative Review
Good-quality product	1	2
Average-quality product	3	4
Poor-quality product	5	6

reviews should belong to which regions, it is hard to assess how much real damage has been done by fake reviews.

Although reviews in regions 1 and 6 do not harm consumers, they nevertheless create an unfair advantage for the product that their reviewers are trying to promote. That is why when some businesses are caught paying for fake reviews, they justify their action by claiming that others are also engaging in the same activity. After all, it is well known that positive reviews help sales. These unethical activities do create an unhealthy environment that can potentially render online reviews completely useless over the long run, because they largely become either implicit or hidden advertisements for products/services, or weapons for businesses to attack each other.

12.1.2 Types of Spammers and Spamming

Fake reviews may be written by many types of people – for example, friends and family, business owners and employees, competitors, freelance fake review writers, businesses that provide fake review writing services, dismissed former employees, unhappy current employees, and even genuine customers (who were given some benefits by businesses in exchange for writing positive reviews for the businesses). In other forms of social media, public or private agencies may employ people to post messages to secretly influence social media conversations and to spread lies and disinformation.

We classify fake reviewers or opinion spammers into two main categories: professional fake reviewers and nonprofessional fake reviewers.

Professional fake reviewers. They write a large number of fake reviews and get paid to do so. They may work as freelance fake review writers or work for companies that write fake reviews as part of their businesses. Professional reviewers are often easier to catch because they write a large number of fake reviews, which can leave linguistic and behavioral patterns easily discoverable by data mining algorithms. However, the issue is that by the time when they are caught, the damage might have already been done: it takes some time and many fake reviews for the system to detect abnormal writing styles and behavioral patterns. Thus, it is important to discover the patterns as soon as possible, which is challenging. To make matters worse, once an account of a fake reviewer is identified as engaging in spamming activities, the fake reviewer may simply abandon the account, register another account, and start spamming again from the new account.

Nonprofessional fake reviewers. These people do not write many fake reviews and often are not paid. They write mainly to help themselves, their businesses, or their friends. These fake reviewers may include friends and family of a business, business owners and their employees, competitors, dismissed former employees, unhappy current employees, and genuine customers who were given some incentives to write. They write fake reviews (1) to promote their own products and services or those of their friends, (2) to discredit their competitors, and (3) to hurt their former or current employers and their businesses. There are also some fake reviewers who just write for fun.

Because nonprofessional fake reviewers do not write many reviews, their reviews may not follow the same patterns as those of professional reviewers. However, this is not to say that there is no pattern at all. For example, suppose someone frequently checks a restaurant review page without writing anything. Then, one day, after seeing a negative review appear on the page, he quickly writes a strongly positive review. Clearly, this positive review is suspicious because the person could be the restaurant owner or someone closely associated with the restaurant who wrote the positive review to mitigate the impact of the negative review.

In addition, another group of people fall on the borderline between real and fake reviewers. These people are normal reviewers or even influencers who have contributed many genuine reviews and in the process built up their reputation. Based on that reputation, they are approached by some businesses and asked to promote their products for financial rewards. Some of these reviewers then start to spam for these businesses, at which point their body of reviews contains a mixture of genuine and fake reviews. Some even sell their accounts to spammers.

We can also categorize spamming into two main types: individual spamming and group spamming (Mukherjee et al., 2011, 2012). They have different characteristics that facilitate their detection.

Individual spamming. A individual spammer does not work with anyone. She just writes fake reviews herself using a single account (or userid) – for example, the author of a book.

Group spamming. A group of spammers or accounts may knowingly or unknowingly work together to promote or disparage some products or services. Group spamming is mainly carried out by professional review writers or fake review writing businesses. However, nonprofessional spammers may do it, too. Group spammers mainly work in the following two models or some ad hoc mixture of the models.

1. A group of spammers (persons) collude to promote a target entity and/ or to damage the reputation of another. The individual spammers in the group may or may not know each other or each other's activities. For example, a book author asks a group of friends to write positive

reviews for one of his new books. The friends may not know one another's activity, and they are normally not professional spammers.

2. A single person or organization registers multiple accounts (each with a different userid) and begins spamming using these accounts. These multiple accounts (or userids) behave just like a group working in collusion. This practice is called *sock puppeting*. In the case of an organization, different submodels are possible – that is, multiple people posting from these accounts, one person in charge of several accounts, or a mixture of both. Some so-called reputation management companies and government agencies work in this way.

Group spamming is highly damaging because due to the sheer number of members in a group, it can take total control of the sentiment on a product and completely mislead potential customers, especially at the beginning of a product launch. Although group spammers can also be seen as many individual spammers, group spamming has some distinctive characteristics that can give it away, as we will see in Section 12.6.

Clearly, a spammer might work individually on some occasions and as a member of a group at other times. She may also be a genuine reviewer in some cases because she also purchases products as a consumer and may write reviews about them based on her true experiences. All these complicated situations make opinion spamming a very challenging problem to solve.

12.1.3   Types of Data, Features, and Detection

Several types of data can be used for review spam detection:

Review content: the actual text content of each review including its title. From the content, we can extract *linguistic features* such as word and POS *n*-grams and other syntactic, semantic, and stylistic clues for deceptions and lies. However, linguistic features are often not sufficient because one can fairly easily craft a fake review that is just like a genuine one. In the extreme case, one can write a fake positive review for a bad restaurant based on one's true experience in a good restaurant.

Metadata about each review: data such as the star rating given to each review, the reviewer's userid, the review id, the time/date when the review was posted, the number of helpfulness votes, and the total number of votes. From these pieces of data, many features can be generated. For example, we can compute the number of reviews written by a reviewer in a day. If the number is too large, the reviewer should be viewed as suspicious. From the review ratings and product information, we may find that a reviewer wrote only positive reviews for a brand and only negative reviews for a competing brand. In Section 12.4, we will see that many such features/patterns can be mined automatically using data mining algorithms.

Web usage data. Every website records the activities that one person performs on the website. The data collected include the sequence of clicks, the time when each click is made, how long a user stays on a page, the time taken to write a review, and so on. Such data, called *side information*, are collected automatically by the web application server and represent the fine-grained navigational behavior of visitors. Specifically, each hit against the server, corresponding to an HTTP request, generates a single entry in the server access logs. Each log entry (depending on the log format) may contain fields such as the time and date of the request, the client's IP address, the resource requested, possible parameters used in invoking a web application, status of the request, HTTP method used, the user agent (browser and operating system type and version), the referring web resource, and, if available, client-side cookies that uniquely identify a repeat visitor. Using the IP address information, it is also possible to find the approximate geolocation of the user's computer. From such raw web usage data, many types of abnormal *behavioral patterns* of reviewers and their reviews can be defined. For example, we may find that multiple userids from the same computer posted multiple positive reviews for a product. These reviews are suspicious. Also, if the positive reviews for a hotel are all from an area nearby to the hotel, they are clearly not trustworthy. If a person monitors the review page of a business constantly and writes a positive review, this person is also suspicious because she cares about the business on the page too much: she may be the business owner.

Product information: information about the entity being reviewed – for example, product brand, model, type/category, and description. These pieces of information can also be exploited to generate abnormal patterns of reviewers and reviews.

Sales information: in general, business-related information such as the sales volume and the sales rank of a product in each period of time. This information is useful for spam detection because the number of products sold should roughly correlate to the number of reviews posted. If a product is not selling well but has many positive reviews, those reviews are hard to believe. Here "product" can also mean a business or a service.

These types of data can not only be used individually to generate useful features but can also be combined to produce more powerful features for spam detection. Furthermore, many of these features can be discovered automatically using rule mining (Section 12.4).

We can also classify the preceding data as either *public data* or *site private data*.

Public data: data displayed on the review pages of the hosting site – for example, review content, review metadata, and possibly some product information that is available.

Site private data: data that the site collects but that are not displayed on the review pages for public viewing. Such data mainly include web usage data, product data, and sales data.

Owing to privacy concerns of review hosting companies, none of the published algorithms has used any site private data so far. All algorithms are based on public data.

    Different types of detection. Existing research has studied three types of detection: *fake review detection, fake reviewer detection,* and *fake reviewer group detection.* These tasks are closely related, as fake reviews are written by fake reviewers and fake reviewers can also form fake reviewer groups. Thus, one type of detection can facilitate the other types of detection. Each type also has its own special characteristics that can be exploited in detection algorithms.

    In the next four sections, we focus on detecting individual fake reviews and reviewers. In Section 12.6, we examine the detection of fake reviewer groups.

12.1.4 Fake Reviews versus Conventional Lies

Fake reviews can be seen as a special form of deception (Newman et al., 2003; Hancock et al., 2007; Pennebaker et al., 2007; Vrij, 2008; Zhou et al., 2008; Mihalcea and Strapparava, 2009). Conventional deception refers to lies about some facts or personal feelings. Researchers have identified many deception signals in text. Many are specific to particular situations and domains, but some are broad signals across domains. Generally, lying/deception communications are characterized by the use of fewer first-person personal pronouns, more negative emotion words, fewer "exclusive" words, and more motion/ action words (Newman et al., 2003). The justification for these conclusions is summarized under three main psychological mindsets exhibited in deception:

Detachment. Several researchers (Knapp and Comaden, 1979; Newman et al., 2003; Vrij, 2008) have hypothesized that liars often try to avoid statements of ownership either to "dissociate" themselves from their words or due to a lack of personal experiences, resulting in fewer uses of first-person pronouns such as *I, me, my,* and so on, and more uses of third-person pronouns such as *she, he,* and *they.* In some cases, liars may also use fewer third-person pronouns (Newman et al., 2003).

Liars feeling guilty. Liars may feel discomfort and guilt either about lying or about the topic they are discussing (Knapp and Comaden, 1979; Vrij, 2008). This often translates into deceptive communications characterized by the use of more negative emotion words (e.g., *hate, worthless, sad*).

Lowering cognitive complexity. Liars need to make up false stories, which is a highly complicated cognitive task (Knapp et al., 1974; Vrij, 2008). Owing to the difficulty of fabricating a story, lies typically exhibit two additional characteristics:

1. *Using fewer exclusive words such as* but, except, *and* without. Sentences using such words often require a person to know the intricate details of a task or situation. Without true experiences, it is hard to know such details and, therefore, to use these words.

2. *Using more motion verbs.* Because lies are fabricated, due to the cognitive complexity required to construct a believable story, the easiest thing to do is to describe some actions using motion words such as *walk, move,* and *go.* It is much harder to create a detailed evaluation and judgment, as this task consumes significantly more cognitive resources if one has not experienced the situation firsthand.

Although fake reviews are related to conventional deception/lying, writing such reviews is a somewhat different cognitive process than lying about facts and feelings in the conventional sense due to the nature of fake reviews.

- In conventional deception, liars tend to use fewer first-person pronouns to "detach" themselves from lies. However, fake reviewers behave completely differently. They actually like to use more first-person pronouns such as *I, me, my, we, us,* and so on, rather than third-person pronouns; their intent is to make their reviews sound more convincing and to give readers the impression that their reviews are based on their true experiences and evaluations. We call this "attachment," as opposed to the "detachment" that characterizes conventional lies.

- Conventional liars may "feel guilty" and, in turn, use more negative emotion words. Fake reviewers may not have such guilty feelings due to their different states of mind and the practical scenarios in which they operate. They often have resolute motivations of inflicting spam. Their use of positive and negative opinion or emotion words is entirely contingent on whether they are writing positive or negative fake reviews. Additionally, in many cases, fake reviews may not be lies. For example, someone who writes a book may pretend to be a reader and write a review to promote the book. The review might express the true feelings of the author. Also, many fake reviewers might have never used the reviewed products/services, but simply tried to give positive or negative opinions. They are not lying about any facts they know or their true feelings.

However, fake reviews and conventional lies also share some similarities. The frequency of action/motion words does seem to be higher in fake reviews than in truthful reviews based on the study performed by Mukherjee et al. (2013a), just as is the case for conventional lies. This is not surprising because writing fake reviews is also a complex and demanding cognitive task. For the same reason, fake reviewers tend to use more general opinion words such as *great, good, wonderful*, and so on, rather than specific opinion words to evaluate specific features of products and services based on their actual performances.

We can also grossly classify fake reviewers into two categories: those who know the products or businesses well (e.g., business owners and their employees) and those who do not know the products or the businesses well (e.g., professional reviewers who are paid to write). Their writings can be quite different. Unfortunately, no studies of their linguistic style or word usage differences have been published as yet. On the basis of my general observations, I find that fake reviews from business owners and their employees often sound too knowledgeable about the business and thus read like advertisements, whereas fake reviews from paid reviewers who know little about the businesses often contain empty praises and lack depth or details. However, if one puts in enough time and effort, crafting a fake review that is just like a genuine review is not hard.

12.2 Supervised Fake Review Detection

Fake review detection can be naturally formulated as a classification problem with two classes, *fake* and *nonfake*. Supervised learning is then applicable. However, as we described earlier, the key difficulty is that it is very hard – if not impossible – to recognize fake reviews reliably by manually reading them because a spammer can carefully craft a fake review that is just like any genuine review (Jindal and Liu, 2008). Owing to this difficulty, there is no reliable fake-review and nonfake-review data set available to train a machine learning model to recognize fake reviews. Despite these difficulties, several supervised detection algorithms have been proposed and evaluated in various ways. This section discusses three such methods. In the next section, we describe a supervised learning experiment using the filtered and unfiltered reviews from Yelp.com.

To account for the unavailability of labeled training data for learning, Jindal and Liu (2008) exploited duplicate reviews. In their study of 5.8 million reviews and 2.14 million reviewers from Amazon.com, a large number of duplicate and near-duplicate reviews were found, indicating that review spam was a widespread phenomenon. Writing new reviews can be taxing, so many spammers use the same reviews or slightly modified reviews for different products. These duplicates and near-duplicates can be divided into four categories:

1. Duplicates from the same reviewer id on the same product
2. Duplicates from different reviewer ids on the same product
3. Duplicates from the same reviewer id on different products
4. Duplicates from different reviewer ids on different products

The first type of duplicates can result from reviewers mistakenly clicking the review submit button multiple times (which can be easily checked based on the submission dates). In contrast, the last three types of duplicates are most likely fake. Thus Jindal and Liu used the last three types of duplicates as fake reviews and the rest of the reviews as nonfake reviews in the training data for machine learning. They employed three sets of features for learning:

Review-centric features. These are features about each review. Example features include length of title, length of review, percentage of positive and negative sentiment words in the review, cosine similarity of the review and product description, percentage of the brand name mentions, percentages of numerals, capital letters and all-capital words in the review, and the number of helpful feedback citations. In the last case, in many review sites (e.g., Amazon.com), readers can provide feedback to each review by answering the question "Do you find this review helpful?"

Reviewer-centric features. These are features about each reviewer. Example features include the average rating given by the reviewer, the mean and the standard deviation of the ratings, the ratio of the number of reviews that this reviewer wrote which were the first reviews of products to the total number of reviews that he has written, and the ratio of the number of cases in which he was the only reviewer.

Product-centric features. These features are about each product. Example features include the price of the product, the sales rank of the product (Amazon.com assigns a sales rank to each product according to its sales volume), and the mean and the standard deviation of review ratings of the product.

Logistic regression was used for model building. The experimental results showed some tentative but interesting results.

- Negative outlier reviews (ratings with large negative deviations from the average rating of a product) tend to be heavily spammed. Positive outlier reviews are less spammed.
- Reviews that are the only reviews of some products are likely to be spam. This can be explained by sellers' tendency to promote their unpopular products with fake reviews.

- Top-ranked reviewers are more likely to be fake reviewers. Amazon.com gives a rank to each reviewer based on its proprietary method. The study analysis showed that top-ranked reviewers generally have written a large number of reviews. People who write a large number of reviews are natural suspects. Some top reviewers had written thousands or even tens of thousands of reviews, which is unlikely for an ordinary consumer.
- Fake reviews can get good feedback and genuine reviews can get bad feedback. This shows that if the quality of a review is defined based on helpful feedback citations, people can be fooled by fake reviews because spammers can easily craft a sophisticated review that receives many helpfulness commendations.
- Products ranked as having lower sales are more likely to be spammed. This indicates that spam activities seem to be limited to poorly selling products. This is intuitive, as it is difficult to damage the reputation of a popular product, while an unpopular product needs a boost to its reputation.

We again stress that these results are tentative because (1) it was not confirmed that the three types of duplicates are definitely fake and (2) many fake reviews are not duplicates, yet were considered as nonfake reviews in model building in the study by Jindal and Liu (2008).

Li et al. (2011a) made another supervised learning attempt to identify fake reviews. These authors built a manually labeled fake review corpus using Epinions reviews. At the Epinions site, after a review has been posted, users can evaluate the review by giving it a helpfulness score. They can also write comments about the reviews. The researchers manually labeled a set of fake or nonfake reviews by reading the reviews and the comments. For learning, several types of features were proposed, similar to those described by Jindal and Liu (2008) with some additions – for example, subjective and objectivity features, positive and negative features, reviewer's profile, authority score computed using PageRank (Page et al., 1999), and so on. For learning, they used naïve Bayes classification, which gave promising results. The authors also experimented with semi-supervised learning, exploiting the idea that a spammer tends to write many fake reviews.

The study by Ott et al. (2011) also employed supervised learning. In this case, the authors used Amazon Mechanical Turk (AMT) to crowdsource fake hotel reviews of twenty hotels. Several provisions were made to ensure the quality of the fake reviews. For example, they allowed each Turker (an anonymous online worker) to make only a single submission, Turkers had to be located in the United States, and so on. The Turkers were also given a scenario – namely, that they worked in the hotels, and their bosses asked them to write fake reviews to promote the hotels. Each Turker was paid US$1 per review. Four hundred fake positive reviews were crafted using AMT for twenty popular Chicago hotels. Four hundred positive reviews from Tripadvisor.com for the same twenty Chicago hotels were used as nonfake reviews.

To analyze these data, Ott et al. (2011) tried several classification approaches used in related tasks such as genre identification, psycholinguistic deception detection, and text classification. All these tasks have some existing features proposed by researchers. Their experiments showed that the best text classification performance was achieved using only unigrams and bigrams based on the 50/50 fake and nonfake class distribution. Traditional features for deceptions (Newman et al., 2003; Hancock et al., 2007; Pennebaker et al., 2007; Vrij, 2008; Zhou et al., 2008; Mihalcea and Strapparava, 2009) did not do well. This work reported 89.6 percent of accuracy using only word bigram features under the balanced class distribution.

Feng et al. (2012b) further used some deep syntax rule–based features to boost the accuracy to 91.2 percent. Deep syntax–based features are lexicalized (e.g., PRP $\rightarrow$ "you") and unlexicalized (e.g., NP2 $\rightarrow$ NP3 SBAR) production rules involving immediate or grandparent nodes of probabilistic context-free grammar (PCFG) sentence parse trees. Similar work was also reported by Xu and Zhao (2012).

The very high accuracy in classification using only word n-gram features is surprising and encouraging. It shows that while writing fake reviews, fake reviewers do exhibit some linguistic differences from genuine reviewers. However, as for the previous studies, a weakness of the study by Ott et al. (2011) was its evaluation data, which were still not perfect. Although the reviews crafted using AMT were fake, they were not *real* "fake reviews" on a commercial website: the Turkers did not know the hotels well and were not likely to have the same psychological state of minds when they wrote fake reviews as the authors of real fake reviews, who have real business interests to promote. If a real fake reviewer is a business owner, he knows the business very well and is able of writing with sufficient details, rather than just giving glowing praise of the business. He will also be very careful in writing to ensure that the review sounds genuine and is not easily spotted as fake by readers. Consequently, the reviews by Turkers and the "real fake reviewers" may be very different. Furthermore, using a balanced data set consisting of 50 percent fake reviews and 50 percent nonfake reviews for training and testing does not reflect the true distribution of the real-life situation. The class distribution can have a significant impact on the precision of the detected fake reviews.

12.3   Supervised Yelp Data Experiment

Yelp.com is a large hosting site of online reviews about businesses. To ensure the credibility and trustworthiness of its reviews, Yelp uses a review filtering algorithm to filter out suspicious reviews and prevent them from showing up on the businesses' pages. According to Yelp's CEO, Jeremy Stoppelman (2009), the filtering algorithm has evolved over the years and is constantly being improved by Yelp engineers. Yelp acknowledges that the filter might catch some false positives, but is ready to accept the cost of filtering out a few legitimate reviews over the infinitely higher cost of not having an algorithm at all – something that would turn it into a *laissez-faire* review site that people would stop using (Luther, 2010; Holloway, 2011). Yelp purposely does not reveal the clues that go into its filtering algorithm, as doing so would lessen the filter's effectiveness (Luther, 2010) – fake reviewers would, in turn, change their strategies in writing reviews to circumvent the filter.

Because Yelp has performed filtering since its launch in 2005 and also make its filtered reviews public, its transparency shows that the company is confident about its filtering accuracy. Yelp's filter was also deemed to be accurate in a study reported in *BusinessWeek* (Weise, 2011). My own group had firsthand experience with Yelp's filter as well. We knew that there were several fake reviews for a business based on some insider information, and these reviews were all filtered by Yelp.

Thus, we believe that Yelp's filtering is at least reasonably reliable. Its filtered and unfiltered reviews are probably the closest to the ground truth labels (fake and nonfake) available in the real-life setting. I am also aware that the Chinese Internet company Dianping.com has a similar filtering system. Apart from filtering, the Dianping system provides evidence in response to reviewers who complain that their "genuine" reviews were filtered.

Yelp does not actually delete the filtered reviews, but rather puts them in a filtered list, which is publicly available. Mukherjee et al. (2013b) crawled both filtered and unfiltered reviews for 85 hotels and 130 restaurants in the Chicago area and conducted an experiment using supervised learning to try to reverse-engineer Yelp's filter algorithm. In their experiment, the filtered reviews were treated as fake and the unfiltered reviews as nonfake. This gave a two-class classification problem. The experiments generated some interesting results. The paper also analyzed the quality of the Yelp data set and showed that the filtered reviews were strongly correlated with abnormal spamming behaviors (Section 12.3.2), which again raises confidence in the quality of fake and nonfake labels identified by Yelp.

12.3.1 Supervised Learning Using Linguistic Features

Two general types of features can be used in classification: *linguistic features* and *behavioral features*. Linguistic features deal with the review text content, while behavioral features focus on behaviors of reviewers and their reviews. This subsection describes the experiment results using only linguistic features.

Table 12.2 *SVM Five-Fold Cross-Validation Accuracy Results for the Hotel and Restaurant Domains*

Feature Setting	Hotel Accuracy (%)	Restaurant Accuracy (%)
Unigram	67.6	67.9
Bigram	64.9	68.5

As noted earlier, in Ott et al.'s (2011) study, unigrams and bigrams performed the best classification of the AMT-generated hotel review data, with an accuracy of 89.6 percent. Subsequently, Mukherjee et al. (2013b) experimented with unigrams and bigrams using Yelp data (only positive reviews about popular Chicago hotels and restaurants) with exactly the same experimental settings. Both papers used SVM as the classifier. However, classification of the Yelp hotel data yielded only 67.6 percent accuracy, and classification of the Yelp restaurant data had only 67.9 percent accuracy (Table 12.2). [Note that Ott et al. (2011) used only hotel reviews in their evaluation.] These results show that (1) *n*-gram features are indeed useful and (2) fake review detection in a real-life setting is considerably harder than using the artificial AMT data. Because both papers used 50 percent fake reviews and 50 percent nonfake reviews in training and testing, by chance the accuracy should be 50 percent.

An interesting and intriguing question is: what exactly is the difference between the AMT fake reviews and the Yelp fake reviews, and how can we find and characterize that difference? Mukherjee et al. (2013b) proposed a principled method based on the information theoretic measure, KL-divergence and its asymmetric property. These authors found the following results:

1. The word distributions of fake reviews generated using AMT and nonfake reviews from Tripadvisor.com were widely different, meaning that a large number of words in the two sets have very different frequencies. That is, Turkers tend to use different words from those of genuine reviewers. This may be because Turkers did not know the hotels well and/or they did not put their hearts into writing their fake reviews. In essence, Turkers did not do a good job at "faking." This explains why the AMT-generated fake reviews were easy to classify.
2. For the real Yelp data, the frequency distributions of a large majority of words in both the fake and nonfake reviews were very similar. In other words, fake reviewers on Yelp did a good job at faking: they used similar words as the genuine (nonfake) reviewers to make their reviews sound convincing. However, the asymmetry of KL-divergence shows that a small number of words in the fake reviews had much higher frequencies than in nonfake reviews. Those high-frequency words imply pretense and deception.

This indicates that Yelp fake reviewers may have *overdone* it in an effort to make their reviews sound genuine. The combination of the two findings explains why the accuracy is better than 50 percent (random guessing) but much lower than that for the AMT data.

The next interesting question is: is it possible to improve the classification accuracy for real-life Yelp data? Mukherjee et al. (2013b) proposed a set of behavioral features of reviewers and their reviews. This set of features gave a large margin of improvement.

12.3.2 Supervised Learning Using Behavioral Features

Because linguistic features did not perform well in classifying Yelp reviews, a set of reviewer and review behavioral features was proposed and tried in the study by Mukherjee et al. (2013a). These features helped improve classification accuracy dramatically. For the behavioral study, the authors crawled profiles of all reviewers in the hotel and restaurant domain data. The features were as follows:

1. *Maximum number of reviews (MNR)*. This is the number of reviews posted by a reviewer in a day.
2. *Percentage of positive reviews (PR)*. This is the percentage of positive (four or five stars) reviews written by a reviewer in the data.
3. *Review length (RL)*. This is the length (assessed by word count) of each review. As opinion spamming involves writing about fake experiences, there is probably not much to write – and at least a (paid) spammer probably does not want to invest too much time in writing.
4. *Reviewer deviation (RD)*. To determine RD, we first computed the absolute rating deviation of a review from other reviews based on their star ratings on the same business. Then, we computed the average deviation of a reviewer by taking the mean of all rating deviations over all his reviews.
5. *Maximum content similarity (MCS)*. Crafting a new fake review every time is time consuming. This feature computes the MCS (using the cosine similarity) between any two reviews of a reviewer.

Each review in the data was represented by these five behavioral features of its reviewer. Note that other pieces of metadata could potentially be extracted from Yelp to generate more features – for example, friendship and fan relations, compliments and usefulness votes, percentage of previous reviews filtered, and so on. However, using these features for classification is not fair because they are somewhat directly or indirectly affected by Yelp's filtering. For example, if a review is filtered, its chance of getting usefulness votes, compliments, and friend and fan requests is automatically reduced. The preceding features were not affected or minimally affected by Yelp's filtering.

Table 12.3 *SVM Five-Fold Cross-Validation Classification Results in Accuracy across Behavioral Features (BF) and n-Gram Features in Two Domains: Hotel and Restaurant*

Feature Setting	Hotel Accuracy (%)	Restaurant Accuracy (%)
Unigrams	65.6	66.9
Bigrams	64.4	67.8
Behavioral features (BF)	83.2	82.8
Unigrams + BF	·83.6	84.1
Bigrams + BF	84.8	86.1

The results are reported in Table 12.3, which used much larger data sets including all hotels and restaurants. We can observe that behavioral features (BF) improve the classification dramatically over the results obtained with linguistic *n*-grams features. Adding linguistic features was useful for the restaurant domain to some extent, but made little difference for the hotel domain. It appears that Yelp might be using behavioral clues in its filtering algorithm. Note that this does not say that Yelp uses supervised learning. An in-depth analysis of Yelp reviews against the preceding behaviors revealed that Yelp's filtering has good precision, but it is not clear what its recall is.

12.4   Automated Discovery of Abnormal Patterns

Owing to the difficulty of manually labeling training examples, most of the published algorithms do not use any labeled fake or nonfake data. In this and the next few sections, we discuss several of these approaches. In this section, we focus on a specific approach that formulates the problem of finding fake reviewers or spammers and many other kinds of abnormalities as a data mining task of discovering unexpected class association rules (Jindal et al., 2010). Specifically, this method is based on automated rule mining and a probabilistic definition of suspicious review and reviewer patterns represented as unexpected rules. The method is general, as the different types of unexpectedness are defined on a general form of rules and thus can be used in any domain. This method is also interesting in the sense that it discovers unexpected patterns automatically without the need to manually design abnormal patterns or scenarios and write corresponding specific codes.

12.4.1   Class Association Rules

Class association rules are a special type of association rules with a fixed class attribute (Liu et al., 1998). The data for mining class association rules (CARs) consist of a set of data records, which are described by a set of normal attributes $A = \{A_1, \ldots, A_n\}$ and a class attribute $C = \{c_1, \ldots, c_m\}$ of m discrete values, called *class labels*. A CAR rule is of the form: $X \rightarrow c_i$, where X is a set of conditions from the attributes in A and c_i is a class label in C. Such a rule computes the conditional probability $\Pr(c_i|X)$ (called *confidence*) and the joint probability $\Pr(X, c_i)$ (called *support*). Note that CARs were originally designed for supervised learning due to the known class labels. However, in this study, CAR mining is not used as a supervised learning method for fake review detection because the class labels here are not "fake" and "nonfake" and are not employed for prediction.

For the spam detection application, one form of data for CAR mining can be as follows. Each review forms a data record with a set of attributes – for example, *reviewer-id*, *product-category*, *IP-address*, *email-address*, *brand-id*, *product-id*, and *a class*. Note that IP-address and email-address (of the reviewer) are usually site private data. The class is the sentiment of the reviewer about the product – that is, *positive*, *negative*, or *neutral* based on the review rating. In most review sites (e.g., Amazon.com), each review has a rating between 1 (lowest) and 5 (highest) assigned by its reviewer. Ratings of 4 or 5 are assigned to the positive class, 3 to the neutral class, and 1 or 2 to the negative class. A discovered CAR rule could be that a reviewer (reviewer-1) gives all positive ratings to a brand (brand-1) of products:

reviewer-1, brand-1 $\rightarrow$ positive (supportCount = 10; confidence = 100 percent)

where supportCount is the number of positive reviews from reviewer-1 about brand-1.

Before going further, we note that the preceding data are just an example. In an application, any attribute can serve as the class attribute. It is also possible not to use any class attribute. In that case, the problem is reduced to mining conventional association rules (Agrawal and Srikant, 1994). Then we may find all kinds of interesting rules. For example, we may find that multiple review ids share a single e-mail address (which is highly suspicious), a particular reviewer id has multiple reviews for a single product, a particular userid reviewed only products of a single product category, and so on.

We now use the example data to find unexpected rules based on the work by Jindal et al. (2010). To find something unexpected, we need to first define what is expected. The definition begins by assuming that the class prior probabilities $[\Pr(c_i)]$ is known; it is easily computed from the data automatically. The priors give the initial natural distribution of the data. Two additional principles govern the definition of expectations:

1. Given no prior knowledge, we expect that the data attributes and classes have no relationships; that is, they are statistically independent. This

assumption is justified because it allows us to find those patterns that show strong relationships.
2. We use shorter rules (with fewer conditions) to compute the expectations of longer rules. This is logical for two reasons. First, it enables the user to see interesting short rules first. Second, and more importantly, unexpected shorter rules may be the cause of abnormality in some longer rules (discussed later), but not the other way around. Thus, knowing such short rules, the longer rules may no longer be unexpected.

On the basis of these two principles, we examine the unexpectedness of one-condition rules, and then two-condition rules. For multicondition rules, see the work by Jindal et al. (2010).

12.4.2   Unexpectedness of One-Condition Rules

Jindal et al. (2010) define four types of unexpectedness. This subsection discusses the unexpectedness of one-condition rules, which are rules with only a single condition – that is, an attribute value pair, $A_j = v_{jk}$.

1. *Confidence unexpectedness.* To simplify the notation, we use a single value v_{jk} [$v_{jk} \in dom(A_j)$] to denote the kth value of attribute A_j. A one-condition rule is thus of the form: $v_{jk} \rightarrow c_i$. The expected confidence of the rule is defined as follows:

   Expectation: Because we consider one-condition rules, we use the information from zero-condition rules to define expectations:
   $$\rightarrow c_i,$$
   which is the class prior probability of c_i, $\Pr(c_i)$. Given $\Pr(c_i)$ and no other knowledge, we should expect that attribute values and the classes are independent. Thus, confidence [$\Pr(c_i|v_{jk})$] in the preceding rule ($v_{jk} \rightarrow c_i$) is expected to be $\Pr(c_i)$. We use $E[\Pr(c_i|v_{jk})]$ to denote the expected confidence:

   $$E[\Pr(c_i|v_{jk})] = \Pr(c_i) \tag{12.1}$$

   Confidence unexpectedness (Cu). Confidence unexpectedness of a rule is defined as the ratio of the deviation of the actual confidence to the expected confidence. Let the actual confidence of the rule be $\Pr(c_i|v_{jk})$. We use $Cu(v_{jk} \rightarrow c_i)$ to denote the unexpectedness of the rule $v_{jk} \rightarrow c_i$.

   $$Cu\left(v_{jk} \rightarrow c_i\right) = \frac{\Pr\left(c_i|v_{jk}\right) - E\left[\Pr\left(c_i|v_{jk}\right)\right]}{E\left[\Pr\left(c_i|v_{jk}\right)\right]} \tag{12.2}$$

   The unexpectedness values can be used to rank rules. For example, if 20 percent of the reviews in the data are negative [$\Pr(negative) = 20$

percent], but a particular reviewer's reviews are all negative, then this reviewer is quite unexpected and suspicious. Note that the unexpectedness value can be positive or negative. In applications, rules with positive unexpectedness are often more useful. Other rules can be discarded if not needed.

2. *Support unexpectedness.* The confidence measure does not consider the proportion of data records involved. We therefore need support unexpectedness.

   Expectation: Given no knowledge, we expect that an attribute value and each class are independent. Thus, we have $\Pr[v_{jk}, c_i)] = \Pr(v_{jk})\Pr(c_i)$. $\Pr(c_i)$ is known, but not $\Pr(v_{jk})$. It is reasonable to expect that it is the average probability of all values of A_j. Thus we have [$\Pr(v_{jk})$ is unknown to the user, but can be computed]:

$$E\left[\Pr\left(v_{jk}, c_i\right)\right] = \Pr(c_i)\frac{\sum_{a=1}^{|A_j|}\Pr\left(v_{ja}\right)}{|A_j|} \qquad (12.3)$$

   Support unexpectedness (Su). Support unexpectedness of a rule is defined as follows:

$$Su\left(v_{jk} \rightarrow c_i\right) = \frac{\Pr\left(v_{jk}, c_i\right) - E\left[\Pr\left(v_{jk}, c_i\right)\right]}{E\left[\Pr\left(v_{jk}, c_i\right)\right]} \qquad (12.4)$$

   This definition of Su [Equations (12.3) and (12.4)] is reasonable, given that it ranks those rules with high supports high, which is what we want. For example, on average each reviewer wrote two negative reviews, but some reviewers wrote hundreds of negative reviews. The latter reviewers are suspicious, and at least worth further investigation.

3. *Attribute distribution unexpectedness.* Confidence or support unexpectedness considers only a single rule. In many cases, a group of rules together shows an interesting scenario. Here we define an unexpectedness metric based on all values of an attribute and a class, which thus covers multiple rules. This unexpectedness shows how skewed the data records are for the class – that is, whether the data records of the class concentrate on only a few values of the attribute or if they are spread evenly to all values, which is expected given no prior knowledge. For example, we may find that most positive reviews for a brand of products come from only one reviewer, even though a large number of reviewers have reviewed products of the brand. This reviewer is clearly a spammer suspect.

   We use supports (or joint probabilities) to define attribute distribution unexpectedness. Let the attribute be A_j and the class of interest be c_i. The attribute distribution of A_j with respect to class c_i is denoted by:

   $$A_j \rightarrow c_i$$

It represents all the rules, $v_{jk} \rightarrow c_i$, $k = 1, 2, \ldots, |A_j|$, where $|A_j|$ is the total number of values of attribute A_j.

Expectation: We can use the expected value of $\Pr(v_{jk}, c_i)$ computed earlier [Equation (12.3)] for our purpose here.

Attribute distribution unexpectedness (ADu). It is defined as the sum of normalized support deviations of all values of A_j.

$$ADu(A_j \rightarrow c_i) = \sum_{v_{jk}: v_{jk} \in dom(A_j) \wedge Dev > 0} \frac{Dev(v_{jk})}{\Pr(c_i)} \tag{12.5}$$

where
$$Dev(v_{jk}) = \Pr(v_{jk}, c_i) - E[\Pr(v_{jk}, c_i)] \tag{12.6}$$

We use $\Pr(c_i)$ in Equation (12.5) because $\sum_{k=1}^{|A_j|} \Pr(v_{jk}, c_i) = \Pr(c_i)$. Note that in this definition, negative deviations are not utilized because positive and negative deviations [$Dev(v_{jk})$] are symmetric or equal since $\Pr(c_i)$ is constant and $\sum_{k=1}^{|A_j|} \Pr(v_{jk}, c_i) = \Pr(c_i)$. Thus, considering one side is sufficient.

4. *Attribute unexpectedness.* In this case, we want to discover how the values of an attribute can predict the classes. This is denoted by

$$A_j \rightarrow C$$

where A_j represents all its values and C represents all classes. Given no knowledge, our expectation is that A_j and C are independent. In the ideal case (or the most unexpected case), every rule $v_{jk} \rightarrow c_i$ has 100 percent confidence. Then, the values of A_j can predict the classes in C completely.

Conceptually, the idea is the same as measuring the discriminative power of each attribute in classification learning. Hence the *information gain* (IG) measure can be used for the purpose (Quinlan, 1993). The expected information is computed based on entropy. Given no knowledge, the entropy of the original data D is [note that $\Pr(c_i)$ is the confidence of the zero-condition rule on class c_i]:

$$entropy(D) = -\sum_{i=1}^{m} \Pr(c_i) \log \Pr(c_i) \tag{12.7}$$

Expectation: The expectation is the entropy of the data D:

$$E(A_j \rightarrow C) = entropy(D)$$

Attribute unexpectedness (Au). Attribute unexpectedness is defined as the information gained by adding the attribute A_j. After adding A_j, we obtain the following entropy:

$$entropy_{A_j}(D) = -\sum_{k=1}^{|A_j|} \frac{|D_k|}{|D|} entropy(D_k) \tag{12.8}$$

Based on the values of A_j, the data set D is partitioned into $|A_j|$ subsets, $D_1, D_2, \ldots, D_{|A_{jl}|}$ (i.e., each subset has a particular value of A_j). The unexpectedness [which is the IG measure (Quinlan, 1993)] is thus computed as:

$$Au\left(A_j \rightarrow C\right) = entropy(D) - entropy_{A_j}(D) \tag{12.9}$$

12.4.3 Unexpectedness of Two-Condition Rules

We now consider two-condition rules. Although we might still assume that the expected confidence of a rule is the class prior probability, as is true for one-condition rules, that assumption is no longer appropriate because a two-condition rule is made up of two one-condition rules. It is possible that the unexpectedness of a two-condition rule is caused by a one-condition rule.

Let us use confidence unexpectedness as an example. We have a data set with two classes and each class has 50 percent of the data; that is, the class prior probabilities are equal, $\Pr(c_1) = \Pr(c_2) = 0.5$. For a rule $v_1 \rightarrow c_1$ with 100 percent confidence [i.e., $\Pr(c_1 | v_1) = 1$], it is highly unexpected based on Equation (12.2).

Now let us look at a two-condition rule, $v_1, v_2 \rightarrow c_1$, which clearly also has 100 percent confidence [i.e., $\Pr(c_1 | v_1, v_2) = 1$]. If we assume no knowledge, its expected confidence should be 50 percent. Then, we say that this rule is highly unexpected. However, because we know $v_1 \rightarrow c_1$ has a 100 percent confidence, the 100 percent confidence for the rule $v_1, v_2 \rightarrow c_1$ is completely expected. The 100 percent confidence of rule $v_1 \rightarrow c_1$ is the cause for rule $v_1, v_2 \rightarrow c_1$ to have the 100 percent confidence.

With the knowledge of one-condition rules, we define different types of unexpectedness of two-condition rules of the form:

$$v_{jk}, v_{gh} \rightarrow c_i.$$

1. *Confidence unexpectedness.* We first compute the expected confidence of the two-condition rule based on two one-condition rules:

$$v_{jk} \rightarrow c_i \text{ and } v_{gh} \rightarrow c_i$$

Expectation: Given the confidences of the two rules, $\Pr(c_i | v_{jk})$ and $\Pr(c_i | v_{gh})$, we compute the expected probability of $\Pr(c_i | v_{jk}, v_{gh})$ using Bayes's rule and obtain:

$$\Pr\left(c_i | v_{jk}, v_{gh}\right) = \frac{\Pr\left(v_{jk}, v_{gh} | c_i\right)\Pr(c_i)}{\sum_{r=1}^{m}\Pr\left(v_{jk}, v_{gh} | c_r\right)\Pr(c_r)} \tag{12.10}$$

The first term of the numerator can be further written as:

$$\Pr\left(v_{jk}, v_{gh}|c_i\right) = \Pr\left(v_{jk}|v_{gh}, c_i\right)\Pr\left(v_{gh}|c_i\right) \tag{12.11}$$

Conditional independence assumption. With no prior knowledge, it is reasonable to expect that all attributes are conditionally independent given class c_i. Formally, we expect that:

$$\Pr\left(v_k|v_{gh}, c_i\right) = \Pr\left(v_{jk}|c_i\right) \tag{12.12}$$

On the basis of Equation (12.10), the expected value of $\Pr(c_i \mid v_{jk}, v_{gh})$ is:

$$E\left[\Pr\left(c_i|v_{jk}, v_{gh}\right)\right] = \frac{\Pr\left(v_{jk}|c_i\right)\Pr\left(v_{gh}|c_i\right)\Pr(c_i)}{\sum_{r=1}^{m}\Pr\left(v_{jk}|c_r\right)\Pr\left(v_{gh}|c_r\right)\Pr(c_r)} \tag{12.13}$$

Because we know $\Pr(c_i \mid v_{jk})$ and $\Pr(c_i \mid v_{gh})$, we finally have:

$$E\left[\Pr\left(c_i|v_{jk}, v_{gh}\right)\right] = \frac{\Pr\left(c_i|v_{jk}\right)\Pr\left(c_i|v_{gh}\right)}{\Pr(c_i)\sum_{r=1}^{m}\dfrac{\Pr\left(c_r|v_{jk}\right)\Pr\left(c_r|v_{gh}\right)}{\Pr(c_r)}} \tag{12.14}$$

Confidence unexpectedness (Cu). Cu is defined as follows:

$$Cu\left(v_{jk}, v_{gh} \rightarrow c_i\right) = \frac{\Pr\left(c_i|v_{jk}, v_{gh}\right) - E\left[\Pr\left(c_i|v_{jk}, v_{gh}\right)\right]}{E\left[\Pr\left(c_i|v_{jk}, v_{gh}\right)\right]} \tag{12.15}$$

Using this measure, one can find reviewers who give all high ratings to products of a brand, when most other reviewers are generally negative about the brand.

2. *Support unexpectedness.* The expected support of v_{jk}, $v_{gh} \rightarrow c_i$ is computed first.

Expectation: The expected support $\Pr(v_{jk}, v_{gh}, c_i)$ is computed based on the following:

$$\Pr\left(v_{jk}, v_{gh}, c_i\right) = \Pr\left(c_i|v_{jk}, v_{gh}\right)\Pr\left(v_{jk}, v_{gh}\right) \tag{12.16}$$

Using the conditional independence assumption, we know the value for $\Pr(c_i \mid v_{jk}, v_{gh})$. Let us compute the value for $\Pr(v_{jk}, v_{gh})$ based on the same assumption:

$$\Pr\left(v_{jk}, v_{gh}\right) = \Pr\left(v_{jk}\right)\Pr\left(v_{gh}\right)\sum_{r=1}^{m}\frac{\Pr\left(c_r|v_{jk}\right)\Pr\left(c_r|v_{gh}\right)}{\Pr(c_r)} \tag{12.17}$$

By combining Equations (12.10) and (12.17), we obtain:

$$E\left[\Pr\left(v_{jk}, v_{gh}, c_i\right)\right] = \frac{\Pr\left(v_{jk}, c_i\right)\Pr\left(v_{gh}, c_i\right)}{\Pr(c_i)} \tag{12.18}$$

Support unexpectedness (Su). It is computed as follows:

$$Su(v_{jk}, v_{gh} \to c_i) = \frac{\Pr(v_{jk}, v_{gh}, c_i) - E[\Pr(v_{jk}, v_{gh}, c_i)]}{E[\Pr(v_{jk}, v_{gh}, c_i)]} \tag{12.19}$$

Using this measure, one can find reviewers who write multiple reviews for a single product, while other reviewers write only one review.

3. *Attribute distribution unexpectedness.* For two-condition rules, two attributes are involved. Thus, to compute attribute distribution unexpectedness, we need to fix an attribute. Without loss of generality, we assume v_{jk} is fixed, and include (or vary) all the values of attribute A_g. We thus compute the unexpectedness of:

$$v_{jk}, A_g \to c_i$$

This attribute distribution represents all rules, $v_{jk}, v_{gh} \to c_i, h = 1, 2, \ldots,$ $|A_g|$, where $|A_g|$ is the number of possible values of attribute A_g. *Expectation:* We can make use of the expected value of $\Pr(v_{jk}, v_{gh}, c_i)$ computed in Equation (12.18).

Attribute distribution unexpectedness (ADu). It is defined as follows:

$$ADu(v_{jk}, A_g \to c_i) = \sum_{v_{gh}:v_{gh} \in dom(A_g) \land Dev>0} \frac{Dev(v_{gh})}{\Pr(v_{jk}, c_i)} \tag{12.20}$$

where $Dev(v_{gh}) = \Pr(v_{jk}, v_{gh}, c_i) - E[\Pr(v_{jk}, v_{gh}, c_i)]$.

Using this measure, we can find that most positive reviews for a brand of products are written by only one reviewer, even though a large number of reviewers have reviewed the products of the brand.

4. *Attribute unexpectedness.* In this case, we compute the unexpectedness of an attribute given a constraint, which is of the form:

$$v_{jk}, A_g \to C$$

Using this measure, one can find reviewers (constraint) who wrote only positive reviews for one brand and only negative reviews for another brand,
Rule1: reviewer-1, brand-1 $\to$ positive (confidence = 100 percent)
Rule2: reviewer-1, brand-2 $\to$ negative (confidence = 100 percent)

12.5 Model-Based Behavioral Analysis

This section describes several model-based methods, ranging from simple behavioral models to sophisticated graph models and Bayesian probabilistic models. They all make use of behaviors of reviewers and their reviews to detect fake reviews and reviewers.

We should note that all behaviors studied in published papers are based on the public data displayed on review pages of their respective review hosting sites. The private data collected by each review hosting site are not visible to the general public, but are very useful – and perhaps even more useful than the public data – for spam detection. For example, if multiple userids from the same IP address posted a number of positive reviews for a product, then these userids are suspicious. If the positive reviews for a hotel all come from an area nearby to the hotel, their veracity is also doubtful. If the site private data are available, they can be incorporated into existing approaches with no or minimum changes to the models.

12.5.1   Spam Detection Based on Atypical Behaviors

The first technique is from Lim et al. (2010), who identified several unusual reviewer behavior models based on different review patterns that suggest spamming. Each model assigns a numeric spamming behavior score to a reviewer by measuring the extent to which the reviewer practices spamming behavior of the type. All the scores are then combined to produce the final spam score. Thus, this method focuses on finding spammers or fake reviewers rather than on identifying fake reviews.

The spamming behavior models are as follows:

1. *Targeting products.* To game a review system, it is hypothesized that a spammer will direct most of her efforts toward promoting or victimizing a few target products. She is expected to monitor the products closely and mitigate the existing ratings by writing fake reviews when time is appropriate.
2. *Targeting groups.* This spam behavior model defines the pattern of spammers manipulating ratings of a set of products sharing some attribute(s) within a short span of time. For example, a spammer may target several products of a brand within a few hours. This pattern of ratings saves the spammers' time, as they do not need to log on to the review system many times. To achieve the maximum impact, the ratings given to these target groups of products are either very high or very low.
3. *General rating deviation.* A genuine reviewer is expected to give ratings similar to other raters of the same product. As spammers attempt to promote or demote some products, their ratings typically deviate a great deal from those of other reviewers.
4. *Early rating deviation.* Early deviation captures the behavior of a spammer contributing a fake review soon after product launch. Such reviews are likely to attract attention from other reviewers, allowing spammers to affect the views of subsequent reviewers.

Wu et al. (2010) also proposed an unsupervised method to detect fake reviews based on a distortion criterion (not on reviewers' behaviors, as the preceding methods). The idea is that fake reviews will distort the overall popularity ranking for a collection of entities. Deleting a set of reviews chosen at random should not overly disrupt the ranked list of entities, whereas deleting fake reviews should significantly alter or distort the ranking of entities to reveal the "true" ranking. This distortion can be measured by comparing popularity rankings before and after the deletions using rank correlation. Along similar lines, Xie et al. (2012) proposed a time series–based detection method, and Feng et al. (2012a) introduced a review rating distribution analysis–based detection method for each product.

12.5.2 Spam Detection Using Review Graphs

Wang et al. (2011) proposed a graph-based method for detecting spam in store or merchant reviews. Such reviews describe purchase experiences and evaluations of stores. Their study was based on a snapshot of all reviews from resellerratings.com, which were crawled on October 6, 2010. After removing stores with no reviews, there were 343,603 reviewers who wrote 408,470 reviews for 14,561 stores.

Although one can borrow some clues from product review spammer detection algorithms, these criteria are insufficient for the store review context. For example, it is unusual for a person to post multiple reviews for the same product, but a person might routinely post more than one review to the same store due to multiple purchasing experiences there. Also, it can be normal to have near-duplicate reviews from one reviewer for multiple stores: unlike the case for products, different stores basically provide the same type of services. Therefore, features or clues proposed in approaches for detecting fake product reviews and reviewers are not all appropriate for detecting spammers of store reviews. Thus, there is a need to look for a more sophisticated and complementary framework.

Wang et al. (2011) developed a heterogeneous review graph-based approach. The graph consists of three types of nodes – reviewers, reviews, and stores – to capture their relationships and to model spamming clues. A reviewer node has a link to each review that he wrote. A review node has an edge to a store node if the review is about that store. A store is connected to a reviewer via this reviewer's review about the store. Each node is also attached to a set of features. For example, a store node has features about its average rating, its number of reviews, and so on.

Based on the review graph, three concepts are defined and computed: the *trustiness* of reviewers, the *honesty* of reviews, and the *reliability* of stores. A reviewer is more trustworthy if she has written more honest reviews; a store is more reliable if it has more positive reviews from trustworthy reviewers; and a review is more honest if it is supported by many other honest reviews. Furthermore, if the honesty of a review decreases, it affects the reviewer's trustiness, which in turn has an impact on the store she reviewed. These intertwined relations are revealed in the review graph and defined mathematically.

An iterative computation method was proposed to compute the three values, which were then used to rank reviewers, stores, and reviews. Those top-ranked reviewers, stores, and reviews are likely to be involved in review spamming. To perform the evaluation, human judges compared scores of stores with data from the Better Business Bureau (BBB), a well-known US corporation that gathers reports on business reliability and alerts the public to business or consumer scams.

Akoglu et al. (2013) proposed another graph-based method for solving a similar problem. The method is based on Markov random fields.

12.5.3   Spam Detection Using Bayesian Models

Most existing detection algorithms are based on different heuristics or hinge on ad hoc fake and nonfake labels for model building. Mukherjee et al. (2013a) proposed a theoretical model to formulate the task as a clustering problem in an unsupervised Bayesian framework. The Bayesian setting enables modeling of *spamicity* of reviewers as a latent characteristic with a set of observed behavioral features. The proposed (graphical) model was called the author spamicity model (ASM). Spamicity here means the degree of being spammed. The key motivation hinges on the hypothesis that opinion spammers differ from other reviewers on behavioral dimensions. This creates a separation margin between population distributions of two naturally occurring clusters: spammers and nonspammers. Inference in ASM results in learning the distributions of the two clusters (or classes) based on a set of behavioral features. Various extensions of ASM have also been proposed to exploit different priors.

More specifically, ASM belongs to the class of generative models for clustering (Duda et al., 2001) based on a set of observed features. It models spamicity s_a (degree/tendency of spamming in the range $[0, 1]$) of an author a, as well as spam/nonspam label π_r of a review r, as latent variables. π_r is essentially the *class* variable reflecting the cluster memberships (two clusters in this case, $K = 2$, for spam and nonspam) for every review instance. Each author/reviewer (and, respectively, each review) has a set of observed features (behavioral clues) emitted according to the corresponding latent prior class distributions. Model inference learns the latent population distributions of the two clusters across various behavioral dimensions, and the cluster assignments of reviews in the unsupervised setting are based on the principle of probabilistic model-based clustering (Smyth, 1999). The reviewer/author features include content similarity, maximum number of reviews, reviewing burstiness, and ratio of first reviews. Review features include duplicate/near-duplicate reviews, extreme rating, rating deviation, early time frame, and rating abuse. This method is highly involved, and interested readers are referred to the original paper by Mukherjee et al. (2013a).

A key advantage of employing Bayesian inference is that because the model characterizes various spamming activities using estimated latent variables and the posteriors, it facilitates both detection and analysis in a single framework, rendering deep insights into the opinion spam problem. This is hard to do using other methods.

12.6   Group Spam Detection

Group spamming refers to a group of reviewers writing fake reviews together to promote or to disparage some target products (Mukherjee et al., 2012). The reason for submitting multiple fake reviews for a single product or service is that, in many cases, just one fake review is not enough to promote a product or service or change the existing sentiment about the product. Hence, a group writes multiple fake reviews and seeks to use their collective might to alter opinions about the product. A spammer group can be highly damaging because it has many people writing fake reviews, and can therefore take total control of the sentiment on a product. It is hard to detect spammer groups using review content features or even indicators for detecting abnormal behaviors of individual spammers, because a group has more people available to post reviews; in turn, each member may no longer appear to behave abnormally. Here by a group of reviewers, we mean a set of reviewer ids. The actual reviewers behind the ids could be a single person with multiple ids (sockpuppets), multiple persons, or a combination of both. We do not distinguish among these configurations here.

Before proceeding further, let us see a spammer group. Figures 12.2, 12.3, and 12.4 show the reviews of a group of three reviewers.[1] The following suspicious patterns can be noted with this group: (1) the group members all reviewed the same three products, giving all five star ratings; (2) they posted reviews within a small time window of four days (two of them posted in the same day); (3) each of them reviewed only the three products (which became evident when the Amazon review data were crawled; Jindal and Liu, 2008); and (4) they were among the early reviewers for the products (to make a big impact). All these patterns occurring together strongly suggest suspicious activities. Note that none of the reviews themselves are similar to any others (i.e., no duplicates) or appear deceptive. Indeed, if we look at the three reviewers individually, they all appear genuine. In fact, five out of nine reviews received 100 percent helpfulness votes by Amazon users, indicating that the reviews were useful. Clearly, these three reviewers have taken total control of

---

[1] www.amazon.com/gp/pdp/profile/A3URRTIZEE8R7W; www.amazon.com/gp/pdp/profile/A254
LYRIZUYXZG; www.amazon.com/gp/cdp/member-reviews/A1O70AIHNS4EIY.

1 of 1 people found the following review helpful:
⭐⭐⭐⭐⭐ **Practically FREE music**, December 4, 2004
This review is from: **Audio Xtract (CD-ROM)**
I can't believe for $10 (after rebate) I got a program that gets me free unlimited music. I was hoping it did half what was ....

3 of 8 people found the following review helpful:
⭐⭐⭐⭐⭐ **Yes – it really works**, December 4, 2004
This review is from: **Audio Xtract Pro (CD-ROM)**
See my review for Audio Xtract - this PRO is even better. This is the solution I've been looking for. After buying iTunes, ...

5 of 5 people found the following review helpful:
⭐⭐⭐⭐⭐ **My kids love it**, December 4, 2004
This review is from: **Pond Aquarium 3D Deluxe Edition**
This was a bargain at $20 - better than the other ones that have no above water scenes. My kids get a kick out of the ....

Figure 12.2 Big John's profile.

the sentiment about the set of reviewed products. In fact, there is a fourth reviewer in the group. Owing to space limitations, we omit it here.

If a group of reviewers work together only once to promote or to disparage a product, it is hard to detect them based on their collective behavior (see also Section 12.7). However, in recent years, opinion spamming has become a business. Put simply, people get paid to write fake reviews. These people cannot just write a single review, as they would not make enough money that

2 of 2 people found the following review helpful: ☆☆☆☆☆ **Like a tape recorder...**, December 8, 2004   This review is from: **Audio Xtract (CD-ROM)**   This software really rocks. I can set the program to record music all day long and just let it go. I come home and my ....
3 of 10 people found the following review helpful: ☆☆☆☆☆ **This is even better than...**, December 8, 2004   This review is from: **Audio Xtract Pro (CD-ROM)**   Let me tell you, this has to be one of the coolest products ever on the market. Record 8 Internet radio stations at once, ...
5 of 5 people found the following review helpful: ☆☆☆☆☆ **For the price you...**, December 8, 2004   This review is from: **Pond Aquarium 3D Deluxe Edition**   This is one of the coolest screensavers I have ever seen, the fish move realistically, the environments look real, and the ....

Figure 12.3 Cletus's profile.

way. Instead, they write many reviews about many products. Such collective behaviors of a group can give them away. This section focuses on detecting such spam groups.

Because reviewers in the group write reviews for multiple products, the data mining technique known as frequent itemset mining (FIM) (Agrawal and Srikant, 1994) can be used to find them. However, the discovered groups in this way are only group spam candidates, because many groups may be coincidental. For example, some reviewers may have happened to review the same set of products due to similar tastes and popularity of the products (e.g.,

⭐⭐⭐⭐⭐ **Wow, Internet music!**
..., December 4, 2004
This review is from: **Audio Xtract (CD-ROM)**
I looked forever for a way to record Internet music. My way took a long time and many steps (frustrtaing). Then I found Audio Xtract. With more than 3,000 songs downloaded in ...

2 of 9 people found the following review helpful:
⭐⭐⭐⭐⭐ **Best music just got** ..., December 4, 2004
This review is from: **Audio Xtract Pro (CD-ROM)**
The other day I upgraded to this TOP NOTCH product. Everyone who loves music needs to get it from Internet ....

3 of 3 people found the following review helpful:
⭐⭐⭐⭐⭐ **Cool, looks great...**, December 4, 2004
This review is from: **Pond Aquarium 3D Deluxe Edition**
We have this set up on the PC at home and it looks GREAT. The fish and the scenes are really neat. Friends and family ....

Figure 12.4 Jake's profile.

many people review all three Apple products: iPod, iPhone, and iPad). Thus, our goal is to identify true spammer groups in the candidate set.

The algorithm described by Mukherjee et al. (2012) works in two steps:

1. *Frequent itemset mining.* The step finds a set of frequent itemsets. Each itemset is a group of reviewers who have all reviewed a set of products. Such a group is regarded as a candidate spam group. FIM (Agrawal and Srikant, 1994) is used to perform the task.

   FIM is conducted as follows. Let I be a set of items, which is the set of all reviewers in our case. Let T be a transaction set. Each transaction t_i ($t_i \in T$) is a subset of items in I ($t_i \subseteq I$), which are the reviewers who have reviewed a particular product. Each product thus generates a transaction, which is the set of all reviewers who have reviewed the product. By mining frequent itemsets, we can discover all frequent itemsets. Each itemset is a set of reviewers who have appeared in the transaction set T at least a minimum number of times (called minimum support count, or minsup_c) and at least two reviewers must be in each itemset (group); that is, each group must have at least two reviewers who have worked together on at least minsup_c products. In the paper, the authors used minsup_c = 3.

2. *Rank groups based on a set of group spam features.* The groups discovered in step 1 may not all be true spammer groups. Many of the reviewers are grouped together in pattern mining simply due to chance. This step uses a relational model, called GSRank (group spam rank), to rank the candidate groups based on their likelihood of being a spam group. This model captures the relationships among individual group members, and with products that they have reviewed. It is defined based on a set of spam indicators or features that aim to capture different types of unusual group and individual member behaviors. In the next two subsections, we will define these features. For details on the relational model, refer to the original paper by Mukherjee et al. (2012).

The FIM method is unsupervised, as it does not use any manually labeled data for training. A set of labeled spammer groups was, however, used to evaluate the proposed model, which showed promising results. Clearly, with the labeled data, supervised learning can be applied as well. Indeed, Mukherjee et al. (2012) also experimented with supervised classification, regression, and learning to rank algorithms for the task.

12.6.1 Group Behavior Features

This subsection describes the set of group features, and the next subsection describes the set of individual member features. These features are indicators or clues of spamming activities.

1. *Group time window (GTW).* Members of a spam group are likely to have worked together in posting reviews for the target products during a short time interval. The degree of active involvement of a group is modeled as its GTW:

$$GTW(g) = \max_{p \in P_g} (GTW_P(g,p)). \tag{12.21}$$

$$GTW_P(g,p) = \begin{cases} 0 & \text{if } L(g,p) - F(g,p) > \tau \\ 1 - \dfrac{L(g,p) - F(g,p)}{\tau} & \text{otherwise} \end{cases}$$

where $L(g, p)$ and $F(g, p)$ are the latest and earliest (respectively) dates of reviews posted for product $p \in P_g$ by reviewers of group g. P_g is the set of all products reviewed by group g. Thus, $GTW_P(g, p)$ gives the time window information of group g for a single product p. This definition says that a group g of reviewers posting reviews on a product p within a short burst of time is more prone to be spamming (attaining a value close to 1). Groups working over a longer time interval than τ (which is a parameter) get a value of 0: they are unlikely to have worked together. The group time window $GTW(g)$ considers all products reviewed by the group, taking max over p ($\in P_g$) as a means to capture the worst behavior of the group. For subsequent behaviors, max is taken for the same reason.

2. *Group deviation (GD)*. A highly damaging group spam occurs when the ratings of the group members deviate a great deal from those of other (genuine) reviewers. The larger the deviation, the worse the group is. This behavior is modeled by GD on a five-star rating scale (with 4 being the maximum possible deviation):

$$GD(g) = \max_{p \in P_g} [D(g,p)] \tag{12.22}$$

$$D(g,p) = \frac{|r_{p,g} - \bar{r}_{p,g}|}{4}$$

where $r_{p,g}$ and $\bar{r}_{p,g}$ are the average ratings for product p given by members of group g and by other reviewers not in g, respectively. $D(g, p)$ is the deviation of the group on a single product p. If there are no other reviewers who have reviewed the product p, $\bar{r}_{p,g} = 0$.

3. *Group content similarity (GCS)*. Group connivance is also exhibited by content similarity (duplicate or near-duplicate reviews) when spammers copy reviews among themselves. In consequence, the victimized products have many reviews with similar content. GCS models this behavior:

$$GCS(g) = \max_{p \in P_g} [CS_G(g,p)] \tag{12.23}$$

$$CS_G(g,p) = \underset{m_i, m_j \in g, i<j}{avg} \left(cosine \left[c(m_i, p), c(m_j, p) \right] \right)$$

where $c(m_i, p)$ is the content of the review written by group member $m_i \in g$ for product p. $CS_G(g, p)$ captures the average pairwise similarity of review contents among group members for a product p by computing the cosine similarity.

4. *Group member content similarity (GMCS)*. Another flavor of content similarity is exhibited when the members of a group g do not know one another (and are contacted by a contracting agency). Because writing a new review every time is taxing, a group member may copy or modify her own previous reviews for similar products. If multiple members of the group do this, the group is more likely to be spamming. This behavior can be captured by GMCS as follows:

$$GMCS(g) = \frac{\sum_{m \in g} CS_M(g,m)}{|g|}$$ (12.24)

$$CS_M(g,m) = \underset{p_i, p_j \in P_g, i<j}{avg} \left(cosine\left[c(m,p_i), c(m,p_j)\right]\right)$$

The group attains a value ≈ 1 (indicating spam) on GMCS when all its members entirely copied their own reviews across different products in P_g. $CS_M(g, m)$ models the average pairwise content similarity of the member $m \in g$ over all products in P_g.

5. *Group early time frame (GETF)*. Spammers usually review a product early – that is, soon after its launch – to make the biggest impact. Similarly, when group members are among the very first people to review a product, they can totally hijack the sentiment on the products. GETF models this behavior:

$$GETF(g) = \max_{p \in P_g} [GTF(g,p)]$$ (12.25)

$$GTF(g,p) = \begin{cases} 0 & \text{if } L(g,p) - A(p) > \beta \\ 1 - \dfrac{L(g,p) - A(p)}{\beta} & \text{otherwise} \end{cases}$$

where $GTF(g, p)$ captures the time frame as how early a group g reviews a product p. $L(g, p)$ and $A(p)$ are the latest date of a review posted for product $p \in P_g$ by group g and the date when p was made available for reviewing, respectively. β is a threshold such that, after β months, GTF attains a value of 0, as reviews posted then are no longer considered to be early.

6. *Group size ratio (GSR)*. The ratio of group size to the total number of reviewers for a product can also indicate spamming. At one extreme (worst case), the group members are the only reviewers of the product and completely control the sentiment on the product. At the other extreme, the total number of reviewers of the product is very large, whereas the group size is very small. Then the impact of the group is small.

$$GSR(g) = \underset{p \in P_g}{avg} [GSR_P(g,p)]$$ (12.26)

$$GSR_P(g,p) = \frac{|g|}{|M_p|}$$

where GSRP(g, p) is the ratio of group size to M_p (the set of all reviewers of product p) for product p.

7. *Group size (GS)*. Group collusion is also related to the group size. For large groups, the probability of members happening to be together by chance is very small. Furthermore, the larger the group, the more damaging it is. GS

is easy to model. We normalize it to [0, 1]. $max(|g_i|)$ is the largest group size of all discovered groups.

$$GS(g) = \frac{|g|}{max\,(|g_i|)} \tag{12.27}$$

8. *Group support count (GSUP).* The group support count is the total number of products for which the group has worked together to review. Groups with high support counts are more likely to be spam groups, as the probability that a group of random people happen to have reviewed many products together is small. GSUP is modeled in the following equation:

$$GSUP(g) = \frac{|P_g|}{max\,(|P_{g_i}|)} \tag{12.28}$$

We normalize GSUP to [0, 1], with $max(|P_{g_i}|)$ being the largest support count of all discovered groups.

These eight group behaviors can be seen as group spamming features that can be used in modeling or learning.

12.6.2   Individual Member Behavior Features

Although group behaviors are important, they hide a lot of details about the group's members. Clearly, individual members' behaviors also give signals indicative of group spamming. We now describe the behaviors of individual members.

1. *Individual rating deviation (IRD).* Like GD, we can model IRD as

$$IRD(m,p) = \frac{|r_{p,m} - \bar{r}_{p,m}|}{4} \tag{12.29}$$

where $r_{p,m}$ and $\bar{r}_{p,m}$ are the rating for product p given by reviewer m and the average rating for p given by other reviewers, respectively.
2. *Individual content similarity (ICS).* Individual spammers may review a product multiple times, posting duplicate or near-duplicate reviews each time, in an effort to increase the product popularity. Similar to GMCS, ICS of a reviewer m is modeled over all his reviews toward a product p as follows:

$$ICS(m,p) = avg(cosine[c(m,p)]) \tag{12.30}$$

The average is taken over all reviews on p posted by m.

3. *Individual early time frame (IETF).* Like GETF, IETF of a group member m for product p is defined as:

$$IETF(m,p) = \begin{cases} 0 & \text{if } L(m,p) - A(p) > \beta \\ 1 - \dfrac{L(m,p) - A(p)}{\beta} & \text{otherwise} \end{cases} \qquad (12.31)$$

where $L(m, p)$ is the latest date of review posted for a product p by member m, $A(p)$ is the date when p was made available for reviewing, and β is a threshold parameter.

4. *Individual member coupling in a group (IMC).* This behavior measures how closely a member works with the other members of the group. If a member m almost always posts at the same date as other group members, then m is said to be tightly coupled with the group. However, if m posts at a date that is far away from the posting dates of the other members, m is not tightly coupled with the group. We can find the difference between the posting date of member m for product p and the average posting date of other members of the group for p. To compute this time, we use the time when the first review was posted by the group for product p as the baseline. Individual member coupling (IMC) is modeled as:

$$IMC(g,m) = \underset{p \in P_g}{avg} \left(\frac{|\, T(m,p) - F(g,p) - avg(g,m)\, |}{L(g,p) - F(g,p)} \right) \qquad (12.32)$$

$$avg(g,m) = \frac{\sum_{m_i \in G - \{m\}} [T(m_i,p) - F(g,p)]}{|\,g\,| - 1}$$

where $L(g, p)$ and $F(g, p)$ are the latest and earliest dates of reviews posted for product $p \in$ by group g, respectively, and $T(m, p)$ is the actual posting date of reviewer m for product p.

12.7 Identifying Reviewers with Multiple Userids

Another way of detecting fake reviewers or spammers is to identify authors who have multiple accounts or userids and use them to write reviews. As mentioned in Section 12.6, in many cases a single review may not be sufficient to establish a desired sentiment or to reverse an existing undesirable sentiment on a product. Although the reviewer can write more than one review for the product, writing multiple reviews from a single account for a product is not a good idea – the pattern it is easily detected. Instead, to avoid detection, a reviewer may register multiple accounts or userids and post one review from each account.

This section describes a technique for detecting such multi-id reviewers. The technique was proposed by Qian and Liu (2013). In addition, variations of this technique can deal with two related problems:

- *Same reviewer posting on multiple sites.* When an author/reviewer promotes a product, she may write fake reviews for the product on multiple sites that sell the product. Then, we want to solve the problem of detecting accounts or userids from multiple sites that may belong to the same author.
- *Author change.* A reviewer with a good reputation on a website may sell his account or userid to a spammer, who then uses the account to post fake reviews. In other cases, a person purposely "raises" a userid (just like raising a child) for sale. That is, the person posts truthful reviews organically for a period of time to establish the reputation for the account, and then sells the account or userid to a spammer. In this case, we need to detect whether there is an author change for the account.

In this section, we first present the technique developed by Qian and Liu (2013) for identifying multi-id authors, and then discuss how the preceding two problems can be tackled.

12.7.1   Learning in a Similarity Space

Problem definition: Given a set of userids $ID = \{id_1, \ldots, id_n\}$, where each id_i has a set of reviews R_i, we want to identify userids in ID that belong to the same physical authors.

One application scenario is that ID is the set of all userids that have posted reviews for a single product. R_i is the set of all reviews that userid id_i has posted on this and other products.

The task has some similarity to *authorship attribution* (AA). Conventional AA aims to identify authors of some given documents, a problem often solved using supervised learning. Let $A = \{a_1, \ldots, a_k\}$ be a set of authors (or classes), and let each author $a_i \in A$ have a set of training documents D_i. A classifier is then built using the training documents that can predict the author a of each test document d, where a must be one of the authors in A. However, this approach is not suitable for our task because we have only userids, not authors. Because some userids may belong to the same author, we cannot treat each userid as a class: in that case, we would be classifying different userids, which does not solve the problem of identify multi-id authors.

The algorithm proposed by Qian and Liu (2013) still uses supervised learning, but it learns in a similarity space (LSS). In LSS, the data consist of a set of similarity vectors, called *s*-vectors. Each feature is a similarity between two reviews. One of the reviews is called the query review q, and the other the sample review d. If q and d are written by the same author, the class label for the s-vector is labeled q-positive (or 1) meaning "d is written by the author of q"; otherwise, the class label is q-negative (or -1), meaning "d is not written by the author of q."

The LSS formulation thus gives a two-class classification problem. Any supervised learning method can be used to build a classifier: SVM was used in the study by Qian and Liu (2013). The resulting classifier can decide whether two reviews were written by the same author – a capability needed to solve the multi-id problem.

12.7.2 Training Data Preparation

For learning, we have the set of training authors $AR = \{ar_1, \ldots, ar_n\}$. Each author ar_i has a set of documents (or reviews) DR_i. Each document in DR_i is first represented with a document vector (or d-vector). The algorithm for producing the training set is given in Figure 12.5.

The algorithm first randomly selects a small set of queries Q_i from documents DR_i of each author ar_i (lines 1 and 2). For each query $q_{ij} \in Q_i$ (line 3), it selects a set of documents DR_{ij} also from DR_i (excluding q_{ij}) of the same author (line 4) to be the q-positive documents for q_{ij} (written by the author of query q_{ij}); they are labeled 1. Then, for each document dr_{ijk} in DR_{ij}, a q-positive training example with the label 1 is generated for dr_{ijk} by computing the similarities of q_{ij} and dr_{ijk} using the similarity function S (lines 5 and 6). In line 7, it selects a set of documents $DR_{ij,rest}$ from other authors to be the q-negative documents for q_{ij} (not written by the author of q_{ij}); they are labeled -1. For each document $dr_{ijk,rest}$ in $DR_{ij,rest}$ (line 8), a q-negative training example with label -1 is generated for dr_{ijk} by computing the similarities of q_{ij} and $dr_{ijk,rest}$ using Sim (line 9). How Q_i, DR_{ij}, and $DR_{ij,rest}$ (lines 2, 4, and 7) are selected is left open intentionally to give flexibility in implementation.

1. **for** each author $ar_i \in AR$ **do**
2.   select a set of query documents $Q_i \subseteq DR_i$
3.   **for** each query $q_{ij} \in Q_i$ **do**
           // produce positive training examples
4.   select a set of documents from author ar_i, $DR_{ij} \subseteq DR_i - \{q_{ij}\}$
5.   **for** each document $dr_{ijk} \in DR_{ij}$ **do**
6.   produce a training example for dr_{ijk}, $(Sim(dr_{ijk}, q_{ij}), 1)$
           // produce negative training examples
7.   select a set of documents from the rest of authors, $DR_{ij,rest} \subseteq (DR_1 \cup \ldots \cup DR_n) - DR_i$
8.   **for** each document $dr_{ijk,rest} \in DR_{ij,rest}$ **do**
9.   produce a training example for $dr_{ijk,rest}$, $(Sim(dr_{ijk,rest}, q_{ij}), -1)$

Figure 12.5 Generating training examples in LSS.

// for d_{12} of author a_1 // for d_{22} of author a_2

$<Sim(d_{12}, q_{11}), 1>$ $<Sim(d_{22}, q_{11}), -1>$

$<Sim(d_{12}, q_{21}), -1>$ $<Sim(d_{22}, q_{21}), 1>$

Figure 12.6 Example training data for LSS.

Let us see an example. Suppose we have two training authors, $\{a_1, a_2\}$. Each author has two documents d_{i1} and d_{i2}. We assume d_{i1} is used as a query and call it q_{i1} for clarity. With two query documents q_{11} and q_{21} and two nonquery documents d_{12} and d_{22}, we obtain the four training examples shown with their class labels in Figure 12.6, where $Sim(d, q)$ represents d's *s-vector* to q.

From these four training examples (*s*-vectors) of two classes, a two-class classifier can be trained, which can be used to determine whether any two documents/reviews were written by the same author. A very important property of LSS is that reviewers/authors used in testing do not have to be used in training, because the classifier simply takes an *s*-vector generated from two documents and determines whether they are written by the same author. Unlike AA, this approach does not decide whether a test document is written by a training author.

12.7.3 d-*features and* s-*features*

d-features. Each feature in the *d*-vector is called a *d-feature* (for *document feature*). Qian and Liu (2013) used four types of *d*-features related to length (Gamon, 2004a; Graham et al., 2005), frequency, *tf.idf*, and richness. For frequency- and *tf.idf*-based *d*-features, the algorithm first extracts word unigrams and syntactic and stylistic tokens from the raw documents and the parsed syntactic trees; it then computes their frequency and *tf.idf* values. Syntactic features are POS *n*-grams ($1 \leq n \leq 3$) (Hirst and Feiguina, 2007) and rewrite rules (Halteren et al., 1996). Besides the *common stylistic features* such as punctuations and function words (Argamon and Levitan, 2004), some review-specific stylistic features were also included: *all-cap word, quotation mark, bracket, exclamatory mark, contraction, two or more consecutive nonalphanumeric characters, modal auxiliary,* and *sentence with the first letter capitalized*. For richness, this model applies the richness metrics in Burrows (1992).

s-features. Each feature in an *s-vector* is called an *s-feature* and is computed using a similarity measure between document *d*'s *d*-vector and query *q*'s *d*-vector. Five types of *s*-features were used: Sim4 length, Sim7 retrieval, Sim3 sentence, SimC tfidf, and SimC richness. Sim7 and Sim3 were defined in the papers by Metzler et al. (2005) and Cao et al. (2006). The two SimC *s*-features used the cosine similarity. Sim4 length *s*-features were defined by Qian and Liu (2013). For more details about all these features, please refer to the original papers.

Let us consider an example. Suppose we have the following d-vector of a query q:

$$q: \quad 1{:}1 \; 2{:}1 \; 6{:}2$$

where $i{:}j$ is a d-feature representing term/token i with frequency count j in q. d-features with the value 0 are omitted. We also have two nonquery documents: d_1 written by the author of q and d_2 not written by the author of q. Their d-vectors are given here:

$$d_1: \quad 1{:}2 \; 2{:}1 \; 3{:}1 \qquad d_2: \quad 2{:}2 \; 3{:}1 \; 5{:}2$$

If we use cosine as one measure of similarity, we can generate one s-feature 1:0.50 for d_1 and one s-feature 1:0.27 for d_2. With more similarity measures, we can generate more s-features. Attaching their class labels (1 or -1), we obtain:

$$(q, d_1): 1 \; 1{:}0.50 \dots \qquad (q, d_2): -1 \; 1{:}0.27 \dots$$

where $x{:}y$ is an s-feature representing the xth similarity measure and its similarity value y between q and d_k.

12.7.4 Identifying Userids of the Same Author

We now use the classifier to solve our problem of identifying userids of the same author. To simplify the problem, Qian and Liu's (2013) algorithm assumes that at most two userids belong to the same author. This algorithm consists of two main steps:

1. *Candidate identification.* For each user id_i, the algorithm first finds the most likely userid id_j ($i \neq j$) that may have the same author as id_i. id_j is called the *candidate* of id_i. This function is called *candid-iden*; that is, $id_j = candid\text{-}iden(id_i)$.
2. *Candidate confirmation.* In the reverse order, the algorithm applies the function *candid-iden* on id_j, which produces id_k; that is, $id_k = candid\text{-}iden$ (id_j).

   Decision making: If $k = i$, the algorithm concludes that id_i and id_j are from the same author; otherwise, id_i and id_j are not from the same author.

The detailed algorithm is given in Figure 12.7. Lines 1–2 partition the document set D_i of each id_i in the given userid set $ID = \{id_1, id_2, \dots, id_n\}$. How the partition is done is flexible. Line 4 performs step 1, candidate identification; line 5 carries out step 2, candidate confirmation. Lines 6–8 provide the decision making for step 2. Line 6 produces a classification score

1. **for** the document set D_i of each $id_i \in ID$ **do**
2.   partition D_i into two subsets:
            (1) query set Q_i and (2) sample set S_i;
3. **for** the document set D_i of each $id_i \in ID$ **do**
4. id_j = candid-iden(id_i, ID), $i < j$;   // step 1: *candidate identification*
5. id_k = candid-iden(id_j, ID), $k \neq j$;   // step 2: *candidate confirmation*
6.   **if** $k = i$ **then** id_i and id_j are from the same author
7.   **else** id_i and id_j are not from the same author

Figure 12.7 Identifying userids from the same authors.

Function candidate-iden(id_i, ID)
1. **for** the sample document set S_j of each $id_j \in ID - \{id_i\}$ **do**
2. $pcount[id_j]$, $psum[id_j]$, $psqsum[id_j]$, $max[id_j] = 0$;
3.   **for** each query $q_i \in Q_i$ **do**
4.   **for** each sample $s_{jf} \in S_j$ **do**
5. $ss_{jf} = <(id_i, q_i), (Sim(s_{jf}, q_i), ?)>$;
6.   Classify ss_{jf} using the classifier built earlier;
7.   **if** ss_{jf} is classified positive, i.e., 1 **then**
8. $pcount[id_j] = pcount[id_j] + 1$;
9. $psum[id_j] = psum[id_j] + ss_{jf}.score$
10. $psqsum[id_j] = psqsum[id_j] + (ss_{jf}.score)^2$
11.   **if** $ss_{jf}.score > max[id_j]$ **then**
12. $max[id_j] = sr_{jf}.score$

    // Four methods to decide which id_j is the candidate for id_i

13. **if** for all $id_j \in ID - \{id_i\}$, $pcount[id_i] = 0$ **then**
14. $cid = \arg\max_{id_j \in ID-\{id_i\}} (max[id_j])$

15. **else** $cid = \arg\max_{id_j \in ID-\{id_i\}} (\dfrac{pcount[id_j]}{|S_j|})$ // **1. Voting**

16. $cid = \arg\max_{id_j \in ID-\{id_i\}} (\dfrac{psum[id_j]}{|S_j|})$ // **2. ScoreSum**

17. $cid = \arg\max_{id_j \in ID-\{id_i\}} (\dfrac{(psum[id_j])^2}{|S_j|})$ // **3. ScoreSqSum**

18. $cid = \arg\max_{id_j \in ID-\{id_i\}} (max[id_j])$ // **4. ScoreMax**

19. return cid;

Figure 12.8 Identifying the candidate.

using the classifier described in Section 12.7.1. The key function here is *candid-iden*. Its algorithm is shown in Figure 12.8.

The *candid-iden* function takes two arguments: the query userid id_i and the whole set of userids ID. It basically classifies each sample ss_{jf} in sample set S_j

of $id_j \in ID\text{-}\{id_i\}$ as positive (q_i-positive) or negative (q_i-negative) (lines 4–6). We then aggregate the classification results to determine which userid is likely to belong to the same author as id_i. Line 2 initializes variables for recording the aggregated values used in the final decision-making process.

One simple aggregation method is voting. That is, we can count the number of positive classifications of the sample documents for each userid in $ID\text{-}\{id_i\}$. The userid id_j with the highest count is the candidate cid that may share the same author as query id_i. cid is returned as the candidate.

Other methods may depend on which output value the classifier produces. Four methods, including the voting method, were proposed in the research by Qian and Liu (2013). The other three methods require the classifier to produce a prediction score to reflect the positive and negative certainty. SVM can produce such as score for each classification.

All four alternative methods are given in Figure 12.8, and briefly described here:

1. *Voting*. For each sample from userid id_j, if it is classified as positive, one vote/count is added to $pcount[id_j]$. The userid with the highest $pcount$ is regarded as the candidate userid, cid (line 15). Note that normalization is applied because the sizes of the sample sets S_j can be different for different userids. In lines 13 and 14, if all documents of all userids are classified as negative ($pcount[id_j] = 0$), that also implies $psum[id_j] = psqsum[id_j] = 0$), and we use method 4.

2. *ScoreSum*. This method works similarly to voting, except that instead of counting positive classifications, it sums all scores of positive classifications in $psum[id_j]$ for each userid (line 9). The decision is also made in a similar way (line 16).

3. *ScoreSqSum*. This method works in the same way as ScoreSum, except that it sums the squared scores of positive classifications in $psqsum[id_j]$ for each userid (line 10). The decision is also made in a similar way (line 17).

4. *ScoreMax*. This method works similarly to the voting method as well. except that it finds the maximum classification score for the documents of each userid (lines 11 and 12). The decision is made in line 18.

The experiments were conducted using a large set of Amazon.com book reviews. The results showed that even with one hundred userids, the F_1 score could reach 0.85. When the number of userids was smaller, the results were almost perfect.

We now turn to the two related problems presented at the beginning of the section:

- *Same reviewer posting on multiple sites*. The preceding algorithm can be directly applied to solve this problem. As an alternative, another method solves this problem purely based on the user behaviors (Zafarani and Liu, 2013).

- *Author change*. This problem can be solved in about the same way. Here, we assume that the review hosting site can detect a major change of IP address used by a userid/account, meaning that either the reviewer has moved to a new place or there is an author change. To find out which is the case, we can use the reviews of the userid before the change as queries and the reviews after the change as samples. If the classification results show that most samples are positive, an author change has likely occurred.

Finally, I would like to point out that the challenge of identifying authors with multiple userids is to some extent related to the problem of finding spamming groups, because an author with multiple userids can be regarded as a group. In Section 12.6, a group was defined as a set of userids that have all posted reviews for a set of products. Because a spamming author with multiple userids usually writes reviews for multiple products (especially the case for paid reviewers), we can use the algorithm in Section 12.6 to find the userid groups. Alternatively, we can perform frequent pattern mining on the transaction data, where each transaction represents a single userid containing all products that the userid has reviewed. However, these methods cannot determine whether the userids in a group belong to the same author or multiple authors. Nevertheless, these methods can also be integrated for accurate detection.

12.8   Exploiting Burstiness in Reviews

This section examines the topic of spamming activities manifested as review bursts. A review burst is a sudden increase in the number of reviews in a short period of time for a product (Fei et al., 2013). In the normal situation, reviews for a product arrive randomly. However, sometimes the reviews for a product are bursty, meaning that concentrations of reviews occur in particular time periods. Review bursts can also occur at the individual reviewer level, meaning that a reviewer posts a large number of reviews in a short period of time. This has been used as a behavioral feature in several existing detection algorithms. In this section, we focus on review bursts for a particular product.

A review burst can be due to either one or both of the following reasons:

- A sudden increase in popularity of the product. For example, a successful TV commercial may cause a product to suddenly become popular. If a large number of customers purchase the product, the product is likely to get more reviews. Most reviewers in this kind of burst are likely to be genuine reviewers. Such bursts can be easily detected by merchant sites such as Amazon.com that sell the product and also host its reviews.
- The product is under a spam attack. In this scenario, a number of spam or fake reviews are posted in a short period of time. As mentioned earlier,

posting a single fake review may not change the overall sentiment for the product if the product already has some negative or positive reviews. Likewise, if a product has no review, posting only a single positive review may not be enough to sway the public, because readers usually do not trust the single positive review. Hence, spam bursts are mainly generated in two main situations:

- A business promotes its products or services by giving its customers discounts, on the condition that they write positive reviews for the products.
- A spammer group uses several accounts or reviewer ids to write fake reviews aimed at promoting or disparaging some target products in a short period of time.

Fei et al. (2013) proposed a fake reviewer detection algorithm based on bursts. Their algorithm rests on the hypothesis that reviewers within the same burst usually have similar states (spam or nonspam). That is, if a burst is deemed to be an attack by spammers, then most reviewers in the burst are likely to be spammers; however, if a burst is not a spam attack, reviewers in it are likely to be genuine reviewers. By exploiting several features of reviewers in bursts, the algorithm is able to capture their spamicity (the degree of being a spammer). The algorithm works in two steps:

1. Detect review bursts for each product using *kernel density estimation* (KDE)
2. Use Markov random fields (MRFs) to model and to detect spammers

Because using KDE to discover bursts is quite standard, here we focus on step 2.

MRF are a class of probabilistic graphical models particularly suited for solving inference problems with uncertainty in observed data. An MRF consists of an undirected graph in which each node can be in any of a finite number of states. The state of a node is assumed to be dependent upon each of its neighbors, but independent of any other node in the graph. This assumption yields a pairwise MRF that is a special case of the general MRF. In pairwise MRF, the joint probability of the network can be written as a product of pairwise factors rather than the maximal cliques used in general MRF.

In the model developed by Fei et al. (2013), a node is a reviewer that can be in any of the three states: Spammer (S), Mixed (M), or NonSpammer (NS). The rationale for using "Mixed" as a state is that some reviewers may write fake reviews sometimes (for various reasons), but write genuine reviews at other times as legitimate buyers. Each edge between any two nodes signifies that the corresponding reviewers have appeared in a burst together. Base on the graph, we want to infer the maximum likelihood assignment of states to nodes – that is, to compute the node marginals. Fei et al. (2013) used the loopy belief propagation (LBP) method to perform the inference with the help of a set of spammer features such as *Amazon verified purchase ratio, rating deviation, burst review ratio, review content similarity,* and *reviewer burstiness,* and burst features such as *burst Amazon verified purchase ratio, burst sharpness, burst content similarity,* and *burst rating deviation.*

Evaluation based on classification. Besides the preceding burst-based spam detection method, Fei et al.'s (2013) paper proposed an objective method for evaluating spam detection results. Owing to the difficulty of obtaining ground truth data on spam (fake) and nonspam (nonfake) that can be used in model building and model testing, researchers have mainly used human evaluation in previous works. However, human evaluation is subjective: different evaluators often have different tolerance levels, even if they are given the same set of behavior indicators and reviews of a reviewer. The proposed method uses supervised classification to evaluate the discovered review spammers, which is complementary to human evaluation, and thus gives us more information about whether the detection algorithm is doing a good job.

First, it assumes that if a reviewer is labeled as a spammer, all his reviews are considered to be spam reviews, and if a reviewer is labeled as a nonspammer, then all his reviews are considered to be nonspam reviews. This gives us a two-class classification problem. Next, a classifier can be built to separate the two classes of reviews. Fei et al. (2013) used SVM with unigram features and Boolean assignment of feature values. A key point here is that in the detection algorithm, only behavior features are employed, but in the review classification, only linguistic features are applied. If the classification shows good accuracy, we know that the reviews written by reviewers labeled as spammers and nonspammers based on their behaviors are also separable based on their review text. This, to some extent, shows that the spam detection algorithm is effective.

Xie et al. (2012) proposed another burst-based method to detect singleton reviewers who are likely to be involved in review spamming. Singleton reviewers write only a single review. These authors' paper used the store review data from the study by Wang et al. (2011). Their technique first detects review bursts for each store. If a burst has many reviews with ratings (e.g., five stars) that are very different from other reviews, and if many of the reviewers are singleton reviewers, the algorithm concludes that these singleton reviewers are likely to be involved in spamming. That is, they probably received some discounts or other benefits from the store in exchange for posting positive reviews about the store.

The preceding algorithms analyzed bursts of reviews only for individual products or services. However, bursts also occur for reviewers; that is, a reviewer may write many reviews in a short period of time. Such a burst may also indicate possible spamming activities. For example, the reviewer might have the task of writing reviews for many products of a brand in a short period of time. However, I am not aware of any study of this problem in the literature.

12.9   Future Research Directions

Although many algorithms have been proposed to detect fake reviews, we have a long way to go before we can confidently weed out opinion spamming activities. There are also many interesting research directions that have not been, or barely been, explored. Here, I describe several such directions.

Multiple-site comparisons. Spammers who promote or disparage some target products may write fake reviews on multiple sites to achieve the maximum effect, as many websites may sell the same products or host reviews about those products. It would be interesting to compare reviews of the same product across these sites to discover abnormalities – for example, similar reviews (contents or ratings) that are written at about the same time, similar userids, and the same/similar IP addresses. It is quite unlikely that a genuine reviewer would bother to post positive reviews for the same product on multiple sites, considering that users often need to register and sign in to post a review at a website.

Language inconsistency. To suit different products and to stress personal experiences, fake reviewers may write something that is inconsistent or against social norms in different reviews. For example, to promote a woman's watch, a paid reviewer might write "I bought this watch for my wife and she simply loves it." Later on, to promote a man's shirt, the same reviewer might write "I bought this shirt for my husband yesterday." To promote a diaper, the reviewer could write "My baby loves the diaper." Later on, to promote a wedding gown, he might write "My girlfriend tried the wedding gown yesterday." The first and the second sentences indicate gender inconsistency, while the third and the fourth sentences show that the reviewer's behavior is against the social norm – in some cultures, people almost never have children before getting married. There are many other possible inconsistencies that can be detected, such as age, with/without children, ethnicity, and so on.

Nature of business. In many cases, the nature of the product or business can help one detect fake reviewing activities. For example, if all positive reviews of a hotel come from people living nearby to the hotel (based on their IP addresses), these positive reviews are clearly suspicious – after all, few people would stay in a hotel if they have homes nearby. However, there are myriad types of businesses. and manually compiling such normal and abnormal behavior patterns is very difficult. The challenge is to design an algorithm that can automatically discover such abnormal behavioral patterns for each domain.

Web usage abnormality. Web servers record almost everything that a person does at a website, which is valuable for detecting fake reviews. For example, using the IP address information and click behaviors, we may find that all positive reviews for a product come from the same or similar IP addresses, or that many reviewers who have never visited the website suddenly come to a product page directly and write positive reviews. In the first case, all the reviews might have come from the same person. In the second case, the seller of the product might have paid people to write reviews for the product and also provided a link to the product page. The fake reviewers simply clicked the link and posted fake reviews.

I believe that the rule mining method presented in Section 12.4 can be extended to find many such abnormal patterns automatically. I am aware that several review hosting sites are using such data to detect fake reviews, but no academic research has been reported that used the web usage data of reviewers to detect fake reviews. The main reason is that academics have difficulty gaining access to such data for research, partly due to privacy concerns and partly due to the fact that review hosting companies do not want to publicize the detection methods that they use: if fake reviewers know the methods, they will change their behaviors and/or writing styles to avoid detection.

Early detection. Most existing algorithms rely on patterns detected from review content and reviewers' behaviors. Most types of patterns take some time to form. However, by the time the patterns finally show themselves, some major damages might have already been done. Thus, it is important to design algorithms that can detect fake reviews as soon as possible, ideally right after they are posted.

12.10   Summary

As social media are increasingly used for critical decision making by organizations and individuals alike, opinion spamming is also becoming more and more sophisticated – and more widespread. For many businesses, posting fake opinions themselves or employing professional fake-review writers to do it for them has become a cheap means of marketing and brand promotion. Fortunately, major online review hosting sites are actively combating fake reviews by detecting them using computer algorithms.

In the past few years, many effective algorithms have been proposed in academia, and some of them or their simplifications (the industry usually uses simpler algorithms) have been used in practice. I believe that we already have the main ideas and algorithms that can catch most fake reviews and reviewers. These algorithms just need to be adapted to the real-life application environment. For example, none of the published research papers have used any site private data, which consist of web usage data (e.g., IP addresses and click behaviors) and reviewer profile data, in their algorithms or in their evaluations. If such private site data are available in an application, existing published algorithms can be augmented with additional features gleaned from them. In certain cases, modifications of the published algorithms will be needed. Companies can also apply a large number of web usage mining algorithms in the existing literature to generate effective features (Liu, 2006, 2011).

Going forward, I believe that the main technical difficulty is how to spot fake reviews right after they are posted. This is a serious challenge because most existing algorithms need sufficient evidence to judge whether a review is suspicious (except text classification algorithms), but such evidences may take a while to accumulate. The effects on a small business can be devastating during the period if it is a nasty negative review. I personally know of two such cases where businesses suffered damage after being targeted by fake reviews.

As detection algorithms are getting smarter in spotting sophisticated fake reviewers, fake reviewers are also becoming more careful and sophisticated in their writing. They also try to guess the strategies that are used by detection algorithms so that they can avoid being detected. This is an arms race between detection algorithms and spammers. I am optimistic that fake reviews will become less of an issue in the future due to the joint efforts involving researchers, practitioners, regulators, and law enforcement agencies. Measures are also being taken by review hosting sites to make it more difficult to post fake reviews. For example, some sites do not allow people to write reviews for a product or service unless they have purchased the product or used the service. However, it will be very hard to completely eradicate fake reviews or deceptive opinions because the incentive is too high.

Finally, I would reiterate that opinion spamming occurs not only in reviews, but also in other forms of social media, such as blogs, forum discussions, commentaries, and microblogs. Although little direct research has investigated these contexts, many algorithms designed for detecting fake reviews are also applicable to detecting opinion spam in these other forms of social media. Some additional complexities do arise with these forms of social media, however. For example, some existing detection algorithms need review ratings, which reflect the sentiments of the reviewers about the products being reviewed – but none of the posts in the other forms of social media has such a rating. If an algorithm needs this information, it has to perform sentiment analysis first.

13   Quality of Reviews

In this chapter, we discuss the quality of reviews. This topic is related to opinion spam detection yet also different, because low-quality reviews may not be spam or fake reviews, and fake reviews may not be perceived as low-quality reviews by readers. Indeed, as we discussed in Chapter 12, it is very difficult to spot fake reviews simply by reading them. For this reason, fake reviews may also be seen as helpful or high-quality reviews if the imposters write their reviews early and craft them well.

The objective of this task is to determine the quality, helpfulness, usefulness, or utility of each review (Kim et al., 2006; Zhang and Varadarajan, 2006; Ghose and Ipeirotis, 2007; Liu et al., 2007). This is a meaningful task because it is desirable to rank reviews based on quality or helpfulness when showing reviews to the user, with the most helpful reviews being presented first. In fact, many review aggregation or hosting sites have used this practice for years. They obtain the helpfulness or quality score of each review by asking readers to provide helpfulness feedback about each review. For example, at Amazon. com, the reader can indicate whether she finds a review helpful by responding to the question "Was the review helpful to you?", which appears just below each review. The feedback results from all responses are then aggregated and displayed right before each review – for example, "15 of 16 people found the following review helpful." Although most review hosting sites already provide this service, automatically determining the quality of each review is still useful because a good number of user feedback ratings may take a long time to accumulate. That is why many reviews have few or no feedback scores, especially new reviews.

13.1   Quality Prediction As a Regression Problem

Determining the quality of reviews is usually formulated as a regression problem. The learned model assigns a quality score to each review, which can be used in review rankings or review recommendations. In this area of research, the ground truth data used for both training and testing are typically the user-helpfulness feedback given for each review, which is provided for

354

each review at many review hosting sites. So, unlike in fake review detection, the training and testing data here are not an issue. Researchers have used many types of features for model building.

Kim et al. (2006) used SVM regression to solve the problem. Their feature sets included the following elements:

Structure features: review length, number of sentences, percentages of question sentences and exclamations, and the number of HTML bold tags <b> and line breaks <br>.

Lexical features: unigrams and bigrams with TFIDF weights.

Syntactic features: age of parsed tokens that are of open class (i.e., nouns, verbs, adjectives, and adverbs), percentage of tokens that are nouns, percentage of tokens that are verbs, percentage of tokens that are verbs conjugated in the first person, and percentage of tokens that are adjectives or adverbs.

Semantic features: product aspects and sentiment words.

Meta-data features: review rating (number of stars).

In the study by Zhang and Varadarajan (2006), the authors also treated this task as a regression problem. They used similar features: review length, review rating, counts of some specific POS tags, sentiment words, TFIDF weighting scores, wh-words, product aspect mentions, comparison with product specifications, comparison with editorial reviews, and so on.

Unlike in the preceding approaches, Liu et al. (2008) considered three main factors: reviewers' expertise, the timeliness of reviews, and review styles based on POS tags. A nonlinear regression model was proposed to integrate the factors. This work focused on movie reviews.

In Ghose and Ipeirotis (2007, 2010), three additional sets of features were used: (1) reviewer profile features, which were available from the review site; (2) reviewer history features, which captured the helpfulness of the person's reviews in the past; and (3) a set of readability features, comprising spelling errors and readability indices from the readability research. For learning, the authors tried both regression and binary classification.

Lu et al. (2010b) looked at the problem from a different angle. They investigated how the social context of reviewers can enhance the accuracy of a text-based review quality predictor. They argued that the social context can reveal a great deal of information about the quality of reviewers, which in turn suggests the quality of their reviews. Specifically, their approach was based on the following hypotheses:

Author consistency hypothesis. Reviews from the same author are of similar quality.

Trust consistency hypothesis. A link from a reviewer r_1 to a reviewer r_2 is an explicit or implicit statement of trust. Reviewer r_1 trusts reviewer

r_2 only if the quality of reviewer r_2 is at least as high as that of reviewer r_1.

Co-citation consistency hypothesis. People are consistent in how they trust other people. So, if two reviewers r_1 and r_2 are trusted by the same third reviewer r_3, then their quality should be similar.

Link consistency hypothesis. If two people are connected in the social network (r_1 trusts r_2, or r_2 trusts r_1, or both), then their review quality should be similar.

These hypotheses were enforced as regularizing constraints and added into the text-based linear regression model to solve the review quality prediction problem. In their experiments, the authors used data from Ciao (www.ciao .co.uk), a community review website. In Ciao, people not only write reviews for products and services, but also rate the reviews written by others. Furthermore, people can add members to their network of trusted members or "Circle of Trust," if they find these members' reviews to be consistently interesting and helpful. Clearly, this technique will not be applicable to websites that do not have a trust-based social network in place.

13.2   Other Methods

O'Mahony and Smyth (2009) proposed a classification approach to classify helpful and nonhelpful reviews. Their model included the following features:

Reputation features. The mean (R1) and standard deviation (R2) of review helpfulness over all reviews authored by the reviewer, the percentage of reviews authored by the reviewer that received a minimum of T feedbacks (R3), and so on.

Content features. Review length (C1), the ratio of uppercase to lowercase characters in the review text (C3), and so on.

Social features. The number of reviews authored by the reviewer (SL1), the mean (SL2) and standard deviation (SL3) of the number of reviews authored by all reviewers, and so on.

Sentiment features. The rating score of the review (ST1), the mean (ST5) and standard deviation (ST6) of the scores assigned by the reviewer over all reviews authored by the reviewer, and so on.

Liu et al. (2007) formulated this task as a two-class classification problem. However, they argued that using the helpfulness votes as the ground truth may not be appropriate because of three biases: (1) vote imbalance (a very large percentage of votes are helpful votes); (2) early bird bias (early reviews tend to get more votes); and (3) winner circle bias (if a review gets many votes, it will be ranked high on the review site, which helps it get even more votes). In particular, lower-ranked reviews may get few votes, but are not necessarily of low quality. The authors then divided reviews into four categories – "best review," "good review," "fair review," and "bad review" – based on whether the reviews discussed many aspects of the product and provided convincing opinions. Manual labeling was carried out to produce the gold-standard training and testing data. In their classification, these authors used SVM to perform binary classification. Only the "bad review" category was regarded as the low-quality class; the other three categories were regarded as belonging to the high-quality class. The features for learning were informativeness, subjectiveness, and readability, each of which contained a set of individual features.

Tsur and Rappoport (2009) studied the helpfulness of book reviews using an unsupervised approach that was quite different from the previously described supervised methods. The method works in three steps. Given a collection of reviews, it first identifies a set of important terms in the reviews. These terms together form a vector representing a virtual optimal or core review. Then, each actual review is mapped or converted to this vector representation based on occurrences of the discovered important terms in the review. Finally, each review is assigned a rank score based on the distance of the review to the virtual review (both are represented as vectors).

Moghaddam et al. (2012) proposed a new problem of personalized review quality prediction for the recommendation of helpful reviews. All of the preceding methods assume that the helpfulness of a review is the same for all users/readers, which, these authors argued, is not true. To solve the new problem, they proposed several factorization models. These models are based on the assumption that the observed review ratings depend on some latent features of reviews, reviewers, raters/users, and products. In essence, their paper treated this task as a personalized recommendation problem. The proposed technique to solve the problem is quite involved. Some background knowledge about this form of recommendation can be found in Chapter 12 of Liu, 2006, 2011).

All the approaches mentioned so far rank reviews based on the computed helpfulness or quality scores. However, Tsaparas et al. (2011) argued that these approaches do not consider an important fact – namely, that the top few high-quality reviews may be highly redundant and repetitive. In their work, they proposed the problem of selecting a *comprehensive* yet *small* set of high-quality reviews that cover many different aspects of the reviewed entity as well as different viewpoints. They formulated the problem as a maximum coverage problem, and presented an algorithm to solve the problem. Earlier work by Lappas and Gunopulos (2010) also studied the problem of finding a small set of reviews that cover *all* product aspects.

13.3   Some New Frontiers

Although the existing research can help identify high-quality reviews to some extent, new problems have also emerged. I have had opportunities to talk to several industrial executives who deal with reviews in their daily work. They revealed that the information overload problem is still not solved. On the consumer side, people still find reviews too long to read even though good reviews are ranked high. Some evidence suggests that the brief pros-and-cons summary for each review used by some review hosting sites is useful because it gives people a quick overview of the review. However, these summaries also have a weakness: they are not detailed enough, and some people still want to selectively see the detailed opinions and the reasons for them regarding those aspects that they really care about (e.g., why products are good or bad, and in what sense). There is no simple way to get there without reading the reviews; in other words, pros and cons do not provide links to the details in the review.

One way to solve this problem is to mine reasons for opinions and summarize them as we discussed in Section 2.1.5, and then provide a link from each pro or con item to the text segment in the review that elaborates on the opinion. This leads to the next problem: how to effectively present opinions and their reasons to users in a visual framework so that they can see this information easily. So far, little work has been done on this task, but I can think of two ways.

First, we can extend the summarization framework described by Hu and Liu (2004) to include a summary of opinion reasons. That is, when presenting positive or negative sentences for each aspect, the system can also summarize them so that the big issues and benefits can be clustered and displayed at the top. The advantage of this approach is that it is brief and focused, and thus easy for users to see. The disadvantage is that the excerpts do not appear in the context from which they were extracted. In many cases, understanding the context in which an opinion or reason appears is very important.

The second solution is to use links and some color scheme to connect and highlight each pro or con, and the detailed reasons for it, in each actual review. The disadvantages and advantages of this approach are just the opposite of those for the first approach. Perhaps a combination of the two will give the user a better experience. Of course, there could also be some other, even better solutions.

On the business side, the reasons behind reviewers' opinions are extremely important: companies want to know the detailed complaints and issues about their products or services as experienced by their customers. That is why, in many applications, negative opinions weigh more heavily than positive ones. Hence, mining, summarizing, and highlighting reasons for opinions are critical.

13.4 Summary

Determining review helpfulness is an important research topic. It is especially useful for products and services that have a large of number reviews. To help the reader get to quality opinions quickly, review sites should rank reviews based on their quality or utility. Many review hosting sites are already doing that.

Some cautionary notes are in order, though. First, as we discussed in Chapter 9 in the context of opinion search and retrieval, the review ranking (rankings) should reflect the natural distribution of positive and negative opinions. It is not a good idea to rank all positive (or all negative) reviews at the top simply because they have high-quality scores. The redundancy issue raised in Tsaparas et al. (2011) is a valid one. In my opinion, both quality and distribution (in terms of positive and negative viewpoints) are important.

Second, readers tend to determine whether a review is helpful or not based on whether the review expresses opinions on many aspects of the product and appear to be genuine. A spammer can satisfy that requirement by carefully crafting a review that appears just like a normal helpful review. In consequence, using the number of helpfulness feedbacks to define review quality or as the ground truth alone can be problematic. Furthermore, user feedback can be spammed. Feedback spam is a subproblem of click fraud in search advertising, where a person or robot clicks on some online advertisements to give the impression of real customer clicks. Here, a robot or a human spammer can click on the helpfulness feedback button to increase the helpfulness counts of a review.

Finally, many people do not want to read long reviews even if they are ranked. Thus, means of finding reasons for opinions, issues/problems, and benefits; summarizing them; and presenting them in a suitable way are required. However, little research has been done in this direction so far.

14   Conclusion

This book introduced the field of sentiment analysis or opinion mining. It presented some basic knowledge and mature techniques in detail and surveyed numerous other state-of-the-art algorithms and techniques. Owing to numerous challenging research problems and a wide variety of practical applications, sentiment analysis has been a very active research area in several computer science fields, including NLP, data mining, web mining, and information retrieval. It has also spread to management science (Hu et al., 2006; Archak et al., 2007; Das and Chen, 2007; Dellarocas et al., 2007; Ghose et al., 2007; Park et al., 2007; Chen and Xie, 2008) and other social science fields such as communications and political science because of its importance to business and society as a whole. With the rapid expansion of social media on the web, the importance of sentiment analysis is also growing by the day.

In the book, I first defined the problem of sentiment analysis (Chapter 2), which provides a common framework to unify different research directions and research problems in the area. It also presents a schema to convert unstructured free text to structured data, which facilitates qualitative and quantitative analysis of opinions. I then discussed the widely studied problem of document-level sentiment classification (Chapter 3), which aims to determine whether an opinion document (e.g., a product review) expresses a positive or a negative sentiment. This was followed by Chapter 4's exploration of sentence-level subjectivity and sentiment classification. These tasks determine whether a sentence is opinionated, and if opinionated, whether it carries a positive or negative opinion.

Chapters 5 and 6 focused on aspect-based sentiment analysis, which employs the full problem definition from Chapter 2. Sentiment analysis is a multifaceted problem with multiple challenging subproblems. Chapter 5 focused on the task of aspect-based sentiment classification, and Chapter 6 was devoted to the task of opinion target extraction, which includes the extraction of entities and their aspects. These are the two core tasks of aspect-based sentiment analysis and have been studied extensively in different communities. Chapter 7 studied the problem of sentiment lexicon generation, including the two dominant approaches proposed to solve it.

Chapter 8 dealt with comparative and superlative opinion mining. Comparisons represent a different type of opinions and require different methods for their analysis. The chapter first defined the problem and then presented some techniques for comparison mining. Chapter 9 addressed opinion summarization and search. Opinion summarization is a special form of multidocument summarization, but differs from the traditional multidocument summarization in that it can be done in a structured manner, which enables both qualitative and quantitative analysis, and the visualization of opinions. The topic of opinion search or retrieval was also introduced in that chapter.

Chapter 10 moved to online debates, discussions, and comments, which represent different types of social media content than reviews. These posts are characterized by dialogues involving user exchanges of opinions and arguments. Such social media forms also introduced another type of sentiment – namely, *agreement* and *disagreement* (or *contention*). In addition to presenting several novel mining tasks, the analysis of debates and discussions also brings us to the social science research fields of communication and political science: researchers in these fields are very interested in online discussions and debates about social and political issues, and the behaviors of people participating in such debates and discussions.

Chapter 11 focused on intent mining, another important social media mining task that is closely related to but also different from sentiment analysis. This topic has not received much attention in academia or the industry so far, but it likely has a great potential for commercial applications. For example, commercial intents expressed in social media are clearly useful to advertisers or recommender systems.

Chapter 12 discussed opinion spam detection. Opinion spamming by writing fake or deceptive reviews and posting bogus comments are increasingly becoming an important issue as more people rely on the opinions found on the web for their decision making. To ensure the trustworthiness of such opinions, combating opinion spamming is an urgent and critical task.

Last but not least, we discussed the quality and utility of online reviews in Chapter 13. Studying the quality of reviews enables websites to rank high-quality reviews at the top, thereby facilitating users to get needed opinions easily.

After reading this book, you probably feel that sentiment analysis is highly challenging from a technical standpoint. Indeed, it is. Although the research community has attempted many subproblems and proposed a large number of approaches to solving the problems, none of the subproblems has been solved satisfactorily as yet. In fact, no standard approach exists for any subproblem. Our understanding and knowledge about sentiment analysis and its solutions remain very limited. The main reason is that this is a NLP task, and NLP has no easy problems. Another reason may be due to the popular ways of doing research, which rely too much on machine learning. Some of the most effective machine learning algorithms – for example, support vector machines (SVMs), naïve Bayes, conditional random fields (CRFs), and deep learning – produce no human-understandable results. Thus, although they may help us achieve improved accuracy, we know little about how and why, apart from some superficial knowledge gained in the manual feature engineering process.

To rectify the situation, I covered a great deal of linguistic knowledge in this book. Such knowledge tells us which expressions people often use to voice their opinions and how we can recognize these expressions from a computational perspective. As explained early on in the book, my presentation of this linguistic information does not follow the linguistic tradition because my objective is computational realization of the linguistic knowledge in a computer program to extract opinions and sentiments from text. I encourage linguists to join this research. After all, sentiment is an important aspect of the semantics of the natural language, and it is also of great practical importance. These ideas should provide linguists with enough motivation to develop a computational linguistic theory of sentiment and opinion, along with their related concepts such as emotion, mood, and affect, from a natural language perspective. Although these concepts have been researched extensively by psychologists, neuropsychologists, and sociologists, they have focused on people's psychological states of mind, not the language constructions used in expressing such states of minds or feelings.

Beyond the applications of mining consumer opinions about products and services and public opinions about politics, such a theory will be very useful for analyzing people's states of mind from their posts on social media platforms such as Facebook and Twitter, which can have a profound impact on the society. For example, schools always want information about the mental health of their students. They want to detect any depression and even suicidal intentions of children. Law enforcement authorities want to identify potential criminals and people with antisocial behaviors who might cause major damage to society. For example, in some mass shooting cases in the United States, those shooters had shown many troubling signs in their social network pages.

We live in an exciting time. The massive amount of social media data being collected is enabling scientists to develop new understandings of both individuals and the larger society. Most past research results in social sciences were derived from small-scale lab experiments. With the big social media data, social scientists can now conduct research on a massive scale. On the one hand, this enables them to gain a better understanding of human nature and society as a whole; on the other hand, it allows them to understand each and every one of us at the individual level. This has not been possible in the past. It is sometimes said that the virtual society may be a truer society in the sense that people hide behind anonymous userids and speak their true feelings without having to follow any social norms such as being polite in front of people. In a familiar story, before knowing that a person has committed a terrible crime, her neighbors believed that she was a very nice person. We now have the capability to analyze everyone's posts on Facebook and Twitter to detect any early warning signs of such impending antisocial behavior.

On the opinion spam detection front, social scientists who study lies and deceptions can potentially contribute a great deal to the detection of deceptions, lies, and rumors in social media. Such unethical posts are widespread on the web. Detecting them is important to ensure healthy growth of social media and to ensure social media act as a trusted source of information rather than just a place for people to spread lies and rumors. Although we have already studied these topics to some extent in the computer science community, we have only scratched the surface, and computer scientists generally lack the necessary training and expertise to do a good job.

In the past two decades, researchers have made significant progress in both research and application of sentiment analysis. This is evident from the large number of start-ups and established companies that offer sentiment analysis services. There is a real – and huge – need in industry for such services – after all, every business wants to know how consumers perceive its products and services, and those of its competitors. The same is often true about consumers: whenever one wants to buy something, one wants to know the opinions and experiences of existing users. In the past few years, government and private organizations have begun showing strong interest in obtaining public opinions about their policies and their images. These practical needs and the technical challenges that accompany them will keep the field vibrant and lively for years to come.

Building on what has been done so far, I believe that two research directions are particularly promising. First, there are many opportunities to design novel machine learning algorithms that can learn from large volumes of text data and mine general as well as domain-specific knowledge that is useful to sentiment analysis. Domain-specific knowledge is very important because every domain has some special desirable and undesirable situations that are different from those of other domains. I also believe that learning to perform a single task is not very productive. Integrated learning of all related tasks simultaneously, made possible by exploiting their interrelations, is an especially interesting area. Learning should also consider prior knowledge, which can guide training to learn much more accurately.

Second, in addition to conducting research, we should build more advanced sentiment analysis systems. Building practical systems and applications will enable us to see the full spectrum of the problem and gain deeper insights. For system building, I believe that a holistic or integrated approach is more likely to be successful. Ideally, such a system will perform and deal with all sub-problems at the same time, because their interactions could help solve each individual subproblem. I am optimistic that this problem will be solved satisfactorily in the near future for widespread practical applications.

By no means do I claim that a fully automated and accurate solution can be designed and implemented very soon. However, it is possible to devise effective semi-automated solutions. The key is to fully understand the whole range of issues and pitfalls, cleverly manage them, and determine which portions can be done automatically and which portions need human assistance. In the continuum between the fully manual solution and the fully automated solution, as time goes by we can push more and more toward automation. I do not see a silver bullet emerging anytime soon. A good bet will be to work hard on a large number of diverse application domains, understand each of them, and design general solutions gradually. After all, a human person also takes many years of continuous learning and experiencing to understand things around him or her.

I also believe that interdisciplinary research from computer scientists and social scientists can potentially make major contributions to research in both fields and to society as a whole. Many social scientists have realized the potential of social media analysis and sentiment analysis and are actively working on related projects. However, their ability to handle large volumes of data is limited. Collaboration with computer scientists, however, can enable novel discoveries. My own group is involved in two such collaborations, and it has been an eye-opening and mutually beneficial experience. Several research problems and their solution techniques described in Chapter 10 have already resulted from these collaborations.

Finally, I would point out that much of the current research on sentiment analysis has been done in English. Although researchers from many countries have conducted research in the field, most of them used English content. This book is also mainly based on research done in English and my own experience in building a sentiment analysis system to analyze English-language opinion text. I am aware of many systems in other languages, but they are mostly based on methods developed for the English language with some customizations and/or additions to handle language-specific issues. I expect that more research in other languages will be reported in the research literature in the future. I also hope that a language-independent platform or system can be built so that a developer can specify opinion- and sentiment-related knowledge of a language to the system, with the system then performing sentiment analysis in that language automatically.

Appendix

Additional categories of sentiment composition rules to those given in Section 5.2.1 are listed here.

11. *Having everything or nothing*: If an entity has everything that one wants, then one is positive about the entity. Conversely, if an entity has nothing that one wants, then one is negative about the entity. For example:

    "This car has everything that my mother really wants."
    "This plan has nothing that I need."
    "This car has all the features."

    We thus have the following composition rules:

PO	:: = HAVE EVERYTHING
NE	:: = HAVE NOTHING
HAVE	:: = have | has | ...
EVERYTHING	:: = everything | all | ...
NOTHING	:: = nothing | ...

    In using these rules, we need to consider some exceptions, which are not difficult to deal with. For example:

    "This car has everything that is bad."
    "This car has nothing bad."
    "This program has all the bad features."

12. *Being exact the way that one wants*: If something is exact the way that one wants, then one is positive about the entity.

    "This phone is designed exactly the way that I wanted."
    "They polished the car exactly the way that I wanted."
    "My hair looks exact the way that I want."

    We then have the following PO rule:

PO	:: = EXACTLY the way ONE WANT
EXACTLY	:: = exact | exactly | ...

```
ONE        :: = I | we | you | one | ...
WANT       :: = want | need | ...
```

Composition rules for this category of sentiment expressions can be diverse. The PO rule covers only a subset of cases.

13. *Having or using some positive or negative potential items, or having something that one wants*: If an entity has some positive potential items (PPIs) or anything that one wants, then one tends to be positive about the entity. If an entity has some negative potential items (NPIs), then one tends to be negative about the entity. For example:

> "Google has the answer."
> "This vacuum cleaner has/uses bag."
> "This store has the shoes that I want."

Here *answer* is the PPI, *bag* is a NPI in the vacuum cleaner domain (as older vacuums use bags to hold dust, and these bags are expensive to buy and troublesome to change), and *shoes* is neither a PPI nor an NPI. See the definitions of PPI and NPI in Section 5.2.1.

```
PO         :: = USE PPI
 | HAVE NOUN-PHRASE ONE WANT
NE         :: = HAVE NPI
USE        :: = use | have | has | ...
NOUN-PHRASE means any noun phrase.
```

14. *Saving or wasting resources*: If an entity saves resources, it is desirable (or positive), but if it wastes resources, it is undesirable (or negative). For example:

> "This device can save electricity."
> "Buying this car is wasting of money."
> "He has wasted a great opportunity."

We thus have the following rules ([] means optional):

```
PO         :: = SAVE RESOURCE
NE         :: = WASTE [PO] RESOURCE
SAVE       :: = save | ...
WASTE      :: = drain | waste | ...
```

15. *Causing or preventing negative or positive effects or situations*: If an entity can cause positive (or negative) effects, it is positive (or negative). If it prevents a negative (or positive) effect from happening, it is positive (or negative). For example:

> "The sensitive brake has prevented a major accident."
> "This drug caused my back pain."

"This device keeps you away from danger."
"This tool protects you from virus attack."

We have the following composition rules:

PO	:: =	CAUSE PO I PREVENT NE
NE	:: =	CAUSE NE I PREVENT PO
CAUSE	:: =	cause I result in I . . .
PREVENT	:: =	prevent something from I keep someone away I protect against I protect from I . . .

16. *Solving problems or making improvements*: These concepts imply positive sentiment.

PO	: =	SOLVE NE
	I	MAKE_IMPROVEMENT [NE]
SOLVE	: =	solve I address I clear up I deal with I fight I fix I handle I help with I give a solution I make up for I tackle I offer a solution I resolve I settle I sort out I tame I . . .
MAKE_IMPROVEMENT	: =	make improvement I improve I make progress I . . .

Again, [] means optional. Here are some example sentences:

"The company has fixed the voice quality problem."
"The noise problem has been addressed."
"The programmer has solved the terrible filtering problem."
"The company has made some major improvements to this phone."

17. *Destroying positive or negative items*: If someone kills a positive item, then the sentiment is negative. If someone kills a negative item, then the sentiment is positive:

PO	: =	DESTROY NE
NE	: =	DESTROY PO
KILL	:: =	kill I destroy I dash I end I put to death I smash I . . .

Some example sentences are:

"They killed a great idea."
"He dashed my hope."
"They killed the goose that laid the golden eggs."

18. *Capable of performing some action*: If an entity is capable of performing a useful or a negative action, it is positive (or negative). We have the following composition rules:

PO	:: = CAPABLE_OF USEFUL_ACTION
NE	:: = CAPABLE_OF NE_ACTION
CAPABLE_OF	:: = can I able to I capable of I have the capability of I . . .

We do not specify USEFUL_ACTION, as they are different in different domains. NE_ACTION is usually indicated by a NE term. Some example sentences are:

> "This car can climb very steep hills."
> "This drug is capable of treating that disease."
> "This software can damage your hard drive."

19. *Keeping or breaking one's promise*: Keeping one's promise is positive and breaking one's promise is negative.

> P :: = keep (promise | word)
> N :: = break promise

Here are some examples:

> "Their service people always keep their promises."
> "Their service people never keep their word."
> "They break their promises all the time."

20. *Taking or enduring pain or abuse*: The following examples show this case:

> "This phone has held up to my daily abuse."
> "He can endure the pain."
> "Due to its large cash reserves, the company can take a beating."

The composition rule is as follows:

> PO   :: = ENDURE NE
> ENDURE   :: = endure | take | stand | hold up | withstand | sustain | resist
> | ...

The negative expressions here are usually related to *suffering, pain, abuse, hardship,* and so on.

21. *Throwing away something*: If something desirable (or undesirable) is thrown away, it is negative (or positive). We have the following composition rules:

> NE   :: = THROW_AWAY (PO | PPI)
> PO   :: = THROW_AWAY [NE | NPI]
> THROW_AWAY :: = do away with | get rid of | sell off | throw way | ...

The following are some example sentences:

> "The company threw away a great idea."
> "I got rid of the phone the second day."
> "I want to throw this phone out of the window."

22. *Staying away from, drifting away, or coming back to something*: If we want to stay away from something, that something is usually undesirable. If we like to come back to something, that something is usually desirable. Drifting away from an undesirable state is positive, while drifting away from a desirable state is negative. We thus have the following rules.

```
NE                 :: =  STAY_AWAY_FROM (ENTITY | ASPECT)
                   |     DRIFT_AWAY_FROM PO
                   |     DRIFT_AWAY_FROM NE
PO                 :: =  COME_BACK_TO ENTITY
STAY_AWAY          :: =  avoid | get away from | run away from | stay away from |
                         steer away from | ...
DRIFT_AWAY         :: =  (drift | move | slip | slide) away from | ...
COME_BACK_TO       :: =  come back to | come to | ...
ENTITY             : =   this ENTITY_TYPE | ENTITY_NAME
ASPECT             : =   ASPECT_NAME
```

ENTITY_TYPE is a product type, such as car, phone, and so on. ENTITY_NAME stands for a named entity, such as *iPhone* and *Motorola*. ASPECT_NAME stands for the name of an aspect of an entity. The following are some example sentences:

"You should stay away from this car."
"I always come back to Dove."
"The company has drifted away from a profitable situation."

The COME_BACK_TO rule needs to be used with care, as in many cases it expresses no opinion – for example, "I will come back to office at 5 pm."

23. *Supporting or voting for something*: If an entity E1 supports another entity E2, then E1 has a positive opinion about E2. If E1 supports a negative (or positive) item, then the opinion about E1 is negative (or positive).

```
PO         :: =  ENTITY SUPPORT ENTITY
           |     ENTITY SUPPORT PO
NE         :: =  ENTITY SUPPORT NE
SUPPORT    :: =  support | always there for | cheer for | give the green light to | root for
                 | stand behind | stand by | vote for | ...
```

Note that we are unable to specify opinion targets using this concept level specification language. Section 5.7 presented an expression-level rule representation language that allows us to specify opinion targets. Some example sentences for this set of rules are:

"I will vote for the Republican Party."
"He gave the green light to some criminal activities."

"They are always there for you."
"They always stand behind their products."

24. *Associated or friendly with something*: The following example shows this case:

"He is friendly with the bad guy."

The sentence is negative about *he* although *friendly* is a positive sentiment word. We have the following rule:

```
NE                  :: =  FRIENDLY_WITH NE
FRIENDLY_WITH  :: =  friendly with I associated with I . . .
```

25. *Choosing this or something else*: When making a recommendation or suggestion, people often say "choose this one" (positive) and "choose something else" (negative).

```
PO          :: =  ENTITY is for you
            I     ENTITY is it
            I     ENTITY is the one
            I     ENTITY is your baby
            I     go (with I for) ENTITY
            I     ENTITY is the way to go
            I     this is it
            I     (search I look) no more
            I     CHOOSE ENTITY
            I     check ENTITY out
NE          :: =  forget (this I it I ENTITY)
            I     keep looking
            I     look elsewhere
            I     CHOOSE (another one I something else)
CHOOSE  :: =  buy I check I check out I choose I get I grab I pick I purchase I select
ENTITY  :: =  this I this ENTITY_TYPE I ENTITY_NAME
```

These rules are commonly used in conditional sentences when making suggestions or recommendations. They were discussed in Section 4.4 and are reproduced here for completeness. ENTITY_TYPE and ENTITY_-NAME were defined in rule set 22. Some example sentences follow:

"If you want a great phone, choose iPhone."
"If you are in the market for a new phone, choose something else."

The second sentence indicates that the phone being reviewed or discussed is not good.

26. *Under control or out of control*: *Under control* is a positive phrase and *out of control* is a negative phrase.

PO   :: = [NE] UNDER_CONTROL
NE   :: = [NE] OUT_OF_CONTROL
UNDER_CONTROL   :: = in control I keep a rein on I under control I . . .
OUT_OF_CONTROL :: = beyond control I out of control I . . .

Some example sentences are:

"The rescue team got the terrible situation under control."
"This vacuum cleaner keeps a rein on dust."
"The federal spending is out of control."

27. *Undercutting or undermining some positive effort*:

NE   :: = UNDERMINE [PO]
UNDERMINE :: = undercut I undermine I . . .

The following are some example sentences:

"The company undercut its own great effort of producing a new smartphone."
"His action is undermining his party's effort to draw more voters."

28. *Cannot wait to do something to a desirable* (PO) *or undesirable* (NE) *item*:

PO :: = cannot wait PO
NE :: = cannot wait NE

The following are some example sentences:

"I cannot wait to get rid of this lousy car."
"I cannot wait to get this beautiful phone."

These rules are included because *cannot* here does not mean negation. Also, when it is not followed by a negative or positive item, it is usually positive – for example, "I cannot wait to get an iPhone" (see Section 5.4).

29. *Positive or negative (potential) items return*: When a positive item (PO) or a PPI returns, it is positive. When a negative item (NE) or a NPI returns, it is negative. Take, for example, the following sentences:

"My pain has returned."
"This drug got my life back."

We then have the following rule:

NE   :: = (NE I NPI) RETURN
PO   :: = (PO I PPI) RETURN
RETURN   :: = bring back I come back I get back I is back I return I . . .

30. *Emerging from undesirable situation*: The following sentences give us some examples. These three sentences are all positive about the company, although the sentences contain negative sentiment words.

"This company has emerged from the poor economy."
"The economy has jumped out of recession."
"The company comes out of the bankruptcy."

We then have the following composition rules:

```
PO                    :: =  COME_OUT_FROM (NE | NPI)
COME_OUT_FROM  :: =  back from | come out | emerge from | . . .
```

We can also have a rule for "get into an undesirable situation," but it is unnecessary because the undesirable situation (NE) already determines the sentiment.

31. *Positive (negative) outweighing negative (positive)*: This concept compares positive and negative sentiments for some entities or aspects.

```
PO           :: =  PO OUTWEIGH NE
NE           :: =  NE OUTWEIGH PO
OUTWEIGH  :: =  outweigh | make up for | more significant than | . . .
```

For example, the following sentences are all positive about the car, although the sentiments are different for different aspects of it:

"For this car, the pros outweigh the cons."
"The beauty of the car well outweighs its high price."
"The beauty of the car makes up for its high price tag."

However, handling these sentences in practice can be tricky, especially for the second and third sentences, because two aspects are involved and the authors are not positive about both. In a practical application, there are a few options, including (1) assigning positive to the aspect *appearance* and the *car* entity, and negative to the aspect *price*; (2) assigning positive to the aspect *appearance* and the *car* entity, ignoring the sentiment on *price*; and (3) assigning positive to the *car* entity, ignoring both aspects.

32. *Changing from positive* (or *negative*) *to negative* (or *positive*): The following sentences illustrate this concept:

"They changed the good policy to a lousy one."
"The company changed the unreliable switch to a highly reliable one."
"The company changed the previous switch to a highly reliable one."

We have the following rules:

```
PO             :: =  CHANGE_FROM [NE] to PO
NE             :: =  CHANGE_FROM [PO] to NE
CHANGE_FROM  :: =  change from | switch from | . . .
```

33. *Something that is going to die*: The following sentences give some examples:

> "This company's days are numbered."
> "This great company may die next year."

We have the following composition rules:

```
NE   :: =   [NE] DIE
PO   :: =   PO DIE
DIE  :: =   days are numbered I die I . . .
```

34. *Extending one's ability or making it difficult*: Something that extends one's ability is positive and something that makes it difficult for one to do something is negative. For example:

> "This tool enables me to do filtering easily."
> "This security hole allows a hacker to destroy your computer easily."
> "This policy makes it very difficult to cheat."
> "This system makes it very hard to take multiple pictures quickly."

We have the following composition rules:

```
PO                 :: =   ENABLE (PPI I PO)
                   I      MAKE_DIFFICULT (NPI I NE)
NE                 :: =   ENABLE (NPI I NE)
                   I      MAKE_DIFFICULT (PPI I PO)
ENABLE             :: =   allow I enable I make it easy I . . .
MAKE_DIFFICULT     :: =   make it (difficult I hard I impossible) I . . .
```

35. *Forced to do something*: The following are some example sentences:

> "The doctor forced me to take the medicine."
> "They made you pay for the lunch."

We have the following composition rules:

```
NE            :: =   FORCE_TO_DO [ PO I NE I PPI I NPI]
FORCE_TO_DO   :: =   forced to I make someone do something I pressurized to I . . .
```

36. Like something desirable or undesirable: The following are some example sentences:

> "This car is similar to or on par with the best car."
> "This furniture is like a piece of art."

We have the following composition rules:

```
NE       :: =   SUB_PAR (PO I NE)
         I      ON_PAR NE
```

```
PO          :: =  ON_PAR PO
SUB_PAR     :: =  subpar I worse than I ...
ON_PAR      :: =  better than I like I on par I the same as I ...
```

This set of rules is related to comparative opinions, which we discussed in Chapter 8.

37. *High or low on a ranked list*: There are many ways to express this situation, but most of them are difficult to recognize. The following sentences give some examples:

> "This car is high on my list."
> "This song is in the top ten list."
> "This song is now near the top of the chart."

We have the following rules:

```
NE  :: =  AT_BOTTOM_OF_LIST
PO  :: =  ON_TOP_OF_LIST
```

The concepts of AT_BOTTOM_OF_LIST and ON_TOP_OF_LIST can be expressed in many diverse ways, which are not easy to specify simply.

38. *Doing things automatically*: Doing desirable things automatically is positive but doing undesirable things automatically is negative.

```
PO              :: =  (PO I PPI) AUTIMATICALLY
NE              :: =  (PE I NPI) AUTIMATICALLY
AUTIMATICALLY   :: =  automatically I by itself I ...
```

The following sentences give some examples:

> "The recorder stops suddenly by itself."
> "The system automatically avoids obstacles."

39. *Positive (negative) initially, but becomes negative (positive) later*: This type of sentence occurs fairly frequently in product reviews, especially for products that are of low quality or do not last. The sentiment in the second part of the sentence overrides the first part. The following sentences give some examples:

> "This car was good in the first two months, and then everything started to fall apart."
> "This phone works quite nicely initially, and then the sound becomes unclear."
> "I did not like the car at the beginning, but then it impressed me more and more."
> "The car worked very well until yesterday."
> "At first this seemed prohibitive to me, but they do give a lot of discounts."

We have the following composition rules:

```
NE  : =  PO INITIAILLY NE LATER
PO  : =  NE INITIAILLY PO LATER
```

There are numerous ways to express INITIALLY and LATER. The example sentences give some such expressions. This type of opinion is hard to detect because typically intrasentential discourse analysis is required.

40. *Positive but not positive enough*: This category is similar to rule set 39, but there is no time or sequence expression to help detect this case. In such a sentence, the sentiment of the second part often overrides the first part. The following are some example sentences:

> "This car is good but not good enough."
> "Although they have made a lot of improvements to the car, it is still lousy."

We have the following composition rule:

```
NE  : =  PO BUT_STILL NE
```

Sentences covered by this rule typically use *but*, *although*, or other similar words or expressions to indicate BUT_STILL. Many such sentences are hard to recognize as they, too, may need the discourse-level analysis.

Bibliography

Aarts, Bas. *Oxford Modern English Grammar*. 2011. Oxford: Oxford University Press.

Abbasi, Ahmed, Hsinchun Chen, and Arab Salem. Sentiment Analysis in Multiple Languages: Feature Selection for Opinion Classification in Web Forums. *ACM Transactions on Information Systems*, 2008. 26(3): 1–34.

Abdul-Mageed, Muhammad, and Ungar Lyle. EmoNet: Fine-Grained Emotion Detection with Gated Recurrent Neural Networks. In Proceedings of the Annual Meeting of the Association for Computational Linguistics (ACL-2017). 2017.

Abdul-Mageed, Muhammad, Mona T. Diab, and Mohammed Korayem. Subjectivity and Sentiment Analysis of Modern Standard Arabic. In Proceedings of the 49th Annual Meeting of the Association for Computational Linguistics: Short Papers. 2011.

Abu-Jbara, Amjad, Ben King, Mona Diab, and Dragomir Radev. Identifying Opinion Subgroups in Arabic Online Discussions. In Proceedings of the Annual Meeting of the Association for Computational Linguistics. 2013.

Abu-Jbara, Amjad, Pradeep Dasigi, Mona Diab, and Dragomir Radev. Subgroup Detection in Ideological Discussions. In Proceedings of the 50th Annual Meeting of the Association for Computational Linguistics. 2012.

Agrawal, Rakesh, and Ramakrishnan Srikant. Fast Algorithms for Mining Association Rules. In Proceedings of VLDB. 1994.

Agrawal, Rakesh, Sridhar Rajagopalan, Ramakrishnan Srikant, and Yirong Xu. Mining Newsgroups Using Networks Arising from Social Behavior. In Proceedings of International World Wide Web Conference. 2003.

Akhtar, Md Shad, Abhishek Kumar, Deepanway Ghosal, Asif Ekbal, and Pushpak Bhattacharyya. A Multilayer Perceptron Based Ensemble Technique for Fine-Grained Financial Sentiment Analysis. In Proceedings of the Conference on Empirical Methods on Natural Language Processing (EMNLP-2017). 2017.

Akhtar, Md Shad, Ayush Kumar, Asif Ekbal, and Pushpak Bhattacharyya. A Hybrid Deep Learning Architecture for Sentiment Analysis. In Proceedings of the International Conference on Computational Linguistics (COLING-2016). 2016.

Akkaya, Cem, Janyce Wiebe, and Rada Mihalcea. Subjectivity Word Sense Disambiguation. In Proceedings of the 2009 Conference on Empirical Methods in Natural Language Processing. 2009.

Akoglu, Leman, Rishi Chandy, and Christos Faloutsos. Opinion Fraud Detection in Online Reviews by Network Effects. In Proceedings of the International AAAI Conference on Weblogs and Social Media. 2013.

Alm, Cecilia Ovesdotter, Dan Roth, and Richard Sproat. Emotions from Text: Machine Learning for Text-Based Emotion Prediction. In Proceedings of the Conference on Human Language Technology and Empirical Methods in Natural Language Processing. 2005.

Alm, Ebba Cecilia Ovesdotter. *Affect in Text and Speech*. 2008. PhD thesis, University of Illinois at Urbana–Champaign.

Almuhareb, Abdulrahman. *Attributes in Lexical Acquisition*. 2006. PhD thesis, University of Essex.

Aly, Mohamed, and Amir Atiya. Labr: A Large Scale Arabic Book Reviews Dataset. In Proceedings of the Annual Meeting of the Association for Computational Linguistics. 2013.

Aman, Saima, and Stan Szpakowicz. Identifying Expressions of Emotion in Text. In Text, Speech and Dialogue, 2007.

Amir, Zadeh, Minghai Chen, Soujanya Poria, Erik Cambria, and Louis-Philippe Morency. Tensor Fusion Network for Multimodal Sentiment Analysis. In Proceedings of the Conference on Empirical Methods on Natural Language Processing (EMNLP-2017). 2017.

Andreevskaia, Alina, and Sabine Bergler. Mining Wordnet for Fuzzy Sentiment: Sentiment Tag Extraction from Wordnet Glosses. In Proceedings of the Conference of the European Chapter of the Association for Computational Linguistics. 2006.

Andreevskaia, Alina, and Sabine Bergler. When Specialists and Generalists Work Together: Overcoming Domain Dependence in Sentiment Tagging. In Proceedings of the Annual Meeting of the Association for Computational Linguistics. 2008.

Andrzejewski, David, and David Buttler. Latent Topic Feedback for Information Retrieval. In Proceedings of the 17th ACM SIGKDD International Conference on Knowledge Discovery and Data Mining (KDD-2011). 2011.

Andrzejewski, David, and Xiaojin Zhu. Latent Dirichlet Allocation with Topic-in-Set Knowledge. In Proceedings of NAACL HLT. 2009.

Andrzejewski, David, Xiaojin Zhu, and Mark Craven. A Framework for Incorporating General Domain Knowledge into Latent Dirichlet Allocation Using First-Order Logic. In Proceedings of International Joint Conference on Artificial Intelligence (IJCAI-2011). 2011.

Andrzejewski, David, Xiaojin Zhu, and Mark Craven. Incorporating Domain Knowledge into Topic Modeling via Dirichlet Forest Priors. In Proceedings of ICML. 2009.

Angelidis, Stefanos, and Mirella Lapata. Multiple Instance Learning Networks for Fine-Grained Sentiment Analysis. In Transactions of the Association for Computational Linguistics (TACL), 2018. 6: 17–31.

Archak, Nikolay, Anindya Ghose, and Panagiotis G. Ipeirotis. Show Me the Money! Deriving the Pricing Power of Product Features by Mining Consumer Reviews. In Proceedings of the ACM SIGKDD Conference on Knowledge Discovery and Data Mining (KDD-2007). 2007.

Argamon, Shlomo, and Shlomo Levitan. Measuring the Usefulness of Function Words for Authorship Attribution. In Proceedings of the 2005 ACH/ALLC Conference. 2005.

Arguello, Jaime, Fernando Diaz, Jamie Callan, and Jean-Francois Crespo. Sources of Evidence for Vertical Selection. In Proceedings of the 32st Annual International ACM SIGIR Conference on Research and Development in Information Retrieval (SIGIR-2009). 2009.

Arnold, Magda B. *Emotion and Personality*. 1960. New York: Columbia University Press.

Asher, Nicholas, Farah Benamara, and Yvette Yannick Mathieu. Appraisal of Opinion Expressions in Discourse. *Lingvisticæ Investigationes*, 2009. 32(1): 279–92.

Asher, Nicholas, Farah Benamara, and Yvette Yannick Mathieu. Distilling Opinion in Discourse: A Preliminary Study. In Proceedings of the International Conference on Computational Linguistics (COLING-2008): Companion volume: Posters and Demonstrations. 2008.

Asur, Sitaram, and Bernardo A. Huberman. Predicting the Future with Social Media. ArXiv:1003.5699, 2010.

Aue, Anthony, and Michael Gamon. Customizing Sentiment Classifiers to New Domains: A Case Study. In Proceedings of Recent Advances in Natural Language Processing (RANLP-2005). 2005.

Banea, Carmen, Rada Mihalcea, and Janyce Wiebe. Multilingual Subjectivity: Are More Languages Better? in Proceedings of the International Conference on Computational Linguistics (COLING-2010). 2010.

Banea, Carmen, Rada Mihalcea, Janyce Wiebe, and Samer Hassan. Multilingual Subjectivity Analysis Using Machine Translation. In Proceedings of the Conference on Empirical Methods in Natural Language Processing (EMNLP-2008). 2008.

Barbosa, Luciano, and Junlan Feng. Robust Sentiment Detection on Twitter from Biased and Noisy Data. In Proceedings of the International Conference on Computational Linguistics (COLING-2010). 2010.

Bar-Haim, Roy, Elad Dinur, Ronen Feldman, Moshe Fresko, and Guy Goldstein. Identifying and Following Expert Investors in Stock Microblogs. In Proceedings of the Conference on Empirical Methods in Natural Language Processing (EMNLP-2011). 2011.

Barnes, Jeremy, Patrik Lambert, and Toni Badia. Exploring Distributional Representations and Machine Translation for Aspect-Based Cross-Lingual Sentiment Classification. In Proceedings of the 27th International Conference on Computational Linguistics (COLING-2016). 2016.

Barrett, L. F., and J. Russell. A. Structure of Current Affect. *Current Directions in Psychological Science*, 1999. 8: 10–14.

Batson, C. Daniel, Laura L. Shaw, and Kathryn C. Oleson. Differentiating Affect, Mood, and Emotion: Toward Functionally Based Conceptual Distinctions. *Review of Personality and Social Psychology*, 1992. 13: 294–326.

Bautin, Mikhail, Lohit Vijayarenu, and Steven Skiena. International Sentiment Analysis for News and Blogs. In Proceedings of the International AAAI Conference on Weblogs and Social Media (ICWSM-2008). 2008.

Becker, Israela, and Vered Aharonson. Last But Definitely Not Least: On the Role of the Last Sentence in Automatic Polarity-Classification. In Proceedings of the ACL 2010 Conference Short Papers. 2010.

Beineke, Philip, Trevor Hastie, Christopher Manning, and Shivakumar Vaithyanathan. An Exploration of Sentiment Summarization. In Proceedings of AAAI Spring

Symposium on Exploring Attitude and Affect in Text: Theories and Applications. 2003.

Benamara, Farah, Baptiste Chardon, Yannick Mathieu, and Vladimir Popescu. Towards Context-Based Subjectivity Analysis. In Proceedings of the 5th International Joint Conference on Natural Language Processing (IJCNLP-2011). 2011.

Bermingham, Adam, and Alan F. Smeaton. On Using Twitter to Monitor Political Sentiment and Predict Election Results. In Proceedings of the Workshop on Sentiment Analysis Where AI Meets Psychology. 2011.

Bertero, Dario, Farhad Bin Siddique, Chien-Sheng Wu, Yan Wan, Ricky Ho Yin Chan, and Pascale Fung. Real-Time Speech Emotion and Sentiment Recognition for Interactive Dialogue Systems. In Proceedings of the Conference on Empirical Methods in Natural Language Processing (EMNLP-2016). 2016.

Bespalov, Dmitriy, Bing Bai, Yanjun Qi, and Ali Shokoufandeh. Sentiment Classification Based on Supervised Latent N-Gram Analysis. In Proceedings of the ACM Conference on Information and Knowledge Management (CIKM-2011). 2011.

Bethard, Steven, Hong Yu, Ashley Thornton, Vasileios Hatzivassiloglou, and Dan Jurafsky. Automatic Extraction of Opinion Propositions and Their Holders. In Proceedings of the AAAI Spring Symposium on Exploring Attitude and Affect in Text. 2004.

Bickerstaffe, A., and I. Zukerman. A Hierarchical Classifier Applied to Multi-Way Sentiment Detection. In Proceedings of the 23rd International Conference on Computational Linguistics (COLING-2010). 2010.

Bilgic, Mustafa, Galileo Mark Namata, and Lise Getoor. Combining Collective Classification and Link Prediction. In Proceedings of Workshop on Mining Graphs and Complex Structures. 2007.

Bishop, C. M. Pattern Recognition and Machine Learning. Vol. 4. 2006. Singapore: Springer.

Blair-Goldensohn, Sasha, Kerry Hannan, Ryan McDonald, Tyler Neylon, George A. Reis, and Jeff Reynar. Building a Sentiment Summarizer for Local Service Reviews. In Proceedings of WWW-2008 Workshop on NLP in the Information Explosion Era. 2008.

Blei, David M., and John D. Lafferty, Visualizing Topics with Multi-Word Expressions. ArXiv:0907.1013, 2009.

Blei, David M., and Jon D. McAuliffe. Supervised Topic Models. In Proceedings of NIPS. 2007.

Blei, David M., Andrew Y. Ng, and Michael I. Jordan. Latent Dirichlet Allocation. Journal of Machine Learning Research, 2003. 3: 993–1022.

Blitzer, John, Mark Dredze, and Fernando Pereira. Biographies, Bollywood, Boom-Boxes and Blenders: Domain Adaptation for Sentiment Classification. In Proceedings of Annual Meeting of the Association for Computational Linguistics (ACL-2007). 2007.

Blitzer, John, Ryan McDonald, and Fernando Pereira. Domain Adaptation with Structural Correspondence Learning. In Proceedings of the Conference on Empirical Methods in Natural Language Processing (EMNLP-2006). 2006.

Blum, Avrim, and Shuchi Chawla. Learning from Labeled and Unlabeled Data Using Graph Mincuts. In Proceedings of International Conference on Machine Learning (ICML-2001). 2001.

Blum, Avrim, John Lafferty, Mugizi R. Rwebangira, and Rajashekar Reddy. Semi-Supervised Learning Using Randomized Mincuts. In Proceedings of International Conference on Machine Learning (ICML-2004). 2004.

Boiy, Erik, and Marie-Francine Moens. A Machine Learning Approach to Sentiment Analysis in Multilingual Web Texts. *Information Retrieval*, 2009. 12 (5): 526–58.

Bollegala, Danushka, David Weir, and John Carroll. Using Multiple Sources to Construct a Sentiment Sensitive Thesaurus for Cross-Domain Sentiment Classification. In Proceedings of the 49th Annual Meeting of the Association for Computational Linguistics (ACL-2011). 2011.

Bollen, Johan, Huina Mao, and Xiao-Jun Zeng. Twitter Mood Predicts the Stock Market. *Journal of Computational Science*, 2011. 2(1): 1–8.

Boyd-Graber, Jordan, and Philip Resnik. Holistic Sentiment Analysis across Languages: Multilingual Supervised Latent Dirichlet Allocation. In Proceedings of the Conference on Empirical Methods in Natural Language Processing (EMNLP-2010). 2010.

Boyer, Kristy Elizabeth, Joseph Grafsgaard, Eun Young Ha, Robert Phillips, and James Lester. An Affect-Enriched Dialogue Act Classification Model for Task-Oriented Dialogue. In Proceedings of the 49th Annual Meeting of the Association for Computational Linguistics (ACL-2011). 2011.

Branavan, S. R. K., Harr Chen, Jacob Eisenstein, and Regina Barzilay. Learning Document-Level Semantic Properties from Free-Text Annotations. In Proceedings of the Annual Meeting of the Association for Computational Linguistics (ACL-2008). 2008.

Breck, Eric, Yejin Choi, and Claire Cardie. Identifying Expressions of Opinion in Context. In Proceedings of the International Joint Conference on Artificial Intelligence (IJCAI-2007). 2007.

Brody, Samuel, and Nicholas Diakopoulos. Cooooooooooooooooollllllllllllll!!!!!!!!!!!!!! Using Word Lengthening to Detect Sentiment in Microblogs. In Proceedings of the Conference on Empirical Methods in Natural Language Processing (EMNLP-2011). 2011.

Brody, Samuel, and Noemie Elhadad. An Unsupervised Aspect–Sentiment Model for Online Reviews. In Proceedings of the 2010 Annual Conference of the North American Chapter of the ACL. 2010.

Brooke, Julian, Milan Tofiloski, and Maite Taboada. Cross-Linguistic Sentiment Analysis: From English to Spanish. In Proceedings of RANLP. 2009.

Burfoot, Clinton, Steven Bird, and Timothy Baldwin. Collective Classification of Congressional Floor-Debate Transcripts. In Proceedings of the 49th Annual Meeting of the Association for Computational Linguistics (ACL-2011). 2011.

Burns, Nicola, Yaxin Bi, Hui Wang, and Terry Anderson. Extended Twofold-LDA Model for Two Aspects in One Sentence. In Advances in Computational Intelligence. In *Advances in Computational Intelligence: IPMU 2012. Communications in Computer and Information Science*, Vol. 298, S. Greco, B. Bouchon-Meunier, G. Coletti, M. Fedrizzi, B. Matarazzo, and R. R. Yager (Eds.). 2012. Berlin/Heidelberg: Springer.

Burrows, John F. Not Unless You Ask Nicely: The Interpretative Nexus between Analysis and Information. *Literary and Linguistic Computing*, 1992. 7: 91–109.

Cambria, Erik, and Amir Hussain. *Sentic Computing: Techniques, Tools, and Applications*. 2012. Berlin/Heidelberg: Springer.

Canini, Kevin R., Lei Shi, and Thomas L. Griffiths. *Online Inference of Topics with Latent Dirichlet Allocation*. In Proceedings of the Twelth International Conference on Artificial Intelligence and Statistics (PMLR). 2009. 5: 65–72.

Cao, Yunbo, Jun Xu, Tie-Yan Liu, Hang Li, Yalou Huang, and Hsiao-Wuen Hon. Adapting Ranking SVM to Document Retrieval. In Proceedings of the Annual International ACM SIGIR Conference (SIGIR-2006). 2006.

Carenini, Giuseppe, Raymond Ng, and Adam Pauls. Multi-Document Summarization of Evaluative Text. In Proceedings of the European Chapter of the Association for Computational Linguistics (EACL-2006). 2006.

Carenini, Giuseppe, Raymond Ng, and Ed Zwart. Extracting Knowledge from Evaluative Text. In Proceedings of the 3rd International Conference on Knowledge Capture (K-CAP-05). 2005.

Carlos, Cohan Sujay, and Madhulika Yalamanchi. Intention Analysis for Sales, Marketing and Customer Service. In Proceedings of COLING 2012: Demonstration Papers. 2012.

Carpenter, Bob. *Integrating out Multinomial Parameters in Latent Dirichlet Allocation and Naive Bayes for Collapsed Gibbs Sampling*. 2010. Brooklyn: LingPipe, Inc.

Carvalho, Paula, Luís Sarmento, Jorge Teixeira, and Mário J. Silva. Liars and Saviors in a Sentiment Annotated Corpus of Comments to Political Debates. In Proceedings of the 49th Annual Meeting of the Association for Computational Linguistics: Short Papers. 2011.

Castellanos, Malu, Umeshwar Dayal, Meichun Hsu, Riddhiman Ghosh, Mohamed Dekhil, Yue Lu, Lei Zhang, and Mark Schreiman. LCI: A Social Channel Analysis Platform for Live Customer Intelligence. In Proceedings of the 2011 International Conference on Management of Data (SIGMOD-2011). 2011.

Castillo, Carlos, and Brian D. Davison. Adversarial Web Search. *Foundations and Trends in Information Retrieval*, 2010. 4(5): 377–486.

Chaffar, Soumaya, and Diana Inkpen. Using a Heterogeneous Dataset for Emotion Analysis in Text. In Proceedings of the 24th Canadian Conference on Advances in Artificial Intelligence. May 2011. 62–7.

Chaudhuri, Arjun. *Emotion and Reason in Consumer Behavior*. 2006. London: Routledge.

Chen, Bi, Leilei Zhu, Daniel Kifer, and Dongwon Lee. What Is an Opinion about? Exploring Political Standpoints Using Opinion Scoring Model. In Proceeedings of AAAI Conference on Artificial Intelligence (AAAI-2010). 2010.

Chen, Huimin, Maosong Sun, Cunchao Tu, and Yankai Lin, Zhiyuan Liu. Neural Sentiment Classification with User and Product Attention. In Proceedings of the Conference on Empirical Methods in Natural Language Processing (EMNLP-2016). 2016a.

Chen, Peng, Zhongqian Sun, Lidong Bing, Wei Yang. Recurrent Attention Network on Memory for Aspect Sentiment Analysis. In Proceedings of the Conference on Empirical Methods on Natural Language Processing (EMNLP-2017). 2017.

Chen, Wei-Fan, Fang-Yu Lin, and Lun-Wei Ku. WordForce: Visualizing Controversial Words in Debates. In Proceedings of the Conference on Empirical Methods in Natural Language Processing (EMNLP-2016). 2016b.

Chen, Yubo, and Jinhong Xie. Online Consumer Review: Word-of-Mouth As a New Element of Marketing Communication Mix. *Management Science*, 2008. 54(3): 477–91.

Chen, Zheng, Fan Lin, Huan Liu, Yin Liu, Wei-Ying Ma, and Wenyin Liu. User Intention Modeling in Web Applications Using Data Mining. *World Wide Web: Internet and Web Information Systems*, 2002. 5: 181–91.

Chen, Zhiyuan, and Bing Liu, Topic Modeling Using Topics from Many Domains, Lifelong Learning and Big Data. In Proceedings of the International Conference on Machine Learning (ICML-2014). 2014a.

Chen, Zhiyuan, and Bing Liu. Mining Topics in Documents: Standing on the Shoulders of Big Data. In Proceedings of the SIGKDD International Conference on Knowledge Discovery and Data Mining (KDD-2014). 2014b.

Chen, Zhiyuan, and Bing Liu. *Lifelong Machine Learning*. 1st ed. 2016. San Rafael, CA: Morgan & Claypool Publishers.

Chen, Zhiyuan, and Bing Liu. *Lifelong Machine Learning*. 2nd ed. 2018. San Rafael, CA: Morgan & Claypool Publishers.

Chen, Zhiyuan, Bing Liu, Meichun Hsu, Malu Castellanos, and Riddhiman Ghosh. Identifying Intention Posts in Discussion Forums. In Proceedings of the 2013 Conference of the North American Chapter of the Association for Computational Linguistics: Human Language Technologies (NAACL-HLT-2013). 2013a.

Chen, Zhiyuan, Nianzu Ma, and Bing Liu. Lifelong Learning for Sentiment Classification. Proceedings of the 53st Annual Meeting of the Association for Computational Linguistics (ACL-2015, short paper). July 26–31, 2015.

Chen, Zhiyuan, Arjun Mukherjee, and Bing Liu, Aspect Extraction with Automated Prior Knowledge Learning. In Proceedings of the 52th Annual Meeting of the Association for Computational Linguistics (ACL-2014). 2014.

Chen, Zhiyuan, Arjun Mukherjee, Bing Liu, Meichun Hsu, Malu Castellanos, and Riddhiman Ghosh. Discovering Coherent Topics Using General Knowledge. In Proceedings of the 22nd ACM International Conference on Information and Knowledge Management (CIKM-2013). 2013b.

Chen, Zhiyuan, Arjun Mukherjee, Bing Liu, Meichun Hsu, Malu Castellanos, and Riddhiman Ghosh. Exploiting Domain Knowledge in Aspect Extraction. In Proceedings of the Conference on Empirical Methods in Natural Language Processing (EMNLP-2013). 2013c.

Chen, Zhiyuan, Arjun Mukherjee, Bing Liu, Meichun Hsu, Malu Castellanos, and Riddhiman Ghosh. Leveraging Multi-Domain Prior Knowledge in Topic Models. In Proceedings of the 23rd International Joint Conference on Artificial Intelligence (IJCAI-2013). 2013d.

Chen, Zhuang, and Tieyun Qian. Transfer Capsule Network for Aspect-Level Sentiment Classification. In Proceedings of the 57th Conference of the Association for Computational Linguistics (ACL-2019). 2019.

Cho, Kyunghyun, Bart van Merrienboer, Dzmitry Bahdanau, and Yoshua Bengio. On the Properties of Neural Machine Translation: Encoder–Decoder Approaches. arXiv preprint arXiv:1409.1259, 2014.

Choi, Yejin, Eric Breck, and Claire Cardie. Joint Extraction of Entities and Relations for Opinion Recognition. In Proceedings of the Conference on Empirical Methods in Natural Language Processing (EMNLP-2006). 2006.

Choi, Yejin, and Claire Cardie. Learning with Compositional Semantics As Structural Inference for Subsentential Sentiment Analysis. In Proceedings of the Conference on Empirical Methods in Natural Language Processing (EMNLP-2008). 2008.

Choi, Yejin, and Claire Cardie. Adapting a Polarity Lexicon Using Integer Linear Programming for Domain-Specific Sentiment Classification. In Proceedings of the 2009 Conference on Empirical Methods in Natural Language Processing (EMNLP-2009). 2009.

Choi, Yejin, and Claire Cardie. Hierarchical Sequential Learning for Extracting Opinions and Their Attributes. In Proceedings of Annual Meeting of the Association for Computational Linguistics (ACL-2010). 2010.

Choi, Yejin, Claire Cardie, Ellen Riloff, and Siddharth Patwardhan. Identifying Sources of Opinions with Conditional Random Fields and Extraction Patterns. In Proceedings of the Human Language Technology Conference and the Conference on Empirical Methods in Natural Language Processing (HLT/EMNLP-2005). 2005.

Chung, Jessica, and Eni Mustafaraj. Cam Collective Sentiment Expressed on Twitter Predict Political Elections? In Proceedings of the 25th AAAI Conference on Artificial Intelligence (AAAI-2011). 2011.

Cilibrasi, Rudi L., and Paul M. B. Vitanyi. The Google Similarity Distance. *IEEE Transactions on Knowledge and Data Engineering*, 2007. 19(3): 370–83.

Crocker, David A. *Tolerance and Deliberative Democracy*. Technical Report. 2005. College Park: University of Maryland.

Cui, Hang, Vibhu Mittal, and Mayur Datar. Comparative Experiments on Sentiment Classification for Online Product Reviews. In Proceedings of AAAI-2006. 2006.

Dahlgren, Peter. In Search of the Talkative Public: Media, Deliberative Democracy and Civic Culture. *Javnost*, 2002. 3: 5–25.

Dahlgren, Peter. The Internet, Public Spheres, and Political Communication: Dispersion and Deliberation. *Political Communication*, 2005. 22: 147–62.

Dahou, Abdelghani, Shengwu Xiong, Junwei Zhou, Mohamed Houcine Haddoud, and Pengfei Duan. Word Embeddings and Convolutional Neural Network for Arabic Sentiment Classification. In Proceedings of the International Conference on Computational Linguistics (COLING-2016). 2016.

Dai, Honghua, Zaiqing Nie, Lee Wang, Lingzhi Zhao, Ji-Rong Wen, and Ying Li. Detecting Online Commercial Intention (OCI). In Proceedings of the 15th International Conference on World Wide Web (WWW-2006). 2006.

Damasio, Antonio, and Carvalho Gil B. The Nature of Feelings: Evolutionary and Neurobiological Origins. *Nature Reviews Neuroscience*, 2013. 14(2):143.

Das, Dipanjan. A Survey on Automatic Text Summarization Single-Document Summarization. *Language*, 2007. 4: 1–31.

Das, Sanjiv, and Mike Chen. Yahoo! for Amazon: Extracting Market Sentiment from Stock Message Boards. In Proceedings of APFA-2001. 2001.

Das, Sanjiv, and Mike Chen. Yahoo! for Amazon: Sentiment Extraction from Small Talk on the Web. *Management Science*, 2007. 53(9): 1375–88.

Dasgupta, Sajib, and Vincent Ng. Mine the Easy, Classify the Hard: A Semi-Supervised Approach to Automatic Sentiment Classification. In Proceedings of the 47th Annual Meeting of the ACL and the 4th IJCNLP of the AFNLP (ACL-2009). 2009.

Dave, Kushal, Steve Lawrence, and David M. Pennock. Mining the Peanut Gallery: Opinion Extraction and Semantic Classification of Product Reviews. In Proceedings of the International Conference on the World Wide Web (WWW-2003). 2003.

Davidov, Dmitry, Oren Tsur, and Ari Rappoport. Enhanced Sentiment Learning Using Twitter Hashtags and Smileys. In Proceedings of COLING-2010. 2010.

Davis, Alexandre, Adriano Veloso, Altigran S. da Silva, Wagner Meira Jr., and Alberto H. F. Laender. Named Entity Disambiguation in Streaming Data. In Proceedings of the 50th Annual Meeting of the Association for Computational Linguistics (ACL-2012). 2012.

Dellarocas, C., X. M. Zhang, and N. F. Awad. Exploring the Value of Online Product Reviews in Forecasting Sales: The Case of Motion Pictures. *Journal of Interactive Marketing*, 2007. 21(4): 23–45.

de Marneffe, Marie-Catherine, and Christopher D. Manning. *Stanford Typed Dependencies Manual*. 2008. Stanford, CA: Stanford University.

Desmet, P. M. A., M. H. Vastenburg, D. Van Bel, and N. Romero. Pick-a-Mood: Development and Application of a Pictorial Mood-Reporting Instrument. In *Proceedings of the 8th International Conference on Design and Emotion*, J. Brassett, P. Hekkert, G. Ludden, M. Malpass, and J. McDonnell (Eds.). 2012. London: Central Saint Martin College of Art & Design.

Dey, Lipika, and S. K. Mirajul Haque. Opinion Mining from Noisy Text Data. In Proceedings of the 2nd Workshop on Analytics for Noisy Unstructured Text Data (AND-2008). 2008.

Diakopoulos, Nicholas A., and David A. Shamma. Characterizing Debate Performance via Aggregated Twitter Sentiment. In Proceedings of the Conference on Human Factors in Computing Systems (CHI-2010). 2010.

Ding, Xiaowen, and Bing Liu. Resolving Object and Attribute Coreference in Opinion Mining. In Proceedings of International Conference on Computational Linguistics (COLING-2010). 2010.

Ding, Xiaowen, Bing Liu, and Philip S. Yu. A Holistic Lexicon-Based Approach to Opinion Mining. In Proceedings of the Conference on Web Search and Web Data Mining (WSDM-2008). 2008.

Ding, Xiaowen, Bing Liu, and Lei Zhang. Entity Discovery and Assignment for Opinion Mining Applications. In Proceedings of the ACM SIGKDD International Conference on Knowledge Discovery and Data Mining (KDD-2009). 2009.

Ding, Ying, Jianfei Yu, and Jing Jiang. Recurrent Neural Networks with Auxiliary Labels for Cross-Domain Opinion Target Extraction. In Proceedings of the AAAI Conference on Artificial Intelligence (AAAI-2017). 2017.

Dong, Li, Furu Wei, Chuanqi Tan, Duyu Tang, Ming Zhou, and Ke Xu. Adaptive Recursive Neural Network for Target-Dependent Twitter Sentiment Classification. In Proceedings of the Annual Meeting of the Association for Computational Linguistics (ACL-2014). 2014.

Dou, Zi-Yi. Capturing User and Product Information for Document Level Sentiment Analysis with Deep Memory Network. In Proceedings of the Conference on Empirical Methods on Natural Language Processing (EMNLP-2017). 2017.

Dowty, David R., Robert E. Wall, and Stanley Peters. *Introduction to Montague Semantics*. Vol. 11. 1981. Berlin/Heidelberg: Springer.

Dragut, Eduard, Hong Wang, Clement Yu, Prasad Sistla, and Weiyi Meng. Polarity Consistency Checking for Sentiment Dictionaries. In Proceedings of the Annual Meeting of the Association for Computational Linguistics (ACL-2012). 2012.

Dragut, Eduard C., Clement Yu, Prasad Sistla, and Weiyi Meng. Construction of a Sentimental Word Dictionary. In Proceedings of the ACM International Conference on Information and Knowledge Management (CIKM-2010). 2010.

Dredze, Mark, Paul McNamee, Delip Rao, Adam Gerber, and Tim Finin. Entity Disambiguation for Knowledge Base Population. In Proceedings of the 23rd International Conference on Computational Linguistics. 2010.

Du, Weifu, and Songbo Tan. Building Domain-Oriented Sentiment Lexicon by Improved Information Bottleneck. In Proceedings of the ACM Conference on Information and Knowledge Management (CIKM-2009). 2009.

Du, Weifu, Songbo Tan, Xueqi Cheng, and Xiaochun Yun. Adapting Information Bottleneck Method for Automatic Construction of Domain-Oriented Sentiment Lexicon. In Proceedings of the ACM International Conference on Web Search and Data Mining (WSDM-2010). 2010.

Duda, Richard O., Peter E. Hart, and David G. Stork. *Pattern Recognition*. 2001. New York: John Wiley.

Duh, Kevin, Akinori Fujino, and Masaaki Nagata. Is Machine Translation Ripe for Cross-Lingual Sentiment Classification? In Proceedings of the 49th Annual Meeting of the Association for Computational Linguistics: Short Papers (ACL-2011). 2011.

Eagly, Alice H., and Shelly Chaiken. Attitude Structure and Function. In D. T. Gilbert, S. T. Fisk, and G. Lindsey (Eds.). *Handbook of Social Psychology*. 1998. New York: McGraw-Hill, 269–322.

Eguchi, Koji, and Victor Lavrenko. Sentiment Retrieval Using Generative Models. In Proceedings of the Conference on Empirical Methods in Natural Language Processing (EMNLP-2006). 2006.

Ekman, Paul. Facial Expression and Emotion. *American Psychologist*, 1993. 48(3): 384–92.

Ekman, P., W. V. Friesen, and P. Ellsworth. What Emotion Categories or Dimensions Can Observers Judge from Facial Behavior? In *Emotion in the Human Face*, P. Ekman (Ed.). 1982. Cambridge: Cambridge University Press, 98–110.

Elkan, Charles. (Patent) Method and System for Selecting Documents by Measuring Document Quality. 2001. www.google.com/patents/about?id=WIp_AAAAEBAJ.

Esuli, Andrea, and Fabrizio Sebastiani. Determining the Semantic Orientation of Terms through Gloss Classification. In Proceedings of the ACM International Conference on Information and Knowledge Management (CIKM-2005). 2005.

Esuli, Andrea, and Fabrizio Sebastiani. Determining Term Subjectivity and Term Orientation for Opinion Mining. In Proceedings of the Conference of the European Chapter of the Association for Computational Linguistics (EACL-2006). 2006a.

Esuli, Andrea, and Fabrizio Sebastiani. SentiWordNet: A Publicly Available Lexical Resource for Opinion Mining. In Proceedings of Language Resources and Evaluation (LREC-2006). 2006b.

Fang, Lei, and Minlie Huang. Fine Granular Aspect Analysis Using Latent Structural Models. In Proceedings of the Annual Meeting of the Association for Computational Linguistics (ACL-2012). 2012.

Fei, Geli, Zhiyuan Chen, and Bing Liu. Review Topic Discovery with Phrases Using the Pólya Urn Model. In Proceedings of the 25th International Conference on Computational Linguistics (COLING-2014). 2014.

Fei, Geli, Bing Liu, Meichun Hsu, Malu Castellanos, and Riddhiman Ghosh. A Dictionary-Based Approach to Identifying Aspects Implied by Adjectives for Opinion Mining. In Proceedings of Computational Linguistics (Coling-2012). 2012.

Fei, Geli, Arjun Mukherjee, Bing Liu, Meichun Hsu, Malu Castellanos, and Riddhiman Ghosh. Exploiting Burstiness in Reviews for Review Spammer Detection. In Proceedings of the 7th International AAAI Conference on Weblog and Social Media (ICWSM-2013). 2013.

Felbo, Bjarke, Alan Mislove, Anders Søgaard, Iyad Rahwan, and Sune Lehmann. Using Millions of Emoji Occurrences to Learn Any-Domain Representations for Detecting Sentiment, Emotion and Sarcasm. In Proceedings of the Conference on Empirical Methods on Natural Language Processing (EMNLP-2017). 2017.

Feldman, Ronen, Benjamin Rosenfeld, Roy Bar-Haim, and Moshe Fresko. The Stock Sonar: Sentiment Analysis of Stocks Based on a Hybrid Approach. In Proceedings of the 23rd IAAI Conference on Artificial Intelligence (IAAI-2011). 2011.

Feng, Shi, Le Zhang, Binyang Li, Daling Wang, Ge Yu, and Kam-Fai Wong. Is Twitter a Better Corpus for Measuring Sentiment Similarity? in Proceedings of the 2013 Conference on Empirical Methods on Natural Language Processing (EMNLP-2013). 2013a.

Feng, Song, Jun Seok Kang, Polina Kuznetsova, and Yejin Choi. Connotation Lexicon: A Dash of Sentiment beneath the Surface Meaning. In Proceedings of the Annual Meeting of the Association for Computational Linguistics (ACL-2013). 2013b.

Feng, Song, Longfei Xing, Anupam Gogar, and Yejin Choi. Distributional Footprints of Deceptive Product Reviews. In Proceedings of the 6th International AAAI Conference on Weblogs and Social Media (ICWSM-2012). 2012a.

Feng, Song, Ritwik Banerjee, and Yejin Choi. Syntactic Stylometry for Deception Detection. In Proceedings of ACL: Short Paper. 2012b.

Feng, Song, Ritwik Bose, and Yejin Choi. Learning General Connotation of Words Using Graph-Based Algorithms. In Proceedings of the Conference on Empirical Methods in Natural Language Processing (EMNLP-2011). 2011.

Fiszman, Marcelo, Dina Demner-Fushman, Francois M. Lang, Philip Goetz, and Thomas C. Rindflesch. Interpreting Comparative Constructions in Biomedical Text. In Proceedings of BioNLP. 2007.

Frantzi, Katerina, Sophia Ananiadou, and Hideki Mima. Automatic Recognition of Multi-Word Terms:. The C-Value/NC-Value Method. *International Journal on Digital Libraries*, 2000. 3(2): 115–30.

Fung, Pascale, Anik Dey, Farhad Bin Siddique, Ruixi Lin, Yang Yang, Dario Bertero, Wan Yan, Ricky Chan Ho Yin, Chien-Sheng Wu. Zara: A Virtual Interactive Dialogue System Incorporating Emotion, Sentiment and Personality Recognition. In Proceedings of the International Conference on Computational Linguistics (COLING-2016). 2016.

Galley, Michel, Kathleen McKeown, Julia Hirschberg, and Elizabeth Shriber. Identifying Agreement and Disagreement in Conversational Speech: Use of Bayesian

Networks to Model Pragmatic Dependencies. In Proceedings of the Annual Meeting of the Association for Computational Linguistics (ACL-2004). 2004.

Gamon, Michael. Linguistic Correlates of Style: Authorship Classification with Deep Linguistic Analysis Features. In Proceedings of the International Conference on Computational Linguistics (COLING-2004). 2004a.

Gamon, Michael. Sentiment Classification on Customer Feedback Data: Noisy Data, Large Feature Vectors, and the Role of Linguistic Analysis. In Proceedings of the International Conference on Computational Linguistics (COLING-2004). 2004b.

Gamon, Michael, Anthony Aue, Simon Corston-Oliver, and Eric Ringger. Pulse: Mining Customer Opinions from Free Text. *Advances in Intelligent Data Analysis*, 2005. VI: 121–32.

Ganapathibhotla, Murthy, and Bing Liu. Mining Opinions in Comparative Sentences. In Proceedings of the International Conference on Computational Linguistics (COLING-2008). 2008.

Ganesan, Kavita, ChengXiang Zhai, and Jiawei Han. Opinosis: A Graph-Based Approach to Abstractive Summarization of Highly Redundant Opinions. In Proceedings of the 23rd International Conference on Computational Linguistics (COLING-2010). 2010.

Ganter, Viola, and Michael Strube. Finding Hedges by Chasing Weasels: Hedge Detection Using Wikipedia Tags and Shallow Linguistic Features. In Proceedings of the ACL-IJCNLP 2009 Conference: Short Papers. 2009.

Gao, Sheng, and Haizhou Li. A Cross-Domain Adaptation Method for Sentiment Classification Using Probabilistic Latent Analysis. In Proceedings of the ACM Conference on Information and Knowledge Management (CIKM-2011). 2011.

Gastil, John. *Communication As Deliberation: A Non-Deliberative Polemic on Communication Theory*. Technical Report. 2005. Seattle: University of Washington.

Gastil, John. *Political Communication and Deliberation*. 2007. Los Angeles: Sage.

Gatti, Lorenzo, and Marco Guerini. Assessing Sentiment Strength in Words' Prior Polarities. In Proceedings of the 24th International Conference on Computational Linguistics (COLING-2012). 2012.

Gayo-Avello, Daniel, Panagiotis T. Metaxas, and Eni Mustafaraj. Limits of Electoral Predictions Using Twitter. In Proceedings of the International Conference on Weblogs and Social Media (ICWSM-2011). 2011.

Ghahramani, Zoubin, and Katherine A. Heller. Bayesian Sets. In Proceedings of Advances in Neural Information Processing Systems 18 (NIPS). 2005.

Ghani, Rayid, Katharina Probst, Yan Liu, Marko Krema, and Andrew Fano. Text Mining for Product Attribute Extraction. *ACM SIGKDD Explorations Newsletter*, 2006. 8(1): 4–48.

Ghose, Anindya, and Panagiotis G. Ipeirotis. Designing Novel Review Ranking Systems: Predicting the Usefulness and Impact of Reviews. In Proceedings of the International Conference on Electronic Commerce. 2007.

Ghose, Anindya, and Panagiotis G. Ipeirotis. Estimating the Helpfulness and Economic Impact of Product Reviews: Mining Text and Reviewer Characteristics. *IEEE Transactions on Knowledge and Data Engineering*. 2010. 23(10): 1498–512.

Ghose, Anindya, Panagiotis G. Ipeirotis, and Arun Sundararajan. Opinion Mining Using Econometrics: A Case Study on Reputation Systems. In Proceedings of the Association for Computational Linguistics (ACL-2007). 2007.

Ghosh, Aniruddha, and Tony Veale. Magnets for Sarcasm: Making Sarcasm Detection Timely, Contextual and Very Personal. In Proceedings of the Conference on Empirical Methods on Natural Language Processing (EMNLP-2017). 2017.

Gibbs, Raymond W. On the Psycholinguistics of Sarcasm. *Journal of Experimental Psychology: General*, 1986. 115(1): 3–15.

Gibbs, Raymond W., and Herbert L. Colston. *Irony in Language and Thought: A Cognitive Science Reader.* 2007. New York: Lawrence Erlbaum.

Girju, Roxana, Adriana Badulescu, and Dan Moldovan. Automatic Discovery of Part–Whole Relations. *Computational Linguistics*, 2006. 32(1): 83–135.

Glorot, Xavier, Antoine Bordes, and Yoshua Bengio. Domain Adaption for Large-Scale Sentiment Classification: A Deep Learning Approach. In Proceedings of the International Conference on Machine Learning (ICML-2011). 2011.

Goldberg, Andrew B., and Xiaojin Zhu. Seeing Stars When There Aren't Many Stars: Graph-Based Semi-Supervised Learning for Sentiment Categorization. In Proceedings of HLT-NAACL 2006 Workshop on Textgraphs: Graph-Based Algorithms for Natural Language Processing. 2006.

González-Ibáñez, Roberto, Smaranda Muresan, and Nina Wacholder. Identifying Sarcasm in Twitter: A Closer Look. In Proceedings of the 49th Annual Meeting of the Association for Computational Linguistics: Short Papers (ACL-2011). 2011.

Gottipati, Swapna, and Jing Jiang. Linking Entities to a Knowledge Base with Query Expansion. In Proceedings of the 2011 Conference on Empirical Methods in Natural Language Processing. 2011.

Graham, Neil, Graeme Hirst, and Bhaskara. Marthi. Segmenting Documents by Stylistic Character. *Natural Language Engineering*, 2005. 11: 397–415.

Graves, Alex, and Schmidhuber Jurgen. *Framewise Phoneme Classification with Bidirectional LSTM and Other Neural Network Architectures.* Neural Networks, 2005. 18(5–6): 602–10.

Gray, Jeffrey A. *The Neuropsychology of Anxiety.* 1982. Oxford: Oxford University Press.

Greene, Stephan, and Philip Resnik. More Than Words: Syntactic Packaging and Implicit Sentiment. In Proceedings of Human Language Technologies: The 2009 Annual Conference of the North American Chapter of the ACL (NAACL-2009). 2009.

Griffiths, Thomas L., and Mark Steyvers. Prediction and Semantic Association. *Neural Information Processing Systems*, 2003. 15: 11–18.

Griffiths, Thomas L., and Mark Steyvers. Finding Scientific Topics. *Proceedings of the National Academy of Sciences of the United States of America*, 2004. 101(Suppl 1): 5228–35.

Griffiths, Thomas L., Mark Steyvers, David M. Blei, and Joshua B. Tenenbaum. Integrating Topics and Syntax. *Advances in Neural Information Processing Systems*, 2005. 17: 537–44.

Groh, Georg, and Jan Hauffa. Characterizing Social Relations via NLP-Based Sentiment Analysis. In Proceedings of the 5th International AAAI Conference on Weblogs and Social Media (ICWSM-2011). 2011.

Guan, Ziyu, Long Chen, Wei Zhao, Yi Zheng, Shulong Tan, and Deng Cai. Weakly-Supervised Deep Learning for Customer Review Sentiment Classification. In

Proceedings of the International Joint Conference on Artificial Intelligence (IJCAI-2016). 2016.

Guerini, Marco, Lorenzo Gatti, and Marco Turchi. Sentiment Analysis: How to Derive Prior Polarities from Sentiwordnet. In Proceedings of the 2013 Conference on Empirical Methods on Natural Language Processing (EMNLP-2013). 2013.

Guggilla, Chinnappa, Tristan Miller, and Iryna Gurevych. CNN-and LSTM-Based Claim Classification in Online User Comments. In Proceedings of the International Conference on Computational Linguistics (COLING-2016). 2016.

Gui, Lin, Jiannan Hu, Yulan He, Ruifeng Xu, Qin Lu, and Jiachen Du. A Question Answering Approach to Emotion Cause Extraction. In Proceedings of the Conference on Empirical Methods on Natural Language Processing (EMNLP-2017). 2017.

Guo, Honglei, Huijia Zhu, Zhili Guo, Xiaoxun Zhang, and Zhong Su. Product Feature Categorization with Multilevel Latent Semantic Association. In Proceedings of ACM International Conference on Information and Knowledge Management (CIKM-2009). 2009.

Guo, Honglei, Huijia Zhu, Zhili Guo, Xiaoxun Zhang, and Zhong Su. Opinionit: A Text Mining System for Cross-Lingual Opinion Analysis. In Proceedings of the ACM Conference on Information and Knowledge Management (CIKM-2010). 2010.

Gutmann, Amy, and Dennis Thompson. *Democracy and Disagreement*. 1996. Cambridge, MA: Harvard University Press.

Habermas, Jürgen. *The Theory of Communicative Action: Vol. 1. Reason and the Rationalization of Society*, Thomas Mccarthy (Trans.). 1984. Boston: Beacon Press.

Hai, Zhen, Kuiyu Chang, and Gao Cong. One Seed to Find Them All: Mining Opinion Features via Assocaition. In Proceedings of the ACM International Conference on Information and Knowledge Management (CIKM-2012). 2012.

Hai, Zhen, Kuiyu Chang, and Jung-jae Kim. Implicit Feature Identification via Co-occurrence Association Rule Mining. *Computational Linguistics and Intelligent Text Processing*, 2011. LNCS 6608: 393–404.

Halteren, Hans van, Fiona Tweedie, and Harald Baayen. Outside the Cave of Shadows: Using Syntactic Annotation to Enhance Authorship Attribution. *Literary and Linguistic Computing*, 1996. 11: 121–32.

Hamilton, William L, Kevin Clark, Jure Leskovec, and Dan Jurafsky. Inducing Domain-Specific Sentiment Lexicons from Unlabeled Corpora. In Proceedings of Empirical Methods in Natural Language Processing (EMNLP-2016). 2016.

Han, Jiawei, Micheline Kamber, and Pei Jian. *Data Mining: Concepts and Techniques*. 3rd ed. 2011. Waltham, MA: Morgan Kaufmann.

Han, Xianpei, and Le Sun. An Entity–Topic Model for Entity Linking. In Proceedings of the 2012 Joint Conference on Empirical Methods in Natural Language Processing and Computational Natural Language Learning. 2012.

Hancock, Jeffrey T., Lauren E. Curry, Saurabh Goorha, and Michael Woodworth. On Lying and Being Lied to: A Linguistic Analysis of Deception in Computer-Mediated Communication. *Discourse Processes*, 2007. 45(1): 1–23.

Hardisty, Eric A., Jordan Boyd-Graber, and Philip Resnik. Modeling Perspective Using Adaptor Grammars. In Proceedings of the 2010 Conference on Empirical Methods in Natural Language Processing (EMNLP-2010). 2010.

Harmon, Amy. Amazon Glitch Unmasks War of Reviewers. *New York Times*, February 14, 2004. www.nytimes.com/2004/02/14/us/amazon-glitch-unmasks-war-of-reviewers.html

Hartung, Matthias and Anette Frank. A Structured Vector Space Model for Hidden Attribute Meaning in Adjective–Noun Phrases. In Proceedings of the 23rd International Conference on Computational Linguistics (COLING-2010). 2010.

Hartung, Matthias, and Anette Frank. Exploring Supervised LDA Models for Assigning Attributes to Adjective–Noun Phrases. In Proceedings of the Conference on Empirical Methods in Natural Language Processing (EMNLP-2011). 2011.

Hassan, Ahmed, Amjad Abu-Jbara, Rahul Jha, and Dragomir Radev. Identifying the Semantic Orientation of Foreign Words. In Proceedings of the 49th Annual Meeting of the Association for Computational Linguistics: Short Papers (ACL-2011). 2011.

Hassan, Ahmed, Vahed Qazvinian, and Dragomir Radev. What's with the Attitude? Identifying Sentences with Attitude in Online Discussions. In Proceedings of the 2010 Conference on Empirical Methods in Natural Language Processing (EMNLP-2010). 2010.

Hassan, Ahmed, and Dragomir Radev. Identifying Text Polarity Using Random Walks. In Proceedings of the Annual Meeting of the Association for Computational Linguistics (ACL-2010). 2010.

Hatzivassiloglou, Vasileios, Judith L. Klavans, Melissa L. Holcombe, Regina Barzilay, Min-Yen Kan, and Kathleen R. McKeown. Simfinder: A Flexible Clustering Tool for Summarization. In Proceedings of the Workshop on Summarization in NAACL-2001. 2001.

Hatzivassiloglou, Vasileios, and Kathleen R. McKeown. Predicting the Semantic Orientation of Adjectives. In Proceedings of the Annual Meeting of the Association for Computational Linguistics (ACL-1997). 1997.

Hatzivassiloglou, Vasileios, and Janyce Wiebe. Effects of Adjective Orientation and Gradability on Sentence Subjectivity. In Proceedings of the Interntional Conference on Computational Linguistics (COLING-2000). 2000.

He, Ruidan, Wee Sun Lee, and Hwee Tou Ng, Daniel Dahlmeier. An Unsupervised Neural Attention Model for Aspect Extraction. In Proceedings of the Annual Meeting of the Association for Computational Linguistics (ACL-2017). 2017.

He, Yulan. Learning Sentiment Classification Model from Labeled Features. In Proceedings of the ACM Conference on Information and Knowledge Management (CIKM-2011). 2010.

He, Yulan, Chenghua Lin, and Harith Alani. Automatically Extracting Polarity-Bearing Topics for Cross-Domain Sentiment Classification. In Proceedings of the 49th Annual Meeting of the Association for Computational Linguistics (ACL-2011). 2011.

Hearst, Marti. Direction-Based Text Interpretation As an Information Access Refinement. In *Text-Based Intelligent Systems*, P. Jacobs (Ed.). 1992. Mahwah, NJ: Lawrence Erlbaum, 257–74.

Heckman, James J. Sample Selection Bias As a Specification Error. *Econometrica: Journal of the Econometric Society*, 1979. 47(1): 153–61.

Heinrich, Gregor. A Generic Approach to Topic Models. In Proceedings of ECML/PKDD-2009: Machine Learning and Knowledge Discovery in Databases. 2009.

Hirst, Graeme, and Ol'ga Feiguina. Bigrams of Syntactic Labels for Authorship Discrimination of Short Texts. *Literary and Linguistic Computing*, 2007. 22: 405–17.

Hobbs, Jerry R., and Ellen Riloff. Information Extraction. In *Handbook of Natural Language Processing*, 2nd ed., N. Indurkhya and F. J. Damerau (Eds.). 2010. Boca Raton, FL: Chapman & Hall/CRC Press, 511–32.

Hoffart, Johannes, Mohamed Amir Yosef, Ilaria Bordino, Hagen Furstenau, Manfred Pinkal, Marc Spaniol, Bilyana Taneva, Stefan Thater, and Gerhard Weikum. Robust Disambiguation of Named Entities in Text. In Proceedings of the 2011 Conference on Empirical Methods in Natural Language Processing. 2011.

Hofmann, Thomas. Probabilistic Latent Semantic Indexing. In Proceedings of the Conference on Uncertainty in Artificial Intelligence (UAI-1999). 1999.

Holloway, D. Just Another Reason Why We Have a Review Filter. 2011. http://officialblog .yelp.com/2011/10/just-another-reason-why-wehave-a-review-filter.html.

Hong, Yancheng, and Steven Skiena. The Wisdom of Bookies? Sentiment Analysis vs. the NFL Point Spread. In Proceedings of the International Conference on Weblogs and Social Media (ICWSM-2010). 2010.

Hu, Jian, Gang Wang, Fred Lochovsky, Jian-Tao Sun, and Zheng Chen. Understanding User's Query Intent with Wikipedia. In Proceedings of the 18th International Conference on the World Wide Web (WWW-2009). 2009.

Hu, Meishan, Aixin Sun, and Ee-Peng Lim. Comments-Oriented Document Summarization: Understanding Documents with Readers' Feedback. In Proceedings of the 31st Annual International ACM SIGIR Conference on Research and Development in Information Retrieval (SIGIR-2008). 2008.

Hu, Minqing, and Bing Liu. Mining and Summarizing Customer Reviews. In Proceedings of ACM SIGKDD International Conference on Knowledge Discovery and Data Mining (KDD-2004). 2004.

Hu, Nan, Paul A. Pavlou, and Jennifer Zhang. Can Online Reviews Reveal a Product's True Quality? Empirical Findings and Analytical Modeling of Online Word-of-Mouth Communication. In Proceedings of Electronic Commerce (EC-2006). 2006.

Hu, Xia, Lei Tang, Jiliang Tang, and Huan Liu. Exploiting Social Relations for Sentiment Analysis in Microblogging. In Proceedings of the ACM Interntional Conference on Web Seatch and Data Mining (WSDM-2013). 2013.

Huang, Minlie, Qiao Qian, and Xiaoyan Zhu. Encoding Syntactic Knowledge in Neural Networks for Sentiment Classification. *ACM Transactions on Information Systems*, 2017. 35(3): 1–27.

Huang, Xuanjing, and W. Bruce Croft. A Unified Relevance Model for Opinion Retrieval. In Proceedings of the ACM Conference on Information and Knowledge Management (CIKM-2009). 2009.

HUMAINE. Emotion Annotation and Representation Language. 2006. http://emotion-research.net/projects/humaine/earl.

Ikeda, Daisuke, Hiroya Takamura, Lev-Arie Ratinov, and Manabu Okumura. Learning to Shift the Polarity of Words for Sentiment Classification. In Proceedings of the 3rd International Joint Conference on Natural Language Processing (IJCNLP-2008). 2008.

Indurkhya, Nitin, and Fred J. Damerau. *Handbook of Natural Language Processing*. 2nd ed. 2010. London: Chapman and Hall.

Izard, Carroll Ellis. *The Face of Emotion*. 1971. Norwalk, CT: Appleton-Century-Crofts.

Jagarlamudi, Jagadeesh, Hal Daumé III, and Raghavendra Udupa. Incorporating Lexical Priors into Topic Models. In Proceedings of EACL-2012. 2012.

Jakob, Niklas, and Iryna Gurevych. Extracting Opinion Targets in a Single- and Cross-Domain Setting with Conditional Random Fields. In Proceedings of the Conference on Empirical Methods in Natural Language Processing (EMNLP-2010). 2010.

James, William. What Is an Emotion? *Mind*, 1884. 9: 188–205.

Ji, Heng, Ralph Grishman, Hoa Trang Dang, Kira Griffitt, and Joe Ellis. Overview of the TAC 2010 Knowledge Base Population Track. 2010.

Jia, Lifeng, Clement Yu, and Weiyi Meng. The Effect of Negation on Sentiment Analysis and Retrieval Effectiveness. In Proceedings of the 18th ACM Conference on Information and Knowledge Management (CIKM-2009). 2009.

Jiang, Jay J., and David W. Conrath. Semantic Similarity Based on Corpus Statistics and Lexical Taxonomy. In Proceedings of Research in Computational Linguistics. 1997.

Jiang, Long, Mo Yu, Ming Zhou, Xiaohua Liu, and Tiejun Zhao. Target-Dependent Twitter Sentiment Classification. In Proceedings of the 49th Annual Meeting of the Association for Computational Linguistics (ACL-2011). 2011.

Jijkoun, Valentin, Maarten de Rijke, and Wouter Weerkamp. Generating Focused Topic-Specific Sentiment Lexicons. In Proceedings of the Annual Meeting of the Association for Computational Linguistics (ACL-2010). 2010.

Jin, Wei, and Hung Hay Ho. A Novel Lexicalized HMM-Based Learning Framework for Web Opinion Mining. In Proceedings of the International Conference on Machine Learning (ICML-2009). 2009.

Jindal, Nitin, and Bing Liu. Identifying Comparative Sentences in Text Documents. In Proceedings of ACM SIGIR Conference on Research and Development in Information Retrieval (SIGIR-2006). 2006a.

Jindal, Nitin, and Bing Liu. Mining Comparative Sentences and Relations. In Proceedings of National Conference on Artificial Intelligence (AAAI-2006). 2006b.

Jindal, Nitin, and Bing Liu. Review Spam Detection. In Proceedings of WWW. 2007.

Jindal, Nitin, and Bing Liu. Opinion Spam and Analysis. In Proceedings of the Conference on Web Search and Web Data Mining (WSDM-2008). 2008.

Jindal, Nitin, Bing Liu, and Ee-Peng Lim. *Finding Atypical Review Patterns to Detect Possible Spammers*. Technical Report. 2010a. Chicago: University of Illinois at Chicago.

Jindal, Nitin, Bing Liu, and Ee-Peng Lim. Finding Unusual Review Patterns Using Unexpected Rules. In Proceedings of the ACM International Conference on Information and Knowledge Management (CIKM-2010). 2010b.

Jo, Yohan, and Alice Oh. Aspect and Sentiment Unification Model for Online Review Analysis. In Proceedings of the ACM Conference on Web Search and Data Mining (WSDM-2011). 2011.

Joachims, Thorsten. Making Large-Scale SVM Learning Practical. In *Advances in Kernel Methods: Support Vector Learning*, B. Schölkopf, C. Burges, and A. Smola (Eds.). 1999. Cambridge, MA: MIT Press.

Johansson, Richard, and Alessandro Moschitti. Reranking Models in Fine-Grained Opinion Analysis. In Proceedings of the International Conference on Computational Linguistics (COLING-2010). 2010.

Johnson, Rie, and Tong Zhang. Effective Use of Word Order for Text Categorization with Convolutional Neural Networks. In Proceedings of the Conference of the North American Chapter of the Association for Computational Linguistics: Human Language Technologies (NAACL-HLT-2015). 2015.

Joshi, Aditya, Ameya Prabhu, Manish Shrivastava, and Vasudeva Varma. Towards Sub-word Level Compositions for Sentiment Analysis of Hindi–English Code Mixed Text. In Proceedings of the International Conference on Computational Linguistics (COLING-2016). 2016a.

Joshi, Aditya, Vaibhav Tripathi, Kevin Patel, Pushpak Bhattacharyya, and Mark Carman. Are Word Embedding-Based Features Useful for Sarcasm Detection? In Proceedings of the Conference on Empirical Methods on Natural Language Processing (EMNLP-2016). 2016b.

Joshi, M., and C. Penstein-Rosé. Generalizing Dependency Features for Opinion Mining. In Proceedings of the ACL-IJCNLP 2009 Conference: Short Papers. 2009.

Joshi, Mahesh, Dipanjan Das, Kevin Gimpel, and Noah A. Smith. Movie Reviews and Revenues: An Experiment in Text Regression. In Proceedings of the North American Chapter of the Association for Computational Linguistics Human Language Technologies Conference (NAACL-2010). 2010.

Kaji, Nobuhiro, and Masaru Kitsuregawa. Automatic Construction of Polarity-Tagged Corpus from HTML Documents. In Proceedings of COLING/ACL 2006 Main Conference Poster Sessions (COLING-ACL-2006). 2006.

Kaji, Nobuhiro, and Masaru Kitsuregawa. Building Lexicon for Sentiment Analysis from Massive Collection of HTML Documents. In Proceedings of the Joint Conference on Empirical Methods in Natural Language Processing and Computational Natural Language Learning (EMNLP-2007). 2007.

Kalchbrenner, Nal, Edward Grefenstette, and Phil Blunsom. A Convolutional Neural Network for Modelling Sentences. In Proceedings of the Annual Meeting of the Association for Computational Linguistics (ACL-2014). 2014.

Kamps, Jaap, Maarten Marx, Robert J. Mokken, and Maarten de Rijke. Using WordNet to Measure Semantic Orientation of Adjectives. In Proceedings of LREC-2004. 2004.

Kamps, Jaap, Maarten Marx, Robert J. Mokken, and Marten de Rijke. Words with Attitude. In Proceedings of the 1st International Conference on Global WordNet. 2002.

Kanayama, Hiroshi, and Tetsuya Nasukawa. Fully Automatic Lexicon Expansion for Domain-Oriented Sentiment Analysis. In Proceedings of the Conference on Empirical Methods in Natural Language Processing (EMNLP-2006). 2006.

Katiyar, Arzoo, and Claire Cardie. Investigating LSTMs for Joint Extraction of Opinion Entities and Relations. In Proceedings of the Annual Meeting of the Association for Computational Linguistics (ACL 2016). 2016.

Kennedy, Alistair, and Diana Inkpen. Sentiment Classification of Movie Reviews Using Contextual Valence Shifters. Computational Intelligence, 2006. 22(2): 110–25.

Kennedy, Christopher. Comparatives, Semantics of. In *Encyclopedia of Language and Linguistics*, 2nd ed. 2005. New York: Elsevier.

Kessler, Jason S., and Nicolas Nicolov. Targeting Sentiment Expressions through Supervised Ranking of Linguistic Configurations. In Proceedings of the 3rd International AAAI Conference on Weblogs and Social Media (ICWSM-2009). 2009.

Kessler, Wiltrud, and Hinrich Schütze. Classification of Inconsistent Sentiment Words Using Syntactic Constructions. In Proceedings of the 24th International Conference on Computational Linguistics (COLING-2012). 2012.

Khabiri, Elham, James Caverlee, and Chiao-Fang Hsu. Summarizing User-Contributed Comments. In Proceedings of the 5th International AAAI Conference on Weblogs and Social Media (ICWSM-2011). 2011.

Khoo, Christopher Soo-Guan, Armineh Nourbakhsh, and Jin-Cheon Na. Sentiment Analysis of Online News Text: A Case Study of Appraisal Theory. *Online Information Review*, 2012. 36(6): 858–78.

Kim, Hyun Duk, and ChengXiang Zhai. Generating Comparative Summaries of Contradictory Opinions in Text. In Proceedings of the ACM Conference on Information and Knowledge Management (CIKM-2009). 2009.

Kim, Jungi, Jin-Ji Li, and Jong-Hyeok Lee. Discovering the Discriminative Views: Measuring Term Weights for Sentiment Analysis. In Proceedings of the 47th Annual Meeting of the ACL and the 4th IJCNLP of the AFNLP (ACL-2009). 2009.

Kim, Jungi, Jin-Ji Li, and Jong-Hyeok Lee. Evaluating Multilanguage-Comparability of Subjectivity Analysis Systems. In Proceedings of the 48th Annual Meeting of the Association for Computational Linguistics (ACL-2010). 2010.

Kim, Seungyeon, Fuxin Li, Guy Lebanon, and Irfan Essa. Beyond Sentiment: The Manifold of Human Emotions. In Proceedings of the 16th International Conference on Artificial Intelligence and Statistics. 2013.

Kim, Soo-Min, and Eduard Hovy. Determining the Sentiment of Opinions. In Proceedings of International Conference on Computational Linguistics (COLING-2004). 2004.

Kim, Soo-Min, and Eduard Hovy. Identifying and Analyzing Judgment Opinions. In Proceedings of Human Language Technology Conference of the North American Chapter of the ACL. 2006a.

Kim, Soo-Min, and Eduard Hovy. Extracting Opinions, Opinion Holders, and Topics Expressed in Online News Media Text. In Proceedings of the Conference on Empirical Methods in Natural Language Processing (EMNLP-2006). 2006b.

Kim, Soo-Min, and Eduard Hovy. Automatic Identification of Pro and Con Reasons in Online Reviews. In Proceedings of COLING/ACL 2006 Main Conference Poster Sessions (ACL-2006). 2006c.

Kim, Soo-Min, and Eduard Hovy. Crystal: Analyzing Predictive Opinions on the Web. In Proceedings of the Joint Conference on Empirical Methods in Natural Language Processing and Computational Natural Language Learning (EMNLP/CoNLL-2007). 2007.

Kim, Soo-Min, Patrick Pantel, Tim Chklovski, and Marco Pennacchiotti. Automatically Assessing Review Helpfulness. In Proceedings of the Conference on Empirical Methods in Natural Language Processing (EMNLP-2006). 2006.

Kim, Su Nam, Lawrence Cavedon, and Timothy Baldwin. Classifying Dialogue Acts in One-on-One Live Chats. In Proceedings of the 2010 Conference on Empirical Methods in Natural Language Processing. 2010.

Kim, Yoon. Convolutional Neural Networks for Sentence Classification. In Proceedings of the Annual Meeting of the Association for Computational Linguistics (ACL-2014). 2014.

Kindermann, Ross, and J. Laurie Snell. *Markov Random Fields and Their Applications*. 1980. Providence, RI: American Mathematical Society.

Kirkpatrick, James, Razvan Pascanu, Neil Rabinowitz, Joel Veness, Guillaume Desjardins, Andrei A. Rusu, Kieran Milan, John Quan, Tiago Ramalho, Agnieszka Grabska-Barwinska, Demis Hassabis, Claudia Clopath, Dharshan Kumaran, and Raia Hadsell. Overcoming Catastrophic Forgetting in Neural Networks. *Proceedings of the National Academy of Sciences of the United States*, 2017. 114: 3521–6.

Kleinberg, Jon M. Authoritative Sources in a Hyperlinked Environment. *Journal of the ACM*, 1999. 46(5): 604–32.

Klinger, Roman, and Philipp Cimiano. Bi-directional Inter-dependencies of Subjective Expressions and Targets and Their Value for a Joint Model. In Proceedings of the Annual Meeting of the Association for Computational Linguistics (ACL-2013). 2013.

Knapp, Mark L., and Mark E. Comaden. Telling It Like It Isn't: A Review of Theory and Research on Deceptive Communications. *Human Communication Research*, 1979. 5: 270–85.

Knapp, Mark L., Roderick P. Hart, and Harry S. Dennis. An Exploration of Deception As a Communication Construct. *Human Communication Research*, 1974. 1: 15–29.

Kobayashi, Nozomi, Ryu Iida, Kentaro Inui, and Yuji Matsumoto. Opinion Mining on the Web by Extracting Subject–Attribute–Value Relations. In Proceedings of AAAI-CAAW'06. 2006.

Kobayashi, Nozomi, Kentaro Inui, and Yuji Matsumoto. Extracting Aspect-Evaluation and Aspect-of Relations in Opinion Mining. In Proceedings of the 2007 Joint Conference on Empirical Methods in Natural Language Processing and Computational Natural Language Learning. 2007.

Kost, Amanda. Woman Paid to Post Five-Star Google Feedback. ABC7 News. September 15, 2012.

Kouloumpis, Efthymios, Theresa Wilson, and Johanna Moore. Twitter Sentiment Analysis: The Good, the Bad, and the OMG! In Proceedings of the 5th International AAAI Conference on Weblogs and Social Media (ICWSM-2011). 2011.

Kovelamudi, Sudheer, Sethu Ramalingam, Arpit Sood, and Vasudeva Varma. Domain Independent Model for Product Attribute Extraction from User Reviews Using Wikipedia. In Proceedings of the 5th International Joint Conference on Natural Language Processing (IJCNLP-2010). 2011.

Kreuz, Roger J., and Gina M. Caucci. Lexical Influences on the Perception of Sarcasm. In Proceedings of the Workshop on Computational Approaches to Figurative Language. 2007.

Kreuz, Roger J., and Sam Glucksberg. How to Be Sarcastic: The Echoic Reminder Theory of Verbal Irony. *Journal of Experimental Psychology: General*, 1989. 118 (4): 374–86.

Ku, Lun-Wei, Yu-Ting Liang, and Hsin-Hsi Chen. Opinion Extraction, Summarization and Tracking in News and Blog Corpora. In Proceedings of AAAI-CAAW'06. 2006.

Labutov, Igor, and Hod Lipson. Re-embedding Words. In Proceedings of the Annual Meeting of the Association for Computational Linguistics (ACL-2013). 2013.

Lafferty, John, Andrew McCallum, and Fernando Pereira. Conditional Random Fields: Probabilistic Models for Segmenting and Labeling Sequence Data. In Proceedings of International Conference on Machine Learning (ICML-2001). 2001.

Lai, Guo-Hau, Ying-Mei Guo, and Richard Tzong-Han Tsai. Unsupervised Japanese–Chinese Opinion Word Translation Using Dependency Distance and Feature–Opinion Association Weight. In Proceedings of the Conference of the 24th International Conference on Computational Linguistics (COLING-2012). 2012.

Lakkaraju, Himabindu, Chiranjib Bhattacharyya, Indrajit Bhattacharya, and Srujana Merugu. Exploiting Coherence for the Simultaneous Discovery of Latent Facets and Associated Sentiments. In Proceedings of the SIAM Conference on Data Mining (SDM-2011). 2011.

Lappas, Theodoros, and Dimitrios Gunopulos. Efficient Confident Search in Large Review Corpora. In Proceedings of ECML-PKDD 2010. 2010.

Lazaridou, Angeliki, Ivan Titov, and Caroline Sporleder. A Bayesian Model for Joint Unsupervised Induction of Sentiment, Aspect and Discourse Representations. In Proceedings of the Annual Meeting of the Association for Computational Linguistics (ACL-2013). 2013.

Le, Quoc, and Tomas Mikolov. Distributed Representations of Sentences and Documents. In Proceedings of the International Conference on Machine Learning (ICML 2014). 2014.

LeDoux, J. Rethinking the Emotional Brain. Neuron, 2012. 73(4):653–76.

Lee, Lillian. Measures of Distributional Similarity. In Proceedings of the Annual Meeting of the Association for Computational Linguistics (ACL-1999). 1999.

Lee, Sophia Yat Mei, Ying Chen, Chu-Ren Huang, and Shoushan Li. Detecting Emotion Causes with a Linguistic Rule-Based Approach. Computational Intelligence, 2013. 29(3): 390–416.

Lei, Tao, Regina Barzilay, and Tommi Jaakkola. Rationalizing Neural Predictions. In Proceedings of the Conference on Empirical Methods on Natural Language Processing (EMNLP-2016). 2016.

Lerman, Kevin, Sasha Blair-Goldensohn, and Ryan McDonald. Sentiment Summarization: Evaluating and Learning User Preferences. In Proceedings of the 12th Conference of the European Chapter of the Association for Computational Linguistics (EACL-2009). 2009.

Lerman, Kevin, and Ryan McDonald. Contrastive Summarization: An Experiment with Consumer Reviews. In Proceedings of NAACL HLT 2009: Short Papers. 2009.

Lerner, Jean-Yves, and Manfred Pinkal. Comparatives and Nested Quantification. CLAUS-Report 21. 1992.

Li, Binyang, Lanjun Zhou, Shi Feng, and Kam-Fai Wong. A United Graph Model for Sentence-Based Opinion Retrieval. In Proceedings of the Annual Meeting of the Association for Computational Linguistics (ACL-2010). 2010a.

Li, Cheng, Xiaoxiao Guo, and Qiaozhu Mei. Deep Memory Networks for Attitude Identification. In Proceedings of the ACM International Conference on Web Search and Data Mining (WSDM-2017). 2017.

Li, Fangtao, Chao Han, Minlie Huang, Xiaoyan Zhu, Ying-Ju Xia, Shu Zhang, and Hao Yu. Structure-Aware Review Mining and Summarization. In Proceedings of the 23rd International Conference on Computational Linguistics (COLING-2010). 2010b.

Li, Fangtao, Minlie Huang, Yi Yang, and Xiaoyan Zhu. Learning to Identify Review Spam. In Proceedings of the International Joint Conference on Artificial Intelligence (IJCAI-2011). 2011a.

Li, Fangtao, Minlie Huang, and Xiaoyan Zhu. Sentiment Analysis with Global Topics and Local Dependency. In Proceedings of the 24th AAAI Conference on Artificial Intelligence (AAAI-2010). 2010c.

Li, Fangtao, Sinno Jialin Pan, Ou Jin, Qiang Yang, and Xiaoyan Zhu. Cross-Domain Co-extraction of Sentiment and Topic Lexicons. In Proceedings of the Annual Meeting of the Association for Computational Linguistics (ACL-2012). 2012a.

Li, Jiwei, and Dan Jurafsky. Do Multi-Sense Embeddings Improve Natural Language Understanding? In Proceedings of the Conference on Empirical Methods in Natural Language Processing (EMNLP-2015). 2015.

Li, Junhui, Guodong Zhou, Hongling Wang, and Qiaoming Zhu. Learning the Scope of Negation via Shallow Semantic Parsing. In Proceedings of the 23rd International Conference on Computational Linguistics (COLING-2010). 2010d.

Li, Shasha, Chin-Yew Lin, Young-In Song, and Zhoujun Li. Comparable Entity Mining from Comparative Questions. In Proceedings of the Annual Meeting of the Association for Computational Linguistics (ACL-2010). 2010e.

Li, Shoushan, Chu-Ren Huang, Guodong Zhou, and Sophia Yat Mei Lee. Employing Personal/Impersonal Views in Supervised and Semi-Supervised Sentiment Classification. In Proceedings of Annual Meeting of the Association for Computational Linguistics (ACL-2010). 2010f.

Li, Shoushan, Shengfeng Ju, Guodong Zhou, and Xiaojun Li. Active Learning for Imbalanced Sentiment Classification. In Proceedings of the 2012 Conference on Empirical Methods on Natural Language Processing (EMNLP-2012). 2012b.

Li, Shoushan, Sophia Yat Mei Lee, Ying Chen, Chu-Ren Huang, and Guodong Zhou. Sentiment Classification and Polarity Shifting. In Proceedings of the 23rd International Conference on Computational Linguistics (COLING-2010). 2010g.

Li, Shoushan, Zhongqing Wang, Guodong Zhou, and Sophia Yat Mei Lee. Semi-Supervised Learning for Imbalanced Sentiment Classification. In Proceedings of International Joint Conference on Artificial Intelligence (IJCAI-2011). 2011b.

Li, Shoushan, and Chengqing Zong. Multi-Domain Sentiment Classification. In Proceedings of ACL-08: HLT, Short Papers (Companion Volume). 2008.

Li, Si, Zheng-Jun Zha, Zhaoyan Ming, Meng Wang, Tat-Seng Chua, Jun Guo, and Weiran Xu. Product Comparison Using Comparative Relations. In Proceedings of SIGIR-2011. 2011c.

Li, Tao, Yi Zhang, and Vikas Sindhwani. A Non-negative Matrix Tri-factorization Approach to Sentiment Classification with Lexical Prior Knowledge. In Proceedings of the Annual Meeting of the Association for Computational Linguistics (ACL-2009). 2009.

Li, Xiao, Ye-Yi Wang, and Alex Acero. Learning Query Intent from Regularized Click Graph. In Proceedings of the 31st Annual International ACM SIGIR Conference on Research and Development in Information Retrieval (SIGIR-2008). 2008.

Li, Xiao-Li, Lei Zhang, Bing Liu, and See-Kiong Ng. Distributional Similarity vs. PU Learning for Entity Set Expansion. In Proceedings of the Annual Meeting of the Association for Computational Linguistics (ACL-2010). 2010h.

Li, Xin, Lidong Bing, Piji Li, Wai Lam, and Zhimou Yang. Aspect Term Extraction with History Attention and Selective Transformation. In Proceedings of the International Confernece on Artificial Intelligence (IJCAI-2018). 2018.

Li, Xin, and Wai Lam. Deep Multi-Task Learning for Aspect Term Extraction with Memory Interaction. In Proceedings of the Conference on Empirical Methods on Natural Language Processing (EMNLP-2017). 2017.

Li, Zheng, Yu Zhang, Ying Wei, Yuxiang Wu, and Qiang Yang. End-to-End Adversarial Memory Network for Cross-Domain Sentiment Classification. In Proceedings of the International Joint Conference on Artificial Intelligence (IJCAI-2017). 2017.

Lim, Ee-Peng, Viet-An Nguyen, Nitin Jindal, Bing Liu, and Hady W. Lauw. Detecting Product Review Spammers Using Rating Behaviors. In Proceedings of the ACM International Conference on Information and Knowledge Management (CIKM-2010). 2010.

Lin, Chenghua, and Yulan He. Joint Sentiment/Topic Model for Sentiment Analysis. In Proceedings of the ACM International Conference on Information and Knowledge Management (CIKM-2009). 2009.

Lin, Dekang. Automatic Retrieval and Clustering of Similar Words. In Proccedings of the 36th Annual Meeting of the Association for Computational Linguistics and the 17th International Conference on Computational Linguistics (COLING-ACL-1998). 1998.

Lin, Dekang. Minipar. 2007: http://webdocs.cs.ualberta.ca/lindek/minipar.htm.

Lin, Kevin Hsin-Yih, Changhua Yang, and Hsin-Hsi Chen. What Emotions Do News Articles Trigger in Their Readers? In Proceedings of the 30th Annual International ACM SIGIR Conference on Research and Development in Information Retrieval (SIGKR-2007). 2007.

Lin, Wei-Hao, Theresa Wilson, Janyce Wiebe, and Alexander Hauptmann. Which Side Are You on? Identifying Perspectives at the Document and Sentence Levels. In Proceedings of the Conference on Natural Language Learning (CoNLL-2006). 2006.

Liu, Bing. *Web Data Mining: Exploring Hyperlinks, Contents, and Usage Data*. 1st ed. 2006. Heidelberg: Springer.

Liu, Bing. Sentiment Analysis and Subjectivity. In *Handbook of Natural Language Processing*, 2nd ed., N. Indurkhya and F. J. Damerau (Eds.). 2010. London: Chapman and Hall, 627–66.

Liu, Bing. *Web Data Mining: Exploring Hyperlinks, Contents, and Usage Data*. 2nd ed. 2011. Heidelberg: Springer.

Liu, Bing. *Sentiment Analysis and Opinion Mining*. 2012. San Rafael, CA: Morgan and Claypool.

Liu, Bing, Wynne Hsu, and Yiming Ma. Integrating Classification and Association Rule Mining. In Proceedings of the International Conference on Knowledge Discovery and Data Mining (KDD-1998). 1998.

Liu, Bing, Minqing Hu, and Junsheng Cheng. Opinion Observer: Analyzing and Comparing Opinions on the Web. In Proceedings of the International Conference on World Wide Web (WWW-2005). 2005.

Liu, Bing, Wee Sun Lee, Philip S. Yu, and Xiao-Li Li. Partially Supervised Classification of Text Documents. In Proceedings of the International Conference on Machine Learning (ICML-2002). 2002.

Liu, Feifan, Bin Li, and Yang Liu. Finding Opinionated Blogs Using Statistical Classifiers and Lexical Features. In Proceedings of the 3rd International AAAI Conference on Weblogs and Social Media (ICWSM-2009). 2009.

Liu, Feifan, Dong Wang, Bin Li, and Yang Liu. Improving Blog Polarity Classification via Topic Analysis and Adaptive Methods. In Proceedings of Human Language Technologies: The 2010 Annual Conference of the North American Chapter of the ACL (HLT-NAACL-2010). 2010.

Liu, Hugo, Henry Lieberman, and Ted Selker. A Model of Textual Affect Sensing Using Real-World Knowledge. In Proceedings of the 2003 International Conference on Intelligent User Interfaces (IUI-2003). 2003.

Liu, Jiangming, and Yue Zhang. Attention Modeling for Targeted Sentiment. In Proceedings of the Conference of the European Chapter of the Association for Computational Linguistics (EACL-2017). 2017.

Liu, Jingjing, Yunbo Cao, Chin-Yew Lin, Yalou Huang, and Ming Zhou. Low-Quality Product Review Detection in Opinion Summarization. In Proceedings of the Joint Conference on Empirical Methods in Natural Language Processing and Computational Natural Language Learning (EMNLP-CoNLL-2007). 2007.

Liu, Jingjing, and Stephanie Seneff. Review Sentiment Scoring via a Parse-and-Paraphrase Paradigm. In Proceedings of the 2009 Conference on Empirical Methods in Natural Language Processing (EMNLP-2009). 2009.

Liu, Kang, Liheng Xu, and Jun Zhao. Opinion Target Extraction Using Word-Based Translation Model. In Proceedings of the 2012 Conference on Empirical Methods on Natural Language Processing (EMNLP-2012). 2012.

Liu, Kang, Liheng Xu, and Jun Zhao. Syntactic Patterns versus Word Alignment: Extracting Opinion Targets from Online Reviews. In Proceedings of the Annual Meeting of the Association for Computational Linguistics (ACL-2013). 2013.

Liu, Pengfei, Shafiq Joty, and Helen Meng. Fine-Grained Opinion Mining with Recurrent Neural Networks and Word Embeddings. In Proceedings of the Conference on Empirical Methods in Natural Language Processing (EMNLP-2015). 2015.

Liu, Qian, Bing Liu, Yuanlin Zhang, Doo Soon Kim, and Zhiqiang Gao. Improving Opinion Aspect Extraction Using Semantic Similarity and Aspect. Associations. In Proceedings of the 30th AAAI Conference on Artificial Intelligence (AAAI-2016). February 12–17, 2016.

Liu, Xiaohua, Ming Zhou, Furu Wei, Zhongyang Fu, and Xiangyang Zhou. Joint Inference of Named Entity Recognition and Normalization for Tweets. In Proceedings of the 50th Annual Meeting of the Association for Computational Linguistics (ACL-2012). 2012.

Liu, Yang, Xiangji Huang, Aijun An, and Xiaohui Yu. ARSA: A Sentiment-Aware Model for Predicting Sales Performance Using Blogs. In Proceedings of the ACM SIGIR Conference on Research and Development in Information Retrieval (SIGIR-2007). 2007.

Liu, Yang, Xiangji Huang, Aijun An, and Xiaohui Yu. Modeling and Predicting the Helpfulness of Online Reviews. In Proceedings of ICDM-2008. 2008.

Liu, Yang, Xiaohui Yu, Zhongshuai Chen, and Bing Liu. Sentiment Analysis of Sentences with Modalities. In Proceedings of the 2013 International Workshop on Mining Unstructured Big Data Using Natural Language Processing. 2013.

Long, Chong, Jie Zhang, and Xiaoyan Zhu. A Review Selection Approach for Accurate Feature Rating Estimation. In Proceedings of COLING 2010: Poster Volume. 2010.

Long, Yunfei, Qin Lu, Rong Xiang, Minglei Li, and Chu-Ren Huang. A Cognition Based Attention Model for Sentiment Analysis. In Proceedings of the Conference on Empirical Methods on Natural Language Processing (EMNLP-2017). 2017.

Lu, Bin. Identifying Opinion Holders and Targets with Dependency Parser in Chinese News Texts. In Proceedings of Human Language Technologies: The 2010 Annual Conference of the North American Chapter of the ACL (HLT-NAACL-2010). 2010.

Lu, Bin, Chenhao Tan, Claire Cardie, and Benjamin K. Tsou. Joint Bilingual Sentiment Classification with Unlabeled Parallel Corpora. In Proceedings of the 49th Annual Meeting of the Association for Computational Linguistics (ACL-2011). 2011.

Lu, Yue, Malu Castellanos, Umeshwar Dayal, and ChengXiang Zhai. Automatic Construction of a Context-Aware Sentiment Lexicon: An Optimization Approach. In Proceedings of the 20th International Conference on World Wide Web (WWW-2011). 2011.

Lu, Yue, Huizhong Duan, Hongning Wang, and ChengXiang Zhai. Exploiting Structured Ontology to Organize Scattered Online Opinions. In Proceedings of the Interntional Conference on Computational Linguistics (COLING-2010). 2010a.

Lu, Yue, Panayiotis Tsaparas, Alexandros Ntoulas, and Livia Polanyi. Exploiting Social Context for Review Quality Prediction. In Proceedings of the International World Wide Web Conference (WWW-2010). 2010b.

Lu, Yue, and ChengXiang Zhai. Opinion Integration through Semi-Supervised Topic Modeling. In Proceedings of the International Conference on the World Wide Web (WWW-2008). 2008.

Lu, Yue, ChengXiang Zhai, and Neel Sundaresan. Rated Aspect Summarization of Short Comments. In Proceedings of the International Conference on World Wide Web (WWW-2009). 2009.

Lui, Marco, and Timothy Baldwin. Classifying User Forum Participants: Separating the Gurus from the Hacks, and Other Tales of the Internet. In Proceedings of the Australasian Language Technology Association Workshop. 2010.

Luo, Huaishao, Tianrui Li, Bing Liu, and Junbo Zhang. DOER: Dual Cross-Shared RNN for Aspect Term-Polarity Co-extraction. In Proceedings of the Annual Meeting of the Association for Computational Linguistics (ACL-2019). July 28–August 2, 2019.

Luther. Yelp's Review Filter Explained. 2010. http://officialblog.yelp.com/2010/03/yelp-review-filter-explained.html.

Lv, Guangyi, Shuai Wang, Bing Liu, Enhong Chen, and Kun Zhang. Sentiment Classification by Leveraging the Shared Knowledge from a Sequence of Domains. In Proceedings of the 24th International Conference on Database Systems for Advanced Applications (DASFAA-2019). April 22–25, 2019.

Ma, Dehong, Sujian Li, Xiaodong Zhang, and Houfeng Wang. Interactive Attention Networks for Aspect-Level Sentiment Classification. In Proceedings of the International Joint Conference on Artificial Intelligence (IJCAI-2017). 2017.

Ma, Tengfei, and Xiaojun Wan. Opinion Target Extraction in Chinese News Comments. In Proceedings of COLING 2010 Poster Volume (COLING-2010). 2010.

Ma, Zongyang, Aixin Sun, Quan Yuan, and Gao Cong. Topic-Driven Reader Comments Summarization. In Proceedings of the 21st ACM International Conference on Information and Knowledge Management (CIKM-2012). 2012.

Maas, Andrew L., Raymond E. Daly, Peter T. Pham, Dan Huang, Andrew Y. Ng, and Christopher Potts. Learning Word Vectors for Sentiment Analysis. In Proceedings of the 49th Annual Meeting of the Association for Computational Linguistics (ACL-2011). 2011.

Macdonald, Craig, Iadh Ounis, and Ian Soboroff. Overview of the TREC 2007 Blog Track. 2007.

Mahmoud, Hosam. *Pólya Urn Models*. 2008. Boca Raton, FL: Chapman and Hall/CRC.

Manevitz, Larry M., and Malik Yousef. One-Class SVMs for Document Classification. *Journal of Machine Learning Research*, 2002. 2: 139–54.

Manning, Christopher D., Prabhakar Raghavan, and Hinrich Schutze. *Introduction to Information Retrieval*. Vol. 1. 2008. Cambridge: Cambridge University Press.

Manning, Christopher D., and Hinrich Schutze. *Foundations of Statistical Natural Language Processing*. Vol. 999. 1999. Cambridge, MA: MIT Press.

Martin, J. R., and P. R. R. White. *The Language of Evaluation: Appraisal in English*. 2005. London: Palgrave Macmillan.

Martineau, Justin, and Tim Finin. Delta TFIDF: An Improved Feature Space for Sentiment Analysis. In Proceedings of the 3rd International AAAI Conference on Weblogs and Social Media (ICWSM-2009). 2009.

Mass, Andrew L., Raymond E. Daly, Peter T. Pham, Dan Huang, Andrew Y. Ng, and Christopher Potts. Learning Word Vectors for Sentiment Analysis. In Proceedings of the Annual Meeting of the Association for Computational Linguistics (ACL-2011). 2011.

Mayfield, Elijah, and Carolyn Penstein Rose. Recognizing Authority in Dialogue with an Integer Linear Programming Constrained Model. In Proceedings of the 49th Annual Meeting of the Association for Computational Linguistics (ACL-2011). 2011.

McDonald, Ryan, Kerry Hannan, Tyler Neylon, Mike Wells, and Jeff Reynar. Structured Models for Fine-to-Coarse Sentiment Analysis. In Proceedings of the Annual Meeting of the Association for Computational Linguistics (ACL-2007). 2007.

McDougall, William. *An Introduction to Social Psychology*. 1926. New York: Luce.

McGlohon, Mary, Natalie Glance, and Zach Reiter. Star Quality: Aggregating Reviews to Rank Products and Merchants. In Proceedings of the International Conference on Weblogs and Social Media (ICWSM-2010). 2010.

McNamee, Paul, and Hoa Trang Dang. Overview of the TAC 2009 Knowledge Base Population Track. In Proceedings of the 2nd Text Analysis Conference. 2009.

Medlock, Ben, and Ted Briscoe. Weakly Supervised Learning for Hedge Classification in Scientific Literature. In Proceedings of the 45th Annual Meeting of the Association of Computational Linguistics. 2007.

Mei, Qiaozhu, Xu Ling, Matthew Wondra, Hang Su, and ChengXiang Zhai. Topic Sentiment Mixture: Modeling Facets and Opinions in Weblogs. In Proceedings of the International Conference on the World Wide Web (WWW-2007). 2007.

Mejova, Yelena, and Padmini Srinivasan. Exploring Feature Definition and Selection for Sentiment Classifiers. In Proceedings of the 5th International AAAI Conference on Weblogs and Social Media (ICWSM-2011). 2011.

Meng, Xinfan, and Houfeng Wang. Mining User Reviews: From Specification to Summarization. In Proceedings of the ACL-IJCNLP 2009 Conference: Short Papers. 2009.

Meng, Xinfan, Furu Wei, Ge Xu, Longkai Zhang, Xiaohua Liu, Ming Zhou, and Houfeng Wang. Lost in Translations? Building Sentiment Lexicons Using Context Based Machine Translation. In Proceedings of the 24th International Conference on Computational Linguistics (COLING-2012). 2012.

Metzler, Donald, Yaniv Bernstein, W. Bruce Croft, Alistair Moffat, and Justin Zobel. Similarity Measures for Tracking Information Flow. In Proceedings of the ACM International Conference on Information and Knowledge Management (CIKM-2005). 2005.

Mihalcea, Rada, Carmen Banea, and Janyce Wiebe. Learning Multilingual Subjective Language via Cross-Lingual Projections. In Proceedings of the Annual Meeting of the Association for Computational Linguistics (ACL-2007). 2007.

Mihalcea, Rada, and Hugo Liu. A Corpus-Based Approach to Finding Happiness. In Proceedings of AAAI Spring Symposium: Computational Approaches to Analyzing Weblogs. 2006.

Mihalcea, Rada, and Carlo Strapparava. The Lie Detector: Explorations in the Automatic Recognition of Deceptive Language. In Proceedings of the ACL-IJCNLP 2009 Conference: Short Papers. 2009.

Mikolov, Tomas, Kai Chen, Greg Corrado, and Jeffrey Dean. Efficient Estimation of Word Representations in Vector Space. arXiv:1301.3781 [cs.CL], 2013a.

Mikolov, Tomas, Ilya Sutskever, Kai Chen, Greg Corrado, and Jeffrey Dean. Distributed Representations of Words and Phrases and Their Compositionality. *Advances in Neural Information Processing Systems*, 2013b. 26: 3111–19.

Miller, George A., Richard Beckwith, Christiane Fellbaum, Derek Gross, and Katherine Miller. *WordNet: An On-Line Lexical Database*. 1990. Oxford: Oxford University Press.

Miller, Mahalia, Conal Sathi, Daniel Wiesenthal, Jure Leskovec, and Christopher Potts. Sentiment Flow through Hyperlink Networks. In Proceedings of the 5th International AAAI Conference on Weblogs and Social Media (ICWSM-2011). 2011.

Milne, David, and Ian H. Witten. Learning to Link with Wikipedia. In Proceedings of the ACM International Conference on Information and Knowledge Management (CIKM-2008). 2008.

Min, Hye-Jin, and Jong C. Park. Detecting and Blocking False Sentiment Propagation. In Proceedings of the 5th International Joint Conference on Natural Language Processing (IJCNLP-2010). 2011.

Mishne, Gilad, and Maarten de Rijke. Capturing Global Mood Levels Using Blog Posts. In Proceedings of the AAAI Spring Symposium on Computational Approaches to Analyzing Weblogs. 2006.

Mishne, Gilad, and Natalie Glance. Predicting Movie Sales from Blogger Sentiment. In Proceedings of the AAAI Spring Symposium on Computational Approaches to Analysing Weblogs. 2006.

Mishra, Abhijit, Kuntal Dey, and Pushpak Bhattacharyya. Learning Cognitive Features from Gaze Data for Sentiment and Sarcasm Classification Using Convolutional Neural Network. In Proceedings of the Annual Meeting of the Association for Computational Linguistics (ACL-2017). 2017.

Mitchell, Margaret, Jacqui Aguilar, Theresa Wilson, and Benjamin Van Durme. Open Domain Targeted Sentiment. In Proceedings of the 2013 Conference on Empirical Methods on Natural Language Processing (EMNLP-2013). 2013.

Mitchell, Tom. *Machine Learning*. 1997. New York: McGraw-Hill.

Moghaddam, Samaneh, and Martin Ester. Opinion Digger: An Unsupervised Opinion Miner from Unstructured Product Reviews. In Proceedings of the ACM Conference on Information and Knowledge Management (CIKM-2010). 2010.

Moghaddam, Samaneh, and Martin Ester. ILDA: Interdependent LDA Model for Learning Latent Aspects and Their Ratings from Online Product Reviews. In Proceedings of the Annual ACM SIGIR International Conference on Research and Development in Information Retrieval (SIGIR-2011). 2011.

Moghaddam, Samaneh, Mohsen Jamali, and Martin Ester. ETF: Extended Tensor Factorization Model for Personalizing Prediction of Review Helpfulness. In Proceedings of the ACM International Conference on Web Search and Data Mining (WSDM-2012). 2012.

Mohammad, Saif. From Once upon a Time to Happily Ever after: Tracking Emotions in Novels and Fairy Tales. In Proceedings of the ACL 2011 Workshop on Language Technology for Cultural Heritage, Social Sciences, and Humanities (LaTeCH-2011). 2011.

Mohammad, Saif M. # Emotional Tweets. In Proceedings of the 1st Joint Conference on Lexical and Computational Semantics (*Sem). 2012.

Mohammad, Saif, Cody Dunne, and Bonnie Dorr. Generating High-Coverage Semantic Orientation Lexicons from Overtly Marked Words and a Thesaurus. In Proceedings of the 2009 Conference on Empirical Methods in Natural Language Processing (EMNLP-2009). 2009.

Mohammad, Saif M., and Peter D. Turney. Emotions Evoked by Common Words and Phrases: Using Mechanical Turk to Create an Emotion Lexicon. In Proceedings of the NAACL HLT 2010 Workshop on Computational Approaches to Analysis and Generation of Emotion in Text. 2010.

Mohammad, Saif, and Tony Yang. Tracking Sentiment in Mail: How Genders Differ on Emotional Axes. In Proceedings of the ACL Workshop on ACL 2011 Workshop on Computational Approaches to Subjectivity and Sentiment Analysis (WASSA-2011). 2011.

Mohtarami, Mitra, Man Lan, and Chew Lim Tan. Probabilistic Sense Sentiment Similarity through Hidden Emotions. In Proceedings of the Annual Meeting of the Association for Computational Linguistics (ACL-2013). 2013.

Moilanen, Karo, and Stephen Pulman. Sentiment Composition. In Proceedings of Recent Advances in Natural Language Processing (RANLP-2007). 2007.

Moldovan, Dan, and Adriana Badulescu. A Semantic Scattering Model for the Automatic Interpretation of Genitives. In Proceedings of the Human Language Technology Conference and the Conference on Empirical Methods in Natural Language Processing (HLT/EMNLP-2005). 2005.

Montague, Richard. *Formal Philosophy: Selected Papers of Richard Montague*. 1974. New Haven, CT: Yale University Press.

Mooney, Raymond J., and Razvan Bunescu. Mining Knowledge from Text Using Information Extraction. *ACM SIGKDD Explorations Newsletter*, 2005. 7(1): 3–10.

Moraes, Rodrigo, João Francisco Valiati, and Wilson P. Gavião Neto. Document-Level Sentiment Classification: An Empirical Comparison between SVM and ANN. *Expert Systems with Applications*, 2013. 40(2): 621–33.

Morbini, Fabrizio, and Kenji Sagae. Joint Identification and Segmentation of Domain-Specific Dialogue Acts for Conversational Dialogue Systems. In Proceedings of the 49th Annual Meeting of the Association for Computational Linguistics (ACL-2011): Short Papers. 2011.

Morinaga, Satoshi, Kenji Yamanishi, Kenji Tateishi, and Toshikazu Fukushima. Mining Product Reputations on the Web. In Proceedings of ACM SIGKDD International Conference on Knowledge Discovery and Data Mining (KDD-2002). 2002.

Mowrer, Orval Hobart. *Learning Theory and Behavior*. 1960. New York: John Wiley.

Moxey, Linda M., and Anthony J. Sanford. Communicating Quantities: A Review of Psycholinguistic Evidence of How Expressions Determine Perspectives. *Applied Cognitive Psychology*, 2000. 14: 197–294.

Mukherjee, Arjun, Abhinav Kumar, Bing Liu, Junhui Wang, Meichun Hsu, Malu Castellanos, and Riddhiman Ghosh. Spotting Opinion Spammers Using Behavioral Footprints. In Proceedings of the 19th ACM SIGKDD Conference on Knowledge Discovery and Data Mining (KDD-2013). 2013a.

Mukherjee, Arjun, and Bing Liu. Aspect Extraction through Semi-Supervised Modeling. In Proceedings of the 50th Annual Meeting of the Association for Computational Linguistics (ACL-2012). 2012a.

Mukherjee, Arjun, and Bing Liu. Mining Contentions from Discussions and Debates. In Proceedings of the SIGKDD International Conference on Knowledge Discovery and Data Mining (KDD-2012). 2012b.

Mukherjee, Arjun, and Bing Liu. Modeling Review Comments. In Proceedings of the 50th Annual Meeting of the Association for Computational Linguistics (ACL-2012). 2012c.

Mukherjee, Arjun, and Bing Liu. Discovering User Interactions in Ideological Discussions. In Proceedings of the 51st Annual Meeting of Association for Computational Linguistics (ACL-2013). 2013.

Mukherjee, Arjun, Bing Liu, and Natalie Glance. Spotting Fake Reviewer Groups in Consumer Reviews. In Proceedings of International World Web Conference (WWW-2012). 2012.

Mukherjee, Arjun, Bing Liu, Junhui Wang, Natalie Glance, and Nitin Jindal. Detecting Group Review Spam. In Proceedings of the International Conference on the World Wide Web (WWW-2011). 2011.

Mukherjee, Arjun, Vivek Venkataraman, Bing Liu, and Natalie Glance. What Yelp's Fake Review Filter Might Be Doing. In Proceedings of the 7th International AAAI Conference on Weblog and Social Media (ICWSM-2013). 2013b.

Mukherjee, Arjun, Vivek Venkataraman, Bing Liu, and Sharon Meraz. Public Dialogue: Analysis of Tolerance in Online Discussions. In Proceedings of the 51st

Annual Meeting of the Association for Computational Linguistics (ACL-2013). 2013c.

Mukund, Smruthi, and Rohini K. Srihari. A Vector Space Model for Subjectivity Classification in Urdu Aided by Co-training. In Proceedings of COLING 2010: Poster Volume. 2010.

Mullen, Tony, and Nigel Collier. Sentiment Analysis Using Support Vector Machines with Diverse Information Sources. In Proceedings of EMNLP-2004. 2004.

Murakami, Akiko, and Rudy Raymond. Support or Oppose? Classifying Positions in Online Debates from Reply Activities and Opinion Expressions. In Proceedings of COLING 2010: Poster Volume. 2010.

Na, Seung-Hoon, Yeha Lee, Sang-Hyob Nam, and Jong-Hyeok Lee. Improving Opinion Retrieval Based on Query-Specific Sentiment Lexicon. In *ECIR: Lecture Notes in Computer Science*, Vol. 5478. 2009. Berlin/Heidelberg: Springer, 734–8.

Nakagawa, Tetsuji, Kentaro Inui, and Sadao Kurohashi. Dependency Tree-Based Sentiment Classification Using CRFs with Hidden Variables. In Proceedings of Human Language Technologies: The 2010 Annual Conference of the North American Chapter of the ACL (HAACL-2010). 2010.

Nalisnick, Eric, and Henry Baird. Character-to-Character Sentiment Analysis in Shakespeare's Plays. In Proceedings of the Annual Meeting of the Association for Computational Linguistics (ACL-2013). 2013.

Narayanan, Ramanathan, Bing Liu, and Alok Choudhary. Sentiment Analysis of Conditional Sentences. In Proceedings of the Conference on Empirical Methods in Natural Language Processing (EMNLP-2009). 2009.

Nasukawa, Tetsuya, and Jeonghee Yi. Sentiment Analysis: Capturing Favorability Using Natural Language Processing. In Proceedings of K-CAP-03, the 2nd International Conference on Knowledge Capture. 2003.

Neviarouskaya, Alena, Helmut Prendinger, and Mitsuru Ishizuka. Compositionality Principle in Recognition of Fine-Grained Emotions from Text. In Proceedings of the 3rd International Conference on Weblogs and Social Media (ICWSM-2009). 2009.

Neviarouskaya, Alena, Helmut Prendinger, and Mitsuru Ishizuka. Recognition of Affect, Judgment, and Appreciation in Text. In Proceedings of the 23rd International Conference on Computational Linguistics (COLING-2010). 2010.

Newman, Matthew L., James W. Pennebaker, Diane S. Berry, and Jane M. Richards. Lying Words: Predicting Deception from Linguistic Styles. *Personality and Social Psychology Bulletin*, 2003. 29(5): 665–75.

Ng, Vincent, and Claire Cardie. Improving Machine Learning Approaches to Coreference Resolution. In Proceedings of the Annual Meeting of the Association for Computational Linguistics (ACL-2002). 2002.

Ng, Vincent, Sajib Dasgupta, and S. M. Niaz Arifin. Examining the Role of Linguistic Knowledge Sources in the Automatic Identification and Classification of Reviews. In Proceedings of COLING/ACL 2006 Main Conference Poster Sessions (COLING/ACL-2006). 2006.

Nigam, Kamal, and Matthew Hurst. Towards a Robust Metric of Opinion. In Proceedings of the AAAI Spring Symposium on Exploring Attitude and Affect in Text. 2004.

Nigam, Kamal, Andrew K. McCallum, Sebastian Thrun, and Tom Mitchell. Text Classification from Labeled and Unlabeled Documents Using EM. *Machine Learning*, 2000. 39(2): 103–34.

Nishikawa, Hitoshi, Takaaki Hasegawa, Yoshihiro Matsuo, and Genichiro Kikui. Opinion Summarization with Integer Linear Programming Formulation for Sentence Extraction and Ordering. In Proceedings of COLING 2010: Poster Volume. 2010a.

Nishikawa, Hitoshi, Takaaki Hasegawa, Yoshihiro Matsuo, and Genichiro Kikui. Optimizing Informativeness and Readability for Sentiment Summarization. In Proceedings of the Annual Meeting of the Association for Computational Linguistics (ACL-2010). 2010b.

Nummenmaa, L., E. Glerean, R. Hari, and J. K. Hietanen. Bodily Maps of Emotions. *Proceedings of the National Academy of Sciences*, 2014. 111(2): 646–51.

Oatley, K., and P. N. Johnson-Laird. Towards a Cognitive Theory of Emotions. *Cognition and Emotion*, 1987. 1: 29–50.

O'Connor, Brendan, Ramnath Balasubramanyan, Bryan R. Routledge, and Noah A. Smith. From Tweets to Polls: Linking Text Sentiment to Public Opinion Time Series. In Proceedings of the International AAAI Conference on Weblogs and Social Media (ICWSM-2010). 2010.

O'Mahony, Michael P., and Barry Smyth. Learning to Recommend Helpful Hotel Reviews. In Proceedings of the 3rd ACM Conference on Recommender Systems. 2009.

Ortony, Andrew, and Terence J. Turner. What's Basic about Basic Emotions? *Psychological Review*, 1990. 97(3): 315–31.

Osgood, Charles E., George J. Succi, and Percy H. Tannenbaum. *The Measurement of Meaning*. 1957. Urbana/Champaign: University of Illinois.

Ott, Myle, Yejin Choi, Claire Cardie, and Jeffrey T. Hancock. Finding Deceptive Opinion Spam by Any Stretch of the Imagination. In Proceedings of the 49th Annual Meeting of the Association for Computational Linguistics (ACL-2011). 2011.

Ounis, Iadh, Craig Macdonald, Maarten de Rijke, Gilad Mishne, and Ian Soboroff. Overview of the TREC-2006 Blog Track. In Proceedings of the 15th Text REtrieval Conference (TREC-2006). 2006.

Ounis, Iadh, Craig Macdonald, and Ian Soboroff. Overview of the TREC-2008 Blog Track. In Proceedings of the 16th Text REtrieval Conference (TREC-2008). 2008.

Page, Lawrence, Sergey Brin, Rajeev Motwani, and Terry Winograd. The Pagerank Citation Ranking: Bringing Order to the Web. 1999.

Paltoglou, Georgios, and Mike Thelwall. A Study of Information Retrieval Weighting Schemes for Sentiment Analysis. In Proceedings of the 48th Annual Meeting of the Association for Computational Linguistics (ACL-2010). 2010.

Pan, Sinno Jialin, Xiaochuan Ni, Jian-Tao Sun, Qiang Yang, and Zheng Chen. Cross-Domain Sentiment Classification via Spectral Feature Alignment. In Proceedings of the International Conference on the World Wide Web (WWW-2010). 2010.

Pang, Bo, and Lillian Lee. A Sentimental Education: Sentiment Analysis Using Subjectivity Summarization Based on Minimum Cuts. In Proceedings of the Meeting of the Association for Computational Linguistics (ACL-2004). 2004.

Pang, Bo, and Lillian Lee. Seeing Stars: Exploiting Class Relationships for Sentiment Categorization with Respect to Rating Scales. In Proceedings of the Meeting of the Association for Computational Linguistics (ACL-2005). 2005.

Pang, Bo, and Lillian Lee. Opinion Mining and Sentiment Analysis. *Foundations and Trends in Information Retrieval*, 2008a. 2(1–2): 1–135.

Pang, Bo, and Lillian Lee. Using Very Simple Statistics for Review Search: An Exploration. In Proceedings of the International Conference on Computational Linguistics (COLING-2008). 2008b.

Pang, Bo, Lillian Lee, and Shivakumar Vaithyanathan. Thumbs Up? Sentiment Classification Using Machine Learning Techniques. In Proceedings of the Conference on Empirical Methods in Natural Language Processing (EMNLP-2002). 2002.

Panksepp, Jaak. Toward a General Psychobiological Theory of Emotions. *Behavioral and Brain Sciences*, 1982. 5(3): 407–22.

Pantel, Patrick, Eric Crestan, Arkady Borkovsky, Ana-Maria Popescu, and Vishnu Vyas. Web-Scale Distributional Similarity and Entity Set Expansion. In Proceedings of the Conference on Empirical Methods in Natural Language Processing (EMNLP-2009). 2009.

Park, Do-Hyung, Jumin Lee, and Ingoo Han. The Effect of On-Line Consumer Reviews on Consumer Purchasing Intention: The Moderating Role of Involvement. *International Journal of Electronic Commerce*, 2007. 11(4): 125–48.

Park, Souneil, KyungSoon Lee, and Junehwa Song. Contrasting Opposing Views of News Articles on Contentious Issues. In Proceedings of the 49th Annual Meeting of the Association for Computational Linguistics (ACL-2011). 2011.

Parrott, W. Gerrod. *Emotions in Social Psychology: Essential Readings*. 2001. New York: Psychology Press.

Paul, Michael J., ChengXiang Zhai, and Roxana Girju. Summarizing Contrastive Viewpoints in Opinionated Text. In Proceedings of the Conference on Empirical Methods in Natural Language Processing (EMNLP-2010). 2010.

Peled Lotem, and Roi Reichart. Sarcasm SIGN: Interpreting Sarcasm with Sentiment Based Monolingual Machine Translation. In Proceedings of the Annual Meeting of the Association for Computational Linguistics (ACL-2017). 2017.

Peng, Wei, and Dae Hoon Park. Generate Adjective Sentiment Dictionary for Social Media Sentiment Analysis Using Constrained Nonnegative Matrix Factorization. In Proceedings of the 5th International AAAI Conference on Weblogs and Social Media (ICWSM-2011). 2011.

Pennebaker, James W., Cindy K. Chung, Molly Ireland, Amy Gonzales, and Roger J. Booth. The Development and Psychometric Properties of LIWC2007. 2007.

Pennington, Jeffrey, Richard Socher, and Christopher D. Manning. GloVe: Global Vectors for Word Representation. 2014.

Perez-Rosas, Veronica, Rada Mihalcea, and Louis-Philippe Morency. Utterance-Level Multimodal Sentiment Analysis. In Proceedings of the Annual Meeting of the Association for Computational Linguistics (ACL-2013). 2013.

Petterson, James, A. J. Smola, Tiberio Caetano, Wray Buntine, and Shravan Narayanamurthy. Word Features for Latent Dirichlet Allocation. In Proceedings of NIPS-2010. 2010.

Picard, Rosalind W. *Affective Computing*. 1997. Cambridge, MA: MIT Press.

Plutchik, Robert. A General Psychoevolutionary Theory of Emotion. In *Emotion: Theory, Research, and Experience*: Vol. 1. Theories of Emotion, R. Plutchik and H. Kellerman (Eds.). 1980. Cambridge, MA: Academic Press, 3–33.

Polanyi, Livia, and Annie Zaenen. Contextual Valence Shifters. In Proceedings of the AAAI Spring Symposium on Exploring Attitude and Affect in Text. 2004.

Ponomareva, Natalia, and Mike Thelwall. Do Neighbours Help? An Exploration of Graph-Based Algorithms for Cross-Domain Sentiment Classification. In Proceedings of the 2012 Conference on Empirical Methods on Natural Language Processing (EMNLP-2012). 2012.

Popat, Kashyap, A. R. Balamurali, Pushpak Bhattacharyya, and Gholamreza Haffari. The Haves and the Have-Nots: Leveraging Unlabelled Corpora for Sentiment Analysis. In Proceedings of the Annual Meeting of the Association for Computational Linguistics (ACL-2013). 2013.

Popescu, Ana-Maria, and Oren Etzioni. Extracting Product Features and Opinions from Reviews. In Proceedings of the Conference on Empirical Methods in Natural Language Processing (EMNLP-2005). 2005.

Poria, Soujanya, Erik Cambria, and Alexander Gelbukh. Deep Convolutional Neural Text Features and Multiple Kernel Learning for Utterance-Level Multimodal Sentiment Analysis. In Proceedings of the Conference on Empirical Methods on Natural Language Processing (EMNLP-2015). 2015.

Poria, Soujanya, Erik Cambria, and Alexander Gelbukh. Aspect Extraction for Opinion Mining with a Deep Convolutional Neural Network. *Journal of Knowledge-Based Systems*, 2016a. 108: 4–49.

Poria, Soujanya, Erik Cambria, Devamanyu Hazarika, Navonil Mazumder, Amir Zadeh, and Louis-Philippe Morency. Context-Dependent Sentiment Analysis in User-Generated Videos. In Proceedings of the Annual Meeting of the Association for Computational Linguistics (ACL-2017). 2017.

Poria, Soujanya, Erik Cambria, Devamanyu Hazarika, and Prateek Vij. A Deeper Look into Sarcastic Tweets Using Deep Convolutional Neural Networks. In Proceedings of the International Conference on Computational Linguistics (COLING-2016). 2016b.

Qian, Qiao, Minlie Huang, Jinhao Lei, and Xiaoyan Zhu. Linguistically Regularized LSTM for Sentiment Classification. In Proceedings of the Annual Meeting of the Association for Computational Linguistics (ACL-2017). 2017.

Qian, Tieyun, and Bing Liu. Identifying Multiple Userids of the Same Author. In Proceedings of the Conference on Empirical Methods in Natural Language Processing (EMNLP-2013). 2013.

Qian, Qiao, Bo Tian, Minlie Huang, Yang Liu, Xuan Zhu, and Xiaoyan Zhu. Learning Tag Embeddings and Tag-Specific Composition Functions in the Recursive Neural Network. In Proceedings of the Annual Meeting of the Association for Computational Linguistics (ACL-2015). 2015.

Qiu, Guang, Bing Liu, Jiajun Bu, and Chun Chen. Expanding Domain Sentiment Lexicon through Double Propagation. In Proceedings of the International Joint Conference on Artificial Intelligence (IJCAI-2009). 2009a.

Qiu, Guang, Bing Liu, Jiajun Bu, and Chun Chen. Opinion Word Expansion and Target Extraction through Double Propagation. *Computational Linguistics*, 2011. 37(1): 9–27.

Qiu, Likun, Weish Zhang, Changjian Hu, and Kai Zhao. SELC: A Self-Supervised Model for Sentiment Classification. In Proceedings of the 18th ACM Conference on Information and Knowledge Management (CIKM-2009). 2009b.

Qu, Lizhen, Georgiana Ifrim, and Gerhard Weikum. The Bag-of-Opinions Method for Review Rating Prediction from Sparse Text Patterns. In Proceedings of the International Conference on Computational Linguistics (COLING-2010). 2010.

Quinlan, J. Ross. *C4.5: Programs for Machine Learning*. 1993. San Mateo, CA: Morgan Kaufmann.

Raaijmakers, Stephan, and Wessel Kraaij. A Shallow Approach to Subjectivity Classification. In Proceedings of ICWSM-2008. 2008.

Raaijmakers, Stephan, Khiet Truong, and Theresa Wilson. Multimodal Subjectivity Analysis of Multiparty Conversation. In Proceedings of the Conference on Empirical Methods in Natural Language Processing (EMNLP-2008). 2008.

Rabiner, Lawrence R. A. Tutorial on Hidden Markov Models and Selected Applications in Speech Recognition. *Proceedings of the IEEE*, 1989. 77(2): 257–86.

Radev, Dragomir R., Simone Teufel, Horacio Saggion, Wai Lam, John Blitzer, Hong Qi, Arda Celebi, Danyu Liu, and Elliott Drabek. Evaluation Challenges in Large-Scale Document Summarization. In Proceedings of the Annual Meeting of the Association for Computational Linguistics (ACL-2003). 2003.

Rao, Delip, and Deepak Ravichandran. Semi-Supervised Polarity Lexicon Induction. In Proceedings of the 12th Conference of the European Chapter of the ACL (EACL-2009). 2009.

Ravichandran, Deepak, and Eduard Hovy. Learning Surface Text Patterns for a Question Answering System. In Proceedings of the Annual Meeting of the Association for Computational Linguistics (ACL-2002). 2002.

Ren, Yafeng, Yue Zhang, Meishan Zhang, and Donghong Ji. Improving Twitter Sentiment Classification Using Topic-Enriched Multi-Prototype Word Embeddings. In Proceedings of the AAAI Conference on Artificial Intelligence (AAAI-2016). 2016.

Riloff, Ellen. Automatically Constructing a Dictionary for Information Extraction Tasks. In Proceedings of AAAI-1993. 1993.

Riloff, Ellen. Automatically Generating Extraction Patterns from Untagged Text. In Proceedings of AAAI-1996. 1996.

Riloff, Ellen, Siddharth Patwardhan, and Janyce Wiebe. Feature Subsumption for Opinion Analysis. In Proceedings of the Conference on Empirical Methods in Natural Language Processing (EMNLP-2006). 2006.

Riloff, Ellen, Ashequl Qadir, Prafulla Surve, Lalindra De Silva, Nathan Gilbert, and Ruihong Huang. Sarcasm As Contrast between a Positive Sentiment and Negative Situation. In Proceedings of the 2013 Conference on Empirical Methods on Natural Language Processing (EMNLP-2013). 2013.

Riloff, Ellen, and Janyce Wiebe. Learning Extraction Patterns for Subjective Expressions. In Proceedings of the Conference on Empirical Methods in Natural Language Processing (EMNLP-2003). 2003.

Robertson, Stephen, and Hugo Zaragoza. The Probabilistic Relevance Framework: Bm25 and Beyond. *Foundations and Trends in Information Retrieval*, 2009. 3 (4): 333–89.

Rosenberg, Sabine, and Sabine Bergler. Uconcordia: CLAC Negation Focus Detection at *SEM 2012. In Proceedings of *SEM 2012: The 1st Joint Conference on Lexical and Computational Semantics. 2012.

Rosenberg, Sabine, Halil Kilicoglu, and Sabine Bergler. CLAC Labs Processing Modality and Negation. In Working Notes for QA4MRE Pilot Task at CLEF 2012. 2012.

Rosen-Zvi, Michal, Thomas Griffiths, Mark Steyvers, and Padhraic Smyth. The Author–Topic Model for Authors and Documents. In Proceedings of the 20th Conference on Uncertainty in Artificial Intelligence. 2004.

Ruder, Sebastian, Parsa Ghaffari, and John G. Breslin. A Hierarchical Model of Reviews for Aspect-Based Sentiment Analysis. In Proceedings of the Conference on Empirical Methods on Natural Language Processing (EMNLP-2016). 2016.

Ruppenhofer, Josef, Swapna Somasundaran, and Janyce Wiebe. Finding the Sources and Targets of Subjective Expressions. In Proceedings of LREC. 2008.

Russell, J. A. A Circumplex Model of Affect. *Journal of Personality and Social Psychology*, 1980. 39: 1161–78.

Russell, James A. Core Affect and the Psychological Construction of Emotion. *Psychological Review*, 2003. 110(1): 145–72.

Sadikov, Eldar, Aditya Parameswaran, and Petros Venetis. Blogs As Predictors of Movie Success. In Proceedings of the 3rd International Conference on Weblogs and Social Media (ICWSM-2009). 2009.

Sakunkoo, Patty, and Nathan Sakunkoo. Analysis of Social Influence in Online Book Reviews. In Proceedings of the 3rd International AAAI Conference on Weblogs and Social Media (ICWSM-2009). 2009.

Salton, Gerard. *The Smart Retrieval System: Experiments in Automatic Document Processing*. 1971. Upper Saddle River, NJ: Prentice Hall.

Sang, Tjong Kim, and Johan Bos. Predicting the 2011 Dutch Senate Election Results with Twitter. In Proceedings of the 13th Conference of the European Chapter of the Association for Computational Linguistics. 2012.

Santorini, Beatrice. *Part-of-Speech Tagging Guidelines for the Penn Treebank Project*. 1990. Philadelphia: University of Pennsylvania, School of Engineering and Applied Science, Department of Computer and Information Science.

Santos, Cícero dos, and Maíra Gatti. Deep Convolutional Neural Networks for Sentiment Analysis for Short Texts. In Proceedings of the International Conference on Computational Linguistics (COLING 2014). 2014.

Sarawagi, Sunita. Information Extraction. *Foundations and Trends in Databases*, 2008. 1(3): 261–377.

Sarawagi, Sunita, and William W. Cohen. Semi-Markov Conditional Random Fields for Information Extraction. In Proceedings of NIPS-2004. 2004.

Sauper, Christina, Aria Haghighi, and Regina Barzilay. Content Models with Attitude. In Proceedings of the 49th Annual Meeting of the Association for Computational Linguistics (ACL-2011). 2011.

Scaffidi, Christopher, Kevin Bierhoff, Eric Chang, Mikhael Felker, Herman Ng, and Chun Jin. Red Opal: Product-Feature Scoring from Reviews. In Proceedings of the 12th ACM Conference on Electronic Commerce (EC-2007). 2007.

Schapire, Robert E., and Yoram Singer. Boostexter: A Boosting-Based System for Text Categorization. *Machine Learning*, 2000. 39(2): 135–68.

Scheible, Christian, and Hinrich Schütze. Sentiment Relevance. In Proceedings of the Annual Meeting of the Association for Computational Linguistics (ACL-2013). 2013.

Scholz, Thomas, and Stefan Conrad. Opinion Mining in Newspaper Articles by Entropy-Based Word Connections. In Proceedings of the 2013 Conference on Empirical Methods on Natural Language Processing (EMNLP-2013). 2013.

Seki, Yohei, Koji Eguchi, Noriko Kando, and Masaki Aono. Opinion-Focused Summarization and Its Analysis at DUC 2006. In Proceedings of the Document Understanding Conference (DUC). 2006.

Sen, Prithviraj, Galileo Namata, Mustafa Bilgic, Lise Getoor, Brian Galligher, and Tina Eliassi-Rad. Collective Classification in Network Data. *AI Magazine*, 2008. 29(3): 93–106.

Shanahan, James G., Yan Qu, and Janyce Wiebe. *Computing Attitude and Affect in Text: Theory and Applications*. Vol. 20. 2006. Dordrecht: Springer.

Sharma, Raksha, Arpan Somani, Lakshya Kumar, and Pushpak Bhattacharyya. Sentiment Intensity Ranking among Adjectives Using Sentiment Bearing Word Embeddings. In Proceedings of the Conference on Empirical Methods on Natural Language Processing (EMNLP-2017). 2017.

Shawe-Taylor, John, and Nello Cristianini. *Support Vector Machines*. 2000. Cambridge: Cambridge University Press.

Shen, Dou, Jian-Tao Sun, Qiang Yang, and Zheng Chen. Building Bridges for Web Query Classification. In Proceedings of the 29th Annual International ACM SIGIR Conference on Research and Development in Information Retrieval (SIGIR-2006). 2006.

Shu, Lei, Bing Liu, Hu Xu, and Annice Kim. Lifelong-RL: Lifelong Relaxation Labeling for Separating Entities and Aspects in Opinion Targets. Proceedings of the 2016 Conference on Empirical Methods in Natural Language Processing (EMNLP-2016). 2016.

Shu, Lei, Hu Xu, and Bing Liu. Lifelong Learning CRF for Supervised Aspect Extraction. In Proceedings of the Annual Meeting of the Association for Computational Linguistics (ACL-2017, short paper). 2017.

Si, Jianfeng, Arjun Mukherjee, Bing Liu, Qing Li, Huayi Li, and Xiaotie Deng. Exploiting Topic Based Twitter Sentiment for Stock Prediction. In Proceedings of the 51st Annual Meeting of the Association for Computational Linguistics. 2013.

Siddharthan, Advaith, Nicolas Cherbuin, Paul J. Eslinger, Kasia Kozlowska, Nora A. Murphy, and Leroy Lowe. WordNet-Feelings: A Linguistic Categorisation of Human Feelings. arXiv:1811.02435 [cs.CL], 2019.

Singh, Push. The Public Acquisition of Commonsense Knowledge. In Proceedings of AAAI Spring Symposium: Acquiring (and Using) Linguistic (and World) Knowledge for Information Access. 2002.

Singhal Prerana, and Bhattacharyya Pushpak. Borrow a Little from Your Rich Cousin: Using Embeddings and Polarities of English Words for Multilingual Sentiment Classification. In Proceedings of the International Conference on Computational Linguistics (COLING-2016). 2016.

Smyth, Padhraic. Probabilistic Model-Based Clustering of Multivariate and Sequential Data. In Proceedings of Artificial Intelligence and Statistics. 1999.

Snyder, Benjamin, and Regina Barzilay. Multiple Aspect Ranking Using the Good Grief Algorithm. In Proceedings of the Conference of the North American Chapter of the Association for Computational Linguistics: Human Language Technologies (NAACL/HLT-2007). 2007.

Socher, Richard, Brody Huval, Christopher D. Manning, and Andrew Y. Ng. Semantic Compositionality through Recursive Matrix-Vector Spaces. In Proceedings of the Conference on Empirical Methods on Natural Language Processing (EMNLP-2012). 2012.

Socher, Richard, Jeffrey Pennington, Eric H. Huang, Andrew Y. Ng, and Christopher D. Manning. Semi-Supervised Recursive Autoencoders for Predicting Sentiment Distributions. In Proceedings of the Conference on Empirical Methods in Natural Language Processing (EMNLP-2011). 2011a.

Socher, Richard, Alex Perelygin, Jean Wu, Christopher Manning, Andrew Ng, and Jason Chuang. Recursive Deep Models for Semantic Compositionality over a Sentiment Treebank. In Proceedings of the 2013 Conference on Empirical Methods on Natural Language Processing (EMNLP-2013). 2013.

Somasundaran, Swapna, Galileo Namata, Lise Getoor, and Janyce Wiebe. Opinion Graphs for Polarity and Discourse Classification. In Proceedings of the 2009 Workshop on Graph-Based Methods for Natural Language Processing. 2009.

Somasundaran, S., J. Ruppenhofer, and J. Wiebe. Discourse Level Opinion Relations: An Annotation Study. In Proceedings of the 9th SIGdial Workshop on Discourse and Dialogue. 2008.

Somasundaran, Swapna, and Janyce Wiebe. Recognizing Stances in Online Debates. In Proceedings of the 47th Annual Meeting of the ACL and the 4th IJCNLP of the AFNLP (ACL-IJCNLP-2009). 2009.

Somasundaran, Swapna, and Janyce Wiebe. Recognizing Stances in Ideological On-Line Debates. In Proceedings of the NAACL HLT 2010 Workshop on Computational Approaches to Analysis and Generation of Emotion in Text. 2010.

Steyvers, Mark, and Thomas L. Griffiths. Probabilistic Topic Models. *Handbook of Latent Semantic Analysis*, 2007. 427(7): 424–40.

Stone, Philip. The General Inquirer: A Computer Approach to Content Analysis. *Journal of Regional Science*, 1968. 8(1): 113–16.

Stoppelman, J. Why Yelp Has a Review Filter. 2009. http://officialblog.yelp.com/2009/10/why-yelp-has-a-reviewfilter.html.

Stoyanov, Veselin, and Claire Cardie. Partially Supervised Coreference Resolution for Opinion Summarization through Structured Rule Learning. In Proceedings of the Conference on Empirical Methods in Natural Language Processing (EMNLP-2006). 2006.

Stoyanov, Veselin, and Claire Cardie. Topic Identification for Fine-Grained Opinion Analysis. In Proceedings of the International Conference on Computational Linguistics (COLING-2008). 2008.

Strapparava, Carlo, and Rada Mihalcea. Learning to Identify Emotions in Text. In Proceedings of the 2008 ACM Symposium on Applied Computing. 2008.

Strapparava, Carlo, and Alessandro Valitutti. WordNet-Affect: An Affective Extension of WordNet. In Proceedings of the International Conference on Language Resources and Evaluation. 2004.

Streitfeld, David. For $2 a Star, an Online Retailer Gets 5-Star Product Reviews. *New York Times*, January 26, 2012. www.nytimes.com/2012/01/27/technology/for-2-a-star-a-retailer-gets-5-star-reviews.html

Streitfeld, David. The Best Book Reviews Money Can Buy. *New York Times*, August 25, 2012. www.nytimes.com/2012/08/26/business/book-reviewers-for-hire-meet-a-demand-for-online-raves.html

Su, Fangzhong, and Katja Markert. From Words to Senses: A Case Study of Subjectivity Recognition. In Proceedings of the 22nd International Conference on Computational Linguistics (COLING-2008). 2008.

Su, Fangzhong, and Katja Markert. Word Sense Subjectivity for Cross-Lingual Lexical Substitution. In Proceedings of Human Language Technologies: The 2010 Annual Conference of the North American Chapter of the ACL (HLT-NAACL-2010). 2010.

Su, Qi, Xinying Xu, Honglei Guo, Zhili Guo, Xian Wu, Xiaoxun Zhang, Bin Swen, and Zhong Su. Hidden Sentiment Association in Chinese Web Opinion Mining. In Proceedings of the International Conference on the World Wide Web (WWW-2008). 2008.

Sutton, Charles, and Andrew McCallum. An Introduction to Conditional Random Fields. *Foundations and Trends in Machine Learning*, 2011. 4(4): 267–373.

Taboada, Maite, Caroline Anthony, and Kimberly Voll. Creating Semantic Orientation Dictionaries. In Proceedings of the 5th International Conference on Language Resources and Evaluation (LREC-2006). 2006.

Taboada, Maite, Julian Brooke, Milan Tofiloski, Kimberly Voll, and Manfred Stede. Lexicon-Based Methods for Sentiment Analysis. *Computational Linguistics*, 2011. 37(2): 267–307.

Täckström, Oscar, and Ryan McDonald. Semi-Supervised Latent Variable Models for Sentence-Level Sentiment Analysis. In Proceedings of the 49th Annual Meeting of the Association for Computational Linguistics: Short Papers (ACL-2011). 2011a.

Täckström, Oscar, and Ryan McDonald. Discovering Fine-Grained Sentiment with Latent Variable Structured Prediction Models. *Advances in Information Retrieval*, 2011b. 368–74.

Takamura, Hiroya, Takashi Inui, and Manabu Okumura. Extracting Semantic Orientations of Words Using Spin Model. In Proceedings of the Annual Meeting of the Association for Computational Linguistics (ACL-2005). 2005.

Takamura, Hiroya, Takashi Inui, and Manabu Okumura. Latent Variable Models for Semantic Orientations of Phrases. In Proceedings of the Conference of the European Chapter of the Association for Computational Linguistics (EACL-2006). 2006.

Takamura, Hiroya, Takashi Inui, and Manabu Okumura. Extracting Semantic Orientations of Phrases from Dictionary. In Proceedings of the Joint Human Language Technology/North American Chapter of the ACL Conference (HLT-NAACL-2007). 2007.

Tan, Pang-Ning, Michael Steinbach, and Vipin Kumar. *Introduction to Data Mining*. 2005. Boston: Addison-Wesley.

Tan, Songbo, Gaowei Wu, Huifeng Tang, and Xueqi Cheng. A Novel Scheme for Domain-Transfer Problem in the Context of Sentiment Analysis. In Proceedings of the ACM Conference on Information and Knowledge Management (CIKM-2007). 2007.

Tang, Duyu, Bing Qin, Xiaocheng Feng, and Ting Liu. Effective LSTMs for Target-Dependent Sentiment Classification. In Proceedings of the International Conference on Computational Linguistics (COLING 2016). 2016a.

Tang, Duyu, Bing Qin, and Ting Liu. Document Modelling with Gated Recurrent Neural Network for Sentiment Classification. In Proceedings of the Conference on Empirical Methods in Natural Language Processing (EMNLP-2015). 2015a.

Tang, Duyu, Bing Qin, and Ting Liu. Learning Semantic Representations of Users and Products for Document Level Sentiment Classification. In Proceedings of the Annual Meeting of the Association for Computational Linguistics (ACL-2015). 2015b.

Tang, Duyu, Bing Qin, and Ting Liu. Aspect Level Sentiment Classification with Deep Memory Network. In Proceedings of the 2016 Conference on Empirical Methods in Natural Language Processing (EMNLP-2016). 2016b.

Tang, Duyu, Furu Wei, Bing Qin, Nan Yang, Ting Liu, and Ming Zhou. Sentiment Embeddings with Applications to Sentiment Analysis. *IEEE Transactions on Knowledge and Data Engineering*. 2016c. 28(2): 496–509.

Tang, Duyu, Furu Wei, Nan Yang, Ming Zhou, Ting Liu, and Bing Qin. Learning Sentiment-Specific Word Embedding for Twitter Sentiment Classification. In Proceedings of the Annual Meeting of the Association for Computational Linguistics (ACL-2014). 2014.

Tata, Swati, and Barbara Di Eugenio. Generating Fine-Grained Reviews of Songs from Album Reviews. In Proceedings of Annual Meeting of the Association for Computational Linguistics (ACL-2010). 2010.

Tay, Yi, Luu Anh Tuan, Siu Cheung Hui. Dyadic Memory Networks for Aspect-Based Sentiment Analysis. In Proceedings of the International Conference on Information and Knowledge Management (CIKM-2017). 2017.

Teng, Zhiyang, Duy-Tin Vo, and Yue Zhang. Context-Sensitive Lexicon Features for Neural Sentiment Analysis. In Proceedings of the Conference on Empirical Methods in Natural Language Processing (EMNLP-2016). 2016.

Thomas, Matt, Bo Pang, and Lillian Lee. Get out the Vote: Determining Support or Opposition from Congressional Floor-Debate Transcripts. In Proceedings of the Conference on Empirical Methods in Natural Language Processing (EMNLP-2006). 2006.

Titov, Ivan, and Ryan McDonald. Modeling Online Reviews with Multi-Grain Topic Models. In Proceedings of the International Conference on the World Wide Web (WWW-2008). 2008a.

Titov, Ivan, and Ryan McDonald. A Joint Model of Text and Aspect Ratings for Sentiment Summarization. In Proceedings of the Annual Meeting of the Association for Computational Linguistics (ACL-2008). 2008b.

Tokuhisa, Ryoko, Kentaro Inui, and Yuji Matsumoto. Emotion Classification Using Massive Examples Extracted from the Web. In Proceedings of the 22nd International Conference on Computational Linguistics (COLING-2008). 2008.

Tomkins, Silvan. Affect Theory. In *Approaches to Emotion*, K. R. Scherer and P. Ekman (Eds.). 1984. Mahwah, NJ: Lawrence Erlbaum, 163–95.

Tong, Richard M. An Operational System for Detecting and Tracking Opinions in On-Line Discussion. In Proceedings of the SIGIR Workshop on Operational Text Classification. 2001.

Toprak, Cigdem, Niklas Jakob, and Iryna Gurevych. Sentence and Expression Level Annotation of Opinions in User-Generated Discourse. In Proceedings of the 48th Annual Meeting of the Association for Computational Linguistics (ACL-2010). 2010.

Tripathi, Samarth, Shrinivas Acharya, Ranti Dev Sharma, Sudhanshi Mittal, and Samit Bhattacharya. Using Deep and Convolutional Neural Networks for Accurate Emotion Classification on DEAP Dataset. In Proceedings of the AAAI Conference on Artificial Intelligence (AAAI-2017). 2017.

Tsaparas, Panayiotis, Alexandros Ntoulas, and Evimaria Terzi. Selecting a Comprehensive Set of Reviews. In Proceedings of the ACM SIGKDD Conference on Knowledge Discovery and Data Mining (KDD-2011). 2011.

Tsur, Oren, Dmitry Davidov, and Ari Rappoport. A Great Catchy Name: Semi-Supervised Recognition of Sarcastic Sentences in Online Product Reviews. In Proceedings of the 4th International AAAI Conference on Weblogs and Social Media (ICWSM-2010). 2010.

Tsur, Oren, and Ari Rappoport. Revrank: A Fully Unsupervised Algorithm for Selecting the Most Helpful Book Reviews. In Proceedings of the International AAAI Conference on Weblogs and Social Media (ICWSM-2009). 2009.

Tumasjan, Andranik, Timm O. Sprenger, Philipp G. Sandner, and Isabell M. Welpe. Predicting Elections with Twitter: What 140 Characters Reveal about Political Sentiment. In Proceedings of the International Conference on Weblogs and Social Media (ICWSM-2010). 2010.

Turney, Peter D. Thumbs Up or Thumbs Down? Semantic Orientation Applied to Unsupervised Classification of Reviews. In Proceedings of the Annual Meeting of the Association for Computational Linguistics (ACL-2002). 2002.

Turney, Peter D., and Michael L. Littman. Measuring Praise and Criticism: Inference of Semantic Orientation from Association. *ACM Transactions on Information Systems*, 2003. 21(4): 315–46.

Utsumi, Akira. Verbal Irony As Implicit Display of Ironic Environment: Distinguishing Ironic Utterances from Nonirony. *Journal of Pragmatics*, 2000. 32(12): 1777–806.

Valitutti, Alessandro, Carlo Strapparava, and Oliviero Stock. Developing Affective Lexical Resources. *PsychNology Journal*, 2004. 2(1): 61–83.

Van Hee, Cynthia, Els Lefever, and Veronique Hoste. Monday Mornings Are My Fave:)# Not: Exploring the Automatic Recognition of Irony in English Tweets. In Proceedings of the International Conference on Computational Linguistics (COLING 2016). 2016.

Velikovich, Leonid, Sasha Blair-Goldensohn, Kerry Hannan, and Ryan McDonald. The Viability of Web-Derived Polarity Lexicons. In Proceedings of the Annual Conference of the North American Chapter of the Association for Computational Linguistics (HAACL-2010). 2010.

Velosoa, Adriano, Wagner Meira Jr., and Mohammed J. Zaki. Lazy Associative Classification. In Proceedings of the 6th IEEE International Conference on Data Mining. 2006.

Vo, Duy-Tin, and Yue Zhang. Target-Dependent Twitter Sentiment Classification with Rich Automatic Features. In Proceedings of the International Joint Conference on Artificial Intelligence (IJCAI-2015). 2015.

Volkova, Svitlana, Theresa Wilson, and David Yarowsky. Exploring Demographic Language Variations to Improve Multilingual Sentiment Analysis in Social Media. In Proceedings of the 2013 Conference on Empirical Methods on Natural Language Processing (EMNLP-2013). 2013a.

Volkova, Svitlana, Theresa Wilson, and David Yarowsky. Exploring Sentiment in Social Media: Bootstrapping Subjectivity Clues from Multilingual Twitter Streams. In Proceedings of the Annual Meeting of the Association for Computational Linguistics (ACL-2013). 2013b.

Vrij, Aldert. *Detecting Lies and Deceit: Pitfalls and Opportunities.* 2008. New York: Wiley-Interscience.

Wallach, Hanna M. Topic Modeling: Beyond Bag-of-Words. In Proceedings of the 23rd International Conference on Machine Learning (ICML-2006). 2006.

Wan, Xiaojun. Using Bilingual Knowledge and Ensemble Techniques for Unsupervised Chinese Sentiment Analysis. In Proceedings of the Conference on Empirical Methods in Natural Language Processing (EMNLP-2008). 2008.

Wan, Xiaojun. Co-training for Cross-Lingual Sentiment Classification. In Proceedings of the 47th Annual Meeting of the ACL and the 4th IJCNLP of the AFNLP (ACL-IJCNLP-2009). 2009.

Wan, Xiaojun. Co-regression for Cross-Language Review Rating Prediction. In Proceedings of the Annual Meeting of the Association for Computational Linguistics (ACL-2013). 2013.

Wang, Bo, and Houfeng Wang. Bootstrapping Both Product Features and Opinion Words from Chinese Customer Reviews with Cross-Inducing. In Proceedings of the International Joint Conference on Natural Language Processing (IJCNLP-2008). 2008.

Wang, Dong, and Yang Liu. A Pilot Study of Opinion Summarization in Conversations. In Proceedings of the 49th Annual Meeting of the Association for Computational Linguistics (ACL-2011). 2011.

Wang, Guan, Sihong Xie, Bing Liu, and Philip S. Yu. Identify Online Store Review Spammers via Social Review Graph. *ACM Transactions on Intelligent Systems and Technology*, 2011. 3(4): 1–21.

Wang, Hao, Bing Liu, Chaozhuo Li, Yan Yang, and Tianrui Li. Learning with Noisy Labels for Sentence-Level Sentiment Classification. In Proceedings of the 2019 Conference on Empirical Methods in Natural Language Processing (EMNLP-2019, short paper). November 3–7, 2019a.

Wang, Hao, Bing Liu, Shuai Wang, Nianzu Ma, and Yan Yang. Forward and Backward Knowledge Transfer for Sentiment Classification. In Proceedings of the Asian Conference on Machine Learning. 2019b.

Wang, Haohan, Aaksha Meghawat, Louis-Philippe Morency and Eric P. Xing. Select-Additive Learning: Improving Generalization in Multimodal Sentiment Analysis. In Proceedings of the International Conference on Multimedia and Expo (ICME-2017). 2017a.

Wang, Hongning, Yue Lu, and Chengxiang Zhai. Latent Aspect Rating Analysis on Review Text Data: A Rating Regression Approach. In Proceedings of the ACM

SIGKDD International Conference on Knowledge Discovery and Data Mining (KDD-2010). 2010.

Wang, Jin, Liang-Chih Yu, K. Robert Lai, and Xuejie Zhang. Dimensional Sentiment Analysis Using a Regional CNN-LSTM Model. In Proceedings of the Annual Meeting of the Association for Computational Linguistics (ACL-2016). 2016a.

Wang, Jingwen, Jianlong Fu, Yong Xu, and Tao Mei. Beyond Object Recognition: Visual Sentiment Analysis with Deep Coupled Adjective and Noun Neural Networks. In Proceedings of the International Joint Conference on Artificial Intelligence (IJCAI-2016). 2016b.

Wang, Leyi, and Rui Xia. Sentiment Lexicon Construction with Representation Learning Based on Hierarchical Sentiment Supervision. In Proceedings of the Conference on Empirical Methods on Natural Language Processing (EMNLP-2017). 2017b.

Wang, Li, Marco Lui, Su Nam Kim, Joakim Nivre, and Timothy Baldwin. Predicting Thread Discourse Structure over Technical Web Forums. In Proceedings of the 2011 Conference on Empirical Methods in Natural Language Processing (EMNLP-2011). 2011.

Wang, Shuai, Guangyi Lv, Sahisnu Mazumder, Geli Fei, and Bing Liu. Lifelong Learning Memory Networks for Aspect Sentiment Classification. Proceedings of the 2018 IEEE International Conference on Big Data (IEEE BigData 2018). December 10–13, 2018a.

Wang, Shuai, Sahisnu Mazumder, Bing Liu, Mianwei Zhou, and Yi Chang. Target-Sensitive Memory Networks for Aspect Sentiment Classification. Proceedings of the Annual Meeting of the Association for Computational Linguistics (ACL-2018). 2018b.

Wang, Wenya, Sinno Jialin Pan, Daniel Dahlmeier, and Xiaokui Xiao, Recursive Neural Conditional Random Fields for Aspect-Based Sentiment Analysis. In Proceedings of the Conference on Empirical Methods on Natural Language Processing (EMNLP-2016). 2016c.

Wang, Wenya, Sinno Jialin Pan, Daniel Dahlmeier, and Xiaokui Xiao. Coupled Multi-Layer Attentions for Co-extraction of Aspect and Opinion Terms. In Proceedings of the AAAI Conference on Artificial Intelligence (AAAI-2017). 2017b.

Wang, Xin, Yuanchao Liu, Chengjie Sun, Baoxun Wang, and Xiaolong Wang. Predicting Polarities of Tweets by Composing Word Embeddings with Long Short-Term Memory. In Proceedings of the Annual Meeting of the Association for Computational Linguistics (ACL-2015). 2015.

Wang, Xingyou, Weijie Jiang, and Zhiyong Luo. Combination of Convolutional and Recurrent Neural Network for Sentiment Analysis of Short Texts. In Proceedings of the International Conference on Computational Linguistics (COLING-2016). 2016c.

Wang, Yasheng, Yang Zhang, and Bing Liu. Sentiment Lexicon Expansion Based on Neural PU Learning, Double Dictionary Lookup, and Polarity Association. In Proceedings of the 2017 Conference on Empirical Methods in Natural Language Processing (EMNLP-2017). September 7–11, 2017c.

Wang, Yequan, Minlie Huang, Li Zhao, and Xiaoyan Zhu. Attention-Based LSTM for Aspect-Level Sentiment Classification. In Proceedings of the Conference on Empirical Methods in Natural Language Processing (EMNLP-2016). 2016e.

Wang, Yequan, Aixin Sun, Jialong Han, Ying Liu, and Xiaoyan Zhu. Sentiment Analysis by Capsules. *WWW*, 2018. 1165–74.

Wang, Yong, and Ian H. Witten. *Pace Regression*. Technical Report 99/12. 1999. Hamilton, NZ: Department of Computer Science, University of Waikato.

Wang, Zhongqing, Yue Zhang, Sophia Yat Mei Lee, Shoushan Li, and Guodong Zhou. A Bilingual Attention Network for Code-Switched Emotion Prediction. In Proceedings of the International Conference on Computational Linguistics (COLING-2016). 2016f.

Watson, D. The Vicissitudes of Mood Measurement: Effects of Varying Descriptors, Time Frames, and Response Formats on Measures of Positive and Negative Affect. *Journal of Personality and Social Psychology*, 1988. 55: 128–41.

Watson, D., L. A. Clark, and A. Tellegen. Development and Validation of Brief Measures of Positive and Negative Affect: The PANAS Scales. *Journal of Personality and Social Psychology*, 1988. 54(6): 1063–70.

Watson, D., and A. Tellegen. Towards a Consensual Structure of Mood. *Psychological Bulletin*, 1985. 98(2): 219–35.

Watson, John B. *Behaviorism*. 1930. Chicago: Chicago University Press.

Wei, Bin, and Christopher Pal. Cross Lingual Adaptation: An Experiment on Sentiment Classifications. In Proceedings of the ACL 2010 Conference Short Papers (ACL-2010). 2010.

Weiner, B., and S. Graham. An Attributional Approach to Emotional Development. In *Emotion, Cognition and Behavior*, C. E. Izard, J. Kagan, and R. B. Zajonc (Eds). 1984. Cambridge: Cambrige University Press, 167–91.

Weise, K. A Lie Detector Test for Online Reviewers. *Businessweek*, 2011. www .businessweek.com/magazine/a-lie-detector-test-for-online-reviewers-09292011.html.

Wen, Miaomiao, and Yunfang Wu. Mining the Sentiment Expectation of Nouns Using Bootstrapping Method. In Proceedings of the 5th International Joint Conference on Natural Language Processing (IJCNLP-2010). 2011.

Wiebe, Janyce. Identifying Subjective Characters in Narrative. In Proceedings of the International Conference on Computational Linguistics (COLING-1990). 1990.

Wiebe, Janyce. Tracking Point of View in Narrative. *Computational Linguistics*, 1994. 20: 233–87.

Wiebe, Janyce. Learning Subjective Adjectives from Corpora. In Proceedings of the National Conference on Artificial Intelligence (AAAI-2000). 2000.

Wiebe, Janyce, Rebecca F. Bruce, and Thomas P. O'Hara. Development and Use of a Gold-Standard Data Set for Subjectivity Classifications. In Proceedings of the Association for Computational Linguistics (ACL-1999). 1999.

Wiebe, Janyce, and Rada Mihalcea. Word Sense and Subjectivity. In Proceedings of the International Conference on Computational Linguistics and 44th Annual Meeting of the ACL (COLING/ACL-2006). 2006.

Wiebe, Janyce, and Ellen Riloff. Creating Subjective and Objective Sentence Classifiers from Unannotated Texts. In *International Conference on Intelligent Text Processing and Computational Linguistics*. 2005. Berlin/Heidelberg: Springer, 486–97.

Wiebe, Janyce, Theresa Wilson, Rebecca F. Bruce, Matthew Bell, and Melanie Martin. Learning Subjective Language. *Computational Linguistics*, 2004. 30(3): 277–308.

Wiebe, Janyce, Theresa Wilson, and Claire Cardie. Annotating Expressions of Opinions and Emotions in Language. *Language Resources and Evaluation*, 2005. 39 (2): 165–210.

Wiegand, M., and D. Klakow. Convolution Kernels for Opinion Holder Extraction. In Proceedings of Human Language Technologies: The 2010 Annual Conference of the North American Chapter of the ACL (HAACL-2010). 2010.

Willcox, Gloria. The Feeling Wheel: A Tool for Expanding Awareness of Emotions and Increasing Spontaneity and Intimacy. *Transactional Analysis Journal*, 1982. 12 (4): 274–6.

Williams, Gbolahan K., and Sarabjot Singh Anand. Predicting the Polarity Strength of Adjectives Using WordNet. In Proceedings of the 3rd International AAAI Conference on Weblogs and Social Media (ICWSM-2009). 2009.

Wilson, Theresa, and Stephan Raaijmakers. Comparing Word, Character, and Phoneme *N*-Grams for Subjective Utterance Recognition. In Proceedings of Interspeech. 2008.

Wilson, Theresa, and Janyce Wiebe. Annotating Attributions and Private States. In Proceedings of the ACL Workshop on Frontiers in Corpus Annotation II: Pie in the Sky. 2005.

Wilson, Theresa, Janyce Wiebe, and Paul Hoffmann. Recognizing Contextual Polarity in Phrase-Level Sentiment Analysis. In Proceedings of the Human Language Technology Conference and the Conference on Empirical Methods in Natural Language Processing (HLT/EMNLP-2005). 2005.

Wilson, Theresa, Janyce Wiebe, and Paul Hoffmann. Recognizing Contextual Polarity: An Exploration of Features for Phrase-Level Sentiment Analysis. *Computational Linguistics*, 2009. 35(3): 399–433.

Wilson, Theresa, Janyce Wiebe, and Rebecca Hwa. Just How Mad Are You? Finding Strong and Weak Opinion Clauses. In Proceedings of the National Conference on Artificial Intelligence (AAAI-2004). 2004.

Wilson, Theresa, Janyce Wiebe, and Rebecca Hwa. Recognizing Strong and Weak Opinion Clauses. *Computational Intelligence*, 2006. 22(2): 73–99.

Wu, Fangzhao, Jia Zhang, Zhigang Yuan, Sixing Wu, Yongfeng Huang, and Jun Yan. Sentence-Level Sentiment Classification with Weak Supervision. In Proceedings of SIGIR, 973–6, 2017.

Wu, Guangyu, Derek Greene, Barry Smyth, and Pádraig Cunningham. Distortion As a Validation Criterion in the Identification of Suspicious Reviews. In Proceedings of Social Media Analytics. 2010.

Wu, Qion, Songbo Tan, and Xueqi Cheng. Graph Ranking for Sentiment Transfer. In Proceedings of the ACL-IJCNLP 2009 Conference" Short Papers (ACL-IJCNLP-2009). 2009a.

Wu, Yuanbin, Qi Zhang, Xuanjing Huang, and Lide Wu. Phrase Dependency Parsing for Opinion Mining. In Proceedings of the Conference on Empirical Methods in Natural Language Processing (EMNLP-2009). 2009b.

Wu, Yuanbin, Qi Zhang, Xuanjing Huang, and Lide Wu. Structural Opinion Mining for Graph-Based Sentiment Representation. In Proceedings of the 2011 Conference on Empirical Methods in Natural Language Processing (EMNLP-2011). 2011.

Wu, Yunfang, and Miaomiao Wen. Disambiguating Dynamic Sentiment Ambiguous Adjectives. In Proceedings of the 23rd International Conference on Computational Linguistics (COLING 2010). 2010.

Xia, Rui, and Zixiang Ding. Emotion-Cause Pair Extraction: A New Task to Emotion Analysis in Texts. In Proceedings of the Annual Meeting of the Association for Computational Linguistics (ACL-2019). 2019.

Xia, Rui, Tao Wang, Xuelei Hu, Shoushan Li, and Chengqing Zong. Dual Training and Dual Prediction for Polarity Classification. In Proceedings of the Annual Meeting of the Association for Computational Linguistics (ACL-2013). 2013.

Xia, Rui, and Chengqing Zong. Exploring the Use of Word Relation Features for Sentiment Classification. In Proceedings of COLING 2010: Poster Volume. 2010.

Xia, Rui, and Chengqing Zong. A POS-Based Ensemble Model for Cross-Domain Sentiment Classification. In Proceedings of the 5th International Joint Conference on Natural Language Processing (IJCNLP-2010). 2011.

Xie, Sihong, Guan Wang, Shuyang Lin, and Philip S. Yu. Review Spam Detection via Temporal Pattern Discovery. In Proceedings of the 18th ACM SIGKDD Conference on Knowledge Discovery and Data Mining (KDD-2012). 2012.

Xiong, Shufeng, Yue Zhang, Donghong Ji, and Yinxia Lou. Distance Metric Learning for Aspect Phrase Grouping. In Proceedings of the International Conference on Computational Linguistics (COLING-2016). 2016.

Xu, G., X. Meng, and H. Wang. Build Chinese Emotion Lexicons Using a Graph-Based Algorithm and Multiple Resources. In Proceedings of the 23rd International Conference on Computational Linguistics (COLING-2010). 2010.

Xu, Hu, Bing Liu, Lei Shu, and Philip S. Yu. Double Embeddings and CNN-Based Sequence Labeling for Aspect Extraction. In Proceedings of the Annual Meeting of the Association for Computational Linguistics (ACL-2018, short paper). July 15–20, 2018.

Xu, Hu, Bing Liu, Lei Shu, and Philip S. Yu. BERT Post-Training for Review Reading Comprehension and Aspect-Based Sentiment Analysis. In Proceedings of the 2019 Annual Conference of the North American Chapter of the Association for Computational Linguistics (NAACL-2019). June 2–7, 2019.

Xu, Jiacheng, Danlu Chen, Xipeng Qiu, and Xuanjing Huang. Cached Long Short-Term Memory Neural Networks for Document-Level Sentiment Classification. In Proceedings of the Conference on Empirical Methods in Natural Language Processing (EMNLP-2016). 2016.

Xu, Liheng, Kang Liu, Siwei Lai, Yubo Chen, and Jun Zhao. Mining Opinion Words and Opinion Targets in a Two-Stage Framework. In Proceedings of the Annual Meeting of the Association for Computational Linguistics (ACL-2013). 2013.

Xu, Qiongkai, and Hai Zhao. Using Deep Linguistic Features for Finding Deceptive Opinion Spam. In Proceedings of the 24th International Conference on Computational Linguistics (COLING-2012). 2012.

Yang, Bishan, and Claire Cardie. Extracting Opinion Expressions with Semi-Markov Conditional Random Fields. In Proceedings of the 2012 Conference on Empirical Methods on Natural Language Processing (EMNLP-2012). 2012.

Yang, Bishan, and Claire Cardie. Joint Inference for Fine-Grained Opinion Extraction. In Proceedings of the Annual Meeting of the Association for Computational Linguistics (ACL-2013). 2013.

Yang, Changhua, Kevin Hsin-Yih Lin Lin, and Hsin-Hsi Chen. Building Emotion Lexicon from Weblog Corpora. In Proceedings of the 45th Annual Meeting of the ACL: Interactive Poster and Demonstration Sessions. 2007.

Yang, Hui, Luo Si, and Jamie Callan. Knowledge Transfer and Opinion Detection in the Trec2006 Blog Track. In Proceedings of TREC. 2006.

Yang, Jufeng, Ming Sun, and Xiaoxiao Sun. Learning Visual Sentiment Distributions via Augmented Conditional Probability Neural Network. In Proceedings of the AAAI Conference on Artificial Intelligence (AAAI-2017). 2017a.

Yang, Min, Wenting Tu, Jingxuan Wang, Fei Xu, and Xiaojun Chen. Attention-Based LSTM for Target-Dependent Sentiment Classification. In Proceedings of the AAAI Conference on Artificial Intelligence (AAAI-2017). 2017b.

Yang, Seon, and Youngjoong Ko. Extracting Comparative Entities and Predicates from Texts Using Comparative Type Classification. In Proceedings of the 49th Annual Meeting of the Association for Computational Linguistics (ACL-2011). 2011.

Yang, Yiming, and Jan O. Pedersen. A Comparative Study on Feature Selection in Text Categorization. In Proceedings of the 14th International Conference on Machine Learning (ICML-1997). 1997.

Yang, Zichao, Diyi Yang, Chris Dyer, Xiaodong He, Alex Smola, and Eduard Hovy. Hierarchical Attention Networks for Document Classification. In Proceedings of the Conference of the North American Chapter of the Association for Computational Linguistics: Human Language Technologies (NAACL-HLT-2016). 2016.

Yano, Tae, and Noah A. Smith. What's Worthy of Comment? Content and Comment Volume in Political Blogs. In Proceedings of the International AAAI Conference on Weblogs and Social Media (ICWSM-2010). 2010.

Yatani, Koji, Michael Novati, Andrew Trusty, and Khai N. Truong. Analysis of Adjective–Noun Word Pair Extraction Methods for Online Review Summarization. In Proceedings of the International Joint Conference on Artificial Intelligence (IJCAI-2011). 2011.

Yessenalina, Ainur, and Claire Cardie. Compositional Matrix-Space Models for Sentiment Analysis. In Proceedings of the Conference on Empirical Methods in Natural Language Processing (EMNLP-2011). 2011.

Yessenalina, Ainur, Yejin Choi, and Claire Cardie. Automatically Generating Annotator Rationales to Improve Sentiment Classification. In Proceedings of the ACL 2010 Conference Short Papers. 2010a.

Yessenalina, Ainur, Yison Yue, and Claire Cardie. Multi-Level Structured Models for Document-Level Sentiment Classification. In Proceedings of the Conference on Empirical Methods in Natural Language Processing (EMNLP-2010). 2010b.

Yi, Jeonghee, Tetsuya Nasukawa, Razvan Bunescu, and Wayne Niblack. Sentiment Analyzer: Extracting Sentiments about a Given Topic Using Natural Language Processing Techniques. In Proceedings of the IEEE International Conference on Data Mining (ICDM-2003). 2003.

Yin, Yichun, Yangqiu Song, and Ming Zhang. Document-Level Multi-Aspect Sentiment Classification As Machine Comprehension. In Proceedings of the Conference on Empirical Methods in Natural Language Processing (EMNLP 2017). 2017.

Yin, Yichun, Furu Wei, Li Dong, Kaimeng Xu, Ming Zhang, and Ming Zhou. Unsupervised Word and Dependency Path Embeddings for Aspect Term Extraction. In Proceedings of the International Joint Conference on Artificial Intelligence (IJCAI-2016). 2016.

Yogatama, Dani, Yanchuan Sim, and Noah A. Smith. A Probabilistic Model for Canonicalizing Named Entity Mentions. In Proceedings of the 50th Annual Meeting of the Association for Computational Linguistics (ACL-2012). 2012.

Yoshida, Yasuhisa, Tsutomu Hirao, Tomoharu Iwata, Masaaki Nagata, and Yuji Matsumoto. Transfer Learning for Multiple-Domain Sentiment Analysis: Identifying Domain Dependent/Independent Word Polarity. In Proceedings of the 25th AAAI Conference on Artificial Intelligence (AAAI-2011). 2011.

You, Quanzeng, Hailin Jin, and Jiebo Luo. Visual Sentiment Analysis by Attending on Local Image Regions. In Proceedings of the AAAI Conference on Artificial Intelligence (AAAI-2017). 2017.

Yu, Chun-Nam, and Thorsten Joachims. Learning Structural SVMs with Latent Variables. In Proceedings of the International Conference on Machine Learning (ICML-2009). 2009.

Yu, Hong, and Vasileios Hatzivassiloglou. Towards Answering Opinion Questions: Separating Facts from Opinions and Identifying the Polarity of Opinion Sentences. In Proceedings of the Conference on Empirical Methods in Natural Language Processing (EMNLP-2003). 2003.

Yu, Jianfei, and Jing Jiang. Learning Sentence Embeddings with Auxiliary Tasks for Cross-Domain Sentiment Classification. In Proceedings of the Conference on Empirical Methods in Natural Language Processing (EMNLP-2016). 2016.

Yu, Jianxing, Zheng-Jun Zha, Meng Wang, and Tat-Seng Chua. Aspect Ranking: Identifying Important Product Aspects from Online Consumer Reviews. In Proceedings of the 49th Annual Meeting of the Association for Computational Linguistics. 2011a.

Yu, Jianxing, Zheng-Jun Zha, Meng Wang, Kai Wang, and Tat-Seng Chua. Domain-Assisted Product Aspect Hierarchy Generation: Towards Hierarchical Organization of Unstructured Consumer Reviews. In Proceedings of the Conference on Empirical Methods in Natural Language Processing (EMNLP-2011). 2011b.

Yu, Liang-Chih, Jin Wang, K. Robert Lai, and Xuejie Zhang. Refining Word Embeddings for Sentiment Analysis. In Proceedings of the Conference on Empirical Methods on Natural Language Processing (EMNLP-2017). 2017.

Zadrozny, Bianca. Learning and Evaluating Classifiers under Sample Selection Bias. In Proceedings of the International Conference on Machine Learning, 2004.

Zafarani, Reza, and Huan Liu. Connecting Users across Social Media Sites: A Behavioral-Modeling Approach. In Proceedings of the SIGKDD International Conference on Knowledge Discovery and Data Mining (KDD-2013). 2013.

Zaidan, Omar F., Jason Eisner, and Christine Piatko. Using "Annotator Rationales" to Improve Machine Learning for Text Categorization. In Proceedings of NAACLHLT-2007. 2007.

Zhai, Shuangfei, and Zhongfei Zhang. Semi-Supervised Autoencoder for Sentiment Analysis. In Proceedings of the AAAI Conference on Artificial Intelligence (AAAI-2016). 2016.

Zhai, Zhongwu, Bing Liu, Hua Xu, and Peifa Jia. Grouping Product Features Using Semi-Supervised Learning with Soft Constraints. In Proceedings of the International Conference on Computational Linguistics (COLING-2010). 2010.

Zhai, Zhongwu, Bing Liu, Hua Xu, and Peifa Jia. Constrained LDA for Grouping Product Features in Opinion Mining. In Proceedings of PAKDD-2011. 2011a.

Zhai, Zhongwu, Bing Liu, Hua Xu, and Peifa Jia. Clustering Product Features for Opinion Mining. In Proceedings of the ACM International Conference on Web Search and Data Mining (WSDM-2011). 2011b.

Zhai, Zhongwu, Bing Liu, Lei Zhang, Hua Xu, and Peifa Jia. Identifying Evaluative Opinions in Online Discussions. In Proceedings of AAAI. 2011c.

Zhang, Lei, and Bing Liu. Extracting Resource Terms for Sentiment Analysis. In Proceedings of IJCNLP-2011. 2011a.

Zhang, Lei, and Bing Liu. Identifying Noun Product Features That Imply Opinions. In Proceedings of the Annual Meeting of the Association for Computational Linguistics (ACL-2011). 2011b.

Zhang, Lei, and Bing Liu. Entity Set Expansion in Opinion Documents. In Proceedings of the ACM Conference on Hypertext and Hypermedia (HT-2011). 2011c.

Zhang, Lei, Bing Liu, Suk Hwan Lim, and Eamonn O'Brien-Strain. Extracting and Ranking Product Features in Opinion Documents. In Proceedings of the International Conference on Computational Linguistics (COLING-2010). 2010a.

Zhang, Lei, Shuai Wang, and Bing Liu. Deep Learning for Sentiment Analysis: A Survey. *Wiley Interdisciplinary Reviews: Data Mining and Knowledge Discovery*, 2018. 8(4). doi: 10.1002/widm.1253.

Zhang, Meishan, Yue Zhang, and Guohong Fu. Tweet Sarcasm Detection Using Deep Neural Network. In Proceedings of the International Conference on Computational Linguistics (COLING-2016). 2016a.

Zhang, Meishan, Yue Zhang, and Duy-Tin Vo. Neural Networks for Open Domain Targeted Sentiment. In Proceedings of the Conference on Empirical Methods in Natural Language Processing (EMNLP-2015). 2015.

Zhang, Meishan, Yue Zhang, and Duy-Tin Vo. Gated Neural Networks for Targeted Sentiment Analysis. In Proceedings of the AAAI Conference on Artificial Intelligence (AAAI-2016). 2016b.

Zhang, Min, and Xingyao Ye. A Generation Model to Unify Topic Relevance and Lexicon-Based Sentiment for Opinion Retrieval. In Proceedings of the Annual ACM SIGIR International Conference on Research and Development in Information Retrieval (SIGIR-2008). 2008.

Zhang, Qi, Jin Qian, Huan Chen, Jihua Kang, and Xuanjing Huang. Discourse Level Explanatory Relation Extraction from Product Reviews Using First-Order Logic. In Proceedings of the Conference on Empirical Methods in Natural Language Processing (EMNLP-2013). 2013.

Zhang, Wei, Lifeng Jia, Clement Yu, and Weiyi Meng. Improve the Effectiveness of the Opinion Retrieval and Opinion Polarity Classification. In Proceedings of the ACM International Conference on Information and Knowledge Management (CIKM-2008). 2008.

Zhang, Wei, Jian Su, Chew Lim Tan, and Wen Ting Wang. Entity Linking Leveraging Automatically Generated Annotation. In Proceedings of the 23rd International Conference on Computational Linguistics (COLING-2010). 2010b.

Zhang, Wei, and Clement Yu, UIC at TREC 2007 Blog Report. 2007.

Zhang, Wei, Quan Yuan, Jiawei Han, and Jianyong Wang. Collaborative Multi-Level Embedding Learning from Reviews for Rating Prediction. In Proceedings of the International Joint Conference on Artificial Intelligence (IJCAI-2016). 2016c.

Zhang, Wenbin, and Steven Skiena. Trading Strategies to Exploit Blog and News Sentiment. In Proceedings of the International Conference on Weblogs and Social Media (ICWSM-2010). 2010.

Zhang, Xue, Hauke Fuehres, and Peter A. Gloor. Predicting Stock Market Indicators through Twitter: "I Hope It Is Not As Bad As I Fear." In Proceedings of the Collaborative Innovations Networks Conference (COINs). 2010c.

Zhang, Zhu, and Balaji Varadarajan. Utility Scoring of Product Reviews. In Proceedings of the ACM International Conference on Information and Knowledge Management (CIKM-2006). 2006.

Zhao, Wayne Xin, Jing Jiang, Jing He, Yang Song, Palakorn Achananuparp, Ee Peng Lim, and Xiaoming Li. Topical Keyphrase Extraction from Twitter. In Proceedings of the Annual Meeting of the Association for Computational Linguistics: Human Language Technologies (ACL-2011). 2011.

Zhao, Wayne Xin, Jing Jiang, Hongfei Yan, and Xiaoming Li. Jointly Modeling Aspects and Opinions with a Maxent-LDA Hybrid. In Proceedings of the Conference on Empirical Methods in Natural Language Processing (EMNLP-2010). 2010.

Zhao, Yanyan, Bing Qin, and Ting Liu. Collocation Polarity Disambiguation Using Web-Based Pseudo Contexts. In Proceedings of the 2012 Conference on Empirical Methods on Natural Language Processing (EMNLP-2012). 2012.

Zhao, Zhou, Hanqing Lu, Deng Cai, Xiaofei He, and Yueting Zhuang. Microblog Sentiment Classification via Recurrent Random Walk Network Learning. In Proceedings of the International Joint Conference on Artificial Intelligence (IJCAI-2017). 2017.

Zhe, Xu, and A. C. Boucouvalas. Text-to-Emotion Engine for Real Time Internet Communication. In Proceedings of International Symposium on Communication Systems, Networks and DSPs. 2002.

Zheng, Zhicheng, Fangtao Li, Minlie Huang, and Xiaoyan Zhu. Learning to Link Entities with Knowledge Base. In Proceedings of Human Language Technologies: The 2010 Annual Conference of the North American Chapter of the ACL. 2010.

Zhou, Hao, Minlie Huang, Tianyang Zhang, Xiaoyan Zhu, and Bing Liu. Emotional Chatting Machine: Emotional Conversation Generation with Internal and External Memory. In Proceedings of AAAI-2018. 2018.

Zhou, Huiwei, Long Chen, Fulin Shi, and Degen Huang. Learning Bilingual Sentiment Word Embeddings for Cross-Language Sentiment Classification. In Proceedings of the Annual Meeting of the Association for Computational Linguistics (ACL-2015). 2015.

Zhou, Lanjun, Binyang Li, Wei Gao, Zhongyu Wei, and Kam-Fai Wong. Unsupervised Discovery of Discourse Relations for Eliminating Intra-sentence Polarity Ambiguities. In Proceedings of the Conference on Empirical Methods in Natural Language Processing (EMNLP-2011). 2011.

Zhou, Lina, Yongmei Shi, and Dongsong Zhang. A Statistical Language Modeling Approach to Online Deception Detection. *IEEE Transactions on Knowledge and Data Engineering*, 2008. 20(8): 1077–81.

Zhou, Shusen, Qingcai Chen, and Xiaolong Wang. Active Deep Networks for Semi-Supervised Sentiment Classification. In Proceedings of COLING 2010: Poster Volume. 2010.

Zhou, Xinjie, Xiaojun Wan, and Jianguo Xiao. Collective Opinion Target Extraction in Chinese Microblogs. In Proceedings of the 2013 Conference on Empirical Methods on Natural Language Processing (EMNLP-2013). 2013.

Zhou, Xinjie, Xiaojun Wan, and Jianguo Xiao. Representation Learning for Aspect Category Detection in Online Reviews. In Proceedings of the AAAI Conference on Artificial Intelligence (AAAI-2015). 2015.

Zhou, Xinjie, Xiaojun Wan, and Jianguo Xiao. Attention-Based LSTM Network for Cross-Lingual Sentiment Classification. In Proceedings of the Conference on Empirical Methods in Natural Language Processing (EMNLP-2016). 2016.

Zhu, Jingbo, Huizhen Wang, Benjamin K. Tsou, and Muhua Zhu. Multi-Aspect Opinion Polling from Textual Reviews. In Proceedings of the ACM International Conference on Information and Knowledge Management (CIKM-2009). 2009.

Zhu, Xiaojin, and Zoubin Ghahramani. *Learning from Labeled and Unlabeled Data with Label Propagation*. Technical Report CMU-CALD-02-107. 2002. Pittsburgh: Carnegie Mellon University.

Zhu, Xinge, Liang Li, Weigang Zhang, Tianrong Rao, Min Xu, Qingming Huang, and Dong Xu. Dependency Exploitation: A Unified CNN-RNN Approach for Visual Emotion Recognition. In Proceedings of the International Joint Conference on Artificial Intelligence (IJCAI-2017). 2017.

Zhuang, Li, Feng Jing, and Xiaoyan Zhu. Movie Review Mining and Summarization. In Proceedings of the ACM International Conference on Information and Knowledge Management (CIKM-2006). 2006.

Zirn, Cäcilia, Mathias Niepert, Heiner Stuckenschmidt, and Michael Strube. Fine-Grained Sentiment Analysis with Structural Features. In Proceedings of the 5th International Joint Conference on Natural Language Processing (IJCNLP-2011). 2011.

Index

Printed in the United States
by Baker & Taylor Publisher Services